HIDDEN®
Southern California

"Excellent."
—*Chicago Tribune*

"A handy paperback."
—*Los Angeles Times*

"A complete guidebook!"
—*San Diego Tribune*

"Breezy and informative."
—*Fresno Bee*

"Covers it all from the obvious to the obscure."
—*San Antonio Express-News*

"A fast-paced, extraordinarily comprehensive, highly readable
guidebook to Southern California."
—*Books of the Southwest*

"This book is superb and is recommended for the seasoned or neophyte
traveler to the area."
—*St. Louis Post-Dispatch*

"A sure-fire clue to a good travel book is if it includes the word 'hidden' in the
title and is written by Ray Riegert."
—*Toronto Sun*

HIDDEN®
Southern California

Ray Riegert

FIFTH EDITION

Ulysses Press®
BERKELEY, CALIFORNIA

For my mother

∾

Published by:
ULYSSES PRESS
P.O. Box 3440
Berkeley, CA 94703-3440

Library of Congress Catalog Card Number 96-60086
ISBN 1-56975-055-6

10 9 8 7 6

EDITORIAL DIRECTOR: Leslie Henriques
MANAGING EDITOR: Claire Chun
PROJECT DIRECTOR: Deema Khorsheed
COPY EDITOR: Lee Micheaux
EDITORIAL ASSOCIATES: Toby Bielawski, Lily Chou,
    Phoebe McClure, Natasha Lay, Ellen Nidy
TYPESETTER: Kenya Ratcliff
CARTOGRAPHERS: Rob March Harper, Phil Gardner,
    Lindsay Mugglestone, Claire Chun
COVER DESIGN: Sarah Levin
INDEXER: Sayre Van Young
COVER PHOTOGRAPHY: Front: Larry Ulrich
    Circle and back: Dennis Junor/Superstock
    Back: Robert Holmes
ILLUSTRATOR: Tim Carroll

Distributed in the United States by Publishers Group West, in Canada by Raincoast Books, and in Great Britain and Europe by World Leisure Marketing

Acknowledgments

If publishing a book is comparable to sailing a boat, the vessel I captain is a cross between *The Good Ship Lollipop* and a *Ship of Fools*. Surprisingly, during the two-year voyage, no one mutinied.

My wife and co-publisher Leslie Henriques is primarily responsible for keeping the project on course. She worked indefatigably on every phase and shares equally in any credit that may be forthcoming.

Claire Chun also weathered the storms, proving that it's really quite easy to simultaneously research a chapter, type notes, and supervise a production team. Deema Khorsheed worked ably and conscientiously as project director. Thanks as well to Lee Micheaux for her work with the red pencil.

Tim Carroll created the illustrations, and the cover was nicely designed by Sarah Levin and Leslie. Over in the production department, Phil Gardner served ably as mapmaker.

Toby Bielawski, Lily Chou, Kenya Ratcliff, Phoebe McClure, Natasha Lay and Ellen Nidy helped with research and production. Sayre Van Young turned out another in a long line of professionally rendered indexes.

In the original edition, Dave Houser ably navigated the San Diego Coast and Jan Butchofsky contributed to the text.

To all of them I want to extend a large, warm, and heartfelt thank you.

Contents

OUTDOOR ADVENTURE SYMBOLS

The following symbols accompany national, state, and regional park listings, as well as beach descriptions throughout the text.

⛰	Camping		🏄	Surfing
🚶	Hiking		🎿	Waterskiing
🚲	Biking		🏄	Windsurfing
🐎	Horseback Riding		🛶	Canoeing or Kayaking
⛷	Downhill Skiing		🚤	Boating
⛷	Cross-country Skiing		🚤	Boat Ramps
🏊	Swimming		🐟	Fishing
🤿	Snorkeling or Scuba Diving			

Maps

Special Features

What's Hidden?

At different points throughout this book, you'll find special listings marked with a hidden symbol:

◀ HIDDEN

This means that you have come upon a place off the beaten tourist track, a spot that will carry you a step closer to the local people and natural environment of Southern California.

The goal of this guide is to lead you beyond the realm of everyday tourist facilities. While we include traditional sightseeing listings and popular attractions, we also offer alternative sights and adventure activities. Instead of filling this guide with reviews of standard hotels and chain restaurants, we concentrate on one-of-a-kind places and locally owned establishments.

Our authors seek out locales that are popular with residents but usually overlooked by visitors. Some are more hidden than others (and are marked accordingly), but all the listings in this book are intended to help you discover the true nature of Southern California and put you on the path of adventure.

Write to us!

If in your travels you discover a spot that captures the spirit of Southern California, or if you live in the region and have a favorite place to share, or if you just feel like expressing your views, write to us and we'll pass your note along to the author.

We can't guarantee that the author will add your personal find to the next edition, but if the writer does use the suggestion, we'll acknowledge you in the credits and send you a free autographed copy of the new edition.

ULYSSES PRESS
P.O. Box 3440
Berkeley, CA 94703-3440
E-mail: ulypress@aol.com

ONE

Southern California

"The lands of the sun," according to an old Spanish proverb, "expand the soul." In the iconography of American life, sunshine is synonymous with Southern California. Life here is lived outdoors. Since the turn of the century the region has been cast as the country's Mediterranean shoreline, picturesque and leisurely. A land without water resources and lacking natural harbors, it has built its reputation on climate. Warm winters and cool summers, ocean breezes and desert warmth, have created a civilization whose foremost symbol is the palm tree.

Geographically Southern California is a place apart, a domain that the historian, Carey McWilliams, termed "an island on the land." Bounded by the Tehachapis to the north and the Sierra Nevada to the east, it is vast but solitary.

Constituting only half a state, Southern California is broader and more diverse than most nations are. Along its western border it nuzzles the Pacific; the interior is a region of piedmont and plain, once given over to cattle ranching and citrus cultivation, but presently being developed into one continuous megalopolis; to the east lies the desert, wind-burnished domain of piñon and palm, Joshua trees and juniper.

Southern California, paradoxically, is a desert facing an ocean. It's a region that has everything—luxurious beaches, dynamic cities, desolate sand dunes, and bald mountains. The highest peak in the contiguous United States rests here just 60 miles from the lowest point.

To capture this diversity in a guidebook, to confine the grandeur of the place within the pages of a single volume, is to square the circle. Los Angeles alone deserves several texts. Here it is covered in two sections—Chapter Two, which extends from Downtown to Hollywood, then out to the San Gabriel and San Fernando valleys; and Chapter Three, which combs the L.A. coastline from Long Beach to Malibu.

Chapter Four is dedicated to Orange County, ranging from the Pacific resorts of Newport Beach and Laguna Beach to theme parks such as Disneyland and Knott's Berry Farm. Then, in a stubborn attempt to find something still "hidden" in this sprawling suburb, it ventures out to the Santa Ana Mountains. San Diego, from city to coast to Mt. Palomar, is the subject of Chapter Five. The Central Coast, Chapter Six, sweeps from Ventura north to Santa Barbara and San Simeon, taking in Ojai and San Luis Obispo along the way.

The California desert is the subject of Chapters Seven and Eight, with the former devoted to the Inland Empire, Palm Springs, and the Sonora desert and the latter covering the central Mojave Desert, Death Valley, and the Sierra Nevada. General information on how, where, when, and why to visit Southern California appears in the chapter you are reading.

Throughout the book I have tried to convey a specific sense of place, providing information on hotels, restaurants, and sightseeing spots, then carrying you several strides further to the beaches, parks, trails, and unknown locales that make adventuring in Southern California high sport. Although the region's hidden realms are rapidly falling to the advance of suburbia, the soul of the place prevails.

What remains hidden in Southern California, underlying every aspect of its outward reality, is the mythology of the region. Southern California is a picture in your mind. Envision an orange—plump, round, and spilling over with the promise of good health—and you think of Southern California. Conversely, if you visualize an automobile, L.A.'s smog-shrouded freeways will occur just as naturally. Think of political conservatism—the presidencies of Richard Nixon and Ronald Reagan—and the nation's southwestern corner will flash to the fore. Or conjure a picture of Mexican culture, saturated with romantic imagery, and your daydreams will lead inevitably to the far edge of the Sunbelt.

To tour Southern California is to experience *déjà vu*. Regardless of your place of origin, the area exists, through the medium of film, somewhere in the psyche. More than being inseparable, myth and reality in the Southland feed on one another. Many times during my explorations I felt as if I were leading both of us back through our own pasts, to locations not yet real, but already behind us.

The first time I saw Southern California I was 18 years old, hitchhiking down the coast to Mexico. A child of the television age, I had grown up on the East Coast believing that major cities were lined with palm trees, the Wild West began in the Mojave and ended in the Sierra Nevada, and that all oceans resembled the Pacific. To kids like me all across the country, the architecture of Southern California represented the building styles of the world and the people of the Southland portrayed populations everywhere. I was hitchhiking along Memory Lane.

For all of us, Hollywood has elevated Southern California to a metaphor for living. The attributes that initially attracted movie makers to Los Angeles—its Italian climate, diverse geography, and leisurely pace—are precisely the features that Hollywood projects onto movie screens and television sets around the globe. It is the greatest act of cultural feedback in history. And it continues today.

To provide you with an unclouded picture, I have included historical information and factual details throughout the text in the hope that you can draw from them substantive ideas for planning and executing a trip. Regardless, you'll find in the end that truth in Southern California is built on a foundation of fiction. The region is living out its own legend. Follow my specific directions to a particular address and you'll discover that the romance rather than the reality of the place sweeps you along. It is the spirit of Southern California that entices and enthralls us all, holding us prisoners in paradise as long as we wish.

Any place the size of Southern California is bound to have several different climates. When it is also a region that ranges from seashore to desert to mountains and climbs from below sea level to over 14,000 feet, the problem is compounded.

▼▼▼▼▼▼▼▼▼
When to Go

SEASONS

In Southern California you can surf and ski in the same day. Temperatures sometimes vary 40 degrees between the beaches and the mountains. In the desert the mercury can fluctuate this drastically in a single location: a balmy 70-degree day can give way to a 30-degree night.

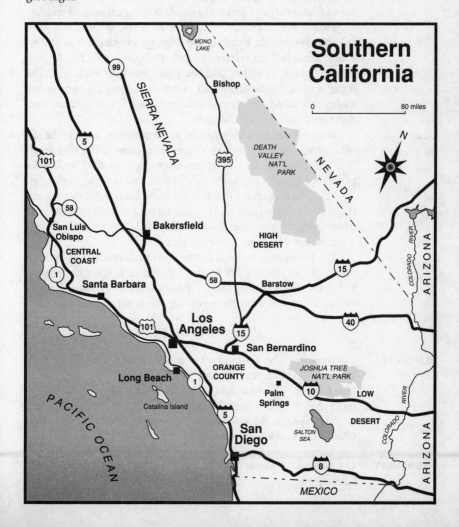

Along the Pacific and on the coastal plain, where most visitors concentrate, the weather corresponds to a Mediterranean climate with mild temperatures year-round. Because the coastal fog creates a natural form of air conditioning and insulation, the mercury rarely drops below 40° or rises above 80°. September and October are the hottest months, and December and January the coolest. In Los Angeles the average temperature is 75° during the warm period and about 50° in mid-winter.

Spring and particularly autumn are the ideal times to visit. Winter represents the rainy season, which extends from November to March, with the heaviest showers from December to February. During the rest of the year there is almost no rain. Summer is the peak tourist season, when large crowds can present problems. Like spring, it's also a period of frequent fog; during the morning and evening, fog banks from offshore blanket the coast, burning off around midday.

Most winter storms sweep in from the north, so the annual rainfall averages and the length of the rainy season diminish as you go south. Santa Barbara receives 17 inches of rain a year, Los Angeles averages about 15 inches, and San Diego gets only ten inches. The ocean air also creates significant moisture, keeping the average humidity around 65 percent and making some areas seem colder than the thermometer would indicate.

Smog is heaviest during August and September. Then in the autumn, the Santa Ana winds kick up out of the desert. Hot, dry winds from the northeast, they sometimes reach velocities of 35 to 50 miles per hour, blowing sand, fanning forest fires, and making people edgy.

It's no secret that the desert is hot in the summer, with temperatures often rising well above 100°. Spring is a particularly pretty time to visit, when the weather is cool and the wildflowers are in bloom. Autumn and winter are also quite pleasant.

The mountains are cold in winter, cool during spring and autumn, and surprisingly hot in summer. You can expect less precipitation than there is along the coast, but the higher elevations receive sufficient snow to make them popular winter ski areas.

CALENDAR OF EVENTS

JANUARY   **Los Angeles**   The Tournament of Roses Parade kicks off the Rose Bowl game in Pasadena on New Year's Day.
Low Desert   The Palm Springs International Film Festival features more than 100 films from 25 countries. Celebrities and pros gather in Palm Springs for the annual Bob Hope Desert Chrysler Golf Classic and Frank Sinatra Invitational.

FEBRUARY   **Los Angeles**   Chinese New Year celebrations snake through L.A.'s Chinatown.

Orange County Arts and crafts displays highlight the **Laguna Beach Winter Fest**. In Dana Point the **Festival of the Whales** features a concert series, sporting competitions, a film fest, and a street fair.
Low Desert The **Riverside County Fair & National Date Festival** at Indio Fairgrounds features camel races and a diaper derby.

MARCH

Orange County The **Fiesta de las Golondrinas** commemorates the return of the swallows to Mission San Juan Capistrano. Meanwhile along the coast crowds gather for seasonal **grunion runs**.
San Diego The **Ocean Beach Kite Festival**, with contests for flying and decorating kites, takes place at Ocean Beach.
Central Coast Stars and stargazers gather for **Santa Barbara's International Film Festival**.
Low Desert Palm Springs hosts the **Nabisco Dinah Shore LPGA Golf Tournament**. Borrego Springs holds a **Circle of Arts** art show and sale.

APRIL

Los Angeles **Easter Sunrise Services** are marked at the famed Hollywood Bowl. In Little Tokyo **Buddha's Birthday** is celebrated; along nearby Olvera Street the **Blessing of the Animals**, a Mexican tradition, is re-enacted. In Palmdale the **Lilac Festival** signals the advent of spring.
Los Angeles Coast Race car buffs train their binoculars on the **Long Beach Grand Prix**.
San Diego **Lakeside Western Days** features a parade and carnival.
Low Desert The **Peg-Leg Liars Contest**, a tall-tale competition, takes place in Borrego Springs. Hemet's **Ramona Pageant** depicts Early California history with American Indian rituals, music, and dance.

MAY

Los Angeles Dancers, revelers, and mariachi bands around Olvera Street and East Los Angeles mark **Cinco de Mayo**, the festival celebrating the Battle of Puebla in the French-Mexican War. The UCLA **Mardi Gras** offers games, entertainment, and food.
San Diego Carlsbad hosts the first of the semiannual **Village Fair** with hundreds of exhibits, an elephant ride, petting zoo, and countless foodstands. Old Town celebrates **Cinco de Mayo** with mariachis, traditional Mexican folk dancers, food, and displays. The **Wildflower Festival** blossoms in Julian.
Central Coast Ventura observes the **Ventura Chamber Music Festival** with a series of chamber music concerts situated in various historic landmarks.
High Desert A parade, steer-roping contest, barbecues, and crafts displays mark **Mule Days** in Bishop.

JUNE

Los Angeles **Gay Pride Week** is celebrated here by a parade through West Hollywood.

San Diego   The National Shakespeare Festival starts its summer run at Balboa Park's Old Globe Theater.

Central Coast   A parade and other festivities highlight Santa Barbara's Summer Solstice Celebration. Lompoc sponsors an annual Flower Festival. The Ojai Music Festival includes concerts of classical and new music.

JULY

Los Angeles   The Hollywood Bowl Summer Festival explodes with a Fourth of July concert.

Los Angeles Coast   Every Thursday evening during July the Santa Monica Pier Twilight Dance Series features a variety of live music from reggae to western swing. Surfers hang ten at the International Surf Festival on Hermosa, Manhattan, Torrance, and Redondo beaches.

Orange County   The Festival of Arts and Pageant of the Masters, one of Southern California's most notable events, occurs in Laguna Beach.

Central Coast   Santa Barbara is busy with its Greek Festival.

Low Desert   Big Bear Lake remembers Old Miners Days with week-long festivities featuring a chili cook-off, parades, and dances.

AUGUST

Los Angeles   Little Tokyo's Nissei Week honors Japanese-American culture with parades, dances, music, and martial arts demonstrations.

San Diego   Crowds sprout up at the Julian Weed Show for an artful display of native plants.

Central Coast   Santa Barbara rounds up everyone for the Old Spanish Days Fiesta, Rodeo, and Stock Show. Food, exhibits, and dancing highlight the Festa Italiana, also in Santa Barbara.

SEPTEMBER

Los Angeles   Los Angeles County Fair, the nation's largest county fair, offers music, food, carnival rides, livestock competitions, and just about everything else you can imagine.

San Diego   The Cabrillo Festival in Point Loma commemorates the discovery of the California coast by Europeans.

Central Coast   Ojai applauds Mexican Independence Day with a grand fiesta. Solvang celebrates Danish Days with food, music, and dance.

OCTOBER

San Diego   In the San Diego area, the La Mesa Oktoberfest features Bavarian bands, beer gardens, and arts and crafts.

Central Coast   Pismo Beach, the "clam capital of the world," presents its annual Pismo Beach Clam Festival with feasting, live entertainment, and arts and crafts booths.

Los Angeles Coast   The St. Katherine Greek Festival in Redondo Beach is a three-day celebration of Greek food, dance, and culture.

Low Desert An arts and crafts fair, barbecue, and parade mark the Borrego Springs' **Desert Festival**.

High Desert Parades, parties, and gunfights commemorate **Calico Days** at Calico Ghost Town near Barstow.

Los Angeles Santa arrives early at the **Hollywood Christmas Parade** and is joined by television and movie stars. In Pasadena, the rollicking **Doo Dah Parade** parodies the city's staid Rose Parade.

San Diego Carlsbad hosts the year's second **Village Fair** (see May listing).

High Desert The **Death Valley Annual Encampment** honors desert pioneers with gold panning contests, liars' competitions, and historical programs.

NOVEMBER

During December Several coastal communities, including Marina del Rey, Naples, Huntington Beach, and San Diego, mark the season with **Christmas Boat Parades**. Hispanic communities in Los Angeles, San Luis Obispo, San Diego, and throughout the Southland celebrate the Mexican yuletide with **Las Posadas**.

DECEMBER

▼▼▼▼▼▼▼▼▼▼▼
Several agencies provide free information to travelers. The California Office of Tourism will help guide you to areas throughout the state. ~ 801 K Street, Suite 1600, Sacramento, CA 95814; 800-862-2543. You'll find information at the Los Angeles Visitors and Convention Bureau. ~ 633 West 5th Street, Suite 6000, Los Angeles, CA 90071; 213-624-7300. The Anaheim Area Visitors and Convention Bureau can be useful. ~ 800 West Katella Avenue, Anaheim, CA 92802; 714-999-8999. In San Diego the San Diego Convention and Visitors Bureau might be a good source. ~ 401 B Street, Suite 1400, San Diego, CA 92101; 619-236-1212. The Palm Springs Desert Resorts Convention and Visitors Bureau can assist travelers. ~ 69-930 Highway 111, Suite 201, Rancho Mirage, CA 92270; 619-770-9000. Also consult local chambers of commerce and information centers, which are mentioned in the area chapters.

Before You Go

VISITORS CENTERS

There are two important guidelines when deciding what to take on a trip. The first is as true for Los Angeles and Southern California as anywhere in the world—pack light. Dress styles here are relatively informal unless you're planning to spend all of your time in Beverly Hills (in which case you should pack an Armani suit and a Dior dress!) Otherwise, try to keep it casual. The airlines allow two suitcases and a carry-on bag.

The second rule is to prepare for temperature variations. While day-time temperatures often hover in the mid-70s, evenings can bring on temperatures as low as 30°, especially in Death Valley. A warm

PACKING

sweater and jacket are absolute necessities year-round, in addition to shorts and T-shirts. Pack a raincoat if you're planning to visit from December to February. And if you're traveling in the high mountains in winter, carry cold weather clothing. Drinking water, flashlights, blankets, and extra gas are essential requirements when you're traveling long distances with very few amenities along the way.

LODGING   Overnight accommodations in Southern California are as varied as the region itself. They range from highrise hotels and neon motels to hostels and bed-and-breakfast inns. Check through the various regional chapters and you're bound to find something to fit your budget and taste.

The neon motels offer bland facilities at low prices and are excellent if you're economizing or don't plan to spend much time in the room. Larger hotels often lack intimacy, but provide such conveniences as restaurants and shops in the lobby. My personal preference is for historic hotels, those slightly faded classics that offer charm and tradition at moderate cost. Bed-and-breakfast inns present an opportunity to stay in a homelike setting. Like hostels, they are an excellent way to meet fellow travelers; unlike hostels, Southern California's country inns are quite expensive.

Southern California is an extremely popular area, particularly in summer, and facilities fill up quickly—reserve well in advance.

To help you decide on a place to stay, I've organized the accommodations not only by area but also according to price (prices listed are for double occupancy during the high season; prices may decrease in low season). *Budget* hotels generally are less than $50 per night for two people; the rooms are clean and comfortable, but not luxurious. The *moderately* priced hotels run $50 to $90 and provide larger rooms, plusher furniture, and more attractive surroundings. At a *deluxe* hotel you can expect to spend between $90 and $130 double. You'll check into a spacious, well-appointed room with all modern facilities; downstairs the lobby will be a fashionable affair, usually with a restaurant, lounge, and cluster of shops. If you want to spend your time (and money) in the city's very finest hotels, try an *ultra-deluxe* facility, which will include all the amenities and cost more than $130.

DINING   It seems as if Southern California has more restaurants than people, particularly in Los Angeles. To establish a pattern for this parade of dining places, I've organized them according to location and cost. Restaurants listed in this book offer lunch and dinner unless otherwise noted.

Within a particular chapter, the restaurants are categorized geographically, with each restaurant entry describing the establishment as budget, moderate, deluxe, or ultra-deluxe in price. Dinner entrées at *budget* restaurants usually cost $8 or less. The ambience is informal café-style and the crowd is often a local one. *Moderately* priced restaurants range between $8 and $16 at dinner and offer pleasant surroundings, a more varied menu, and a slower pace. *Deluxe* establishments tab their entrées above $16, featuring sophisticated cuisines, plush decor, and more personalized service. *Ultra-deluxe* dining rooms, where $24 will only get you started, are gourmet gathering places in which cooking (one hopes) is a fine art form and service is a way of life.

Breakfast and lunch menus vary less in price from restaurant to restaurant. Even deluxe kitchens usually offer light breakfasts and lunch sandwiches, which place them within a few dollars of their budget-minded competitors. These early meals can be a good time to test expensive restaurants.

TRAVELING WITH CHILDREN

Visiting Southern California with kids can be a real adventure, and if properly planned, a truly enjoyable one. To ensure that your trip will feature the joy, rather than the strain, of parenthood, remember a few important guidelines.

Use a travel agent to help with arrangements; they can reserve spacious bulkhead seats on airlines and determine which flights are least crowded. Also plan to bring everything you need on board— diapers, food, toys, and extra clothes for kids and parents alike. If the trip to Southern California involves a long journey, plan to relax and do very little during the first few days.

Always allow extra time for getting places. Book reservations well in advance and make sure the hotel has the extra crib, cot, or bed you require. It's smart to ask for a room at the end of the hall to cut down on noise. Be aware that many bed-and-breakfast inns do not allow children.

Most towns have stores that carry diapers, food, and other essentials; in cities and larger towns, 7-11 stores are sometimes open all night (check the yellow pages for addresses). Hotels often provide access to babysitters, or check the yellow pages for state licensed and bonded babysitting agencies. A first-aid kit is always a good idea. Consult with your pediatrician for special medicines and dosages for colds and diarrhea.

Finding activities to interest children in Southern California couldn't be easier. Especially helpful in deciding on the day's outing is the "Calendar" section of the Sunday *Los Angeles Times*.

WOMEN TRAVELING ALONE

Several Southern California communities offer women's resource centers, referral numbers, and health centers. In the Los Angeles and Orange County area consult the **Women's Yellow Pages** (818-995-6646) or **Family Planning Associates** (213-738-7283). Feminist bookstores are also good sources of information.

GAY & LESBIAN TRAVELERS

Although Southern California is often known for its social and political conservatism, the tolerance that accompanies the booming entertainment industry makes certain areas inviting and exciting for gay and lesbian travelers. Southern California's largest gay area is centered in and around West Hollywood, the first city in the nation to boast a gay city government. Here you'll find hotels, shops, restaurants, and nightclubs catering to gay and lesbian travelers. (See "West Hollywood Gay Scene" in Chapter Two.)

Farther south, San Diego's Hillcrest district is the focus of that city's gay scene, with guesthouses, stores, and cafes. (See "San Diego Gay Scene" in Chapter Five.)

An oasis in more ways than one, Palm Springs beckons to the gay or lesbian traveler from the heart of the desert. While the resort town may be more famous as the home of previous Republican mayor Sonny Bono and the spring break destination of rowdy college students, it's also the locale of the largely lesbian Dinah Shore Golf Tournament. (See "Palm Springs Gay Scene" in Chapter Seven.)

There are other gay and lesbian bars and nightclubs sprinkled throughout Southern California.

If you're a fan of cozy lodgings, you can arrange book a room ahead of time by calling **Caritas Bed & Breakfast Network**, a national reservation service that works exclusively with gay- and lesbian-owned bed and breakfasts. ~ 75 East Wacker Drive, Chicago, IL 60601; 312-857-0801, 800-227-4827, fax 312-857-0805. After arriving in town, visitors may want to make their first stop the **Los Angeles Gay & Lesbian Center**, a resource center with informative bulletin boards, brochures, counseling, and, for the long-term visitor, job placement services. Should you get slapped with one of L.A.'s famous jaywalking tickets, they also offer legal services. ~ 1625 North Schrader Boulevard; 213-993-7400. Pick up a copy of the *Edge*, which comes out twice a month—almost as often as the average Sunset Strip pedestrian—and covers the goings-on in L.A. County. ~ 6434 Santa Monica Boulevard, West Hollywood; 213-962-6994. Also look for the bimonthly *Nightlife Entertainment Magazine*; it's full of movie, theater, and club reviews. ~ 6363 Santa Monica Boulevard, West Hollywood; 213-462-5400. Women may consult *Female FYI*, a monthly publication based in L.A. that covers the statewide entertainment scene. Along with reviews, interviews, health, and travel, the magazine has a comprehensive club guide and calendar of events. ~ 8033 Sunset Boulevard, Suite 2013, Los Angeles; 310-657-5592.

For information on services aimed at gay travelers, see "Gay and lesbian travelers" in the index.

In San Diego, get a copy of *Gay & Lesbian Times*, a weekly publication with local and world news, business, sports, weather, and arts sections. It also contains a calendar of events, and a directory of gay-friendly businesses and establishments. ~ 3911 Normal Street, San Diego; 619-299-6397. *Update* is another weekly which covers gay and lesbian news, and gives you a feel of San Diego and Southern

California. ~ 2801 4th Avenue, San Diego; 619-299-4104. **The Lesbian and Gay Men's Community Center** is open for drop-in counseling, mental health services, or support groups—or stop by on Thursday nights for bingo. Closed Sunday. ~ 3916 Normal Street, San Diego; 619-692-2077. The Center also runs a **phone line** that provides information around the clock about upcoming events, community resources and visitor information. ~ 619-294-4636.

In Palm Springs, look for the bimonthly *MEGA-Scene* for worldwide and local gay news. It also has maps that come in handy when you're attempting to visit all the highlights within the folds of its entertainment guide. ~ 611 South Palm Canyon Drive #7-B, Palm Springs; 619-327-5178. *The Bottom Line*, a bimonthly magazine, publishes a detailed roster of desert eateries, bars, hotels, and nightspots that gay travelers will find essential. It also includes reviews of movies, books, and theater. ~ 1243 Gene Autry Trail, Suite 121, Palm Springs; 619-323-0552. *Hijinx*, a tour guide for the Palm Springs/Cathedral City gay scene, comes out yearly with listings of hotels, bars, restaurants, and things to do in the area. Maps are also included. ~ Attn: Georgia Peach Publications, 15685 Palm Drive #3-B, Desert Hot Springs; 619-329-2421. **Palm Springs Lesbian & Gay Pride** has live people manning this 24-hour referral line, which is perfect for travelers in search of gay-friendly dining, lodging, and organizations. ~ 619-322-8769. For support groups, rap sessions, and monthly meetings in the desert area, **P-FLAG Palm Springs** is the place to call. ~ 68277 Farrell Lane, Cathedral City; 619-321-0135.

SENIOR TRAVELERS

Southern California is ideal for older vacationers. The mild climate makes touring in the off-season possible, helping to cut down on expenses. Many museums, theaters, restaurants, and hotels have senior discounts (with a driver's license, Medicare card, or other age-identifying card). Ask your travel agent when booking reservations.

The **American Association of Retired Persons** (AARP) offers members travel discounts and provides escorted tours. ~ 3200 East Carson Street, Lakewood, CA 90712; 310-496-2277. For those 60 or over, **Elderhostel** provides educational programs in California. ~ 75 Federal Street, Boston, MA 02110; 617-426-7788.

Be extra careful about health matters. Bring along any medications you ordinarily use, together with the prescriptions for obtaining more. Consider carrying a medical record with you—including your medical history and current medical status as well as your doctor's name, phone number, and address. Also be sure to confirm that your insurance covers you away from home.

DISABLED TRAVELERS

California stands at the forefront of social reform for travelers with disabilities. During the past decade, the state has responded with a series of progressive legislative measures to the needs of the blind, wheelchair-bound, and others.

The **Department of Motor Vehicles** provides special parking permits for the disabled (check the phone book for the nearest location). Many local bus lines and other public transit facilities are wheelchair accessible.

There are also agencies in Southern California assisting persons with disabilities. For tips and information about the Los Angeles area, contact the **Westside Center for Independent Living.** ~ 12901 Venice Boulevard, Los Angeles; 310-390-3611. In the San Diego area, try the **Access Center.** ~ 1295 University Avenue, Suite 10, San Diego; 619-293-3500.

There are numerous organizations offering general information. Among these are:

The **Society for the Advancement of Travel for the Handicapped.** ~ 347 5th Avenue, #610, New York, NY 10016; 212-447-7284, fax 212-725-8253.

The **Travel Information Center.** ~ Corman Building, 12th Street and Tabor Road, Philadelphia, PA 19141; 215-456-9603.

Mobility International USA. ~ P.O. Box 10767, Eugene, OR 97440; 503-343-1284.

Flying Wheels Travel. ~ P.O. Box 382, Owatonna, MN 55060; 800-535-6790.

Travelin' Talk, a network of people and organizations, also provides assistance. ~ P.O. Box 3534, Clarksville, TN 37043; 615-552-6670.

Or consult the comprehensive guidebook, *Access to the World—A Travel Guide for the Handicapped*, by Louise Weiss (Holt, Rinehart & Winston).

Be sure to check in advance when making room reservations. Many hotels and motels feature facilities for travelers in wheelchairs.

FOREIGN TRAVELERS

Passports and Visas Most foreign visitors need a passport and tourist visa to enter the United States. Contact your nearest U.S. Embassy or Consulate well in advance to obtain a visa and to check on any other entry requirements.

Customs Requirements Foreign travelers are allowed to carry in the following: 200 cigarettes (1 carton), 50 cigars, or 2 kilograms (4.4 pounds) of smoking tobacco; one liter of alcohol for personal use only (you must be 21 years of age to bring in alcohol); and US$100 worth of duty-free gifts that can include an additional quantity of 100 cigars. You may bring in any amount of currency, but must fill out a form if you bring in over US$10,000. Carry any prescription drugs in clearly marked containers. (You may have to produce a written prescription or doctor's statement for the custom's officer.) Meat or meat products, seeds, plants, fruits and narcotics are not allowed to be brought into the United States. Contact the **United**

States Customs Service for further information. ~ 1301 Constitution Avenue NW, Washington, DC 20229; 202-927-6724.

Driving If you plan to rent a car, an international driver's license should be obtained before arriving in the United States. Some car rental agencies require both a foreign license and an international driver's license. Many also require a lessee to be at least 25 years of age; all require a major credit card.

Currency United States money is based on the dollar. Bills generally come in denominations of $1, $5, $10, $20, $50, and $200. Every dollar is divided into 100 cents. Coins are the penny (1 cent), nickel (5 cents), dime (10 cents) and quarter (25 cents). Half-dollar and dollar coins are rarely used. You may not use foreign currency to purchase goods and services in the United States. Consider buying traveler's checks in dollar amounts. You may also use credit cards affiliated with an American company such as Interbank, Barclay Card, VISA, and American Express.

Electricity Electric outlets use currents of 110 volts, 60 cycles. For appliances made for other electrical systems, you need a transformer or other adapter.

Weights and Measurements The United States uses the English system of weights and measures. American units and their metric equivalents are: 1 inch = 2.5 centimeters; 1 foot (12 inches) = 0.3 meter; 1 yard (3 feet) = 0.9 meter; 1 mile (5280 feet) = 1.6 kilometers; 1 ounce = 28 grams; 1 pound (16 ounces) = 0.45 kilogram; 1 quart (liquid) = 0.9 liter.

Outdoor Adventures

CAMPING

The state government oversees 285 camping facilities. Amenities at each campground vary, but there is a standard day-use fee of $5 per vehicle plus $14 per campsite ($12 in winter). For a complete listing of all state-run campgrounds, send $2 for the *Official Guide to California State Parks* to the **California Department of Parks and Recreation.** ~ P.O. Box 942896, Sacramento, CA 94296; 916-653-6995. For campground reservations call 800-444-7275.

For general information on National Park campgrounds, contact the **National Park Service.** ~ Western Information Center, Fort Mason, Building 201, San Francisco, CA 94123; 415-556-0561. To reserve a National Park campsite call the individual park directly or call 800-365-2267.

Reservations for **U.S. Forest Service** campsites must be made by calling DESTINET at 800-365-2267. ~ 630 Sansome Street, San Francisco, CA 94111; 415-705-2874. A fee is charged at these facilities and the length of stay varies from park to park. It's best to reserve in advance, though many parks keep some sites open to be filled daily on a first-come, first-served basis.

Southern California also offers numerous municipal, county, and private facilities. See the "Beaches & Parks" sections in each area chapter for the locations of these campgrounds.

PERMITS   For camping and hiking in the wilderness and primitive areas of national forests, a wilderness permit is required. Permits are free and are issued for a specific period of time, which varies according to the wilderness area. Information is available through the **U.S. Forest Service.** ~ 630 Sansome Street, San Francisco, CA 94111; 415-705-2874. You can obtain permits from ranger stations and regional information centers, as described in the "Beaches & Parks" sections in each area chapter.

FISHING   For current information on the fishing season and state license fees, contact the **Department of Fish and Game.** ~ 3211 S Street, Sacramento, CA 95816; 916-227-2244.

TWO

Los Angeles

Naturally it began as fiction. California, according to the old Spanish novel, was a mythical island populated by Amazons and filled with gold, a place "very near to the terrestrial paradise." The man who set off to pursue this dream was Juan Rodríguez Cabrillo. The year was 1542 and Cabrillo, a Portuguese navigator in the employ of the Spanish crown, sailed north from Mexico, pressing forward the boundaries of empire.

Failing to find either royalty or gilded cities, Cabrillo discovered a land which in the contrary course of its history produced kings of industries not yet invented and cities wealthy beyond the imaginings of even the conquistadors. California, a mythical land indeed, with a cultural capital called Los Angeles.

If California is the land of dreams, L.A. is the dream factory, that worldly workshop where the impossible takes form. Since its founding as a pueblo in 1781, the city has continually recast itself as a promised land, health haven, agricultural paradise, movie capital, and world financial center.

Second largest city in the country, it rests in a bowl surrounded by five mountain ranges and an ocean and holds within its ambit sandy beaches, tawny hills, and wind-ruffled deserts. At night from the air Los Angeles is a massive gridwork, an illuminated checkerboard extending from the ink-colored Pacific to the dark fringe of the mountains.

The religious dream of this "city of angels" began way back in 1769 when Padre Junípero Serra and Gaspar de Portolá ventured north from Mexico to establish the first of California's 21 missions. Two years later Mission San Gabriel Archangel was founded several miles from Los Angeles.

The first settlers comprised a mixed bag of Spaniards, Indians, mestizos, and blacks, among them a surprising number of women and children. They planted vines, olives, and grains, and spent 50 years expanding their population to 700.

Today, with a census numbering almost four million urban dwellers and over nine million throughout Los Angeles County, it remains a multicultural city. In Los Angeles minorities are becoming the majority. Over 80 different languages are spoken in the schools. Neighborhoods are given over to Latinos, blacks, Chinese, Japanese, Koreans, Jews, Laotians, Filipinos, and Armenians. There are gay communities and nouveau riche neighborhoods, not to mention personality sects such as low riders, Valley girls, punks, and hippies.

One group which never became part of this sun-baked melting pot were the Indians. For American Indians, Padre Serra's dream of a New World became a nightmare. Before the advent of Westerners, as many as 300,000 indigenous people populated California. Around Los Angeles the Gabrieleños held sway.

Like other groups west of the Sierra Nevada they were hunter-gatherers, exploiting the boundless resources of the ocean, picking wild plants, and stalking local prey. Primitive by comparison with the agricultural tribes of the American Southwest, they fashioned dome-shaped dwellings from woven grasses and wooden poles.

The conquistadors eventually overcame American Indian resistance, forcibly converting these native spiritualists to Catholicism and pressing them into slavery. Eventually American Indians built a chain of missions that formed the backbone of the Spanish empire and broke the back of the Indian nation. While their slaves were dying in terrible numbers, the Spanish, dangerously overextended, fell plague to problems throughout the empire. Finally, in 1821 Mexico declared its independence and seized California from Spain.

Then in 1846 American settlers, with assistance from the United States government, fomented the Bear Flag Revolt. That summer Captain John C. Fremont pursued Governor Pío Pico from Los Angeles south to San Juan Capistrano, forcing the Mexican official to flee across the border. Finally in February, 1848, at a home in the San Fernando Valley, a treaty was signed and the Stars and Stripes flew over California.

The Latinos, who were driven from Los Angeles, now number almost 40 percent of the population and represent the largest concentration of Mexicans outside Mexico. The countryside they departed was a region of ranchos, land grants often measuring 75 square miles, which were used for cattle ranching.

The metropolis they now inhabit will be the world's twelfth largest city by the turn of the century. Once a pastoral realm of caballeros and señoritas, greater metropolitan L.A. now leads the nation in aerospace, boasts one of the country's largest concentrations of high-tech industries and possesses the fastest growing major port in the country. In raw economic terms it is the twelfth largest "nation" in the world, with a gross national product higher than Australia, Switzerland, and India.

Disparagingly referred to as the "cow counties" by Northern Californians in the 19th century, metropolitan L.A. is a megalopolis unified by a convoluted freeway system—a congeries of cloverleafs, overpasses, and eight-lane speedways that lies snarled with traffic much of the day.

A distinctly Western city, it has grown *out* toward the open range, not *up* within tightly defined perimeters. A collection of suburbs in search of a city, it has broken all the rules, leading urban experts to describe Los Angeles as a series of constellations creating a metropolitan galaxy. A schizophrenic among cities, it is comprised of many facets, many cities. In fact, there are 88 incorporated cities in Los Angeles County, as well as 1500 miles of freeways and 19,000 miles of surface streets.

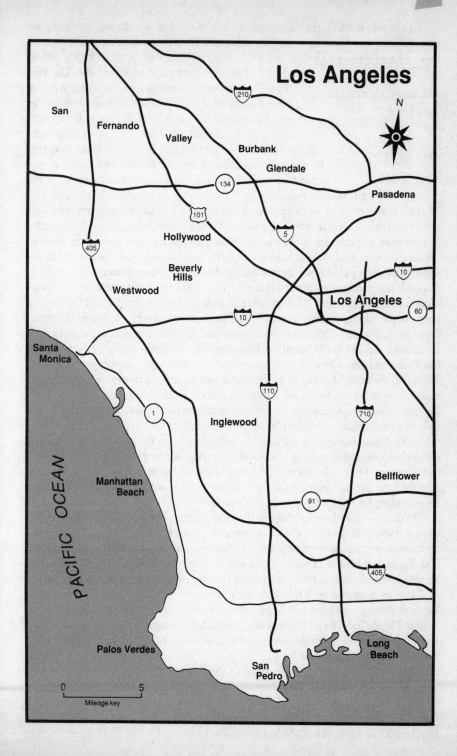

To simplify matters, the urban quiltwork is divided in this chapter into eight geographic sections. Creating an arc around central *Downtown* is *Greater Los Angeles*, an expansive area that sweeps from Inglewood to East Los Angeles, then north to Silver Lake. The *Wilshire District* forms a narrow corridor along Wilshire Boulevard, running west from Downtown toward the ocean. *Hollywood* and *Beverly Hills* require little introduction; both border the *Westside*, an upscale area comprised of Westwood and Bel Air. To the northeast, bounded by mountains and desert, lies the *San Gabriel Valley*, whose cultural center is Pasadena. Northwest of Los Angeles is the *San Fernando Valley*.

> The city that today has a scandalously deficient transit system once possessed the finest electric trolley network in the world.

This entire territory is a region with unhealthy air, healthy crime statistics, and one of the highest divorce rates in the world. Known for traffic and smog, Los Angeles has the most polluted air in the country. One out of every three days some place in the metropolitan area violates federal air quality standards. In L.A. the proverbial silver lining in every cloud may be just that—a layer of airborne metal.

Little more than a century ago this mega-city was a tough Western town. The population totaled less than 3000 but L.A. still managed to average a murder a day. By the time the transcontinental railroad connected California with the rest of the country in 1869, Southern California's economy trailed far behind its northern counterpart.

During the 1870s the South began to rise. The Southern Pacific railroad linked San Pedro and Santa Monica with interior valleys where citrus cultivation was flourishing. Southern California's rich agriculture and salubrious climate led to a "health rush." Magazines and newspapers romanticized the region's history and beauty, leading one writer to proclaim that "if the Pilgrim fathers had landed on the Pacific Coast instead of the Atlantic, little old New York wouldn't be on the map."

Santa Monica became a fashionable resort town and the port of San Pedro expanded exponentially, making Los Angeles a major shipping point. Around the turn of the century Henry Huntington, nephew of railroad baron Collis P. Huntington, established the Pacific Electric Railway Company and created a series of land booms by extending his red trolley lines in all directions.

When oil was discovered early in the 20th century, Southern California also became a prime drilling region. Oil wells sprang up along Huntington Beach, Long Beach, and San Pedro, adding to coastal coffers while destroying the aesthetics of the shore. The Signal Hill field in Long Beach, tapped by Shell Oil in the 1920s, turned out to be the richest oil deposit in the world and Los Angeles became the largest oil port.

Little wonder that by 1925, flush with petroleum just as the age of the automobile was shifting into gear, Los Angeles became the most motor-conscious city in the world. The Pacific Coast Highway was completed during the 1930s, "auto camps" and "tourist cabins" mushroomed, and motorists began exploring Southern California in unprecedented numbers.

This burgeoning city, with its back to the desert, had already solved its water problems in 1913 when the Los Angeles Aqueduct, bleeding water from the distant Owens Valley, was completed. An engineering marvel, stretching almost 250 miles from the Sierra Nevada, the controversial pipeline supplied enough water to enable Los Angeles to annex the entire San Fernando Valley.

Ironically, the semi-arid Los Angeles Basin was once underwater. Built by volcanic activity, the geologic area is so young that the Palos Verdes Peninsula was a chain of offshore islands just one million years ago. Earthquakes still rattle the region with disturbing frequency. The last colossal quake was back in the 1850s when almost every building in Los Angeles collapsed. In 1971 an earthquake in the San Fernando Valley killed 64 people and caused more than $1 billion damage. Then, on January 17, 1994, a 6.8 magnitude earthquake rocked the Los Angeles basin. Centered again in the San Fernando Valley, this time in Northridge, it resulted in 61 deaths and over $10 billion in damage.

Perhaps with an eye to earthquakes, not to mention Southern California's flaky reputation, architect Frank Lloyd Wright developed a theory of "continental tilt" by which all the loose nuts slid into Hollywood. Its penchant for health, fitness, and glamour have always rendered L.A.'s hold on reality a bit shaky, but it is the city's appeal to religious sects that has particularly added to its aura of unreality.

The first book printed in Los Angeles was a religious tract by a heretical Scotsman. Aimee Semple McPherson preached her Four Square Gospel here in the 1920s and other groups have included everything from the Theosophists and Krishnamurtis to the Mankind United and Mighty I Am movements. Televangelism is now big business throughout the area and Hollywood serves as headquarters for Scientology.

In the end L.A. is a city that one comes to love or scorn. Or perhaps to love and scorn. It is either Tinseltown or the Big Orange, Smogville or the City of Angels. To some it is the Rome of the West, a megalopolis whose economic might renders it an imperial power. To others Los Angeles is the American Athens, an international center for cinema, music, and art.

Culturally speaking, the sun rises in the west. L.A., quirky but creative, sets the trends for the entire nation. It has been admired and self-admiring for so long that the city has swallowed its own story, become a reflection of its mythology. Beautifully crazed, pulsing with electric energy, Los Angeles is living its own dream.

▼▼▼▼▼▼▼▼
Downtown

Contrary to the opinion of Los Angeles bashers, the city does indeed possess a center. Ever since the town was settled in 1781, the focus of the community has been near Olvera Street and the Civic Center, along the Los Angeles River.

While there's barely enough water in the river these days to cause a ripple, the Downtown district is inundated with people. About 20,000 people live in this vital neighborhood and more than 200,000 commuters arrive daily. Adding to the smog and congestion, they also make Downtown the center for politics, finance, and culture.

SIGHTS

For walking tours of the Downtown district contact the **Los Angeles Conservancy**. Closed Saturday and Sunday. ~ 727 West 7th Street, Suite 925; 213-623-2489.

To help you navigate around this urban core, I've divided the district into several sections: Olvera Street, Chinatown, Little Tokyo, the Civic Center, and Central Downtown (which includes the financial district). In exploring each neighborhood, remember that the DASH shuttle, a purple-striped minibus, serves most of Downtown for just 25 cents a ride. Downtown is also served by the **Metro Red Line,** Los Angeles' first subway. Starting at Union Station, the 4.4-mile line runs between Union Station and MacArthur Park, at the corner of Wilshire and Alvarado boulevards.

CIVIC CENTER   Art and politics have always been odd bedfellows, but they make a cozy couple around the Los Angeles Civic Center. Here an impressive group of government buildings combines with an array of museums to create a complex well worth touring.

The centerpiece of the ensemble is **City Hall,** a vintage 1928 building. Rendered famous by the old "Dragnet" television show, this pyramid-topped edifice is also a frequent backdrop in many contemporary movies. The tile-and-marble rotunda on the third floor is a study in governmental architecture. But the most impressive feature is the **observation deck** on the 27th floor, from which you can enjoy a 360° view of Los Angeles' smog banks. At last report, the observation deck and all floors above the fifth were closed indefinitely for restoration. ~ 200 North Spring Street; 213-485-2121.

Those who report on City Hall reside across the street at the **Los Angeles Times Building.** One of the nation's largest and finest newspapers, the *Times* sits in a classic 1934 moderne-style building to which latter day architects, in a fit of ego and insanity, added a glass box monstrosity that appears to be devouring the original. The older structure, housing the newspaper, is open to guided tours; the glass accretion contains corporate offices. Closed Saturday and Sunday. ~ 202 West 1st Street; 213-237-5000.

Cultural counterpoint to these centers of power is the nearby **Music Center.** Gathered into one stunningly designed complex are the **Dorothy Chandler Pavilion,** a marble-and-black-glass music hall which hosts the opera and symphony; the **Mark Taper Forum,** a world-renowned theater that presents contemporary and experimental drama; and the **Ahmanson Theatre,** a 2000-seat auditorium where touring Broadway plays are staged. Not to be outdone, the visual arts are represented by a pulsating fountain with more than 100 rhythmically timed streams. Guided tours are available. ~ Grand Avenue between 1st and Temple streets; 213-972-7211.

This last art form reaches flood tide at the **Museum of Contemporary Art.** Affectionately dubbed "the MOCA," this ultramodern showplace was designed by Japanese architect Arata Isozaki. It's an exotic mix of red sandstone and pyramidal skylights with a sunken courtyard. The galleries consist of expansive open spaces displaying a variety of traveling exhibits and the works of Mark Rothko, Robert Rauschenberg, Jackson Pollock, and others. Closed Monday. Admission. ~ 250 South Grand Avenue; 213-621-2766.

It's the noisiest museum in the world. The **Los Angeles Children's Museum,** with countless hands-on and hands-all-over-everything ex-

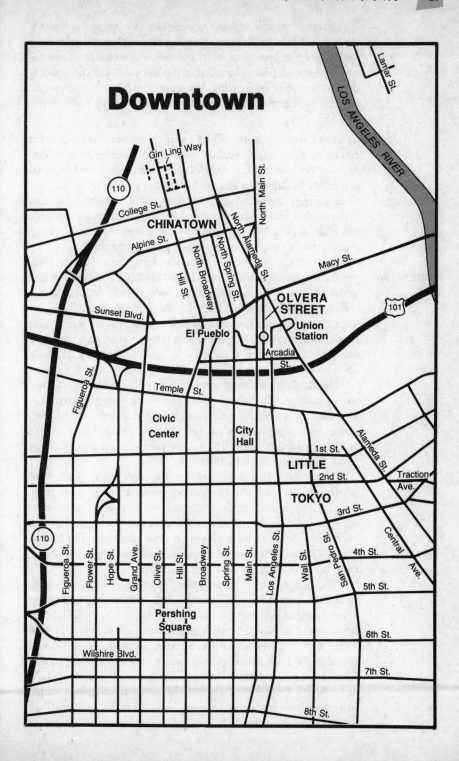

Downtown

Lamar St.

LOS ANGELES RIVER

110

Gin Ling Way

College St.

CHINATOWN

Alpine St.

North Main St.

North Alameda St.

North Broadway

North Spring St.

Hill St.

Macy St.

Sunset Blvd.

OLVERA STREET

101

El Pueblo

Union Station

Arcadia St.

Figueroa St.

Temple St.

Civic Center

City Hall

1st St.

Alameda St.

LITTLE

2nd St.

Traction Ave.

TOKYO

3rd St.

110

Figueroa St.

Flower St.

Hope St.

Grand Ave.

Olive St.

Hill St.

Broadway

Spring St.

Main St.

Los Angeles St.

Wall St.

San Pedro St.

Central Ave.

4th St.

5th St.

Pershing Square

6th St.

Wilshire Blvd.

7th St.

8th St.

hibits, is probably the happiest as well. There's a bus and police motorcycle for kids to ride; make-up rooms for them to paint their faces; a hospital bed, x-ray table, and dentist chair for practicing future professions; plus a recording studio and video cameras for children to tape their own antics. Always open weekends; open weekdays by appointment only. Admission. ~ 310 North Main Street; 213-687-8800.

CENTRAL DOWNTOWN While social classes may be miles apart culturally, their neighborhoods often stand shoulder to shoulder. Midway between the Los Angeles centers of political and financial power sits **Broadway**, a vibrant Latino shopping district. This, not Olvera Street, is where today's Mexican population shops. A cross between New York's 42nd Street and the boulevards of Mexico City, this multiblock strip is crowded with cut-rate clothing stores, swap meets, pawn shops, and stands selling pizza by the slice.

HIDDEN ►   Start at the South 300 block and wander uptown. The first place you'll encounter is **Grand Central Public Market**, a fresh food bazaar in the tradition of Mexico's *mercados*. More than 50 fruit stalls, vegetable stands, butchers, and fresh fish shops line the aisles. There are juice stands dispensing dozens of flavors and vendors selling light meals. More than 30,000 people pass through every day, making it one of the city's most vital scenes. ~ 317 South Broadway; 213-624-2378.

The **Bradbury Building** across the street has undergone a massive restoration. The interior features an extraordinary courtyard illuminated by a skylight, with wrought-iron grillwork, and winding stairs surrounding an open cage elevator. Add flourishes of marble and brick to finish off this 1893 masterpiece. Closed Sunday. ~ 304 South Broadway; 213-626-1893.

During the 1940s Broadway was the city's Great White Way, where stars mingled and Hollywood premiered its greatest films. Today the boulevard's diminished glory is evident in the old theaters between 3rd and Olympic streets. Once the pride of the studios that built them, they are now in varying stages of disrepair. **The Million Dollar Theater**, where movie mogul Sid Grauman began as a showman, is now a church. ~ 310 South Broadway.

Also of note are the **Los Angeles Theatre**, located at 615 South Broadway, with its gaudy Versailles-style architecture, that shows Spanish-language films; the magnificent **Orpheum**, at 842 South Broadway, a 2000-seat Spanish and French Gothic hybrid built in 1926; and the **United Artists Theatre**, situated on 933 South Broadway, a 1926 Spanish Gothic structure with murals depicting Charlie Chaplin and Mary Pickford, now restored for service as Dr. Gene Scott's University Cathedral. Many of these grande dames presently show Spanish films from noon 'til night, but most will allow you to glance inside.

Recapturing part of this past is the nearby **Los Angeles Conservancy**, a preservation group that on Saturday conducts tours of the theaters and other places of historic interest. ~ 727 West 7th Street, Suite 955; 213-623-2489.

Crowds from Broadway in search of greenery inevitably head to **Pershing Square**. This centrally located five-acre park of palm trees and flower beds has a small amphitheater and food concessions. ~ Bounded by Olive, Hill, 5th, and 6th streets.

If Broadway was once The Great White Way, **Spring Street** was the Wall Street of the West. Like its theatrical counterpart, this faded financial district is now the venue of historians and sentimentalists. ~ Between 4th and 7th streets. The former **Pacific Coast Stock Exchange**, a 1930 masterpiece of moderne architecture, has been closed. ~ 618 South Spring Street. Among the other hallowed halls of finance is the **Design Center of Los Angeles**, a 1928 building with tile murals and zigzag facade. ~ 433 South Spring Street. Another worthy stop is the **Banco Popular**, a 1903 Beaux-Arts office building. ~ 354 South Spring Street.

Today the focus of finance has shifted to a highrise district between Grand Avenue and Figueroa, 3rd, and 8th streets. Here the **First Interstate World Center** rises 74 stories. ~ 633 West 5th Street. Around the corner at the **Wells Fargo History Museum**, you can view displays re-creating more than a century of Western history. Closed Saturday and Sunday. ~ 333 South Grand Avenue; 213-253-7166. The **World Trade Center**, another architectural extravaganza, looms nearby. ~ 350 South Figueroa Street; 213-489-3337.

At ARCO **Plaza**, a twin-tower, 52-story behemoth, you'll encounter the MTA (Metropolitan Transportation Authority, Level C), where you can obtain route maps of the city's largest transportation agency. ~ Flower Street between 5th and 6th streets; 213-626-4455.

The **Greater Los Angeles Convention & Visitors Bureau** is the city's main information center. There you'll find maps, leaflets, and

---

✔ **CHECK THESE OUT—UNIQUE SIGHTS**

• Take in both masterpieces and mastodons with a visit to the **L.A. County Museum of Art** and the adjacent **La Brea Tar Pits**. *page 49*

• Find out which celebrity's footprint matches your own by stepping over to Hollywood's most famous landmark, **Mann's Chinese Theater**. *page 61*

• Catch your breath viewing the beauty of the **Watts Tower**, set amid the urban scene of 1965's catastrophic race riots. *page 39*

• Explore the **Huntington Library and Gardens**, where you can examine a hand-painted manuscript from 1410 and then roam the acres of exquisite gardens. *page 103* a friendly staff to help point the way through this urban maze. Closed Sunday. ~ 685 South Figueroa Street; 213-689-8822.

Amid all these elite and expensive office buildings, one structure stands forth like a visitor from the future. Its five mirror-glass cylinders resembling a space station with legs, the **Westin Bonaventure Hotel** is easily the city's most imaginative skyscraper. Because of its unique design, together with an interior of reflecting pools and bubble elevators, the 1976 building is a favorite backdrop for sci-fi movies. ~ 404 South Figueroa Street; 213-624-1000.

Across the street from this symbol of tomorrow stands an emblem of the past. The **Los Angeles Central Library**, built in the 1920s, incorporates Egyptian, Roman, and Byzantine elements into a Beaux-Arts design. The most striking feature of all is the pyramid tower inlaid with colorful tile patterns. In 1986, fire gutted the interior and the city closed the library for repairs—and expansion. Seven years later, it reopened its doors, doubling the floor space with the addition of a new wing and a one-and-a-half-acre garden atop the parking garage—an oasis of greenery replete with five fountains. It is now the third largest central library in the nation. ~ 5th and Hope streets; 213-612-3200.

HIDDEN ▶ For a view of blue-collar Los Angeles, depart Central Downtown for the **Southern California Flower Market**, where wholesale flower merchants line an entire block and the air is redolent with fragrant merchandise. ~ 742 Maple Avenue; 213-627-2482. Over at the **Produce Markets**, the bounty from California's interior valleys goes on the block every morning. The place is a beehive of business, a fascinating area where the farm meets the city. ~ Central Avenue and 7th Street; or San Pedro and 11th streets.

LODGING   **Hotel Stillwell**, a competitively priced hostelry, offers 232 rooms in a vintage 1920 building. The lobby is decorated with Asian wallhangings, matching the hotel's Indian restaurant. Each guest room has been refurbished with pastel colors, trim carpeting, and modern furniture throughout. ~ 838 South Grand Avenue; 213-627-1151, 800-553-4774, fax 213-622-8940. BUDGET.

In the reasonable price range it's hard to top the **Figueroa Hotel**. A 1927 Spanish-style building, it offers a beautiful lobby with tile floor and hand-painted ceiling. The palm-fringed courtyard contains a swimming pool, jacuzzi, and lounge. The rooms are very large, adequately furnished, and decorated with wallhangings. Tile baths add a touch of class to this very appealing establishment. Coffee shop and restaurants on the premises. ~ 939 South Figueroa Street; 213-627-8971, 800-421-9092, fax 213-689-0305. MODERATE.

What can you say about a place that became a landmark as soon as it was built? To call the **Westin Bonaventure** ultramodern would belittle the structure. "Post Future" is a more appropriate tag. Its dark glass silos rise 35 stories from the street like a way station on the road to the 21st century. Within are five levels of shops, 1364 rooms, 20 restaurants, and a revolving cocktail lounge. The atrium lobby furthers the Buck Rogers theme with reflecting pools, glass shaft elevators, and lattice skylights. Considering all this, the guest rooms seem almost an afterthought; because of the building's configuration they are small and pie-shaped but offer good views of the surrounding financial district. ~ 404 South Figueroa Street; 213-624-1000, 800-228-3000, fax 213-612-4800. DELUXE TO ULTRA-DELUXE.

The past rests safely ensconced a few blocks distant at **The Biltmore Hotel.** Here the glamour and elegance of the Roaring '20s endure in a grand lobby replete with stately pilasters and floor-to-ceiling mirrors. A classic in the tradition of grande-dame hotels, the Biltmore conveys an Old World ambience with hand-oiled wood panels, frescoes, and ornamental molding. Its gourmet restaurants and sumptuous lounges reflect the rich Spanish–Italian Renaissance style that makes this 700-room hostelry a kind of museum for overnight guests. The bedrooms are moderate-sized, adorned with contemporary artworks and provided with traditional French furniture. Among the other amenities is an elegant health club with swimming pool, jacuzzi, and sauna. ~ 506 South Grand Avenue; 213-612-1575, 800-245-8673, fax 213-612-1545. ULTRA-DELUXE.

Located downtown is the European-style **Wyndam Checkers Hotel.** This 188-room luxury hostelry originally opened in 1927 as the Mayflower Hotel. Its impressive modeled art stone facade of two carved ships, the Mayflower and the Santa Maria, made it one of the most strikingly beautiful buildings of its time. A massive renovation has restored it beyond its original elegance into one of the swankier hotels in town. Posh rooms come complete with original artwork, marble bathrooms, and three telephones. A gourmet restaurant, comfortable lounge, library, and rooftop spa make Checkers well

---

✔ CHECK THESE OUT—UNIQUE LODGING

- *Budget:* Peer out at MacArthur Park from your room in the 1920s deco-style **Park Plaza Hotel,** where the marble-floor lobby and grand stairway recall the glory of bygone days. *page 50*
- *Moderate:* Hang your sombrero in the **Figueroa Hotel,** a 1927 Spanish-style hostelry with a beautiful lobby and spacious rooms. *page 24*
- *Deluxe:* Relax in the European ambience of the **Beverly House Hotel,** with its friendly staff and free continental breakfast. *page 87*
- *Ultra-deluxe:* Snooze with the stars, past and present, at **Château Marmont,** Hollywood's historic celebrity haunt. *page 67*

Budget: under $50 Moderate: $50–$90 Deluxe: $90–$120 Ultra-deluxe: over $120

worth the price tag. ~ 535 South Grand Avenue; 213-624-0000, 800-996-3426, fax 213-626-9906. ULTRA-DELUXE.

The first major new hotel downtown in over a decade, the tasteful and contemporary 17-story **Hotel Inter-Continental**, is perched on Bunker Hill next to California Plaza's one-and-a-half-acre Watercourt (check out the dancing waters). Sunlight streams through the lobby's glass walls, creating a bright, open atmosphere that is enhanced by an indoor garden and modern sculpture on loan from the adjacent Museum of Contemporary Art. The 439 guest rooms are large, comfortably furnished, and decorated in shades of peach or teal. Guests can also enjoy the health club that has a sauna, hot tub, and an outdoor swimming pool. ~ 251 South Olive Street; 213-617-3300, 800-327-0200, fax 213-617-3399. ULTRA-DELUXE.

DINING

HIDDEN ►

To dine in the true style of Mexico the place to go is not a restaurant at all. **Grand Central Public Market**, a block-long produce market, features stands selling Mexican finger foods. Tacos, tostadas, and burritos are only part of the fare. Try the *chile rojo* (pork in red chile sauce), *machaca* (shredded beef), and *lengua* (tongue). If you're really daring there's *rellena* (blood sausage), *buche* (hog maws), and *tripas* (intestines). *Mucho gusto!* ~ 317 South Broadway; 213-624-2378. BUDGET.

Another funky but fabulous low-priced eating place is **Clifton's Brookdale Cafeteria**, a kind of steam-tray vistarama. The second floor of this cavernous place displays illuminated photos of California's sightseeing spots. The ground floor resembles a redwood forest, with tree trunks bolted to the walls, fake rocks stacked on the floor, and a waterfall tumbling through a cement funnel. A scene you cannot afford to miss. ~ 648 South Broadway; 213-627-1673. BUDGET.

✦✦

✔ CHECK THESE OUT—UNIQUE DINING

- *Budget:* Munch on one of the myriad offerings at the sprawling and festive **Grand Central Public Market** in the heart of downtown. *page 26*
- *Moderate:* Opt for old-fashioned lounge dining with a Dublin broil in a curtained booth at **Casey's Bar and Grill**. *page 27*
- *Moderate to deluxe:* Tempt yourself with **Tokyo Kaikan**'s tasty Japanese offerings, many of which are cooked at your table. *page 35*
- *Ultra-deluxe:* Practice your French—or at least your attitude—at Hollywood's famous **L'Orangerie**, where *foie gras* is served in an elegant setting. *page 75*

Budget: under $8   Moderate: $8–$16   Deluxe: $16–$24   Ultra-deluxe: over $24

Casey's Bar and Grill is one of those marvelous old dining lounges with dark paneling, trophy cases, and graying photographs. One room displays antique song sheets, another is covered with sports photos; my personal favorite is the back room, where you can request a private booth with curtain. Lunch consists of hamburgers, sandwiches, and entrées such as Dublin broil (steak with mushrooms, spinach, and mashed potatoes). For dinner there are pasta dishes, fish and chips, and barbecued ribs. Bottoms up! Closed Saturday and Sunday. ~ 613 South Grand Avenue; 213-629-2353. MODERATE.

Gill's Cuisine of India, set in the lobby of the 1920-era Hotel Stillwell, conveys an air of South Asia. Indian fabrics adorn the walls, complementing a menu of chicken marsala, *tandoori* shrimp, lamb *vindallo*, and curry dishes. There's also a buffet-style lunch. ~ 838 South Grand Avenue; 213-623-1050. BUDGET TO MODERATE.

Incomparable is the perfect adjective to describe **Rex Il Ristorante**. Set in a landmark art deco building and modeled after a 1930s Italian luxury liner, it represents one of Los Angeles' loveliest restaurants. This Italian dining room is furnished in burgundy colors and enhanced by a sweeping staircase that curves up to a black marble dancefloor. The decorative glass is Lalique, the silverware Ricci, and the china Ginori, each element adding subtle flair. Not to be upstaged by the appurtenances, the cuisine is exceptional and the wine list is one of the most formidable in the country. The ultimate dining experience is the fixed-price menu, a stunning six-course meal that demonstrates chef Gino Angelini's limitless skills. Among the à la carte selections, he prepares an array of rotisserie meats, pasta, and rack of lamb with porcini mushrooms. Closed Sunday. ~ 617 South Olive Street; 213-627-2300. ULTRA-DELUXE.

It is, quite simply, Everyperson's Eating Place. **The Original Pantry**, short on looks but long on soul, has been serving meals 24 hours a day since 1924 without missing a beat. When forced to relocate in 1950, they prepared lunch in the old building and served dinner at the new place. It simply consists of a counter with metal stools and a formica dining area decorated with grease-stained paintings. The cuisine is a culinary answer to heavy metal—ham hocks, navy bean soup, standing rib roast, sirloin tips with noodles, and roast pork. ~ 877 South Figueroa Street; 213-972-9279. BUDGET.

◄ *HIDDEN*

SHOPPING

Los Angeles' downtown business district is experiencing a major renaissance which has elevated the area to its former status. The shopping scene has blazed back to life with the development of malls like the **Atlantic Richfield Shopping Center**, where 55 shops and restaurants create one of the largest subterranean shopping centers in the country. ~ ARCO Plaza, 5th and Flower streets.

In a space age linkup, this mall connects via glass footbridge with the **Westin Bonaventure Shopping Gallery**, where numerous other stores, located on three levels, surround the Bonaventure's vaulting atrium lobby. ~ 404 South Figueroa Street. Among these elegant shops is **August Moon**, which houses a beautiful selection of Oriental arts and jewelry. ~ 213-626-4395.

Broadway Plaza lies at the heart of the downtown shopping hub and features **Macy's** (213-628-9311) department store as well as a galleria of specialty shops. ~ 700 South Flower Street.

A charming European-style center, **Seventh Market Place** has dozens of shops and restaurants in an open-air setting. With an emphasis on fashion, the mall is highlighted by stores such as **G. B. Harb** (213-624-4785) and **Ann Taylor** (213-629-2818). ~ Citicorp Plaza, 735 South Figueroa Street; 213-955-7150.

The city's old jewelry district still houses a variety of shops selling goods at competitive prices. ~ Hill Street between 5th and 7th streets. Historic **St. Vincent Jewelry Center** is reputed to be the world's largest jewelry outlet, covering an entire square block. ~ 650 South Hill Street; 213-629-2124. Here and at the **International Jewelry Center**, another mammoth complex, you'll find items in every price range, from ten dollars to ten thousand. ~ 550 South Hill Street; 213-624-3201.

As in many urban areas, warehouses and industrial districts around Los Angeles have become home to young artists seeking low rents. Among the small galleries which have resulted is **Cirrus Gallery**, where contemporary works by West Coast artists are displayed. ~ 542 South Alameda Street; 213-680-3473. **Los Angeles Artcore** is a nonprofit artists' organization where you'll find outstanding contemporary works. Closed Monday and Tuesday. ~ 420 East 3rd Street; 213-617-3274.

The former Theater District, which served as Los Angeles' Great White Way during the 1930s, is now the main shopping district for the Hispanic community. Today, discount clothing, luggage, and electronic stores line this crowded boulevard. Latino sounds and the spicy aroma of Mexican food fills the air. ~ Broadway between 3rd and 10th streets. The **Old Globe Theater**, once a legitimate theater, has been converted into a swap meet. ~ 744 South Broadway.

EVERYTHING'S COMING UP ROSES—AND LILIES AND TULIPS . . .

You can watch the city work through its paces in the **Flower District**. Huge warehouses are filled with flowers and potted plants in one of the region's most amazing floral displays. There are proteas from Southern California, New Zealand calla lilies, lilacs from Holland, Columbian roses, and French tulips, all fresh and blooming with pride. ~ Wall Street between 7th and 8th streets.

Grand Central Public Market, a huge indoor public market dat-   ◄ HIDDEN
ing back to 1917, is filled with Spanish-speaking crowds shopping
for fresh produce, ethnic goods, and Mexican specialties. Here you
can sample a glass of *jamica* (flower drink) at the juice bar, taste tripe
soup, or indulge in Mexican sweet candies. Stroll the aisles of this
classic old market and you'll swear you've been transported to
Mexico City. ~ 317 South Broadway; 213-624-2378.

You can literally shop until you drop in Los Angeles' bustling
Garment District. Known as a major manufacturing center since the
1930s, the district today lies concentrated along Los Angeles Street
between 4th and 10th streets.

The **Cooper Building** offers six floors of name brand clothes and
accessories, with prices as much as 70 percent below retail. Among
the highlights is **International Design** (213-489-7601), which features ladies' designer and contemporary wear. ~ 860 South Los Angeles Street; 213-622-1139.

Across the street at **Academy Award Clothes**, they stock thousands of quality men's suits at very reasonable prices. ~ 821 South
Los Angeles Street; 213-622-9125.

The Garment District does not begin and end on Los Angeles
Street, but rather extends along side streets and down alleyways. A
bargain hunter's delight, **The Alley** is part and parcel of this busy
neighborhood. Boxes, bins, and mannequins line the two-block-long
alleyway where hawkers and vendors vie for your attention. ~ Located between Santee Street and Maple Avenue.

Consider **Bell of California**, which displays a beautiful selection
of silks and cottons for ladies and juniors. Happy hunting! ~ 1018
South Santee Street; 213-748-5716.

At the **Produce Markets**, you can purchase produce by the lug or
bushel. Even if a box of lettuce doesn't sound like the perfect souvenir
from your Los Angeles' sojourn, plan to visit these early-morning
markets. Burly truckers, out-of-town farmers, and Hispanic workers
are all part of this urban tableau. ~ Central Avenue and 7th Street;
or San Pedro and 11th streets.

Located nearby, **Basket World & Supply** is floor to ceiling with
baskets (sold at wholesale, even to retail buyers). ~ 741 South Maple
Avenue; 213-622-8640. **Nuts To You** has been selling nuts to the
public (also at wholesale) in the same location since early in the century. ~ 901 South San Pedro Street; 213-627-8855.

Its dual role as music center of the United States and film capital of   **NIGHTLIFE**
the world makes Los Angeles one very hot entertainment destina-
tion. There are nightclubs frequented by Hollywood stars, movie
theaters premiering major films, and dancehalls headlining top musicians from local recording studios. With so much talent concentrated in one city, the performing arts also flourish. Attending the

theater in Los Angeles often means seeing a famous movie star playing the lead in a new drama.

Located on the ground floor of the Dorothy Chandler Pavilion, **Otto Rothschild's Bar & Grill** is *the* place to meet before and after the theater. Sixty years of theatrical photos, taken by the club's namesake, cover the walls. ~ 135 North Grand Avenue; 213-972-7322.

A lovely place for evening cocktails, **Bonavista** offers a revolving 360-degree panorama of the city from the 34th floor of the Westin Bonaventure Hotel. One floor up, the lounge at the **Top of Five** restaurant also sports a tremendous although non-revolving view. ~ 404 South Figueroa Street; 213-624-1000.

The **Grand Avenue Bar** offers 13 TV screens broadcasting sports events in the stately Biltmore Hotel. For a more upscale scene, check the hotel's **Rendezvous Court**. ~ 506 South Grand Avenue; 213-612-1532.

To find out what's happening all over town, check out the "Calendar" section, the *L.A. Reader*, the *L.A. Weekly*, and *Los Angeles* magazine.

Located below street level, **Casey's Bar and Grill** may well be the most popular downtown bar. A comfortable pub filled with sports memorabilia, it draws business people on weekdays until 10 p.m. ~ 613 South Grand Avenue; 213-629-2353.

At **Karma**, the scene is decidedly postmodern. The decor is a combination of wood and metal, and the large dancefloor pulsates with the sounds of techno and house music. Cover. ~ 333 South Boylston Street; 213-747-4849.

Brightly painted terra cotta warrior priests welcome guests to **The Mayan Nightclub**. Here a young and fashionable crowd dances to deejay tunes and live salsa bands in a grandiose Mayan tomb. Cover. ~ 1038 South Hill Street; 213-746-4287.

The most prestigious performing arts complex on the West Coast, the **Music Center** consists of three major theaters located within a massive, white marble plaza. The elegant **Dorothy Chandler Pavilion**, home to the Los Angeles Philharmonic Orchestra, is a spectacular 4000-seat facility. The concert hall also hosts performances by the Joffrey Ballet and American Ballet Theatre. The 2000-seat **Ahmanson Theatre** presents classic dramas and comedies as well as West Coast premieres like *Phantom of the Opera*. The more intimate, 700-seat **Mark Taper Forum** is ideal for contemporary dramatic and musical performances. The resident Center Theater Group, associated with the Ahmanson Theatre and the Mark Taper Forum, is committed to the development of new works and artists and has produced such award-winning plays as *Zoot Suit*, *Children of a Lesser God*, and *The Shadow Box*. ~ 135 North Grand Avenue; 213-972-7211.

Tickets for performances at all three theaters are available through Ticketmaster. ~ 213-480-3232, 800-755-4000.

The 6200-seat **Shrine Civic Auditorium** hosts major musical events, including classical, opera, jazz, pop, rock, and ethnic folk music presentations. ~ 665 West Jefferson Boulevard; 213-749-5123. Advance tickets are available through Ticketmaster. ~ 213-480-3232, 800-755-4000. For same-day tickets, you'll need to go to the Shrine ticket booth.

The historic heart of the city is El Pueblo de Los Angeles, a 44-acre outdoor museum centered around Olvera Street. In 1781 a few dozen Spanish settlers established hardscrabble farms and built adobes here, breaking ground for what eventually became one of the world's largest metropolitan areas.

▼▼▼▼▼▼▼▼▼▼
Olvera Street

The **visitors center**, providing maps, brochures, and walking tours, sits in one of the pueblo's vintage buildings, an 1887 brick-faced Victorian called the Sepulveda House. ~ 622 North Main Street; 213-628-1274.

SIGHTS

Heart of hearts is the **Plaza**, a tree-shaded courtyard adorned with statues and highlighted by a wrought-iron bandstand. A colorful gathering place, it's a frequent site for fiestas and open-air concerts. ~ North Main and Los Angeles streets.

Anchoring one corner of the plaza is **Firehouse No. 1**, Los Angeles' original fire station. Built in 1884, the brick structure served the fire department for little more than a decade, after which it became a saloon, boarding house, and store. Today it's a miniature museum filled with horse-drawn fire wagons, old-time helmets, and an ample inventory of memories. ~ 134 Paseo de la Plaza.

The plaza's most prestigious building, **Pico House** was built in 1870 by Pío Pico, the last Mexican governor of California. Italianate in style, it represented the grandest hotel of its era. ~ Paseo de la Plaza and North Main Street.

Old Plaza Church, first dedicated as a church in 1822, also faces the square. The city's oldest Catholic church, it is unassuming from the outside but displays an interior that is a study in wrought iron and gold leaf. Murals cover the ceiling of the diminutive chapel and a collection of religious canvases adorns the altar. ~ 535 North Main Street.

Mexicans with more worldly matters in mind gather in large crowds outside the **Biscailuz Building**, a whitewashed structure decorated with brightly hued murals by Leo Politi, El Pueblo's resident artist for over 30 years. ~ 125 Paseo de la Plaza, northeast corner of the plaza.

For the full flavor of Spanish California, wander down **Olvera Street**. Lined with *puestos* (stands) selling Mexican handicrafts, it provides a window into Mexican culture. The brick-paved alleyway is also one of the West's first pedestrian shopping malls.

Among the antique buildings bordering this narrow corridor is the **Ávila Adobe**, a classic mud-brick house constructed around

1818. The oldest house in Los Angeles, it has undergone numerous incarnations, serving as a private residence, boarding house, and restaurant and surviving several earthquakes. Today it's a museum, fully restored and filled with period pieces.

A nearby historical marker points out the vital water source for early Los Angeles. La Zanja Madre, the mother ditch, channeled the precious waters of the Los Angeles River to the fledgling community for more than a century.

Located just off the plaza is **Masonic Hall**, an 1858 building which houses a museum of Masonic Order memorabilia. With wrought-iron balcony and ornate facade it follows an Italianate design. ~ 416½ North Main Street. Even more elaborate, though of later vintage, the neighboring **Merced Theatre** was constructed in 1870 and represents the city's first theatrical center.

The **San Antonio Winery** represents the last of a disappearing breed. Years ago vineyards dotted the San Gabriel foothills, but Los Angeles' phenomenal urbanization steadily displaced them. Somehow this family-operated facility remained, situated surprisingly close to the center of the city. Today second- and third-generation members of the Riboli clan lead tasting tours through the vintage 1917 building. ~ 737 Lamar Street; 213-223-1401.

DINING

Olvera Street, where the Spanish originally located the pueblo of Los Angeles, is still a prime place for Mexican food. Tiny **taco stands** line this brick-paved alley. Little more than open-air kitchens, they dispense fresh Mexican dishes at budget prices. You'll also find bakeries and candy stands, where old Mexican ladies sell *churros* (Mexican donuts) and candied squash. BUDGET.

La Golondrina provides something more formal. Set in the historic Pelanconi House, an 1850-era home built of fired brick, it features an open-air patio and a dining room with stone fireplace and *viga* ceiling. The bill of fare includes a standard selection of tacos, tostadas, and enchiladas as well as specialties such as fajitas, crabmeat enchiladas, and grilled jumbo shrimp. ~ West 17 Olvera Street; 213-628-4349. MODERATE.

SENTIMENTAL JOURNEY

Union Station, one of the country's great train depots, has been a Los Angeles landmark since 1939. With a Spanish-Mexican exterior, the station is a cavernous structure boasting marble floors, a beam ceiling 52 feet high, arched corridors, and walls of inlaid tile. Embodying the romance and promise of travel, it is a destination with a distinct identity, a point of departure for the far fringes of the imagination. ~ 800 North Alameda Street.

Across from Union Station, midway between Olvera Street and Chinatown, stands one of the city's most famous cafeterias. **Philippe The Original** has been around since 1908, serving pork, beef, turkey, and lamb sandwiches in a French-dip style. With sawdust on the floors and memories tacked to the walls, this antique eatery still serves ten-cent cups of coffee. ~ 1001 North Alameda Street; 213-628-3781. BUDGET.   ◄ *HIDDEN*

Historic **Olvera Street**, the site of Los Angeles' original pueblo, is the setting for a traditional Mexican marketplace. Its brick-paved walkways are lined with shops and stalls selling Mexican artworks and handicrafts. You can shop at **Casa de Sousa** for Mexican Indian folk art, then stroll the plaza where food vendors serve homemade *maza* (cornmeal) tortillas, fresh tropical fruits, and tempting *nopales* (fresh diced cactus candies). ~ West 19 Olvera Street; 213-626-7076.   **SHOPPING**

Mariachi music and margaritas draw Angelenos and outlanders alike to **La Golondrina**. You can sit by the fireplace or out on the patio of this historic adobe building. ~ West 17 Olvera Street; 213-628-4349.   **NIGHTLIFE**

Back in 1870, when the Chinese population numbered perhaps 200, "Orientals" were sequestered in a rundown neighborhood southeast of the original plaza. As that area was torn down during the 1930s to build Union Station, they moved in increasing numbers to modern-day Chinatown, a multiblock neighborhood which has become the cultural and commercial center for Chinese throughout the city.   ▼▼▼▼▼▼▼▼ **Chinatown**

For an authentic view, stroll the **600 block of North Spring Street** past the herb shops and fresh fish stores. Here local residents buy goat meat and fresh produce and choose from among the racks of roast ducks that hang forlornly in store windows.   **SIGHTS**

Don't miss **Kong Chow Temple**, a tiny chapel tucked away on the second floor of an assuming building. Crowded with elderly Chinese, the place is heavy with incense and handwoven tapestries. Gilded altars and bas-relief figures add a touch of the exotic. Closed Monday. ~ 931 North Broadway; 213-626-1955.   ◄ *HIDDEN*

The commercial heart of the district lies along Broadway and Hill Street, with stores lining both boulevards for several blocks. Connecting these two thoroughfares is **New Chinatown** (Gin Ling Way), a two-block-long pedestrian mall. Traditional gates with swirling outlines mark the entranceways to this enclave. Figures of animals and ceremonial fish adorn the buildings and dragons breathe fire from the rooftops.

Chinatown's latest addition to the downtown hotel scene is an 80-room establishment, the **Metro Plaza Hotel**. Close to Union Station   **LODGING** and across the street from the historic Olvera Street complex, this four-story hostelry offers rooms and suites decorated in a blend of contemporary and Oriental styles. Downstairs you'll find a small lobby with two sitting rooms. ~ 711 North Main Street; 213-680-0200, 800-223-2223, fax 213-620-0200. MODERATE.

DINING

Chinese Friends Restaurant is a postage-stamp eatery with plastic chairs, formica tables, and a mural-sized photo portraying water and trees. In addition to the standard selection of shrimp, pork, and vegetable dishes they offer several unusual specials such as shredded pig stomach and hot-and-sour chicken. There's little else to note except one salient point: the place is inevitably crowded with Chinese. ~ 984 North Broadway; 213-626-1837. BUDGET TO MODERATE.

One of Chinatown's dim sum dining rooms, Ocean Seafood is a voluminous second-floor establishment. The dim sum service, in which you choose finger foods from passing carts, is only during lunch. At dinner there's a comprehensive Cantonese menu. With its fragile lamps and molded woodwork, Ocean Seafood has established a solid reputation for good food in sumptuous surroundings. ~ 747 North Broadway; 213-687-3088. MODERATE.

An anomaly in an Asian neighborhood, Little Joe's is a throwback to the days when Italians in the area outnumbered Chinese. Long since departed, the southern Europeans left an impressive landmark, a sprawling restaurant with six dining rooms and a spacious lounge. The place is covered with murals of Italia and adorned with knickknacks from the Old Country. The menu, as you might expect, is a mix of cannelloni, ravioli, and fettuccine dishes, with specialties such as veal piccata, beef medallions, scampi, *saltimbocca*, and butterflied halibut. Closed Sunday. ~ 900 North Broadway; 213-489-4900. MODERATE.

HIDDEN ►

Thanh My Restaurant, also in Chinatown, is a small Vietnamese plastic-chair-and-linoleum floor eatery. Here the dishes include barbecued pork with steamed rice, chicken bamboo rice noodles, and pork tips with steamed noodles. What this café lacks in atmosphere it makes up with good food at great prices. ~ 406 Sunset Boulevard; 213-680-1950. BUDGET.

SHOPPING

The heart of Chinatown, where local Chinese shop at food emporiums, markets, and cookware stores, rests along North Spring Street.

Ornate Chinese-style roofs in reds and greens adorn Chinatown Plaza, the focal point of Chinatown. Along this promenade, well-stocked gift shops offer everything from imported trinkets to very fine, very ancient antiques and artworks. ~ 900 block of North Broadway.

Walk through the Plaza, then cross Hill Street, and you'll discover a treasure trove of antique stores dotting Chung King Road.

Fong's carries a fine array of Chinese antique pieces. ~ 943 Chung King Road; 213-626-5904. For beautiful screens and antique teapots, check out **The Jade Tree.** ~ 957 Chung King Road; 213-624-3521. The smell alone will lure you into the **Phoenix Bakery.** A Chinatown institution since 1938, this Asian-style bakery prepares whimsical confections that seem inevitably to attract a long line to its door. ~ 969 North Broadway; 213-628-4642.

Mandarin Plaza is a "modern" pedestrian mall, which houses **Asian Craft Imports** (213-626-5386), an imaginative shop filled with a large selection of import gift items. ~ 970 North Broadway.

The Japanese response to Chinatown is Little Tokyo, a discrete neighborhood bounded by Los Angeles Street, Central Avenue, 1st Street, and 3rd Street. Located near the Downtown district, it represents the center of Japanese culture in Los Angeles.

Little Tokyo

At the heart of the district is the **Japanese American Cultural and Community Center,** a stoic plate-glass-and-poured-concrete structure designed by Buckminster Fuller and Isamu Noguchi. The complex, which houses dozens of Asian organizations, faces a spacious brick-paved courtyard. ~ 244 South San Pedro Street; 213-628-2725. Next door sits the **Japan America Theatre,** an important showcase for kabuki theater, Asian music, and other performing arts. ~ 244 South San Pedro Street; 213-680-3700.

SIGHTS

Follow the brick paving stones from the cultural center through **Japanese Village Plaza,** a two-block shopping mall adorned with fountains and sculptures. At the end of the plaza stands Little Tokyo's tile-roofed **fire tower,** an ornamental but practical structure which has become a local landmark.

Another cultural gathering place is the lovely **Higashi Buddhist Temple.** With its pagoda roof, the temple represents Japanese architecture adapted to a Western cityscape. ~ 505 East 3rd Street; 213-626-4200.

Catering largely to an international clientele, the **New Otani Hotel & Garden** is a 434-room extravaganza with restaurants, shops, lounges, spa, and a tranquil half-acre Japanese "garden in the sky." The hotel offers small rooms, many decorated in traditional Japanese style with shoji screens. Standard accommodations are painted in pastel hues and decorated with ultramodern furniture in curvilinear designs. Finest feature of all is the lobby, a vaulted-ceiling affair with a skylight and an eye-catching sculpture. ~ 120 South Los Angeles Street; 213-629-1200, 800-421-8795, fax 213-622-0980. ULTRA-DELUXE.

LODGING

One of the district's most popular restaurants, **Tokyo Kaikan** is a warren of woodframe rooms, each highly stylized and decorated

DINING

with lanterns and masks. Particularly inviting is one room that has been divided into private bamboo booths. Dinner includes several dishes cooked at your table as well as specialties such as *wafu* steak and tofu broth. Closed Sunday. ~ 225 South San Pedro Street; 213-489-1333. MODERATE TO DELUXE.

The oak trees at **Little Tokyo Bonsai Nursery** might be 200 years old, but they're only a few inches in height. These amazing miniatures are displayed outside the shop. ~ 622 East 1st Street; 213-626-4079.

The most elaborate of Little Tokyo's addresses is **Horikawa**, a restaurant with many faces. This beautifully appointed establishment serves meals in four separate locations—a sushi bar, a dining room, a *teppan* room where meals are prepared at your table and a luxurious teahouse with private rooms. Dining behind *shoji* screens in the teahouse you will experience *kaiseki* cooking, a 14-course meal which represents the pinnacle of Japanese cuisine. The dining room menu is quite varied, mixing staples like tempura with such specials as *isoyaki* (baked seafood combination) and chicken *amiyaki* (grilled with soy-sake sauce); the *teppan* room offers grilled steak, chicken, scallops, and lobster. The dining and *teppan* rooms are deluxe; the teahouse rooms are priced in the ultra-deluxe range and require a four-day advance reservation. Closed Sunday. ~ 111 South San Pedro Street; 213-680-9355. DELUXE TO ULTRA-DELUXE.

Suehiro offers a largely Japanese menu in an American-style setting, complete with blue vinyl booths and counter service. You'll find such Japanese standards as chicken teriyaki, tempura and sukiyaki. ~ 337 East 1st Street; 213-626-9132. BUDGET TO MODERATE.

SHOPPING Little Tokyo is a busy shopping district centered along 1st Street between Main Street and Alameda Boulevard. **Japanese Village Plaza**, right in the heart of the neighborhood at 327 East 2nd Street, is a commercial expression of the sights, sounds, smells, and flavors of Japan. Enter at the site of the Fire Tower, a traditional fireman's lookout facing 1st Street, and walk the Plaza's winding brick pathways while browsing its tile-roofed shops. One such store, **Mikawaya Sweet Shop**, tempts you with subtle Japanese candies. ~ 213-624-1681.

Just beyond the Plaza, **Bun-ka Do** offers an interesting collection of Japanese art objects, records, and magazines. ~ 340 East 1st Street; 213-625-1122.

Weller Court, situated at South Onizuka and 3rd streets, a modern tri-level shopping arcade, boasts among its tenants **Matsuzakaya America, Inc.** (213-626-2112), a branch of Japan's oldest and largest department store. Also featured is **Kinokuniya Book Store of America** (213-687-4447), with a complete selection of books on Japan.

Conveniently, Weller Court is connected via walking bridges to the **New Otani Hotel Shopping Arcade**, where a series of specialty shops showcase everything from fine jewelry to tourist trinkets. ~ 110 South Los Angeles Street.

The **Genji Bar** at the New Otani Hotel is a restful piano bar in the heart of Little Tokyo. ~ 120 South Los Angeles Street; 213-629-1200.

NIGHTLIFE

Housed in the Japanese American Cultural and Community Center in Little Tokyo, the **Japan America Theatre** presents traditional and contemporary Japanese productions. Performances include Grand Kabuki, Bugaku, and Noh dramas as well as Japanese puppet theater. In addition, western dance troupes and chamber orchestras are sometimes featured. ~ 244 South San Pedro Street; 213-680-3700.

Home to impressive architecture, major museums, an athletic palace, and one of the city's fine universities, the Exposition Park area lies just southwest of downtown Los Angeles. Whatever your interests, you'll find more than enough outdoor and indoor activities to entice you in and around Exposition Park.

▼▼▼▼▼▼▼▼▼▼▼▼▼▼▼
Exposition Park Area

Minutes from Los Angeles' ultramodern downtown, where real estate sells by the square foot, sits the spacious, Romanesque campus of the **University of Southern California**. Lined with sycamore and maple trees, this red-brick-and-ivy enclave features a park-like setting filled with historic buildings.

SIGHTS

The movie location for everything from *The Hunchback of Notre Dame* to *The Graduate*, it's an ideal spot for a stroll. Among the many features of the USC campus are the **Fisher Gallery** (213-740-8229), with an excellent collection of European and New World art from the 15th century to the present, and the **Hancock Memorial Museum** (213-740-9119), containing the furnishings of a 1907 mansion which was modeled after the Villa de Medici. Open by appointment only.

Of course it is athletics, not academics and architecture, for which USC is famous. More concerned with quarterbacks than quasars, the school has produced four Heisman trophy winners and more than 100 All-Americans while leaving the Nobel prizes to UCLA and Berkeley. Marcus Allen, not Socrates, is the role model for this 28,000-student university. ~ Bounded by Jefferson Boulevard, Vermont Avenue, Exposition Boulevard, and Figueroa Street; 213-740-2311.

Exposition Park—a multiblock extravaganza—is long on exposition and short on park. There *is* an enchanting **sunken garden** with a fountain, gazebos, and almost 20,000 rose bushes representing nearly 200 varieties of roses. Otherwise the park blooms with museums and sports arenas. ~ Bounded by Exposition Boulevard, Menlo Avenue, Martin Luther King, Jr. Boulevard, and Figueroa Street.

The **California Museum of Science and Industry** is one of those hands-on, great-for-kids-of-all-ages complexes. Rambling between several buildings, it has halls devoted to health and economics and displays demonstrating everything from simple laws of science to the latest advances in high technology. ~ Exposition Park; 213-744-7400.

Over in the **Aerospace Complex** there are exhibits explaining the principles of aerodynamics as well as planes, jets, and space capsules suspended from the ceiling in mock flight. Climbing a catwalk-like series of staircases, you'll have a bird's-eye view of a 1920 glider, Air Force T-38, an F-20 Tiger Shark, and Gemini II spacecraft. ~ Exposition Park; 213-744-2533.

The five-story-high screen in the IMAX **Theater** takes viewers on film adventures of stunning, you-are-there realism. Several different films are screened daily. You might find yourself aboard the Space Shuttle, rafting through the Grand Canyon, or flying into the eye of a hurricane. Admission. ~ Exposition Park; 213-744-2014.

The **Natural History Museum of Los Angeles County**, reputedly the largest and most popular museum in California, is a world (and an afternoon) unto itself. Among the three-dozen galleries are rock and gem displays; dioramas of bears, wolves, and bison; set pieces from the American past, including a cut-away Conestoga wagon demonstrating life on the frontier; and, of course, the dinosaur skeletons required of every self-respecting natural history museum. If this is not enough, the museum contains bird specimens and a "discovery center" where you can play scientist. Closed Monday. Admission. ~ 900 Exposition Park; 213-744-3466.

Prettiest of all the buildings in this museum park is the **California Afro-American Museum** with its glass-roofed sculpture court and bright, airy galleries. Devoted to black culture and history, the center displays the work of artists from around the world. Closed Monday. ~ 600 State Drive, Exposition Park; 213-744-7432.

Surprisingly enough, Exposition Park's most notable architectural achievement is not the museum buildings, but rather the **Los Angeles Memorial Coliseum**, a 92,000-seat arena built in 1923. One of the most beautiful stadiums in the country, site of the 1932 and 1984 Olympics, the Coliseum is a classic arena with arched entranceways and rainbow-colored seats. Today it is home to the University of Southern California football team. ~ Exposition Park; 213-748-6131.

▼▼▼▼▼▼▼▼
Watts Area

Television cameras arrived in Watts in 1959 to broadcast an amazing event: The spire-like sculptures known as *Watts Towers*, made of steel and found objects, were being subjected to a pull-test ordered by the City of Los Angeles, which had been threatening to demolish the structures since their completion in 1954. As art aficionados around the world held their breath, a force equal to a 120-mile-an-hour gale was applied to the tallest tower. Only one seashell fell off, and the Watts Towers were allowed to stand.

When the television cameras returned in 1965, the occasion was a tragic one—they were there to document the devastating Watts race riots, during which 43 people were killed and 4000 arrested. Watts was to the 1960s what South-Central later became to the 1990s in the wake of the 1992 riots: a poverty-stricken area with an ominous reputation. Watts is still one of L.A.'s poorest areas, filled with blocks of decrepit bungalows and bisected by Southern Pacific railroad tracks. Yet both artists from local communities and visitors from around the world come here to take inspiration from the beauty of the Towers. And while you're on your way there or back, stop and explore some off-the-beaten-path sights of L.A.'s urban industrial areas.

SIGHTS

◄ *HIDDEN*

One of the seven wonders of Los Angeles is located northeast of Watts in the industrial town of Vernon, where **Farmer John's Pig Mural** covers an entire city block. Probably the biggest mural you'll ever see, it's also one of the funniest, picturing hundreds of pigs running through open fields. This idyllic landscape, in the midst of miles of factories, was begun in 1957 by a movie-industry artist named Les Grimes. For years Grimes gave everything to the project and in the end sacrificed his life, falling from a scaffold while working on the mural. His legacy is a romping, rollicking, technicolor creation. ~ 3049 East Vernon Avenue.

After priming your eyes with this porcine art, head down to L.A.'s legendary folk-art wonder, also the result of an individual artist with an uncommon vision—**Watts Towers**. Fashioned by Simon Rodia over a three-decade period, these delicate, curving towers, inlaid with *objets trouvés*, rise nearly 100 feet. Encrusted with tile shards, stones, and more than 70,000 sea shells, they form a work of unsettling beauty. After half a lifetime of work Rodia finished the sculpture in 1954, gave the property to a neighbor, and left Los Angeles, never to visit his towers again. After five years of being untended and vandalized, the towers were purchased by a group of volunteers, who set up a committee to oversee their maintenance. ~ 1765 East 107th Street, in Simon Rodia State Historic Park.

The **Watts Towers Arts Center** next door features a rotating series of exhibits by artists in the black and Asian community. Closed Monday. ~ 213-847-4646.

◄ *HIDDEN*

Continuing farther south, Los Angeles' industrial district also contains some of California's early creations. The **Dominguez Ranch Adobe**, in the heavy-metal town of Compton, is a 19th-century Spanish rancho which now doubles as a seminary and historic museum. The grounds of this sprawling hacienda are landscaped with lovely flower and cactus gardens. The museum features the original furniture and effects of the Dominguez family, the Spanish dons who first built a home here in 1826. Open Monday and Tuesday from 1 p.m. to 3 p.m. and the second and third Sunday of each month. ~ 18127 South Alameda Street; 310-631-5981.

When you've had your fill of history and art, head up to **Hollywood Park,** one of the Southland's great tracks, where you'll find thoroughbred racing from the end of April until the end of July. Beautifully laid out, the track features a landscape complete with palm trees, lagoon, and children's play area. Admission. ~ 1050 South Prairie Avenue, Inglewood; 310-419-1500.

DINING   A good spot for a basic meal is **The Main Event.** Decorated in peach and green with beautiful emerald tiles lining the entrance, this establishment offers everything from Italian dishes to soul food. Among their popular dishes are fried chicken bits, stir-fry, prime rib, and pork chops served with yams. ~ 230 North La Brea Avenue, Inglewood; 310-674-2255. MODERATE.

▼▼▼▼▼▼▼▼▼▼▼▼▼
East Los Angeles
The spirit of Mexico is alive and shimmering in the *barrio* of East L.A. With a population that is 90 percent Latino, this sprawling neighborhood represents the country's largest concentration of Hispanics. Originally settling Los Angeles in the 18th century, Mexicans emigrated en masse following the Mexican Revolution of 1910.

Today they are a rapidly growing minority group flexing political muscle and demonstrating cultural pride. As playwright Luis Valdez explains, "No Statue of Liberty ever greeted our arrival in this country. We did not in fact come to the United States at all. The United States came to us."

SIGHTS   **Brooklyn Avenue,** a major thoroughfare in the Boyle Heights district, represents "Little Mexico," a region rich in Mexican restaurants, candy stores, and family shops. If Brooklyn Avenue is the heart of the *barrio*, **Whittier Boulevard** is the spine, a neon ganglion charged with electric color. It is here that a guy goes to show off his girl, his car, and himself. Lined with discount stores, *tacquerías*, and auto body shops, Whittier is the Sunset Strip of East L.A.

The life of the *barrio* is also evident at **El Mercado,** an indoor market crowded with shoppers and filled by the strains of Spanish songs. There are clothing shops, fresh food markets, and stores selling everything from cowboy boots to Spanish-language videos. The signs are bilingual and the clientele represents a marvelous multicultural mix. ~ 3425 East 1st Street; 213-268-3451.

Of course the full flavor of the Chicano community is found among the murals which decorate the streets of East Los Angeles. Exotic in design, vibrant with color, they are a vital representation of the inner life of the *barrio*, a freeform expression of the Mexican people and their 400-year residence in the United States.

HIDDEN ►   A spectacular series of murals adorn the walls of the **Estrada Courts Housing Project.** Here dozens of bright-hued images capture the full sweep of Latin history. ~ Olympic Boulevard between Grande Vista Avenue and Lorena Street.

Two other buildings also provide a panoramic image of Mexican history. In a succession of panels, the **First Street Store** re-creates prehistoric Mexican society, then progresses through the Aztec area to modern times. ~ 3640 East 1st Street. With a series of surreal tile murals, the nearby **Pan American Bank** carries the saga into the future, portraying Latins in the post-atomic age. ~ 3626 East 1st Street.

"El Corrido de Boyle Heights" ("The Ballad of Boyle Heights"), another color-soaked mural, painted in 1983, captures the community at work and play, with the family and on the road. A succession of overlapping scenes, it's an anecdotal expression of the *barrio*, done with a flair unique to Chicano culture. ~ Corner of Brooklyn Avenue and Soto Street.

Mexican restaurants are on parade at **El Mercado**, a two-story indoor market adorned with tile floors and colorful murals. Along the mezzanine of this Spanish emporium are chili bars, taco stands, seafood restaurants, and cafés from south of the border. Adding to your dining pleasure, Mexican bands perform love songs and ballads. ~ 3425 East 1st Street; 213-268-3451. BUDGET.

DINING

The greatest of all East L.A.'s Mexican restaurants is **El Tepeyac Café**, a hole-in-the-wall with so much soul people migrate across the city to feast on its legendary burritos. Consisting of a small dining room with take-out window and side patio, the place serves everything—*machaca*, tacos, steak *picado*, enchiladas, *chile colorado*, *huevos con chorizo*, and so on. The food is delicious, and the portions are overwhelming. Closed Tuesday. ~ 812 North Evergreen Avenue; 213-268-1960. BUDGET.

◄ HIDDEN

For neighborhood shopping in an ethnic environment, just traverse the Macy Street Bridge over the Los Angeles River and enter East Los Angeles. Affectionately known as "Little Mexico," the area around Brooklyn Avenue is chockablock with restaurants, markets, bridal

SHOPPING

THE HEARTBEAT OF A COMMUNITY

Many of the muralists decorating East Los Angeles' streets started at **Plaza de la Raza**. This Chicano cultural center is intimately involved in the artistic life of the community, sponsoring classes in dance, music, theater, and visual arts. For visitors there's a variety of regularly scheduled events. ~ 3540 North Mission Road; 213-223-2475. Adjacent to the cultural center, **Lincoln Park** features a lake and tree-studded picnic area.

shops, and toy stores. **El Mercado** is an enclosed marketplace filled with shops and stalls. Vendors here sell cowboy boots and Mexican blankets, restaurants serve up tacos *de cabeza* and strolling mariachis create an atmosphere of Old Mexico. ~ 3425 East 1st Street.

NIGHTLIFE The **Margo Albert Theatre**, part of the Plaza de la Raza arts center, hosts drama, music, and dance programs which are often related to Mexican holidays. ~ 3540 North Mission Road; 213-223-2475.

The East L.A. theater scene is dominated by the **Bilingual Foundation of the Arts**, which presents plays in English and Spanish. ~ 421 North Avenue 19; 213-225-4044.

A perfect place for a "girls night out," **Chippendale's** features exotic male dancers and a ladies-only crowd. The scene gets wild as the dancers strut about while the women stuff greenbacks into their G-strings. Cover. ~ 310-442-0025.

▼▼▼▼▼▼▼▼▼▼▼▼
Elysian Park– Silver Lake Area

Set along sloping hillsides and separated by parks and eucalyptus groves are several suburban neighborhoods. Once a favored spot among Yang-Na Indians, this hill-and-dale district is now inhabited by an intriguing mix of blue-and white-collar workers. While the areas around Elysian and Echo parks have become Hispanic neighborhoods, the heights above Silver Lake are given over to young white professionals, including a significant gay population. In fact, together with West Hollywood, Silver Lake has emerged as one of Los Angeles' major centers of gay culture. With its curving mountain roads, tile-topped houses, jogging paths, and city vistas, this last neighborhood is also popular with artists.

SIGHTS For the outdoor-minded, 575-acre **Elysian Park**, the city's second largest park, is a forested region of rolling hills and peaceful glens. There are picnic areas, meadows planted with exotic palm trees and numerous nature trails offering views of central Los Angeles and the San Gabriel Valley, as well as basketball, volleyball, and tennis courts. For the sports-minded, the park contains 56,000-seat **Dodger Stadium**, home of the Los Angeles Dodgers. ~ Located near the intersection of Routes 110 and 5; 213-224-1500.

Nearby, **Echo Park** features a palm-fringed lake complete with footbridge and ducks. There are rental boats for exploring the fountain and lotus flowers, which highlight this 15-acre body of water. There's also a playground. ~ Glendale Boulevard and Echo Park Avenue; 213-250-3578.

That circular structure with the imposing white columns across the street is **Angelus Temple**. Modeled after London's Royal Albert Hall, it served the congregation of spiritualist Aimee Semple McPherson during the 1920s and 1930s. Open Sunday, Wednesday, and Friday. ~ 1100 Glendale Boulevard; 213-484-1100.

The nearby neighborhood of **Angelino Heights** was the city's first suburb, built during the 1880s on a hill overlooking Downtown and connected to the business district by cable car. Today the once elegant borough, ragged along the edges, still retains vestiges of its glory days. Foremost is the **1300 block of Carroll Avenue**, where a string of gingerbread Victorians have been gussied up in the fashion of the Gay Nineties. Representing Los Angeles' largest concentration of Victorian houses, the street is an outdoor museum lined with turrets, gables, and fanciful woodwork.

Another noteworthy housing colony surrounds the reservoir at **Silver Lake**. Built after World War II, the homes are generally of stucco construction. Since they cover nearby hills, the best way to tour the neighborhood is by winding through the labyrinth of narrow streets which ascend from the lake. ~ Silver Lake Boulevard.

Of architectural note, though unappealing to my taste, is the row of houses on the **2200 block of East Silver Lake Boulevard**. Designed by Austrian architect Richard Neutra, they are stucco-and-plate-glass structures representative of the International Style.

DINING

Sunset Boulevard, particularly around Echo Park and Silver Lake, is a veritable restaurant row. Traveling northwest on this famous street you'll come upon restaurants of every ethnic persuasion. **Les Frères Taix** is a huge, common-denominator restaurant serving French country cuisine in several dining rooms. The lunch and dinner *cartes* include roast pork, trout almondine, chicken breast, and lamb chops. The interior is attractive, if crowded. ~ 1911 West Sunset Boulevard; 213-484-1265. BUDGET TO MODERATE.

Probably the cheapest place to dine is **Burrito King**, a take-out stand serving tacos, tostadas, enchiladas, and its namesake, as well as burgers. ~ 2109 West Sunset Boulevard; 213-413-9444. BUDGET.

◄ HIDDEN

Seafood Bay is the best type of seafood restaurant, one with an adjacent fish market, ensuring freshness. Just a naugahyde café with formica tables, it offers sole, swordfish, trout, calamari, shrimp, and practically everything else that swims. ~ 3916 West Sunset Boulevard; 213-664-3902. BUDGET TO MODERATE.

SHOPPING

You can browse the stacks or snuggle up in a reading chair at **Skylight Books** in Los Feliz. This marvelous facility has an extensive selection of foreign and American literature as well as literary periodicals. ~ 1818 North Vermont Avenue; 213-660-1175.

NIGHTLIFE

The **Dresden**, a stately brick-and-stained-glass restaurant, hosts an elegant piano bar. ~ 1760 North Vermont Avenue; 213-665-4294.

Get into the Latin swing of things at **La Fogata**, a sizzling Colombian restaurant and nightclub. Cover. ~ 3000 Los Feliz Boulevard; 213-664-2955.

The Bavarian-style **Red Lion Tavern**, a friendly German rathskeller, serves lagers in two-liter boots. The German bartenders occasionally initiate impromptu sing-alongs, especially after games at nearby Dodger Stadium. ~ 2366 Glendale Boulevard; 213-662-5337.

There are two small theaters of note in Silver Lake. **Colony Studio Theatre Playhouse**, originally built in 1927 as a movie palace, hosts classic dramas, musicals, and new plays. ~ 1944 Riverside Drive; 213-665-3011. The **Celebration Theatre** presents gay and lesbian productions. ~ 7051-B Santa Monica Boulevard; 213-857-8085.

The Hyperion, known locally as Woody's, is a casual Levis bar with deejay music. Cover. ~ 2810 Hyperion Avenue; 213-660-1503.

▼▼▼▼▼▼▼▼▼▼▼▼▼▼
Mt. Washington Area

If an entire neighborhood could qualify as an outdoor museum, the Mt. Washington district would probably charge admission. Here within a few blocks are several picture-book expressions of desert culture.

SIGHTS

The **Lummis House**, or El Alisal, is the work of one man, Charles Fletcher Lummis, whose life is inextricably bound to the history of the region. Though born in the Northeast, Lummis fell in love with the Southwest, devoting his life to defending the region's Indian tribes and promoting local arts and crafts. A writer and magazine editor, he built this stone house himself, using granite from the nearby arroyo, carving the doors by hand and placing his Indian photos everywhere, even embedding pictures in the windows where the sun still shines through them. Surrounded by a cactus garden, the house is an excellent example of turn-of-the-century Southwestern sensibilities. ~ 200 East Avenue 43; 213-222-0546.

HIDDEN ►

Perhaps Charles Lummis' most important role was as founder of the **Southwest Museum**. Set in a Mission-style structure overlooking downtown Los Angeles, this important facility contains exquisite jewelry, basketry, weaving, and other handicrafts from Pueblo Indian tribes. California's Indians are represented by their petroglyphs, pottery, weapons, and decorative beadwork. In fact, the museum has so expanded its collection since Lummis' day that the current theme focuses more on American Indians in general than on the Southwest. There are bead papooses, a tepee, and leather clothing hand-painted by Plains Indians; totem poles and artifacts from the Pacific Northwest tribes; and an excellent research library. Admission. ~ 234 Museum Drive; 213-221-2163.

That antique neighborhood on the other side of the Pasadena Freeway is **Heritage Square**, an eclectic collection of historic buildings. Several impressive Victorian buildings, a Methodist church, and the old Palms Railroad Depot rest here. Carted from all over the city, they constitute a kind of architectural graveyard. Open on weekends and most major holidays. Admission. ~ 3800 Homer Street; 818-449-0193.

There are hundreds, perhaps thousands of
reasons to visit Los Angeles. But could any be
as important as a Richard Nixon pilgrimage?

Think about it, a sacred visit to the hometown of the only president
who ever resigned from office, "Tricky Dick" himself, the first national leader ever compelled to assure the American public that "I
am not a crook."

Anyone who has ever heard a maudlin Nixon speech knows Whittier,
where the 37th President of the United States was raised, schooled,
and elected to Congress. The **Whittier Chamber of Commerce** is a
source of information. ~ 8158 Painter Avenue; 310-698-9554.

Among the highlights are **East Whittier Elementary School** (Whittier Boulevard and Gunn Avenue); **Whittier Union High School** (Philadelphia Street and Pierce Avenue), where young Richard graduated
in 1930; and the Spanish-style campus of **Whittier College** (Painter
Avenue and Philadelphia Street), from which he received his diploma
four years later.

The **Whittier Museum and Historical Society** has displays on
local history from the 1800s and early 1900s. Permanent exhibits include "Main Street in the 1890s," complete with shop windows, and
a working replica of the original 1905 "Old Red Car," which carries passengers into the children's room. Here, kids play with turn-
of-the-century typewriters, telephones, and clothes. There are also
temporary exhibits such as the recent retrospective of Richard Nixon's
early life. Open Saturday and Sunday to the public. ~ 6755 Newlin
Street, Whittier; 310-945-3871.

The Nixon family store was tragically converted into a gas station, but the **Pat Ryan Nixon House**, where the future First Lady
lived when she met her husband, still stands. ~ 13513 Terrace Place.

The couple married in 1940; after the future President was elected
to Congress in 1946, the **Nixon residence** became a modest, low-
slung stucco house. Characteristic of the esteem in which Nixon is
held these days, none of these places acknowledge the Watergate
President. Not to worry, for those of us who remain true believers,
each location is an immortal shrine. ~ 14033 Honeysuckle Lane.

Of course the true pilgrimage is to the **Richard Nixon Library and
Birthplace**. Here you'll find the 900-square-foot home (that "made up
in love what it lacked in size") where Nixon was born "on the coldest day of one of the coldest winters in California history." Indeed.

The library itself, with barely a book to be seen, is a marvelous
succession of movies, interactive videos and touch-screen presentations that rewrite American history in a fashion that would make
even a novelist blush. Admission. ~ 18001 Yorba Linda Boulevard,
Yorba Linda; 714-993-3393.

Another famous politician, who eventually died in poverty, made
his home nearby. **Pío Pico State Historic Park** contains the 13-room

adobe house built by Pío Pico, the last governor of California under Mexican rule. Surrounded today by freeways and railroad tracks, the home was once a vibrant center of Mexican life during the 19th century. For the time being the adobe is being completely restored and can only be viewed by reserving appointments for guided tours. ~ 6003 Pioneer Boulevard, Whittier; 310-695-1217.

In the summer of 1997 the area code for the city of Whittier will change from 310 to 562.

A natural island in a sea of commerce, **Whittier Narrows Nature Center** is a 277-acre preserve near the San Gabriel and Rio Hondo rivers. Over 275 bird species have been sighted within this quiltwork of rivers, lakes, and open fields. To help you get back to the basics, there are nature trails and an interpretive center. ~ 1000 North Durfee Avenue, South El Monte; 818-575-5523.

Another point of interest, the **El Monte Historic Museum** resides in a classic Spanish-style building which was actually part of a 1936 WPA project. In addition to a typical 19th-century El Monte home, the facility contains representations of the town's old general store, school, and barber shop, as well as an art gallery. Rich in historic lore, the surrounding area was the terminus of the Santa Fe Trail; as a result, the museum has countless photographs, maps, and diaries from the pioneer era. Closed Saturday and Monday. ~ 3150 North Tyler Avenue, El Monte; 818-444-3813.

Who could have imagined that the City of Industry, located deep in the industrial outlands of Los Angeles, would remember its roots with a tree-lined historic park? **The Workman and Temple Family Homestead Museum**, an impressive six-acre site, contains the Workman House (a 19th-century adobe), a Victorian-style gazebo, and the county's oldest private cemetery. The centerpiece of the park is La Casa Nueva, a 1920s-era Spanish Colonial Revival mansion complete with stained-glass windows, hand-carved ornaments, decorative tiles, and intricate iron fittings. Tours of this intriguing complex concentrate primarily on the 1840s, 1870s, and 1920s, when the various buildings were being constructed. Closed Monday. ~ 15415 East Don Julian Road, Industry; 818-968-8492.

HIDDEN ►

Carrying you forward to the tacky architecture of the 1950s, in the equally tacky town of La Puente, is **The Donut Hole**. This drive-through snack bar consists of two structures in the shape of giant donuts. Though these architectural accretions look more like overinflated truck tires than anything edible, visitors drive through the first donut hole, place their orders, then exit via the second donut. ~ 15300 East Amar Road, La Puente; 818-968-2912.

DINING

HIDDEN ►

You wouldn't expect to find a Chinese seafood restaurant of gourmet caliber in a suburban mall. Granted, the **Dragon Regency** is located in the Chinatown section of Monterey Park. But snake soup in a shopping center? Not to mention sea cucumber with straw, braised fish snouts, pan-fried eel, and other adventurous dishes. There are also crab, lobster, oyster, shrimp, conch, clam, and fresh fish entrées, plus selections of duck, beef, and squab. The interior completes the theme of unpredictability, with delicate Chinese paintings and a large aquarium. Outstanding! ~ 120 South Atlantic Boulevard, Monterey Park; 818-282-1089. BUDGET TO MODERATE.

FRANK G. BONELLI REGIONAL PARK 🚶🚲🐎 🛶 🏊 🚤 **PARKS**
🛥️ This 2200-acre facility is a combination of tree-covered hills and theme park attractions. For the outdoor-minded there are trails, stables, and a 250-acre lake with boating and fishing facilities. There are also picnic areas, restrooms, a snack bar, and groceries. The rest of the crowd beelines to **Raging Waters** (909-592-6453), an aquatic theme park with waterslides and simulated surfing waves. Open spring and summer. Visitors who can't decide between the natural and artificial head for the golf course and hot tubs. ~ 120 Via Verde in San Dimas; 909-599-8411.

▲ Permitted at **East Shore RV Park** located within the park. There are 519 sites (with full hookups), $23 to $26 per night, and 25 tent sites, $24 per night. ~ 909-599-8355.

Extending from Downtown all the way to the Pacific, Wilshire Boulevard reaches for 16 miles through the ▼▼▼▼▼▼▼▼▼▼ **Wilshire District** western heart of Los Angeles. In its course the grand avenue passes Jewish, Korean, Southeast Asian, Filipino, Mexican, and Central American neighborhoods. Originally an Indian trail leading from the downtown area to the La Brea tar pits, the boulevard was developed during the 1890s by H. Gaylord Wilshire, a socialist with an ironic knack for making money in real estate.

Not far from Wilshire's street stands an institution which would **SIGHTS** have offended his socialist sensibilities while piquing his interest in profits. Smaller and more sedate than its New York counterpart, the **Pacific Stock Exchange** nevertheless conveys a sense of financial drama. Peering through windows in the visitors' gallery, you can look down on the confetti-strewn floor, banks of computers, and crowds in business suits. ~ 233 South Beaudry Avenue, 12th floor; 213-977-4500.

Several stately Victorians, built in the 19th century when the Westlake district was a wealthy neighborhood, remain along the **800 and 1000 blocks of South Bonnie Brae Street**. Particularly dramatic are the Queen Anne confection at 818 and the onion-domed house next door.

MacArthur Park, a 32-acre greensward bisected by Wilshire Boulevard, is one of Los Angeles' oldest parks. Today the place has become a gathering place for local immigrants, who enjoy the shady picnic areas, playground, and snack bar. Home to more than 80 plant species, the park's central feature is a small lake complete with fountain, boat rental, and palm-fringed island inhabited by ducks. ~ Alvarado Street between 6th and 7th streets.

One of Los Angeles' truly exquisite structures, the former **I. Magnin Building**, a 1929 art deco extravaganza, is marked by a solitary tower. Built on several tiers in a series of thin, fluted columns, the building is faced with ornamental copper. ~ 3050 Wilshire Boulevard.

Another art deco masterpiece, the **Wiltern Center**, lies a few blocks away. A towering building with wings flaring from either side, the structure was built in 1931 and is covered in green terra cotta. ~ 3780 Wilshire Boulevard.

Not to be outclassed, the residential architecture of **Hancock Park** includes posh estates once owned by the Crocker, Huntington, and Doheny families. Developed during the 1920s, this well-tended neighborhood contains a variety of architectural styles. With wide boulevards and manicured lawns, it's a perfect place for a Sunday drive (even on a Tuesday). ~ Between Wilshire Boulevard and Melrose Avenue, centered around the Wilshire Country Club.

One of the highlights of the district, politically if not architecturally, is the **Getty House**. A 1921 Tudor home with leaded-glass windows and slate roof, it is the official residence of the mayor of Los Angeles. ~ 605 South Irving Boulevard.

HIDDEN ► **St. Elmo Village** marks another breed of neighborhood entirely. Here a complex of cottages has been transformed into a kind of creative art center. The simple bungalows are painted nursery colors and adorned with murals and sculptures. Containing private residences and art studios, the settlement is luxuriously landscaped. Houses are open to the public. ~ 4830 St. Elmo Drive; 213-931-3409.

Back in the 1920s and 1930s the showcase for commercial architecture rested along the **Miracle Mile**. That was when an enterprising developer turned the area into a classy corridor for shops and businesses. The magnificent art deco towers that lined the strip still survive, particularly between the 5200 and 5500 blocks of Wilshire, but Wilshire's early glory has faded as the area has changed from popular to historic. ~ Wilshire Boulevard between La Brea and Fairfax avenues.

Still retaining its luster and heritage is **Carthay Circle**, a cluster of small 1930-era homes. This antique neighborhood is shaped more like a triangle than a circle. The Spanish stucco and art deco homes create an island surrounded by streets streaming with traffic. ~ Bounded by Fairfax Avenue and Wilshire and San Vicente boulevards.

HIDDEN ► L.A.'s vernacular architecture is alive and well at **Tail O' The Pup**, a hot dog stand shaped (how else?) like a hot dog. Created in 1946, the hot dog was actually moved to its present location, where it stands in humorous contrast to its well-heeled neighbors. ~ 329 North San Vicente Boulevard; 310-652-4517.

If you're fascinated by wee things, you'll marvel at the displays in the **Caroline and Barry Kaye Museum of Miniatures**. This museum is a fantasy world of priceless miniatures in every conceivable setting, from Old West scenes to a Japanese imperial palace. Closed Monday. Admission. ~ 5900 Wilshire Boulevard; 310-277-8108.

The West's largest museum is a multibuilding complex with an international art collection. Providing a thumbnail tour of the entire history of art, the **Los Angeles County Museum of Art** ranges from pre-Columbian gold objects and African masks to post–World War II minimalist works. Stops along the way include sculpture, paintings, and stained-glass windows from the Middle Ages; a Renaissance gallery featuring Rembrandt and other Masters; Impressionist paintings by Cézanne, Gauguin, and Monet; and early-20th-century creations by Magritte, Chagall, and Miró. The Pavilion for Japanese Art, houses the well-known Shin'enkan collection of paintings as well as Japanese screens, scrolls, ceramics, and sculpture. The entire complex is beautifully laid out around a central courtyard adorned with terra cotta pillars and four-tiered waterfall. Admission. ~ 5905 Wilshire Boulevard; 213-857-6111.

Beauty gives way to the beast at the adjacent **George C. Page Museum**. This paleontological showplace features displays of mammoths, mastodons, and ground sloths. There are also extinct camels, ancient horses, and ancestral condors. Admission. ~ 5801 Wilshire Boulevard; 213-936-2230.

Altogether, there are more than 200 varieties of other creatures that fell victim to the **La Brea Tar Pits**, which surround the museum. Dating to the Pleistocene Era, these oozing oil pools trapped birds, mammals, insects, and reptiles, creating fossil deposits which are still being discovered by scientists. Indians once used the tar to caulk boats and roofs. Today you can wander past the pits, which bubble menacingly with methane gas and lie covered in globs of black tar.

The **Craft & Folk Art Museum** nearby is a small gallery with a rotating exhibit. Arts and crafts from all over the world are displayed. Admission. ~ 5814 Wilshire Boulevard; 213-937-5544.

OY TOGETHER NOW

A favorite gathering place of the Jewish community is the intersection of Fairfax and Oakwood avenues. Here one corner supports a mural depicting Jewish life in Los Angeles and another corner contains **Al's Newsstand**, which sells periodicals from around the world. ~ 370 North Fairfax Avenue; 213-935-8525.

HIDDEN ►   Another tiny but intensely powerful exhibit is the **Martyrs Memorial & Museum of the Holocaust.** Devoted to the tragedy of World War II, it is filled with images from the Nazi extermination camps. The ovens of Buchenwald, the gas chambers of Auschwitz, and skeletal figures from other camps are captured in terrifying detail. The photos portray masses being executed; tiny children, their hands in the air, surrounded by storm troopers; and a mother being shot while clutching a child in her arms. Many of the docents are Holocaust survivors with personal stories to recount as they lead visitors through these harrowing halls. Closed Saturday. ~ 6505 Wilshire Boulevard; 213-852-3242.

Nearby, **Fairfax Avenue** is the center of the city's Jewish community. Since World War II this middle-class neighborhood has been a local capital for Los Angeles Semites. Filled with delicatessens, bakeries, and kosher grocery stores, it is occupied by Orthodox, Hasidic, and Reform Jews. ~ Located between Beverly Boulevard and Melrose Avenue.

Back in 1934 local farmers created a cooperative market where they could congregate and sell their goods. Today the **Farmers Market** is an open-air labyrinth of stalls, shops, and vendor stands. There are tables overflowing with vegetables, fruits, meats, cheeses, and baked goods, a total of over 160 outlets. Stop by for groceries, gifts, and finger foods or simply to catch Los Angeles at its relaxed and informal best. ~ 6333 West 3rd Street; 213-933-9211.

The Asian answer to gentrification is evident in **Koreatown,** a burgeoning neighborhood that is rapidly redefining the Wilshire District. Colorful storefronts, refurbished cottages, and Korean calligraphy have transformed the entire area into a unique enclave. ~ Centered between 4th Street and Olympic Boulevard, Western Avenue and Vermont Avenue.

In fact, if you take a long drive down Pico Boulevard or Olympic Boulevard from the Harbor Freeway (Route 110) to Fairfax Avenue, you'll pass through a succession of **ethnic neighborhoods** including Indonesian, Japanese, Taiwanese, Vietnamese, and Thai sections.

LODGING   The **Park Plaza Hotel,** a bulky art deco building constructed during the 1920s, was a fabulous hostelry back in the days when the Westlake district was in its prime. Today the aging establishment is a 160-room, Grade B hotel in a scruffy neighborhood. Vestiges of old glory remain, however, in the vaulted lobby with its arched columns and fresco ceiling. Cathedral-like in atmosphere, the room contains marble floors, stately chandeliers, and a grand stairway. Located across the street from MacArthur Park, the Park Plaza may be the most lavish low-priced hotel you'll ever encounter. ~ 607 South Park View Street; 213-384-5281, fax 213-480-1928. BUDGET.

Best Western, The Mayfair Hotel, located on the fringes of the Downtown district, is a 295-room hostelry. Built in 1928 and beautifully refurbished, it offers a touch of luxury at a price lower than the five-star hotels. There's a restaurant and lounge as well as an attractive skylit lobby. The guest rooms are average size and feature contemporary furnishings, textured wallpaper, and pastel color schemes. ~ 1256 West 7th Street; 213-484-9614, 800-821-8682, fax 213-484-2769. MODERATE TO DELUXE.

Another 1920s-era art deco building, the **Wilshire Royale Hotel** has been fashionably refurbished and transformed into a contemporary 200-room facility. The lobby is a beamed-ceiling affair with piano, fresh flowers, and upholstered armchairs. Rooms, decorated in a peach-colored motif, have tile baths and standard furnishings. Restaurant, lounge, pool, spa. This historic hotel is an excellent choice. ~ 2619 Wilshire Boulevard; 213-387-5311, 800-421-8072, fax 213-380-8174. MODERATE TO DELUXE.

The **Chancellor Hotel** is a residence hotel occupied primarily by students and young professionals. This 1924 Romanesque building also accommodates individual travelers, who share the lobby and recreation room with permanent residents. A five-story complex one block from Wilshire Boulevard, the Chancellor is well maintained. The price includes breakfast and dinner. ~ 3191 West 7th Street; 213-383-1183, 800-446-5552. MODERATE.

Wilshire Crest Inn is one of those terribly modern hotels with track lighting, black trim, and fabric wall coverings. The 34 rooms, built around an interior courtyard, are done in oak and furnished with platform beds. The color scheme, naturally, is pastel. There's a dining room where continental breakfast is served and a sitting area complete with potted plants and trimly upholstered armchairs. The hotel is conveniently located near Wilshire Boulevard in the Fairfax district. ~ 6301 Orange Street; 213-936-5131, 800-654-9951, fax 213-936-2013. MODERATE.

For cut-rate lodging consider the **Wilshire Orange Hotel**, a funky stucco resting place just off Wilshire Boulevard. Expect plaster walls, spotty carpets, damaged furniture, and some rooms that share baths. But generally the place is clean and neat (some rooms have been repainted and recarpeted); hot plates and refrigerators. ~ 6060 West 8th Street; 213-931-9533. BUDGET TO MODERATE.

MID-WILSHIRE DISTRICT   Elegance 24 hours a day? In a restaurant on wheels? Somehow all-night restaurants conjure visions of truckstop dives, but at **Pacific Dining Car** 'round-the-clock service is provided in dark wood surroundings. Modeled after an old-style railroad dining car, with plush booths and outsized plate-glass windows, this destination has been a Los Angeles landmark since 1921. The cuisine is well-heeled all-American: breakfast includes eggs Benedict and eggs Sardou, and the dinner menu features Maine lobster and some of the best steaks in the city. ~ 1310 West 6th Street; 213-483-6000. DELUXE TO ULTRA-DELUXE.

DINING

The reason for the balcony at **La Fonda** becomes stirringly evident every evening when Los Camperos strikes up a Spanish song. One of the city's best mariachi bands, they lure dinner guests by the dozens to this hacienda-style restaurant. In addition to the sound of Los Camperos, diners enjoy the flavor of Veracruz-style shrimp, steak *picado*, chicken flautas, and *chile verde*. No lunch on Saturday and Sunday. ~ 2501 Wilshire Boulevard; 213-380-5055. MODERATE.

The interior of **Casa Carnitas** is tiny but overwhelming. Colorful as an old mission chapel, the walls are covered with murals portraying Mayan warriors. Naturally, the food is Yucatecan and includes a variety of beef, chicken, and shrimp dishes prepared with tasty *ranchera* sauce. Considering the imaginative decor and low prices, Casa Carnitas is an excellent find. ~ 4067 West Beverly Boulevard; 213-667-9953. BUDGET.

HIDDEN ▶   **Tommy's Hamburgers** is a Los Angeles landmark. In fact at last count there were 17 such landmarks. But the original Tommy's, dating back to 1946, is at 2575 West Beverly Boulevard. Here you can enjoy "while you watch" service as they prepare hamburgers, hot dogs, and tamales before your hungry eyes. Open 24 hours, this is the place where they give you paper towels instead of napkins and still charge cheap prices. (Ain't L.A. amazing?) ~ 2575 West Beverly Boulevard; 213-389-9060. BUDGET.

The Original Sonora Café is a Southwestern restaurant decorated with earth tones, *viga* ceilings, and potted cactus. The patio in front is covered with wrought-iron lattice-work. Lunch and dinner include fajitas, duck tamales, chicken tostadas, and blue corn enchiladas. There are also fresh fish and steak dishes. Outdoor seating available with a view of the city skyline. ~ 180 South La Brea Avenue; 213-857-1800. MODERATE TO DELUXE.

Well-known for its Thai cuisine, **Chan Dara** is a modern restaurant with mirrored bar and brass-rail dining room. The specialties vary from spicy barbecue to vegetable entrées. Patio dining is available. ~ 310 North Larchmont Boulevard; 213-467-1052. MODERATE.

Also consider **La Fonda Antioqueña**, a Columbian restaurant that comes recommended by a former Consul General of Colombia. Here you will discover about 15 different platters, each prepared with South American flair. This intriguing ethnic restaurant offers everything from fish, chicken, beef, and pork dishes to liver and tongue. For an adventure in south-of-the-border dining, La Fonda Antioqueña is the place. ~ 4903 Melrose Avenue; 213-957-5164. MODERATE.

FAIRFAX DISTRICT   Angular beam ceiling, bright contemporary paintings, plain white walls, pipe sculpture aquarium, and candles. Sound chic? That's **Muse**, a California-cuisine restaurant with the feel of an offbeat art gallery. They serve pasta dishes as well as a changing repertoire of entrées. Examples: salmon with caviar and basmati rice, fusilli pasta with duck, honey-marinated pork with deep-fried won tons, and flame-broiled New York steak with shiitake mushrooms. It's the only menu I've ever seen written in English but still requiring translation. Closed Sunday and Monday. ~ 7360 Beverly Boulevard; 213-934-4400. MODERATE TO DELUXE.

Also out along the edge is **The Farm Café**, a healthy gourmet restaurant decorated in Southwestern fashion. With blond wood furniture, and changing contemporary artwork, it represents one of the city's few upscale vegetarian-oriented dining rooms. The bill of fare features baked egg rolls, corn and pinto bean griddle cakes, lentil chili, fresh fish, and organic chicken dishes. ~ 8009 Beverly Boulevard; 213-655-8895. MODERATE.

The Authentic Cafe is truly trendy, but the food merits its popularity. It raises the nebulous designation "Southwest cuisine" to something real and tasty: try the designer pizzas, Szechuan fire dumplings, chicken casserole in cornbread crust, or the chilaquiles. ~ 7605 Beverly Boulevard; 213-939-4626. MODERATE.

A restaurant inside a flower shop is unique enough, but it's the clever concoctions, healthfully prepared, that account for the popularity of **Flora Kitchen**. Sandwiches and salads are the specialties, with ingredients such as olive tapenade, roasted peppers, fresh herbs, buffalo mozzarella, and fresh ahi tuna. They do breakfast, lunch, and dinner (with special hot entrées in the evening), cappuccino, and espresso. Flora also does a booming gourmet takeout business, and you can pick up fresh flowers at the same time. ~ 460 South La Brea Boulevard; 213-931-9900. BUDGET TO MODERATE.

Farmers Market, a sprawling open-air collection of vendor stands, is a good spot to visit and an even better place to eat. The takeout stands lining each corridor dispense burritos, egg rolls, jambalaya, corned beef, hot dogs, fish and chips, and every other type of ethnic food imaginable. Simply order at the counter, then find a table in the sun. ~ 6333 West 3rd Street; 213-933-9211. BUDGET.

Also in the Farmers Market area are two critically acclaimed ethnic restaurants. **Sofi Greek Restaurant** is a family-run Greek restaurant with a potful of grandmother's recipes. Open for lunch and din-

---

THE WURST IS THE BEST

L.A.'s best known delicatessen lies at the heart of the Jewish neighborhood around Fairfax Avenue. **Canter's**, a casual 24-hour restaurant, doubles as local landmark and ethnic cultural center. As you might have guessed, lox and bagels, hot pastrami, corned beef, and matzo ball soup are the order of the day. When in doubt, go kosher. ~ 419 North Fairfax Avenue; 213-651-2030. BUDGET TO MODERATE.

ner, they serve moussaka in the dining room or out on the patio. No lunch on Sunday. ~ 8030¾ West 3rd Street; 213-651-0346. MODERATE TO DELUXE.

Siamese Princess is a fashionable Thai bistro oddly decorated with unmatched antiques and pictures of international royalty. There are 160 wines on the four-star wine list. But remember, you came for the spicy Asian cuisine. ~ 8048 West 3rd Street; 213-653-2643. MODERATE.

SOUTH OF WILSHIRE   El Izalqueño is a plain, naugahyde café offering a multitude of Salvadoran dishes. The interior is a strange blend of tacky oil paintings and an overly loud jukebox. But the food—varying from breaded chicken to shredded beef, shrimp with garlic to steamed gizzards—is very inviting. ~ 1830 West Pico Boulevard; 213-387-2467. BUDGET.

One of Koreatown's best restaurants is a multiroom complex named **Dong Il Jang**. The place contains several dining rooms as well as a sushi bar, each decorated with bamboo screens and Asian statuary. The Korean dinners include *maewoon tahng* (spicy codfish casserole), *kalbi* (marinated ribs), and *jun bok juk* (abalone porridge). A complete offering of Japanese dishes is also presented. ~ 3455 West 8th Street; 213-383-5757. MODERATE.

HIDDEN ▶   Favored among savvy locals, **Rosalind's West African Cuisine** serves plantains, yam balls, and *akara* (deep-fried black-eyed peas). Main courses include Niger-style goat (sautéed with African herbs and spices), sautéed beef with onions and herbs, and groundnut stew (with nuts, beef, chicken, and spices). Added to the exotic cuisine is a complete wall mural depicting a waterfall on the Nile river. ~ 1044 South Fairfax Avenue; 213-936-2486. MODERATE.

SHOPPING   A spate of new art galleries, and restaurants has attracted a flood of shoppers along **La Brea Avenue**. The La Brea corridor, as the area between Wilshire Boulevard and Melrose Avenue has come to be called, is home to a collection of innovative galleries. **Jan Baum** presents national and international contemporary art exhibits. ~ 170 South La Brea Avenue; 213-932-0170. **Frank Lloyd Gallery** offers much of the same. ~ 170 South La Brea Avenue; 213-939-2189. **Jack Rutberg Fine Arts** features modern paintings, drawings, sculptures, original prints, and museum-quality collectibles. ~ 357 North La Brea Avenue; 213-938-5222.

Along Wilshire Boulevard, stop in at the gift shop at the **Los Angeles County Museum of Art**, where you'll find art books, photographic items, and graphic reproductions. ~ 5905 Wilshire Boulevard; 213-857-6146. Or visit the **Craft & Folk Art Museum** where contemporary folk art is the theme. In addition to arts and crafts items, this gallery-cum-museum stocks books and unusual gift items. ~ 5800 Wilshire Boulevard; 213-937-5544.

Farmers Market, an informal, open-air market which originated during the Depression to help farmers sell eggs and produce, has evolved into a giant shopping complex. Frequented by Angelenos and tourists alike, Farmers Market is a European boulevard, Oriental bazaar, and Mexican market all in one. In addition to fruit and vegetable stands, there are crafts shops, clothing outlets, and sundry shops in this urban marketplace. ~ 6333 West 3rd Street; 213-933-9211.

Nearby Fairfax Avenue, the center of L.A.'s Jewish community, is a neighborhood steeped in religious tradition and filled with delis, bakeries, and kosher grocery stores. **Canter's,** with its sumptuous baked goods and delicious sandwiches, is by far the most popular deli in the district. ~ 419 North Fairfax Avenue; 213-651-2030.

Journeying from the ethnic to the futuristic, you'll arrive at the **Beverly Center,** a neon-laced shopping mall with signature clothing stores, world-class restaurants, and a multiplex entertainment center. Exterior glass-enclosed elevators move shoppers quickly through this eight-acre complex. ~ 8500 Beverly Boulevard; 310-854-0070.

Among the center's 200 international shops and restaurants is **Following Sea,** a gift shop selling many items you didn't know you wanted and a few that you didn't know existed. ~ 310-659-0592.

The city's burgeoning **Koreatown** is a warren of small shops and markets, each brightly painted in the calligraphy of the East. While many sell Korean foodstuffs and cater to local clientele, each provides a small glimpse into the life of this energetic community. ~ Centered between 4th Street and Olympic Avenue, Western Avenue and Vermont Avenue.

The **Korean Shopping Center** is a small shopping arcade housing quality shops. Inside is an exceptional boutique, **Marie France** (213-480-0013). ~ 3300 West 8th Street.

NIGHTLIFE

The Mexican food may be good at **El Cholo,** but the famed margaritas really draw the crowds to this lively bar scene. ~ 1121 South Western Avenue; 213-734-2773.

Tom Bergin's, a traditional Irish pub dating to the 1930s, was voted one of the top 100 bars in the United States by *Esquire* magazine. Judging from the 7500 patron-inscribed shamrocks mounted on the wood-paneled walls, the regular crowd confirms *Esquire's* vote. ~ 840 South Fairfax Avenue; 213-936-7151.

Actors, musicians, and writers meet in the small **Coronet Pub,** a comfortable and unpretentious spot to carouse. ~ 370 North La Cienega Boulevard; 310-659-4583.

The **Hard Rock Cafe,** a wildly popular gathering place in the Beverly Center, features the loud music and rock memorabilia decor for which this nightclub chain is renowned. A Cadillac protruding from the roof and walls covered with Beatles artifacts and Madonna icons add to the ambience. ~ 8600 Beverly Boulevard; 310-276-7605.

The **Wiltern Theater** opened its doors in 1931 as a Warner Brothers movie house. Now restored to its art deco splendor, the terra cotta structure is a center for the performing arts. Rock and classical music, drama, and opera programs are regularly scheduled. ~ 3790 Wilshire Boulevard; 213-380-5005.

A beautiful 1927 Renaissance-style building, the **Wilshire Ebell Theatre** is the setting for television specials and live theater, opera, and dance presentations. ~ 4401 West 8th Street; 213-939-1128.

The **Coronet Theatre** presents comedies, musicals, and occasional dramas. ~ 366 North La Cienega Boulevard; 310-657-7377.

Here in the land of celluloid, where movies began, what could be more appropriate than the **Silent Movie**. This imaginative movie house shows old silent films complete with organ accompaniment. ~ 611 North Fairfax Avenue; 213-653-2389.

▼▼▼▼▼▼▼▼
Hollywood

It was farm country when Horace and Daeida Wilcox first moved to Cahuenga Valley. Originally part of the Rancho La Brea land grant, the dusty hills lay planted in bell peppers, watermelons, and citrus trees. Then in 1887 Horace had a brainstorm: he subdivided the family farm, Daeida christened the spread "Hollywood," and they put lots on the market for $150 an acre.

By 1910, the cow town's population had grown to 4000 middle-class, god-fearing souls. Like the Wilcoxes, they were staid and sober folk, drawn predominantly from Midwestern stock.

Then came the deluge. The fledgling movie industry—attracted by warm weather and natural locations and conspiring to avoid the royalties levied by Thomas Edison's east coast company for use of his moving picture inventions—began relocating to Hollywood. The first studio arrived in 1911. Two years later the trio of Jesse Lasky, Samuel Goldfish (later Goldwyn), and Cecil B. De Mille set up shop. De Mille soon began shooting *Squaw Man*, the first full-length motion picture, in a barn on the corner of Selma Avenue and Vine Street.

The townsfolk termed these studios "gypsy camps" and posted signs declaring, "No dogs, No actors." Movie people were Easterners, morally suspect and in many cases Jewish, defining characteristics guaranteed to stir unease among the local Protestant majority.

But if there is no stopping progress, it is simply impossible to halt a tidal wave. During the 1920s the movie industry became a billion-dollar business, with Hollywood its capital. Picture palaces mushroomed along Hollywood Boulevard beside glamorous restaurants and majestic hotels and by 1930 the population totaled 150,000.

Hollywood's glory days lasted until the 1960s, when development gave way to decline. The boulevard of dreams became a byway for bikers; Chevys with hydraulic lifters replaced limousines; punks with flaming hair supplanted platinum starlets; and movie studios moved to the San Fernando Valley. Prostitutes worked side streets,

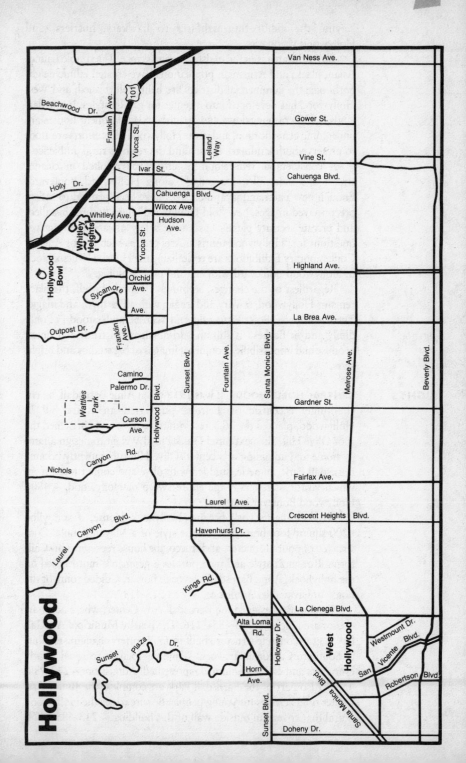

leaving the major thoroughfares to hawkers, hustlers, and Hollywood visionaries.

Today the area is in the midst of a renaissance. The sizable Latino, Asian, black, and Armenian populations have created ethnic neighborhoods; the commercial districts are being refurbished; and West Hollywood has developed into a center for gay lifestyles. In the flatlands, 1920-era bungalows and Spanish-style apartment houses are undergoing gentrification, and in the Hollywood Hills efforts are afoot to preserve both landmark homes and the region's rural ambience.

A considerable redevelopment effort has resulted in cleaner streets and sidewalks, particularly along Hollywood Boulevard. Enough new palm and jacaranda trees have been planted to satisfy preconceived images, new "old Hollywood" light fixtures installed, and private security patrols ensure the safety of (and even answer questions for) Hollywood tourists. Arts groups such as Los Angeles Contemporary Exhibitions are revitalizing the Hudson-Wilcox block of Hollywood Boulevard with cultural programming.

Regardless of the changes, seemingly in spite of itself, the place remains Hollywood, tawdry and tragic, with all its myth and magic. The town that F. Scott Fitzgerald said "can be understood . . . only dimly and in flashes" is still an odd amalgam of truth and tinsel, promise and impossibility, conjuring images of big studios and bright stars.

SIGHTS

CENTRAL HOLLYWOOD   It was 1918 when Aline Barnsdall, an enchantingly eccentric oil heiress, purchased an entire hill in Hollywood, planted the 36 acres with olive trees and christened the spot Olive Hill. She next hired Frank Lloyd Wright to design a family home and adjoining arts center. Olive Hill subsequently became **Barnsdall Park**, an aerie, studded with olive and conifer trees, from which visitors can survey the entire sweep of Hollywood. ~ 4800 Hollywood Boulevard.

Wright's masterwork became **Hollyhock House**, a sprawling 6200-square-foot home built in the style of a Mayan temple. Constructed of poured concrete and stucco, the house represents his California Romanza style and incorporates a geometric motif based on the hollyhock, Aline Barnsdall's favorite flower. Guided tours of the house are available. Admission. ~ 213-913-4157.

Wright also designed the **Barnsdall Arts Center**, where adult art classes are taught. ~ 213-485-2116. The nearby **Municipal Art Gallery**, a gray concrete structure built in 1971, offers changing exhibits of Southern California artwork. While the focus is regional, nearly every arts and crafts medium is represented. Admission. ~ 213-485-4581. Also part of the Barnsdall Park art complex, the **Junior Arts Center** offers classes for young people. Be sure to see the Hollywood mural that covers an outside wall of this building. ~ 213-485-4474.

Until recently, the public wasn't allowed behind the famous wrought-iron gate, at **Paramount Studios**. A subject for countless newsreels and Hollywood movies, the portal's most memorable appearance was in *Sunset Boulevard* (1950) when Erich von Stroheim drove Gloria Swanson onto the lot for her tragic encounter with Cecil B. De Mille.

Paramount is the last of the great studios to remain in Hollywood. Established during the silent era, the production company signed stars such as Rudolph Valentino and Clara Bow in the 1920s, Gary Cooper and Marlene Dietrich during the 1930s, and later headlined Dorothy Lamour, Betty Hutton, Bob Hope, and Bing Crosby. Tours consist of a behind-the-scenes view of this vast studio. Tours are offered Monday through Friday. Admission. ~ 5555 Melrose Avenue; 213-956-5575.

Many of these same legends lie buried just north of the studio in **Hollywood Memorial Park Cemetery**. Surrounded by high walls and shaded with palm trees, the 60-acre greensward is a kind of museum park crowded with Greek statues, Egyptian temples, and Roman memorials. Marble urns and obelisks adorn the place, and the Paramount water tower rises above the south wall.

Along the eastern side of the cemetery, Rudolph Valentino rests in Cathedral Mausoleum, crypt number 1205; Peter Finch is across the aisle in number 1224. Around the nearby pond are the graves of Tyrone Power, Marion Davies, Adolphe Menjou, and the double tomb of Cecil B. De Mille and his wife, Constance Adam De Mille. Next to the Cathedral Mausoleum, a staircase leads to the reflecting pool and tomb of Douglas Fairbanks. ~ 6000 Santa Monica Boulevard.

Despite numerous incarnations, including the most recent as headquarters for A & M Records, the **Charlie Chaplin Studios** have weathered the years relatively unchanged. This row of Tudor cottages, built by Chaplin in 1918, housed the star's sound stage, dressing rooms, carpentry shop, and stables. ~ 1416 North La Brea Avenue.

No one can quite figure how Movieland's most famous address became so prominent. Most of the action occurred elsewhere, but somehow the corner of **Hollywood and Vine** has come to symbolize Hollywood. But Hollywood is good at making the most of fables, so

GRAVE MATTERS

For a tour of the truly macabre there's **Graveline Tours**. From your resting place in a Cadillac hearse you'll see the hotel where John Belushi died, the spot where George "Superman" Reeves shot himself, and the sites of other infamous Hollywood deaths. Heavy, man. Closed Monday. ~ P.O. Box 931694, Hollywood, CA 90093; 213-469-4149.

new "skytracker" lights at each of the four corners create an archway of light above the vaunted intersection.

Maybe its the many radio studios that lined the thoroughfare during the 1930s, or perhaps because the **Pantages Theater** is just down the street. One of the nation's finest art deco theaters, the Pantages was built in 1930, with a vaulted-ceiling lobby and a monumental auditorium. ~ 6233 Hollywood Boulevard; 213-468-1770.

The Mediterranean-style **Alto Nido Apartments** at 1851 North Ivar Street was the fictional home of the down-and-out screenwriter played by William Holden in *Sunset Boulevard*.

Gazing down on all the commotion is the **Capitol Records Building**, a building you have seen in countless photographs. Resembling a squadron of flying saucers piggy-backed on one another, the 13-story structure was actually designed to look like a stack of records with a stylus protruding from the top. ~ 1750 Vine Street.

In a tribute to the great studios once occupying the area, **Home Savings of America** adorned its facade with the names of hundreds of stars and added a tile mural depicting the most noteworthy. The interior contains a marvelous stained-glass window with scenes from Hollywood's early movies. ~ 1500 North Vine Street.

Eschewing nostalgia, a nonprofit gallery, the **Los Angeles Contemporary Exhibitions** (LACE) provides space for performance art, video productions, and film forums. ~ 6522 Hollywood Boulevard; 213-957-1777.

During the halcyon days of the 1920s, as silent movies gave way to talkies, Hollywood Boulevard was door-to-door with mansions. **The Janes House**, one of the last of this long-vanished breed, is a Queen Anne Victorian complete with turret, gable, and stained-glass windows. This architectural grande belle rests at the end of a plastic shopping mall and houses the **Hollywood Visitors Information Center**. Perhaps they can tell you where to find the lost beauty of Hollywood. Closed Sunday. ~ 6541 Hollywood Boulevard; 213-236-2331.

Today, Hollywood Boulevard has been taken over by taco vendors, cut-rate video stores, T-shirt shops, and souvenir stands. More like New York's 42nd Street than the Great White Way, it's a cheap strip where photo galleries take tourists' pictures next to cardboard cutouts of stars.

The perfect expression of this high-camp neighborhood is **Frederick's of Hollywood**, a lingerie shop located in an outrageous purple and pink art deco building. With a naughty reputation and a selection of undergarments that leave nothing to the imagination, Frederick's is one of those places we visit in spite of ourselves. Be sure to make your way to the back of the store and visit **Frederick's of Hollywood Lingerie Museum**, rich in Hollywood's version of cultural treasures. On display are a tassles-and-leather bustier from Madonna, the bra Marilyn Monroe wore in *Let's Make Love*, a more modest (but autographed) 32B from Cher, and celebrity undergarments worn by such icons as Mae West and Zsa Zsa Gabor. ~ 6608 Hollywood Boulevard; 213-466-8506.

Then there's the **Hollywood Wax Museum**, a melancholy place where you can "see your favorite stars in living wax." Here they are— Marilyn Monroe and Elvis Presley, Clint Eastwood and Sylvester Stallone—looking just as they would three days after rigor mortis set in, that classic grin or sneer frozen forevermore into a candle with arms. Admission. ~ 6767 Hollywood Boulevard; 213-462-8860.

Built by Sid Grauman in 1927, **Mann's Chinese Theater** is a fabulous movie palace, fashioned in a kind of Oriental Baroque style with pagoda roof, stone guard dogs, metal towers, Asian masks, and beautiful bas-reliefs. The interior is equally as lavish with its ornate columns, murals, and Asian vases.

Though the architecture is splendid, the theater is actually known for its sidewalk. Embedded in the cement forecourt are the handprints and footprints of Hollywood's greatest stars. Jean Harlow, Rock Hudson, Cary Grant, and Jimmy Stewart have left their signatures in this grandest of all autograph collections. Not every celebrity simply signed and stepped, however: there are also cement images of Jimmy Durante's nose, Betty Grable's leg, Harpo Marx's harp, Sonja Henie's ice skates, Harold Lloyd's glasses, and the webbed feet of Donald Duck. ~ 6925 Hollywood Boulevard; 213-464-8111.

Throughout this area—extending for three and a half miles along Hollywood Boulevard from Gower Street to La Brea Boulevard and on Vine Street between Sunset Boulevard and Yucca Street—is the **Walk of Fame**, of star-studded terrazzo, commemorating notables from the film, television, radio, theater, and music industries. The names of over 1850 legends appear on brass-rimmed stars embedded in the sidewalk. Pride of Hollywood, it represents the only walkway in Los Angeles to be washed several times weekly.

The new sculpture at the intersection of Hollywood and La Brea boulevards defies simple characterization. It's a gleaming, 30-foothigh gazebo supported at each corner by a statue of a Hollywood legend (Dolores del Rio, Anna May Wong, Mae West, and Dorothy Dandridge) and crowned with what is supposed to be Marilyn Monroe but looks more like an angel atop the Eiffel Tower. Check it out.

Above Hollywood Boulevard, the **1800 block of North Ivar Street** is lined with apartment buildings reflecting the architecture of the 1920s and 1930s. Nathaniel West lived in the mock-Tudor Parua Sed Apartments at #1817 in 1935. Here he wrote screen plays and began work on his great Hollywood novel *The Day of the Locust*.

HOLLYWOOD HILLS The lower slopes of the enchanting Santa Monica Mountains contain some of Los Angeles' most fashionable

Text continued on page 64.

Hollywood in Action

The tram is filled with innocent people, a random collection of folks from all walks, some with little kids in tow. Suddenly it is blasted by aliens and hijacked onto a giant spaceship. As the Cyclons prepare to destroy the tram, a laser battle of galactic proportions breaks out.

Escaping one peril, the passengers cross a collapsing wooden bridge, dodge a flash flood and are swept up in an avalanche. This is all child's play compared to the next adventure, when the tram crosses the Brooklyn Bridge with flames erupting, sirens screaming, and King Kong clinging to the trembling girders.

Sound like Hollywood? Actually it's **Universal Studios Hollywood**, a Disneyesque introduction to one of the nation's biggest motion picture and television facilities. Founded in 1912 when Carl Laemmle, a Bavarian immigrant, converted a chicken farm into a production lot for silent films, Universal is a mammoth 420-acre complex complete with 36 sound stages, a 15-story administration building, and a staff of over 10,000 filmmakers. Admission. ~ 100 Universal City Plaza, Universal City; 818-508-9600.

More like an amusement park than an authentic studio tour, Universal offers visitors an ersatz introduction to Hollywood. The tram passes the locations for classic films such as *My Little Chickadee* (1940) and *The Sting* (1973) and explores the backlot with its street sets of Europe, Texas, New York, and Mexico. If Hollywood is one step away from reality, the Universal Tour is two steps. It's a staging of a staging, a Hollywood version of Hollywood.

Among the most exciting rides at this movie-studio-cum-theme-park are "Jurassic Park: The Ride," "Backdraft," "Back to the Future" and "E.T.'s Adventure," based on some of Universal's most popular films. Be prepared for long lines!

The **NBC Studio Tour** provides a similar view of the television industry. Though only 75 minutes long (in contrast to Universal's half-day extravaganza), it takes in a special-effects center and visits a mini-studio where visitors participate in a mock game show. The wardrobe area, set-construction shop, and make-up room are also on the itinerary. Admission. ~ 3000 West Alameda Avenue, Burbank; 818-840-3537. Here and at **CBS Ticket Information**, free tickets to television shows are available. ~ 7800 Beverly Boulevard, Los Angeles; 213-852-2458.

The **Warner Brothers Studios**, by contrast, takes you behind the scenes to see the day-to-day activities of a multimedia complex. It's also home to the Warner Brothers Museum, where memorabilia from the 75-year history of the studio is displayed. The studio accepts only small groups; tours are mostly technical and educational and change daily. Admission. ~ 4000 Warner Boulevard, Burbank; 818-954-1744.

Paramount Studios operates weekday tours in a behind-the-scenes fashion with a historical overview. Admission. ~ 5555 Melrose Avenue, 213-956-5575.

KCET, the Los Angeles public television station, also conducts technical tours of its studio. ~ 4401 Sunset Boulevard, Hollywood; 213-666-6500.

Dozens of television programs are taped in Los Angeles. The prime production season runs from August through March. For information on tickets call: **Audiences Unlimited** (818-506-0067); **Paramount Guest Relations** (213-956-1777); **CBS-TV** (213-852-2458); **NBC-TV** (818-840-4444).

That's Hollywood!

addresses. These rugged foothills, divorced from the glitter of Hollywood by serpentine roads, provide a pricey escape valve from the pressures of Tinseltown. But for those with a car and an afternoon, it costs no more to explore Hollywood's vaunted upcountry than to browse Beverly Hills' Rodeo Drive.

Beachwood Canyon, one of the town's prettiest residential areas, is a V-shaped valley with 1920- and 1930-era homes on either side. First developed as "Hollywoodland" by *Los Angeles Times* publisher Harry Chandler, the neighborhood is now popular with screenwriters. When Chandler broke ground, he hoped to create an urban utopia "above the traffic congestion, smoke, fog, and poisonous gas fumes of the lowlands." (It seems that even in the 1920s, long before Los Angeles had a name for it, the city suffered from smog.) ~ Beachwood Drive.

To advertise "Hollywoodland" the developer erected a huge sign on the hillside. Eventually "land" was removed, the fixture was refurbished, and Chandler's billboard became the **Hollywood Sign,** a 45-foot-tall, 450-foot-long landmark that is now the foremost symbol of Movieland. (Head up Beachwood Drive toward the sign and you'll pass through the stone entrance gates of Hollywoodland at Westshire Drive.)

Los Angeles has little space for idyllic retreats. One of the city's HIDDEN ► more placid places is **Lake Hollywood,** a forest-framed reservoir created by the Mulholland Dam. Popular with hikers and joggers, the lake is surrounded by a chain-link fence but still offers splendid views. The reservoir was built in 1925 by Water Commissioner William Mulholland as part of Los Angeles' scandalous water program. Scenes from *Chinatown* (1974), the movie that exposed the civic corruption behind Mulholland's project, were shot around the lake. The dam was also used in *Earthquake,* another 1974 flick in which the dike collapses, inundating the city. ~ Southern entrance is at Weidlake Drive; northern entrance is at Lake Hollywood Drive.

HIDDEN ► For stars living in **Whitley Heights** during the 1920s, life was much like it is in Beverly Hills today. This hilltop neighborhood, with its tile-roofed Mediterranean homes, was the premier residential area for the silent-movie set. Rudolph Valentino lived here, and later stars included Gloria Swanson, Bette Davis, and Janet Gaynor. Today the realm is as unspoiled as it was when H. J. Whitley, a Los Angeles developer with an eye to Europe, first built his "Italian hilltown." To explore the landmark neighborhood, drive up Whitley Avenue to Whitley Terrace and Wedgewood Place, following all three streets as they spiral around the hilltop.

One of Hollywood's most enduring symbols is the **Hollywood Bowl,** a concrete band shell built in 1929. Situated in a sylvan glade called Daisy Dell, the concert hall is an amphitheater within an amphitheater, surrounded by a circle of wooded hills. ~ 2301 North Highland Avenue; 213-850-2000.

The Los Angeles Philharmonic performs here and a regular series of concerts is presented. Many movies have used the shell as a backdrop, including *Anchors Aweigh* and the 1937 version of *A Star Is Born*. The adjacent **Hollywood Bowl Museum** hosts a showcase of the history of the Hollywood Bowl and a changing series of exhibits on the culture of music. ~ 213-850-2058.

◄ HIDDEN

A part of Hollywood's history stands just across the street. Back in 1913, a young director named Cecil B. De Mille found a farm town called Hollywood with an empty barn he could convert into a studio. The barn, a kind of woodframe keepsake, moved around with De Mille over the years, seeing use as an office, a set, and even a gymnasium for stars like Gary Cooper and Kirk Douglas. Eventually moved to its present site, the historic building became the **Hollywood Studio Museum**, a showplace dedicated to the era of silent films and containing a replica of De Mille's original office. Admission. ~ 2100 North Highland Avenue; 213-874-2276.

Château Marmont is a brooding presence amid the glitter. Constructed around 1929 in the pattern of a Norman castle, the place has numbered Boris Karloff, Greta Garbo, and Jean Harlow among its guests. With its petite gardens, imposing colonnade, and arched-window lobby, the hotel is a study in European elegance. Little wonder it is still favored by Hollywood stars as a hometown hideaway. ~ 8221 Sunset Boulevard; 213-656-1010.

If that French Renaissance mansion above Hollywood Boulevard begins to levitate, you'll know the residents are busy at work. The **Magic Castle**, built in 1925, is "the only club in the world devoted to magicians and lovers of magic." Home over the years to several movie stars, the private estate now plays host to a secret membership comprised of the town's top tricksters. ~ 7001 Franklin Avenue.

Further up the hill lies another dream house, a magnificent replica of a Japanese palace called **Yamashiro**. Built of cedar and teak in 1913, the former estate is presently a restaurant complete with ceremonial gardens and a 600-year-old pagoda. Of the many films shot here perhaps the most famous was *Sayonara* (1958), in which Yamashiro was cast as the American Officers' Club. ~ 1999 North Sycamore Avenue; 213-466-5125.

From here it's an easy jaunt up Outpost Drive through **Outpost Estates**. Another of Hollywood's picture-perfect neighborhoods, this residential canyon was developed during the 1920s by a creative contractor who placed the utilities underground and built Mediterranean-style homes. The result is a lovely, tree-shaded community, an unpretentious version of Beverly Hills.

Tucked into a narrow canyon lies **Wattles Park**, part of the old Gurdon Wattles Estate, a 49-acre preserve. While the Wattles Mansion and formal gardens can be viewed by appointment only, the adjacent park is open on a regular basis. A pond, palm grove, and teahouse occupy the property. ~ 1850 North Curson Avenue; 213-874-4005.

◄ HIDDEN

The real spirit of the Hollywood Hills resides in the deep canyons which climb from Hollywood Boulevard into the Santa Monica Mountains. **Nichols Canyon,** a chaparral-coated valley adorned with million-dollar homes, represents one of the toniest parts of town. A narrow two-lane road winds through dense forest to bald heights. ~ Nichols Canyon Road.

Possessing the same cachet and even greater fame, **Laurel Canyon** became known as a hippie hideaway during the 1960s. With its sinuous side streets and modest bungalows, the wooded vale has a decidedly rustic atmosphere. ~ Laurel Canyon Boulevard.

Both Nichols and Laurel canyons rise sharply into the mountains, eventually reaching the rim of Los Angeles, a 50-mile-long country road called **Mulholland Drive,** which extends from Hollywood to Malibu. Tracing a course along the ridge of the Santa Monicas, Mulholland is a spectacularly beautiful road, curving through forests and glades, climbing along sharp precipices, and offering magnificent views of the Los Angeles Basin and San Fernando Valley.

LODGING

All those rising stars have to have some place to sleep, so sections of Hollywood have always been low-rent districts. The **Hollywood YMCA,** located off Sunset Boulevard, provides 55 rooms that are clean and share baths. Guests can also use the pools, gym, sauna, and exercise facilities. ~ 1553 Schrader Avenue; 213-467-4161. BUDGET.

The **Hollywood Celebrity Hotel** occupies a 1930s art deco building located just above Hollywood Boulevard. The 40 guest rooms are nicely refurbished, furnished in neo-deco style and decorated in a Hollywood motif. The rooms are quite spacious and include a continental breakfast. There's a sitting room off the lobby. ~ 1775 North Orchid Avenue; 213-850-6464, 800-222-7090, fax 213-850-7667. MODERATE.

The **Orchid Suites Hotel** a few doors down is another 40-unit facility. Lacking the character of its neighbor, it substitutes space and amenities for personality. Every room is a suite and includes a kitchen; there's also a pool. Rooms are fashioned in contemporary style. The building itself is a bland, modern stucco. ~ 1753 North Orchid Avenue; 213-874-9678, 800-537-3052, fax 213-467-7649. MODERATE.

Hollywood Boulevard is one of several strips lined with motels. Representative of the species is the **Hollywood Premiere Motel.** This L-shaped building contains standard rooms, some with kitchens. Pool. ~ 5333 Hollywood Boulevard; 213-466-1691. BUDGET.

HIDDEN ►   One of Hollywood's best bargains is found at the **Magic Hotel,** a 40-unit establishment next to the famed Magic Castle, a private club for magicians. Suites with kitchens are priced moderately, furnished in oak, and decorated (presto!) with magic posters. They are quite spacious and well maintained. Pool and sundeck. ~ 7025 Franklin Avenue; 213-851-0800, 800-741-4915, fax 213-467-7649. MODERATE.

Coral Sands Motel is a 58-unit establishment serving the gay community. The guest rooms look out on a central courtyard with pool, jacuzzi, sauna, and exercise area. Each is carpeted wall-to-wall and sentimentally furnished with standard appointments. Continental breakfast is included in the price. Gay-friendly. ~ 1730 North Western Avenue; 213-467-5141, 800-367-7263, fax 213-467-4683. MODERATE.

Château Marmont is where John Belushi died of a drug overdose.

It's as much a part of Hollywood as the Academy Awards. In fact, the very first Oscars were presented at the **Clarion Hollywood Roosevelt Hotel**. Built in 1927, the Spanish Revival building has been completely refurbished and now offers 320 rooms, a restaurant, lounges, and a palm-studded courtyard with pool and sauna. Priced below many of the city's five-star hotels, this classic caravansary has many features of the finest hostelries. The lobby is a recessed-ceiling affair with colonnades and hand-painted beams. Guest rooms are small but commodiously furnished with plump armchairs and hardwood pieces. Historic and luxurious. ~ 7000 Hollywood Boulevard; 213-466-7000, 800-950-7667, fax 213-469-7006. DELUXE.

The traditional Hollywood resting place is **Château Marmont**, a Norman-style castle built in 1929. Formerly home to Jean Harlow and Howard Hughes, the hotel still lures Hollywood luminaries such as Robert DeNiro, Dustin Hoffman, and Diane Keaton. They come for the privacy and quirky charm of the place, which offers rooms, suites, and cottages. Around its beautifully maintained grounds are flower gardens, shade trees, and a heated swimming pool. More than anything, the Marmont possesses cachet, as if the hotel itself were a celebrity, holding within its cloistered lobby a thousand tales of Hollywood. ~ 8221 Sunset Boulevard; 213-656-1010, 800-222-8328, fax 213-655-5311. ULTRA-DELUXE.

DINING

Jitlada is one of those great ethnic restaurants that L.A. likes to tuck away in minimalls. Just a funky little café, it serves an array of Thai dishes; the most notable are seafood entrées such as squid, mussels, and scallops. ~ 5233 Sunset Boulevard; 213-667-9809. MODERATE.

The best of France and California meet in **Patina**—beautiful, intimate, expensive, and worth it. Specialties include shrimp with mashed potatoes and potato truffle chips and peppered tournedos of tuna with Chinese vegetables and ponzu sauce. Try the chocolate plate for dessert. Dinner is served daily; lunch is served on Tuesday only. ~ 5955 Melrose Avenue; 213-467-1108. DELUXE.

◄ HIDDEN

The Hollywood address for righteous soul food is **Roscoe's House of Chicken & Waffles**, a tiny wood-slat café with overhead fans and an easy atmosphere. Ask for an "Oscar" and they'll bring chicken wings and grits; "E-Z Ed's Special" is a chicken liver omelette; and a "Lord Harvey" is a half chicken smothered in gravy and onions. Very hip. ~ 1514 North Gower Street; 213-466-7453. MODERATE.

La Poubelle means "garbage pail," but it is anything but. This small candlelit restaurant serves up delicate French and Italian cuisine with a style (and a local following) all its own. Dinner only. ~ 5907 Franklin Avenue; 213-465-0807. MODERATE TO DELUXE.

Popular with entertainers from nearby studios, **Pinot Hollywood and the Martini Bar** is the last word in sleek. From the brick patio with topiary trees and peaked skylight to the pullman booths and green-glass shades, the place is designed with a delicate touch. The American regional cuisine menu changes weekly and offers fresh fish, pasta, pizza, assorted steaks, chops, and chicken for lunch and dinner. No lunch on Saturday; closed Sunday. ~ 1448 North Gower Street; 213-461-8800. DELUXE.

Hollywood's oldest restaurant, **Musso & Frank's Grill** is a 1919 original with dark paneling, murals, and red leather booths. A bar and open grill create a clubby atmosphere that reflects the eatery's long tradition. Among the American-style dishes are cracked crab, fresh clams, sea bass, prime rib, roast lamb, plus assorted steaks and chops. Closed Sunday and Monday. ~ 6667 Hollywood Boulevard; 213-467-7788. ULTRA-DELUXE.

Hampton's may be the world's only hamburger joint with valet parking. This well-known noshing spot has transformed the art of hamburger-cooking to a science, preparing over two dozen varieties. You can order them with sour plum jam, peanut butter, or creamed horseradish. If you disagree with the when-in-Rome philosophy, there are broiled shrimp, chicken, pasta, and vegetarian platters. ~ 1342 North Highland Avenue; 213-469-1090. MODERATE.

HIDDEN ► If Hampton's proves too health-conscious, try **Pink's Famous Chili Dogs**. This popular takeout stand has hamburgers and tamales; but at Pink's, not ordering a dog slapped with sauce is like going to Hampton's for waffles. ~ 709 North La Brea Avenue; 213-931-4223. BUDGET.

The fish they serve at **Seafood Village** are not only fresh, they are right there in the display cases of the adjacent market. This nondescript café features several dozen fish dishes plus about a dozen meat entrées. Red snapper, orange roughy, rex sole, sea bass, shark steak, calamari, fried oysters, scallops, shrimp, Alaskan king crab, and Maine lobsters are only some of the offerings. ~ 5732 Melrose Avenue; 213-463-8090. MODERATE.

The celebrity photos covering every inch of **Formosa Cafe** tell a tale of Hollywood that reaches back to the 1940s. This crowded café, originally fashioned from a streetcar, has seen more stars than heaven. Over the years they've poured in from the surrounding studios, leaving autographs and memories. Today you'll find a Chinese-American restaurant serving low-priced lunches and dinners, a kind of museum with meals. No lunch on Sunday. ~ 7156 Santa Monica Boulevard; 213-850-9050. BUDGET.

Hollywood's prettiest restaurant is a re-created Japanese palace called **Yamashiro**. Set in the hills overlooking Los Angeles, the mansion was built earlier in the century, modeled after an estate in the high mountains of Japan, and trimmed with ornamental gardens. Dine here and you are surrounded by hand-carved columns, *shoji* screens, and Asian statuary. The courtyard garden contains a waterfall, koi pond, and miniature trees. For dinner they serve a complete Japanese menu as well as Western-style entrées. Dinner only. ~ 1999 North Sycamore Avenue; 213-466-5125. DELUXE TO ULTRA-DELUXE.

SHOPPING

Nowhere is the nostalgic heartbeat of Hollywood more evident than along Hollywood Boulevard's Walk of Fame. Although the past couple of decades have witnessed the street's decline, the neighborhood is currently being revitalized and signs of rebirth are everywhere.

Most tourist attractions revolve around **Mann's Chinese Theater**, where the souvenir shops, poster studios, T-shirt stores, and postcard vendors are packed tight as a crowd on opening night. ~ 6925 Hollywood Boulevard; 213-464-8111.

Head over to **Supply Sergeant** and stock up on military gear. A favorite among survivalists, bargain hunters, and pink-coiffed punks, this civilian commissary has everything from the subtle to the bizarre. ~ 6664 Hollywood Boulevard; 213-463-4730.

Universal News Agency, reputedly the country's oldest outdoor newsstand, has newspapers and magazines from around the world. ~ 1655 North Las Palmas Avenue; 213-467-3850.

Hollywood Boulevard probably has more bookstores than movie theaters. **Larry Edmonds Bookshop** claims to have the world's largest collection of books and memorabilia on cinema and theater. ~ 6644 Hollywood Boulevard; 213-463-3273. If any place can challenge their claim, it's **Collectors Bookstore** with its museum-quality inventory of stills, posters, books, and scripts from the movies and TV. ~ 1708 North Vine Street; 213-467-3296.

Frederick Mellinger started a tiny mail-order company in 1946 based on the philosophy that "fashion may change but sex appeal is always in style." Today, **Frederick's of Hollywood**, strikingly set in a purple art deco building, continues to entice and enrage onlookers with its fantasy lingerie. ~ 6608 Hollywood Boulevard; 213-466-8506.

A-bigger-than-life mural of Marilyn Monroe marks **Cinema Collectors**. Selling film and television collectibles from every period, they have over 18,000 movie posters and two million photos. ~ 1507 Wilcox Avenue; 213-461-6516.

NIGHTLIFE

Reminiscent of the 1930s, the Hollywood Roosevelt Hotel's deco-style **Cinegrill** is putting glamour back into Hollywood nightlife. Crème de la crème cabaret entertainers perform here in an intimate, sophisticated atmosphere. Cover. ~ 7000 Hollywood Boulevard; 213-466-7000.

Following a $6 million remodel, Pacific's **El Capitan Theatre** has been returned to its early glory as one of Hollywood's classic theaters. Opened in 1926, the El Capitan is part of the newly conceived "Cinema District," an eight-block section along Hollywood Boulevard filled with historic landmarks, including several vintage theaters. If you're going to the movies, this is the place! ~ 6838 Hollywood Boulevard; 213-467-7674.

The Palace also has a colorful history dating back to 1927. Today the luxurious complex showcases popular names in rock and jazz. Several bars, dancefloors, a restaurant, and an open courtyard add to the luxury. Cover. ~ 1735 North Vine Street; 213-462-3000.

Another of Hollywood's jazz clubs, **Catalina Bar & Grill** draws a relaxed crowd. This intimate room features name performers. Cover. ~ 1640 North Cahuenga Boulevard; 213-466-2210.

For sunset panoramas, nothing quite matches **Yamashiro**. Set in a Japanese palace, the lounge overlooks gracious Asian gardens from a perch in the Hollywood Hills. ~ 1999 North Sycamore Avenue; 213-466-5125.

Starmax Productions offers audience-participation whodunits at both the **Cat and the Fiddle Pub and Restaurant**, which is located at 6530 Sunset Boulevard, and **Les Frères Taix** at 1911 West Sunset Boulevard. ~ 310-278-7712.

THEATER Theater in Hollywood varies from tiny storefront establishments to famous stages. In a city filled with actors, the playhouses inevitably are loaded with talent. Professionals from local television and movie studios continually hone their skills on stage, and the area's "equity-waiver" theaters provide an opportunity to see these veterans perform at affordable prices.

The **Hollywood Arts Council** publishes *Discover Hollywood*, calendar listings of all Hollywood theaters. The paper is available at newsstands throughout the city. ~ P.O. Box 931056, Hollywood, CA 90093; 213-462-2355.

To secure tickets for productions, call ticket agencies to charge by phone. Major ticket agencies include **Ticketmaster** (213-480-3232), **Goodtime Tickets** (213-464-7383), and **Murray's Tickets** (213-234-0123). Or contact the theater directly; oftentimes day-of-the-event tickets are available for as much as 50 percent off.

Pantages Theatre, one of Hollywood's largest playhouses, offers major productions, including Broadway musicals. ~ 6233 Hollywood Boulevard; 213-468-1770.

The refurbished **James Doolittle Theatre**, built in 1926, features top shows from Broadway and London. ~ 1615 North Vine Street; 213-972-0700. **The John Anson Ford Theatre**, an outdoor amphitheater, produces Shakespearean and experimental dramas as well as dance and jazz concerts from May to October. ~ 2580 Cahuenga Boulevard; 213-974-1343. One of Hollywood's oldest legitimate theaters, the **Henry Fonda Theatre** also hosts dramatic and musical performances. ~ 6126 Hollywood Boulevard; 213-468-1770. One of Hollywood's oldest playhouses, **Cast Theatre** presents a varied bill of musicals, comedies, and dramas. ~ 804 North El Centro Avenue; 213-462-0265.

One of the world's largest natural amphitheaters, seating 17,620, the **Hollywood Bowl** dates back to the 1920s. The concert shell hosts the Los Angeles Philharmonic and features top-bill pop, jazz, and dance concerts. Bring a cushion, sweater, and picnic, and come join the festivities in this park-like setting. ~ 2301 North Highland Avenue; 213-850-2000.

The **Hollywood Palladium**, which once headlined the swing bands of the '40s, now features new wave, rock, and Latin groups. ~ 6215 Sunset Boulevard; 213-962-7600.

▼▼▼▼▼▼▼▼▼▼▼
West Hollywood

If a time traveler from the 21st century landed in our era, the voyager would easily feel at home along Melrose Avenue. He could go shopping. The chic corridor is door-to-door with designer stores purveying space-age fashions. What Beverly Hills' Rodeo Drive is to classical fashion, Melrose has become to the avant-garde.

Then he could dine. The restaurants lining this strip are tile-and-copper cafés with bare-duct ceilings and Post-Midnight Modern architecture. They serve sushi and whip up recipes on file at the U.S. Patent Office.

Trendy is too lame a term to capture this neighborhood. Melrose Avenue is the cutting edge for L.A.'s young adults, a place to experience and be experienced, the Venice Boardwalk in high heels. The hottest section is from the 6900 to 7700 blocks, though that will probably change by the time this ink dries. Lately the borders of trendiness have been edging south along Beverly Boulevard and West 3rd Street. Stay tuned for future developments.

SIGHTS

If you need a landmark to lead you through this tony part of town, consider a whale. The "Blue Whale" to be precise; that's the nickname for the blue-glass monstrosity on Melrose Avenue and San Vicente Boulevard. Formally known as the **Pacific Design Center**, it's a mammoth mall catering to the interior design industry. Since opening in 1975, it has spawned a Green Whale next door. Rumor has it that Moby Blue is pregnant with a Red Whale, due sometime in the 21st century. ~ 310-657-0800.

Melrose Avenue ends in **West Hollywood**, the first city in the nation to be governed by avowed homosexuals. Much more than a gay city, West Hollywood is a free-form laboratory for social experiment, a place where the spirit of the '60s is transformed into the art form of a later era. Now that Berkeley has become a haven for revolutionaries-turned-real-estate-speculators, and Madison, Wisconsin, is again a quiet campus town, West Hollywood carries on the bohemian ideal of being crazy as a way of life.

The **Nelson House**, where the entire family lived during the 1950s, was used as the model for their TV home on *The Ozzie and Harriet Show*. Harriet sold the house several years after Ozzie died in 1975. ~ 1822 Camino Palermo Drive.

Like the Silver Lake neighborhood to the east, Ventura Boulevard in Studio City and Burbank Boulevard near Vineland, West Hollywood is a major gathering place for Los Angeles' gay population. There are countless clubs here, as well as excellent restaurants, good bookstores, and an array of fashionable shops.

The street scene centers along Sunset Boulevard, a flashy avenue studded with nightclubs and fresh cuisine restaurants. During the 1930s and 1940s, the section between Crescent Heights Boulevard and Doheny Drive formed the fabled **Sunset Strip**. Center of Los Angeles night action, it was an avenue of dreams, housing nightclubs like Ciro's, the Trocadero, Mocombo, and the Clover Club. As picture magazines of the times illustrated, starlets bedecked with diamonds emerged from limousines with their leading men. During the 1950s, Ed "Kookie" Byrnes immortalized the street on the television show *77 Sunset Strip*.

Today, the two-mile strip is chockablock with the offices of agents, movie producers, personal managers, and music executives. The street's most artistic achievement is the parade of **vanity boards** which captivate the eye with their colors and bold conception. These outsize billboards, advertising the latest movie and record releases, represent the work of the region's finest sign painters and designers. Often done in three dimensions, with lights and *trompe l'oeil* devices, they create an outdoor art gallery.

An artist with equal vision was at work here in 1936. That's when architect Robert Derrah built the **Crossroads of the World**. Designed as an oceanliner sailing across Sunset Boulevard, the prow of this proud ship is topped by a tower complete with rotating globe. ~ 6671 Sunset Boulevard.

That streamlined art deco tower nearby is the old Sunset Tower Apartments, refurbished and rechristened the **Argyle Hotel**. Completed in 1931, this moderne palace contained 46 luxury apartments, leased to luminaries like Errol Flynn, the Gabor sisters, Zasu Pitts, Clark Gable, and Howard Hughes (who seems to have slept in more places than George Washington). ~ 8358 Sunset Boulevard; 213-654-7100.

Hollywood might be noted for its art deco towers, but it also contains architectural works by other schools. The **Schindler House**, a house-studio with concrete walls, canvas covers, and sleeping lofts, was designed by Viennese draftsman Rudolph Schindler in 1921. Modeled on a desert camp, the house has been a gathering place for avant-garde architects since the 1920s. ~ 835 North Kings Road; 213-651-1510.

F. Scott Fitzgerald fans will want to see the garden court apartments at 1401 North Laurel Avenue where the Roaring '20s novelist spent the final years of his life. Recovering from alcoholism, his career in decline, the author worked here on a film script and his unfinished novel, *The Last Tycoon*.

The **Colonial House** two blocks away was home to celebrities and fictional characters alike. Bette Davis resided in the red brick building, as did Carole Lombard and her husband, William Powell. They were joined, in the imagination of Hollywood novelist Budd Schulberg, by Sammy Glick, the overly ambitious protagonist in *What Makes Sammy Run?* ~1416 North Havenhurst Drive.

LODGING

Several streamlined and ultramodern hotels are located within a ten-block radius here in West Hollywood. The hallmark of the Mondrian, Bel Âge, Le Parc, Le Dufy, and Le Rêve hotels is the artwork, which hangs seemingly everywhere—in the lobby, public areas, corridors, and guest rooms. You can expect ultramodern furnishings, creative appointments, and personal service at each address.

The **Mondrian Hotel** is a stylized tribute to the Dutch painter Piet Mondrian. The exterior of this 12-story highrise has been painted sherbet colors by a contemporary artist, while the interior is filled with works of modern art. This hotel boasts a restaurant, lounge, pool terrace, spa, and fitness center. ~ 8440 Sunset Boulevard; 213-650-8999, 800-525-8029, fax 213-650-9241. ULTRA-DELUXE.

Somewhat more offbeat is the **Bel Âge Hotel** in West Hollywood. This all-suite hotel offers similar amenities in a complex that is positively laden with artwork. ~ 1020 North San Vicente Boulevard; 310-854-1111, 800-996-3426, fax 213-854-0926. ULTRA-DELUXE.

Located in a quiet residential neighborhood, **Le Parc** offers 154 spacious rooms. Among the amenities are a restaurant, bar, swimming pool, and gym. ~ 733 West Knoll Drive; 310-855-8888, 800-578-4873, fax 310-359-7812. ULTRA-DELUXE.

Summerfield Suites features suites with a kitchen, fireplace, and balcony. This establishment also has a rooftop garden with pool, spa, city views, and a restaurant open exclusively to hotel guests. ~ 1000 Westmount Drive; 310-657-7400, 800-833-4353, fax 310-854-6744. ULTRA-DELUXE.

Le Rêve offers similar accommodations but manages to bring the room tabs in at deluxe rates by substituting room service for a private restaurant. ~ 8822 Cynthia Street; 310-854-1114, 800-835-7997, fax 310-657-2623. DELUXE.

The elegant **Argyle Hotel** treats guests to an upper-crust club atmosphere. Completed in 1931 as Sunset Towers and now restored to its art deco magnificence, the Club once was home to screen luminaries from nearby studios. There are 63 beautifully appointed rooms. ~ 8358 Sunset Boulevard; 213-654-7100, 800-225-2637, fax 213-654-9287. ULTRA-DELUXE.

Another chic Hollywood resting spot, the **Sunset Marquis Hotel and Villas** is a Mediterranean-style hotel frequented by beautiful people with big purses. Guest rooms surround a terrace pool, creating a tropical ambience enhanced by pastel colors and potted plants. The rooms are furnished in contemporary style and range from standard facilities to lavish villas. High in snob appeal, the hotel offers complete amenities. ~ 1200 North Alta Loma Road; 310-657-1333, 800-858-9758, fax 310-652-5200. ULTRA-DELUXE.

DINING

Melrose Avenue, where the fashion-conscious can dress to dine and then shop for their next dinner outfit, has vaulted to prominence as one of L.A.'s leading restaurant rows. Among the more savvy gourmets, many squeeze into **Citrus**, a white-wall-and-track-lighting dining room where indoor umbrellas protect patrons from the harsh rays of the skylights. Affected as this spot can be, it *is* beautifully highlighted with fresh flowers and *does* serve other-worldly dishes. The theme is California cuisine (what else?) with a focus on fresh fish. Where but Citrus can one go for grilled baby salmon with potato garlic purée, mini goat cheese ravioli, duck breast with couscous and figs, or a tuna burger? Sarcasm aside, it's a great restaurant (with a pricey tab). Who knows, perhaps the maître d' will kiss your cheek? No lunch on Saturday. Closed Sunday. ~ 6703 Melrose Avenue; 213-939-5354. ULTRA-DELUXE.

Angeli Caffe/Pizzeria is the archetypal Melrose address. Its high-tech interior is a medley of flying buttresses, wood-slat ceilings, exposed ducts, and whitewashed walls. The menu matches this edge design with pizza, calzone, and daily specials like spaghetti *alla carbonara*, linguine with mussels, and mushrooms in garlic. ~ 7274 Melrose Avenue; 213-936-9086. MODERATE.

Try **Tommy Tang's** when next you have an inclination for Thai finger food. Here you'll find a full sushi bar draped in canvas. The ever-changing gallery of artwork reflects the trendy crowd. The food is delicious, the portions are small. Happily, everyone is rich. ~ 7313 Melrose Avenue; 213-937-5733. MODERATE.

Modern art and pastel walls are also standard issue in the neighborhood's best Chinese restaurant. **Genghis Cohen** serves gourmet dishes to an appreciative crowd at its multiroom complex off Melrose Avenue. Not your ordinary Asian restaurant, specialties here are "scallops on fire," candied shrimp, garlic catfish, soft-shelled shrimp, and "no-name" duck. ~ 740 North Fairfax Avenue; 213-653-0640. DELUXE.

When you tire of the tinsel along Melrose Avenue you can always retreat to **Noura Café**, one of the street's few down-home restaurants. Here the food is Middle Eastern with a Mediterranean touch. Just order shish kebab, falafel, grape leaves, or salad at the counter, then enjoy it in a comfortable dining room or out on the patio. ~ 8479 Melrose Avenue; 213-651-4581. BUDGET.

Barney's Beanery is the only place around where you can shoot pool while eating chili, burritos, and hamburgers. Or where you can choose from more than 200 varieties of beer. A dive with character, Barney's has rainbow-colored booths, license plates on the ceiling, and a road sign decor. Native funk at low prices. ~ 8447 Santa Monica Boulevard; 213-654-2287. BUDGET.

An old favorite celebrity-watching restaurant, **Dan Tana's** is small and crowded, making reservations a must. The fare is Italian, pricey but excellent. The New York steak may well be the best served anywhere. Veal, chicken, and pasta dishes round out the fare. Dinner only. ~ 9071 Santa Monica Boulevard; 310-275-9444. DELUXE TO ULTRA-DELUXE.

Duke's is another legendary watering hole, especially popular with music industry figures. A crowded coffee shop bedecked with posters, it also attracts West Hollywood's underground population. People with purple hair pile into the communal tables, order meatloaf or Chinese vegetables, and settle down for the day. That's what makes Duke's Duke's: it's a scene, a flash, a slice of unreality. A colorful breakfast stop, with dozens of omelette selections; also hamburgers, sandwiches, diet plates, and a few American dinners. ~ 8909 Sunset Boulevard; 310-652-3100. BUDGET.

With the possible exception of Berkeley's Chez Panisse, **Spago** is California's most famous restaurant. Owner Wolfgang Puck helped originate California cuisine, which achieves its pinnacle at his West Hollywood restaurant. Set on a hill overlooking the city, the dining room is dominated by an open-view brick oven. The furnishings are informal, fresh flowers predominate and a back patio is shaded with umbrellas. Everything that can be painted is painted white. The pastas include sweet potato ravioli and angelhair pasta with wild mushrooms; there are pizzas with duck sausage, Louisiana shrimp, or prosciutto. Among the entrées are roasted Cantonese duck, grilled calf's liver with polenta, and whole black bass roasted in a wood-burning oven. Dinner only; reservations required. ~ 8795 Sunset Boulevard; 310-652-4025. DELUXE TO ULTRA-DELUXE.

L'Orangerie possesses all the pretensions you would expect from one of Los Angeles' finest, most expensive French restaurants. The building has the look of a château, with imposing arches and finials atop the roof. The dining areas are appointed with oil paintings and outsized wall sconces; fresh flowers and the scent of money proliferate. Food, decor, service, all are the finest. The *foie gras* and seafood are flown in fresh from France. Life, or dinner at least, doesn't get much better than this classic French restaurant. Reservations are required. Closed Monday. ~ 903 North La Cienega Boulevard; 310-652-9770. ULTRA-DELUXE.

SHOPPING   The section of Sunset Boulevard between Crescent Heights Boulevard and Doheny Drive, commonly known as Sunset Strip, is marked by creatively designed billboards announcing the latest Hollywood releases. Amid this skein of signs is a series of star-studded cartoon characters signaling the way to **Dudley Do-Right Emporium.** Jay Ward's cartoon characters come to life at this Bullwinkle enthusiast's mecca. ~ 8200 Sunset Boulevard; 213-656-6550.

Hollywood's chic leather crowd frequents **North Beach Leather,** where original designs attract a celebrity clientele. ~ 8500 West Sunset Boulevard; 310-652-3224.

Sunset Plaza, a two-block cluster of shops located on Sunset Boulevard between Sunset Plaza Drive and Sherbourne Drive, offers some of the most luxurious shopping on the Strip. Among the nearby stores, **Boulmiche** carries imported French clothing for women. ~ 8641 Sunset Boulevard; 310-652-6446.

Book Soup, a small but special bookstore, offers a top-notch selection of art books, classic literature, current fiction, and international magazines. ~ 8818 West Sunset Boulevard; 310-659-3110.

Step over to **Aahs!** for a selection of greeting cards, informal gifts, and crazy toys. ~ 8878 West Sunset Boulevard; 310-657-4221.

Don't worry, you won't miss **Aida's Flowers.** If the festive mural doesn't catch your eye, the character on the corner (dressed as Santa, the Easter Bunny, or Uncle Sam) will flag you down. Once inside, if you dare to enter, you'll find flowers, cards, produce and piano music in an exotic setting. ~ 1261 North La Brea Avenue; 213-876-6482.

Ultramodern shoppers make a beeline for **Melrose Avenue.** West Hollywood's proving ground for innovative style, Melrose is the smartest street in all L.A., a multiblock mélange of signature boutiques, fresh cuisine restaurants, and heartthrob nightspots. Peopled by visionaries and voluptuaries, it's sleek, fast, and very, very chic. Shops and galleries, with names as trendy as their concepts, come and go with tidal regularity in this super-heated environment. ~ Between Sycamore Avenue and Ogden Drive.

Of course the most futuristic element of all is the past. At **Chic-A-Boom,** the "Mother Lode" of vintage retail, you'll find such shards of American history as a Davy Crockett lamp, a Howdy Doody cookie jar, a drugstore display from the '50s, vintage *TV Guides,* plus movie memorabilia. ~ 6817 Melrose Avenue; 213-931-7441.

Off The Wall is known for "weird stuff" and unusual antiques. ~ 7325 Melrose Avenue; 213-930-1185.

The bold exterior of **Soap Plant/Wacko** hints at the crazy collection of gift items and clothes within this duplex store. The wild interior is jam-packed with wacky toys and keepsakes, L.A. style. ~

7400-7402 Melrose Avenue; Soap Plant: 213-651-5587; Wacko: 213-651-3811.

Occupying an entire block, **Fred Segal** is a series of stores within stores. Seeming to specialize in everything, this consumer labyrinth has clothes for men, women, and children, plus lingerie, luggage, shoes, electronic gear, and cosmetics. There's even a café at hand when you tire of browsing or simply become lost. ~ 8100 Melrose Avenue; 213-651-3342.

The Bodhi Tree is the place for books on mysticism, metaphysics, nature, health, and religion. ~ 8585 Melrose Avenue; 310-659-1733. Behind the main store, **The Used Book Ranch** displays used books as well as herbs, teas, and homeopathic remedies.

A section of West Hollywood within whistling distance of the glass-encased Pacific Design Center, **Designer's Row** consists of classy interior design shops and high-ticket antique stores. **Jebejian Enterprises** displays elaborate handmade furniture and custom-finished antiques. ~ 7403 Melrose Avenue; 213-651-4550.

Clustered nearby around Robertson Boulevard are several prestigious art galleries. At **Margo Leavin,** two large buildings house an impressive collection of contemporary American and European art. ~ 812 North Robertson Boulevard and 817 North Hilldale Avenue; 310-273-0603. Artworks in ceramic and bronze are displayed in a delightful outdoor sculpture garden at **Asher/Fauré,** an important gallery that handles both established and emerging talents. ~ 612 North Almont Drive; 310-271-3665.

For free travel advice, browse through **Traveler's Bookcase,** a friendly bookstore for people on the move. Here you'll discover a collection of hard-to-find regional titles as well as literature for the new breed of adventure traveler. Take a sojourn on one of the plush couches and flip through a few vacations. ~ 8375 West 3rd Street; 213-655-0575.

◄ **HIDDEN**

Another constellation of galleries lies along the 600-to-800-block stretch of North La Cienega Boulevard. Most venerable of all these art centers is **Gallery 825,** which showcases talents from the Los Angeles Art Association. A great place to discover the up and coming while they are still down and out. ~ 825 North La Cienega Boulevard; 310-652-8272.

Gemini GEL is one of the country's top art publishers. Producing limited-edition prints and sculptures, it features two display galleries. ~ 8365 Melrose Avenue; 213-651-0513.

The lounge at **The Roxbury** is a rendezvous for record company executives and show business figures. Cover. ~ 8225 Sunset Boulevard; 213-656-1750.

NIGHTLIFE

The level of talent at the **Comedy Store** is evident from the celebrity signatures covering the building's black exterior and photo-lined interior. The Main Room features the best comedians, the Original Room showcases new talent, and the Belly Room presents a wide range of alternative comics. Cover. ~ 8433 West Sunset Boulevard; 213-656-6225.

Three long-standing rock clubs dominate Sunset Strip. **Whiskey A Go Go** features live music on a nightly basis. Cover. ~ 8901 Sunset Boulevard; 310-652-4202. **The Roxy** headlines known rock-and-roll and alternative rock performers in an art deco–style room. ~ 9009 Sunset Boulevard; 310-276-2222.

Doug Weston's Troubadour, another of West Hollywood's many rock-and-roll clubs, headlines heavy metal bands. No age requirement. Cover. ~ 9081 Santa Monica Boulevard; 310-276-6168.

One of the hottest trends in Hollywood nightlife is the coffeehouse. With plump armchairs, weatherbeaten tables and walls covered by contemporary art, the **Insomnia Cafe** serves cappuccino and desserts until the wee hours of the morning. ~ 7286 Beverly Boulevard; 213-931-4943. **Bourgeois Pig** offers more of the same. ~ 5931 Franklin Avenue; 213-962-6366.

A cozy view lounge, **Café Mondrian** features live jazz in a comfortable setting. ~ 8440 Sunset Boulevard; 213-650-8999.

There are often as many comedians in the bar as on stage at the **Improvisation**. This spacious brick-walled club, patterned after the New York original, draws top-name comics as well as local talent. Cover. ~ 8162 Melrose Avenue; 213-651-2583.

Who would imagine that a neighborhood saloon could survive the gentrification of Melrose Avenue? **J. Sloan's**, with its sawdust floor and old movie props, has not only survived but flourished in the shadow of Melrose's chrome-and-tile nightspots. ~ 8623 Melrose Avenue; 310-659-0250.

THEATER It's really the smaller theaters and local playwrights that make sections of West Hollywood the Off-Broadway of the West. Dozens of talented companies perform regularly on these less-known stages.

A CURE FOR THE HOLLYWOOD BLUES

If you haven't been to the **House of Blues**, you're missing out on one of the best nightspots around. This establishment combines a Delta-inspired restaurant with a live music club. The specialty is blues, although other musical traditions are also featured. Buddy Guy and Jeff Healey have played here as well as Al Green and Melissa Etheridge. The walls at this nightspot are adorned with the portraits of legendary bluesmen including Stevie Ray Vaughan, Robert Johnson, and Albert King. Gospel brunch on Sunday. Cover. ~ 8430 Sunset Boulevard; 213-848-2583.

The **Coast Playhouse** specializes in original musicals and new dramas. ~ 8325 Santa Monica Boulevard; 213-650-8507. A replica of the British original, the **Globe Playhouse** stages Shakespearean plays and other dramas of historical significance. ~ 1107 North Kings Road; 213-654-5623. The **Matrix Theatre** is home to Joseph Stern's award-winning troupe, Actors for Themselves. ~ 7657 Melrose Avenue; 213-653-3279. Comedy and improvisation top the bill at the **Groundling Theatre**. ~ 7307 Melrose Avenue; 213-934-9700.

▼▼▼▼▼▼▼▼▼▼▼▼
West Hollywood Gay Scene

One of the nation's quintessentially queer communities, West Hollywood is probably second only to the San Francisco Bay Area as a West Coast gay and lesbian center; even the AAA map colors it pink! This was the first city in the country to boast a largely gay city government, and combined with the presence of an experimental and tolerant art and entertainment population, West Hollywood became a destination for gay men and women. Along the boulevards and backstreets, especially the main drags of Sunset and Santa Monica boulevards, you'll find restaurants, clubs, and guesthouses catering to a clientele that is both out and outré.

LODGING

The **Grove Guesthouse** offers just one bright and airy room decorated with contemporary leather furniture and high ceilings. There's a distinct home-away-from-home atmosphere here. As a guest, you have kitchen, pool, and hot tub privileges as well as access to a comfortable living room. You're welcome to create your own meals from the goodies available in the overflowing pantry. Hopefully, the oranges on the tree out back will be ready for plucking. ~ 1325 North Orange Grove Avenue; 213-876-7778, fax 213-876-3170. DELUXE.

Located right in the heart of West Hollywood, the **Holloway Motel** is a haven for gays and lesbians. Rooms are comfortably furnished; suites have kitchenettes. ~ 8465 Santa Monica Boulevard; 213-654-2454. MODERATE.

A beige building trimmed with green, the **Ramada West Hollywood** offers classy lodging within its art deco exterior. Straights and gays alike can be found relaxing on the sundeck and around the heated pool. Rooms are appointed in pastels and contemporary furniture. Suites come equipped with kitchens and two-story sleeping lofts. ~ 8585 Santa Monica Boulevard; 310-652-6400, 800-845-8585, fax 310-652-2135. DELUXE.

The gay bed-and-breakfast scene is well served by **San Vicente Inn**. Guests stay in two cottages and a converted horse-and-carriage barn that are adjacent to an 1889 historic landmark house. This ten-unit complex features an attractive courtyard and offers a room with a kitchenette and shared bath or a cottage with private bath. ~ 845 North San Vicente Boulevard; 310-854-6915, fax 310-289-5929. MODERATE.

Upon entering **Le Montrose**, guests will be greeted by friendly attendants along with fresh fruit and mineral water. The posh, art nouveau accommodations consist of fireplaces, fax machines, and Nintendo sets; some include full kitchens and balconies. This all-suite hotel, where 20 percent of the clientele is gay, also makes it easy to keep fit while traveling. There's a pool, a hot tub, a fully equipped fitness center, free bike use, and a rooftop tennis court with tennis instructors to help you perfect your serve. Afterward, schedule an appointment with the on-staff masseuse to work out those knots. Cookies and milk await guests at check-out time. ~ 900 Hammond Street; 310-855-1115, 800-776-0666, fax 310-657-9192. ULTRA-DELUXE.

DINING

The late-night gay crowd heads to **Yukon Mining Co.**, an All-American, booth-and-counter-service eatery that's open 24 hours. The motif, in case you couldn't guess, is mining, and the menu is one of those hamburger-sandwich-and-breakfast-all-day affairs that make choosing an entrée simple. ~ 7328 Santa Monica Boulevard; 213-851-8833. BUDGET.

Located inside the French Quarter Market Place is the **French Quarter Restaurant**, festooned with hanging plants among wrought-iron appointments. Breakfast is served all day for those who don't feel like having one of the many choices of sandwiches, steaks, and pasta dishes. Specialties include pot roast, salmon, and angelhair pasta with shrimp. Its late hours also make it a great nightspot. About 75 percent of the clientele is gay. Breakfast, lunch, and dinner are served daily. ~ 7985 Santa Monica Boulevard; 213-654-0898. MODERATE.

A predominately gay crowd shows up for Argentinean tantalizers at the **Tango Grill**—authenticity furnished courtesy of the chef from Buenos Aires. The brick walls, Mexican tile floors, and wooden tables do much for the South American atmosphere, and diners may choose to take their sizzling dishes out on the patio under large umbrellas. Chicken, seafood, beef, and vegetables are marinated in special blends of citrus juice and garlic. ~ 8807 Santa Monica Boulevard; 310-659-3663. MODERATE.

More upscale but equally popular with West Hollywood's gay population is **Café D'Etoile**. The cuisine here is a Continental mix of pasta, steak, chicken, and roast pork dishes, and the decor is a mix of antique furniture and contemporary artwork. ~ 8941½ Santa Monica Boulevard; 310-278-1011. MODERATE TO DELUXE.

Mark's serves elegant California cuisine in a casual, contemporary setting. Along with tasty entrées such as grilled rare ahi with sesame-ginger sauce, there are Maryland crab cakes with corn purée and tomato-basil sauce, and turkey-vegetable potstickers. The primarily gay clientele also previews large canvases of local art that adorn the walls. No lunch; Sunday brunch. ~ 861 North La Cienega Boulevard; 310-652-5252. MODERATE TO DELUXE.

You'll find sandwiches, quiches, salads, burgers, pot pies, pizzas, and pastas prepared in a variety of ways at **The Abbey**. Although the regulars tend to be gay men, lesbians and straight couples frequently come to chat over coffee and a huge assortment of desserts (which, by the way, outnumber the regular menu). Outdoor seating is available. ~ 692 North Robertson Boulevard; 310-289-8410. BUDGET.

SHOPPING

Not only is **A Different Light** a "full service gay and lesbian bookstore," it also serves as a focal point for West Hollywood's gay population, complete with community bulletin board and an ongoing schedule of events. ~ 8853 Santa Monica Boulevard; 310-854-6601.

Specializing in erotica, **The Pleasure Chest** offers an unparalleled array of leather goods, lingerie, latex clothing, novelties, and gay literature. ~ 7733 Santa Monica Boulevard; 213-650-1022.

NIGHTLIFE

The high-energy atmosphere is complimented with high-tech appointments at **Axis**, a popular, male-oriented gay disco. Cover. ~ 652 North La Peer Drive; 310-659-0471. The adjoining **Love Lounge** caters to a lesbian crowd with live musical acts in a rococo-style setting. Cover. ~ 657 North Robertson Boulevard.

The Abbey transforms into a gay hangout at night and offers a live jazz ensemble on Sunday night. Amateurs can show off their talent during Monday open-mike nights. ~ 692 North Robertson Boulevard; 310-289-8410.

Rage is a spacious dance club that spills onto the sidewalk; inside there are outrageous videos plus sounds ranging from rap to rock. Cover on weekends. ~ 8911 Santa Monica Boulevard; 310-652-7055.

The "videotainment" program at **Revolver** means color monitors on every wall. With two bars, an espresso bar, and a lively crowd, the place is hot. Cover on weekends. ~ 8851 Santa Monica Boulevard; 310-659-8851.

It is primarily gay men who frequent **Micky's**, a West Hollywood nightspot that offers dancing to a deejay video. Occasional cover. ~ 8857 Santa Monica Boulevard; 310-657-1176.

Palms is the oldest women's bar in Los Angeles. It features pool playing, a dancefloor, music videos, a deejay, and (occasionally) a live band. Cover. ~ 8572 Santa Monica Boulevard; 310-652-6188.

An English pub located in the heart of West Hollywood, **Mother Lode** is ideal for those looking for a cozy place to hang out and have a stout or two. Nightly deejays spin tunes ranging from rock-and-roll to dance music; ironically, there's no dancefloor to let loose on. But the crowd, which mainly consists of gay men, doesn't seem to mind. ~ 8944 Santa Monica Boulevard; 310-659-9700

▼▼▼▼▼▼▼▼▼
Beverly Hills
Back in 1844 a Spanish woman named Maria Rita Valdez acquired controlling interest over 4500 acres of sagebrush and tumbleweed. Luckily she spent only $17.50 on the transaction. The land was of little worth. Even by the turn of the century it consisted only of lima bean fields, sheep meadows, and a few isolated farmhouses. Plans for wheat cultivation, oil drilling, and a community of German immigrants failed.

Finally in 1912 a group of entrepreneurs, struggling to sell this barren real estate, happened on the idea of building a big hotel to publicize their new housing development. Happily, the fledgling movie industry was already attracting people to neighboring Hollywood and the Beverly Hills Hotel became a rendezvous for rising stars.

Then in 1920, when the undisputed King and Queen of Hollywood, Douglas Fairbanks and Mary Pickford, built their palace on a hill above the hotel, the community's future was secure. Within a few years Gloria Swanson, Charlie Chaplin, Rudolph Valentino, Buster Keaton, John Barrymore, and Will Rogers were neighbors. The dusty farmland, now a town named Beverly Hills, had finally blossomed.

It's a rags-to-riches town with a lot of Horatio Alger stories to tell. The world capital of wealth and glamour, Beverly Hills is a place in which driving a BMW makes you a second-class citizen and where the million-dollar houses are in the poorer part of town. The community with more gardeners per capita than any other United States city, Beverly Hills is one of the few spots outside Texas where flaunting your money is still considered good taste. A facelift here is as common as a haircut and many of the residents look like they've been embalmed for the past 30 years.

Still, it's Beverly Hills. The town has style, history, and an indomitable sense of magic. It's a void that became a constellation; a place where everyone—whether in movies, television, clothes design, or business—is a star.

SIGHTS
It seems only fitting that the gateway to this posh preserve should be along **Santa Monica Boulevard**, a greenbelt with an exotic array of plant life. Each block of this blooming corridor is alive with a variety of vegetation. Trees are closely pruned, shrubs carefully shaped, and the flowers are planted in a succession of colorful beds. Most impressive of all is the landscape of cactus and succulents between Camden and Bedford drives. ~ Between Doheny Drive and Wilshire Boulevard.

Rising near the center of the promenade is **Beverly Hills City Hall**, a Spanish Baroque structure capped with a tile cupola. The foyer of this 1932 building has a recessed ceiling with scroll ornaments and hand-painted panels. ~ North Rexford Drive and Santa Monica Boulevard.

A contemporary commentary on City Hall, the adjacent **Beverly Hills Civic Center** features a stepped design in Spanish deco style. The tile trim and palm landscape further reflect the earlier building.

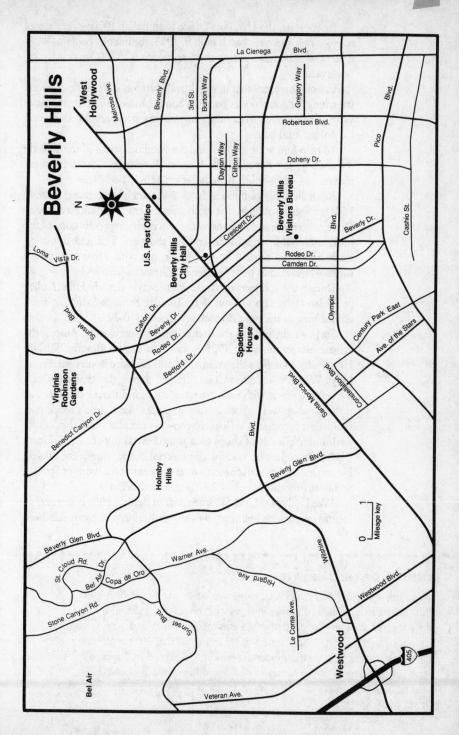

Beverly Hills

West Hollywood

La Cienega Blvd.
Beverly Blvd.
Melrose Ave.
3rd St.
Burton Way
Gregory Way
Blvd.
Pico
Robertson Blvd.
Dayton Way
Clifton Way
Doheny Dr.
Cashio St.
U.S. Post Office
Beverly Hills City Hall
Crescent Dr.
Beverly Hills Visitors Bureau
Blvd.
Beverly Dr.
Rodeo Dr.
Camden Dr.
Loma Vista Dr.
Sunset Blvd.
Cañon Dr.
Beverly Dr.
Rodeo Dr.
Bedford Dr.
Spadena House
Olympic
Century Park East
Ave. of the Stars
Santa Monica Blvd.
Constellation Blvd.
Virginia Robinson Gardens
Benedict Canyon Dr.
Blvd.
Holmby Hills
Beverly Glen Blvd.
Beverly Glen Blvd.
Warner Ave.
St. Cloud Rd.
Bel Air Dr.
Copa de Oro
Hilgard Ave.
Wilshire
Stone Canyon Rd.
Sunset Blvd.
Le Conte Ave.
Westwood Blvd.
Bel Air
Westwood
405
Veteran Ave.

0 1 Mileage key

By contrast, the **U.S. Post Office** is an Italian Renaissance structure of brick and terra cotta. Built in 1933, the interior contains WPA-type murals popular during the Depression. ~ 9300 Santa Monica Boulevard.

Cañon Drive, another horticultural corridor, is a parade of palms stretching for four blocks between Santa Monica and Sunset boulevards. The 80-foot trees lining this august street are Mexican and California sand palms.

To help find your way around the winding streets of this hillside community, the **Beverly Hills Visitors Bureau** provides printed information. ~ 239 South Beverly Drive; 310-271-8174.

Regardless of its famous faces and stately residences, Beverly Hills has a single address that symbolizes the entire community. **Rodeo Drive**, where would-be's walk with the wealthy, represents one of the most fashionable strips in the world of shopping. This gilded row extends only from the 200 to 400 block, but within that enclave are shops whose names have become synonymous with style.

During the summer, catch the classic-style **Beverly Hills Trolley** at Rodeo Drive and Dayton Way, Tuesday through Saturday, for a guided tour of the posh downtown area. ~ 310-271-8174.

Surprisingly, little of the architecture is noteworthy. Among the artistic exceptions is the 1928 Beaux-Arts **Regent Beverly Wilshire Hotel**, which anchors the avenue. ~ 9500 Wilshire Boulevard. Frank Lloyd Wright's **Anderton Court**, created during the 1950s, projects a fractured effect with each part angling in a different direction, as if the building were about to split in pieces like a child's block pile. Holding it together is a Guggenheim-type circular ramp that curves past multiple levels of shops to a jagged metal tower. ~ 332 North Rodeo Drive. Just beyond the commercial district stands the **O'Neill House**, an art nouveau confection reminiscent of the work of Spanish architect Antonio Gaudi. ~ 507 North Rodeo Drive.

Like Hollywood, the favorite sport in Beverly Hills is stargazing. Synonymous with glamour, wealth, and fame, the town has been

ANNALS OF THE AIRWAVES

If you missed President Franklin D. Roosevelt's first fireside chat in 1933, don't despair. It, along with other events of historical and cultural importance, can be seen and heard at the **Museum of Television and Radio**. You can access over 75,000 TV and radio programs from the '20s to the '90s. This sleek, three-story, classic-modernist building, designed by Richard Meier, is the outpost of the Museum of Television and Radio in Manhattan. Closed Monday and Tuesday. Admission. ~ 465 North Beverly Drive; 310-786-1000.

home to actors since the era of silent films. In fact, the best way to discover Hollywood is by driving through Beverly Hills.

That Elizabethan cottage at 508 North Palm Drive was home to **Marilyn Monroe and Joe DiMaggio** in 1954 during their stormy marriage. The couple moved in around April, but by September, when Marilyn was filming *The Seven Year Itch*, the tumultuous tie had already been broken.

The couple who lived on the next street had a happier and far more enduring marriage. If **George Burns and Gracie Allen's** place looks familiar, that's because a model of the home was used for their 1950s television show. ~ 720 North Maple Drive.

Beverly Hills is nothing if not the story of marriages. The bond between **Elizabeth Taylor and Mike Todd** ended tragically in 1958 when Todd's private plane crashed over New Mexico. The couple was occupying this Mediterranean-style mansion when the movie producer died. ~ 1330 Schuyler Road.

Lana Turner and Johnny Stompanato's relationship didn't last long either. It seems that Lana's daughter Cheryl Crane stabbed him to death in their prim Colonial house. Stompanato had threatened Turner's life during a heated argument. The even more heated trial that followed drew tremendous press coverage and exposed secrets of the star's love life. ~ 730 North Bedford Drive.

For over 60 years the winding side streets off Benedict Canyon Drive have housed a who's who of Hollywood celebrities. Today many of movieland's greatest talents still live in this wooded retreat.

Roxbury Drive, a residential street trimmed with trees, has several 1930-era estates which celebrities once called home. **Marlene Dietrich** lived in the squarish, art deco mansion at number 822. **Jimmy Stewart** (921) set up residence in the brick Tudor house one block away, while **Lucille Ball** (1000) and **Jack Benny** (1002) lived next door to one another. Benny's brick Colonial home, like Burns and Allen's house, was sometimes filmed in his television show.

Newspaper baron William Randolph Hearst purchased the mansion at 1700 Lexington Road during the 1920s for his mistress, **Marion Davies**. Later in the decade **Greta Garbo** moved into the neighborhood at 1027 Chevy Chase Drive with a parrot, four cats, and a chow chow.

Tower Road around the corner also saw its share of stars. **Juliet Prowse** lived behind the mullioned windows at 1136; **Arthur Rubinstein** occupied 1139; and actor **Spencer Tracy** called 1158 Tower Road home.

Greenacres, the estate of silent film comedian **Harold Lloyd**, has been reduced to a mere five acres. When Lloyd moved here in 1928 the grounds included 20 acres and were planted with 12 gardens, each following a different theme. The house he occupied until his death in 1971 has 44 rooms, including 26 bathrooms. ~ 1740 Green Acres Place.

Rudolph Valentino chose the distant reaches of Benedict Canyon to escape his adoring fans. In 1925 he moved to Falcon Lair (named for his movie *The Hooded Falcon*), a magnificent mansion appointed with Renaissance art, Oriental carpets, and medieval armor. Little did the young actor realize when he finally found his retreat that he would die from ulcers the next year. ~ 1436 Bella Drive.

Marilyn Monroe reportedly entertained John and Robert Kennedy in a very private bungalow at the Beverly Hills Hotel.

For years Hollywood's chief gossip factory was the **Beverly Hills Hotel**, a pink Mission Revival building dating to 1912. During the 1930s the hotel's Polo Lounge attracted Darryl Zanuck, Will Rogers, and other polo enthusiasts. Later its private bungalows became trysting places for celebrities. Clark Gable, Carole Lombard, Howard Hughes, Marilyn Monroe, and Sophia Loren rented them. John Lennon and Yoko Ono holed up for a week here, and Elizabeth Taylor and Richard Burton made love and war. Today the hotel's manicured grounds are tropically landscaped and well worth visiting, even when the stars are not out. ~ 9641 Sunset Boulevard; 310-276-2251.

The most famous homes in Beverly Hills may be those of the stars, but its most intriguing residence is the **Spadena House**. Built in 1921 as a movie set and office, this "Witch's House" resembles something out of a fairy tale. Its sharp peaked roof, mullioned windows, and cobweb ambience evoke images of Hansel and Gretel. ~ 516 Walden Drive.

By calling in advance you can tour the **Virginia Robinson Gardens**, a six-acre estate landscaped with king palm trees and a variety of gardens. The home here (also open by appointment) is the oldest house in Beverly Hills, a 1911 Mediterranean Revival structure. Admission. ~ 1008 Elden Way; 310-276-5367.

Greystone Park Mansion, a 55-room English Tudor manor, was built during the 1920s by oil tycoon Edward L. Doheny. While the house is closed to the public, visitors can tour the 18-acre grounds, which are landscaped in a succession of balustraded terraces complete with pools and fountains. ~ 905 Loma Vista Drive; 310-550-4654.

LODGING   Despite its standing as one of the wealthiest communities in the nation, Beverly Hills offers at least one low-cost lodging facility. The **Beverly Terrace Motor Hotel** is a 39-unit facility, with accommodations typical of motel digs. Among the amenities are a pool and sundeck as well as a location one block from Melrose Avenue. ~ 469 North Doheny Drive; 310-274-8141. MODERATE.

On a knoll overlooking Beverly Hills is the **Beverly Prescott Hotel**, a 12-story building with 140 rooms. The hotel offers a range of amenities including an outdoor swimming pool, health club, and restaurant. The lobby has an airy feel with a front desk inlaid with onyx and mother of pearl. ~ 1224 South Beverwil Drive; 310-277-2800, 800-421-3212, fax 310-203-9537. DELUXE TO ULTRA-DELUXE.

Among the deluxe-priced hostelries my personal favorite is the **Beverly House Hotel**. A brick Colonial-style structure, it lacks the extra amenities of its competitors but possesses the ambience of a European hotel. Each of the 50 guest rooms is furnished with hardwood pieces and stylishly decorated. Add a friendly staff, comfortable lobby, and free continental breakfast to round out this fine small Beverly Hills hotel. ~ 140 South Lasky Drive; 310-271-2145, 800-432-5444, fax 310-276-8431. DELUXE.

The **Summit Hotel on Rodeo Drive** possesses one very important feature, location. It sits at the center of Rodeo Drive, a step away from the country's finest shops. Space in this neighborhood is precious and the hotel suffers from lack of it. The lobby is tiny and the rooms are cramped; extra facilities are limited to a sundeck and sidewalk café. With unremarkable washed-pine furniture and a flower decor that is overwhelming, the Beverly Rodeo needs all the location it can muster. ~ 360 North Rodeo Drive; 310-273-0300, 800-468-3541, fax 310-859-8730. ULTRA-DELUXE.

Small and elegant, the all-suite **L'Ermitage** is tucked away on a quiet tree-lined street. Only the discreet sign reveals that it's a hotel. A rooftop garden terrace with a 360° view has a heated pool for guests' use. Although L'Ermitage is expensive, you're not dollared to death. ~ 9291 Burton Way; 310-278-3344, 800-800-2113, fax 310-278-8247. ULTRA-DELUXE.

The **Regent Beverly Wilshire Hotel**, a 1928 Beaux-Arts building, is another grand old hotel in Beverly Hills. Located at the foot of Rodeo Drive, this landmark features a Wilshire wing with 146 rooms and suites and an adjacent Beverly wing, built during the 1970s. Guest rooms in the Wilshire wing are quite spacious, designed with flair, and possess the character that makes this a great hotel. The new wing is decorated in a Southern California contemporary style. Both sections draw on a full line of amenities, including shops, restaurants, lounges, fitness center, and pool. ~ 9500 Wilshire Boulevard; 310-275-5200, 800-427-4354, fax 310-274-2851. ULTRA-DELUXE.

DINING

The place to nosh in Beverly Hills is **Nate 'n' Al's Deli**, a traditional delicatessen with a complete assortment of kosher dishes. There are bagels, sandwiches on rye and pumpernickel, and a smoked fish plate that includes lox, cod, and whitefish. ~ 414 North Beverly Drive; 310-274-0101. MODERATE.

Owned and frequented by celebrities, minimalist in decor, **Maple Drive** has emerged as one of Beverly Hills' top trysts. Here you can dine on a number of gourmet tidbits while catching the flash and dance of Hollywood on parade. No lunch on Saturday; closed on

Sunday. ~ 345 North Maple Drive; 310-274-9800. DELUXE TO ULTRA-DELUXE.

Most Beverly Hills restaurants are places to be seen; **Kate Mantílini** is a place to see. A kind of *Star Wars* diner, this 21st-century rendezvous is an artwork in steel and tile. Jagged edges and angular beams are everywhere; a boxing mural covers an entire wall; and in the center a sundial/skylight rises from floor to dome. For dinner there's rotisserie chicken, meatloaf, lamb shank, calves' brains, frogs' legs, a half dozen steaks, and fresh fish daily. ~ 9101 Wilshire Boulevard; 310-278-3699. MODERATE TO DELUXE.

Ed Debevic's is a neon-and-naugahyde diner with a taste for the 1950s. The place is loaded with period chatchkas—pink flamingos, Elvis albums, bowling balls, and a Coca Cola clock. You already know the menu (meat, eggs, more meat). ~ 134 North La Cienega Boulevard; 310-659-1952. BUDGET.

Opulence Chinese-style is the most appealing feature of **The Mandarin**. Beautifully appointed with colored tile and carved wallhangings, this Oriental dining room is illuminated by Chinese lanterns. Among the offerings are Mongolian beef, smoked tea duck, spring crêpes, and steamed fish. ~ 430 North Camden Drive; 213-272-0267. MODERATE TO DELUXE.

Gourmet food, chic surroundings, and beautiful people combine to make **Prego** a popular rendezvous. This Italian trattoria serves pizza, pasta, and several entrées. Among the pizzas are calzones, folded pizzas with smoked mozzarella, and stracchino cheese pizzas. Pasta dishes include *fusilli con luganega* (corkscrew noodles with sausage); entrées feature Italian sausage, veal chops, and fresh fish. The kitchen is open to view and the decor consists of modern artwork along brick walls, track lights, and hardwood trim. No lunch on Sunday. ~ 362 North Camden Drive; 310-277-7346. MODERATE TO DELUXE.

Ranking among Los Angeles' finest restaurants, **La Scala** is an intimate and well-appointed dining room. Upholstered booths add to an elegant interior where statues and oil paintings are combined with decorative plates and fresh flowers. The gourmets and celebrities frequenting this address also come for the excellent Italian cuisine. Among the entrées are *saltimbocca*, swordfish *rosemarino* (grilled swordfish marinated in aromatic herbs), scampi, *pollo galleto* (chicken with rosemary and white wine), *penne alla arrabbiata* (pasta tubes in a spicy chili sauce), and fresh fish dishes. Closed Sunday. ~ 410 North Cañon Drive; 310-275-0579. ULTRA-DELUXE.

SHOPPING   Without doubt, the capital of consumerism is Beverly Hills. In the mythic order of things, this gilded neighborhood is a kind of shopper's heaven, where everything sparkles just out of reach. Often the fun of shopping in Beverly Hills (especially if you're on a budget) is in the people watching.

At the heart of the capital lies the "golden triangle," an exclusive shopping district bounded by Wilshire Boulevard, Rexford Drive, and Santa Monica Boulevard. The heart within the heart is, you guessed it, **Rodeo Drive**. World-famous designer showcases like Gucci, Van Clef and Arpels, Cartier, Vitton, Giorgio, and Ralph Lauren are part of the scenery on Rodeo Drive. Some are soooo exclusive they open only by appointment.

The **Rodeo Collection**, a pink marble shopping complex, houses an array of designer boutiques, including **Jantan** (310-276-6064), which carries Stephanie Anais and Thalian designs, and **Bijan** (310-273-6544). ~ 421 North Rodeo Drive.

The **Barakat** collection of jewelry features an amazing combination of Old World antiquities, such as 5th-century B.C. Greek coins. This magnificent shop also holds an extensive pre-Columbian art collection. Even the catalog is a collector's item. ~ 433 North Rodeo Drive; 310-859-8408.

Among the town's chic spots is **Fred Hayman Beverly Hills**. Owned by the man who launched Giorgio, it features European men's and women's fashions. ~ 273 North Rodeo Drive; 310-271-3000.

Or consider **Giorgio Beverly Hills** itself, boasting an array of haute couture and perfume. ~ 327 North Rodeo Drive; 310-274-0200.

Frances Klein Antique & Estate Jewelry could be the world's most exclusive mom-and-pop store; and there may be enough fine jewelry here to make it the world's first mom-and-pop museum. ~ 310 North Rodeo Drive; 310-276-1839.

Two Rodeo Drive is a $200-million cobblestone mall featuring about two dozen shops. Built along three levels, it's a brass-door-and-antique-street-lamp promenade reminiscent of a European boulevard.

Tiffany's continues to awe and inspire. ~ 210 North Rodeo Drive; 310-273-8880.

Beverly Hills supports several dozen art galleries, many located along Rodeo Drive. Most galleries stay open until 10 p.m.

The breathtaking etchings of Rembrandt are among the rare selections at **Galerie Michael**. ~ 430 North Rodeo Drive; 310-273-3377. American and international artists are represented at **Dyansen Gallery**. ~ 337 North Rodeo Drive; 310-275-0165.

"Little" Santa Monica Boulevard has less formal, less expensive shops, such as **Alexander Brown**, which carries a feminine line of new "vintage" clothing. ~ 9523 Little Santa Monica Boulevard; 310-275-7484. **The Cockpit** has unisex apparel and accessories. ~ 9609 Little Santa Monica Boulevard; 310-274-6900. **Suzanna** features haute couture designs for day and evening wear. ~ 9647 Little Santa Monica Boulevard; 310-276-7510.

Some of the country's most famous department stores line Wilshire Boulevard between the 9600 and 9900 blocks. **Neiman Marcus** (310-550-5900) and **Saks Fifth Avenue** (310-247-9419) are only part of this elite company.

South Robertson Boulevard, by contrast, is home to dozens of small boutiques. **Cynthia Rowley** carries fashionable clothing for women. You'll find everything from sportswear to evening dresses. ~ 112 South Robertson Boulevard; 310-276-9020. At **Lisa Klein**, you can browse through an array of antique and new clothing. ~ 136 South Robertson Boulevard; 310-246-0907.

NIGHTLIFE   A ritzy spot for celebrity voyeurs is **Jimmy's**, a lively art deco piano bar. ~ 201 Moreno Drive; 213-879-2394.

For a European-style disco, check out the scene at **Orsini's**. Every Friday and Saturday, a deejay spins lively dance tunes to the delight of the crowd. Cover. ~ 9575 West Pico Boulevard; 310-277-6229.

▼▼▼▼▼▼▼▼▼
Westside

Like Horace Greeley's proverbial pioneer, wealth in Los Angeles has gone west. With its elite country clubs and walled estates, the Westside has developed during the 20th century into the city's golden ghetto. Cultural diversity is defined here not so much by race and class as by whether one is already rich or simply striving to be. Business mavens from Bel Air whiz along in Maseratis and co-eds buzz by in battered Toyotas.

At UCLA in Westwood, more than 35,000 students are squeezed into one of the most valuable real estate districts in the nation. While this campus town is an odd mix of blocky apartment buildings and mundane office towers, Bel Air and Brentwood are exclusive colonies marked by manicured lawns and lofty mansions.

Nearby Century City, a former film studio, has been transformed into a futuristic city with plazas, greenswards, and vaulting highrises. Culver City, the self-proclaimed "Motion Picture Capital of the World," which produced more than half the movies released in the United States during the 1930s and 1940s, still clings to its aging glory with several studios.

SIGHTS   **CENTURY CITY** If Beverly Hills is the ultimate in residential communities, Century City represents the final word in business centers. Bland as a three-piece suit, this 180-acre highrise heaven is built of office towers and broad boulevards. The only hint of character is the **ABC Entertainment Center**, a mega-sized complex with theaters, movie houses, shops, and restaurants. ~ 2040 Avenue of the Stars; 310-556-3096. **The Century Plaza Hotel** across the street is a twin-tower city in itself, a 1000-room hotel that vies with Century City's other metal-and-glass palaces for prominence.

What today is a corporate version of Las Vegas was once the fabled backlot of Twentieth Century Fox. While the studio still holds ground in part of the city, it has lost the glamour of its Darryl Zanuck days and is closed to the public.

WESTWOOD To students everywhere, Westwood is the scholastic capital of California. Home to UCLA, one of the largest universities in the country, the town was little more than ranch land in the early 20th century. Originally developed during the 1920s as a Mediterranean-style complex with shops and restaurants, Westwood boomed when UCLA opened in 1929. Now, with highrises continually springing up along Wilshire Boulevard, it's a major commercial center.

A sense of the old Westwood pervades **Westwood Village**, near the university. Here you can stroll past a succession of shops, many located in 1920s-era buildings of brick and wood. The Village's true identity, however, is revealed on Friday and Saturday nights when major movies are previewed and the place becomes a world of bumper people, with traffic gridlocked and crowds milling everywhere. ~ Centered around Westwood Boulevard.

Of Westwood's countless movie houses, the most inventive by far is **Mann's Village Theatre**, with its lofty tower and Spanish Moderne design. Built in 1931, the landmark features elevated pillars, ornamental scrollwork, and a free-standing box office. ~ 961 Broxton Avenue; 310-208-5576. The proximity of the 1937 **Mann's Bruin Theatre** across the street makes this the city's busiest crosswalk. ~ 948 Broxton Avenue; 310-208-8998.

Just across Le Conte Avenue from this cinema center lies the **UCLA Campus**, an impressive 419-acre enclave. A true multiversity, UCLA has 12 libraries and boasts 73 separate departments. The grounds are a labyrinth of grand staircases and brick walkways leading past 85 buildings that (as on most major campuses) constitute an architectural hodge-podge. Next door to classic structures are blocky metal-and-glass highrises reflective of the Bauhaus movement; modern masterpieces stand cheek-by-jowl with utilitarian monstrosities.

For a walking tour of this tree-shaded campus call ahead and make reservations with the Admissions Office. ~ 1147 Murphy Hall, 405 Hilgard Avenue; 310-825-8764. They can also tell you about the **Campus Express**, a shuttle service around campus. ~ 310-206-2908.

THE O.J. PILGRIMAGE

Can't get thoughts of the white Bronco, the black glove, and the Brown family out of your head? The surest cure is—you guessed it—a visit to those infamous addresses on Bundy and Rockingham. If you're still irritated at Ito, furious at Fuhrman, and actually remember who Rosa Lopez is, it's time to make this pilgrimage and put the trial of the century behind you. Search for clues around "the house on Rockingham." ~ 360 North Rockingham Avenue. Then record the melting times of various ice cream flavors at Nicole Brown's home. ~ 879 Bundy Drive. For the seriously afflicted, a visit to **Mezzaluna**, the restaurant where Ron Goldman worked, may be required—just don't leave your glasses there! ~ 11750 San Vicente Boulevard; 310-447-8667.

Ackerman Student Union represents the center of campus activity. **Kerckhoff Hall** next door is the only Gothic-style building on campus, a brick imitation of King Edward VII's Westminster chapel.

The geographic center of UCLA lies along the quadrangle at the top of **Janss Steps**. Anchoring the corners of the quad are the school's original buildings, magnificent Italian Romanesque structures dating to 1929. **Royce Hall**, a cloister-like building with twin towers and loggia, contains a public auditorium. The **Fowler Museum of Cultural History**, located next to Royce Hall, offers a changing series of ethnological exhibits. Admission. ~ 310-825-4361.

Powell Hall across the rectangle is an ornate, gargoyled Moorish masterwork housing the **Archive Research and Study Center**. This important cultural resource, an extension of the Film and Television Archive, has a collection of over 25,000 movies and television shows dating as far back as the silent film era. With at least one week's advance reservation, visitors can view any of the archive films at no change. ~ 310-206-5388.

Prettiest place on the entire campus is the **Franklin Murphy Sculpture Garden**, a five-acre park planted with jacaranda trees. Among the more than 60 artworks adorning this greensward are pieces by Arp, Calder, Matisse, Moore, and Rodin. ~ Located near the University Research Library.

The **Mildred Mathias Botanical Garden**, an enchanted spot in the southeastern corner of campus, displays nearly 4000 plant species within its eight-acre domain. Focussing on tropical and subtropical vegetation, the glade is filled with lilies and rhododendrons, palms, and cactus. Visits to the **Hannah Carter Japanese Garden**, a Kyoto-style rock garden with teahouse and footbridges, can be arranged through the visitors center.

Because of its reputation as a university town, Westwood's beautiful residential areas are frequently overlooked. Explore the neighborhood just west of campus and you'll discover the **Tischler House**, a contemporary home designed by Austrian architect Rudolph Schindler in 1949. With a geometric layout and plate-glass prow, the home is like a ship moored in a hillside port. ~ 175 South Greenfield Avenue.

The **Strathmore Apartments**, located several blocks away, were built by Schindler's Viennese colleague, Richard Neutra, in 1937. Among the former tenants of this glass-and-stucco court were Orson Welles and Clifford Odets. ~ 11005 Strathmore Drive.

Nearby you'll encounter the **Armand Hammer Museum**, which features lithographs and sculptures by Honoré Daumier and a collection of Leonardo da Vinci's original manuscripts as well as paintings by Rembrandt, Van Gogh, Monet, Cassatt, and Chagall. Admission. ~ 10899 Wilshire Boulevard; 310-443-7000.

In the same building as the Armand Hammer Museum, you'll find the **Grunwald Center for the Graphic Arts**. Dedicated to "works on paper," the collection contains more than 35,000 prints, drawings, and photos. There are works by Cézanne, Toulouse-Lautrec, and Picasso, as well as contemporary artists such as June Wayne and Carlos Almaraz. ~ 310-443-7076.

The **Skirball Cultural Center and Museum** focuses on the Jewish experience in the Old and New Worlds. The displays include exhibits on the Torah and the Jewish holy days. The archaeology of the Middle East is also represented in a series of artifacts. One very imaginative exhibit features simulated dig sites as well as a cut-away that shows how different strata of a hill contain remnants from earlier and earlier civilizations. Closed Monday. Admission. ~ 2701 North Sepulveda Boulevard; 310-440-4500.

BEL AIR AND BRENTWOOD   Seeming extensions of Beverly Hills, the hillside towns of Bel Air and Brentwood are sleek residential communities filled with winding roads that curve past palatial homes. Developed during the 1920s by an entrepreneur with a sense of elegance, Bel Air was 'originally subdivided into plots of several acres, guaranteeing that only the wealthy would need apply.

At first even movie people, many of whom were Jewish, were excluded from this elite area. Then during the Depression, with other businesses dying while Hollywood flourished, Bel Air's greed proved stronger than its bigotry. Movie stars began moving in en masse and by the 1940s were rapidly becoming the area's most notable residents.

Humphrey Bogart and Lauren Bacall, who met on the set of *To Have and Have Not* in 1944, settled down together in a brick Colonial house in Bel Air. Bogey was 25 years older than Bacall, but they became one of America's most legendary couples, starring together in *The Big Sleep* (1946), *Dark Passage* (1947), and *Key Largo* (1948). ~ 232 South Mapleton Drive.

The stone mansion at 750 Bel Air Road served for eight seasons as the **"Beverly Hillbillies" House.** This French estate was the primetime home for one of television's oddest families.

A real-life family, **Judy Garland** and her mother, lived in the red brick house at 1231 Stone Canyon Road. The childhood star of *The*

TEACHING PEACE

The horrors of racism are the focus of the **Museum of Tolerance.** Here enlightening displays reveal the terrible impact of prejudice throughout history; from Nazi Germany to segregation in America. The center utilizes modern multimedia techniques to create stunning audio, visual and interactive presentations. It includes a special exhibit on the 1992 Los Angeles riots complete with computers that quiz observers about social justice and responsible citizenship. Admission. ~ 9786 West Pico Boulevard; 310-553-9036.

Wizard of Oz built the place in 1940, equipping it with a badminton court, pinball machines, and her own top-floor suite.

One of Hollywood's most infamous families, **Joan Crawford** and her *Mommie Dearest* daughter Christina, lived in the sprawling Brentwood house at 426 North Bristol Avenue. Crawford moved here in 1929 with her first husband, Douglas Fairbanks, Jr., divorced him in 1934, and went on to marry three more husbands while raising four adopted children. Following the death of her last husband she sold the place in 1959.

A far happier child lived just one block away. During the 1930s **Shirley Temple** and her family moved into the Brentwood mansion at 209 North Rockingham Road. The young actress had already blossomed into the country's archetypal little girl, destined to play the curly-haired beauty in over 20 films and then to become, incongruously, a right-wing politician as an adult.

Cowboys may be buried on Boot Hill, but movie stars are interred in a site overlooking the MGM studios. The celebrities in **Holy Cross Cemetery** have one thing in common—they were all Catholic. Rosalind Russell of Auntie Mame fame is here along with Bing Crosby, Jimmy Durante, and Charles Boyer. Bela Lugosi rests nearby; the most macabre tombstone, however, is that of Sharon Tate Polanski and her unborn son Paul, murdered in 1969 by the Charles Manson gang. (Rosalind Russell's grave is marked by the large crucifix near the center of the park; most of the other resting places are near the "grotto" to the left of the entrance.) ~ 5835 West Slauson Avenue, Culver City.

Shirley Temple's house is next door to the home of O. J. Simpson. If you slow down for some innocent sightseeing, you may get a ticket for causing congestion.

LODGING

Just one block from the UCLA campus, the **Hotel Claremont** has 54 rooms. These are plain, clean accommodations that share a large lobby. ~ 1044 Tiverton Avenue, Westwood; 310-208-5957, 800-266-5957, fax 310-208-2386. BUDGET TO MODERATE.

The **Ramada Limited** next door offers 36 guest rooms, many with kitchens. These units are also well maintained and feature private patios. ~ 1052 Tiverton Avenue, Westwood; 310-208-6677, 800-631-0100, fax 310-824-3732. MODERATE TO DELUXE.

Nearby **Hilgard House Hotel** is a spiffy brick building with 47 rooms and two suites. Accommodations in this three-story structure are furnished with facsimile antiques, plushly carpeted, and attractively decorated with wall hangings; many come equipped with jacuzzi tubs. ~ 927 Hilgard Avenue, Westwood; 310-208-3945, 800-826-3934, fax 310-208-9972. DELUXE TO ULTRA-DELUXE.

Directly across the street, but a big step uptown, stands the **Westwood Marquis Hotel and Garden**, a 15-floor, all-suite hotel. This liveried-doorman establishment is beautifully appointed with fine furnishings and antique decorations. There are restaurants and lounges steps away from a sumptuous lobby, two pools set in a landscaped garden, plus a complete health spa facility. ~ 930 Hilgard Avenue, Westwood; 310-208-8765, 800-421-2317, fax 310-824-0355. ULTRA-DELUXE.

Hotel Del Capri is a bright, cozy complex complete with two tiers of rooms encircling a pool terrace. The lobby and many of the guest rooms contain modern curvilinear furniture. The tile baths include jacuzzi bathtubs; continental breakfast is served in your room; some accommodations have kitchenettes. In sum, a very attractive establishment. ~ 10587 Wilshire Boulevard, Westwood; 310-474-3511, 800-444-6835, fax 310-470-9999. DELUXE.

Los Angeles' most Eden-like address lies in a forested canyon surrounded by peach and apricot trees. A classic country inn, the Hotel Bel-Air is an exclusive 92-room complex and private haven for show business celebrities and European royalty. The 1920s Mission-style buildings are shaded by a luxuriant garden of silk floss trees and redwoods. A stream tumbles through the property, creating small waterfalls and a pool with swans. All around is a mazework of archways and footbridges, colonnades, and fountains. Numbering among the nation's finest hotels, the Bel-Air also provides an oval swimming pool, gourmet restaurant, lounge, and a patio terrace. ~ 701 Stone Canyon Road, Bel Air; 310-472-1211, 800-648-4097, fax 310-476-5890. ULTRA-DELUXE.

DINING

Mario's is a Westwood institution, an oil-tablecloth Italian restaurant one block from UCLA. You've seen the menu in a hundred similar places—spaghetti, fettuccine, chicken cacciatore, steak, and pizza. The only difference is that the prices here are a little steeper than elsewhere. ~ 1001 Broxton Avenue, Westwood; 310-208-7077. MODERATE TO DELUXE.

Another campus hangout, Madison's Neighborhood Grill is a turn-of-the-century saloon with a spectacular marble-and-hardwood bar. Selections range from sandwiches, salads, pizza, and pasta to grilled steak and fish. ~ 1037 Broxton Avenue, Westwood; 310-824-6250. BUDGET TO MODERATE.

Sepi's makes the best submarine sandwiches on the West Side. Long a hangout for UCLA athletes, Sepi's walls are festooned with pictures of such athletic heroes as Bill Walton and Lew Alcindor (Kareem Abdul-Jabbar). Half a sandwich is a meal for most humans. ~ 10968 Le Conte Avenue, Westwood; 310-208-7171. BUDGET.

At Caramba!, the Spanish villa theme goes a long way. High ceilings, wrought-iron railings, and brightly painted murals make up the interior. This Mexican eatery serves grilled red snapper in lime-cilantro butter sauce, shrimp tostada with spicy dressing, and carne asada with a smoked-tomato corn relish. ~ 1043 Westwood Boulevard, Westwood; 310-208-3171. MODERATE.

The cheapest place to eat in the entire Westside district is on the UCLA campus. You'll find cafeterias at **Ackerman Student Union** and the **North Campus Student Center** (for visitor information call 310-206-0616). The food will fill your stomach without emptying your purse; beyond that I guarantee nothing. ~ 310-825-4321. BUDGET.

Farther out on Westwood Boulevard, proceeding south from the UCLA campus, there is a string of ethnic restaurants worth trying. **La Bruschetta** serves high Italian cuisine. This gourmet address is filled along several walls with wine racks. Vibrant artwork of recent vintage decorates the place. ~ 1621 Westwood Boulevard, Westwood; 310-477-1052. MODERATE TO DELUXE.

The flavor is Persian at **Shamshiry Restaurant,** a pleasant restaurant with latticework booths and hanging plants. The shish kebab and other Middle Eastern dishes, served at lunch and dinner, are reasonably priced. ~ 1916 Westwood Boulevard, Westwood; 310-474-1410. MODERATE.

Enjoy *tandoori* chicken and a host of curry dishes prepared in **India's Oven.** It isn't the Taj Mahal. At lunch and dinner you'll dine from plastic plates, but at these prices, who can complain? ~ 11645 Wilshire Boulevard, Westwood; 310-207-5522. BUDGET.

For standard old American fare, head farther out to **The Apple Pan,** a clapboard cottage that contains a single U-shaped counter. Renowned for great burgers, The Apple Pan also serves sandwiches (as in ham, Swiss cheese, and tuna salad) and pies (as in apple, berry, and pecan). Closed Monday. ~ 10801 West Pico Boulevard, West Los Angeles; 310-475-3585. BUDGET.

All those two-wheelers suspended from the ceiling give the **Bicycle Shop Café** its name. This casual bistro offers a pasta and quiche menu that also includes a dozen entrées such as scampi, swordfish, red snapper, salisbury steak, and chicken with béarnaise sauce. A great place for slumming. ~ 12217 Wilshire Boulevard, West Los Angeles; 310-826-7831. MODERATE.

Commercial establishments are rare in residential Bel Air. Finding a restaurant with reasonable prices is an even more challenging feat, especially as you ascend the hills. It seems like the farther you climb, the higher the prices become. At **Four Oaks Restaurant** you encounter a French restaurant that's comfortable and understated. This intimate dining room is illuminated through skylights and features a brick patio for dining alfresco. The constantly evolving fare consists of organically grown ingredients prepared in a contemporary French-Californian style. No lunch on Monday. ~ 2181 North Beverly Glen Boulevard, Bel Air; 310-470-2265. DELUXE TO ULTRA-DELUXE.

The restaurant at the **Hotel Bel-Air** is so low-key it doesn't even have a name. This is no glitzy, glamorous monument to gastronomy. At the end of a graceful arcade in the hotel's Mission-style main building, its understated decor soothes diners who settle into comfortable Queen Anne chairs. A menu of topnotch Continental/American food caters to the worldly, well-heeled patron looking for a traditional meal in a comfortable atmosphere. ~ 701 Stone Canyon Road, Bel Air; 310-472-1211. ULTRA-DELUXE.

SHOPPING

Over in Century City, where broad boulevards and highrise buildings rest on the former lot of 20th Century Fox, there's a 100-store mall complete with boutiques, markets, crafts shops, and international food pavilions. **Century City Shopping Center** sprawls across 18 acres, counting among its most inviting addresses **Cottura** (310-277-3828), with a beautiful line of imported ceramics from Italy; **Lolita's** (310-277-7148), an emporium filled with crystal and porcelain; and **Imaginarium** (310-785-0227), a toy store for kids with creativity and imagination. Also here is **Brookstone** (310-284-8444), a chain store specializing in innovative and marginally practical gizmos, gadgets, games, and toys. ~ 10250 Little Santa Monica Boulevard, Century City.

There is also a shopping section in the nearby ABC **Entertainment Center**. Contained within this sky-tower setting are numerous specialty shops. ~ 2040 Avenue of the Stars, Century City.

Westwood might house UCLA, but this highrise city is a far cry from the typical campus town. Among its cosmopolitan attributes is a shopping district large enough to wear a hole in any shopper's shoes (and purse). **Westwood Village**, located along Westwood Boulevard adjacent to UCLA, is the Westside's premier shopping and entertainment district. Designed with the pedestrian in mind, "the village" is frequented by college crowds and fashionable Westside residents alike. Student-oriented shops devoted to books, clothes, and accessories combine with cafés and first-run movie theaters to keep the district hopping day and night.

Bookstores, of course, are a Westwood specialty. Large chain stores and small specialty shops proliferate throughout the neighborhood. Among the finest is **Butler/Gabriel Books**. ~ 10930 Weyburn Avenue, Westwood; 310-208-4424. If you can't find what you're looking for here, browse the 2000 to 2300 blocks of Westwood Boulevard, affectionately known as "Booksellers Row."

THE WIDE, WIDE WORD

The largest bookstore in the city, **Dutton's** is a bibliophile's dream come true (not to mention lovers of CDs and CD-ROMs). The store is furnished with chairs for comfortable perusing, features a café, and has an annex with one of the best selections of greeting cards around. ~ 11975 San Vicente Boulevard; 310-476-6263.

Westside Pavilion, an urban mall designed by the architects of the 1984 Olympics, is a glass atrium affair that spans Westwood Boulevard and contains nearly 200 shops. Department stores anchor this triple-tiered mall. ~ 10800 West Pico Boulevard, West Los Angeles; 310-474-6255. **William's Design** is a poster art gallery selling prints, lithographs, and original paintings by local artists. ~ 310-474-4570.

Boys and girls with dreams of the great outdoors can chart a course to **Adventure 16, Inc.** ~ 11161 West Pico Boulevard, West Los Angeles; 310-473-4574. Catering to the wilderness enthusiast, this shop can outfit you for rock climbing and backpacking. The inventory for adventurers includes clothing, luggage, and travel gear.

For specialty foods at discount prices, there's no place quite like **Trader Joe's**, with its endless array of nuts, cheeses, wines, and gourmet items. ~ 10850 National Boulevard, West Los Angeles; 310-470-1917.

Not far from Westwood, in a hillside setting complete with country estates, lies the town of Brentwood. Commercial establishments in this well-heeled community center around San Vicente Boulevard, a beautiful tree-lined street. **P. J. London** is Brentwood's ultimate resale shop, offering designer clothes handed down from wealthy Westside and Malibu residents. ~ 11661 San Vicente Boulevard; 310-826-4649. **Brentwood Country Mart**, a village-style shopping complex, features several dozen stores. ~ 26th Street and San Vicente Boulevard.

Shopping in Culver City, on the other hand, centers around **Fox Hills Mall**, a modern, 140-store center anchored by large department stores. ~ Slauson Avenue and Sepulveda Boulevard. The old Helms Bakery building, another Culver City institution, was converted into **The Antique Guild**, an entire warehouse filled with period furniture and antiques. Each section of this sprawling building is a different style. ~ 3225 Helms Avenue; 310-838-3131. There are more dads than lads at **Allied Model Trains**, a toy wonderland and replica of the Los Angeles Union Station that's filled with every type of model train imaginable. ~ 4411 South Sepulveda Boulevard; 310-313-9353.

Westchester Faire Antique Mall, a massive marketplace, houses about 70 shops selling antiques, collectibles, and jewelry. ~ 8655 South Sepulveda Boulevard, Westchester; 310-670-4000. **The Place and Company**, one of the best resale stores in the city, carries a large selection of top-designer fashions. ~ 8820 South Sepulveda Boulevard, Westchester; 310-645-1539.

NIGHTLIFE   In Century City, the expansive **ABC Entertainment Center** offers a variety of entertainment options. ~ 2020 Avenue of the Stars, Century City. The **Schubert Theatre** can pack 1829 people into its cavernous facility for Broadway plays with top-bill casts. ~ 800-233-3123. **Harry's Bar and American Grill**, a replica of Harry's Bar in Florence complete with wood paneling and brass detailing, caters to the after-theater crowd (not all 1829 of them at once). ~ 310-277-2333. Also in the ABC Entertainment Center, the New York–style **Harper's** features an open-air patio with views of the city lights. ~ 310-553-1855.

Westwood Village, located at the heart of Westwood a few strides from the UCLA campus, bubbles with nighttime activity. Students and moviegoers crowd the sidewalks and spill into the streets. While many are headed to the first-run movie theaters for which this college town is known, some frequent the local clubs.

Madison's Neighborhood Grill is an old-time saloon complete with marble bar, mahogany railings, and people-watching mezzanine. A popular campus hangout. ~ 1037 Broxton Avenue, Westwood; 310-824-6250.

For escaping the college crowds, there's **Marquis Lounge,** a restful piano bar in the gracious Westwood Marquis Hotel. ~ 930 Hilgard Avenue, Westwood; 310-208-8765.

San Francisco Saloon and Grill is a small, intimate bar. Wood paneling, historic photos of San Francisco, and comfortable surroundings create a sense of intimacy. ~ 11501 West Pico Boulevard, West Los Angeles; 310-478-0152.

Igby's Comedy Cabaret headlines known and unknown comedians in a cozy, contemporary club. Cover. ~ 11637 Tennessee Place, at West Pico Boulevard and Barrington Avenue, West Los Angeles; 310-477-3553.

Hidden in a forested Bel Air canyon, **The Bar** at the Bel Air Hotel is the perfect place for an intimate cocktail. Piano music from this wood-paneled den wafts onto the patio and out across the garden, waterfall, and pond. ~ 701 Stone Canyon Road, Bel Air; 310-472-1211.

Geffin Playhouse, a 500-seat Egyptian-style "event theater," often showcases new plays. ~ 10866 Le Conte Avenue, Westwood; 310-208-5454.

The **UCLA Center for the Performing Arts** holds performances on campus. ~ 405 Hilgard Avenue, Westwood; 310-825-2101.

The "equity-waiver" **Odyssey Theatre** offers avant-garde productions by a variety of playwrights. ~ 2055 South Sepulveda Boulevard, West Los Angeles; 310-477-2055.

▼▼▼▼▼▼▼▼▼▼
Pasadena Area

Tucked between the Downtown district and the lofty San Gabriel Mountains lies the San Gabriel Valley. Extending east from the San Fernando Valley toward San Bernardino, this former orange-growing empire has developed into a suburban realm noted for its wealth, botanic gardens, and smog.

Back in 1771, when 14 soldiers, two priests, and several mule drivers founded a mission in San Gabriel, they laid claim to an outpost that controlled the entire countryside, including Los Angeles Pueblo. The priests became land barons as the region was divided into vineyards, cattle ranches, and olive groves. In the mid-19th century

American settlers further transformed the valley into an oasis of lemon and orange trees.

By the late-19th century Pasadena was supplanting San Gabriel as the cultural heart of the San Gabriel Valley. Boasting an ideal climate, it billed itself as a health lover's paradise and became a celebrated resort area. Its tree-trimmed boulevards were lined with Beaux-Arts, Mediterranean, Italian Renaissance, and Victorian houses, making the town a kind of open-air architectural museum.

Eventually visitors became residents, hotels were converted to apartments, and by the mid-20th century paradise became suburbia. In the process, Pasadena's overweening wealth and stubborn sense of tradition left the town with a reputation for stodgy conservatism. The Beach Boys captured the sense of the place with their 1964 hit record, "The Little Old Lady from Pasadena." But in recent years the world-famous Rose Parade has been challenged by the annual Doo Dah Parade, a motley gathering of "briefcase drill teams" and "lawnmower marching groups," where the queen of the parade is liable to be in drag.

SIGHTS   The decaying downtown district has been transformed into **Old Town**, a ten-square-block neighborhood of modern galleries and gourmet restaurants. Pasadena, it seems, is rapidly proceeding from the 19th to the 21st century. ~ Bordered by Holly and Green streets, Pasadena Avenue and Arroyo Parkway.

Orienting visitors to the old and the new is the **Pasadena Convention and Visitors Bureau.** Closed Sunday. ~ 171 South Los Robles Avenue, Pasadena; 818-795-9311. They will tell you that the best place to begin touring the town is **Pasadena City Hall,** a 1925 Baroque building with a spectacular tile dome. A prime example of the city's classical architecture, the edifice features a colonnaded courtyard with fountain and formal gardens. ~ 100 North Garfield Avenue, Pasadena.

The **Pasadena Public Library,** completed two years later, is a Renaissance-style building with sufficient palm trees and red roof tiles to create a quintessentially Southern California setting. ~ 285 East Walnut Street, Pasadena; 818-405-4052. The **Pasadena Post Office** is a 1913 Italian Renaissance beauty. ~ 281 East Colorado Boulevard, Pasadena. Another point of local pride is the **Pasadena Civic Auditorium,** an attractive building that dates to 1932 and hosts television's Emmy awards. ~ 300 East Green Street, Pasadena; 818-449-7360.

The public sector can never compete with its private counterpart when money is concerned. Pasadena displays its real wealth on the west side of town, where civic gives way to civilian.

HIDDEN ►   First stop at the **Pacific Asia Museum,** a Chinese palace–style building originally owned by a wealthy Pasadena art collector. Dedicated to Asian art and culture, the museum showcases 18th-century

Japanese paintings and Southeast Asian ceramics. In addition to art from India, Afghanistan, and the Philippines, there are anecdotal artworks re-creating the religion and philosophy of the East. Take time to contemplate the Chinese garden and koi fish pond in the courtyard. Admission. ~ 46 North Los Robles Avenue, Pasadena; 818-449-2742.

Then drive out Colorado Boulevard, route of the Rose Parade held every New Year's Day, to the **Norton Simon Museum of Art**. Housed in this odd edifice, which looks more like it was planned by a camera maker than an architect, is one of the finest collections of European and Asian art in the country.

Touring the Simon's several galleries is like striding through time and space. The works span 2500 years, traveling from ancient India and Southeast Asia to the world of contemporary art. The Old Masters are represented by Rembrandt, Reubens, and Raphael. There are Goya etchings, 17th-century watercolors, and Impressionist pieces by Cézanne and Van Gogh. Closed Monday, Tuesday, and Wednesday. Admission. ~ 411 West Colorado Boulevard, Pasadena; 818-449-6840.

Art on a grander scale is evident at the **Colorado Street Bridge**, an antique causeway arching high above an arroyo. ~ Colorado Boulevard west of Orange Grove Boulevard, Pasadena. Not far from this engineering wonder, the old Wrigley mansion, a splendid Mission-style estate, now serves as the **Tournament House**, headquarters of the Rose Parade. Situated on four princely acres, the gardens are open daily. For a tour of the house, which contains Rose Bowl memorabilia, you'll have to arrive between 2 and 4 p.m. on a Thursday afternoon during the months of February through August. ~ 391 South Orange Grove Boulevard, Pasadena; 818-449-4100.

Another mansion with meaning is the imposing 1905 edifice that plays host to the **Pasadena Historical Museum**. Containing furnishings and keepsakes from Pasadena's early days, this Neo-Classical house with an Edwardian interior was once home to the Finnish Consul. As a result the museum expresses a second theme: Finland, represented on the grounds by Finnish gardens, a facsimile 16th-century farmhouse, and an exhibit of Finnish folk art. Closed Monday, Tuesday, and Wednesday. Admission. ~ 470 West Walnut Street, Pasadena; 818-577-1660.

Humbling all these estates is the **Gamble House**, jewel of Pasadena, a Craftsman-style bungalow designed by the famous architectural firm of Greene and Greene in 1908. Heavily influenced by such Japanese innovations as overhanging roofs and pagoda flourishes, the wood shingle home is a warm blend of hand-rubbed teak and Tiffany glass. Built for the Cincinnati-based Gamble family (as in Proctor & Gamble), the house displays crafted woodwork and the original furnishings. A veritable neighborhood of these elegantly

◄ HIDDEN

understated Greene and Greene bungalows lines the **Arroyo Terrace** loop next to the Gamble House. Closed Monday, Tuesday, and Wednesday. Admission. ~ 4 Westmoreland Place, Pasadena; 818-793-3334.

Even the gardens at the Norton Simon Museum of Art are landscaped with 19th- and 20th-century-sculptures by Rodin and Henry Moore.

To continue the architectural tour follow nearby **Prospect Boulevard** and **Prospect Crescent** along their tree-lined courses. The neighborhood entranceway and several local structures were designed by Charles and Henry Greene, the brothers who fashioned the Gamble House. Another architect, one Frank Lloyd Wright, enters the picture at **La Miniatura** (the Millard House), an unusual assemblage of crosses and concrete blocks resembling a pre-Columbian tower. ~ 645 Prospect Crescent.

Grandest of all the area's architectural achievements is the **Rose Bowl**. Built in 1922, this 100,091-seat stadium is the home for UCLA's football team and the site of the New Year's Day clash between the Big Ten and the Pac-10. If you don't have tickets for a game, remember that the stadium is open to the public on weekdays. Admission. ~ 1001 Rose Bowl Drive, Pasadena; 818-577-3100.

The future Frank Lloyd Wrights of the world reside up the hill at the **Art Center College of Design**. An excellent school of industrial design, the college has galleries displaying work by both students and established artists. It also rests on 175 hillside acres which provide marvelous views of Pasadena and the San Gabriel Mountains. ~ 1700 Lida Street, Pasadena; 818-584-5035.

Students with a more scientific bent are cracking the books at **Cal Tech**, an internationally renowned science and engineering school whose faculty have won 23 Nobel prizes and once included Albert Einstein. These hallowed halls, in case you were wondering, were modeled on a medieval cloister. There are campus tours Monday through Friday. ~ California Institute of Technology, 1201 East California Boulevard, Pasadena; 818-395-6811.

While the big kids play with numbers, the little ones are fidgeting with hands-on exhibits at **Kidspace Museum**. This innovative facility has a television studio, a fire station, and everything else a futuristic child might desire. Admission. ~ 390 South El Molino Avenue, Pasadena; 818-449-9144.

HIDDEN ▶

El Molino Viejo, the Old Mill, represents a vital part of the area's Spanish tradition. Built in 1816 by Indians from San Gabriel Mission, it was Southern California's first water-powered grist mill. Only the millstones remain from the actual mill, but the building, an adobe beauty with red tile roof, is still intact. With its courtyard setting and flowering fruit trees, the place is thoroughly enchanting. Down in the basement you'll find a working scale model of the mill's machinery. Closed Monday. ~ 1120 Old Mill Road, San Marino; 818-449-5450.

One of the Southland's most spectacular complexes and certainly the premier attraction in the San Gabriel Valley is the **Huntington Library, Art Collections, and Botanical Gardens**. This incredible cultural preserve was once presided over by a single individual, Henry E. Huntington (1850–1927), a shrewd tycoon who made a killing in railroads and real estate, then consolidated his fortune by marrying the widow of his equally rich uncle.

The focal point of Huntington's 207-acre aesthetic preserve, the **Huntington Gallery**, was originally his home. Today the mansion is dedicated to 18th- and 19th-century English and French art and houses one of the finest collections of its kind in the country. Gainsborough's "Blue Boy" is here, as well as paintings by Turner and Van Dyck, tapestries, porcelains, and furniture. Another gallery contains Renaissance paintings and French sculpture from the 18th century; the **Virginia Steele Scott Gallery of American Art**, housed in an enchanting building, traces American painting from 1730 to 1930.

Moving from oil to ink, and from mansion to mansion, the **Huntington Library** contains one of the world's finest collections of rare British and American manuscripts and first editions. Representing nine centuries of literature, the exhibit includes a Gutenberg bible, the Ellesmere Chaucer (a hand-painted manuscript dating from 1410), classics such as Ovid's *Metamorphosis* and Milton's *Paradise Lost*, and latter-day works by James Joyce and Henry James. The Founding Fathers are present with original manuscripts by Washington, Franklin, and Jefferson; and the American Renaissance is evident in the literary works of such classic authors as Poe, Hawthorne, and Twain.

This describes only the *buildings* on the property! There are also the grounds, a heavenly labyrinth of gardens ranging from a verdant jungle setting to the austerely elegant Desert Garden. Rolling lawns are adorned with Italian statuary and bordered by plots of roses and camellias. The Shakespearean garden is filled with plants mentioned by the playwright; the Japanese garden features an arched bridge, koi pond, and 19th-century teahouse. All are part of the amazing legacy of a philanthropist with a vision equal to his wealth. Closed Monday. Admission. ~ 1151 Oxford Road, San Marino; 818-405-2141.

EASTERN SAN GABRIEL VALLEY Fourth in California's historic chain of missions, **Mission San Gabriel Archangel** is an oasis in an urban setting. Built in 1771, the church is fashioned from cut stone, brick, and mortar. Its buttressed walls and vaulted roof indicate Moorish influences and lend a fortress-like quality, but inside the sanctuary peace reigns: the grounds are covered in cactus gardens and grape arbors and flanked by a cemetery. The chapel features an 18th-century altar built in Mexico City as well as colorful statues from Spain. The winery next door was once the largest in California. Admission. ~ 537 West Mission Drive, San Gabriel; 818-457-3035.

Rarely does a racecourse represent a work of art, but **Santa Anita Park**, built in 1934, is one of the country's most beautiful tracks. Surrounded by landscaped gardens and ornamented with wrought-iron fixtures, the clubhouse is a local landmark. Added to the aesthetics is another unique attraction: the park is family oriented, featuring picnic areas and playgrounds and offering free admission to children accompanied by parents. During the morning from 7:30 to 9:30 the public is admitted free and, during race season, visitors can take a guided tour on weekends and watch the horses work out. Thoroughbred racing season is from October to mid-November and from Christmas through April. Admission. ~ 285 West Huntington Drive, Arcadia; 818-574-7223.

The **Arboretum of Los Angeles County** may be the most photographed location in the world. Everything from Tarzan movies to Bing Crosby's *Road to Singapore* to television's *Fantasy Island* has been filmed in this 127-acre garden. Wander past the duck pond, tropical greenhouse, fountain, and waterfall and you'll be retracing the steps of Humphrey Bogart, Cary Grant, Ingrid Bergman, and Dustin Hoffman.

> With plants from every corner of the globe, the Arboretum has portrayed Hawaii, Burma, Africa, Samoa, and Devil's Island.

The history of the surrounding region, captured in several historic structures still standing on the grounds, long precedes the movies. There are **wickiups** similar to those of the original Gabrieleño Indians, who used the local spring-fed pond as a watering hole. Representing the Spanish era is the **Hugo Reid Adobe**, an 1840 structure built with over 3000 mud bricks. Crudely furnished in 19th-century Mexican fashion, the adobe dates to the days when the area was part of a huge Mexican land grant. E. J. "Lucky" Baldwin, the silver-mining magnate who helped introduce horse racing to Southern California, bought the ranch in 1875, and built a **Queen Anne Cottage**. His castle-in-the-sky dream house, painted white with red stripes and topped by a bell tower, is a gingerbread Victorian often featured on the *Fantasy Island* television show. The interior, decorated in period, is a masterwork of hardwoods and crystal, stained glass and marble.

Also part of this never-ending complex is the **Santa Anita Depot**. Built in 1890, it's a classic brick train station filled with equipment and memorabilia from the great age of railroads. Open Tuesday, Wednesday, and Sunday only. Admission. ~ 301 North Baldwin Avenue, Arcadia; 818-821-3222.

In the trim little town of Claremont, near the foothills of the San Gabriel Mountains, you can tour another idyllic enclave. The **Claremont Colleges**, a collection of six independent colleges, including the famous Harvey Mudd engineering school, form a continuous campus studded with shade trees. There are walking tours of turn-of-the-century buildings and strolls through pretty parks. ~ From Route 10 take the Indian Hill Boulevard North exit; go right on 1st Street; go left on College Avenue, Claremont; 909-621-8000.

Several hundred yards closer to the mountains, **Rancho Santa Ana Botanic Garden** boasts the largest collection of native California plants in the world. This enchanting 85-acre preserve is dedicated to desert plants, coastal vegetation, wildflowers, and woodlands. Wandering its nature trails is like touring a miniature version of natural California. A particularly pretty time to visit is during spring when the California poppies are in bloom. ~ 1500 North College Avenue, Claremont; 909-625-8767.

◄ *HIDDEN*

SAN GABRIEL MOUNTAINS   **Eaton Canyon**, set in the foothills, is a 184-acre park laced with hiking trails which traverse an arroyo and four different plant communities. Sufficiently close to the ocean and mountains to support flora from both regions, the park is a mix of coastal sage scrub, chaparral, oak woodland, and riparian vegetation. Trails meander through the park and lead deep into the adjacent Angeles National Forest. In 1993 about half of Eaton Canyon, including the interpretive center, burned in a fire. A temporary trailer is staffed to greet visitors, and a fire ecology trail shows the amazing regeneration of foothill flora. ~ 818-398-5420.

Another of the region's botanic preserves, **Descanso Gardens** stretches across 165 acres at the foot of the San Gabriel Mountains. This former estate has one of the largest camellia gardens in the world, numbering 100,000 plants, as well as a rose garden where droves of the species' strains are cultivated. There is also a Japanese teahouse and garden, a section devoted to native California plants, and iris and lilac gardens. Unifying this restful hideaway is a tumbling stream that meanders through an oak forest past bird preserves and duck ponds. Admission. ~ 1418 Descanso Drive, La Cañada; 818-952-4400.

◄ *HIDDEN*

To fully explore the San Gabriel Mountains, follow the Angeles Crest Highway (Route 2) in its sinuous course upward from La Cañada. With their sharp-faced cliffs and granite outcroppings, the San Gabriels form a natural barrier between the Los Angeles Basin and the Mojave Desert. Embodied in the 691,000-acre **Angeles National Forest**, these dry, semi-barren mountains are a mix of high chaparral, pine forest, and rocky terrain. Hiking trails crisscross the heights and wildflowers bloom in spring.

A side road from Route 2 leads to 5710-foot **Mount Wilson**, from which you can gaze across the entire expanse of Los Angeles to the Pacific. **Mount Wilson Observatory**, the region's most famous landmark, supports a 100-inch reflecting telescope credited years ago with the discovery that the universe consists of more than a single galaxy. Today the telescope can be seen through an observation window. The observatory is open weekends only. ~ 818-793-3100.

For complete information on the mountains and the Angeles National Forest, stop by the **Chilao Visitors Center**. Located on

Route 2 about 14 miles past the turnoff for Mount Wilson, this small facility has its own nature center and two miles of self-guided nature trails. ~ 818-796-5541.

LODGING   Motel row in Pasadena lies along Colorado Boulevard, route of the famous Rose Parade. **Pasadena Central Travelodge**, a 53-unit stucco complex, is typical of the accommodations. It offers standard rooms with cinderblock walls, stall showers, wall-to-wall carpeting, and other basic amenities. ~ 2131 East Colorado Boulevard, Pasadena; 818-796-3121, 800-578-7878, fax 818-793-4713. BUDGET.

Over $100 million was poured into the revered **Ritz-Carlton Huntington Hotel**, returning the 1907 grande dame to her turn-of-the-century glory. Situated on 20 manicured acres, this 383-room hotel combines modern amenities with the style and charm of another era. The Olympic-size swimming pool (reputed to be the first in California) has been restored, as have the hotel's Japanese and horse-shoe gardens. If you are seeking Old World elegance, this is the address. ~ 1401 South Oak Knoll Avenue, Pasadena; 818-568-3900, fax 818-568-3700. ULTRA-DELUXE.

DINING   One of the San Gabriel Valley's best food bargains is the **Restaurant Mérida**. Serving Yucatán-style dishes, this brick-walled eatery offers *birria de chivo* (goat in spicy sauce), *oriental de pavo* (turkey, onions, and garlic in rich broth), and *cochinita pibil* (pork wrapped in banana leaves). For those accustomed to dining closer to Mexico City there are enchiladas, burritos, and tostadas. Serving three meals daily, with a menu numbering over 100 items, it's an exceptional place. Patio courtyard. ~ 20 East Colorado Boulevard, Pasadena; 818-792-7371. BUDGET TO MODERATE.

For another great buy, try **Burger Continental**, a congested and crazy café where you order at the counter, then dine indoors or on a patio. Portions are bountiful and the prices ridiculously low. In addition to hamburgers they serve steaks, seafood, sandwiches, and an enticing array of Middle Eastern dishes. Best bargain is the "Armenian feast," a combination of kebab dishes and Mid-Eastern appetizers capable of feeding a large family or small army. ~ 535 South Lake Avenue, Pasadena; 818-792-6634. BUDGET TO MODERATE.

You can people watch from the sidewalk dining area while feasting on delectable dishes at the **Crocodile Café**. Try the Chinese pot stickers or the roasted poblano relleno to start. The Cobb salad is also very tasty. Inside seating is a little noisy, but the food makes up for it. Highly recommended. ~ 140 South Lake Avenue, Pasadena; 818-449-9900. BUDGET TO MODERATE.

Tucked away in an art deco building on a side street, **Bistro 45** is a gathering spot for Pasadena's "elegancia." The airy high-tech atmosphere, pastel walls and contemporary art match the handsomely presented French-Californian cuisine. The menu includes roasted chicken with fresh herbs and garlic, grilled ahi, and grilled beef tenderloin. No lunch on Saturday and Sunday. ~ 45 South Mentor Avenue, Pasadena; 818-792-2535. DELUXE.

Specializing in Mandarin and Szechuan cuisine, **Panda Inn** is a dimly lit restaurant with Chinese prints and an atmosphere of intimacy. The spicy Szechuan dishes include hot braised shrimp, sweet and pungent chicken, spicy bean curd, and twice-cooked pork. There are also chow mein, egg foo yung, and noodle entrées, as well as a full inventory of Mandarin-style beef, fowl, seafood, and vegetable dishes. ~ 3488 East Foothill Boulevard, Pasadena; 818-793-7300. MODERATE.

Any town as wealthy and prone to gentrification as Pasadena is bound to have numerous California-cuisine cafés. One of note is **Parkway Grill**, a brick-wall-and-bare-beam restaurant with track lights and stained glass. The antique bar is hardwood; the kitchen, *naturalement*, sits in the center of the complex, completely open to view. The chefs prepare gourmet pizza and pasta dishes such as calzone with bacon and smoked chicken, pizza with duck, fettuccine with grilled chicken, and angelhair primavera. Entrées include catfish in lime-soy sauce, pork tenderloin with apple and shallot marmalade, and veal chops with porcini mushrooms in a red wine sauce. No lunch on Saturday. ~ 510 South Arroyo Parkway, Pasadena; 818-795-1001. MODERATE TO DELUXE.

Italian food is hot in Pasadena. There's always an exuberant and bustling crowd in Old Town's three popular *ristorantes*.

For alfresco dining, be sure to delve into the pleasures of **Sorriso**. Decorated with a stunning art collection, this trattoria-style eatery serves authentic Italian cuisine. Try their delicious *linguine saporose* (linguine served with a zesty tomato sauce and lightly breaded pan-fried calamari and shrimp). The food is outstanding, and the ambience is *molto* Italian. ~ 46 East Colorado Boulevard, Pasadena; 818-793-2233. MODERATE.

At **Mi Píace**, the cuisine is exquisite. Try their chicken lasagne with a sweet pepper cream sauce, and you'll be very *contento*. The airy interior is further enhanced by simple pine-colored chairs, a wrought-iron bar, and fresh flowers. ~ 25 East Colorado Boulevard, Pasadena; 818-795-3131. MODERATE.

Regional Italian cuisine is the name of the game at **Il Fornaio**. Will it be Tuscany, Sicily, or Sardinia? The menu changes monthly, but there are always wood-fired pizzas and mesquite-grilled steaks, chicken, and seafood. With its white marble floors, oak wood bar, and sleek, contemporary Italian feel, this eatery comes highly praised. Patio dining is also available. ~ 24 West Union Street, Pasadena; 818-683-9797. MODERATE.

If you are the former head chef at L'Orangerie and the person who replaced Wolfgang Puck at Los Anges when he left to open

Spago, you can rightfully name your restaurant after yourself. That is exactly what Hideo "Shiro" Yamashiro did. **Shiro Restaurant** combines French and Asian influences with California cuisine to produce an everchanging menu that might include lamb chops marinated in mint and garlic, scallops in ginger and lime sauce, and steamed whitefish with capers. Dinner only. Closed Monday. ~ 1505 Mission Street, South Pasadena; 818-799-4774. DELUXE.

East conquers West at **Chez Sateau**, where a Japanese chef prepares French meals with special flair. The frosted-glass-and-private-booth dining room features a menu that changes seasonally, including specialties such as "rainbow beef" and rack of lamb. Filling out the carte are outlandish desserts like soufflés and crêpes suzettes. No lunch on Saturday. Closed Monday. ~ 850 South Baldwin Avenue, Arcadia; 818-446-8806. MODERATE TO DELUXE.

HIDDEN ► Way up in the San Gabriel Mountains, where Angeles National Forest creates an ideal retreat, you'll find **Newcomb's Ranch Inn**. This remote restaurant, set in a rustic wooden building, specializes in authentic Mexican food but serves an array of American dishes, burgers, and sandwiches. Little more than a log diner, it's a welcome sight for anyone wandering the mountains. ~ Route 2, one-quarter mile past Chilao Visitors Center, Chilao; 818-440-1001. BUDGET.

SHOPPING Shopping in the San Gabriel Valley centers around Pasadena. **South Lake Avenue**, the oldest and once the most prestigious shopping district in town, had its origins in 1947 when Bullocks department store opened for business. Today the venerable establishment has been replaced by **Macy's**.

Stop by **The Colonnade**, a small arcade which houses **Kokila's Boutique**. At this shop you'll find natural fiber fashions for women. ~ 818-584-1157. **Dirk Cable, Bookseller** specializes in rare books on California and the West. ~ 350 South Lake Avenue; 818-449-7001. **Burlington Arcade**, modeled after The Burlington in London, is another elegant gallery of specialty shops. ~ 380 South Lake Avenue.

Just west of South Lake Avenue, visit **Haskett Court**, a charming group of English-style cottages. Here at the **Rose Tree Cottages** (818-793-3337), you can browse for fine British imports or enjoy afternoon tea in a traditional setting. Reservations for tea should be made one day in advance. ~ 824 East California Boulevard, Pasadena.

Another major Pasadena shopping district lies along **Colorado Boulevard**, the town's main artery and the route of the annual Rose Parade. **Vroman's Bookstore**, one of the area's oldest and finest bookstores, is among the revered shops along this boulevard. ~ 695 East Colorado Boulevard, Pasadena; 818-449-5320. Just doors away, the **House of Fiction** projects an atmosphere of the '30s with its disheveled book stacks. ~ 663 East Colorado Boulevard, Pasadena; 818-449-9861.

Nearby, there's also **Page One Bookstore**, a women's bookstore that features scheduled readings and a community bulletin board. ~ 1196 East Walnut Street, Pasadena; 818-796-8418.

Pasadena's current beautification and redevelopment program reaches its apogee in **Old Town Pasadena**, a lively historic district that is fast becoming the pride of the city. ~ Bordered by Holly and Green streets, Pasadena Avenue and Arroyo Parkway. Particularly prevalent in this gentrified ghetto are antique stores.

Exquisite museum-quality antiques are elaborately displayed at **Design Center Antiques**, which also has a fabric showroom with over 100,000 designs. ~ 70 North Raymond Avenue, Pasadena; 213-681-6230.

Touted as the world's largest swap meet, the **Rose Bowl Flea Market** is held on the second Sunday of each month. You'll find everything from collectibles to contemptibles. Admission. ~ 1001 Rose Bowl Drive; 213-588-4411.

del Mano Gallery displays three-dimensional artwork and fine crafts by American artists. Here you'll find a beautiful collection of ceramics, blown glass, hand-painted silks, and jewelry. ~ 33 East Colorado Boulevard, Pasadena; 818-793-6648.

Pasadena Antique Center, the city's largest gallery of shops, houses more than 60 antique dealers. Among them is **Djanet**, with a collection of antique glassware, and **Things of Interest**, specializing in Mission-style furniture and accessories. ~ 480 South Fair Oaks Avenue, Pasadena; 818-449-7706.

The colorful exterior of **The Folk Tree** will inevitably draw you in to see the shop's amazing collection of folk art. Originating from Mexico and South America, the inventory includes a fascinating collection of dolls. ~ 217 South Fair Oaks Avenue, Pasadena; 818-795-8733.

For more international folk art, head three doors down to **The Folk Tree Collection** where there's a large selection of beads, jewelry and clothing from all over the world, as well as changing art exhibits. ~ 199 South Fair Oaks Avenue, Pasadena; 818-793-4828.

Elsewhere in the San Gabriel Valley, there's **Santa Anita Fashion Park**, a colossal 150-store mall adjacent to Santa Anita Racetrack. ~ Baldwin Avenue and Huntington Drive, Arcadia.

Behind the rustic Northwoods Inn, a small group of merchants has opened a cluster of imaginative shops. ~ Rosemead Boulevard and Huntington Drive, Pasadena. If it's baseball cards you're after, consider a trip to **Kenrich Co.**, where you'll find everything in paper collectibles, from maps to autographs. ~ 9418 East Las Tunas Drive, Temple City; 818-286-3888.

Like almost everything else in the San Gabriel Valley, the entertainment scene centers around Pasadena.

NIGHTLIFE

The Ice House presents new and established comedians nightly. Another section of the 1920-era ice house, **The Ice House Annex**, features stand-up comedy. Cover. ~ 24 North Mentor Avenue, Pasadena; 818-577-1894. **Barney's Ltd.**, an old-style saloon with village charm and friendly spirit, pours over 50 brands of beer from all over the world. ~ 93 West Colorado Boulevard, Pasadena; 818-577-2739.

At **Dodsworth Bar and Grill**, a New York–style restaurant and lounge, you'll find a tony crowd at the marble bar listening to live jazz. ~ 2 West Colorado Boulevard, Pasadena; 818-578-1344.

Or consider the **Pasadena Playhouse**, a historic theater which has been the birthplace for numerous stars of stage and screen. Dramatic performances are produced on the 680-seat central stage. ~ 39 South El Molino Avenue, Pasadena; 818-356-7529.

During the thoroughbred horse-racing season, beautiful Santa Anita Park attracts huge crowds every day. At night the bawdy track crowd goes to sing along karaoke-style at the **100 to 1 Club**. ~ 100 West Huntington Drive, Arcadia; 818-445-3520.

PARKS

ANGELES NATIONAL FOREST Nature is rarely reducible to statistics, but numbers are unavoidable in describing this 691,000-acre preserve. Stretching from San Bernardino County across the entire northern tier of Los Angeles County, the park encompasses the San Gabriel Mountains and separates the Los Angeles Basin from the desert. There are two rivers, eight lakes, a 10,000-foot peak, and 189 miles of fishing streams. The 36,000-acre San Gabriel Wilderness is contained within the National Forest. Overall the forest attracts more than 15 million visitors annually. Most are daytrippers intent on sightseeing and picnicking, but campers and hikers, enjoying over 60 campgrounds and 556 miles of trails, are also prevalent. Flora and fauna range from green-winged teal to black bear to horned toads and rattlesnakes. This is also a prime ski area, with nine winter sports centers. Other facilities include picnic areas and restrooms; restaurants, except for a few small cafés, are many miles away. ~ Route 2 is the main highway through the southern sector of the forest; the northern region is located east of Route 5; 818-574-5200.

▲ There are 60 campgrounds for tents and RVs (no hookups); $5 to $12 per night.

▼▼▼▼▼▼▼▼▼▼▼▼▼▼
San Fernando Valley
Sprawling across 220 square miles and containing a population of more than 1.3 million suburbanites, the San Fernando Valley is an inland version of Los Angeles. This mirror image across the mountains, known simply as "The Valley," is a smog-shrouded gridwork of tract homes and shopping malls, a kind of stucco version of the American Dream. The dream was disturbed in January 1994 when a devastating 6.8 earthquake rolled through the region, but today life is steadily returning to normal.

Bounded by the Santa Monica Mountains to the south and the San Gabriels on the east, The Valley first entered the history books in 1796 when Spanish padres established the San Fernando Mission, an isolated outpost which became a cultural center for the *ranchos* that soon sprang up between the mountains.

During the 1870s, when the Spanish land grants were subdivided and the railroad entered the area, the San Fernando region enjoyed its first boom. But the major escalation in population and real estate prices came early the next century during one of the biggest scandals in Los Angeles history.

When Los Angeles voters passed a $1.5 million bond issue in 1905 to buy water-rich land in the distant Owens Valley, they believed they were bringing water to their own parched city. In fact much of this liquid gold poured into the San Fernando Valley, filling the coffers of a cabal of civic leaders who bought up surrounding orange groves and transformed them into housing developments.

In 1914, when Universal turned a 230-acre chicken ranch into a world-acclaimed movie studio, The Valley found a home industry. With its stark mountains and open spaces, the place proved an ideal location for filming Westerns. Columbia, Warner Brothers, and other television and movie studios eventually arrived, as the San Fernando Valley began rivaling that celluloid center on the far side of the Hollywood Hills.

By the post–World War II era, the aerospace industry had landed in The Valley, adding money and glamour to an area fast becoming a kind of promised land for the middle class. With its checkerboard lawns, prefab houses, and predominantly white population, the place is now the West Coast answer to middle America, with parents who commute to Los Angeles and kids who commute to the nearest shopping mall.

GLENDALE   The portal to the land of the living, some say, is through the gates of death. In the San Fernando Valley that would be **Forest Lawn**, one of the most spectacular cemeteries in the world.

SIGHTS

Within the courtyards of this hillside retreat are replicas of Michelangelo's "David," Ghiberti's "Baptism of Jesus," and a mosaic of John Trumbull's painting "The Signing of the Declaration of Independence." There are also re-creations of a 10th-century English church and another from 14th-century Scotland. The museum houses a collection consisting of every coin mentioned in the Bible. "The Crucifixion," the nation's largest religious painting, a tableau 195 feet long and 45 feet high, is also on display.

Death has never been prouder or had more for which to be prideful. On the one hand, Forest Lawn is quite beautiful, a parkland of the dead with grassy slopes and forested knolls, a garden planted with tombstones. On the other, it is tasteless, a theme park of the dead where the rich are buried amid all the pomp their heirs can muster. ~ 1712 South Glendale Avenue; 818-241-4151.

Every great city boasts a great park. Consider New York's Central Park, Golden Gate Park in San Francisco, and in Los Angeles, **Griffith Park** (entrances near Western Canyon Road, Vermont Avenue, Riverside Drive, and Route 5). Set astride the Hollywood Hills between the Westside and the San Fernando Valley, this 4043-acre facility offers a flatlands area complete with golf courses, playgrounds, and picnic areas, plus a vast hillside section featuring meadows, forests, and miles of mountain roads.

Local bird species nest in **Fern Dell**, a shady glade in Griffith Park with a spring-fed stream. The picnic tables lining the dell create an inviting spot to while away an afternoon. ~ Western Canyon Road.

Along Crystal Springs Drive, traversing the eastern edge of the park, you'll pass the **Griffith Park & Southern Railroad**, a miniature train ride. Admission. ~ 213-664-6788. Nearby is a track offering **pony rides**. ~ 213-664-3266. The **ranger station** will provide maps and information while directing you across the street to the **merry-go-round**, a beautiful 1926-vintage carousel. The merry-go-round is open weekends only. ~ 213-665-5188.

Featuring real life versions of these whirling animals, the **L.A. Zoo** is among the highlights of the park. Over 1200 animals inhabit this 113-acre facility, many in environments simulating their natural habitats. The African exhibit houses elephants, rhinos, zebras, and monkeys; Eurasia is represented by tigers and black leopards; there are jaguars from South America as well as kangaroos and koalas from Australia. Admission. ~ 5333 Zoo Drive; 213-666-4650.

The adjacent **Adventure Island** is where newborn animals are bottle-fed. You can see the baby animals in an exhibition area.

Travel Town is a transportation museum featuring a train yard full of cabooses, steam engines, and passenger cars from the glory days of the railroad. The exhibit also includes a fleet of 1920-era fire trucks and old milk wagons. For the kids there are narrow-gauge train rides here and at **Live Steamers** next door. ~ 5200 West Zoo Drive; 213-662-5874.

For Hollywood's version of American history, there's the **Autry Museum of Western Heritage**. The focus here is more on Westerns than the West. There are displays of saloons and stagecoaches, silver saddles and ivory-handled six-shooters, plus photos and film clips of all your favorite stars, kids. Closed Monday. Admission. ~ 4700 Western Heritage Way; 213-667-2000.

Standing above the urban fray at the southern end of the park is the **Griffith Observatory and Planetarium**, a copper-domed beauty that perfectly represents the public-monument architecture of the 1930s. With its bas-reliefs and interior murals, this eerie site also resembles a kind of interplanetary temple. In fact it has been the setting for numerous science fiction films such as *When Worlds Collide* (1951). The Observatory's most famous appearance, however, was in *Rebel Without a Cause* (1955) when James Dean was confronted by the neighborhood gang.

Apart from a movie setting, the Observatory features a Planetarium Theatre and a space-age Laserium complete with high-tech light shows. The Hall of Sciences offers museum displays on astronomy and meteorology. A lot of people come simply for the view, which on clear days (in Los Angeles?) extends from the Hollywood Hills to the Pacific. Closed Monday from September through March. Admission (Laserium). ~ Observatory Drive; 213-664-1191.

High on a slope overlooking Los Angeles stands the **Ennis-Brown House**, a squarerigged, Mayan temple–style home designed by Frank Lloyd Wright in 1924. You need a reservation to visit. Admission. ~ 2655 Glendower Avenue, Los Feliz; 213-660-0607. The Ennis-Brown mansion resides in the same neighborhood as the **Lovell House**, a prime example of Richard Neutra's International Style of architecture, circa 1929. ~ 4616 Dundee Drive, Los Feliz.

Another of Frank Lloyd Wright's pre-Columbian block houses is the **Derby House**, dating to 1926, which was fashioned from precast concrete. ~ 2535 East Chevy Chase Drive, Glendale. One of the master architect's more traditional designs, a Mediterranean-style house, lies up the street. ~ 3021 East Chevy Chase Drive, Glendale.

Far simpler in effect is the **Casa Adobe de San Rafael**, a single-story, mud-brick home built in the 19th century. Once occupied by the Los Angeles County Sheriff, the hacienda's chief feature is the grounds, which are trimly landscaped and covered with shade trees. The house itself is furnished in early-California style. ~ 1330 Dorothy Drive, Glendale.

◄ HIDDEN

Rising above them all, situated in the foothills overlooking Glendale, is the **Brand Library & Art Center**. Neither the library nor the galleries are exceptional, but both are set in **El Miradero**, a unique 1904 mansion modeled after the East Indian Pavilion of the 1893 Columbian World Exposition. With bulbous towers, crenelated archways, and minarets, the building is Saracenic in concept, combining Spanish, Moorish, and Indian motifs. The grounds also include a spacious park with nature trails and picnic areas as well as "The Doctor's House," a heavily ornamented 1890 Queen Anne Eastlake Victorian. Closed Sunday and Monday. ~ 1601 West Mountain Street, Glendale; 818-548-2051.

VENTURA BOULEVARD   Only in the San Fernando Valley could a single street define an entire geographic area. Running from east to west along the southern edge of The Valley, Ventura Boulevard parallels the Santa Monica Mountains as it passes through Universal City, Studio City, Sherman Oaks, and Encino, then continues to the distant towns of Calabasas and Agoura.

Along the way you'll encounter a house called **Campo de Cahuenga,** a 1923 re-creation of a building constructed in 1845. Of little architectural interest, the place is noteworthy because the treaty ending the Mexican War was signed here by Lt. Col. John C. Fremont and General Andrés Pico in 1848. ~ 3919 Lankershim Boulevard, Universal City; 818-763-7651.

Universal Citywalk is a three-block-long pedestrian mall that connects the Universal Studios Hollywood theme park and Amphitheater to the Cineplex Odeon movie theaters. Although the emphasis is on shops and restaurants, you can stroll down the middle of this "city street" and enjoy a collection of vintage neon signs and wacky, eclectic architecture. Occasionally street performers entertain, and in the central court, kids enjoy darting in and out of jets of water shooting up from the sidewalk fountain. You may also want to check out the Panasonic Pavilion, a "high-tech carnival" created by Steven Spielberg that uses multimedia products from Panasonic. ~ 1000 Universal Center Drive, Universal City; 818-622-4455.

Several phases of San Fernando Valley life are preserved at **Los Encinos State Historical Park.** This five-acre facility is studded with orange trees, which covered the valley at the turn of the century. The De La Osa Adobe, built in 1850 and utilized as a resting place along El Camino Real, is a squat eight-room ranch house. Nearby stands the Garnier Building, a two-story limestone residence constructed in 1873 after the fashion of a French farmhouse. With its duck pond and shaded lawns the park is also a choice spot for a picnic. Closed Monday and Tuesday. ~ 16756 Moorpark Street, Encino; 818-784-4849.

Making these old houses seem like youngsters is the **Encino Oak Tree.** With branches spreading 150 feet and a trunk eight feet thick this magnificent specimen dates back about 1000 years. ~ Ventura Boulevard and Louise Avenue, Encino.

Farther out in The Valley lies the town of Calabasas, which prides itself on a Wild West heritage but looks suspiciously like surrounding suburban towns. It does possess a few remnants from its romantic past, including the **Leonis Adobe,** an 1844 mud-brick house which was expanded around 1879 into a stately two-story home with porches on both levels. This Monterey-style beauty stands beside the **Plummer House,** an antique Victorian home. Closed Monday and Tuesday. ~ 23537 Calabasas Road, Calabasas; 818-222-6511.

An ersatz but enchanting version of the Old West awaits at **Paramount Ranch,** a 335-acre park which once served as the film location for Westerns. Paramount owned the spread for two decades beginning in the 1920s, using it as a set for *Broken Lullaby* (1932) with Lionel Barrymore, *Thunder Below* (1932) with Tallulah Bankhead, and *Adventures of Marco Polo* (1937), the Samuel Goldwyn extravaganza which included a fortress, elephants, and 2000 horses. During the heyday of TV Westerns in the 1950s, the property was a location for *The Cisco Kid, Bat Masterson,* and *Have Gun, Will Travel.*

Today you can hike around the ranch, past the rolling meadows, willow-lined streams, grassy hillsides, and rocky heights that made it such an ideal set. "Western Town" still stands, a collection of false-front buildings that change their signs depending on what's being filmed. If you're lucky a film crew will be shooting a commercial or even producing the last of that dying breed of movie, a Western. ~ In Santa Monica Mountains National Recreation Area; 818-597-9192.

Orcutt Ranch Horticultural Center, once a private estate, is now an outdoor museum in full bloom. In addition to farm equipment, horticultural displays, and a ranch house, this 25-acre reserve is landscaped with rose gardens and citrus orchards. Nature trails wind through the oak groves, providing a vision of the San Fernando Valley before the advent of suburbia. ~ 23600 Roscoe Boulevard, West Hills; 818-883-6641.

NORTH SAN FERNANDO VALLEY The **Tujunga Wash Mural**, one   ◄ HIDDEN
of the Southland's local wonders, is reputedly the world's longest mural. Extending for one-half mile along the wall of a flood control channel, it portrays the history of California from prehistoric times to the present. Bright-hued panels capture the era of American Indians and early Spanish explorers, the advent of movies, and the terrors of World War II. ~ On Coldwater Canyon Boulevard between Burbank Boulevard and Oxnard Street, North Hollywood.

Among the finest of California's missions, **Mission San Fernando Rey de España** has been beautifully restored and reconstructed. Exploring the gardens and courtyards of this 1796 institution, visitors encounter the workshops of resident weavers, blacksmiths, and carpenters, as well as an excellent collection of altar furnishings and religious oil paintings. The wine cellar—deep, cool, and dark—has ironically been placed next to the convent. One of the chapels, rebuilt after an earthquake, is decorated with *trompe l'oeil* murals while another is literally covered with gilded appointments, as if God were somehow more receptive to baroque icons. At the rear of this complex lies the site which best symbolizes the experience of the neophyte Indians who struggled and suffered here—the cemetery. Admission. ~ 15151 San Fernando Mission Boulevard, Mission Hills; 818-361-0186.

Nearby stands Los Angeles' second oldest house. Built before 1834 by mission Indians, the **Andrés Pico Adobe** is a prime example of Spanish architecture. Possessing both beauty and strength, it's a simple rectangular structure with a luxurious courtyard. At last report, the building was closed for earthquake repairs. ~ 10940 Sepulveda Boulevard, Mission Hills; 818-365-7810.

Just in case you thought Los Angeles County was entirely urban, there are 350 acres of oak forest and native chaparral at **Placerita Canyon State and County Park**. A stream runs through the property and there are hiking trails and a nature center. ~ 19152 Placerita Canyon Road, Newhall; 805-259-7721.

Over at **William S. Hart Regional Park** there's another 265-acre spread once owned by a great star of silent Westerns. A Shakespearean actor who turned to cinema—starring in his last feature, *Tumbleweeds*, in 1925—William S. Hart left his mansion and estate to the movie-going public.

While much of the property is wild, open to hikers and explorers, the most alluring features are the buildings. The old ranch house, once Hart's office, contains photos of friends and mementoes from his career. The central feature is Hart's home, a 22-room Spanish hacienda filled with guns, cowboy paintings, and collectibles from the early West. ~ 24151 North San Fernando Road, Newhall; 805-259-0855.

HIDDEN ►   California's haunting history of earthquakes is evident at **Vasquez Rocks County Park**, where faulting action has compressed, folded, and twisted giant slabs of sandstone. Tilted to 50° angles and rising 150 feet, these angular blocks create a setting that has been used for countless Westerns as well as science fiction films such as *Star Trek* (1979) and *Star Wars* (1977).

Shoshone Indians first lived among these natural rock formations over 2000 years ago. During the 1870s the infamous bandito Tiburcio Vasquez hid amid the caves and outcroppings to elude sheriff's deputies. A kind of Mexican Robin Hood, Vasquez gave his name to the rocks when he shot it out with lawmen here and escaped, only to be captured and hanged later. ~ Escondido Road, northeast of Newhall off Route 14; 805-268-0840.

To explore this parched and rocky terrain further, head up into **Bouquet Canyon** (Bouquet Canyon Road), a curving, lightly wooded valley with hiking trails and picnic areas. **San Francisquito Canyon** (San Francisquito Canyon Road) is a river-carved valley that parallels Bouquet Canyon. Back in 1928 the Saint Francis Dam collapsed, inundating this quiet canyon and killing more than 400 people in one of the worst natural disasters in United States history. Today it's a placid mountain valley providing ample opportunities to wander. Like Bouquet Canyon it lies outside Saugus near a region appropriately tagged Canyon Country.

Six Flags California encompasses Six Flags Magic Mountain, a quintessential roller-coaster park and Six Flags Hurricane Harbor, a family-oriented water park featuring water slides and a wave pool. Though adjacent to one another, Magic Mountain and Hurricane Harbor are separate parks with their own entrances and admission fees not to mention distinct personalities.

Spreading across 260 acres and featuring more than 100 rides, shows, and attractions, *Six Flags Magic Mountain* is an entertainment center featuring everything from picnic areas to dance clubs to super-thrill rides. Take for instance "Superman the Escape." It's an exceptional adventure-filled ride which accelerates from 0 to 100 miles per hour in seven seconds and rockets up a 41-story tower, then freefalls back down. "Viper," a 188-foot-high megacoaster, takes you on three vertical loops, plus a boomerang and corkscrew, all experienced at 70 miles per hour. There are also gentler rides for small children such as the classic 1912 carousel.

Hurricane Harbor is a fantasy entertainment environment of lost lagoons and pirate coves that was designed with children in mind; one attraction doesn't even allow adults. Of the five themed areas there's "Castaway Cove," a large water play area with sides, waterfalls, and swings. On a raft, you can float along on the "River Cruise," a 1300-foot-long lazy river that surrounds Castaway Cove and Shipwreck Shores. A wave pool called "Forgotten Sea" generates two-foot waves and is up to six feet deep. "Taboo Tower," with a 325-foot enclosed spiraling slide, is one of the four water slides in Hurricane Harbor. Admission. ~ 26101 Magic Mountain Parkway, Valencia; 805-255-4100.

The Safari Inn is that rarest of creatures, a motel with soul. In fact this 103-room facility also possesses a pool, jacuzzi, restaurant, lounge, and an adjacent hotel. The film location for several movies, it offers motel rooms at moderate prices and hotel accommodations, some with kitchens. The amenities and accouterments here are definitely a step above those of a roadside motel. ~ 1911 West Olive Avenue, Burbank; 818-845-8586, 800-782-4373, fax 818-845-0054. MODERATE TO DELUXE.

LODGING

Set in a quiet North Hollywood residential neighborhood, **La Maida House and Bungalows** is a gracious Old World villa built in the early 1920s by Italian immigrant Antonio La Maida. The house boasts extensive use of marble, oak, mahogany, tile, and stained glass. Eleven airy rooms and suites, all with private baths, are decorated eclectically; many feature private patios. Personal touches such as cut flowers (from the house's own gardens), a solarium, and gourmet dining make La Maida a rare alternative to the typical hotel. There's a pool and gymnasium. ~ 11159 La Maida Street, North Hollywood; 818-769-3857, fax 818-753-9363. DELUXE TO ULTRA-DELUXE.

◄ *HIDDEN*

Universal City, the center for tours of Universal Studio, is big on highrise hotels. Among the most luxurious is the **Universal City Hilton and Towers**, a 24-story steel-and-glass structure overlooking the San Fernando Valley. With a vaulting lobby illuminated through skylights and trimmed in chrome, it's an ultramodern facility. Guest rooms are contemporary in decor and feature plate-glass views of the surrounding city. Among the amenities are one restaurant, two lounges, shops, pool, jacuzzi, and exercise room. The good life gilded. ~ 555 Universal Terrace Parkway, Universal City; 818-506-2500, fax 818-509-2031. ULTRA-DELUXE.

A subtle charm pervades the atmosphere at **Sportsmen's Lodge Hotel**. Hidden within this English country–style establishment are gardens with waterfalls and foot-bridges, as well as a swan-filled lagoon. The interior courtyard contains an Olympic-sized swimming pool and the lobby features shops, restaurants, and a pub. Numbering about 200 rooms (each with private patio and room service), the hotel is worth its price. ~ 12825 Ventura Boulevard, Studio City; 818-769-4700, 800-821-8511, fax 213-877-3898. DELUXE.

Ventura Boulevard, a major thoroughfare in The Valley, is chockablock with motels. Passing through Sherman Oaks, Encino, and Tarzana, you'll find a multitude of possibilities. Among the more upscale motels is **St. George Motor Inn,** a 57-unit, mock-Tudor facility. A pool and spa are on the premises. ~ 19454 Ventura Boulevard, Tarzana; 818-345-6911. BUDGET.

Adding to the Valley's hospitality industry is the 15-story **Woodland Hills Hilton and Towers.** The updated art deco look extends from the lobby to the 318 soft pastel guest rooms and suites. The concierge level features a two-story lounge with sweeping mountain views. Suites offer wet bars; other amenities include a restaurant and sports bar. ~ 6360 Canoga Avenue, Woodland Hills; 818-595-1000, 800-445-8667. DELUXE TO ULTRA-DELUXE.

DINING

A small Japanese restaurant, **Aoba,** contains a sushi bar and fewer than a dozen tables. The menu offers a standard array of Japanese dishes, including teriyaki entrées, tempura specials, and, of course, sushi. ~ 239 North Brand Boulevard, Glendale; 818-247-9789. MODERATE.

One of Southern California's great restaurant strips, Ventura Boulevard stretches for miles along the southern rim of The Valley, offering fine kitchens all along the route.

The decor at **Teru Sushi** is as inviting as the cuisine. Handpainted walls and carved figures combine with slat booths and a long dark wood sushi bar. The sushi menu includes several dozen varieties; they also serve a selection of traditional dishes. There is a beautiful garden dining area with a koi pond. No lunch on Saturday and Sunday. ~ 11940 Ventura Boulevard, Studio City; 818-763-6201. MODERATE TO DELUXE.

All the critics agree that the food at **Anajak Thai** is outstanding. The menu features more than four dozen noodle, curry, beef, and chicken dishes. Small and comfortable, the restaurant is painted dark blue and decorated with white latticework and Asian art. No lunch on Saturday and Sunday. ~ 14704 Ventura Boulevard, Sherman Oaks; 818-501-4201. BUDGET.

For French food and charming intimacy try **Mon Grenier.** With a name which translates as "my attic," this whimsical dining room has a solid reputation for fine cuisine. Entrées include pepper steak, crispy duck, and salmon in crust. Dinner only. Closed Sunday. ~ 18040 Ventura Boulevard, Encino; 818-344-8060. DELUXE TO ULTRA-DELUXE.

The **Sagebrush Cantina** is a sprawling restaurant and bar with a sawdust-floor dining room and ample patio space. In addition to an assortment of Mexican dishes they feature steak, ribs, Texas-style link sausage, barbecued brisket, and seafood. ~ 23527 Calabasas Road, Calabasas; 818-222-6062. MODERATE.

Way up in the Santa Monica Mountains, that rocky spine separating the San Fernando Valley from the ocean, you'll uncover a rare find at **Saddle Peak Lodge**. A true country lodge, this antique building is constructed of logs lashed together with leather straps. Flintlocks and trophy heads adorn the walls and leather upholstered chairs surround a stone fireplace. Open for dinner and Sunday brunch, the restaurant offers quail, buffalo burgers, game hen, duckling, venison, pheasant, veal chops, rack of lamb, and "kick-ass chili." If you have the time, it merits the mountain drive. Closed Monday and Tuesday. ~ 419 Cold Canyon Road, Calabasas; 818-222-3888. DELUXE TO ULTRA-DELUXE.

◄ HIDDEN

Over at **Delhi Place** you can dine on affordable Indian cuisine. Cloth napkins and Asian decor are part of the bargain at this excellent restaurant. The dishes include lamb curry, chicken *tandoori*, and numerous vegetarian dishes. ~ 22323 Sherman Way, Canoga Park; 818-992-0913. BUDGET.

If these seem inappropriate just **Follow Your Heart** to a vegetarian restaurant popular with folks from miles around. Specialties at this gathering place include wok stir-fry, deep-dish pizza, nutburgers, black bean and tofu tacos, and steamed organic vegetables. ~ 21825 Sherman Way, Canoga Park; 818-348-3240. BUDGET.

Ask anyone in the Valley where to go for downhome cooking and they will tell you **Dr. Hogly Wogly's Tyler Texas Bar-B-Que**. It's just a regular old café which happens to serve delicious brisket of beef and stick-to-the-ribs ribs. Dinner comes with half a loaf of home-baked bread, baked beans, cole slaw, and macaroni salad. Chow down! ~ 8136 Sepulveda Boulevard, Van Nuys; 818-780-6701. MODERATE TO DELUXE.

◄ HIDDEN

Another conversation piece is the **94th Aero Squadron**, a wildly imaginative establishment obliquely modeled after a World War I aviation headquarters in France. The building resembles a provincial French farmhouse, but it's surrounded by charred airplanes and other artifacts of war. The interior is a sandbagged warren with wings and propellers dangling from the ceiling. The cuisine, which somehow seems irrelevant, is American. Prime rib, Cajun shrimp, and "farmhouse" chicken with ham and cheese are regulars on the menu. The view, naturally, is of Van Nuys Airport. Sunday brunch. ~ 16320 Raymer Avenue, Van Nuys; 818-994-7437. MODERATE TO DELUXE.

Out in "The Valley," shopping is such popular sport that the area has bred a new species—"mallies"—who inhabit the shopping malls from the moment the stores open until the second they close.

SHOPPING

GLENDALE AND BURBANK   Shopping in Glendale centers around the **Glendale Galleria**, a mammoth 240-store complex anchored by such heavies as **Macy's** (818-240-8411) and **Nordstrom** (818-502-9922). A host of apparel stores, specialty shops, knickknack stores, and restaurants offer variety, if not imagination. ~ Central Avenue and Broadway, Glendale.

A promised land for browsers is **Glendale Costumes**, which rents over 60,000 costumes from the tights of Renaissance dandies to the tights of Batman. ~ 746 West Doran Street, Glendale; 818-244-1161.

If it happens to be the first Sunday of the month, add the **Glendale Civic Auditorium** to your list of must-see addresses. That's when more than 80 antique dealers gather to sell their wares. ~ 1401 North Verdugo Road, Glendale; 818-548-2147.

Burbank is not really geared to shopping, with the exception of San Fernando Boulevard between San Jose and Tujunga avenues. Home to several used bookstores, the area includes **Movie World**, which adds movie memorabilia to its inventory of books. ~ 212 North San Fernando Boulevard, Burbank; 818-846-0459.

For New Age titles consider stopping in at the **Psychic Eye Book Store**. Decorated with crystals and Asian statuary, it sells volumes on metaphysics, palmistry, numerology, and the occult. ~ 1011 West Olive Avenue, Burbank; 818-845-8831.

VENTURA BOULEVARD   Cities blend into one another on Ventura Boulevard, the busy east–west corridor that stretches across the entire southern rim of the San Fernando Valley. Shops line every point along the thoroughfare, with only subtle distinctions marking changes in locale. Start in Studio City and you'll find your credit cards still working in Sherman Oaks, Encino, Tarzana, and points west.

Traders of Studio City may not look like a pawnshop, but a hock shop it is. You'll find everything from bangles to cameras at this secondhand store. ~ 12238 Ventura Boulevard, Studio City; 818-985-6136.

The Valley's answer to Melrose Avenue is a three-block stretch of Ventura Boulevard where Valley girls (and guys) hang out, hook up, and put down their bucks. Clothing stores here are even equipped with live disc jockeys. The shops pop every night 'til 10 or 11, with the largest clothiers drawing the biggest crowds. ~ 14500 block of Ventura Boulevard, Sherman Oaks.

The **Sherman Oaks Galleria** is an atrium-style mall with a host of high-class shops as well as big department stores. ~ 15301 Ventura Boulevard, Sherman Oaks.

Strange as it may sound here in Shopperland, there are no department stores at **Encino Town Center** and **Plaza de Oro**. These beautifully landscaped, multitiered plazas provide for more relaxed shopping. Within these open-air facilities are several novel stores offering everything from clothing to chocolate. ~ 17200 and 17171 Ventura Boulevard, Encino.

Specializing in 19th-century works, **Charles Hecht Gallery** offers a museum-quality selection of Impressionist paintings. This exemplary gallery also features work by other artistic schools. ~ 18555 Ventura Boulevard, Tarzana; 818-881-3218.

Out in the Western-style town of Calabasas, a two-block shopping area offers a chance to browse in a sedate environment. Wander Calabasas Road and you'll discover a variety of small, one-of-a-kind shops.

NORTH SAN FERNANDO VALLEY   A life-size model horse stands at the entrance to **Manny's Cowboy Tailors.** Much more than a Western-wear outlet, this store was once a showcase for Nudie, the internationally renowned rodeo tailor. Even today the walls are filled with photos of celebrities like Roy Rogers and Gene Autry strutting about in Nudie's elaborate designs. For you, pardner, they have patterned boots, cowboy hats, and embroidered suits, all designed with the well-heeled cowboy in mind. ~ 5043 Lankershim Boulevard, North Hollywood; 818-763-2726.

Nearby **Sam's Book City** stocks over 100,000 used, out of print, and scarce books. ~ 5245 Lankershim Boulevard, North Hollywood; 818-985-6911.

GLENDALE AND BURBANK   The giant 6000-seat **Greek Theatre,** nestled in the rolling hills of Griffith Park, is patterned after a classical Greek amphitheater. The entertainment in this enchanting spot ranges from stellar jazz, classical, pop, and rock music to dance and dramatic performances. Bring a sweater and picnic. ~ 2700 North Vermont Avenue, Glendale; 213-665-1927.

NIGHTLIFE

Jax Bar & Grill, with its brass elephants and local clientele, is a supper club that headlines notable jazz musicians nightly. ~ 339 North Brand Boulevard, Glendale; 818-500-1604.

For sophisticated entertainment there's the **Glendale Center Theatre,** which presents musicals and comedies. ~ 324 North Orange Street, Glendale; 818-244-8481. **The Third Stage** is a comedy venue. ~ 2811 West Magnolia Boulevard, Burbank; 818-842-4755.

Chadney's, popular with entertainment people from nearby NBC Studio, offers live jazz Tuesday through Saturday. ~ 3000 West Olive Avenue, Burbank; 818-843-5333.

Named after Shirley Temple, **Dimples** is a showcase for fledgling singers. Dance music alternates every half hour with musical auditions. Sing for your drinks while pursuing those dreams of stardom! ~ 3413 West Olive Avenue, Burbank; 818-842-2336.

The after-work crowd pedals over to **Bombay Bicycle Club,** where antique bikes decorate a large cocktail lounge. ~ 321 South 1st Street, Burbank; 818-846-8711.

Just up the block, the **Lobby Lounge** at the Universal City Hilton and Towers represents another choice piano bar. ~ 555 Universal Terrace Parkway, Universal City; 818-506-2500.

Telly's Sporting Bar is named in honor of the late Telly Savalas, a long-term resident of the Sheraton Universal Hotel. The bar is decorated in sports memorabilia. ~ 333 Universal Terrace Parkway, Universal City; 818-509-2791.

The **Baked Potato** serves up contemporary jazz every night. If you want to rub shoulders with L.A. music heavies, this is the place. Cover and minimum drink order. ~ 3787 Cahuenga West Boulevard, Studio City; 818-980-1615.

VENTURA BOULEVARD Representative of the gay scene in The Valley are four Studio City clubs. **Oil Can Harry's** is a country-and-western club. ~ 11502 Ventura Boulevard, Studio City; 818-760-9749. **Apache** is the area's most popular disco. ~ 11608 Ventura Boulevard, Studio City; 818-506-0404. **Oasis** is a piano bar with a pool table and back patio. ~ 11916 Ventura Boulevard, Studio City; 818-980-4811. **Queen Mary's** is a pretty pastel club with a campy weekend floor show that features a parade of queens dressed in their finest regalia. Cover; reservations are recommended. ~ 12449 Ventura Boulevard, Studio City; 818-506-5619.

The **L.A. Connection Comedy Theatre** developed a unique comedy concept several years back. They show camp film classics with house comedians ad-libbing the dialogue. Other shows include regular audience participation improvisation. Cover. ~ 13442 Ventura Boulevard, Sherman Oaks; 818-784-1868.

The **L.A. Cabaret Comedy Club** also features stand-up comedy. Showcased on the lounge's two stages are top entertainers ranging from Milton Berle to Robin Williams. Cover. ~ 17271 Ventura Boulevard, Encino; 818-501-3737.

The outdoor patio and country atmosphere at **Sagebrush Cantina** draw steady crowds. Here you can sip margaritas, linger after sunset and workout on the sawdust floors to the sound of rock bands. ~ 23527 Calabasas Road, Calabasas; 818-222-6062.

NORTH SAN FERNANDO VALLEY The Valley is a prime place for jazz. For live jazz try **The Money Tree**, located just outside of Burbank. ~ 10149 Riverside Drive, Toluca Lake; 818-769-8800.

Norah's Place is an altogether different experience. This lively Bolivian supper club serves up tango music. In between sets by the resident band the dancefloor fills with dancers moving to merengue, cumbia, and salsa tunes on Friday and Saturday nights. Cover on Saturday. ~ 5667 Lankershim Boulevard, North Hollywood; 818-980-6900.

PARKS

CASTAIC LAKE Set at the foot of the Castaic Mountains, this 2300-acre manmade lake is surrounded by rugged slopes. The countryside—covered with chemise, sage, and chaparral—is stark but beautiful. Along the lake, which carves a V in the hills, are facilities for picnicking, boating, and waterskiing. Castaic is stocked with bass, trout, and bluegill. Other facilities are restrooms, picnic areas, and playgrounds; restaurants and groceries are located nearby in Castaic. ~ Castaic Lake is at 32132 Ridge Route Road in Castaic. The Vista del Lago visitors center (805-294-0219) is located 14 miles north of Castaic Lake in Pyramid Lake.

Outdoor Adventures

Though the beach isn't far away, Los Angeles also contains several lakes which provide ample opportunity for water sports. If you'd like to waterski or windsurf, try **Frank G. Bonelli Park**. ~ 120 Via Verde Park Road, San Dimas; 909-599-8411. Or try **Castaic Lake Recreation Area**. ~ 32132 Ridge Route Road, Castaic; 805-257-4050. Remember to bring your own equipment!

WATER SPORTS

For those who are happier lolling about in a boat, there are rentals at **Frank G. Bonelli Park**. ~ 120 Via Verde Park Road, San Dimas; 909-599-8411. **Santa Fe Dam** also offers rentals. ~ 15501 East Arrow Highway, Irwindale; 818-334-1065. In Castaic, visit the **Castaic Lake Recreation Area**. ~ 32132 Ridge Route Road, Castaic; 805-257-2049.

Paddle boating is a big sport at **MacArthur Park**. ~ 2230 West 6th Street, Los Angeles.

SWIMMING

From the air, Los Angeles seems to have a swimming pool for every family. For those without access to backyard water holes, there are several public pools. Among the more notable is **Los Angeles Swim Stadium**, just outside Exposition Park. Although the stadium was damaged during the 1994 Northridge earthquake, the pool behind the stadium is still open to the public. ~ 3980 South Menlo Avenue, Los Angeles.

JOGGING

Though driving seems almost an addiction in the city, many Angelenos still manage to exercise. Filling your lungs with smoggy air might not be the healthiest thing to do, but if you're interested in jogging anyway, join the troopers at **Exposition Park** at 39th and Figueroa streets or at **Elysian Park**, located near the intersection of Routes 110 and 5, both in Los Angeles. Visit **San Vicente Boulevard** in the Brentwood area or **Lacy Park** at 1485 Virginia Road in San Marino. Another popular area is the **arroyo** near the Rose Bowl in Pasadena, or **Griffith Park** at 4730 Crystal Springs Road in Los Angeles.

GLIDING

What better way to let yourself go than by coasting or floating on high? The adventurous can try hang gliding at **Windsports International**. ~ 16145 Victory Boulevard, Van Nuys; 818-988-0111.

GOLF

In Los Angeles it's as easy to tee off at a golf course as it is to get teed off in a traffic jam. One of the many challenging or interesting courses is the **Montebello Country Club**. ~ 901 Via San Clemente,

Montebello; 213-887-4565. In West Los Angeles, try **Rancho Park Golf Course**. ~ 10460 West Pico Boulevard; 310-838-7373. If you are in Pasadena, stop by the **Brookside Golf Course**. ~ 1133 North Rosemont Avenue; 818-796-0177. In Los Angeles, try **Wilson-Harding Golf Course**. ~ Griffith Park; 213-663-2555. Another L.A. area course is **Westchester Golf Course**. ~ 6900 West Manchester Boulevard; 310-670-5110.

In the eastern end of the county try **Marshall Canyon Golf Course**. ~ 6100 North Stephens Ranch Road, La Verne; 909-593-8211. **Diamond Bar Golf Course** is another possibility. ~ 22751 East Golden Springs Drive, Diamond Bar; 909-861-8282. In San Dimas, there's the **San Dimas County Golf Course**. ~ 2100 Terrebonne Avenue, San Dimas; 818-966-8547. Duffers in Pomona head to **Mountain Meadows Golf Course**. ~ 1875 Fairplex Drive, Pomona; 909-623-3704. Rosemead's **Whittier Narrows Golf Course** is also a good choice. ~ 8640 East Rush Street, Rosemead; 818-280-8225.

In the San Fernando Valley consider **Knollwood Golf Course**. ~ 12040 Balboa Boulevard, Granada Hills; 818-363-8161. Another option is **Sepulveda Golf Complex**. ~ 16821 Burbank Boulevard, Encino; 818-995-1170.

TENNIS   Most public parks have at least one tennis court; the city's largest facility, **Griffith Park,** has many. ~ 4730 Crystal Springs Road, Los Angeles; 213-662-7772 or 213-665-5188. Or try **Elysian Park**. ~ Near the intersection of Route 5 and Route 110, Los Angeles.

Tennis clubs dot the county; one such club (with two locations) is the **Racquet Center**. ~ 10933 Ventura Boulevard, Studio City, 818-760-2303; and 920 Lohman Lane, South Pasadena, 213-258-4178. For further information about clubs and tournaments, contact the **Southern California Tennis Association**. ~ P.O. Box 240015, Los Angeles, CA 90024; 310-208-3838.

✔ CHECK THESE OUT—UNIQUE OUTDOOR ADVENTURES

- Get above it all on a hang gliding excursion from **Van Nuys**, where your takeoff will far surpass any departures from LAX. *page 123*
- Go for a leisurely spin in a paddle boat—and get a little leg workout at the same time—on the lake in **MacArthur Park**. *page 123*
- Saddle a steed and explore 4000-acre **Griffith Park**, along trails that wind up hillsides to stunning views. *page 125*
- Hike the trails around **Stoney Point**, where you can watch—or join— top climbers as they practice their moves on the rocks. *page 128*

For further information on other local parks and their facilities, contact the nearest Los Angeles City and County Parks and Recreation Department office.

RIDING STABLES

With its curving hills and flowering meadows, Griffith Park is a favorite spot among urban equestrians. Several places on the edge of the park provide facilities. Try **Sunset Ranch** in Hollywood. ~ 3400 North Beachwood Drive, Hollywood; 213-464-9612. In Burbank consider **Circle K Stables**. ~ 914 Mariposa Street; 818-843-9890. Another Burbank offering is **Griffith Park Livery Stables**. ~ 480 Riverside Drive; 818-840-8401. **Bar S Stables** is another possibility. ~ 1850 Riverside Drive, Glendale; 818-242-8443.

BIKING

Bikeways in Los Angeles are almost as plentiful as freeways. Unlike the freeways, few of them are normally congested. Many run parallel to parks, rivers, aqueducts, and lakes, offering a different view of this diverse area. For example, a flat, nine-mile bike path circumnavigates the **Sepulveda Dam Recreation Area** in the heart of the San Fernando Valley.

Over 14 miles of bike routes wind through Griffith Park. Two notable excursions skirt many of the park attractions: **Crystal Springs Loop**, which follows Crystal Springs Road and Zoo Drive along the park's eastern edge, passes the merry-go-round and Travel Town; **Mineral Wells Loop**, an arduous uphill climb, passes Harding Golf Course, then coasts downhill to Zoo Drive, taking in Travel Town and the zoo.

The most scenic bike path in the L.A. area is the **West Fork Trail** in the San Gabriel Mountains—6.7 miles of gentle, paved path that parallels the west fork of the San Gabriel River. Take Route 210 to Azusa, then Route 39 ten miles north to a parking lot a little past the Rincon Ranger Station.

For a trip from the mountains to the sea, try the **San Gabriel River Bike Trail**. It begins in Azusa and extends 38 miles to the Pacific near Long Beach.

In the Whittier–El Monte area, bicyclists can choose a long jaunt along the **Upper Rio Hondo Bike Trail** or a leisurely go-round on the **Legg Lake Loop** in Whittier Narrows Recreation Area.

In the Mt. Washington area, the **Arroyo Seco Bike Trail** includes a loop past Heritage Square, the Lummis House, and Casa de Adobe. The trail begins at the Montecito Heights Recreation Center on Homer Street and runs along an arroyo.

The **Kenneth Newell Bikeway** begins on Arroyo Boulevard in Pasadena, then dips down to Arroyo Seco and the famed Rose Bowl. The bikeway follows a flood basin, climbs a steep hill into Linda Vista and continues to Devil's Gate Dam and the world-renowned Jet Propulsion Laboratory.

For a look at the good life, check out the route from **San Gabriel Mission to the Huntington Library**, which winds from San Gabriel through the exclusive town of San Marino.

A strenuous but worthwhile excursion is a bike ride along **Mulholland Drive**. Not recommended during commuter hours, this route traverses the spine of the Santa Monica Mountains and offers fabulous views of the city and ocean.

For more information on bicycle routes contact the **Transportation Commission** for a brochure. ~ 213-623-1194.

HIKING

The idea of natural areas in Los Angeles seems to be a contradiction in terms. But the city is so vast—sprawling from the Pacific Ocean to the mountains—that even ambitious developers have been unable to pave it all. For backpackers and daytrippers alike, miles of hiking trails still lace the hills and canyons that lie just beyond the housing tracts and shopping malls. Use of Los Angeles County trails requires a pass. Both annual and three-day passes are available; call 818-855-5384 for details. All distances listed are one way unless otherwise noted.

WHITTIER-EL MONTE AREA   Near Roland Heights, in Schabarum Regional County Park, the **Skyline Trail: Schabarum Park to Hacienda Boulevard** (6 miles) traverses the Puente Hills. The hike leads through wild mustard fields to an overlook with views of the San Gabriel Valley.

Miles of trails abound in **Frank G. Bonelli Regional Park** in San Dimas. To get an overview of the park, hike along the southern hills above Puddingston Reservoir. Maps are available at the park headquarters.

PASADENA AREA   The San Gabriel Mountains are crisscrossed with hiking trails ripe for exploring.

Several years ago the San Gabriel portion of the **Pacific Crest Trail**, which leads from Canada to Mexico, was completed. One part of that great system, the **Mill Creek Summit to Pacifico Mountain Trail** (4 miles) follows a route through spruce and oak forests to a view overlooking the Mojave Desert.

At the end of Chaney Trail Road in Altadena there's a lovely spot for a family hike through a tree-shrouded canyon. **Lower Millard Canyon Falls Trail** (.5 mile) leads to a 50-foot waterfall surrounded by huge boulders. If you're a little more adventurous, try **Upper Millard Canyon Trail** (2.5 miles).

An even more ambitious hike from the same trailhead is the **Mount Lowe Railway Trail** (3.5 miles). At the end you'll discover an abandoned rail line, the old "Railway to the Clouds," and the ruins of Ye Alpine tavern. It's a moderate trek offering spectacular views of Los Angeles.

In Altadena's Eaton Canyon, the **Altadena Crest Trail** (3 miles) explores the foothills of the San Gabriels. A side trip to **Eaton Falls** (.5 mile) follows the stream bed.

Big Santa Anita Canyon north of Sierra Madre is another popular area for hiking. **Sturtevant Falls Trail** (1.8 miles) leads upstream to a 50-foot waterfall. The trailhead is located in Chantry Flat. (Don't climb on the rocks at the waterfall; several people have been seriously hurt here.)

Not as well-known as popular Mount Wilson is a neighboring peak, 5994-foot **Mount Disappointment** (2.8 miles), which offers another opportunity to view Los Angeles from on high. You'll walk through Douglas fir and Coulter pine forests and climb along chaparral-covered ridges. The trailhead is just beyond Red Box off the Mount Wilson Road.

It's all downhill to begin with when you hike **Devil's Canyon Trail** (5.5 miles). This trek through an alder-studded canyon, with a bubbling creek for company, goes from Upper Chilao Campground in the San Gabriel Wilderness.

The **Arroyo Seco Canyon Trail** (9.8 miles), beginning at Switzer's Picnic Area (off Route 2), is a challenging way to explore the serene canyons of the San Gabriels. The trail overlooks Switzer Falls, joins the **Gabrieleño Trail** (3.5 miles), then descends to the tree-laden floor of the canyon. En route is Oakwilde Trail Camp, an ideal spot for an overnight visit. The trail continues to the mouth of the canyon, which overlooks the massive Jet Propulsion Laboratory.

GRIFFITH PARK   Los Angeles' outback is found a few miles from the center of Downtown amid the forested hills of Griffith Park. With more than 55 miles of trails to explore, the park rests along the Hollywood Hills at the edge of the Santa Monica Mountains. For information and maps contact the local ranger station. ~ 213-665-5188.

Among the best hikes here is the **Mt. Hollywood Loop Trail** (6 miles). Beginning near the merry-go-round, the path follows a stream,

SCALING THE TOPS

There are many ways to scale 5710-foot Mount Wilson. One particularly pleasant route is the **Mount Wilson Trail** (7.5 miles), beginning from Miramonte Avenue in Arcadia. This path leads up Little Santa Anita Canyon past oak and spruce trees to Orchard Camp, a way station offering a perfect place for a picnic. From here the trail ascends through dense chaparral to the ridge and Mount Wilson Road. This is also a popular mountain-biking road.

passes deer and coyote habitats, then leads up out of the canyon onto the chaparral-covered slopes of Mt. Hollywood.

For a combination sightseeing-hiking venture take the **Mineral Wells Trail** (4.3 miles). The hike begins on a level bridle trail, then wends its way down toward the zoo, and back to Mineral Wells.

The **Pacific Electric Quarry–Bronson Cave Trail** (2.3 miles) snakes through Brush Canyon to an abandoned rock quarry and the Bronson Caves, an area ripe for exploring. If it seems like you've been here before, that's because this was the location for such shows as *Bonanza, Mod Squad,* and *Star Trek.*

SAN FERNANDO VALLEY Leading up a 5074-foot peak, the highest within the Los Angeles city limits, **Mount Lukens Stone Canyon Trail** (3.3 miles) is a hearty uphill trek. On a clear day the Pacific looms in the distance, beyond a jigsaw puzzle of housing tracts and rolling hills. The trailhead is located in Sunland off Doske Road; be sure to bring water.

At the northern edge of the San Fernando Valley, **Placerita Canyon to Sylmar Trail** (9 miles) offers conditioned hikers an opportunity to climb along a chaparral-covered hillside to an oak-studded canyon. The hike begins in Placerita Canyon State and County Park and goes along the Wilson Canyon Saddle. Another challenging trek is the climb up **Manzanita Mountain** (1 mile), with its picturesque views. For the family, there's **Placerita Canyon Loop Hike** (8 miles), an easygoing jaunt through a shady canyon and along a creek.

The old stage road that connected the San Fernando and San Joaquin valleys is now the route of **Beale's Cut Trail** (.3 mile). This short but steep hike cuts through the San Fernando Pass, with its earthquake fault and twisted rock formations.

HIDDEN ▸ One of Los Angeles' hidden gems is **O'Melveny Park**, a 672-acre preserve in the Santa Susana Mountains at the north end of the San Fernando Valley. **O'Melveny Park Trail** (2.5 miles) begins in Bee Canyon and follows an old fire road past a stream, then climbs through fields of wildflowers to a series of bluffs. After the steep climb, you are rewarded with a panoramic view of Los Angeles, the Santa Clarita Valley, and the San Gabriel Mountains. The trailhead is near Sesnon Boulevard in Granada Hills. (This park is currently closed for earthquake repairs; it will reopen in the summer of 1997.)

In Chatsworth, **Devil's Canyon Trail** (1.5 miles) offers a peaceful walk along a streambed through stands of sycamore and oak trees. Look for the caves which have been etched into the sides of the canyon. Also in Chatsworth is a honeycomb of hiking trails winding around **Stoney Point**, located at the north end of Topanga Boulevard just before it meets Route 118. This huge rock outcropping draws some of the country's best rock climbers, so there's an aspect of theater here as well.

▼▼▼▼▼▼▼▼▼▼
Transportation

CAR

Arriving in Los Angeles by car means entering a maze of freeways. For most Angelenos this is an every day occurrence; they know where they are going and are accustomed to spending a lot of time getting there. It's an intimate affair, a personal relationship between car and driver; they even refer to their freeways by name rather than number.

For the visitor the experience can be very intimidating. The best way to determine a path through this labyrinth is by learning the major highways to and from town.

From the north and west, **Route 101**, the Ventura Freeway, extends from Ventura to Sherman Oaks, then turns southeast to become the Hollywood Freeway.

The Santa Monica Freeway, **Route 10**, cuts through the heart of Los Angeles. It begins in Santa Monica and then becomes the San Bernardino Freeway in downtown Los Angeles.

From Northern California, **Route 5**, the Golden State Freeway, runs south into the center of the city where it changes its name to the Santa Ana Freeway. **Route 405**, better known as the San Diego Freeway, cuts through the San Fernando Valley, the Westside, and then curves east towards Orange County.

AIR

Two airports bring visitors to the L.A. area: the very big, very busy Los Angeles International Airport and the less crowded Burbank-

NORTH–SOUTH FREEWAYS		EAST–WEST FREEWAYS	
(405) San Diego		(14) Antelope Valley	
(5) Golden State	north of Downtown	(118) San Fernando	
Santa Ana	south of Downtown		
(170) Hollywood		(101) Ventura	west of Hollywood
(101) Hollywood	south of Hollywood	(134) Ventura	
(210) Foothill		(210) Foothill	
(2) Glendale		(10) Santa Monica	west of Downtown
		San Bernardino	east of Downtown
(110) Pasadena	north of Downtown	(60) Pomona	
Harbor	south of Downtown		
(710) Long Beach		(91) Redondo Beach	west of Route 710
		Artesia	Route 710 to Route 5
(605) San Gabriel		Riverside	east of Route 5
(57) Orange		(22) Garden Grove	

Glendale-Pasadena Airport. Los Angeles International is convenient if you are headed for the downtown area or out to the coast. Traffic around this major hub is generally ferocious. Those planning to stay around Hollywood and Beverly Hills, in the San Fernando Valley, or out around Pasadena, are better advised to fly in to the Burbank-Glendale-Pasadena Airport.

Los Angeles International Airport, better known as LAX, is served by many domestic and foreign carriers. Currently (and this seems to change daily) the following airlines fly into LAX: Alaska Airlines, American Airlines, America West Airlines, Continental Airlines, Delta Air Lines, Hawaiian Airlines, Morris Air, Northwest Airlines, Southwest Airlines, United Airlines, and USAir.

International carriers are also numerous: Air Canada, Air France, Air New Zealand, All Nippon Airways, British Airways, China Airlines, Canadian Airlines International, Japan Airlines, KLM, Royal Dutch Airlines, Lufthansa German Airlines, Mexicana Airlines, Philippine Airlines, Qantas Airways, Singapore Airlines, and TACA International Airlines.

Flights to and from **Burbank-Glendale-Pasadena Airport** are currently provided by Alaska Airlines, American Airlines, America West Airlines, Skywest Airlines, Southwest Airlines, United Airlines, and United Shuttle.

Taxis, limousines, and buses line up to take passengers from LAX and Burbank. **SuperShuttle** travels between hotels, businesses, and residences to both Burbank and Los Angeles airports. ~ 818-556-6600.

BUS

Greyhound Bus Lines (800-231-2222) has service to the Los Angeles area from all around the country. The main Los Angeles terminal is at 1716 East 7th Street (213-629-8400). Other stations are found in Hollywood at 1409 North Vine Street (213-466-6381); Pasadena at 645 East Walnut Street (818-792-5116); Glendale at 400 West Cerritos Avenue (818-244-7295); and North Hollywood at 11239 Magnolia Boulevard (818-761-5119).

Green Tortoise is an alternative bus company that runs funky (and sometimes unreliable) buses equipped with sleeping platforms. It stops at unusual sightseeing spots and offers an experience in group living. The bus leaves San Francisco for Los Angeles once a week. ~ 494 Broadway, San Francisco, CA 94133; 415-821-0803.

TRAIN

Amtrak will carry you into Los Angeles via the "Coast Starlight" from the North, the "San Diegan" from San Diego, the "Desert Wind" and "Southwest Chief" from Chicago, the "Eagle" from Chicago by way of Texas, and the "Sunset Limited" from New Orleans. The L.A. station, Union Station, is at 800 North Alameda Street. There are also stations in Pasadena at 150 South Los Robles Avenue and Glendale at 400 West Cerritos Avenue. ~ 800-872-7245.

Having a car in Los Angeles is practically a must. Distances are great and public transportation leaves much to be desired. As you can imagine, it's not difficult to find a car rental agency. The challenge is to find the best deal. Be sure to request a mileage-free rental, or one with at least some free mileage. One thing is certain in the Los Angeles area, you'll be racking up mileage on the odometer.

CAR RENTALS

If you arrive by air, consider renting a car at the airport. These cost a little more but eliminate the hassles of getting to the rental agency.

Looking for a car at Los Angeles International Airport will bring you to **Avis Rent A Car** (310-646-5600, 800-331-1212), **Budget Rent A Car** (310-645-4500, 800-527-0700), **Hertz Rent A Car** (310-568-5100, 800-654-3131), or **National Interrent** (310-670-4950, 800-227-7368).

Agencies providing free airport pick-up service include **Enterprise Rent A Car** (310-649-5400, 800-325-8007) and **Thrifty Car Rental** (310-645-1880, 800-367-2277).

At the Burbank airport several companies rent autos: **Avis Rent A Car** (818-566-3001, 800-331-1212), **Enterprise Rent A Car** (818-846-4471, 800-325-8007), **Hertz Rent A Car** (818-846-8220, 800-654-3131), **National Interrent** (818-842-4847, 800-227-7368), and **American Eagle Car and Truck Rental** (818-840-8816).

Among the used car rentals in the Los Angeles area are **Rent A Wreck** (310-478-0676, 800-423-2158) and **G & R Rent A Car** (310-478-4208).

If there was ever a place to rent a limousine, Los Angeles is it. Dozens of companies specialize in "elegant service for elegant people." Check the Yellow Pages for listings.

If you arrive in Los Angeles without a car, believe it or not you can still get around. **Los Angeles County Metropolitan Transportation Authority,** or MTA, has over 200 bus routes covering more than 2200 square miles. "Rapid" transit may be a misnomer, but buses do get you where you want to go. Seven customer service centers are located throughout Los Angeles; call for the nearest location. ~ 213-626-4455.

PUBLIC TRANSIT

The **Metro Red Line** runs between Downtown (from the Union Station rail passenger terminal) and the MacArthur Park area in seven minutes. The Red Line has also been extended along Wilshire Boulevard and into Western Avenue. The train runs from Union Station to Western Avenue in 13 minutes. (Plans are underway for extensions into Hollywood and the San Fernando Valley.) The **Metro Blue Line,** with trains operating daily between Downtown and Long Beach, is the first part of a 300-mile light rail system under development. The **Green Line** trains travel from Norwalk to Los Angeles International Airport.

Before arriving in Los Angeles, write for a free **Rider's Kit**. These have information on routes and fares. One brochure, "MTA Self-Guided Tours," covers the traditional sights. When using the bus for an extended period, you can save money by purchasing an MTA Monthly Pass. ~ MTA, P.O. Box 194, Los Angeles, CA 90053.

For traveling around downtown Los Angeles or Westwood, the DASH shuttle service is available Monday through Saturday (except holidays). ~ 213-626-4455.

TAXIS

Several cab companies serve Los Angeles International Airport, including **United Independent Taxis** (213-934-6700), **L.A. Taxi** (310-412-8000), and **Yellow Cab** (213-627-7000).

From Burbank Airport, **Checker Cab** (818-843-8500), **Red Top Cab** (818-242-3131), and **Universal Cab** (818-558-3000) provide taxi service.

THREE

Los Angeles Coast

L.A., according to a popular song, is a great big freeway. Actually, this sprawling metropolis by the sea is a great big beach. From Long Beach north to Malibu is a 74-mile stretch of sand that attracts visitors in the tens of millions every year. Life here reflects the culture of the beach, a freewheeling, pleasure-seeking philosophy that combines hedonism with healthfulness.

Perfectly fitted to this philosophy is the weather. The coastal climatic zone, called a maritime fringe, is characterized by cooler summers, warmer winters, and higher humidity than elsewhere in California. Sea breezes and salt air keep the beaches relatively free from smog. During summer months the thermometer hovers around 75° or 80° and water temperatures average 67°. Winter carries intermittent rain and brings the ocean down to a chilly 55°.

Add a broadly ranging coastal topography and Los Angeles has an urban escape valve just minutes from downtown. The shoreline lies along the lip of the Los Angeles basin, a flat expanse interrupted by the sharp cliffs of the Palos Verdes Peninsula and the rocky heights of the Santa Monica Mountains. There are broad strands lapped by gentle waves and pocket beaches exploding with surf. Though most of the coast is built up, some sections remain raw and undeveloped.

Route 1, the Pacific Coast Highway, parallels the coast the entire length of Los Angeles County, tying its beach communities together. To the south lie Long Beach and San Pedro, industrial enclaves which form the port of Los Angeles, a world center for commerce and shipping. Embodying 50 miles of heavily developed waterfront, the port is a maze of inlets, islets, and channels protected by a six-mile breakwater. It is one of the world's largest manmade harbors; over $55 billion in cargo crosses its docks every year, making it the country's most profitable port. Despite all this hubbub, the harbor supports over 125 fish species and over 90 types of birds, including several endangered species.

The great port dates to 1835 when a small landing was built on the shore. Following the Civil War an imaginative entrepreneur named Phineas Banning developed the area, brought in the railroad, and launched Los Angeles into the 20th century. Now Long Beach wears several hats. In addition to being a major port and manufacturing center, it is the site of a naval base and a revitalized tourist center.

Home to the retired ocean liner *Queen Mary*, Long Beach also contains the neighborhood of Naples, a system of islands, canals, and footbridges reminiscent of Italy's gondola cities.

Once an amusement center complete with airship, carousel, and sword swallowers, the city became one big oil field during the 1920s. That's when wildcat wells struck rich deposits and the region was transformed into a two-square-mile maze of derricks. Even today the offshore "islands" hide hundreds of oil wells.

Commercial fishing, another vital industry in Long Beach and San Pedro, supports an international collection of sailors. Mariners from Portugal, Greece, and elsewhere work the waterfront and add to the ethnic ambience.

Just a few miles north, along the Palos Verdes Peninsula, blue collar gives way to white collar and the urban surrenders to the exotic. A region of exclusive neighborhoods and striking geologic contrasts, Palos Verdes possesses Los Angeles' prettiest seascapes. A series of 13 marine terraces, interrupted by sheer cliffs, descend to a rocky shoreline. For 15 miles the roadway rides high above the surf past tidepools, rocky points, a lighthouse, and secluded coves.

This wealthy suburban environment is replaced in turn by another type of culture, typified by blond-haired surfers. Santa Monica Bay, the predominant feature of the Los Angeles Coast, is a single broad crescent of sand extending 30 miles from Redondo Beach through Venice and Santa Monica to Point Dume. South Bay—comprising the towns of Redondo Beach, Hermosa Beach, and Manhattan Beach—is the surfing center of Southern California, where the sport was first imported from Hawaii. This strip of coast is also home to Los Angeles International Airport and is considered the world's top aerospace research center.

Like most of the coastal communities, South Bay didn't take off as a beach resort until the turn of the century, after railroad lines were extended from the city center to the shore and several decades after downtown Los Angeles experienced its 1880s population boom.

It was well into the 20th century, 1962 to be exact, that neighboring Marina del Rey, the largest manmade small boat harbor in the world, was developed. Nearby Venice, on the other hand, was an early 1900s attempt to re-create its Italian namesake. Built around plazas and grand canals, Venice originally was a fashionable resort town with oceanfront hotels and an amusement park. Today studios and galleries have replaced canals and gondolas in this seaside artist colony. The place has become a center for thinkers at the cutting edge and street people who have stepped over it. Zany and unchartable, modern-day Venice is an open ward for artists, the place where bohemians go to the beach, where roller skating is an art form and weight lifting a way of life.

The town of Santa Monica next door was originally developed as a beachside resort in 1875. Back in 1769 explorer Gaspar de Portolá had claimed the surrounding area for the Spanish crown. Over the years this royal domain has served as a major port, retirement community, and location for silent movies; today it is a bastion of brown-shingle houses, flower-covered trellises, and left-wing politics.

Bordering it to the north are the Santa Monica Mountains, a succession of rugged peaks which are part of the Transverse Range, the only mountains in California running east and west. Extending to the very edge of the sea, the Santa Monicas create

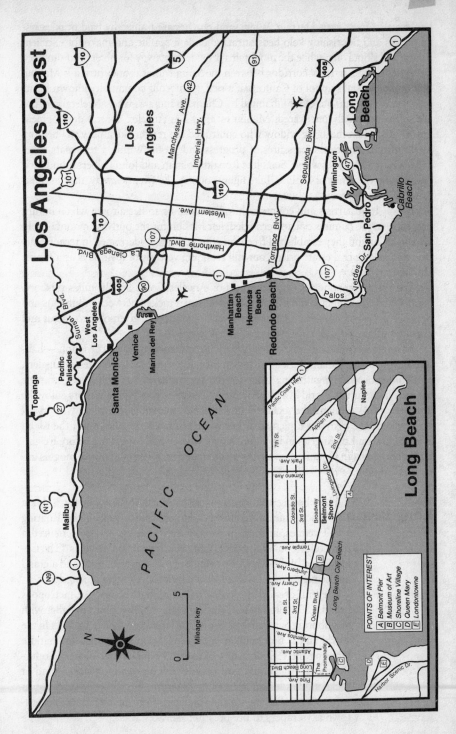

Los Angeles Coast

Los Angeles

Long Beach

Topanga

Malibu

Pacific Palisades

West Los Angeles

Santa Monica

Venice

Marina del Rey

Manhattan Beach

Hermosa Beach

Redondo Beach

Palos Verdes Dr.

San Pedro

Wilmington

Cabrillo Beach

Sunset Blvd.

Sepulveda Blvd.

Manchester Ave.

Imperial Hwy.

Western Ave.

Hawthorne Blvd.

La Cienega Blvd.

Torrance Blvd.

PACIFIC OCEAN

N

Mileage key

0   5

Long Beach

Pacific Coast Hwy.

Naples

Appian Wy.

7th St.

Park Ave.

Ximeno Ave.

Colorado St.

Broadway

3rd St.

2nd St.

Livingston Dr.

Belmont Shore

Temple Ave.

Junipero Ave.

Cherry Ave.

4th St.

3rd St.

Ocean Blvd.

Alamitos Ave.

Atlantic Ave.

Long Beach Blvd.

Pine Ave.

The Promenade

Long Beach City Beach

Harbor Scenic Dr.

POINTS OF INTEREST

A Belmont Pier
B Museum of Art
C Shoreline Village
D Queen Mary
E Londontowne

Los Angeles' most varied terrain. White sand beaches are framed by bald peaks, crystal waters and flourishing kelp beds attract abundant sea life and make for excellent fishing and skindiving, while the mountains provide a getaway for hikers and campers.

Lying along a narrow corridor between the Santa Monicas and the sea is Malibu, that quintessential symbol of California, a rich, glamorous community known for its movie stars and surfers. Once inhabited by Chumash Indians, whose skeletal remains are still occasionally uncovered, Malibu escaped Los Angeles' coastal development until 1928, when the aging widow who controlled the region like a personal fiefdom finally succumbed to the pressures of progress and profit. Within a few years it became a haven for Hollywood. Stars like Ronald Colman and John Gilbert found their paradise on the sands of Malibu. Like figures out of *The Great Gatsby*, they lived insouciant lives in movie-set houses.

By the 1960s artists and counterculturalists, seeking to flee a town which in turn had become too commercial and crowded, left Malibu for the outlying mountains. In Topanga Canyon they established freeform communities, undermined in recent years by breathtaking real estate prices, but still retaining vestiges of their days as a flower children's retreat.

The most romantic locale along the Los Angeles Coast lies 22 miles offshore. Santa Catalina, highlighted by Avalon, a resort town tucked between mountains and ocean, is a 28-mile-long island almost entirely undeveloped, given over to cactus and grazing buffalo.

Through the centuries this solitary island has undergone many incarnations—habitat for Stone Age Indians; base for Russian fur hunters; center for pirates, smugglers, and gold prospectors; gathering place for the big bands of the 1930s; and strategic military base during World War II. Today it's a singular spot where visitors enjoy the amenities of Avalon and the seclusion of the island's outback. If Avalon, with its art deco waterfront, provides a picture of Los Angeles circa 1933, the rest of the island is a window on Los Angeles in its natural state, wild and alluring, long before freighters embarked from Long Beach, surfers worked the South Bay, and movie moguls uncovered Malibu.

▼▼▼▼▼▼▼▼▼
Long Beach

Anchoring the southern end of Los Angeles County is Long Beach, one of California's largest cities. Back in the Roaring Twenties, after oil was discovered and the area experienced a tremendous building boom, Long Beach became known as "The Coney Island of the West." Boasting five miles of beachfront and a grand amusement park, it was a favorite spot for daytripping Angelenos.

Several decades of decline followed, but recently the metropolis began a $2 billion redevelopment plan. Today it ranks together with neighboring San Pedro as one of the largest manmade harbors in the world and is becoming an increasingly popular tourist destination. Ignoring the Chamber of Commerce hoopla about the city's refurbishment, you should find Long Beach a revealing place, a kind of social studies lesson in modern American life. Travel Ocean Boulevard as it parallels the sea and you'll pass from quaint homes to downtown skyscrapers to fire-breathing smokestacks.

For a dynamic example of what I mean, visit the enclave of **Naples** near the south end of town. Conceived early in the century, modeled on Italy's fabled canal towns, it's a tiny community of three islands separated by canals and linked with walkways. Waterfront greenswards gaze out on Alamitos Bay and its fleet of sloops and motorboats. You can wander along bayside paths past comfortable homes, contemporary condos, and humble cottages. Fountains and miniature traffic circles, alleyways and boulevards, all form an incredible labyrinth along which you undoubtedly will become lost.

Adding to the sense of old Italia is the **Gondola Getaway**, a romantic hour-long cruise through the canals of Naples. For a hefty price (less, however, than a ticket to Italy), you can climb aboard a gondola, dine on hors d'oeuvres, and be serenaded with Italian music. ~ 5437 East Ocean Boulevard; 310-433-9595.

The **Long Beach Museum of Art** is a must. Dedicated to 20th-century art, this avant-garde museum has ever-changing exhibitions ranging from German Expressionism to contemporary Southern California work. Particularly noted for its video presentations, the museum is a window on modern culture. Closed Monday and Tuesday. Admission. ~ 2300 East Ocean Boulevard; 310-439-2119.

For a touch of early Mexican culture, plan on visiting the region's old adobes. Built in the 1800s with walls more than three feet thick, **Rancho Los Alamitos** is Southern California's oldest remaining house. In its gardens which cover more than three acres, are brick walkways and majestic magnolias. You can tour old barns, a blacksmith shop, and a feed shed. There's also a chuck wagon with a coffeepot still resting on the wood-burning stove. Closed Monday and Tuesday. ~ 6400 Bixby Hill Road; 310-431-3541.

Rancho Los Cerritos, a two-story Mission Revival home, once served as headquarters for a 27,000-acre ranch. Now the 19th-century adobe is filled with Victorian furniture and surrounded by gardens. Closed Monday and Tuesday. ~ 4600 Virginia Road; 310-570-1755.

✔ CHECK THESE OUT—UNIQUE SIGHTS

- Step aboard the **Queen Mary** and explore the deco beauty of the 1000-foot-long "grand lady" from poop deck to pump room. *page 138*
- Flex your biceps at Muscle Beach—or just ogle others—in the roiling activity of Venice's **boardwalk.** *page 156*
- Get on your high horse and ride the antique carousel that was featured in the movie *The Sting* at the **Santa Monica Pier.** *page 162*
- Commune with ancient Rome amid the Classical art and architecture of the **Getty Museum**, where views of the Pacific compete with manmade wonders. *page 173*

HIDDEN ►

The Pacific Ocean may be Long Beach's biggest natural attraction, but many birds in the area prefer the **El Dorado Nature Center**. Part of the 450-acre El Dorado Park complex, this 85-acre wildlife sanctuary offers one- and two-mile hikes past a lake and creek. About 150 bird species as well as numerous land animals can be sighted. Though located in a heavily urbanized area, the facility encompasses several ecological zones. Closed Monday. Admission. ~ 7550 East Spring Street; 310-570-1745.

Chapter Two in the Long Beach civics lesson is the steel-and-glass downtown area, where highrise hotels vie for dominance. The best way to tour this crowded commercial district is to

In the summer of 1997, the 310 area code for the Long Beach area will change to 562.

stroll **The Promenade**, a six-block brick walkway leading from 3rd Street to the waterfront. There's a **tile mosaic** (Promenade and 3rd Street) at the near end portraying an idyllic day at the beach complete with sailboats, sunbathers, and lifeguards. Midway along the landscaped thoroughfare sits the **Long Beach Area Convention & Visitors Bureau**, home to maps, brochures, and other bits of information. ~ 1 World Trade Center, #300; 310-436-3645. Then you'll arrive at a park shaded with palm trees and adjacent to **Shoreline Village**, a shopping center and marina disguised as a 19th-century fishing village. ~ 407 Shoreline Village Drive.

Long Beach Part III rises in the form of oil derricks and industrial complexes just across the water. To view the freighters, tankers, and warships lining the city's piers, gaze out from the northern fringes of Shoreline Village.

Fittingly, the climax of a Long Beach tour comes at the very end, after you have experienced the three phases of urban existence. Just across the Los Angeles River, along Harbor Scenic Drive ("scenic" in this case meaning construction cranes and cargo containers), lies one of the strangest sights I've ever encountered. The first time I saw it, peering through the steel filigree of a suspension bridge, with harbor lights emblazoning the scene, I thought something had gone colossally wrong with the world. An old-style ocean liner, gleaming eerily in the false light, appeared to be parked on the ground. Next to it an overgrown geodesic dome, a kind of giant aluminum breast, was swelling up out of the earth.

Unwittingly I had happened upon Long Beach's top tourist attraction, the *Queen Mary*, once the world's largest ocean liner. Making her maiden voyage in 1936, the **Queen Mary** was the pride of Great Britain. Winston Churchill, the Duke and Duchess of Windsor, Greta Garbo, and Fred Astaire sailed on her, and during World War II, she was converted to military service.

Today she is the pride of Long Beach, a 1000-foot-long "city at sea" transformed into a floating museum and hotel that brilliantly re-create shipboard life. An elaborate walking tour carries you down into the engine room (a world of pumps and propellers), out along the decks, and up to each level of this multistage behemoth. There's a parking fee and admission to the boat (the admission fee is waived for hotel guests).

The *Queen Mary* is expertly refurbished and wonderfully laid out, an important addition to the Long Beach seafront and the anchor attraction for Queen Mary Seaport, which also includes The Queen's Marketplace shopping and dining area and The Queen's Playland children's area. Her neighbor is the world's largest clear-span geodesic dome. The dome, now empty, once housed Howard Hughes' *Spruce Goose*, the largest plane ever built. ~ 1126 Queen's Highway; 310-435-3511.

Beyond all the shoreline hubbub, the venerable Pacific gray whales migrate along the "Whale Freeway" between late December and mid-April, and enterprises in Long Beach offer whale-watching opportunities. The **Long Beach Area Convention & Visitors Bureau** can put you in touch with a whale-watching operator. ~ 310-436-3645.

LODGING

Beach Terrace Manor Motel is a 43-unit complex which occupies both sides of a side street off Long Beach's main drag. Mock-Tudor in design, the facility has some units fronting the beach; most are equipped with kitchen facilities. Guest rooms are comfortable if undistinguished. At a reasonable price for a room with a kitchen, the Beach Terrace provides a fair bargain. ~ 1700 East Ocean Boulevard; 310-436-8204, fax 310-436-2474. MODERATE.

The **Surf Motel**, with a similar layout, has 39 units, some with ocean views, many offering kitchens and all with easy access to the beach. Each room is furnished in contemporary fashion. There's a pool and jacuzzi. ~ 2010 East Ocean Boulevard; 310-437-0771. MODERATE.

Granted I'm a fool for gimmicks, but somehow the opportunity to stay aboard a historic ocean liner seems overwhelming. Where else but at the **Hotel Queen Mary** can you recapture the magic of British gentility before World War II? What other hotel offers guests a "sunning deck?" Staying in the original staterooms of this grand old ship, permanently docked on the Long Beach waterfront, you are surrounded by the art deco designs for which the *Queen Mary* is famous. Some guest rooms are small (this *is* a ship!) and dimly illuminated through portholes, but the decor is classic. There are also restaurants, lounges, and shops on board. ~ 1126 Queen's Highway; 310-432-6964. MODERATE TO ULTRA- DELUXE.

DINING

One of the first small brewery-restaurants in the Long Beach area, the **Belmont Brewing Company** brews pale and amber ales, seasonal beers, and a dark, rich porter—Long Beach Crude—which closely resembles the real stuff pumped from nearby coastal oil derricks. Gourmet pizzas, fresh seafood, and pastas are served in the dining area, at the bar, and outside on the patio. I'd opt for the patio where you can enjoy watching the sun set over the water. ~ 25 39th Place; 310-433-3891. MODERATE.

If you don't like hamburgers, you are fated never to set foot in **Hamburger Henry**. It's a cosmic center for burger lovers everywhere, a diner decorated in neon and painted with murals of '50s-era convertibles. The counter has a formica top and swivel stools and booths line the walls. Get the picture? We're talking vintage cuisine in a local hotspot that's open until 10 p.m. on weekdays and until midnight on weekends. There are hamburgers served with pineapple or peanut butter, blue cheese or deep-fried bananas, asparagus or ice cream, eggs or apples. Will you consider the hamburgers with ice cream? They also serve breakfast dishes, salads, chili, special dinner platters, and beer and wine. Definitely a scene; patio dining. ~ 4700 East 2nd Street; 310-433-7070. BUDGET TO MODERATE.

HIDDEN ▶   Southern cooking at the **Shenandoah Café** is becoming a tradition among savvy shore residents. The quilts and baskets decorating this understated establishment lend a country air to the place. Add waitresses in aprons dishing out hot apple fritters and it gets downright homey. Lunch and dinner are special events occasioned with "riverwalk steak" (sirloin steak in mustard caper sauce), shrimp in beer batter, country-style sausage, gumbo, "granny's fried chicken," and Texas-style beef brisket. Try it! ~ 4722 East 2nd Street; 310-434-3469. MODERATE TO DELUXE.

In downtown Long Beach the **King's Pine Avenue Fish House** is a prime spot for seafood. The private booths and dark wood trim lend an antique atmosphere to this open-kitchen establishment. The seafood platters are too numerous to recite (besides, the menu changes daily); suffice it to say that you can have them baked, broiled, sautéed, or grilled. ~ 100 West Broadway; 310-432-7463. MODERATE TO DELUXE.

Birds of Paradise Café, drawing a largely gay clientele, specializes in California cuisine. This eatery serves up an assortment of chicken, steak, and seafood dishes. Original artwork adorns the walls. No lunch Thursday, Friday, and Saturday. ~ 1800 East Broadway; 310-590-8773. MODERATE.

For Italian fare, there's **L'Opera**, a plate-glass dining room with views of the Blue Line train. The chef is from Rome and the menu represents a mixture of classical and modern dishes. There's a seafood, chicken, rice, and pasta dish of the day, everyday. ~ 101 Pine Avenue; 310-491-0066. MODERATE TO DELUXE.

Back in the world of good eats and frugal budgets, **Acapulco Mexican Restaurant & Cantina** offers standard as well as innovative dishes. Tacos, burritos, and enchiladas are only the beginning; this comfortable eatery also serves several Mexican-style seafood dishes. ~ 6270 East Pacific Coast Highway; 310-596-3371. BUDGET.

The **Reef** is rambling, ramshackle, and wonderful. Built of rough-sawn cedar, it sits along the waterfront on a dizzying series of levels. The walls may be decorated with rusty signs and old farm implements, but the cuisine includes such contemporary choices as seafood collage and beer batter shrimp. For the traditionalists, there are steaks and swordfish. ~ 880 Harbor Scenic Drive; 310-435-8013. DELUXE.

The *Queen Mary* carried so many troops across the Atlantic Ocean that Adolf Hitler offered $250,000 and the Iron Cross to the U-boat captain who sank her.

What more elegant a setting in which to dine than aboard the *Queen Mary*. There you will find everything from snack kiosks to coffee shops to first-class dining rooms. The **Promenade Café** offers a well-priced menu of chicken, steak, seafood, and vegetarian dishes. They also have salads, sandwiches, and hamburgers. The coffee shop is a lovely art deco room featuring period lamps and wicker furnishings. ~ 1126 Queen's Highway; 310-435-3511. MODERATE.

For a true taste of regal life aboard the old ship, cast anchor at **Sir Winston's**. The Continental cuisine in this dining emporium includes lamb chops macadamia, breast of capon, beef-stuffed phyllo, roast duckling with loganberry sauce, sautéed scallops, and broiled swordfish with caviar. Sir Winston's is a wood-paneled dining room with copper-rimmed mirrors, white tablecloths, and upholstered armchairs. The walls are adorned with photos of the great prime minister and every window opens onto a full view of Long Beach. Dinner only. ~ 310-435-3511. ULTRA-DELUXE.

SHOPPING

The best street shopping in Long Beach is near the Naples neighborhood along East 2nd Street. This 15-block strip between Livingston Drive and Bayshore Avenue is a gentrified row. Either side is lined with art galleries, book shops, boutiques, jewelers, and import stores.

Shoreline Village is one of those waterfront malls Southern California specializes in. With a marina on one side, the buildings are New England–style shingle and clapboard structures designed to recreate an Atlantic Coast port town. My favorite spot here is not a shop at all but the carousel, a vintage turn-of-the-century beauty awhirl with colorful animals. ~ 407 Shoreline Village Drive; 310-435-2668.

There are more than a dozen stores onboard the **Queen Mary**. There is a fee charged to board the ship. Concentrated in the Piccadilly Circus section of the old ship are several souvenir shops as well as stores specializing in articles and artifacts from Great Britain. Perhaps the prettiest shopping arcade you'll ever enter, it is an art deco masterpiece with etched glass, dentil molding, and brass appointments. ~ 1126 Queen's Highway; 310-435-3511.

Adjacent to the *Queen Mary*, **The Queen's Marketplace** is a shopping plaza styled after a 19th-century British village and offering a variety of specialty and souvenir shops.

NIGHTLIFE   **Panama Joe's** cooks seven nights a week. The bands are jazz ensembles, rock groups, and assorted others, which create an eclectic blend of music. Your average Tiffany-lamp-and-hanging-plant nightspot, the place is lined with sports photos and proudly displays an old oak bar. ~ 5100 East 2nd Street; 310-434-7417.

    E. J. Malloy's is a small sports bar with a comfortable pub-style interior including a long wood bar, brick walls, and plenty of televisions for watching a Kings hockey game with the locals. There's also an outdoor courtyard with a fireplace, bar, and patio seating. The sports fans can get loud and rambunctious on game nights. ~ 3411 East Broadway; 310-433-3769.

    Located right along the promenade in downtown Long Beach is **The Blue Café**. This tavern serves up live blues and swing music seven nights a week and tasty dishes from the deli. Hip hustlers hang out upstairs where there's plenty of billiard tables. ~ 210 Promenade North; 310-983-7111.

    Over at **The Reef**, a sprawling waterfront establishment, there's a piano bar adjoining the dining room with live entertainment every weekend. ~ 880 Harbor Scenic Drive; 310-435-8013.

    No matter how grand, regardless of how much money went into its design, despite the care taken to assure quality, any Long Beach nightspot is hard pressed to match the elegance of the **Observation Bar** aboard the *Queen Mary*. Once the first-class bar for this grand old ship, the room commands a 180° view across the bow and out to the Long Beach skyline. The walls are lined with fine woods, a mural decorates the bar, and art deco appointments appear everywhere. Besides that, they feature live jazz and '30s and '40s on weekends. For softer sounds you can always adjourn aft to **Sir Winston's Piano Bar**, a cozy and elegant setting decorated with memorabilia of the World War II British leader. ~ 1126 Queen's Highway; 310-435-3511.

THE GAY SCENE   Long Beach's gay community frequents the piano bar at the **Birds of Paradise Café**. ~ 1800 East Broadway; 310-590-8773. Another popular gay gathering place is **Ripples**, which has a dance club upstairs and a piano bar downstairs. There's also a game room, pool table, and patio. Live entertainment and cover on Sunday. ~ 5101 East Ocean Boulevard; 310-433-0357. **Mineshaft** is a third gay club with pool tables, pinball machines, and deejay music. ~ 1720 East Broadway; 310-436-2433.

    The Falcon is a gay bar complete with pool table, CD player, pinball machines, and dart board. ~ 1435 East Broadway; 310-432-4146.

BEACHES & PARKS   **ALAMITOS PENINSULA** 🏊 🎣 ⬩ The ocean side of this slender salient offers a pretty sand beach looking out on a tiny island. Paralleling the beach is an endless string of woodframe houses. The sand corridor extends all the way to the entrance of Alamitos Bay where a stone jetty provides recreation for anglers, surfers, swimmers and strollers. Facilities include restrooms, lifeguards, and volleyball courts; restaurants and groceries are nearby. ~ Located along Ocean Boulevard between 54th Place and 72nd Place; park at the end of the road.

ALAMITOS BAY BEACH 🏊 🚣 This hook-shaped strand curves along the eastern and southern shores of a narrow inlet. Houses line the beach along most of its length. Protected from the ocean by a peninsula and breakwater, the beach faces the waterfront community of Naples. Protected from surf and tide, this is a safe, outstanding spot for swimming, and conditions are perfect for windsurfing. Fishing is also good here. Restrooms are available at the beach; restaurants and groceries are nearby. ~ Located along Bayshore Avenue and Ocean Boulevard; 310-432-4496.

LONG BEACH CITY BEACH 🚴 🏊 🎣 🚣 🚤 They don't call it Long Beach for nothing. This strand is broad and boundless, a silvery swath traveling much the length of the town. There are several islets parked offshore. Along the miles of beachfront you'll find numerous facilities and good size crowds. Belmont Pier, a 1300-foot-long, hammerhead-shaped walkway, bisects the beach and offers boat tours and fishing services. Fishing is good from the pier, and the beach is protected by the harbor breakwater, making for safe swimming. Along the beach you'll find restrooms, lifeguards, a snack bar, a playground, and volleyball courts. ~ Located along Ocean Boulevard between 1st and 72nd places. Belmont Pier is at Ocean Boulevard and 39th Place; 310-432-4496.

▼▼▼▼▼▼▼▼
San Pedro

Overlooking the busy Port of Los Angeles and scored by shipping channels, San Pedro lies at the eastern end of the rocky Palos Verdes Peninsula. In 1542 Portuguese explorer Juan Cabrillo sailed into the bay and named it "Bay of Smokes," inspired by the hillside fires of the Gabrieleño Indians; San Pedro was given its current name by Spanish navigator Sebastian Vizcaino in 1602. The city began to develop its reputation as a major port in the mid-19th century, when the railroad came to town. Almost 100 years later, during World War II, Fort MacArthur was built on the bluff to protect the bustling harbor from invasion. Now, the fort houses a small museum and a youth hostel. All manner of boats, from tankers to fishing vessels, cruise the bay in peace.

SIGHTS

The Los Angeles Harbor, a region of creosote and rust, is marked by 28 miles of busy waterfront. This landscape of oil tanks and cargo containers services thousands of ships every year and houses one of the country's largest commercial fishing fleets.

◄ *HIDDEN*

Head over to the **22nd Street Landing** and watch sportfishing boats embark on high sea adventures. Then wander the waterfront and survey this frontier of steel and oil. Here awkward, unattractive ships glide as gracefully as figure skaters and the machinery of civilization goes about the world's work with a clatter and boom. The most common shorebirds are cargo cranes. ~ At the foot of 22nd Street.

Ports O' Call Village, a shopping mall in the form of a 19th-century port town, houses several outfits conducting harbor cruises. ~ The entrance is at foot of 6th Street; 310-831-0287. The boats sail around the San Pedro waterfront and venture out for glimpses of the surrounding shoreline; for information, call Spirit Cruises. ~ Ports O' Call Village; 310-548-8080.

Extending along 6th Street between Mesa Street and Harbor Boulevard is the Sportswalk, featuring plaques dedicated to Olympic medalists as well as great collegiate and professional athletes.

Moored serenely between two bustling docks is the S.S. Lane Victory. This World War II cargo ship, a 455-foot-long National Historic Landmark, has undergone a 2.5-million-dollar restoration and offers weekend cruises in the summer as well as daily tours. Admission. ~ Berth 94; 310-519-9545.

For more of our history on the sea, stop by the Los Angeles Maritime Museum. This dockside showplace displays models of ships ranging from fully rigged brigs to 19th-century steam sloops to World War II battleships. There's even an 18-foot re-creation of the ill-starred *Titanic* and the ocean liner model used to film *The Poseidon Adventure*. Closed Monday. ~ Berth 84; 310-548-7618.

HIDDEN ►

Another piece in the port's historic puzzle is placed several miles inland at the Phineas Banning Residence Museum. This imposing Greek Revival house, built in 1864, was home to the man who dreamed, dredged, and developed Los Angeles Harbor. Today Phineas Banning's Mansion, complete with a cupola from which he watched ships navigate his port, is furnished in period pieces and open for guided tours. Closed Monday and Friday. ~ 401 East M Street, Wilmington; 310-548-7777.

By definition any shipping center is of strategic importance. Head up to Fort MacArthur and discover the batteries with which World War II generals planned to protect Los Angeles Harbor. From this cement-and-steel compound you can inspect the bunkers and a small military museum, then survey the coast. Once a site of gun turrets and grisly prospects, today it is a testimonial to the invasion that never came. ~ Angel's Gate Park, 3601 South Gaffey Street; 310-548-2631.

Another war, the Korean, will be commemorated in a monument being built nearby, but until it's completed you can visit the Bell of Friendship, which the people of South Korea presented to the United States during its 1976 bicentennial. Housed in a multicolor pagoda and cast with floral and symbolic images, it rests on a hilltop looking out on Los Angeles Harbor and the region's sharply profiled coastline.

Down the hill at the Cabrillo Marine Aquarium, there is a modest collection of display cases with samples of shells, coral, and shorebirds. Several dozen aquariums demonstrate local fish and marine plants. Closed Monday. ~ 3720 Stephen M. White Drive; 310-548-7562. Nearby stretches 1200-foot **Cabrillo Fishing Pier**.

Of greater interest is **Point Fermin Park**, a 37-acre blufftop facility resting above spectacular tidepools and a marine preserve. The tidepools are accessible from the Cabrillo Marine Aquarium, which sponsors exploratory tours, and via steep trails from the park. Also of note (though not open to the public) is the **Point Fermin Lighthouse**, a unique 19th-century clapboard house with a beacon set in a rooftop crow's nest. From the park plateau, like lighthouse keepers of old, you'll have open vistas of the cliff-fringed coastline and a perfect perch for sighting whales during their winter migration. ~ 807 Paseo del Mar; 310-548-7756.

Then drive along Paseo del Mar, through arcades of stately palm trees and along sharp sea cliffs, until it meets 25th Street. The sedimentary rocks throughout this region have been twisted and contorted into grotesque shapes by tremendous geologic pressures.

Hostelling International—Los Angeles South Bay is located in the army barracks of old Fort MacArthur. Set in Angel's Gate Park on a hilltop overlooking the ocean, it's a pretty site with easy access to beaches. Men and women are housed separately in dorms but couples can be accommodated; kitchen facilities are provided; guests cannot occupy rooms during the day. ~ 3601 South Gaffey Street, Building 613; 310-831-2836. BUDGET.

LODGING

The vintage shopping mall at **Ports O' Call Village** is Los Angeles Harbor's prime tourist center. It's situated right on the San Pedro waterfront and houses numerous restaurants. Try to avoid the high-ticket dining rooms, as they are overpriced and serve mediocre food to out-of-town hordes. But there are a number of take-out stands and ethnic eateries, priced in the budget and moderate ranges, which provide an opportunity to dine inexpensively on the water. ~ The entrance is at the foot of 6th Street; 310-831-0287.

DINING

Of course local fishermen rarely frequent Ports O' Call. The old salts are over at **Canetti's Seafood Grotto**. It ain't on the waterfront, but it is within casting distance of the fishing fleet. Which means it's the right spot for fresh fish platters at good prices. Dinner Friday and Saturday; breakfast and lunch all week. ~ 309 East 22nd Street; 310-831-4036. MODERATE.

◄ HIDDEN

Trade the Pacific for the Aegean and set anchor at **Papadakis Taverna**. The menu features moussaka, Greek-style cheese dishes, and daily specials like stuffed eggplant, fresh seafood, and regional delicacies. Dinner only. ~ 301 West 6th Street; 310-548-1186. DELUXE.

Los Angeles Harbor's answer to the theme shopping mall craze is **Ports O' Call Village**, a mock 19th-century fishing village. There are

SHOPPING

clapboard stores with shuttered windows, New England–style structures with gabled roofs, and storehouses of corrugated metal. Dozens of shops here are located right on the water, giving you a chance to view the harbor while browsing the stores. It's one of those hokey but inevitable places that I swear to avoid but always seem to end up visiting. ~ The entrance is located at the foot of 6th Street; 310-831-0287.

NIGHTLIFE   Landlubbers can enjoy a quiet drink on the waterfront at **Ports O' Call Restaurant**. In addition to a spiffy oak bar, they have a dockside patio. ~ Ports O' Call Village; 310-833-3553. Better yet, **Hornblower Dining Yachts** runs dinner cruises with live music and dancing aboard a turn-of-the-century steamboat. ~ Catalina Landing, Long Beach; 310-519-9400.

BEACHES & PARKS   **CABRILLO BEACH**   The edge of Los Angeles harbor is an unappealing locale for a beach, but here it is, a two-part strand, covered with heavy-grain sand and bisected by a fishing pier. One half faces the shipping facility; the other half looks out on the glorious Pacific and abuts on the Point Fermin Marine Life Refuge, a rocky corridor filled with outstanding tidepools and backdropped by dramatic cliffs. You'll also find restrooms, picnic areas, lifeguards, a snack bar on the pier, a museum, a playground, and volleyball courts. Fires are permitted, and restaurants and groceries are available in nearby San Pedro. Fishing can be done from the pier, and for surfing try in front of the beach and near the jetty; windsurfing is great in this area, as well. People do swim here, but I saw a lot of refuse from the nearby shipping harbor. If you like tidepooling, beeline to Cabrillo, if not—there are hundreds of other beaches in the Golden State. ~ Located at 3720 Stephen M. White Drive; 310-832-1179.

ROYAL PALMS STATE BEACH   Situated at the base of a sedimentary cliff, this boulder-strewn beach gains its name from a grove of elegant palm trees. Before it was swallowed by a 1920s storm, the Royal Palms Hotel was located here. Today the guests of honor are surfers and tidepoolers. While the location is quite extraordinary, I prefer another beach, Point Fermin Park's **Wilder Annex**, located to the south. This little gem also lacks sand, but is built on three tiers of a cliff. The upper level is decorated with palm trees, the middle tier has a grassy plot studded with shady magnolias, and the bottom floor is a rocky beach with promising tidepools and camera-eye views of Point Fermin. Fishing is very good at both parks, but for swimming stick with Royal Palms, since there are lifeguards. Surfing is popular at Royal Palms and off White Point, a peninsula separating the two parks. Facilities are limited to restrooms; restaurants and groceries are nearby in San Pedro. Day-use fee, $6. ~ Both parks are located along Paseo del Mar in San Pedro. Royal

Palms is near the intersection with Western Avenue and Wilder Annex is around the intersection with Meyler Street; 310-832-1179.

Just a few miles west of San Pedro, along the Palos Verdes Peninsula, blue collar gives way to white collar, and the urban surrenders to the exotic. A region of exclusive neighborhoods and striking geologic contrasts, Palos Verdes possesses Los Angeles' prettiest seascapes. A series of 13 marine terraces, interrupted by sheer cliffs, descend to a rocky shoreline. For 15 miles the roadway rides high above the surf past tidepools, rocky points, a lighthouse and secluded coves.

▼▼▼▼▼▼▼▼▼▼▼▼▼▼▼
Palos Verdes Peninsula

The forces of nature seem to dominate as you proceed out along the Palos Verdes Peninsula from San Pedro. Follow 25th Street, then Palos Verdes Drive South and encounter a tumbling region where terraced hills fall away to sharp coastal bluffs.

As you turn **Portuguese Bend**, the geology of this tumultuous area becomes startlingly evident when the road begins undulating through landslide zones. The earthquake that underlie the Los Angeles basin periodically fold and collapse the ground here. To one side you'll see the old road, fractured and useless. Even the present highway, with more patches than your favorite dungarees, is in a state of constant repair.

SIGHTS

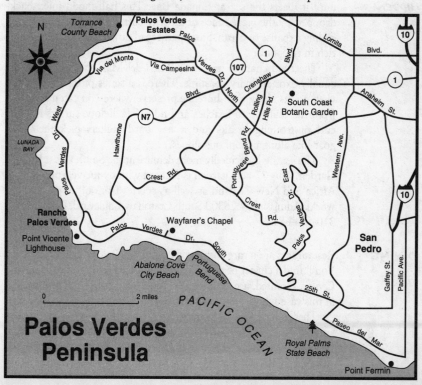

Palos Verdes Peninsula

Of course the terrible power of nature has not dissuaded people from building here. Along the ridgetops and curving hills below are colonies of stately homes. With its rocky headlands, tidepool beaches and sun-spangled views, the place is simply so magnificent no one can resist.

Most lordly of all these structures is **The Wayfarer's Chapel,** a simple but extraordinary center designed by the son of Frank Lloyd Wright. Nestled neatly into the surrounding landscape, the sunlit chapel is built entirely of glass and commands broad views of the terrain and ocean. With its stone altar and easy repose the temple was built to honor Emanuel Swedenborg, the 18th-century Swedish philosopher and mystic. ~ 5755 Palos Verdes Drive South, Rancho Palos Verdes; 310-377-1650.

The **Point Vicente Lighthouse** rises further down the coast, casting an antique aura upon the area. While the beacon is not open to the public, the nearby **Point Vicente Interpretive Center** offers a small regional museum. This is a prime whale-watching spot in the winter when onlookers gather in the adjacent park to catch glimpses of migrating gray whales. Admission. ~ 31501 Palos Verdes Drive West, Rancho Palos Verdes; 310-377-5370.

For a vision of how truly beautiful this region is, turn off Palos Verdes Drive West in Palos Verdes Estates and follow Paseo Lunado until it meets the sea at **Lunada Bay.** This half-moon inlet, backdropped by the jagged face of a rocky cliff, looks out upon an unending expanse of ocean. Steep paths lead down to a rocky shoreline rich in tidepools.

HIDDEN ►

The road changes names to Paseo del Mar but continues past equally extraordinary coastline. There is a series of open fields and vista points along this **shoreline preserve** where you can gaze down from the blufftop to beaches and tidepools. Below, surfers ride the curl of frothing breaks and a few hardy hikers pick their way goat-like along precipitous slopes.

The setting is decidedly more demure at the **South Coast Botanic Garden.** This 87-acre garden is planted with exotic vegetation from Africa and New Zealand as well as species from other parts of the world. Admission. ~ 26300 South Crenshaw Boulevard, Palos Verdes; 310-544-6815.

DINING

Restaurants are a rare commodity along the Palos Verdes Peninsula. You'll find a cluster of them, however, in the Golden Cove Shopping Center. Granted, a mall is not the most appetizing spot to dine, but in this case who's complaining?

There's **Italy One,** a homey little café with congenial staff. Here you can order pizza, sandwiches, and a variety of pasta dishes. Closed Monday. ~ 31218 Palos Verdes Drive West, Rancho Palos Verdes; 310-541-3350. BUDGET.

Then there's **The Admiral Risty**. It's one of those nautical cliché restaurants decorated along the outside with ropes and pilings and on the interior with brass fixtures. Know the type? Normally I wouldn't mention it, but the place has a full bar, a knockout view of the ocean, and happens to be the only member of its species in the entire area. My advice is to play it safe and order fresh fish (or never leave the bar). The menu is a surf-and-turf inventory of local fish (prepared four ways), steaks, chicken dishes, and so on. Dinner and Sunday brunch. ~ 31250 Palos Verdes Drive West, Rancho Palos Verdes; 310-377-0050. DELUXE.

For genuine elegance, make lunch, or dinner reservations at **La Rive Gauche**, an attractively appointed French restaurant. With its upholstered chairs, brass wall sconces, and vintage travel posters, this cozy candlelit dining room is unique to the peninsula. The three-course dinner menu is a study in classic French cooking including veal chop with *foie gras* and truffles, boneless duck in pearl onion sauce, venison in brandy cream sauce, rack of lamb in garlic, and a selection of fresh seafood like Norway salmon and Dover sole. A pianist adds to the romance. The lunch offerings, while more modest, follow a similar theme. In sum, excellent gourmet cuisine, warm ambience and a world-class wine list. No lunch on Monday. ~ 320 Tejon Place, Palos Verdes Estates; 310-378-0267. DELUXE TO ULTRA-DELUXE.

BEACHES & PARKS

ABALONE COVE CITY BEACH The Palos Verdes Peninsula is so rugged and inaccessible that any beach by definition will be secluded. This gray sand hideaway is no exception. It sits in a natural amphitheater guarded by sedimentary rock formations and looks out on Catalina Island. There are tidepools to ponder and a marine ecological reserve to explore, and the fishing and swimming are good. For surfing, try the east end of the cove. There are also picnic areas, restrooms, and part-time lifeguards; restaurants and groceries are several miles away in San Pedro. ~ Located off Palos Verdes Drive South in Rancho Palos Verdes. From the parking lot a path leads down to the beach; 310-541-4566.

TORRANCE COUNTY BEACH This beach is a lengthy stretch of bleach-blond sand guarded on one flank by the stately Palos Verdes Peninsula and on the other by an industrial complex and colony of smokestacks. Just your average middle-class beach; it's not one of my favorites, but it has the only white sand hereabouts. Also consider adjacent Malaga Cove (nicknamed "RAT" beach because it's "right after Torrance"), a continuation of the strand, noted for tidepools, shells, and rock-hounding. Prettier than its pedestrian partner, Malaga Cove is framed by rocky bluffs. At Torrance there are restrooms, some concession stands, and lifeguards; around Malaga Cove you're on your own. Fishing is good at both beaches, and surfing is very good at Malaga Cove. For swimming I recommend Torrance, where lifeguards are on duty. Restaurants and groceries are in downtown Torrance. ~ Paseo de la Playa in Torrance parallels the beach. To reach Malaga Cove, walk south from Torrance toward the cliffs; 310-372-2166.

▼▼▼▼▼▼▼▼▼▼
South Bay

The birthplace of California's beach culture lies in a string of towns on the southern skirt of Santa Monica Bay—Redondo Beach, Hermosa Beach, and Manhattan Beach. It all began here in the South Bay with George Freeth, "the man who can walk on water." It seems that while growing up in Hawaii, Freeth resurrected the ancient Polynesian sport of surfing and transplanted it to California. Equipped with a 200-pound, solid wood board, he introduced surfing to fascinated onlookers at a 1907 event in Redondo Beach.

It wasn't until the 1950s that the surfing wave crested. That's when a group of local kids called The Beach Boys spent their days catching waves at Manhattan Beach and their nights recording classic beach songs. The surrounding towns became synonymous with the sport and a new culture was born, symbolized by blond-haired, blue-eyed surfers committed to sun, sand, and the personal freedom to ride the last wave.

Sightseeing spots are rather scarce in these beach towns. As you can imagine, the interesting places are inevitably along the waterfront. Each town sports a municipal pier, with rows of knickknack shops, cafés, and oceanview lounges, either along the pier or on the nearby waterfront.

SIGHTS

In Redondo Beach, **Fisherman's Wharf** is home to surfcasters and hungry seagulls. Walk out past the shops, salt breeze in your face, and you can gaze along the waterfront to open ocean. Waves wash against the pilings. Beneath the wood plank walkway, sea birds dive for fish. These sights and sounds are repeated again and again on the countless piers that line the California coast.

In fact you'll find them recurring right up in Hermosa Beach at the **Municipal Pier**. Less grandiose than its neighbor, this 1320-foot concrete corridor is simply equipped with a snack bar and bait shop. From the end you'll have a sweeping view back along Hermosa Beach's low skyline. ~ Located at the foot of Pier Avenue, Hermosa Beach.

Similarly, the **Manhattan Beach Pier** extends 900 feet from the beach and offers the generic bait store and take-out stand. Not so generic are the ocean vistas and views of Manhattan Beach's pretty neighborhoods. ~ At the foot of Manhattan Beach Boulevard, Manhattan Beach.

The other sightseeing diversion in these parts is the stroll. The stroll, that is, along the beach. **Esplanade** in Redondo Beach is a wide boulevard paralleling the waterfront. Wander its length and take in the surfers, sunbathers, and swimmers who keep this resort town on the map. Or walk down to the waterline and let the cool Pacific bathe your feet.

In Hermosa Beach you can saunter along **The Strand**. This pedestrian thoroughfare borders a broad beach and passes an endless row of bungalows, cottages, and condominiums. It's a pleasant walk with shops and restaurants along the way.

The Strand continues along Manhattan Beach but lacks the commercial storefronts of Hermosa Beach. Wide and wonderful, the beach is lined by beautiful homes with plate-glass windows that reflect the blue hues of sea and sky. Together, these oceanfront walkways link the South Bay towns in a course that bicyclists can follow for miles.

LODGING

Route 1 barrels through Los Angeles' beach towns and serves as the commercial strip for generic motels. As elsewhere, these facilities are characterized by clean, sterile rooms and comfortable, if unimaginative surroundings. Located within walking distance of the beach, the **Starlite Motel** offers 25 standard, motel-style units. ~ 716 South Coast Pacific Highway, Redondo Beach; 310-540-2406. BUDGET.

East West Inn features 40 rooms with refrigerators, microwaves and TVs. This establishment is two blocks from the beach. ~ 435 South Coast Pacific Highway, Redondo Beach; 310-540-5998. BUDGET.

The Portofino Hotel and Yacht Club is a big, brassy hotel set on King Harbor. The 163 units are decorated in contemporary fashion and look out either on the ocean or the adjoining marina. There is a decorous lobby as well as a waterside swimming pool; restaurants and other facilities are nearby in the marina. ~ 260 Portofino Way, Redondo Beach; 310-379-8481. ULTRA-DELUXE.

The best bargain on lodging in South Bay is found at **Sea Sprite Motel & Apartments**. Located right on Hermosa Beach, this multi-building complex offers oceanview rooms with kitchenettes at moderate to deluxe prices. The accommodations are tidy, well furnished, and fairly attractive. There is a swimming pool and sundeck overlooking the beach. The central shopping district is just two blocks away, making the location hard to match. You can also rent suites at deluxe prices or a two-bedroom beach cottage at an ultra-deluxe price. Be sure to ask for an oceanview room in one of the beachfront buildings. ~ 1016 The Strand, Hermosa Beach; 310-376-6933, fax 310-376-4107. MODERATE TO ULTRA-DELUXE.

At the **Hi View Motel**, you're only a step away from the beach, shopping malls, and restaurants. There are standard rooms and studio apartments for rent. ~ 100 South Sepulveda Boulevard, Manhattan Beach; 310-374-4608. BUDGET TO MODERATE.

The **Sea View Inn at the Beach** is an 14-unit stucco hotel a block up from the beach. There's a swimming pool and two floors of guest rooms. You'll find comfortable furniture, wall-to-wall carpeting, refrigerator, and cable television in accommodations that are tidy. In addition, it is close to the surf and lodging is rare in these parts. ~ 3400 Highland Avenue, Manhattan Beach; 310-545-1504, fax 310-545-4052. MODERATE.

Far from the South Bay beach scene, though only a mile inland, is **Barnabey's Hotel**, a sprawling 128-room Edwardian-style hostelry. Re-creating turn-of-the-century England, Barnabey's provides stylish guest rooms with antique furnishings, floral-patterned carpets, and vintage wallpaper. The lobby is finished in dark woods and appointed with gilded clocks and crystal light fixtures. There's a restaurant and British pub, and guests also enjoy a pool and jacuzzi. ~ 3501 North Sepulveda Boulevard, Manhattan Beach; 310-545-8466, 800-552-5285. DELUXE.

DINING   In downtown Redondo Beach, just a couple blocks from the water, are several small restaurants serving a diversity of cuisines. **Greens at the Beach** specializes in all-organic and vegetarian delights. ~ 247 Avenida del Norte, Redondo Beach; 310-316-9451. BUDGET.

Petit Casino, a French bakery, serves quiche, *croque monsieur*, soups, salads, and sandwiches. ~ 1767 South Elena Avenue, Redondo Beach; 310-543-5585. BUDGET.

At **Kikusui** there is a sushi bar as well as a menu featuring other Japanese dishes. ~ 1809 South Catalina Avenue, Redondo Beach; 310-375-1244. MODERATE.

In addition to serving good Asian food, **Thai Thani** is an extremely attractive restaurant. Black trim and pastel shades set off the blond wood furniture and etched glass. There are fresh flowers all around plus a few well-placed wall prints. The lunch and dinner selections include dozens of pork, beef, vegetable, poultry, and seafood dishes. Unusual choices like spicy shrimp coconut soup, whole pompano smothered in pork, and whole baby hen make this a dining adventure. ~ 1109 South Pacific Coast Highway, Redondo Beach; 310-316-1580. BUDGET TO MODERATE.

✔ **CHECK THESE OUT—UNIQUE LODGING**

- *Budget:* Curl up in the barracks of Fort MacArthur, where the price is right at **Hostelling International—Los Angeles South Bay**. *page 145*
- *Moderate:* Come home to a comfortable cottage and watch the surfers at **Topanga Ranch Motel**, near the beach in Malibu. *page 174*
- *Moderate to deluxe:* Slumber in your bunk and peek out your porthole in a stateroom aboard the historic **Queen Mary**. *page 139*
- *Ultra-deluxe:* Succumb to island magic at **The Inn on Mt. Ada**, overlooking the ocean on Santa Catalina island. *page 186*

Budget: under $50   Moderate: $50–$90   Deluxe: $90–$120   Ultra-deluxe: over $120

One wall of **Millie Riera's Seafood Grotto** is entirely filled with a plate-glass view of the ocean. The rest of this family-run eatery is decorated with flowers and traditional wallhangings. Open for lunch and dinner (dinner only on weekends), the "grotto," true to its title, specializes in seafood. Expect to find bouillabaisse, cracked crab, lobster Newburg, sea bass, and a few steak entrées. ~ 1700 Esplanade, Redondo Beach; 310-375-1483. MODERATE TO DELUXE.

The capital of "in" dining around the South Bay is **Chez Melange**. As the name suggests, and as current trends demand, the cuisine is eclectic. You'll find a hip crowd ordering everything from Cajun to seafood Mexican-style. ~ 1716 Pacific Coast Highway, Redondo Beach; 310-540-1222. MODERATE TO DELUXE.

The Strand, a pedestrian byway paralleling the waterfront in Hermosa Beach, is lined with small restaurants. Among these is **Good Stuff on the Strand**, which serves a standard fare for breakfast; hamburgers, turkey burgers, pita-bread sandwiches, and salads at lunch; and, in the evening, entrées like stuffed spuds, teriyaki, chicken, and linguine with green and red bell peppers served in a white wine sauce. ~ 1286 The Strand, Hermosa Beach; 310-374-2334. BUDGET.

There is excellent thin-crust pizza at **Pedone's**. Popular with the beach crowd, it's a good spot for a quick meal in a convenient locale. ~ 1501 Hermosa Avenue, Hermosa Beach; 310-376-0949. BUDGET.

Café Pierre is another excellent choice for budget-minded gourmets. This fashionable French bistro—with art prints, pastel walls, and skylight—offers the same menu at lunch and dinner. You can feast on veal sweetbreads cognac, marinated chicken on a bed of spinach, garlic-infused broiled shrimp served with jalapeño-covered mashed potatoes, roast duckling, and homemade pasta. There are daily specials at lunch and dinner, which in the evening may include stuffed swordfish or venison. Closed for lunch on Saturday and Sunday. ~ 317 Manhattan Beach Boulevard, Manhattan Beach; 310-545-5252. MODERATE.

No restaurants line the strand in Manhattan Beach, so you'll have to make do with the pier's snack shop or trot a half-block uphill to **Hibachi**. Here is a take-out stand with a full bar and a patio crowded with picnic tables. Beachgoers chow down on hamburgers and hot dogs while table diners feast on stir-fry, seafood platters, teriyaki dishes, and other Japanese entrées. ~ 120 Manhattan Beach Boulevard, Manhattan Beach; 310-374-9493. BUDGET.

SHOPPING

If they weren't famous Pacific beach communities, the South Bay enclaves of Redondo, Hermosa, and Manhattan beaches would seem like small-town America. Their central shopping districts are filled with pharmacies, supply shops, and shoe stores.

There are a few places of interest to folks from out of town. In Redondo Beach, scout out Catalina Avenue, particularly along its southern stretches. Shops in Hermosa Beach concentrate along Pier and Hermosa avenues, especially where they intersect. Likewise in Manhattan Beach, Manhattan Beach Boulevard is traversed by Highland and Manhattan avenues.

NIGHTLIFE

The Comedy & Magic Club features name acts nightly. Many of the comedians are television personalities with a regional, if not national, following. Jay Leno, for instance, frequently tests his new *Tonight Show* material on the club's Sunday night crowd. The supper club atmosphere is upscale and appealing. Reservations are required. Cover. ~ 1018 Hermosa Avenue, Hermosa Beach; 310-372-1193.

The Lighthouse Café spotlights blues, reggae, rock-and-roll, and '60s-style surf bands. Cover on Friday and Saturday. ~ 30 Pier Avenue, Hermosa Beach; 310-372-6911.

Orville & Wilbur's Restaurant is a lush, wood-paneled establishment with an upstairs bar that looks out over the ocean. Live music, ranging from relaxing tunes to dance-inspiring beats, is offered nightly. ~ 401 Rosecrans Boulevard, Manhattan Beach; 310-545-6639.

BEACHES & PARKS

REDONDO STATE BEACH Surfers know this strand and so should you. Together with neighboring Hermosa and Manhattan beaches, it symbolizes the Southern California beach scene. You'll find a long strip of white sand bordered by a hillside carpeted with ice plants. In addition to surfers, the area is populated by bicyclists and joggers, while anglers cast from the nearby piers. Not surprisingly, fishing is particularly good from nearby Fisherman's Wharf. The swimming at Redondo is good, and surfing is even better. Facilities include restrooms, lifeguards, and volleyball courts; restaurants can be found on the pier, and groceries are nearby. ~ Located along the Esplanade in Redondo Beach; 310-372-2166.

HERMOSA CITY BEACH One of the great beaches of Southern California, this is a very, very wide (and very, very white) sand beach extending the entire length of Hermosa Beach. Two miles of pearly sand are only part of the attraction. There's also

PYNCHON'S PICK

Be sure to stop in at the **Either/Or Bookstore**. Situated on a hillside above the ocean, it's a multilevel affair built in a series of terraces. With an outstanding inventory of books and magazines, the store is also endowed with an intriguing history. It seems that years ago Thomas Pynchon—the brilliant, reclusive, rarely photographed author of *V* and *Gravity's Rainbow*—stopped in regularly to buy books and talk contemporary literature. ~ 124 Pier Avenue, Hermosa Beach; 310-374-2060.

The Strand, a pedestrian lane that runs the length of the beach; Pier Avenue, an adjacent street lined with interesting shops; a quarter-mile fishing pier; and a local community known for its artistic creativity. Personally, if I were headed to the beach, I would head in this direction. The swimming is good and the surfing is very good around the pier and all along the beach. Lifeguards are on duty, and facilities include restrooms, volleyball courts, and a playground; restaurants and groceries can be found nearby. ~ Located at the foot of Pier Avenue in Hermosa Beach; 310-372-2166.

MANHATTAN STATE BEACH 🚲 🏊 🏃 🏄 🚣 Back in those halcyon days when their first songs were climbing the charts, the Beach Boys were regular fixtures at this silvery strand. They came to surf, swim, and check out the scene along The Strand, the walkway that extends the length of Manhattan Beach. What can you say, the gentlemen had good taste—the surfing here is some of the best in Southern California. This sand corridor is wide as a desert, fronted by an aquamarine ocean and backed by the beautiful homes of the very lucky. If that's not enough, there's a fishing pier and an adjacent commercial area door-to-door with excellent restaurants. The swimming here is good, and the surfing is tops. Other facilities include restrooms, lifeguards, and volleyball courts. ~ Located at the foot of Manhattan Beach Boulevard in Manhattan Beach; 310-372-2166.

DOCKWEILER STATE BEACH 🚲 🏊 🏃 🏄 🚣 It's long, wide, and has fluffy white sand—what more could you ask? Rather, it's what less can you request. Dockweiler suffers a minor problem. It's right next to Los Angeles International Airport, one of the world's busiest terminals. Every minute planes are taking off, thundering, reverberating, right over the beach. To add insult to infamy, there is a sewage treatment plant nearby. Nevertheless, swimming and surfing are good, fires are permitted, and fishing is good from the jetties. You'll also find picnic areas, restrooms, and a playground; restaurants and groceries are nearby in Playa del Rey. Parking fee, $5. ~ Located at the foot of Imperial Highway, along Vista del Mar Boulevard in Playa del Rey; 310-372-2166.

▲ There is an RV park with 82 sites with full hookup and 35 without. They cost $15 to $25 per night.

Venice

Venice, California, was the dream of one man, a tobacco magnate named Albert Kinney. He envisioned a "Venice of America," a Renaissance town of gondoliers and single-lane bridges, connected by 16 miles of canals.

After convincing railroad barons and city fathers, Kinney dredged swampland along Santa Monica Bay, carved a network of canals, and founded this dream city in 1905. The place was an early-20th-century answer to Disneyland with gondola rides and amusement parks. The canals were lined with vaulted arches and rococo-style hotels.

Oil spelled the doom of Kinney's dream. Once black gold was discovered beneath the sands of Venice, the region became a landscape of drilling rigs and oil derricks. Spills polluted the canals and blackened the beaches. In 1929 the city of Los Angeles filled in the canals and during the subsequent decades Venice more resembled a tar pit than a cultural center.

> Venice, to quote Bob Dylan, represents "life and life only," but a rarefied form of life, slightly, beautifully askew.

But by the 1950s latter-day visionaries—artists and bohemians—rediscovered "Kinney's Folly" and transformed it into an avant-garde community. It became a magnet for Beats in the 1950s and hippies during the next decade. Musician Jim Morrison of The Doors lived here and Venice developed a reputation as a center for the cultural renaissance that Albert Kinney once envisioned.

Today Venice retains much of the old flavor. Palatial hotels have given way to beach cottages and funky wood houses, but the narrow streets and countless alleyways remain. More significant, the town is filled with galleries and covered by murals, making it one of the region's most important art centers.

SIGHTS   The revolution might have sputtered elsewhere, but in Venice artists have seized control. City Hall has become the **Beyond Baroque Literary Arts Center**, housing a library and bookstore devoted to small presses. Admission. ~ 681 Venice Boulevard; 310-822-3006.

Next door, the **Venice City Jail** is home to SPARC, or the Social and Public Art Resource Center. The prison is an imposing 1923 art deco-style building with a cell block converted into an art gallery. Many of the cells are intact and you'll walk through an iron door to view contemporary artwork by alternative, cutting-edge artists. The center also sponsors lectures, mural tours, and mural projects around Los Angeles. ~ 685 Venice Boulevard; 310-822-9560.

Both the Venice City Hall and Jail are great places to learn about what's going on in the community. Also consider the **Venice Chamber of Commerce**. If you can find someone there (which is not always easy), you can obtain maps, brochures, and answers. ~ 2904 Washington Boulevard, Suite 100; 310-827-2366.

The commercial center of Venice rests at the intersection of Windward Avenue and Main Street. Windward was the central boulevard of Kinney's dream city and the Traffic Circle, marked today by a small sculpture, was to be an equally grand lagoon. Continue along Windward Avenue to the arcades, a series of Italian-style colonnades which represent one of the few surviving elements of old Venice.

The heart of modern-day Venice pulses along the **boardwalk**, a two-mile strip that follows Ocean Front Walk from Washington Street to Rose Avenue. **Venice Pier**, an 1100-foot fishing pier, anchors one

end. Between Washington Street and Windward Avenue, the promenade is bordered by a palisade of beachfront homes, two- and three-
story houses with plate-glass facades. The pier is temporarily closed
to the public. ~ Ocean Front Walk and Washington Street.

Walking north, the real action begins around 18th Avenue, at
Muscle Beach, where rope-armed heavies work out in the weight pen,
smacking punching bags and flexing their pecs, while gawking onlookers dream of oiling their bodies and walking with a muscle-
bound strut.

The rest of the boardwalk is a grand open-air carnival which you
should try to visit on the weekend. It is a world of artists and anar-
chists, derelicts and dreamers, a vision of what life would be if
heaven were an insane asylum. Guitarists, jugglers, conga drummers,
and clowns perform for the crowds. Kids on roller skates and bicycles whiz past rickshaws and unicycles. Street hawkers and panhand-
lers work the unwary while singers with scratchy voices pass the hat.
Vendors dispense everything from corn dogs to cotton candy, T-
shirts to wind-up toys. Up the coast, **Marina del Rey** represents the
largest manmade small-boat harbor in the world. Over 6000 pleasure boats and yachts dock here. Harbor cruises are provided aboard
a mock Mississippi riverboat by the **Hornblower Dining Yachts.** ~
13755 Fiji Way; 310-301-9900.

The entire region was once a marsh inhabited by a variety of waterfowl. Personally I think they should have left it to the birds. Marina del Rey is an ersatz community, a completely fabricated place
where the main shopping area, **Fisherman's Village,** resembles a New
England whaling town, and everything else attempts to portray something it's not. ~ 13755 Fiji Way; 310-823-5411. With its endless condominiums, pretentious homes, and overpriced restaurants, Marina
del Rey is an artificial limb appended to the coast of Los Angeles.

There's nothing quite like **The Venice Beach House.** That may well
be because there are so few bed and breakfast inns in the Los Angeles
area. But it's also that this is such a charming house, an elegant and
spacious California craftsman-style home built in 1911 by Albert
Kinney. The living room, with its beam ceiling, dark wood paneling,
and brick fireplace, is a masterwork. Guests also enjoy a sunny al-
cove, patio, and garden. The stroll to the Venice boardwalk and
beach is only one-half block. The nine guest rooms are beautifully
appointed and furnished with antiques; each features patterned wallpaper and period artwork. I can't recommend the place highly enough.
~ 15 30th Avenue; 310-823-1966. MODERATE TO DELUXE.

LODGING

◄ *HIDDEN*

Also consider the **Marina Pacific Hotel.** Located in the commercial center of Venice only 100 yards from the sand, this three-story,
92-unit hostelry has a small lobby and café downstairs. The guest
rooms are spacious, nicely furnished, and well maintained; very large
one-bedroom suites, complete with kitchen and fireplace, are also

available. Most rooms have small patios. ~ 1697 Pacific Avenue; 310-452-1111, fax 310-452-5479. DELUXE TO ULTRA-DELUXE.

For the international hostel-hopper, Venice Beach is a veritable heaven by the ocean. Among the many places offering discount lodging are three hotels run by InterClub, an international hostelry organization. The **Venice Beach Cotel** offers both private and shared rooms. ~ 25 Winward Avenue; 310-305-7649. BUDGET.

Hostel California features ten units with private and shared baths. Other amenities include kitchen and laundry facilities. Free airport pickup is also provided. ~ 2221 Lincoln Boulevard; 310-305-0250. BUDGET.

Located right on the beach, the **Cadillac Hotel** is quite a catch. This establishment features a gym, sauna, sundeck, and laundry facilities. ~ 401 Ocean Front Walk; 310-399-8876. BUDGET TO MODERATE.

DINING

The best place for finger food and junk food in all Southern California might well be the **boardwalk** in Venice. Along Ocean Front Walk are vendor stands galore serving pizza, yogurt, hamburgers, falafel, submarine sandwiches, corn dogs, etc.

Regardless, there's really only one spot in Venice to consider for dining. It simply *is* Venice, an oceanfront café right on the boardwalk, **The Sidewalk Café**. Skaters whiz past, drummers beat rhythms in the distance, and the sun stands like a big orange wafer above the ocean. Food is really a second thought here, but eventually they're going to want you to spend some money. So, on to the menu . . . Breakfast, lunch, and dinner are what you'd expect—omelettes, sandwiches, hamburgers, pizza, and pasta. There are also fresh fish dishes plus platters of wok-fried vegetables, steak, spicy chicken, and fried shrimp. ~ 1401 Ocean Front Walk; 310-399-5547. BUDGET TO MODERATE.

HIDDEN ►

Take a walk down the boardwalk to **Venice Bistro**. This beachfront establishment is a casual dining room with a tile floor and brick walls. Cozy and comfortable, it features a menu that includes hamburgers, salads, pasta, and some Mexican dishes. There's a full bar. ~ 323 Ocean Front Walk; 310-392-7472. BUDGET.

Or check out **Jody Maroni's Sausage Kingdom**, a beach stand with over a dozen types of sausage, all natural. There's sweet Italian, Yucatán chicken, Louisiana hotlinks, and, of course, Polish. No dinner. ~ 2011 Ocean Front Walk; 310-306-1995. BUDGET.

HIDDEN ►

The landing ground for Venetians is a warehouse dining place called **The Rose Café**. There's a full-scale deli, bakery counter, and a restaurant offering indoor and patio service. The last serves three meals daily, including reasonably priced dinners from an everchanging menu that may include entrées like linguine with smoked salmon, sautéed chicken, crab cakes, and a couple of vegetarian dishes. A good spot for pasta and salad, The Rose Café, with its wall murals

The Murals of Venice & Santa Monica

Nowhere is the spirit of Venice and Santa Monica more evident than in the murals adorning their walls. Both seaside cities house major art colonies and the numerous galleries and studios make them important centers for contemporary art.

Over the years, as more and more artists made their homes here, they began decorating the twin towns with their art. The product of this creative energy lives along street corners and alleyways, on storefronts and roadways. Crowded with contemporary and historic images, these murals express the inner life of the city.

Murals adorn nooks and crannies all over Venice. You'll find a cluster of them around Windward Avenue between Main Street and Ocean Front Walk. The interior of the **Post Office** is adorned with public art. There's a *trompe l'oeil* mural nearby on the old St. Marks Hotel that beautifully reflects the street along which you are gazing. Don't miss the woman in the upper floor window. ~ Main Street and Windward Avenue.

On the other side of the building stands a large mural facing the ocean. **Venice Reconstituted** depicts the unique culture of Venice Beach. ~ Windward Avenue and Speedway.

At last count Santa Monica boasted about two dozen outdoor murals. Route 1, or Lincoln Boulevard, is a corridor decorated with local artworks. **John Muir Woods** portrays a redwood forest. ~ Lincoln and Ocean Park boulevards. **Early Ocean Park and Venice Scenes** captures the seaside at the turn of the century. ~ Located two blocks west of Lincoln Boulevard along Kensington Road in Joslyn Park. Nearby Marine Park features **Birthday Party**, with a Noah's ark full of celebratory animals. ~ Marine and Frederick streets.

Ocean Park Boulevard is another locus of creativity. At its intersection with the 4th Street underpass you'll encounter **Whale Mural**, illustrating whales and underwater life common to California waters, and **Unbridled**, which pictures a herd of horses fleeing from the Santa Monica Pier carousel. One of the area's most famous murals awaits you at Ocean Park Boulevard and Main street, where **Early Ocean Park** vividly re-creates scenes from the past.

If you'd like more information or a tour of these and other murals around the city, contact the **Social and Public Art Resource Center**. ~ 685 Venice Boulevard; 310-822-9560. The **Santa Monica Cultural Affairs Division** can also help. ~ 310-458-8350. Los Angeles has earned a reputation as the mural capital of the United States, making this tour a highpoint for admirers of public art.

and paintings, is also a place to appreciate the vital culture of Venice. ~ 220 Rose Avenue; 310-399-0711. MODERATE.

In the mood for Asian cuisine? **Hama Restaurant** is a well-respected Japanese restaurant in the center of Venice. The place features an angular sushi bar, a long, narrow dining room, and a patio out back. The crowd is young and the place is decorated to reflect Venice's vibrant culture. There are paintings on display representing many of the area's artists. In addition to scrumptious sushi, Hama offers a complete selection of Japanese dishes including tempura, teriyaki, and sashimi. ~ 213 Windward Avenue; 310-396-8783. MODERATE.

For dining with flair, **West Beach Café** is quite the place. Decorated in the style of the well-known California artist Billy Al Bengston, the interior is a medley of vibrant colors portraying the beauty of the ocean. Eames chairs, track lighting, and skylights add flourish. The restaurant offers a seasonal menu that always includes a variety of fresh seafood like salmon, swordfish, or sea bass, New York steaks, and chicken and turkey dishes, all prepared with a host of delicious sauces. The lunch menu is equally creative and in the evening after 11:30 they serve gourmet pizza. *Très chic*, *très* California. Dinner is served daily; lunch weekdays only; weekend brunch. ~ 60 North Venice Boulevard; 310-823-5396. MODERATE TO DELUXE.

72 Market Street could be the last word in modern art restaurants. The place is a warren of brick, mirrors, opaque glass, and studio lights. It's adorned with striking art pieces and equipped with a sound system that seems to be vibrating from the inner ear. Moderne to the max, the restaurant serves spicy meatloaf and other regional dishes. It also hosts an oyster bar. ~ 72 Market Street; 310-392-8720. DELUXE TO ULTRA-DELUXE.

SHOPPING   To combine slumming with shopping, be sure to wander the **boardwalk** in Venice. Ocean Front Walk between Windward and Ozone avenues is lined with low-rent stalls selling beach hats, cheap jewelry, sunglasses, beach bags, and souvenirs. You'll also encounter **Small World Books and the Mystery Annex**, a marvelous beachside shop with books, magazines, and mysteries (novels, that is) galore. ~ 1407 Ocean Front Walk; 310-399-2360.

L.A. Louver is one of Venice's many vital and original galleries. It represents David Hockney and other contemporary American and European artists. ~ 45 North Venice Boulevard; 310-822-4955. There is also a covey of art galleries and antique shops along the 1200 to 1500 blocks of West Washington Boulevard.

The **Native American Art Gallery** offers a fascinating collection of pottery, rugs, woven baskets, turquoise jewelry, and kachina dolls. ~ 215 Windward Avenue; 310-392-8465.

The **Beyond Baroque Literary Arts Center**, a clearinghouse for local talent, sponsors poetry readings, dramatic revues, lectures, and concerts. It's located in the old Venice City Hall. ~ 681 Venice Boulevard; 310-822-3006. Next door, in the town's erstwhile jail, the **Social and Public Art Resource Center**, or SPARC, has a store offering Latin American and Southwestern folk art. ~ 685 Venice Boulevard; 310-822-9560.

The Townhouse, set in a '20s-era speakeasy, has live music as well as deejays spinning Top-40 platters. Cover. ~ 52 Windward Avenue; 310-392-4040. **NIGHTLIFE**

Across the street, **Saint Mark's** bills live rhythm-and-blues, world beat, jazz, and flamenco music Tuesday through Sunday. Closed Monday. Cover. ~ 23 Windward Avenue; 310-452-2222.

The Venice Bistro features live rock-and-roll Thursday through Sunday. Cover on Saturday and Sunday. ~ 323 Ocean Front Walk; 310-392-7472.

The Sidewalk Café is also a popular night spot and gathering place, more for its central location than anything else. ~ 1401 Ocean Front Walk; 310-399-5547.

VENICE BEACH If you visit only a single Southern California beach, this should be the one. It's a broad white sand corridor that runs the entire length of Venice and features Venice Pier (which is temporarily closed). But the real attraction—and the reason you'll find the beach described in the "Restaurants," "Sightseeing," and "Shopping" sections—is the boardwalk. A center of culture, street artistry, and excitement, the boardwalk parallels Venice Beach for two miles. As far as beach facilities, you'll find picnic areas, restrooms, showers, lifeguards, playgrounds, basketball courts, and paddle ball courts. If you can tear yourself away from the action on the boardwalk, the swimming and surfing are good here, too. ~ Ocean Front Walk in Venice parallels the beach; 310-399-2775. **BEACHES & PARKS**

Pass from Venice into Santa Monica and you'll trade the boardwalk for a promenade. It's possible to walk for miles along Santa Monica's fluffy beach, past pastel-colored condominiums and funky woodframe houses. Roller skaters and bicyclists galore crowd the byways and chess players congregate at the picnic tables. **Santa Monica**

A middle-class answer to mod Malibu, Santa Monica started as a seaside resort in the 1870s when visitors bumped over long, dusty roads by stagecoach from Los Angeles. After flirting with the film industry in the age of silent movies, Santa Monica reverted in the 1930s to a quiet beach town that nevertheless was notorious for the gambling ships moored offshore. It was during this period that detective writer Raymond Chandler immortalized the place as "Bay City" in his brilliant Philip Marlowe novels.

Today Santa Monica is *in*. Its clean air, pretty beaches, and attractive homes have made it one of the most popular places to live in Los Angeles. As real estate prices have skyrocketed, liberal politics have ascended. Santa Monica, it seems, has become Southern California's answer to Berkeley.

SIGHTS

Highlight of the beach promenade (and perhaps all Santa Monica) is the **Santa Monica Pier**. No doubt about it, the place is a scene. Acrobats work out on the playground below, surfers catch waves offshore, and street musicians strum guitars. And I haven't even mentioned the official attractions. There's a turn-of-the-century carousel with hand-painted horses that was featured in that cinematic classic, *The Sting*. There are video parlors, pinball machines, skee ball, bumper cars, and a restaurant. ~ Located at the foot of Colorado Avenue.

At the Santa Monica Pier is **Pacific Park**, a two-acre family amusement park featuring 11 rides and a food plaza. Reaching up to 55 feet in height, the Santa Monica West Coaster cruises around the park at 35 miles per hour and makes two 360-degree turns. The nine-story-high Ferris wheel offers a bird's-eye view of the beach and coastline. Other attractions include adult and kid bumper cars and a swinging ship. ~ 380 Santa Monica Pier; 310-260-8744.

From here it's a jaunt up to the **Santa Monica Visitors Center** information kiosk. Here are maps, brochures, and helpful workers. ~ 1400 Ocean Avenue; 310-393-7593.

The booth is located in **Palisades Park**, a pretty, palm-lined greensward that extends north from Colorado Avenue more than a mile along the sandstone cliffs fronting Santa Monica beach. One of the park's stranger attractions here is the **Camera Obscura**, a periscope of sorts through which you can view the pier, beach, and surrounding streets. ~ In the Senior Recreation Center, 1450 Ocean Avenue.

For a glimpse into Santa Monica's past, take in the **California Heritage Museum**. Heirlooms and antiques are housed in a grand American Colonial Revival home. The mansion dates to 1894 and is furnished entirely in period pieces. There are photo archives, historic artifacts galore, and other exhibits ranging from contemporary artwork to antique toys. Closed Monday and Tuesday. Admission. ~ 2612 Main Street; 310-392-8537.

The **Museum of Flying** is a miniature Smithsonian. Tracing the history of aviation in a single, brightly painted hangar, the museum houses everything from a 1924 Douglas World Cruiser (built in Santa Monica, it was the first plane to circle the globe) to a Douglas A-4 Skyhawk flown by the Blue Angels. Closed Monday. Admission. ~ Santa Monica Airport, 2772 Donald Douglas Loop North; 310-392-8822.

Sympathetic as it is to liberal politics, Santa Monica is nonetheless an extremely wealthy town. In fact it's a fusion of two very different neighbors, mixing the bohemian strains of Venice with the monied elements of Malibu. For a look at the latter influence, take a drive from Ocean Avenue out along **San Vicente Boulevard**. This fashionable avenue, with its arcade of magnolias, is lined on either side with lovely homes. But they pale by comparison with the estates you will see by turning left on **La Mesa Drive**. This quiet suburban street boasts a series of marvelous Spanish Colonial, Tudor, and contemporary-style houses.

At first glance, the **Self Realization Fellowship Lake Shrine** in nearby Pacific Palisades is an odd amalgam of pretty things. ◄ *HIDDEN* Gathered along the shore of a placid pond are a Dutch windmill, a houseboat, and a shrine topped with something resembling a giant artichoke. In fact, the windmill is a chapel, the houseboat is a former stopping place of yogi and Self Realization Fellowship founder Paramahansa Yogananda, and the oversized artichoke is a golden lotus archway near which some of Indian leader Mahatma Gandhi's ashes are enshrined. A strange but potent collection of icons in an evocative setting. Closed Monday. ~ 17190 Sunset Boulevard; 310-454-4114.

Several miles inland at **Will Rogers State Historic Park**, on a hillside overlooking the Pacific, you can tour the ranch and home of America's greatest cowboy philosopher. Will Rogers, who started as a trick roper in traveling rodeos, hit the big time in Hollywood during the 1920s as a kind of cerebral comedian whose humorous wisdom plucked a chord in the American psyche.

From 1928 until his tragic death in 1935, the lariat laureate occupied this 31-room home with his family. The house is deceptively large but not grand; the woodframe design is basic and unassuming, true to Will Rogers' Oklahoma roots. Similarly the interior is decorated with Indian rugs and ranch tools. Western knickknacks adorn the tables and one room is dominated by a full-sized stuffed calf which Rogers utilized for roping practice. Well worth visiting, the "house that jokes built" is a simple expression of a vital personality. Admission. ~ 1501 Will Rogers Road, Pacific Palisades; 310-454-8212.

HELLO, DOLLY

Angels Attic is more than a great name. Contained in this 1895 Victorian is a unique museum of antique dolls and dollhouses. There's a Noah's ark worth of miniature animals plus a gallery of precious dolls. In keeping with the spirit of the museum, they serve tea on the front porch (by reservation). Closed Monday, Tuesday, and Wednesday. Admission. ~ 516 Colorado Avenue; 310-394-8331.

LODGING   Ocean Avenue, which runs the length of Santa Monica, paralleling the ocean one block above the beach, boasts the most hotels and the best location in town. Among its varied facilities are several generic motels. These are all-American type places furnished in veneer, carpeted wall-to-wall, and equipped with telephones and color televisions. If you book a room in one, ask for quiet accommodations since Ocean Avenue is a busy, noisy street.

One such establishment, the **Pacific Sands Motel**, a 52-unit facility, features a small, heated swimming pool. ~ 1515 Ocean Avenue; 310-395-6133. MODERATE.

A better bargain by far is the **Bayside Hotel**. Laid out in motel fashion, this two-story complex offers plusher carpets and plumper furniture than motels hereabouts. More important, it's just 50 yards from the beach across a palm-studded park. Some rooms have ocean views but none has a phone; no pool. ~ 2001 Ocean Avenue; 310-396-6000, fax 310-451-1111. MODERATE.

Of course the ultimate bargain is found at **Hostelling International—Santa Monica**. This four-story, dorm-like structure boasts 30,000 square feet, room for 228 beds. There are several common rooms, a central courtyard, library, and kitchen. In addition to facilities for independent travelers, the hostel has set aside six private rooms for couples and families. ~ 1436 2nd Street; 310-393-9913, 800-444-6111, fax 310-393-1769. BUDGET.

Despite its location on a busy street, **Channel Road Inn** conveys a cozy sense of home. Colonial Revival in style, built in 1910, this sprawling 14-room bed and breakfast offers guests a living room, library, and dining room as well as a jacuzzi and hillside garden. The guest rooms vary widely in decor—some traditional, others contemporary; some florid, others demure. ~ 219 West Channel Road; 310-459-1920. DELUXE TO ULTRA-DELUXE.

The **Pacific Shore Hotel** looks the part of a contemporary Southern California hotel. Across the street from the beach, this sprawling 168-room facility boasts a pool, sauna, jacuzzi, exercise room, and sundeck. There's a restaurant off the lobby as well as a lounge and gift shop. Guests are whisked to their rooms in a glass elevator. The accommodations are furnished with modular pieces painted in brilliant enamels; the appointments are art deco and the wallpaper has been roughed to resemble raw fabric; some rooms have ocean views. Slightly plastic, but what the hell. ~ 1819 Ocean Avenue; 310-451-8711, 800-622-8711, fax 310-394-6657. ULTRA-DELUXE.

Think of sunflowers backdropped by a deep blue Mediterranean sky. That's what the **Oceana Hotel** evokes. From its magnificent oceanfront setting to its lush courtyard planted with fragrant flowers, this exquisite hotel—reminiscent of the beauty of the Côte d'Azur—is a lesson in understated elegance. The lobby is decorated with a wrought-iron registration desk and floor-to-ceiling murals.

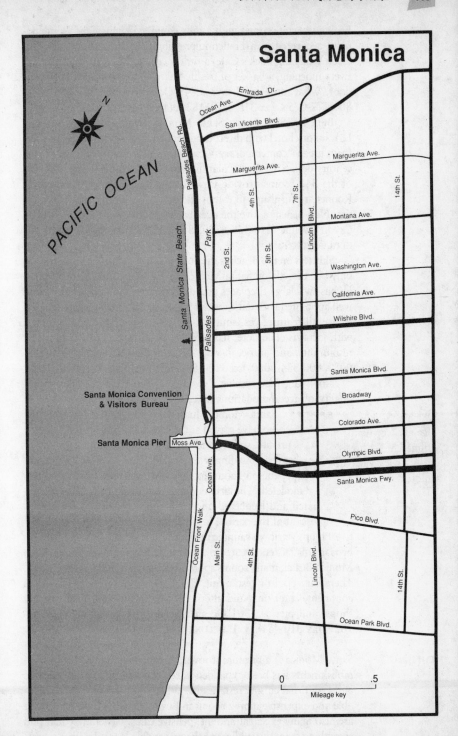

Each guest suite comes with a fully equipped kitchen and is individually decorated in a French-impressionist style. The amenities include Wolfgang Puck's Cafe, a fitness center, and a swimming pool. Every morning, a basket of freshly baked breads is delivered to your door. What more can I say? ~ 849 Ocean Avenue; 310-393-0486, 800-777-0758, fax 310-458-1182. ULTRA- DELUXE.

Built in 1989, **Loews Santa Monica Beach Hotel** was the first L.A. luxury hotel with direct beach access. The peach, beige, and seafoam green "contemporary Victorian" features a mock turn-of-the-century design. Its spectacular five-story glass atrium lobby and most of the 347 rooms provide views of the famed Santa Monica Pier. Rooms are furnished in rattan and wicker and offer special amenities. Non-beachies love the oceanview indoor/outdoor pool. ~ 1700 Ocean Avenue; 310-458-6700, 800-235-6397, fax 310-458-6761. ULTRA-DELUXE.

Shutters on the Beach is the newest L.A. beachfront hotel and the only one directly on Santa Monica Beach. Cozy and sedate, the lobby has two large fireplaces and the 198 green-and-white rooms are well appointed with dark walnut furniture. Most rooms have coastal views; all feature, yes, shutters, as well as marble baths complete with jacuzzis. The hotel has a lovely pool terrace, two ocean-view restaurants, and an ocean-view bar. ~ 1 Pico Boulevard; 310-458-0030, 800-334-9000, fax 310-458-4589. DELUXE TO ULTRA-DELUXE.

Now forget everything I've said. Never mind the variety and quality of accommodations here, there's only one place to stay in Santa Monica. Just ask the many Hollywood stars who have stayed at the **Hotel Shangri-La**. The place is private, stylish, and nothing short of beautiful. A 1939 art deco building with a facade like the prow of a steamship, the 55-room home-away-from-paparazzi is entirely remodeled. The art moderne-era furniture has been laminated and lacquered and each appointment is a perfect expression of the period. You get the sense that you'll see detective Philip Marlowe saunter in with liquor on his lips and a bulge beneath his jacket. Located on the palisades one block above Santa Monica Beach, many rooms sport an ocean view and have a kitchen. There's no pool or restaurant, but the hotel has a sundeck, serves continental breakfast and afternoon tea, and is close to the beach, shops, and pier. ~ 1301 Ocean Avenue; 310-394-2791, 800-345-7829, fax 310-451-3351. DELUXE TO ULTRA-DELUXE.

Randy Newman filmed his "I Love L.A." rock video at Hotel Shangri-La.

DINING

Santa Monica is a restaurant town. Its long tradition of seafood establishments has been expanded in recent years by a wave of ethnic and California cuisine restaurants. While some of the most fashionable and expensive dining rooms in Los Angeles are right here, there are also many excellent and inexpensive cafés. Generally you'll find everything from the sublime to the reasonable located within several commercial clusters—near the beach along Ocean Avenue, downtown on Wilshire and Santa Monica boulevards, and in the chic, gentrified corridors of Main Street and Montana Avenue.

One of the best places in Southern California for stuffing yourself with junk food while soaking up sun and having a whale of a good time is the **Santa Monica Pier**. There are taco stands, fish-and-chips shops, hot dog vendors, oyster bars, snack shops, pizzerias, and all those good things guaranteed to leave you clutching your stomach. The prices are low to modest and the food is amusement park quality. ~ Located at the foot of Colorado Avenue.

There's a sense of the Mediterranean at the sidewalk cafés lining Santa Monica's Ocean Avenue: palm trees along the boulevard, ocean views in the distance, and (usually) a warm breeze blowing. Any of these bistros will do (since it's atmosphere we're seeking), so try **Ivy at the Shore**. It features a full bar, serves espresso, and, if you want to get serious about it, has a full lunch and dinner menu with pizza, pasta, steaks, and Cajun dishes. ~ 1541 Ocean Avenue; 310-393-3113. DELUXE.

Every type of cuisine imaginable is found on the bottom level of **Santa Monica Place**. This multitiered shopping mall has an entire floor of take-out food stands. It's like the United Nations of dining, where everything is affordably priced. ~ On Broadway between 2nd and 4th streets. BUDGET.

Along the Third Street Promenade there is **Benita's Frites**, a Belgian french-fry stand. This diminutive entry in Santa Monica's rough-and-tumble restaurant race does not just serve plain old fries, however. They feature 20 different dips, including spicy barbecue, peanut sauce, and garlic mayonnaise, as well as full lunch and dinner fare. ~ 1437 3rd Street; 310-458-2889. BUDGET.

Benita's, however, is only one of many excellent eateries along Santa Monica's vaunted Third Street Promenade. This three-block-long walkway, filled with movie theaters and located in the downtown district, boasts some of the best coffeehouses and restaurants in the area.

For a Berkeley-style café, complete with funky furniture and creative clientele, there's **California Wrapp**, where you can order espresso and cappuccino, hunker down over a sandwich, and listen to live music, poetry readings, or other acts. ~ 1238 3rd Street Promenade; 310-395-5606. BUDGET.

Nearby, **Broadway Bar and Grill** features spacious booths indoors and curbside tables outside. A perfect spot for checking out the scene, this classic bar and grill serves steaks, fresh fish, and grilled chicken. ~ 1460 3rd Street Promenade; 310-393-4211. MODERATE.

If steak-and-kidney pie, bangers and mash, or shepherds pie sound appetizing, head over to **Ye Olde King's Head**. You won't see a king's head on the wall of this British pub, but there are several trophy animals adorning the place. You'll find them beside photographs of the celebrities who inhabit the pub. Like you, they are drawn here by the cozy ambience and the lively crowd. ~ 116 Santa Monica Boulevard; 310-451-1402. BUDGET TO MODERATE.

Sabor Too offers a wonderfully eclectic mélange of Creole and Latin cuisine. Set in a Mission-style building with whitewashed walls and Latin sculpture, this restaurant serves up such exotic fare as Salvadoran *pupusa* and Brazilian *coxinha* (a buttermilk puff pastry filled with chicken, goat cheese, and fresh herb mousse). No lunch on Saturday and Sunday. ~ 3221 Pico Boulevard; 310-829-3781. MODERATE.

In the world of high chic, **Chinois on Main** stands taller than most. Owned by famous restaurateur Wolfgang Puck, the fashionable dining room is done in nouveau art deco–style with track lights, pastel colors, and a central skylight. The curved bar is hand-painted; contemporary artworks adorn the walls. Once you drink in the glamorous surroundings, move on to the menu, which includes Shanghai lobster with curry sauce, whole sizzling catfish, grilled Szechuan beef, and barbecued quail. The appetizers and other entrées are equal in originality, a medley of French, Chinese, and California cuisine. This is an excellent restaurant with high standards of quality. No lunch Saturday through Tuesday. ~ 2709 Main Street; 310-392-9025. DELUXE TO ULTRA- DELUXE.

HIDDEN ► The spot for breakfast in Santa Monica is **Rae's Restaurant**, a diner on the edge of town several miles from the beach. With its formica counter and naugahyde booths, Rae's is a local institution, always packed. The breakfasts are hearty American-style feasts complete with buttermilk biscuits and country-style gravy. At lunch they serve the usual selection of sandwiches and side orders. Come dinner time they have fried shrimp, pork chops, veal, liver, fried chicken, steaks, and other hot platters at prices that seem like they haven't

---

✔ CHECK THESE OUT—UNIQUE DINING

- *Budget:* Have your hamburger with pineapple, peanut butter, or whatever you like at **Hamburger Henry**, a diner with a '50s atmosphere. *page 140*
- *Moderate:* Watch the world skate by at **The Sidewalk Café** on the Venice boardwalk, where you can refuel with omelettes and sandwiches. *page 158*
- *Deluxe:* Brighten your aura with a meal at the **Inn of the Seventh Ray**, a hippie haven in Topanga, the canyon that time forgot. *page 176*
- *Ultra-deluxe:* Feast your eyes and stomach at **Michael's**, where the walls contain original Hockneys, and the menu is filled with scrumptious masterpieces. *page 169*

Budget: under $8   Moderate: $8–$16   Deluxe: $16–$24   Ultra-deluxe: over $24

changed since the place opened in 1958. ~ 2901 Pico Boulevard; 310-828-7937. BUDGET.

The word has spread about **Louise's**. In fact, Louise's itself has spread all over L.A., but this is the original. A friendly trattoria atmosphere, creative Italian fare, and reasonable prices account for its popularity. ~ 1008 Montana Avenue; 310-394-8888. MODERATE.

There are many who believe the dining experience at **Michael's** to be the finest in all Los Angeles. Set in a restored stucco structure and decorated with original artworks by David Hockney and Jasper Johns, it is certainly one of the region's prettiest dining rooms. The menu is French-American, with original entrées such as squab on duck liver, duck with Grand Marnier sauce, and scallops on watercress purée. At lunch there is charbroiled salmon, chicken on watercress, and several elaborate salads. Haute cuisine is the order of the evening here. The artistry that has gone into the restaurant's cuisine and design have permanently established Michael's reputation. There is a cozy lounge and a garden terrace. Closed Sunday and Monday. ~ 1147 3rd Street; 310-451-0843. DELUXE TO ULTRA-DELUXE.

SHOPPING

Montana Avenue is Santa Monica's version of designer heaven, making it an interesting, if inflationary, strip to shop. From 7th to 17th Street chic shops and upscale establishments line either side of the thoroughfare.

For men's clothing, try **Weathervane For Men**. ~ 1132 Montana Avenue; 310-395-0397.

Sara up the street is like a miniature department store with fashions, jewelry, art pieces, and distinctive gifts. ~ 1324 Montana Avenue; 310-394-2900. The **Quilt Gallery** has handwoven quilts, folk art, and other items of Americana. ~ 1025 Montana Avenue; 310-393-1148.

The **Brenda Cain Store** features vintage jewelry, pottery, rugs, and turn-of-the-century decorative accessories. ~ 1211 Montana Avenue; 310-395-1559.

At **Federico** the merchandise ranges from textiles to jewelry to antiques in a variety of American Indian and Mexican styles. ~ 1522 Montana Avenue; 310-458-4134.

Browse Main Street and you'll realize that Montana Avenue is only a practice round in the gentrification of Santa Monica. Block after block of this thoroughfare has been made over in trendy fashion and filled with stylish shops. Main Street was even the focus of a civic campaign which highlighted its upscale amenities.

On the 2400 block of Main Street, the Frank Geary–designed Edgemar Building houses the **Santa Monica Museum of Art**. ~ 2437 Main Street; 310-399-0433.

The shopper's parade stretches most of the length of Main Street, but the center of action resides around the 2700 block. **Galleria Di**

Maio is an art deco mall with several spiffy shops including **Suji**, which carries fun, romantic women's clothing. ~ 2525 Main Street; 310-396-7614. **Just in Case** features cruelty-free bags and gifts. You won't find any leather or other animal skins—everything is made from recycled rubber, vinyl, and fabric. ~ 2718 Main Street; 310-399-3096.

Tortue Gallery could be better described as a museum of contemporary California art than a shop selling art. The canvases hanging here are brilliant and the gallery provides a singular insight into the local art scene. ~ 2917 Santa Monica Boulevard; 310-828-8878.

Bronson Fine Arts features turn-of-the-century American and European works of art as well as antiquities and tribal art. They also carry contemporary sculpture and artwork on canvas and paper. ~ 1410 2nd Street; 310-587-2577.

The last of Santa Monica's several shopping enclaves is in the center of town. Here you'll find **Santa Monica Place**, a mammoth triple-tiered complex with about 160 shops. This flashy atrium mall has everything from clothes to books to sporting goods to luggage to leather work, jewelry, toys, hats, and shoes. ~ On Broadway between 2nd and 4th streets; 310-394-5451.

Step out from this glittery gathering place and you'll immediately encounter the **Third Street Promenade**, a three-block walkway lined on either side with shops, upscale cafés, and movie theaters. ~ Located between Broadway and Wilshire Boulevard.

Close to museum status is the array of crystals, shells, and fossils at **Jurassic**. ~ 1340 3rd Street Promenade; 310-393-9622.

Muskrat Clothing specializes in vintage items like aloha shirts, bowling shirts, velour jackets, and silk coats with maps of Japan embroidered on the backs. (Thought you'd never find one, eh?) ~ 1238 3rd Street Promenade; 310-394-1713.

Also consider **Na Na**, where the future is happening in the form of alternative accouterments like skull-and-crossbone earrings and motorcycle boots. ~ 1228–30 3rd Street Promenade; 310-394-9690.

For the outward bound, **California Map & Travel Center** has it all—maps, directories, and guidebooks. Or, if you're planning a little armchair traveling at home, there are globes and travelogues. ~ 3312 Pico Boulevard; 310-829-6277.

FOR LOVERS OF LIBERAL LANGUAGE . . .

There is one shop in particular that exemplifies Santa Monica's liberal politics. **Midnight Special Bookstore** specializes in politics and social sciences. Rather than current bestsellers, the window displays will feature books on Latin America, world hunger, Africa, or disarmament. ~ 1318 3rd Street Promenade; 310-393-2923.

Ye Olde King's Head might be the most popular British pub this side of the Thames. From dart boards to dark wood walls, trophy heads to draft beer, it's a classic English watering hole. Known throughout the area, it draws crowds of local folks and expatriate Brits. ~ 116 Santa Monica Boulevard; 310-451-1402.

McCabe's Guitar Shop is a folksy spot with live entertainment on weekends. The sounds are almost all acoustic and range from Scottish folk bands to jazz to blues to country. The concert hall is a room in back lined with guitars. Get down. Cover. ~ 3101 Pico Boulevard; 310-828-4497.

For a raucous good time try **O'Briens**. This bar is a loud, brash place that draws hearty crowds. There are live bands from Irish rock to Texas blues. The decor is Early Insanity—mannequins combined with wagon wheels on the ceiling and alligator skins on the wall. Cover on Friday and Saturday. ~ 2941 Main Street; 310-396-4725.

Abiding by a "fashionable" dress code, **The Pink** is a weekend club featuring deejay-generated hip-hop house music and occasional live acts. Cover. ~ 2810 Main Street; 310-392-1077.

For blues, try **Harvelle's**. Cover. ~ 1432 4th Street; 310-395-1676. If it's reggae you're after then **Kingston 12** is the spot. Cover. ~ 814 Broadway; 310-451-4423.

SANTA MONICA STATE BEACH If the pop song is right and "L.A. is a great big freeway," then truly Santa Monica is a great big beach. Face it, the sand is very white, the water is very blue, the beach is very broad, and they all continue for miles. From Venice to Pacific Palisades, it's a sandbox gone wild. Skaters, strollers, and bicyclists pass along the promenade, sunbathers lie moribund in the sand, and volleyball players perform acrobatic shots. At the center of all this stands the Santa Monica Pier with its amusement park atmosphere. If it wasn't right next door to Venice this would be the hottest beach around. Lifeguards are on duty, and facilities include picnic areas, restrooms, and snackbars; restaurants and groceries are nearby. Swimming and surfing are good, and anglers usually opt for the pier. Parking fee, $7. ~ Located along Route 1, at the foot of Colorado Avenue in Santa Monica; 310-458-8311.

WILL ROGERS STATE BEACH Simple and homespun he might have been, but humorist Will Rogers was also a canny businessman with a passion for real estate. He bought up three miles of beachfront property that eventually became his namesake park. It's a wide, sandy strand with an equally expansive parking lot running the length of the beach. Route 1 parallels the parking area and beyond that rise the sharp cliffs that lend Pacific Palisades its name. You'll find good swimming here, and surfing is best in the area where Sunset Boulevard meets the ocean. Lifeguards are on duty. Facilities include restrooms, volleyball courts, and playgrounds; restaurants and groceries are nearby. Day-use fee, $6.75. ~ Located south along Route 1 from Sunset Boulevard in Pacific Palisades; 310-451-2906.

WILL ROGERS STATE HISTORIC PARK 🚶🚴🐎 The former ranch of humorist Will Rogers, this 186-acre spread sits in the hills of Pacific Palisades. The late cowboy's home is open to visitors and there are hiking trails leading around the property and out into adjacent Topanga Canyon State Park. Facilities include picnic areas, a museum, and restrooms; restaurants and groceries are located nearby in Pacific Palisades. Day-use fee, $5. ~ Located at 1501 Will Rogers Ranch Road, Pacific Palisades; 310-454-8212.

HIDDEN ► **SANTA MONICA MOUNTAINS NATIONAL RECREATION AREA** 🚶 🚴🐎 One of the few mountain ranges in the United States to run transversely (from east to west), the Santa Monicas reach for fifty miles to form the northwestern boundary of the Los Angeles basin. This federal preserve, which covers part of the mountain range, encompasses about 150,000 acres between Routes 1 and 101, much of which is laced with hiking trails; in addition to high country, it includes a coastal stretch from Santa Monica to Point Mugu. Considered a "botanical island," the mountains support chaparral, coastal sage, and oak forests; mountain lions, golden eagles, and many of California's early animal species still survive here. ~ Several access roads lead into the area; Mulholland Drive and Mulholland Highway follow the crest of the Santa Monica Mountains for about 50 miles from Hollywood to Malibu. The information center is located at 30401 Agoura Road, Suite 100, Agoura Hills (just outside the park boundaries off Route 101); 818-597-9192.

▲ There are 23 sites for primitive camping only; $6 per night.

▼▼▼▼▼▼
Malibu

Malibu is a 27-mile-long ribbon lined on one side with pearly beaches and on the other by the Santa Monica Mountains. Famed as a movie star retreat and surfer's heaven, it is one of America's mythic communities.

It has been a favored spot among Hollywood celebrities since the 1920s when a new highway opened the region and film stars like Clara Bow and John Gilbert publicized the idyllic community. By the 1950s Malibu was rapidly developing and becoming nationally known for its rolling surf and freewheeling lifestyle. The 1959 movie *Gidget* cast Sandra Dee and James Darren as Malibu beach bums and the seaside community was on its way to surfing immortality.

Paradise can be precarious in Malibu—witness the massive fires that swept across the Santa Monica Mountains in the fall of 1993. Many canyon dwellers tragically lost their homes, but coastal structures were spared. Thousands of hilly acres burned, but such apparent disasters are natural (necessary, actually) for the endemic chaparral landscape. Evidence of the fires will linger for a long time, but the regeneration of chaparral and wildflowers is a wondrous sight to behold.

Today blond-mopped surfers still line the shore and celebrities continue to congregate in beachfront bungalows. Matter of fact, the most
popular sightseeing in Malibu consists of ogling the homes of the
very rich. Malibu Road, which parallels the waterfront, is a prime
strip. To make it as difficult as possible for common riffraff to reach
the beach, the homes are built townhouse-style with no space between them. It's possible to drive for miles along the water without
seeing the beach, only the backs of baronial estates. Happily there are
a few accessways to the beach, so it's possible to wander along the
sand enjoying views of both the ocean and the picture-window palaces. Among the accessways is one that local wags named after the
"Doonesbury" character, Zonker Harris.

What's amazing about these beachfront colonies is not the houses,
which really can't compare to the estates in Beverly Hills, but the fact
that people insist on building them so close to the ocean that every
few years several are demolished by high surf and others sink into
the sand.

One of Malibu's loveliest houses is open to the public. The **Ad-
amson House**, located at Malibu Lagoon State Beach is a stately
Spanish Colonial Revival–style structure adorned with ceramic tiles.
With its bare-beam ceilings and inlaid floors, the house is a study in
early-20th-century elegance. Outstanding as it is, the building is upstaged by the landscaped grounds, which border the beach at Malibu
and overlook a lagoon alive with waterfowl and are open to the public. Though there is an admission for the house, there is no fee to
stroll the gardens. Closed Sunday, Monday, and Tuesday. Admission.
~ 23200 Pacific Coast Highway; 310-456-8432.

The town's most prestigious address is that of the **J. Paul Getty
Museum**, one of the wealthiest art museums in the world. Set on a
hillside overlooking the sea, the building re-creates a 2000-year-old
Roman villa in the most splendid manner imaginable.

The colonnaded entranceway, which greets the visitor with a reflecting pool and fountains, is nothing short of magnificent. This grand
passage is adorned by bronze sculptures and lined with hedgerows.
The floors are inlaid with tile, and the walls are painted fresco style.

The galleries are equally beautiful. Focusing on Greek and Roman antiquities, Renaissance and Baroque art, and French furniture,
the museum reflects the taste of founder J. Paul Getty. Some of the
world's finest artworks are displayed here and the relatively young
museum has already established an awesome reputation in the art
world. Advance reservation required for parking. Closed Monday. ~
17985 Pacific Coast Highway; 310-458-2003.

Another seafront attraction is **Malibu Pier** where you can walk
out over the water, cast for fish, or gaze back along Malibu's heavily developed coastline. If you're in a sporting mood, they rent fishing tackle here; if you prefer less strenuous sports, there's a bar at the
foot of the pier. ~ 23000 Pacific Coast Highway.

When you tire of Malibu's sand and surf, take a drive along one of the canyon roads which lead from Route 1 up into the Santa Monica Mountains. This chaparral country is filled with oak and sycamore forests and offers sweeping views back along the coast. Topanga Canyon Boulevard, perhaps the best known of these mountain roads, curves up to the rustic town of **Topanga**. Back in the '60s it was a fabled retreat for flower children. Even today vestiges of the hip era remain in the form of health food stores, New Age shops, and natural restaurants. Many of the woodframe houses are hand-crafted and the community still vibrates to a slower rhythm than coastal Malibu and cosmopolitan Los Angeles.

To reach the top of the world (while making a mountain loop of this uphill jaunt), take Old Topanga Canyon Road from town and turn left out on **Mulholland Highway**. With its panoramic views of the Los Angeles Basin and San Fernando Valley, Mulholland is justifiably famous. (To complete the circle follow Kanan–Dume Road back down to the ocean.)

LODGING

There are several motels scattered along the coastal highway in Malibu, two of which I can recommend. **Topanga Ranch Motel** is a 30-unit complex that dates back to the 1920s. Here are cute little cottages painted white with red trim and clustered around a circular drive. Granted they're somewhat timeworn, but each is kept neat and trim with plain furnishings and little decoration. A few have kitchens. A good deal for a location right across the highway from the beach. ~ 18711 Pacific Coast Highway; 310-456-5486, 800-200-0019. MODERATE.

At **Casa Malibu Inn on the Beach**, you'll be in a 21-room facility that actually overhangs the sand. Located smack in the center of Malibu, the building features a central courtyard with lawn furniture and ocean view plus a balcony dripping with flowering plants. The rooms are decorated in an attractive but casual fashion; some have private balconies, kitchens, and/or ocean views. ~ 22752 Pacific Coast Highway; 310-456-2219, 800-831-0858, fax 310-456-5418. DELUXE TO ULTRA-DELUXE.

The **Malibu Beach Inn** is posh and each of its 47 guest rooms offers spectacular ocean views from private balconies. Fireplaces, jacuzzis, and minibars round out the amenities. The location on the beach, one block from the Malibu Pier, makes this an ideal getaway. ~ 22878 Pacific Coast Highway; 310-456-6444, 800-462-5428. ULTRA-DELUXE.

DINING

Malibu's best-known eating spot sits at the foot of Malibu Pier. **Alice's Restaurant** is a trim, glass-encased dining room with views extending across the beach and out over the ocean. A gathering place for locals in the know and visitors on the make, it serves a lunch and dinner menu of seafood and pasta dishes. Salads—including roasted goat cheese and warm duck—are another specialty. The good food, friendly bar, and lively crowd make it a great place for carousing. ~ 23000 Pacific Coast Highway; 310-456-6646. MODERATE TO DELUXE.

The **Reel Inn** is my idea of heaven—a reasonably priced seafood restaurant. Located across the highway from the beach, it's an oilcloth restaurant with an outdoor patio and a flair for serving good, healthful food at low prices. Among the fresh fish lunches and dinners are salmon, snapper, lobster, and swordfish. ~ 18661 Pacific Coast Highway; 310-456-8221. MODERATE.

On weekend nights, Mulholland Drive, as it's known in town, is a rendezvous for lovers and a drag strip for daredevil drivers, but the rest of the time you'll find it a sinuous country road far from the madding mobs.

There's nothing fancy about **Malibu Fish & Seafood**. It's just a fish and chips stand with a few picnic tables outside, but the menu includes such tantalizing specialties as ahi tuna burgers and steamed lobster. The price is hard to beat when you add the ocean view. ~ 25653 Pacific Coast Highway; 310-456-3430. BUDGET.

Beau Rivage Mediterranean Restaurant, another gourmet gathering place, located across the highway from the ocean, boasts a cozy dining room and ocean-view terrace. With exposed-beam ceiling, brick trim, and copper pots along the wall, it has the feel of a French country inn. The dinner menu, however, is strictly Mediterranean. In addition to several fettuccine and linguine dishes, there is white fish meunière, baby lamb chops, Norwegian salmon, and daily specials that range from grilled shark with persimmon sauce to ragoût of wild boar. ~ 26025 Pacific Coast Highway; 310-456-5733. DELUXE TO ULTRA-DELUXE.

The quintessential Malibu dining experience is **Geoffrey's**, a cliff-top restaurant overlooking the ocean. The marble bar, whitewashed stucco walls, stone pebble tiles, and flowering plants exude wealth and elegance. The entire hillside has been landscaped and beautifully terraced, creating a Mediterranean atmosphere. The menu features a variation on California cuisine, and includes swordfish with roasted pasilla chili and cucumber-mint salsa, and salmon with angelhair pasta. The lunch and dinner menus are almost identical and on Saturday and Sunday they also serve brunch. The setting, cuisine, and high prices make Geoffrey's a prime place for celebrity gazing. ~ 27400 Pacific Coast Highway; 310-457-1519. DELUXE TO ULTRA-DELUXE.

When you're out at the beaches around Point Dume or elsewhere in northern Malibu, there are two adjacent roadside restaurants worth checking out. **Coral Beach Cantina** is a simple Mexican restaurant with a small patio. The menu contains standard south-of-the-border fare. ~ 29350 Pacific Coast Highway; 310-457-5503. BUDGET.

◀ HIDDEN

Over at **Zuma Sushi** they have a sushi bar and table service. In addition to the house specialty there are tempura and teriyaki dishes.

Like its neighbor, this is a small, unassuming café. Dinner only. ~ 29350 Pacific Coast Highway; 310-457-4131. MODERATE TO DELUXE.

For a good meal near the beach there's **Neptune's Net Seafood.** Located across the highway from County Line Beach (at the Los Angeles–Ventura county border), it's a breezy café frequented by surfers. There are egg dishes for breakfast; during the rest of the day they serve sandwiches, burgers, clam chowder, as well as shrimp, oyster, clam, and scallop baskets. Ocean views at beach bum prices. ~ 42505 Route 1; 310-457-3095. BUDGET.

Cutting-edge Continental cuisine can be found at **Granita,** where chef Wolfgang Puck's culinary cohorts whip up original creations. You can watch as they prepare dry-roasted Sonoma lamb with goat cheese polenta or grilled free-range chicken served on a potato purée with sizzling lime butter. Yow! The art deco interior, highlighted by mosaic tiling, completes the progressive effect. No lunch on Monday and Tuesday. ~ Malibu Colony Plaza; 310-456-0488. DELUXE.

Up in the Santa Monica Mountains, high above the clamor of Los Angeles, rests the **Inn of the Seventh Ray.** A throwback to the days when Topanga Canyon was a hippie enclave, this mellow dining spot serves "energized" foods to "raise your body's light vibrations." These auricly charged entrées include "artichoke queen of light" (artichokes stuffed with tofu) and "five secret rays" (steamed veggies with organic brown rice and five sauces). There is also a selection of fresh seafood, duckling, and lamb dishes. Open for lunch and dinner, the restaurant features dining indoors or outside on a pretty, tree-shaded patio, where coyotes can often be seen from your table. Far out. ~ 128 Old Topanga Canyon Road; 310-455-1311. DELUXE TO ULTRA-DELUXE.

SHOPPING   Somehow the name **Malibu Country Mart** doesn't quite describe this plaza shopping mall. There's not much of the "country" about the pricey boutiques and galleries here. The parking lot numbers more Porsches than pickup trucks. But these two dozen stores will provide a sense of the Malibu lifestyle and give you a chance to shop (or window shop) for quality. ~ 3835 Cross Creek Road; 310-456-2047.

Zuma Canyon Orchids offers elegant and exquisite prize-winning orchids that can be shipped anywhere in the world. If you call ahead for a reservation, they will even provide a tour of the greenhouses. ~ 5949 Bonsall Drive; 310-457-9771.

Up in the secluded reaches of Topanga Canyon there are numerous artists and craftspeople who have traded the chaos of the city for the serenity of the Santa Monica Mountains. Craft shops come and go with frustrating regularity here, but it's worth a drive into the hills to see who is currently selling their wares.

NIGHTLIFE   For some easy listening, check out the scene at **Beau Rivage Mediterranean Restaurant.** There's a piano player Monday through Wednesday, a singing couple Thursday through Friday, and a guitar player Saturday through Sunday. A cozy bar and fireplace add charm to the scene. ~ 26025 Pacific Coast Highway; 310-456-5733.

Across from the Malibu Pier is the **Malibu Inn**, a burger joint and beer hall that's the prime nighttime mustering spot for Pepperdine students and local surfers. Live entertainment may include karaoke and local bands. Cover for live shows. ~ 22969 Pacific Coast Highway; 310-456-6106.

TOPANGA CANYON STATE PARK 🚶🚵🏇 Not much sand here, but you will find forests of oak and fields of rye. This 10,000-acre hideaway nestles in the Santa Monica Mountains above Malibu. Along the 35 miles of hiking trails and fire roads are views of the ocean, San Gabriel Mountains, and San Fernando Valley. There are meadows and a stream to explore. The park climbs from 200 to 2100 feet in elevation, providing an introduction to one of Los Angeles' few remaining natural areas. Facilities include an equestrian camp and trails, picnic areas, and restrooms; restaurants and groceries are several miles away. Parking fee, $5. ~ Located at 20825 Entrada Road; from Route 1 in Malibu take Topanga Canyon Road up to Entrada Road; 310-455-2465.

BEACHES & PARKS

▲ There are eight hike-in sites, tents only; $3 per person.

TOPANGA BEACH 🏊 🏄 This narrow sand corridor extends for over a mile. The adjacent highway breaks the quietude, but the strand

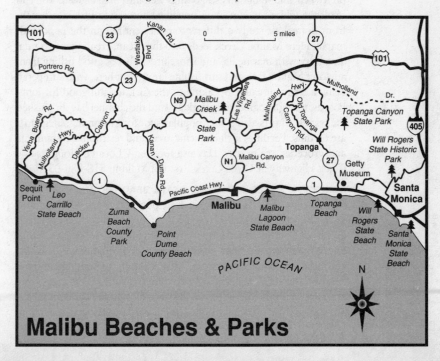

Malibu Beaches & Parks

is still popular with surfers and those wanting to be close to Malibu services. The swimming is good, and the surfing is excellent around Topanga Creek. Lifeguards are on duty; facilities are limited to restrooms. Restaurants and stores are located nearby. ~ Located along Route 1 near Topanga Canyon Road in Malibu; 310-451-2906.

MALIBU CREEK STATE PARK 🏃🚴🐎 🏕 🛶 Once the location site for *M.A.S.H.* and *Planet of the Apes*, this 6600-acre facility spreads through rugged, virgin country in the Santa Monica Mountains. Among its features are 15 miles of hiking trails, four-acre Century Lake, and Malibu Creek, which is lined with willow and cottonwood. In spring the meadows explode with wildflowers; at other times of the year you'll encounter squirrels, rabbits, mule deer, and bobcats. The bird life ranges from aquatic species such as ducks and great blue herons along the lake to hawks, woodpeckers, and golden eagles. The lava hills, sloping grasslands, and twisted sedimentary rock formations make it an intriguing escape from the city. Facilities here include picnic areas, restrooms, and showers; restaurants and groceries are located several miles away. Day-use fee, $6. ~ Located off Mulholland Highway and Las Vírgenes Road above Malibu; 818-880-0350.

▲ There are 60 sites for tents and trailers or RVs (no hookups); $14 per night in season.

MALIBU LAGOON STATE BEACH 🏃 🛶 🏊 🛶 Not only is there a pretty beach here but an estuary and wetlands area as well. You can stroll the white sands past an unending succession of lavish beachfront homes, or study a different species entirely in the park's salt marsh. Here Malibu Creek feeds into the ocean, creating a rich tidal area busy with marine life and shorebirds. There's good fishing from adjacent Malibu Pier, and surf fishing is excellent here, with surf perch being a frequent catch. Speaking of the surf, it's still good for longboards, though engineering work around the channel has diminished the waves. This is also a very popular spot for swimming; lifeguards are on duty. Facilities include picnic areas and restrooms; restaurants and groceries are nearby. Day-use fee, $6. ~ Located along Pacific Coast Highway at Cross Creek Road in Malibu; 818-880-0350.

ROBERT H. MEYER MEMORIAL STATE BEACHES 🏃 🏊 This unusual facility consists of three separate pocket beaches—**El Pescador**, **La Piedra**, and **El Matador**. Each is a pretty strand with sandy beach and eroded bluffs. Together they are among the nicest beaches in Malibu. My favorite is El Matador with its rock formations, sea stacks, and adjacent Malibu mansions. Use caution swimming at these beaches; there are no lifeguards. Facilities include toilets and picnic areas; restaurants and groceries are several miles away. Parking for all beaches is $5. ~ Located on Route 1 about 11 miles west of Malibu; 818-880-0350.

WESTWARD BEACH POINT DUME STATE PARK 🏃 🏊 ⛵ 🚶
This long narrow stretch is really a southerly continuation of Zuma
Beach. Unlike its neighbor, it is conveniently located away from the
highway and bordered by lofty sandstone cliffs. There are tidepools
here and trails leading up along the bluffs. For white sand serenity
this is a choice spot. Matter of fact, on the far side of Point Dume
you'll encounter what was once a popular nude beach in **Pirate's**   ◀ *HIDDEN*
Cove. Swimming is good, but beware of dangerous currents. Surfing
is good along Westward Beach and off Point Dume. Lifeguards are
on duty and restrooms are available; restaurants and groceries are
located nearby. ~ The park entrance is adjacent to the southern entrance to Zuma Beach County Park; take Westward Beach Road off
Highway 1 about six miles west of Malibu. To reach the beach at
Pirate's Cove, take the trail over the Point Dume Headlands; 310-
457-9891.

ZUMA BEACH COUNTY PARK 🏊 ⛵ 🚶 🏖 This long, broad
beach is a study in the territorial instincts of the species. Los Angeles
County's largest beach park, it is frequented in one area by Chicanos;
"Vals," young residents of the San Fernando Valley, have staked claim
to another section, while families and students inhabit another stretch
(Zuma 3 and 4). Not as pretty as other Malibu beaches, Zuma offers
more space and better facilities, such as restrooms, lifeguards, playgrounds, volleyball courts, and proximity to restaurants and stores.
Swimming and surfing are good; for information on surf conditions,
call 310-457-9701. ~ Located along Route 1 approximately six miles
west of Malibu; 310-457-9891.

LEO CARRILLO STATE BEACH 🏃 🏊 🏄 🚶 🏖 Extending more
than a mile, this white sand corridor rests directly below Route 1.
Named after Leo Carrillo, the TV actor who played sidekick Pancho
in *The Cisco Kid*, the beach offers sea caves, tidepools, interesting
rock formations, and a natural tunnel. Nicer still is Leo Carrillo
Beach North, a sandy swath located just beyond Sequit Point and
backdropped by a sharp bluff. This entire area is a prime whale-
watching site. At the south end of this 1600-acre park you can bathe
in the buff—but beware, if caught you will be cited. Facilities here
include limited picnic areas, restrooms, showers, and lifeguards; restaurants and groceries are several miles away. Swimming and surfing
are both good; the best waves break around Sequit Point, and there's
also excellent surfing a few miles north at County Line Beach. Day-
use fee, $6. ~ On Route 1 about 14 miles west of Malibu. There's
access to Leo Carrillo Beach North from the parking lot at 35000
Pacific Coast Highway; 818-880-0350.

▲ There are 136 sites for tents and trailers or RVs (no hookups); $14 to $16 per night. Reservations through DESTINET (800-
444-7275).

▼▼▼▼▼▼▼▼▼▼▼▼▼▼▼
Santa Catalina Island

Twenty-six miles across the sea, (You know the song.) *Santa Catalina is a waitin' for me,* (Everyone has heard it.) *Santa Catalina, the island of Romance, romance, romance, romance.*

Actually this Mediterranean hideaway is parked just 22 miles off the Los Angeles coastline. But for romance, the song portrays it perfectly. Along its 54 miles of shoreline Catalina offers sheer cliffs, pocket beaches, hidden coves, and some of the finest skindiving anywhere. To the interior, mountains rise sharply to over 2000 feet elevation. Island fox, black antelope, mountain goats, and over 400 bison range the island while its waters teem with marlin, swordfish, and barracuda.

Happily, this unique habitat is preserved for posterity and adventurous travelers by an arrangement under which 70 percent of the island lies undeveloped, protected by the Santa Catalina Conservancy. Avalon, the famous coastal resort enclave, is the only town on the island. The rest is given over to mountain wilderness and pristine shoreline.

As romantic as its setting is the history of the island. Originally part of the Baja coastline, it broke off from the mainland eons ago and drifted 100 miles to the northwest. Its earliest inhabitants arrived perhaps 4000 or 5000 years ago, leaving scattered evidence of their presence before being supplanted by the Gabrieleño Indians around 500 B.C. A society of sun worshippers, the Gabrieleños constructed a sacrificial temple, fished island waters, and traded ceramics and soapstone carvings with mainland tribes, crossing the channel in canoes.

Juan Rodríguez Cabrillo discovered Catalina in 1542, but the place proved of such little interest to the Spanish that other than Sebastian Vizcaíno's exploration in 1602 they virtually ignored it.

By the 19th century Russian fur traders, attracted by the rich colonies of sea otters, succeeded in exterminating both the otters and the indigenous people. Cattle and sheep herders took over the Gabrieleños' land while pirates and smugglers, hiding in Catalina's secluded coves, menaced the coast.

Later in the century Chinese coolies were secretly landed on the island before being illegally carried to the mainland. Even during Prohibition it proved a favorite place among rumrunners and bootleggers.

Other visionaries, seeing in Catalina a major resort area, took control. After changing hands several times the island was purchased in 1919 by William Wrigley, Jr. The Wrigley family—better known for their ownership of a chewing gum company and the Chicago Cubs baseball team—developed Avalon for tourism and left the rest of the island to nature.

SIGHTS   Attracting big-name entertainers and providing an escape from urban Los Angeles, **Avalon** soon captured the fancy of movie stars and wealthy Californians. Today Avalon is the port of entry for the island. Set in a luxurious amphitheater of green mountains, the town is like a time warp of Southern California early in the century. The architecture is a blend of Mediterranean and Victorian homes as well as vernacular structures designed by creative locals who captured both the beautiful and whimsical.

From the ferry dock you can wander **Crescent Avenue**, Avalon's oceanfront boulevard. Stroll out along the **Avalon Pleasure Pier**, located at Crescent Avenue and Catalina Street, for a view of the entire town and its surrounding crescent of mountains. Located along this wood plank promenade are food stands, the harbormaster's office, and bait-and-tackle shops. The **Santa Catalina Island Chamber of Commerce and Visitors Bureau** has an information center here that will help orient you to Avalon and the island. ~ #1 Green Pier; 310-510-1520.

Among the pier kiosks are some offering **glass-bottom boat tours** out to a nearby cove filled with colorful fish and marine plant life. Known as Catalina's "undersea gardens," the area is crowded with rich kelp beds and is a favorite haunt of brilliant red goby, golden adult Garibaldi, and leopard sharks. **Santa Catalina Island Company** features tours during the day and also at night when huge floodlights are used to attract sea life. During summer months they seek out the spectacular phosphorescent flying fish that seasonally inhabit these waters. ~ Avalon Harbor Pier; 310-510-2000.

Further along the waterfront, dominating the skyline, sits the **Avalon Casino**. A massive circular building painted white and capped with a red tile roof, it was built in 1929 after a Spanish Moorish design. What can you say other than that the place is famous: it has appeared on countless post cards and travel posters. The ballroom has heard the big band sounds of Count Basie and Tommy Dorsey and the entire complex is a study in art deco with fabulous murals and tile paintings. ~ On Casino Way at the end of Crescent Avenue; 310-510-2000.

Downstairs is the **Catalina Island Museum** with a small collection of local artifacts. Of particular interest is the contour relief map of the island which provides an excellent perspective for anyone venturing into the interior. Admission. ~ Avalon Casino; 310-510-2414.

Another point of particular interest, located about two miles inland in Avalon Canyon, is the **Wrigley Memorial and Botanical Garden**, a tribute to William Wrigley, Jr. The monument, an imposing 130-foot structure fashioned with glazed tiles and Georgia marble, features a spiral staircase in a solitary tower. The gardens, a showplace for native island plants, display an array of succulents and cactus. Admission. ~ 1400 Avalon Canyon Road; 310-510-2288.

The most exhilarating sightseeing excursion in Avalon lies in the hills around town. Head out Pebbly Beach Road along the water, turn right on Wrigley Terrace Road, and you'll be on one of the many terraces that rise above Avalon. The old Wrigley Mansion (currently the Inn on Mt. Ada, Wrigley Road), an elegant estate with sweeping views, was once the (ho hum) summer residence of the Wrigley family. Other scenic drives on the opposite side of town lie along Stage and Chimes Tower roads. Here you'll pass the **Zane Grey Hotel**, a 1926 pueblo adobe that was formerly the Western novel writer's home. ~ 199 Chimes Tower Road; 310-510-0966.

Both routes snake into the hills past rocky outcroppings and patches of cactus. The slopes are steep and unrelenting. Below you blocks of houses run in rows out to a fringe of palm trees and undergrowth. Gaze around from this precarious perch and you'll see that Avalon rests in a green bowl surrounded by mountains.

When it comes time to venture further afield, you'll find that traveling around Santa Catalina Island is more complicated than it first seems. You can hike or bicycle to most places on the island. **Brown's Bikes** rents bicycles, tandems, and mountain bikes. ~ 107 Pebbly Beach Road; 310-510-0986. In Avalon proper it's possible to rent golf carts from outfits like **Cartopia Cars**. ~ 615 Crescent Avenue; 310-510-2493. Also try **Catalina Auto Rental**. ~ 301 Crescent Avenue; 310-510-0111. There are also taxis in town.

Santa Catalina Island Company has a visitor information center and conducts tours around the island. They offer coastal cruises and inland motor tours. ~ 423 Crescent Avenue; 310-510-2000.

Catalina Safari Bus provides drop-offs for people. ~ 310-510-2800. **Santa Catalina Island Conservancy**, the agency charged with overseeing the island, shuttles visitors to the airport and provides jeep tours. ~ 125 Claressa Avenue; 310-510-1421. To hike independently outside Avalon you will need a permit from the Santa Catalina Island Conservancy. ~ 125 Claressa Avenue; 310-510-1421. Permits are also available at The Airport in the Sky. ~ 310-510-0143. You can also call the Catalina Cove and Camp Agency. ~ P.O. Box 5044, Two Harbors, CA 90704; 310-510-0303.

The other thing to remember about Catalina is that perhaps more than any other spot along the California coast, its tourism is seasonal. The season, of course, is summer, when mobs of people descend on the island. During winter everything slows down, storms wash through intermittently, and some facilities close. Spring and fall, when the crowds have subsided, the weather is good, and everything is still open, may be the best seasons of all.

Regardless of how you journey into Catalina's outback, there's only one way to get there, Airport Road. This paved thoroughfare climbs steadily from Avalon, offering views of the rugged coast and surrounding hills. Oak, pine, and eucalyptus dot the hillsides as the road follows a ridgetop with steep canyons falling away on either side. **Mt. Orizaba**, a flat-topped peak which represents the highest point on the island, rises in the distance.

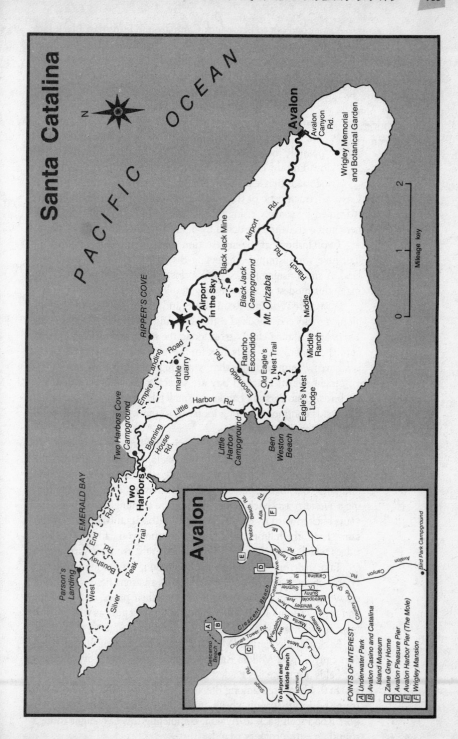

Santa Catalina

PACIFIC OCEAN

N

Avalon

Avalon Canyon Rd.

Wrigley Memorial and Botanical Garden

RIPPER'S COVE

Black Jack Mine

Airport Rd.

Airport in the Sky

Black Jack Campground

Mt. Orizaba

Middle Ranch Rd.

Middle Ranch

Road

Landing

Empire

marble quarry

Escondido Rd.

Rancho Escondido

Old Eagle's Nest Trail

Eagle's Nest Lodge

Little Harbor Rd.

Two Harbors Cove Campground

Banning House Rd.

Little Harbor Campground

Ben Weston Beach

EMERALD BAY

Two Harbors

Parson's Landing

End Rd.

Boushay Rd.

West Rd.

Silver Peak Trail

Mileage key

0   1   2

Avalon

Pebbly Beach Rd.

Ada Rd.

Mt.

F

E

D

Crescent Ave

Catalina St

Summer St

Sunny Ln

Lower Terrace Rd

Avalon Canyon Rd

Bird Park Campground

Crescent Beach

Chimes Tower Rd.

Descanso Beach

A

B

C

Metropole Ave

East Whitley Ave

Sunny Ave

Whitley Ave

Marilla Ave

Mesa Ave

La

Mesa

Ave

State

Rd

Isthmus Rd.

To Airport and Middle Ranch

POINTS OF INTEREST
A | Underwater Park
B | Avalon Casino and Catalina
    Island Museum
C | Zane Grey Home
D | Avalon Pleasure Pier
E | Avalon Harbor Pier (The Mole)
F | Wrigley Mansion

A side road out to Black Jack Campground leads past **Black Jack Mine**, a silver mine closed since early in the century. Today little remains except tailing piles and a 520-foot shaft. Then the main road climbs to Catalina's **Airport in the Sky**, a small landing facility located at 1600-foot elevation.

Gold fever swept Santa Catalina in 1863 as miners swept onto the island, but the rush never panned out.

From the airport you might want to follow a figure eight course in your route around the island, covering most of the island's roads and taking in as much of the landscape as possible (beyond the airport all the roads are dirt). Just follow Empire Landing Road, a curving, bumping track with side roads that lead down past an **old marble quarry** to **Ripper's Cove**. Characteristic of the many inlets dotting the island, the cove is framed by sharply rising hills. There's a boulder-and-sand beach here and a coastline bordered by interesting rock formations.

Two Harbors, at the intersection of the figure-eight's loops, is a half-mile wide isthmus connecting the two sections of Catalina Island. A small fishing pier, several tourist facilities, and a boat harbor make this modest enclave the only developed area outside Avalon.

From here West End Road curves and climbs, bends and descends along a rocky coast pocked with cactus and covered by scrub growth. There are Catalina cherry trees along the route and numerous coves at the bottom of steep cliffs. Not for the faint-hearted, West End Road is a narrow, bumpy course that winds high above the shore.

Anchored off **Emerald Bay** are several rock islets crowded with sea birds. From **Parson's Landing**, a small inlet with a gray sand beach, dirt roads continue in a long loop out to the west end of the island, then back to Two Harbors.

Catalina possesses about 400 species of flora, some unique to the island, and is rich in wildlife. Anywhere along its slopes you are likely to spy quail, wild turkey, mountain goats, island fox, mule deer, and wild boar. Bison, placed on the island by a movie company filming a Western way back in the 1920s, graze seemingly everywhere. En route back toward Avalon, Little Harbor Road climbs into the mountains. From the hilltops around **Little Harbor** you can see a series of ridges which drop along sheer rockfaces to the frothing surf below.

Take a detour up to **Rancho Escondido**, a working ranch that boards champion Arabian horses. There's an arena here where trainers work these exquisite animals through their paces, and a "saddle and trophy room" filled with handcrafted riding gear as well as prizes from major horse shows.

Back at Little Harbor, Middle Ranch Road cuts through a mountain canyon past **Middle Ranch**, a small spread with livestock and oat fields. En route lies **Eagles' Nest Lodge**, a stagecoach stop dating to 1890. Numbered among the antique effects of this simple wood-frame house are wagon wheels and a split-rail fence. Carry on to Airport Road then back to Avalon, completing this easy-eight route around an extraordinary island.

One fact about lodging in Catalina everyone seems to agree upon is that it is overpriced. Particularly in the summer, when Avalon's population swells from under 3000 to over 10,000, hotels charge stiff rates for rooms. But what's a traveler to do? The island is both pretty and popular, so you have no recourse but to pay the piper.

LODGING

It's also a fact that rates jump seasonally more than on the mainland. Summer is the most expensive period, winter the cheapest, with spring and fall somewhere in between. Weekend rates are also sometimes higher than weekday room tabs and usually require a two-night minimum.

The last fact of life for lodgers to remember is that since most of the island is a nature preserve, the hotels, with one lone exception, are located in Avalon.

Low-price lodgings are as rare as snow in Avalon. But at the **Hotel Atwater** you'll find accommodations priced in the moderate-to-deluxe category (budget during winter months). What that buys is a room with a veneer dresser, nicked night tables, soft mattress, spotty carpet, postage stamp bathroom, and, if it's like the room I saw, a hole in the wall. But, hey, the place *is* clean and this *is* Catalina. Besides it has a friendly lobby with oak trim and naugahyde furniture plus dozens of rooms to choose from. Good luck. ~ 125 Sumner Street; 310-510-1788, 800-322-3434. MODERATE TO DELUXE.

One of Santa Catalina's most popular hotels is the **Pavilion Lodge**, a 72-room facility on Avalon's waterfront street. Designed around a central courtyard, it offers guests a lawn and patio for sunbathing. The rooms contain modern furniture, wall-to-wall carpeting, and stall showers. If you want to be at the heart of downtown in a comfortable if undistinguished establishment, this is the place. ~ 513 Crescent Avenue; 310-510-1788, 800-322-3434. DELUXE TO ULTRA-DELUXE.

Plainly put, the **Hotel Vista del Mar** is a gem. Each of the 15 spacious Mediterranean-style rooms is decorated in soft pastels and features a wet bar, fireplace, and full tiled bath. All surround an open-air atrium courtyard lobby, where guests enjoy ocean breezes and views from comfortable wicker rockers. One smaller room is priced moderate to deluxe, while courtyard rooms command deluxe to ultra-deluxe rates. ~ 417 Crescent Avenue; 310-510-1452, fax 310-510-2917. MODERATE TO ULTRA DELUXE.

Farther along the same street is **Hotel Villa Portofino** with 34 rooms situated around a split-level brick patio. The accommodations are small but have been stylishly decorated with modern furniture, dressing tables, and wallpaper in pastel shades. There are tile baths with stall showers. A small lobby downstairs has been finished with potted plants and marble. ~ 111 Crescent Avenue; 310-510-0555, fax 310-510-0839. MODERATE TO DELUXE.

It's a big, bold, blue and white structure rising for five levels above the hillside. **Hotel Catalina** has been a fixture on the Avalon skyline since 1892. The 32-unit facility features a comfortable lobby complete with overhead fans, plus a sundeck and jacuzzi. The sleeping rooms are small but comfy with standard furnishings; many offer ocean views. There are also four trim little cottages that are warmly decorated. A bright, summer atmosphere pervades the place. ~ 129 Whittley Avenue; 310-510-0027, 800-540-0184. MODERATE TO DELUXE.

La Paloma Cottages, a rambling complex consisting of several buildings, features a string of eight contiguous cottages. These are cozy units with original decor and comfortable furnishings. There are also larger family units (with kitchens) available in a nearby building. Set on a terraced street in a quiet part of town, La Paloma is attractively landscaped. There are no phones or daily maid service in the rooms. However, at La Flores, an addition to the original hotel, you can get pricier rooms with maid service, phones and a whirlpool bath to boot. ~ 326 Sunny Lane; 310-510-0737, 800-310-1505, fax 310-510-2424. DELUXE TO ULTRA-DELUXE.

No rental cars operate on the island, and visitors are not permitted to drive.

Catalina Canyon Hotel is a chic, modern 80-room complex complete with pool, jacuzzi, sauna, restaurant, and bar. This Mediterranean-style hotel sits on a hillside in Avalon Canyon. The grounds are nicely landscaped with banana plants and palm trees. Each guest room is furnished in white oak, adorned with art prints, and decorated in a motif of soft hues. ~ 888 Country Club Drive; 310-510-0325, 800-253-9361, fax 310-510-0900. DELUXE.

The romantic Hotel St. Lauren rises with a pink blush a block from the sand above Catalina's famed harbor. The Victorian-style hotel is a honeymoon paradise, with spacious rooms and jacuzzi tubs in minisuites. ~ Metropole and Beacon streets; 310-510-2299. DELUXE TO ULTRA-DELUXE.

Rare and incredible is the only way to describe The Inn on Mt. Ada. Nothing on the island, and few places along the California coast, compare. Perched on a hillside overlooking Avalon and its emerald shoreline, this stately hostelry resides in the old Wrigley mansion, a 7000-square-foot Georgian Colonial home built by the chewing gum baron in 1921. A masterwork of french doors and elegant columns, curved ceilings, and ornamental molding, the grande dame is beautifully appointed with antiques and plush furnishings. The entire ground floor—with rattan-furnished sitting room, oceanfront veranda, formal dining room, and spacious living room—is for the benefit of visitors. Wine and hors d'oeuvres are served in the afternoon and there's a full breakfast, deli lunch, and dinner served to guests and a limited number of visitors. The wonder of the place is that all this luxury is for just six guest rooms, guaranteeing personal service and an atmosphere of intimacy. The private rooms are stylishly furnished in period pieces and adorned with a creative selection of artwork. All meals are included. Reserve at least two months in advance. ~ 398 Wrigley Road, P.O. Box 2560, Avalon, CA 90704; 310-510-2030, 800-884-1186, fax 310-510-2237. ULTRA-DELUXE.

As with Catalina hotels, there are a few points to remember when shopping for a restaurant. Prices are higher than on the mainland. With very few exceptions the dining spots are concentrated in Avalon; services around the rest of the island are minimal. Also, business is seasonal, so restaurants may vary their schedules, serving three meals daily during summer and weekends but dinner only during winter. The wisest course is to check beforehand.

DINING

Antonio's Pizzeria is a hole-in-the-wall, but a hole-in-the-wall with panache. It's chockablock with junk—old pin-up pictures, record covers, dolls, trophies, fish nets. There's sawdust on the floor and a vague '50s theme to the place. The food—pizza, pasta, and hot sandwiches—is good, filling, and served daily at lunch and dinner. "Come on in," as the sign suggests, "and bask in the ambience of the decaying 1950s." ~ 114 Sumner Avenue; 310-510-0060. BUDGET TO MODERATE.

The Busy Bee, established in 1923, is a local gathering place located right on the beach. It's hard to match the views from the patio of this simple café. This is one place in Catalina that's open for breakfast, lunch, and dinner year-round. For lunch you can dine on vegetable platters, tacos, tostadas, salads, and sandwiches while gazing out at the pier and harbor. The dinner menu offers buffalo burgers, fried shrimp, teriyaki chicken, and steak. ~ 306-B Crescent Avenue; 310-510-1983. MODERATE.

◄ **HIDDEN**

The other half of the vintage stucco-and-red-tile building housing the Busy Bee is the site of **Armstrong's Seafood Restaurant and Fish Market**. The interior is trimly finished in knotty pine and white tile with mounted gamefish on the walls. Since the establishment doubles as a fish market you can count on fresh seafood. The menu is the same at lunch and dinner with only the portions and prices changing. Mesquite-grilled dishes include mahimahi, scallops, swordfish, skewered shrimp, and steak. They also feature lobster, abalone, and orange roughy. You can dine indoors or on the patio right along the waterfront, making Armstrong's reasonable prices a bargain. ~ 306-A Crescent Avenue; 310-510-0113. MODERATE.

Café Prego, a small Italian bistro complete with oilcloth tables and stucco arches, comes highly recommended. The specialties are seafood and pasta; you'll find a menu offering fresh swordfish, sea bass, halibut, and snapper, plus manicotti, rigatoni, lasagna, and fettuccine. There are also steak and veal dishes at this waterfront nook. It features good food and a cozy ambience. ~ 609 Crescent Avenue; 310-510-1218. MODERATE TO DELUXE.

For a step upscale head down the street to **Ristorante Villa Portofino**. Here a baby grand piano is set off by pink stucco walls and the candlelit tables are decorated with flowers. With art deco curves and colorful art prints the place has an easy Mediterranean feel about it. The Continental cuisine includes several veal dishes, scampi, grilled filet mignon, swordfish, and a selection of pasta dishes. This is the place for a romantic dinner. ~ 111 Crescent Avenue; 310-510-0508. MODERATE TO DELUXE.

The **Runway Café**, situated up in the mountains at 1600 feet, is part of Catalina's Airport in the Sky complex. This facility serves egg dishes, hot cakes, buffalo burgers, and a variety of sandwiches. There's not much to the self-service restaurant itself, but it adjoins a lobby with stone fireplace and a tile patio that overlooks the surrounding mountains. No dinner. ~ 310-510-2196. BUDGET.

HIDDEN ►   Catalina's remotest dining place is **Doug's Harbor Reef Restaurant**, located way out in the Two Harbors area. This rambling establishment has a dining room done in nautical motif with fish nets, shell lamps, and woven *lauhala* mats. There's also an adjoining patio for enjoying the soft breezes that blow through this isthmus area. Doug's offers pork ribs, shrimp tempura, and chicken teriyaki. Prime rib and swordfish are local favorites and at lunch in the summer there are buffalo burgers. ~ Two Harbors; 310-510-0303. MODERATE TO DELUXE.

Next to Doug's there's an adjoining **snack bar** serving three meals daily; breakfast and lunch in winter months. It offers egg dishes, sandwiches, burgers, and burritos. ~ Two Harbors. BUDGET.

SHOPPING   No one sails to Santa Catalina Island searching for bargains. Everything here has been shipped from the mainland and is that much more expensive as a result. The town of Avalon has a row of shops lining its main thoroughfare, Crescent Avenue, and other stores along the streets running up from the waterfront. Within this commercial checkerboard are also several mini-malls, one of which, **Metropole Market Place**, is a nicely designed, modern complex. ~ Crescent and Whitney avenues.

Half the stores in town are either souvenir or curio shops. I'd wait until you return to that shopping metropolis 26 miles across the sea.

NIGHTLIFE   Like all other Catalina amenities, nightspots are concentrated in Avalon. During summer months the **Santa Catalina Island Company** conducts buffet cruises along the coastline in an old paddlewheeler. There are splendid sunsets, pretty views of the shore, music, and dancing. ~ Avalon Harbor Pier; 310-510-2000.

The **Chi Chi Club** is one of the hottest dance clubs on the island with live and deejay music (ranging from Top-40 and hip-hop to retro) and an enthusiastic crowd. ~ 107 Sumner Avenue; 310-510-2828.

There's also dancing to deejay tunes during the summer at **The Landing**. The motif is decidedly Mexican. ~ 101 Marilla Avenue; 310-510-1474.

Antonio's Cabaret hosts karaoke every night. ~ 230 Crescent Avenue; 310-510-0008. Also check the schedule for Avalon Casino. This fabulous vintage ballroom still hosts big bands and most of the island's major events. ~ Located at the end of Crescent Avenue; 310-510-2000.

If you are planning to camp on Catalina, there are a few things to know. First, there is a fee for camping and reservations are a must (reservation numbers are listed under the particular park).

BEACHES & PARKS

In addition to designated beaches, camping is permitted in many of the island's coves. These are undeveloped sites with no facilities; most readily accessible by boat. Patrolling rangers collect the fees here.

For information on hiking permits, camping, and transportation to campgrounds, contact the Santa Catalina Island Conservancy (125 Claressa Avenue, Avalon; 310-510-1421), the Catalina Cove and Camp Agency (P.O. Box 5044, Two Harbors; 310-510-0303), or the agent at Two Harbors Campground (310-510-2800) who seems to know just about everything relating to camping in the area.

CRESCENT BEACH About as relaxing as Coney Island, this beach is at the center of the action. Avalon's main drag parallels the beach and a pier divides it into two separate strips of sand. Facing Avalon Harbor, the strand is flanked on one side with a ferry dock and along the other by the famous Avalon Casino. Full service facilities (including restrooms, showers, and beach rentals) are available on the street adjacent to the beach; lifeguards are also on duty. Fishing is good from the pier, and the harbor provides protection from the surf, making it an excellent swimming area. ~ Located along Crescent Avenue in Avalon.

DESCANSO BEACH CLUB Somehow the appeal of this private enclave escapes me. A rock-strewn beach on the

TALLY HO. . .TEL!

Banning House Lodge, the only hotel on the island located outside Avalon, is a turn-of-the-century hunting lodge. Set in the isthmus that connects the two sections of Santa Catalina, it's a low-slung shingle building with a dining room, bar, and a mountain-lodge atmosphere. The living room boasts a brick fireplace and is adorned with a dozen trophy heads. Staring out dolefully from the wood-paneled walls are deer, bison, fox, wild turkey, boar, and mountain goats. The guest rooms are trimly decorated with throw rugs and rustic wood furniture. The lodge provides an excellent opportunity to experience the island's outback. Continental breakfast is served in the lodge's dining room. ~ Two Harbors; 310-510-0303. DELUXE TO ULTRA-DELUXE.

far side of the Avalon Casino, it seconds as a mooring facility for sailboats. Granted, there is a rolling lawn dotted with palm trees and the complex is nicely surrounded by hills. But with all the commotion at the snack bar and volleyball courts it's more like being on an amusement pier than a beach. Besides that, you have to pay to get onto the beach. Once there, you'll find good swimming, restrooms, a playground, and showers. The beach is closed weekdays during the winter. ~ Located off Crescent Avenue past the Avalon Casino; 310-510-2780.

HERMIT GULCH CAMPGROUND 🚶 This grassy field, dotted with palm and pine trees, is the only campground serving the Avalon area. Located up in Avalon Canyon inland from the beach, it provides a convenient and inexpensive way to visit Avalon and utilize its many services. There are pretty views of the surrounding hills and hiking trails are nearby. Facilities include picnic areas, restrooms, and showers; restaurants and groceries are nearby in Avalon. ~ On Avalon Canyon Road a mile from downtown Avalon; 310-510-2780.

▲ There are extensive camping facilities, ranging from A-frames to teepee sites to equipment rentals. There are 63 tent sites, $7.50 per person per night.

HIDDEN ► **BLACK JACK CAMPGROUND** 🚶🚵🏇 Situated at 1500 feet elevation, this facility sits on a plateau below Mt. Black Jack, the island's second highest peak. It's a lovely spot shaded by pine and eucalyptus trees and affording views across the rolling hills and out along the ocean. Among backcountry facilities this is about the most popular on the island. The campground has picnic areas, toilets, and showers; restaurants and groceries are way back in Avalon. ~ Located south of The Airport in the Sky off Airport Road. Seasonal shuttle available from Avalon to Black Jack trail junction; 310-510-2800.

▲ There is a hike-in campground; $6.50 per person per night.

HIDDEN ► **BEN WESTON BEACH** 🚶🏄🎣🎣 A favorite among locals, this pewter-colored beach is surrounded by rocky hills. Located at the end of a long canyon road, it is serene and secluded. Avalon residents come here to flee the tourists, so you might consider making it your hideaway. This is a day-use beach only. Fishing and swimming are good, and it is one of the island's best spots for surfing. Facilities are limited to toilets. ~ Located about two miles south of Little Harbor off Middle Ranch Road.

LITTLE HARBOR CAMPGROUND 🏄🛶🎣🎣 On the southwest shore of the island, this camp sits near a sandy beach between rocky headlands. It's studded with palm trees and occasionally filled with grazing bison, making it one of the island's prettiest facilities. In addition, Shark Harbor, a section of Little Harbor, is excellent for shell collecting and bodysurfing. Fishing, swimming and skindiving are good here; facilities include picnic areas, toilets, and cold showers.

Restaurants and groceries are in Two Harbors. ~ Located about six miles south of Two Harbors along Little Harbor Road; 310-510-2800.

▲ The campground has a 150-person maximum; tents only; $7.50 per person per night.

TWO HARBORS CAMPGROUND 🏃🚴🏊 ⚓ Set along a series of terraces above a brown sand beach, this facility is adjacent to the services at Two Harbors. It's also a convenient base camp from which to hike out along the island's west end. Facilities include picnic areas, restrooms, showers, lockers, laundry, and volleyball; restaurants and groceries are nearby. The fishing and swimming are good, and the colorful waters here make skindiving especially rewarding. ~ Located next to Two Harbors in Little Fisherman's Cove; 310-510-0303.

▲ The facilities here are extensive and include: 55 tent sites, tent cabins and teepees with added amenities, a 24-hour-a-day ranger, and more. Prices vary; call for information.

PARSON'S LANDING 🏃🚴🏊 ⚓ The most remote of Catalina's campgrounds, this isolated facility sits along a small brown sand beach with grass-covered hills in the background. Fishing, swimming, and skindiving are all good; facilities include picnic areas and toilets; restaurants and groceries are several miles away. ~ It's 6.8 miles west of Two Harbors along West End Road; 310-510-2800.

▲ The campground holds a maximum of 50 people with no assigned sites; tents only; $7.50 per person nightly.

Outdoor Adventures

SPORT-FISHING

Fish the waters around Los Angeles and you can try your hand at landing a barracuda, calico bass, halibut, white croaker, or maybe even a relative of Jaws.

For sportfishing outfits call **Belmont Pier Sportfishing**. ~ Termino and Ocean avenues, Belmont Shore; 310-434-6781. In San Pedro try **L.A. Harbor Sportfishing**. ~ Berth 79, San Pedro; 310-547-9916, 310-832-2274. In Long Beach, the place to call is **Long Beach Sportfishing**. ~ 555 Pico Avenue, Long Beach; 310-432-8993. **Redondo Sportfishing** serves the Redondo-Hermosa area. ~ 233 North Harbor Drive, Redondo Beach; 310-372-2111. In Marina del Rey go with **Marina del Rey Sportfishing**. ~ 13759 Fiji Way, Marina del Rey; 310-822-3625.

In Catalina you can contact the **Santa Catalina Island Chamber of Commerce and Visitors Bureau** for listings of private boat owners who outfit sportfishing expeditions. ~ 310-510-1520.

DIVING

If you'd rather search for starfish than stars along L.A.'s coastline, you'll find an active diving scene.

To explore Los Angeles' submerged depths, call **Pacific Sporting Goods**. ~ 11 39th Place, Long Beach; 310-434-1604. In San Pedro dive with **Pacific Wilderness Ocean Sports**. ~ 1719 South Pacific Avenue, San Pedro; 310-833-2422. In Redondo Beach, try **Dive 'n Surf**. ~ 504 North Broadway, Redondo Beach; 310-372-8423. Another option is **Sea D Sea**. ~ 1911 South Catalina Avenue, Redondo Beach; 310-373-6355. **Blue Cheer Ocean Water Sports** runs trips from Santa Monica. ~ 1110 Wilshire Boulevard, Santa Monica; 310-828-1217. Or call **Scuba Haus**. ~ 2501 Wilshire Boulevard, Santa Monica; 310-828-2916. In Malibu call **Malibu Divers** to rent gear and/or take a dive trip. ~ 21231 Pacific Coast Highway, Malibu; 310-456-2396.

Without doubt Santa Catalina offers some of the finest scuba diving anywhere in the world. Perfectly positioned to attract fish from both the northern and southern Pacific, it teems with sea life. Large fish ascend from the deep waters surrounding the island while small colorful species inhabit rich kelp forests along the coast. There are caves and caverns to explore as well as the wrecks of rusting ships.

Several outfits rent skindiving and scuba equipment and/or sponsor dive trips. In Avalon call **Catalina Divers Supply**. ~ 310-510-0330. There's also **Island Charters, Inc.** ~ 310-510-0600. A third option is **Argo Diving Service**. ~ 310-510-2208. In Two Harbors try the **Dive Shop**. ~ 310-510-2800.

WHALE WATCHING

If you're visiting Los Angeles during the late fall or winter, hop aboard a whale-watching vessel and keep your eyes peeled for plumes and tails.

During the annual whale migration several outfits offer whale-watching trips. **Mickey's Belmont, Inc.** can take you from Long Beach. ~ Belmont Pier, Long Beach; 310-434-6781. So can **Long Beach Sportfishing**. ~ 555 Pico Avenue, Long Beach; 310-432-8993. Another outfitter is **Catalina Cruises**. ~ 320 Golden Shore, Long Beach; 310-436-5006. Out of San Pedro, try **Los Angeles Harbor Cruise**. ~ Berth 78, San Pedro; 310-831-0996. Or have a whale of a time with **Spirit Cruises**. ~ Berth 77, San Pedro; 310-831-1073. There's also **L.A. Harbor Sportfishing**. ~ Berth 79, San Pedro; 310-547-9916.

WIND-SURFING & SURFING

"Surfing is the only life," so when in the southland, sample a bit of Los Angeles' seminal subculture; remember, it's more fun to hang ten than just hang out. Grab a board from **Fun Bunns**. ~ 1116 Manhattan Avenue, Manhattan Beach; 310-372-8500. In Hermosa Beach, there's **Jeffers**. ~ 39 14th Street, Hermosa Beach; 310-372-9492. Up in Malibu try **Zuma Jay Surfboards**. ~ 22775 Pacific Coast Highway, Malibu; 310-456-8044.

SKATING & SKATE BOARDING

Los Angeles may well be the roller skating capital of California, and skateboarding, of course, is the closest thing to surfing without waves. Between the two of them, you can't get much more L.A., so find a way to put yourself on wheels.

To rent skates or a skate board call **Fun Bunns**. ~ 1116 Manhattan Avenue, Manhattan Beach; 310-372-8500. Or try **Rollerskates of America**. ~ 1312 Hermosa Avenue, Hermosa Beach; 310-372-8812. **Spokes 'n Stuff** has three convenient locations. ~ At the parking lot on Admiralty Way at Jamaica Bay Inn Hotel, Marina del Rey, 310-306-3332; 36 Washington Boulevard, Venice; and near the Santa Monica Pier in Loews Santa Monica, 310-395-4748. Also in Santa Monica is **Sea Mist Skate Rentals**. ~ 1619 Ocean Front Walk, Santa Monica Pier, Santa Monica; 310-395-7076.

GOLF

Tee off in the gentle sea breeze—L.A.'s coastal climate is ideal for spending a day on the greens. Just don't swing too hard, because those golf balls don't float!

Try **El Dorado Park Municipal Golf Course**. ~ 2400 Studebaker Road, Long Beach; 310-430-5411. **Skylink Golf Course** is a duffer's delight. ~ 4800 East Wardlow Road, Long Beach; 310-421-3388. Also in Long Beach is **Recreation Park**. ~ 5000 East Anaheim Street, Long Beach; 310-494-5000. On the Palos Verdes Peninsula, there's **Los Verdes Golf Course**. ~ 7000 West Los Verdes Drive, Rancho Palos Verdes; 310-377-7370. If you can take a break from the action in Venice, head to **Penmar Golf Course**. ~ 1233 Rose Avenue, Venice; 310-396-6228. In Catalina call **Catalina Visitors Golf Club**. ~ 1 Country Club Drive, Avalon; 310-510-0530.

TENNIS

A visit to the Los Angeles coast is reason enough to re-string your racquet and start enjoying the weather; these waterfront communities sport an abundance of courts.

There are public tennis courts available in **El Dorado Park**. ~ 2800 Studebaker Road, Long Beach; 310-425-0553. Also in Long Beach is **Billie Jean King Tennis Center**. ~ 1040 Park Avenue, Long Beach; 310-438-8509. Try **Alta Vista Tennis Courts** in Redondo Beach. ~ 715 Julia Avenue, Redondo Beach; 310-318-0670. Or serve and swing at **The Sport Center at King Harbor**. ~ 819 North Harbor Drive, Redondo Beach; 310-372-8868. **Marina Tennis Center** is the place in Marina del Rey. ~ 13199 Mindanao Way, Marina del Rey; 310-822-2255. In Santa Monica, check out **Lincoln Park**. ~ 1133 7th Street, Santa Monica; 310-394-6011. There's also **Memorial Park**. ~ Colorado Boulevard at 14th Street, Santa Monica; 310-394-6011. Another option is **Ocean View Park**. ~ Barnard Way south of Ocean Park Boulevard, Santa Monica; 310-394-6011.

BIKING

Though Los Angeles might seem like one giant freeway, there are scores of shoreline bike trails and routes for scenic excursions. Whether you're up for a leisurely and level beachfront loop, or a more strenuous trek through coastal cliffside communities, the weather and scenery make this area a beautiful place for a bike ride.

Foremost is the **South Bay Bike Trail**, with over 22 miles of coastal vistas. The trail, an easy ride and extremely popular, runs from RAT Beach in Torrance to Will Rogers State Beach in Pacific Palisades. The path intersects the Ballona Creek Bikeway in Marina Del Rey, which extends seven miles east and passes the Venice Boardwalk, as well as piers and marinas along the way.

Naples, a Venice-like neighborhood in Long Beach, provides a charming area for freeform bike rides. There are no designated paths but you can cycle with ease past beautiful homes, parks, and canals.

Of moderate difficulty is the **Palos Verdes Peninsula** coastline trail. Offering wonderful scenery, the 14-mile round trip ride goes from Malaga Cove Plaza in Palos Verdes Estates to the Wayfarers Chapel. (Part of the trail is a bike path, the rest follows city streets.)

The **Santa Monica Loop** is an easy ride starting at Ocean Avenue and going up San Vicente Boulevard, past Palisades Park and the Santa Monica Pier. Most of the trail is on bike lanes and paths; ten miles round trip.

In **Catalina**, free use of bikes is allowed only in Avalon. Elsewhere permits are required: they may be obtained free of charge from the **Catalina Conservancy**. ~ P.O. Box 2739, Avalon, CA 90704; 310-510-1421. Cross-channel carriers have special requirements for transporting bicycles and must be contacted in advance for complete details.

For maps, brochures, and additional information on bike routes in Los Angeles contact the **Department of Transportation**. ~ 207 South Broadway; 213-485-4277.

Bike Rentals To rent bikes try **Fun Bunns**. ~ 1116 Manhattan Avenue, Manhattan Beach; 310-372-8500. In Hermosa Beach there's **Jeffers**. ~ 39 14th Street, Hermosa Beach; 310-372-9492. **Spokes 'n Stuff** has three locations. ~ At the parking lot on Admiralty Way at Jamaica Bay Inn Hotel, Marina del Rey, 310-306-3332; 36 Washington Boulevard, Venice; and near the pier in Loews Santa Monica, 310-395-4748. Also in Santa Monica is **Sea Mist Skate Rentals**. ~ 1619 Ocean Front Walk, Santa Monica; 310-395-7076. In Catalina try **Brown's Bikes**. ~ 107 Pebbly Beach Road, Avalon; 310-510-0986.

HIKING

Depending on where you go for your hike, you may want your boots, spiffy street shoes, or Tevas. The terrain of this region offers a wide array of pedestrian options, from beaches and tidepools to busy boardwalks to the trails of the rugged coast range. For a unique foray, try exploring a beached shipwreck or hiking in to the familiar-looking filming location of *M.A.S.H.* The only common denominators for hiking around here are the fine weather and sweeping vistas. All distances listed are one way unless otherwise noted.

The Los Angeles portion of the **California Coastal Trail** begins on Naples Island in Long Beach. From here the trail is a varied journey across open bluffs, boat basins, rocky outcroppings accessible only at low tide, along beachwalks filled with roller skaters, jugglers, and skate boarders, and up goat trails with stunning views of the Pacific Ocean.

PALOS VERDES PENINSULA   Set beneath wave-carved bluffs, the **Palos Verdes Peninsula Trail** (5 miles) takes you along a rocky beachside trail past coves and teeming tidepools. The trail begins at Malaga Cove and ends at Point Vicente Lighthouse.

If you're interested in exploring a shipwreck, head to Palos Verdes Estate Shoreline Preserve, near Malaga Cove, and hike the **Seashore–Shipwreck Trail** (2.25 miles). The trail hugs the shoreline (and requires an ability to jump boulders), skirting tidepools and coves, until it arrives at what is left of an old Greek ship, the *Dominator*.

SANTA MONICA MOUNTAINS   It is difficult to imagine, but Los Angeles does have undeveloped mountain wilderness areas prime for trekking. The Santa Monica Mountains offer chaparral-covered landscapes, grassy knolls, mountain streams, and dark canyons.

When visiting Will Rogers State Historic Park, take a walk down **Inspiration Point Trail** (2 miles) for a view overlooking the Westside.

Topanga Canyon State Park has over 32 miles of trails. The **Musch Ranch Loop Trail** (4 miles) passes through five different types of plant communities. Or try the **Santa Ynez Canyon Trail** (6.6 miles), which guides you along the Palisades Highlands with views of the ocean and Santa Ynez Canyon. In spring wildflowers add to the already spectacular scenery.

Several trails trace the "backbone" of the Santa Monica Mountains. In fact, conservationists are trying to secure a trail that extends from Will Rogers State Historic Park to Point Mugu State Park. Presently, you will have to be happy with routes that hop, skip, and jump through the area.

Eagle Rock to Eagle Springs Loop Trail (4 miles), for instance, begins in Topanga State Park and traverses oak and chaparral countryside on its way to Eagle Spring. Another section of the "Backbone

◆◆◆

✔ CHECK THESE OUT—UNIQUE OUTDOOR ADVENTURES

- Exercise your soles and your sole by hiking the **California Coastal Trail**, with its beautiful bluffs, basins, and beachwalks. *page 194*
- Take the plunge in the waters off **Santa Catalina Island**, where scuba divers discover kelp forests, sunken ships, and underwater caverns. *page 192*
- Roll past the scene on the **Venice boardwalk**, where roller skating and biking offer you a way to see the most in the shortest time. *page 156*
- Get in the middle of the most amazing commute in Southern California, the annual migration of the big greys, on a whale-watching cruise from **Long Beach** or **San Pedro**. *page 192*

Trail," **Tapia Park–Malibu Creek State Park Loop** (12 miles) begins near Tapia Park, just off of Malibu Canyon Road. The trail follows fire roads and offers choice views of the ocean and Channel Islands before it winds into Malibu Creek Canyon. **Charmlee Park** is a little-visited wildflower paradise in the hills overlooking the ocean. A 1.75-mile trail offers great coastal views. Take Encinal Canyon Road four miles into the mountains from Pacific Coast Highway. **Solstice Canyon Park**, operated by the Santa Monica Mountains Conservancy, is another hidden beauty with trails offering hikes of up to six miles. The three-mile round trip to the Roberts Ranch House ruins follows a perennial stream and ends at the burned-out remains of a terraced dream house that retains a palm-shaded charm. Take Corral Canyon Road a quarter-mile north from Pacific Coast Highway.

HIDDEN ►

HIDDEN ►

For a nostalgic visit to the location of many movie and television shows, including *M.A.S.H.* and *Love Is A Many Splendored Thing*, check out the **Century Ranch Trail** (2.3 miles) in Malibu Creek State Park. The trail travels along Malibu Creek to Rock Pool, the Gorge, and Century Lake.

An easy climb up **Zuma Ridge Trail** (6.3 miles) brings you to the center of the Santa Monica Mountains and affords otherworldly views of the Pacific. The trail begins off Encinal Canyon Road, 1.5 miles from Mulholland Highway.

MALIBU **Zuma-Dume Trail** (1 mile) in Malibu takes you from Zuma Beach County Park, along Pirate's Cove (which used to be a nude beach) to the Point Dume headlands and Paradise Cove, a popular diving spot.

For a pleasant hike along part of the Malibu coast dotted with coves and caves and providing terrific swimming, surfing, and skindiving, head out the **Leo Carrillo Trail** (1.5 miles), located at Leo Carrillo State Beach. Or to hike up a gently sloping hill for a view of the coastline, take the nearby **Oceanview Loop Trail** (2 miles).

SANTA CATALINA ISLAND For a true adventure in hiking, gather your gear and head for Santa Catalina. A network of spectacular trails crisscrosses this largely undeveloped island. Bring plenty of water and beware of rattlesnakes and poison oak. You'll also need a hiking permit (see the "Santa Catalina Island" section in this chapter).

Empire Landing Road Trail (11.5 miles) begins at Black Jack Junction and ends up at Two Harbors. The path passes a lot of interesting terrain and provides glimpses of island wildlife, especially buffalo. (You can arrange with the ferry service to ride back to the mainland from Two Harbors.)

Other routes to consider are **Sheep Chute Trail** (3.3 miles), a moderate hike between Little Harbor and Empire Landing; and **Boushay Road** (2.1 miles), a strenuous trek between Silver Peak Trail and Parsons Landing.

Route 1, which parallels the coast throughout Los Angeles County, undergoing several name changes during its course, is the main coastal route. Route 101 shadows the coast further inland, while Route 405 provides access to the Los Angeles basin from San Diego and Route 10 arrives from the east.

▼▼▼▼▼▼▼▼▼▼
Transportation

CAR

Two airports bring visitors to the Los Angeles coast area: the small Long Beach Airport and the very big, very busy Los Angeles International Airport (LAX). (See Chapter Two for information pertaining to LAX.)

AIR

Presently, carriers into Long Beach are America West, Great America Airways, SunJet International, and United Airlines.

The Airport in the Sky, set at 1600-foot elevation in the mountains of Santa Catalina, may be the prettiest landing strip anywhere. The small terminal building conveys a mountain lodge atmosphere with a stone fireplace adorned by a trophy bison head. ~ 310-510-0143. National Air, also called Catalina Vegas Airlines, services the airport from the mainland. ~ 619-292-7311.

Another means of transportation to Catalina is Island Express, a helicopter service from Long Beach and San Pedro. They also offer around-the-island tours. ~ 310-510-2525.

Several companies provide regular transportation to Catalina by boat. The island is just "26 miles across the sea," but it's still necessary to make advance reservations. Catalina Express has service to Avalon and Two Harbors from the Catalina Terminal in San Pedro, from Long Beach next to the *Queen Mary* and from the Redondo Beach Marina. ~ 310-519-1212. Catalina Cruises travels from the Catalina Landing in Long Beach to Two Harbors and Avalon. ~ San Pedro; 310-436-5006. Catalina Passenger Service has service from Orange County. Catalina Passenger Service provides transportation only from Easter through October with weekend service December 26 to Easter. ~ 400 Main Street, Newport Beach; 714-673-5245.

BOAT

Greyhound Bus Lines has service to the Los Angeles area from around the country. The Long Beach terminal is at 464 West 3rd Street (310-432-1842), and the Los Angeles terminal is at 1716 East 7th Street (213-629-8400).

BUS

At the Long Beach Airport are Avis Rent A Car (310-988-3255, 800-331-1212), Budget Rent A Car (310-421-0143, 800-527-0700), Enterprise Rent A Car (310-421-8841, 800-325-8007), Hertz Rent A Car (310-420-2322, 800-654-3131), and National Interrent (310-421-8877, 800-227-7368). Located outside the Long Beach Airport, Enterprise Rent A Car (310-496-1230, 800-325-8007) will pick you up from the airport and deliver you to their car lot.

CAR RENTALS

To save even more money, try agencies that rent used cars. In the Long Beach area this includes **Robin Hood Rent A Car**. ~ 310-518-9807.

In Catalina, golf carts are the only vehicles permitted for sightseeing in Avalon. Check with **Catalina Auto and Bike Rental**. ~ 301 Crescent Avenue; 310-510-0111. **Island Rentals** is another option. ~ 125 Pebbly Beach Road; 310-510-1456. For further information on vehicle rentals on Catalina see the "Santa Catalina Island" section in this chapter.

PUBLIC TRANSIT

Long Beach Transit transports riders throughout the Long Beach area. Among the services is the Long Beach Runabout Shuttle Van, which carries visitors between major points of interest. ~ 1300 Gardenia Avenue, Long Beach; 310-591-2301. MTA **Bus Line** serves the Los Angeles area from Topanga Beach south; disabled riders can call a hotline for information, 800-621-7828 (this number is functional only within the designated area). ~ 425 South Main Street, Los Angeles; 213-626-4455. In Santa Monica, call the **Big Blue Bus**. ~ Santa Monica Municipal Bus Lines, 1660 7th Street; 310-451-5444. In Catalina, **Catalina Safari Bus** provides daily buses from Avalon to Two Harbors and all campgrounds. This shuttle service also takes passengers from Avalon to the Airport in the Sky. ~ 310-510-2800.

TAXIS

Long Beach Yellow Cab provides taxi service in Long Beach. ~ 310-435-6111. In Catalina you'll find the **Catalina Cab Company**. ~ 310-510-0025.

FOUR

Orange County

Places are known through their nicknames. More than official titles or proper names, sobriquets reveal the real identity of a region. "Orange Coast" can never describe the 42 miles of cobalt blue ocean and whitewashed sand from Seal Beach to San Clemente. That moniker derives from the days when Orange County was row on row with orchards of plump citrus. Today prestigious homes and marinas sprout from the shoreline. This is the "Gold Coast," habitat of beachboys, yachtsmen, and tennis buffs, the "American Riviera."

The theme that ties the territory together and gives rise to these nicknames is money. Money and the trappings that attend it—glamour, celebrity, elegance, power. Orange County is a sun-blessed realm of beautiful people, where politics is rightwing and real estate sells by the square foot.

Some half-dozen freeways crisscross the broad coastal plane where Spain's Gaspar de Portolá led the first overland expedition into present-day Orange County in 1769. Today, more than two million people live, work, and play where during the mid-19th century a few hundred Mexican ranchers tended herds of livestock on a handful of extensive land grants.

Ever since Walt Disney founded his fantasy empire here in the 1950s, Orange County has exploded with population and profits. In Disney's wake came the crowds, and as they arrived they developed housing projects and condominium complexes, mini-malls and business centers. To the interior, towns now look alike and Orange County, once an empire of orange groves, has become a cookie-cutter civilization. Only in the distant mountain areas to the south and east does any wilderness remain. Here the granite escarpments, oak-studded valleys, and chaparral-covered hillsides of the Santa Ana Mountains continue to hold out against the encroachment of suburban blight.

Along the coast progress also levied a tremendous toll but has left intact some of the natural beauty, the deep canyons and curving hills, soft sand beaches and sharp escarpments. The towns too have retained their separate styles, each projecting its own identifying image.

Seal Beach, Orange County's answer to small-town America, is a pretty community with a sense of serenity. To the south lies Huntington Beach, a place that claims the nickname "Surfing Capital of the World." The social capital of this beachside society is Newport Beach, a fashion-conscious center for celebrities, business mavens, and those to whom God granted little patience and a lot of money.

Corona del Mar is a model community with quiet streets and a placid waterfront. Laguna Beach is an artist colony so *in* that real estate prices have driven the artists *out*. Dana Point represents a marina development in search of a soul. San Juan Capistrano, a small town surrounding an old mission, is closer to its roots than any place in this futuristic area. San Clemente, which served as President Nixon's Western White House, is a trim, strait-laced residential community. Linking this string of beach towns together is Route 1, the Pacific Coast Highway, which runs south from Los Angeles to Capistrano Beach.

The geography throughout Orange County is varied and unpredictable. Around Newport Beach and Huntington Beach, rugged heights give way to low-lying terrain cut by rivers and opening into estuaries. These northerly towns, together with Dana Point, are manmade harbors carved from swamps and surrounded by landfill islands and peninsulas. Huntington Harbor, the first of its kind, consists of eight islands weighted down with luxury homes and bordered by a mazework of marinas. To the south, particularly around Laguna Beach, a series of uplifted marine terraces create bold headlands, coastal bluffs, and pocket coves.

Land here is so highly prized that it's not surprising the city fathers chose to create more by dredging it from river bottoms. The Gabrieleño and Juañero Indians who originally inhabited the area considered the ground sacred, while the Spanish who conquered them divided it into two immense land grants, the San Joaquin and Niguel ranchos.

Establishing themselves at the San Juan Capistrano mission in 1776, the Spanish padres held sway until the 19th century. By the 1830s American merchants from the East Coast were sending tall-masted trading ships up from Cape Horn. Richard Henry Dana, who sailed the shoreline, giving his name to Dana Point, described the area in *Two Years Before the Mast* as "the most romantic spot along the coast."

Orange County's first real spurt of growth came in the late 1850s when European immigrants, inspired by the agricultural successes of Franciscan missionaries, left the worked-out gold fields of the north to try their luck farming the fertile soil of the Santa Ana River Valley. German immigrants formed a successful winegrowing colony at Anaheim in 1857 and soon began planting the citrus trees which would eventually give the county its name.

By the 1860s, after California became a state, the Spanish ranchos were joined into the Irvine Ranch, a land parcel extending ten miles along the coast and 22 miles inland, and controlled with a steel fist by a single family.

They held in their sway all but Laguna Beach, which was settled in the 1870s by pioneers developing 160-acre government land grants. A freestyle community, Laguna developed into an artist colony filled with galleries and renowned for its cliff-rimmed beaches. Over the years artists and individualists—including LSD guru Timothy Leary and a retinue of hippies, who arrived during the 1960s—have been lured by the simple beauty of the place.

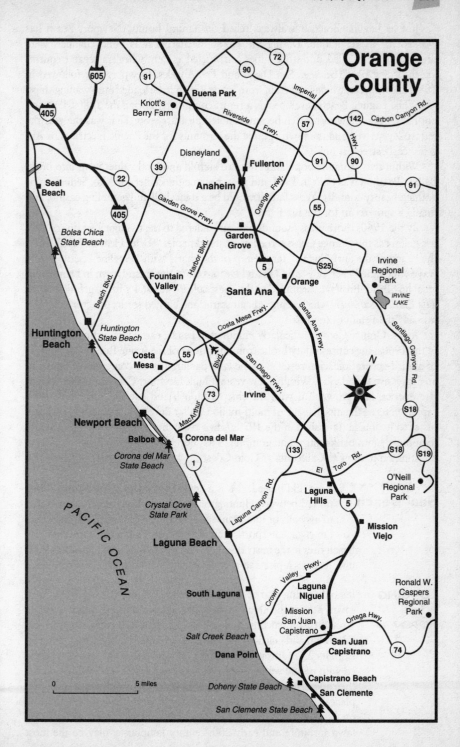

Orange County

Just as Laguna Beach has always relied on natural beauty, Newport Beach has worked for its reputation. During the 1870s the harbor was built; channels were dredged, marshes filled, and stone jetties constructed as stern-wheelers began frequenting the "new port" between San Diego and Los Angeles. Newport Pier followed in 1888, allowing cattle hides and grain from Irvine Ranch to be loaded onto waiting ships.

While Laguna Beach developed as a resort community during the 1880s, it wasn't until 1904 that Newport Beach became a noted pleasure stop. That was the year the red trolley arrived and the town became the terminus for the Pacific Electric, Los Angeles' early streetcar line.

Within two years the population jumped sixfold and land values went into orbit. Balboa Pavilion was built in 1905 and soon became the center for Max Sennett–type bathing beauty contests. Years later it would be a dancehall and gambling casino, and finally a showroom for the Big Bands.

By the 1960s those brassy sounds had surrendered to the twanging strains of electric guitars as the Orange Coast earned its final nickname, "Surfer Heaven." Dick Dale, the "King of the Surf Guitar," hit the top of the charts with "Pipeline," setting off a wave which the Beach Boys and Jan and Dean rode to the crest. Down in Dana Point local boy Bruce Brown contributed to the coast culture in 1964 with a surf flick called *The Endless Summer*, which achieved cult status and earned for its director a reputation as "the Fellini of foam."

As the Orange Coast, particularly Huntington Beach, earned its surfing reputation in the 1960s, the entire county broke from the power of the Irvine Ranch. The suicide of a third-generation scion resulted in the land passing from a conservative family to an aggressive foundation. Within a few years it built Newport Center, the area's high-rise district, and crowned it with the chic Fashion Island enclave. Orange County rapidly entered the modern age of multi-million-dollar development, adding a certain luster to its image (tarnished in the 1990s when risky investments forced the county temporarily into bankruptcy) and granting to its shoreline, for better or worse, an everlasting reputation as California's "Gold Coast."

▼▼▼▼▼▼▼▼▼
Seal Beach

Rare find indeed, this is a small town with a small-town beach tucked between Huntington Beach and Long Beach. In addition to a swath of fine-grain sand, there is a fishing pier from which you can engage in sportfishing. Oil derricks loom offshore and Long Beach rises in the misty distance. The beach, located along Ocean Avenue, features a pier and is popular with swimmers and surfers alike.

LODGING

HIDDEN ►

It's only fitting that Seal Beach, Orange County's answer to a small town, houses the area's most appealing bed and breakfast. With its wrought-iron balcony, ornate fence, and garden ambience, the **Seal Beach Inn and Gardens** has garnered a reputation for style and seclusion. Its 23 rooms are furnished in hardwood antiques and appointed with period wallhangings. Guests breakfast in a cozy "tea room," then adjourn to the parlor with its upholstered armchairs and tile fireplace. The guest rooms are named for flowers, many of which grow on the grounds. Indeed the landscaping, which includes wrought-iron lawn furniture and early-20th-century lampposts, may be the most appealing feature of this fine old inn. ~ 212 5th Street; 310-493-2416, 800-443-3292, fax 310-799-0483. DELUXE TO ULTRA-DELUXE.

Dating back to 1930, the **Glide 'er Inn** is an unusual landmark indeed. The motif is aviation, as in model airplanes dangling from the ceiling and aeronautical pictures covering every inch of available wall space. The menu is covered with biplanes and, almost as an afterthought, includes an extensive list of seafood selections as well as European dishes like wienerschnitzel, bouillabaisse, and veal *smetana* (sautéed in light cream and mushrooms). ~ 1400 Coast Highway; 310-431-3022. MODERATE.

DINING

Walt's Wharf restaurant specializes in creative seafood dishes but there's also Walt's oyster bar with a premium well and over 40 imported beers. Start off with appetizers such as the blackened ahi sashimi or the oak-grilled artichoke. Entreés vary with the catch of the day but may include oak-grilled Chilean sea bass with roasted macadamia nut sauce and steamed asparagus, or blackened Louisiana catfish with cilantro cream and fried polenta. ~ 201 Main Street; 310-598-4433. MODERATE TO DELUXE.

Hennessey's Tavern is Seal Beach's neighborhood meetingplace and watering hole (especially on St. Patrick's Day). Serving breakfast, lunch, and dinner, it specializes in hamburgers, hot sandwiches and fish and chips. ~ 140 Main Street; 310-598-4419. BUDGET.

▼▼▼▼▼▼▼▼▼▼▼▼
Huntington Beach

In most of Orange County, a reference to "Duke" will conjure images of John Wayne, former resident and namesake of the airport here; in Huntington Beach, however, natives are more likely to assume you're talking about Duke Kahanamoku, the Hawaiian Olympic swimmer who brought the sport of surfing to the mainland in 1911. His bust stands at the foot of the Huntington Beach Pier, and his legacy continues through the international surfing competitions held here. At the surfing museum, located a few blocks from the beach, you can learn anything else you want to know about the history and culture of the sport. There are, of course, many other ways to enjoy the beautiful coastline here: you can pedal the bike paths, dig for Pismo clams, hike in a wetlands preserve, and warm up at beach bonfires in the evening. But no matter what you do, you'll encounter surfing in some shape or form, even if it's only to admire a wave rider in the distance or watch a "woody," loaded with boards, driving through the streets. While the official story is that the discovery of offshore oil made Huntington Beach the largest city in Orange County, beach bums will argue that it was the discovery of how to ride the onshore breaks.

As Route 1 buzzes south from Los Angeles it is bordered on one side by broad beaches and on the other by **Bolsa Chica Ecological Reserve**. An important wetlands area dotted with islands and overgrown

SIGHTS

in cord grass and pickleweed, this 300-acre preserve features a mile-and-a-half-long loop trail. Among the hundreds of animal species inhabiting or visiting the marsh are egrets, herons, and five endangered species. There are raucous seagulls as well as rare Belding's savannah sparrows and California least terns. There is an Interpretive Center with scientific displays, educational material, and trail guides. ~ The accessways are across from the entrance to Bolsa Chica State Beach and at Warner Avenue.

Leave this natural world behind and you will enter the surf capital of California. In the mythology of surfing, Huntington Beach rides with Hawaii's Waimea Bay and the great breaks of Australia. Since the 1920s boys with boards have been as much a part of the seascape as blue skies and billowing clouds.

Synonymous with Huntington Beach is the **Huntington Beach Pier**. First built in 1904 for oil drilling purposes, it has been damaged by storms and extensively repaired four times. The last monster storm hit in 1988, when 20-foot waves tore 250 feet from the end of the pier. The new pier, which opened in July 1992, is 1856 feet long, 38 feet above the water, and has a life expectancy of 100 years. But, as anyone who has lived by the ocean will agree, that century-long life span could be shortened dramatically by the next winter storm. ~ At the end of Main Street.

Stop in at the **International Surfing Museum Huntington Beach** for a historic perspective on Southern California's favorite pastime. The showplace sits two blocks from the beach and features boards, boards, and more boards as well as an array of surfing paraphernalia. For those with a keen interest in the surfing culture, the museum gift shop sells the one and only *Surfin'ary* by Trevor Cralle (Ten Speed Press), a dictionary of surfing terminology that will teach you how to do the "Huntington Hop" and explain why they're calling you "ho'daddy" down at the beach. Closed Monday and Tuesday in the winter. Admission. ~ 411 Olive Avenue; 714-960-3483.

✔ CHECK THESE OUT—UNIQUE SIGHTS

At the **Newland House Museum** visitors can see what life in 19th-century Huntington Beach was all about. Listed on the National Register of Historic Places and built in 1898, the grand dame is filled with furnishings and antiques from the town's early days. Closed Monday, Tuesday, and Friday. ~ 19820 Beach Boulevard; 714-962-5777.

LODGING

The **Colonial Inn Youth Hostel** is a cavernous three-story house located four blocks from the beach. Capable of accommodating couples and families as well as individual travelers, its many rooms each contain two to eight beds. The house is in a residential neighborhood and has a kitchen, dining room, TV room, washer, dryer, yard and barbecue. ~ 421 8th Street; 714-536-3315, fax 714-536-9485. BUDGET.

Sunset Bed and Breakfast is a tiny six-room hostelry right on the highway in Huntington Beach. Decorated in bed-and-breakfast fashion, it has individual rooms as well as accommodations with bedroom-sitting room combinations. Features like overhead fans, oak armoires, and handwrought headboards add to the ambience. ~ 16401 Coast Highway; 310-592-1666. BUDGET TO MODERATE.

DINING

For a quick meal near the water, try **Maxie's**. This easygoing eatery is an all-American establishment serving omelettes in the morning, then hamburgers, hot dogs, sandwiches, and pizza the rest of the day. ~ 317 Pacific Coast Highway; 714-536-5127. BUDGET.

At **Louise's Trattoria** you can dine on fine Italian cuisine for reasonable prices. Try one of their fresh pasta dishes, such as rigatoni with grilled vegetables tossed in olive oil, or a California-style pizza with one of their inventive salads. The restaurant is open and airy with modern decor, plenty of windows, and a patio overlooking the ocean for open-air dining. ~ 300 Pacific Coast Highway; 714-960-0996. BUDGET TO MODERATE.

◀ *HIDDEN*

Harbor House Café is one of those hole-in-the-wall places packed with local folks. In this case it's "open 24 hours, 365 days a year" and has been around since 1939. Add knotty-pine walls covered with black-and-whites of your favorite movies stars and you've got a coastal classic. The menu, as you have surmised, includes hamburgers and sandwiches. Actually, it's pretty varied—in addition to pita bread and croissant sandwiches there are Mexican dishes, seafood platters, chicken entrées, and omelettes. ~ 16341 Coast Highway; 310-592-5404. BUDGET TO MODERATE.

Bonadonna's Cornerstone offers an alternative to the casual Huntington Beach scene. Their specialties come straight out of rustic Italia—*scallopini marsala* (thinly sliced veal topped with marsala wine sauce) or scampi over angelhair pasta. ~ 520 Main Street; 714-960-8091. BUDGET TO MODERATE.

NIGHTLIFE

Located at the Waterfront Hilton Beach Resort, the **West Coast Club** is what one might call a gentlemen's club. Featuring light jazz and a fireplace, it's a perfect spot for unwinding. ~ 21100 Pacific Coast Highway, Huntington Beach; 714-960-7873.

BEACHES & PARKS

SURFSIDE BEACH 🏖️ 🐟 🏊 🛶 **AND SUNSET BEACH** 🏖️ 🏊 🛶 These contiguous strands extend over three miles along the ocean side of Huntington Harbor. Broad carpets of cushioning sand, they are lined with beach houses and lifeguard stands. Both are popular with local people. But Surfside, which fronts a private community and lacks facilities, is still a great beach to get away from the crowds. Sunset Beach has restrooms and lifeguards; restaurants and groceries are nearby. Swimming and surfing are good at both beaches, although spectacular winter breaks near the jetty at the end of Surfside Beach make it the better choice during that season. For fishing, Sunset is the best bet. ~ Surfside runs north from Anderson Street, which provides the only public access to the beach; Sunset is off the Pacific Coast Highway, extending from Warner Avenue to Anderson Street in Huntington Beach.

BOLSA CHICA STATE BEACH 🏃 🚴 🏖️ 🏊 🛶 With three miles of fluffy sand, this is another in a series of broad, beautiful beaches. There are seasonal grunion runs and rich clam beds here; the beach is backdropped by the **Bolsa Chica Ecological Reserve**, an important wetlands area. Since the summer surf is gentler here than at Huntington Beach, Bolsa Chica is ideal for swimmers and families. You'll find picnic areas, restrooms, lifeguards, outdoor showers, snack bars, and beach rentals—and all these facilities do come with a cost. Restaurants and groceries are nearby in Huntington Beach. The fishing is good year-round at Bolsa Chica; swimming is better in the summer. For surfing, there are small waves in summer and big breaks in winter. Day-use fee, $5. ~ Located along Coast Highway between Warner Avenue and Huntington Pier in Huntington Beach; 714-846-3460.

▲ There are 63 sites for self-contained vehicles only (no hookups); $18 per night. Reservations may be made by calling DESTINET at 800-444-7275.

HUNTINGTON CITY BEACH 🚴 🏖️ 🏊 🛶 An urban continuation of the state beach to the south, this strand runs for several miles. This is one of the most famous surfing spots in the world. The Huntington Pier, completely renovated and extended to over 600 yards in length, is the pride of the city. The surrounding waters are crowded with surfers in wet suits. A great place for water sports and people-watching. This surfer heaven gives way to an industrial inferno north of the pier where the oil derricks that plague offshore waters climb right up onto the beach, making it look more like the Texas coast than the blue Pacific.

So stay south of the pier and make use of the fire pits, lifeguards, restrooms and outdoor showers, volleyball courts, and beach rentals. Swimming is good here if you can find a time when the swells aren't too big, but the surf pumps year-round here, and international competitions are held throughout the summer months and in September. Restaurants and fishing tackle shops are nearby in Huntington Beach; if you're aiming to angle, try the pier. Day-use fee, $6. ~ Located along Coast Highway in Huntington Beach with numerous accesses; 714-536-5280.

▲ At Sunset Vista (714-536-5280) there are spaces for 25 self-contained vehicles (no hookups); $15 per night.

HUNTINGTON STATE BEACH 🚲 🏊 ⛵ 🎣 ⚓ One of Southern California's broadest beaches, this strand extends for three miles. In addition to a desert of soft sand, it has those curling waves that surfer dreams (and movies) are made of. Pismo clams lie buried in the sand, a bike path parallels the water, and there is a five-acre preserve for endangered least terns. Before you decide to move here permanently, take heed: these natural wonders are sandwiched between industrial plants and offshore oil derricks. Nonetheless, your visit will be made more comfortable by the restrooms, fire rings, lifeguards, outdoor showers, dressing rooms, snack bars, volleyball, and beach rentals; if you need more, restaurants and groceries are located about two miles away in Huntington Beach. The fishing is good here, and the surfing is excellent. Swimming is prime when the surf is low. Day-use fee, $5. ~ Located along Coast Highway in Huntington Beach; entrances are at Beach Boulevard, Newland Street, Brookhurst Street and Magnolia Street; 714-536-1454.

▼▼▼▼▼▼▼▼▼▼▼
Newport Beach

Newport Beach is a mélange of manmade islands and peninsulas surrounding a small bay, and as a result, boating is the order of the day here. One of the largest pleasure harbors in the state, Newport Bay is the starting point for the famous Ensenada Race, a 125-mile sailboat race to Baja held every May. There is also an annual Christmas Festival of Lights, a nighttime procession of lighted boats. In addition to recreational boats, fishing boats are a common sight; Newport Pier, the oldest in Southern California, is where the fishing boats return every morning to sell the day's catch. If you don't buy from them directly, you can still sample local seafood at the myriad waterfront area restaurants. Although virtually the entire shoreline of the lower bay is developed, the upper bay, a narrow channel carved by a Pleistocene river, is a protected wetlands, and it offers perhaps the only escape from the constant flow of boat traffic and manmade vistas of the lower bay.

SIGHTS

For help finding your bearings around this labyrinth of waterways, contact the **Newport Harbor Area Chamber of Commerce.** ~ 1470 Jamboree Road; 714-729-4400. The **Newport Beach Conference & Visitors Bureau** can also provide information. ~ 3300 West Coast Highway; 714-722-1611, 800-942-6278.

While it cannot compete with Laguna Beach as an art center, the town does offer the **Orange County Museum of Art**. Specializing in contemporary art, this facility possesses perhaps the finest collection of post–World War II California art in existence. Admission. ~ 850 San Clemente Drive; 714-759-1122.

Further evidence of Newport's creativity can be found at the **Lovell Beach House**. This private residence, set on the beach, is a modern masterpiece. Designed by Rudolf Schindler in 1926, it features a Bauhaus-like design with columns and cantilevers of poured concrete creating a series of striking geometric forms. ~ 13th Street and West Ocean Front.

One of Newport Beach's prettiest neighborhoods is **Balboa Island**, comprised of two manmade islets in the middle of Newport Bay. It can be reached by bridge along Marine Avenue or via a short ferry ride from Balboa Peninsula. Walk the pathways that circumnavigate both islands and you will pass clapboard cottages, Cape Cod homes, and modern block-design houses that seem made entirely of glass. While sailboats sit moored along the waterfront, streets that are little more than alleys lead into the center of the island.

Another landfill island, **Lido Isle**, sits just off Balboa Peninsula. Surrounded by Newport Bay, lined with sprawling homes and pocket beaches, it is another of Newport Beach's wealthy residential enclaves.

Nearby **Lido Peninsula** seems like yet one more upscale neighborhood. But wait a minute, doesn't that house have a corrugated roofline? And the one next to it is made entirely of metal. Far from an ordinary suburban neighborhood, Lido Peninsula is a trailer park. In Newport Beach? Granted they call them "mobile homes" here, and many are hardly mobile with their brick foundations, flower boxes, and shrubs. But a trailer park it is, probably one of the fanciest in the country, with tin homes disguised by elaborate landscape designs, awnings, and wooden additions. Surreal to say the least.

The central piece in this jigsaw puzzle of manmade plots is **Balboa Peninsula**, a long, narrow finger of land bounded by Newport Bay and the open ocean. High point of the peninsula is **Balboa Pavilion** located at the end of Main Street, a Victorian landmark that dates back to 1905, when it was a bathhouse for swimmers in ankle-length outfits. Marked by its well-known cupola, the bayfront building hosted the nation's first surfing tournament in 1932 and gave birth to its own dance sensation, the "Balboa." Today it's a mini-amusement park with carousel, Ferris wheel, photograph booths, skee ball, video games, and pinball machines.

Cruise ships to Catalina Island debark from the dock here and there are harbor cruises offered by **Catalina Passenger Service** aboard the *Pavilion Queen*, a mock riverboat that motors around the mazeway that is Newport Bay. Admission. ~ 714-673-5245.

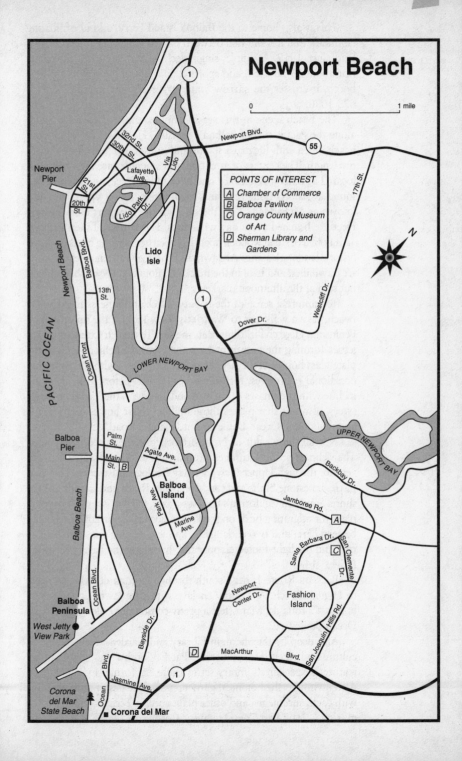

Newport Beach

0   1 mile

POINTS OF INTEREST

A Chamber of Commerce
B Balboa Pavilion
C Orange County Museum of Art
D Sherman Library and Gardens

This is also home to the **Balboa Island Ferry**, a kind of floating landmark that has shuttled between Balboa Peninsula and Balboa Island since 1919. A simple, single-deck ferry that carries three cars (for about $1.50 each) and sports a pilot house the size of a phone booth, it crosses the narrow waterway every few minutes. ~ 714-673-1070.

The beach scene in this seaside city extends for over five miles along the Pacific side of Balboa Peninsula. Here a broad white sand beach, lined with lifeguard stands and houses, reaches along the entire length. The centers of attention and amenities are **Newport Pier**, located at Balboa Boulevard and McFadden Place, and **Balboa Pier** found at Balboa Boulevard and Main Street. At Newport Pier, also known as McFadden's Pier, the skiffs of the **Newport Dory Fishing Fleet** are beached every day while local fishermen sell their catches. This flotilla of small wooden boats has been here so long it has achieved historic landmark status. At dawn the fishermen sail ten miles offshore, set trawl lines, and haul in the mackerel, flounder, rock fish, and halibut sold at the afternoon market.

To capture a sense of the beauty which still inheres in Newport Beach, take a walk out to **West Jetty View Park** at the tip of Balboa Peninsula. Here civilization meets the sea. To the left extend the rock jetties forming the mouth of Newport Harbor. Behind you are the plate-glass houses of the city. A wide beach, tufted with ice plants and occasional palm trees, forms another border. Before you, changing its hue with the phases of the sun and clouds, is the Pacific, a single sweep of water that makes those million-dollar homes seem fragile and tenuous. ~ Ocean Boulevard at Channel Road.

HIDDEN ▶ Not all the wealth of Newport Beach is measured in finances. The richness of the natural environment is evident as well when you venture through **Upper Newport Bay Ecological Reserve**. The road passes limestone bluffs and sandstone hills. Reeds and cattails line the shore. Southern California's largest estuary, the bay is a vital stopping place for migrating birds on the Pacific Flyway. Over 200 species can be seen here; and two endangered species, Belding's savannah sparrow and the light-footed clapper rail, live along the bay. ~ Back Bay Drive; 714-640-6746.

Back on Route 1, head south through Corona del Mar en route to Laguna Beach. A wealthy enclave with trim lawns and spacious homes, Corona del Mar offers a pretty **coastal drive** along residential Ocean Boulevard.

Also drop by the **Sherman Library and Gardens**. Devoted to the culture and recent history of the "Pacific Southwest," this complex features a specialized library set in Early California–style buildings. Also inviting is the botanical garden, a 2.3-acre desert museum alive with cacti, succulents, and other plant species. Free on Monday. Admission. ~ 2647 East Coast Highway, Corona del Mar; 714-673-2261.

You'd have a hell of a time docking your boat at the **Sail Inn Motel.**   **LODGING**
Actually it's on an island, but the island is a median strip dividing the
two busiest streets on the Balboa Peninsula. Offering standard motel
accommodations, the Sail Inn is a block from the beach and walking
distance from many restaurants. ~ 2627 Newport Boulevard; 714-
675-1841, fax 714-673-1057 [let it ring seven times]. BUDGET TO
MODERATE.

The **Balboa Inn,** next to the beach at Balboa Pier, is a Spanish-
style hotel built in 1929. With its cream-colored walls and tile-roofed
tower this 34-room hostelry is vintage Southern California. Adding
to the ambience is a swimming pool that looks out on the water. The
rooms, some of which have ocean views, are furnished in knotty pine,
decorated with colorful prints, and supplied with jacuzzi tubs, brass
fixtures, and fireplaces. ~ 105 Main Street; 714-675-3412, fax 714-
673-4587. DELUXE TO ULTRA-DELUXE.

Portofino Beach Hotel, a 15-room bed-and-breakfast inn, rests on
the beach in an early-20th-century building. Richly appointed with
brass beds, armoires, and antique fixtures, the Portofino has a wine
bar downstairs and two oceanfront parlors overlooking Newport
Pier. Each room is decorated with antiques and equipped with a private bath; many have jacuzzis, skylights, fireplaces, and ocean views.
~ 2306 West Ocean Front; 714-673-7030, fax 714-723-4370. DELUXE
TO ULTRA-DELUXE.

The *only* hotel on tiny Balboa Island is the **Balboa Island Hotel,**
a family-operated, three-bedroom, bed-and-breakfast affair. Set in a
1925 house, it's about one block from the water (of course on Balboa Island everything is one block from the water). Each room of this
bed-and-breakfast inn has been decorated in period and furnished
with antiques. The place has a small, intimate, homey feel. Guests share
bathrooms and there are two porches which serve as sitting rooms. ~
127 Agate Avenue; 714-675-3613. MODERATE.

◆◆

✔ CHECK THESE OUT—UNIQUE LODGING

- *Budget:* Save your bucks for surfing lessons when you bunk at **Colonial Inn Youth Hostel,** which has laundry and kitchen facilities and, most impor-
tantly, is only four blocks from the beach. *page 205*
- *Moderate:* Check into Balboa's only lodge, the 1925 **Balboa Island Hotel,** a quaint bed and breakfast just a block from the beach. *page 211*
- *Deluxe:* Select a suite at **The Carriage House,** a New Orleans–style bed and breakfast built around a brick courtyard. *page 219*
- *Ultra-deluxe:* Ride the monorail back to the 1131-room **Disneyland Hotel,** which has its very own beach and light show. *page 239*

Budget: under $50 Moderate: $50–$90 Deluxe: $90–$120 Ultra-deluxe: over $120

By way of full-facility destinations, Southern California–style, few places match the **Hyatt Newporter Resort**. Situated on a hillside above Upper Newport Bay, it sprawls across 26 acres and sports three swimming pools, three jacuzzis, a nine-hole pitch-and-putt course, and a tennis club. There are restaurants, a lounge, a lavishly decorated lobby, and a series of terraced patios. Guest rooms are modern in design, comfortably furnished, and tastefully appointed. An inviting combination of elegance and amenities. ~ 1107 Jamboree Road; 714-729-1234, 800-233-1234, fax 714-644-1552. ULTRA-DELUXE.

DINING

Everything in Newport Beach was built last week. Everything, that is, except **The Cannery Restaurant and Cruises**. This 1921 fish cannery is today much as it was way back when. The conveyor belts and pulleys are still here, their gears exposed; and there are fire wagons, a fierce-looking boiler, and more tin cans than you can imagine. All part of a waterfront seafood restaurant that serves lunch, dinner, and weekend brunch. Ultra-deluxe weekend brunch cruises aboard a 58-foot boat are also offered. ~ 3010 Lafayette Avenue; 714-675-5777. MODERATE TO DELUXE.

21 Ocean Front is a gourmet seafood dining place known for fine cuisine. Located on the beach overlooking Newport Pier, the interior is done (or rather, overdone) in a kind of shiny Victorian style with black trim and brass chandeliers. The secret is to close your eyes and surrender to the senses of taste and smell. At dinner the chef prepares *ono*, *opakapaka*, and other Hawaiian fish specials as well as abalone, Maine lobster, and bouillabaisse. For those who miss the point there's rack of lamb, veal piccata, and filet mignon. Dinner only. ~ 2100 West Ocean Front; 714-675-2566. DELUXE TO ULTRA-DELUXE.

Around **Balboa Pavilion** you'll find snack bars and amusement park food stands.

A place nearby that's worth recommending is **Newport Landing**, a double-decker affair where you can lounge downstairs in a wood-paneled dining room or upstairs on a deck overlooking the harbor. Serving lunch, dinner, and weekend brunch, it specializes in fresh fish selections and also features hickory-smoked prime rib and chicken with artichokes. ~ 503 East Edgewater Avenue; 714-675-2373. MODERATE TO DELUXE.

Who could imagine that at the end of Balboa Pier there would be a vintage 1940s-era diner complete with art deco curves and red plastic booths. **Ruby's Diner** is a classic. Besides that it provides 270° views of the ocean. Of course the menu, whether breakfast, lunch, or dinner, contains little more than omelettes, hamburgers, sandwiches, chili, and salads. But who's hungry anyway with all that history and scenery to savor? ~ 1 Balboa Pier; 714-675-7829. BUDGET.

What's Cooking? is a locals' favorite for reasonably priced Italian food in an informal, trattoria setting. All the pastas and gnocchi are homemade, the seafood fresh, the daily specials interesting (quail, for example), and the biscotti superb. ~ 2632 San Miguel Drive; 714-644-1820. MODERATE.

Because there are very few restaurants on Balboa Island, one place stands out: **Amelia's**, a family-run restaurant serving Italian ◄ HIDDEN dishes and seafood, is a local institution. At lunch you'll find them serving a multitude of pasta dishes, fresh fish entrées, sandwiches, and salads. Then in the evening the chef prepares calamari stuffed with crab, scallops, Icelandic cod, bouillabaisse, veal piccata, and another round of pasta platters. Sunday brunch. ~ 311 Marine Avenue; 714-673-6580. MODERATE TO DELUXE.

If you were hoping to spend a little less money, **Wilma's Patio** is just down the street. It's a family-style restaurant—open morning, noon, and night—that serves multicourse American and Mexican meals. ~ 225 Marine Avenue; 714-675-5542. BUDGET TO MODERATE.

It's people-watching *par excellence* at **Bistro 201**—and the food's pretty good, too. Here the chef combines New York chic with healthy California cuisine, most notably, fresh seafood such as salmon wrapped in a crispy potato crust served with vegetable ragout and basil sauce. Locals flock here for happy hour. With views of the harbor, who could ask for more? ~ 333 Pacific Coast Highway; 714-631-1551. MODERATE TO DELUXE.

For a multicourse feast, Moroccan-style, reserve a tent at **Marrakesh**. Decorated in the fashion of North Africa with tile floor and cloth drapes, this well-known dining room conveys a sense of Morocco. There are belly dancers Thursday through Sunday and any night of the week you can experience *harira* (an aromatic soup), *jine fassi* (chicken with marinated lemon rinds), couscous, and a host of rabbit, lamb, quail, duck, and chicken dishes. Dinner only. ~ 1100 West Coast Highway; 714-645-8384. DELUXE.

Ironically enough, one of Newport Beach's top dining bargains lies at the heart of the region's priciest shopping malls. Encircling the lower level of **Fashion Island** is a collection of stands dispensing sushi, soup and sandwiches, Mexican food, pasta salads, hamburgers,

CRUSTACEAN CELEBRATION

You won't miss **The Crab Cooker**. First, it's painted bright red; second, it's located at a busy intersection near Newport Pier; last, the place has been a local institution since the 1950s. Actually, you don't *want* to miss The Crab Cooker. This informal eatery, where lunch and dinner are served on paper plates, has fish, scallops, shrimp, crab, and oysters. There's a fish market attached to the restaurant, so freshness and quality are assured. ~ 2200 Newport Boulevard; 714-673-0100. MODERATE TO DELUXE.

and other light fare. ~ Newport Center, 401 Newport Center Drive; 714-721-2000. BUDGET TO MODERATE.

A local favorite in Corona del Mar, the small town adjacent to Newport Beach, is **The Quiet Woman**, a small, dark, friendly place serving mesquite-grilled food. The lunch and dinner menus both feature steak and seafood. Live entertainment accompanies evening meals Wednesday through Saturday. ~ 3224 East Coast Highway; 714-640-7440. MODERATE TO ULTRA-DELUXE.

SHOPPING   The streets radiating out from **Balboa Pavilion** (end of Main Street) are lined with beachwear stores, sundries shops, and souvenir stands. While there's little of value here, it is a good place to shop for knick-knacks. The scene is much the same around **Newport Pier**, located at Balboa Avenue and McFadden Place.

For more upscale shopping, cast anchor at **Lido Marina Village**. This well-heeled complex features a host of shops lining a brick courtyard and adjacent boardwalk. ~ Via Oporto; 714-675-8662.

Another Newport Beach shopping enclave lies along Marine Avenue on Balboa Island. This consumer strip is door-to-door with card shops, gift shops, and sundries stores. Without exaggerating, I would estimate that more than half the outlets here sell beachwear.

After all is said and done, but hopefully before the money is all spent, the center for Newport Beach shopping is Fashion Island. Situated at the heart of Newport Center, the town's highrise financial district, it is also the best place for beautiful-people watching. Every self-respecting department store is here. **Neiman Marcus, Macy's, Robinson's-May,** and **Bloomingdale's** are all represented. ~ Newport Center Drive; 714-721-2000.

There's an outdoor plaza filled with fashion outlets and an atrium displaying one floor of designer dreams. If you don't believe Newport Beach is a match for Beverly Hills in flash and cash, take a tour of the parking lot. It's a showplace for Rolls Royces, Jaguars, and Mercedes, as well as more plebeian Volvos and Audis.

NIGHTLIFE   For an evening on Newport Bay, climb aboard the *Pavilion Queen* or *Pavilion Paddy*, two double-deck boats which depart from the Balboa Pavilion on a **harbor cruise**. ~ End of Main Street; 714-673-5245.

There's live music every night at the **Studio Cafe**, a waterfront watering hole near Balboa Pier. ~ 100 Main Street; 714-675-7760.

I doubt that John Wayne ever danced here, but **Duke's** is dubbed in his honor. The club features country-and-western hits spun by a deejay. ~ Hyatt Newporter, 1107 Jamboree Road; 714-644-1700.

The Cannery Restaurant and Cruises, an old fish cannery that's been converted into a restaurant-cum-museum (and a fascinating one at that), has entertainment nightly. Live rock music is performed by local bands on Friday and Saturday, and there's karaoke on Monday and Wednesday. Cover on weekends. ~ 3010 Lafayette Avenue; 714-675-5777.

NEWPORT BEACH 🏊 🏄 ⛱ Narrow at the northern end and widening to the south, this sandy strip extends for several miles along the base of the Balboa Peninsula. Newport Pier (also known as McFadden's Pier) and the surrounding facilities serve as the center of the strand. Here fishermen from the Newport Dory Fishing Fleet beach their boats and sell their daily catches. A wonderful beach, with entrances along its entire length, this is an important gathering place for the crowds that pour into town. There are restrooms, lifeguards, and beach rentals; at the foot of the pier you'll find restaurants, groceries, and all amenities imaginable. The pier is also the place for fishing. Swimming and surfing are both good. If you want to ride the waves, try in the morning around Newport Pier and then in the afternoon at the 30th Street section of the beach. There are year-round breaks near the Santa Ana River mouth at the far north end of the beach. ~ The beach parallels Balboa Boulevard in Newport Beach. Newport Pier is between 20th and 21st streets.

BEACHES & PARKS

BALBOA BEACH 🏊 🏄 ⛱ This broad sandy strip forms the ocean side of Balboa Peninsula and extends along its entire length. There are entrances to the beach from numerous side streets, but the center of the facility is around Balboa Pier, a wooden fishing pier. With a palm-shaded lawn and many nearby amenities, this beach, together with neighboring Newport Beach, is the most popular spot in town. Facilities include restrooms, showers, lifeguards, a playground, and beach rentals; restaurants, groceries, etc. are near the pier. Fishing is good from the pier, and swimming and surfing are good in different spots at different times. ~ The beach parallels Balboa Boulevard; Balboa Pier is at the end of Main Street.

WEST JETTY VIEW PARK 🏄 Set at the very end of the Balboa Peninsula, this triangle of sand is perfectly placed. From the tip extends a rock jetty that borders Newport Harbor. You can climb the rocks and watch boats in the bay, or turn your back on these trifles and wander across the broad sand carpet that rolls down to the ocean. There are wonderful views of Newport Beach and the coast. You can stock up for your hike or fuel up afterwards at the restaurants and grocery stores about a half mile away. If you're daring enough, you can challenge the waves at **The Wedge**. Known to bodysurfers around the world, the area between the jetty and beach is one of the finest and most dangerous shore breaks anywhere, the "Mount Everest of bodysurfing." If it's any comfort, there are lifeguards. Swimming is very dangerous; the shore break here is fierce. Bodysurfing is the main sport; surfing is permitted further down the beach. But take heed, these breaks are only for veteran bodysurfers. ~ At the end of Balboa and Ocean boulevards at the tip of the Balboa Peninsula.

NEWPORT DUNES RV RESORT 🧍🚲🐎 ⚓🚤🛥 This private facility is a broad, horseshoe-shaped beach about one-half mile in length. It curves around the lake-like waters of Upper Newport Bay, one mile inland from the ocean. Very popular with families and campers, it offers a wide range of possibilities, including playground activities, volleyball, a swimming pool, jacuzzi, and boat rentals. Lifeguards are on duty in the summer. Other facilities include restrooms, a café, groceries, picnic areas, and laundry. The park is very popular, so plan to come for the attractions, not peace and quiet. Day-use fee, $5. ~ Located at 1131 Back Bay Drive in Newport Beach; 714-729-3863.

▲ There are 405 sites for freestanding tents and RVs (all with hookups); $29 to $65 per night.

CORONA DEL MAR STATE BEACH 🏊🎣⚓ Located at the mouth of Newport Harbor, this park offers an opportunity to watch sailboats tacking in and out from the bay. Bounded on one side by a jetty, on the other by homes, with a huge parking lot behind, it is less than idyllic, yet it is also inevitably crowded. Throngs congregate because of its easy access, landscaped lawn, and excellent facilities, which include restrooms, picnic areas, lifeguards, showers, concession stands, beach rentals, and volleyball courts. It's well protected for swimming and also popular for surfing and fishing—cast from the jetty bordering Newport Harbor. Skindiving is also good around the jetty. If the crowds are driving you crazy, you will find one possible escape valve: there are a pair of pocket beaches on the other side of the rocks next to the jetty. Parking fee, $6. ~ Located at Jasmine Avenue and Ocean Boulevard in Corona del Mar; 714-644-3047.

LITTLE CORONA DEL MAR STATE BEACH 🏊🎣🤿⚓ Another in the proud line of pocket beaches along the Orange Coast, this preserve features the **Corona del Mar Tidepool Reserve**, which organizes tours and classes around the beach's tidepools. The bluff to the north consists of sandstone that has been contorted into a myriad of magnificent lines. There's a marsh behind the beach thick with reeds and cattails. Unfortunately you won't be the first explorer to hit the sand; Little Corona is known to a big group of local people. The beach is also popular with swimmers, surfers, snorkelers and skindivers; for anglers, try casting from the rocks. Restaurants and groceries are nearby in Corona del Mar. ~ There is an entrance to the beach at Poppy Avenue and Ocean Boulevard in Corona del Mar; 714-644-3047.

▼▼▼▼▼▼▼▼▼
Laguna Beach
Next stop on this cavalcade of coastal cities is Laguna Beach. Framed by the San Joaquin hills, the place is an intaglio of coves and bluffs, sand beaches and rock outcroppings. It conjures images of the Mediterranean with deep bays and greenery running to the sea's edge.

Little wonder that Laguna, with its wealthy residents and leisurely beachfront, has become synonymous with the chic but informal style of Southern California. Its long tradition as an artist colony adds to this sense of beauty and bounty, aesthetics and aggrandizement.

Laguna's traditional tranquility was shattered in the fall of 1993 by arson-torched fires that burned hundreds of homes. The fire swept through Laguna Canyon along the north side of Route 133, but you won't see much evidence of the fire, which primarily affected the rugged residential canyons. Businesses, parks, and galleries were untouched.

Part of Laguna's artistic tradition is the **Festival of Arts and Pageant of the Masters,** staged every year during July and August. While the festival displays the work of 160 local artists and craftspeople, the Pageant of the Masters is the high point, an event which you *absolutely must not miss*. It presents a series of *tableaux vivants* in which local residents, dressed to resemble figures from famous paintings, remain motionless against a frieze that re-creates the painting. Elaborate make-up and lighting techniques flatten the figures and create a sense of two-dimensionality. Admission. ~ Irvine Bowl, 650 Laguna Canyon Road; 714-494-1145.

SIGHTS

During the 1960s freelance artists, excluded from the more formal Festival of the Arts, founded the **Sawdust Festival** across the street. Over the years this fair too has become pretty established, but it still provides an opportunity to wander along sawdust-covered paths past hundreds of arts and crafts displays accompanied by musicians and jugglers from late June to late August. Admission. ~ 935 Laguna Canyon Road; 714-494-3030.

Laguna Beach's artistic heritage is evident in the many studios around town. The **Laguna Beach Visitors Bureau and Chamber of Commerce**, with its maps and brochures, can help direct you. They can also assist with hotel and restaurant reservations. ~ 252 Broadway; 714-494-1018.

The **Laguna Art Museum** has a wonderfully chosen collection of historic and contemporary California paintings. Complementing the Chamber of Commerce, it will help you find your way through the local art world. Admission. ~ 307 Cliff Drive; 714-494-6531.

Beauty in Laguna is not only found on canvases. The coastline too is particularly pretty and well worth exploring (see the "Beaches & Parks" section below). One of the most enchanting areas is along **Heisler Park**, a winding promenade set on the cliffs above the ocean. Here you can relax on the lawn, sit beneath a palm tree, and gaze out on the horizon. There are broad vistas out along the coast and down to the wave-whitened shoreline. Paths from the park descend to a series of coves with tidepools and sandy beaches. The surrounding rocks, twisted by geologic pressure into curving designs, rise in a series of protective bluffs. ~ Located on Cliff Drive.

Cliff Drive streams along Heisler Park and then past a series of entranceways to sparkling coves and pocket beaches. At the north end of this shoreline street take a left onto Coast Highway, then another quick left onto Crescent Bay Drive, which leads to **Crescent Bay Point Park.** Seated high upon a coastal cliff, this landscaped facility offers magnificent views for miles along the Laguna shore.

For a lighthouse keeper's view of the harbor and outlying coastline, take in either of the **lookout points** at the ends of Old Golden Lantern and Blue Lantern streets in Dana Point.

When you're ready to leave the beach behind and head for the hills, take Park Avenue up from the center of Laguna Beach, turn right at the end onto Alta Laguna Boulevard, and right again to head back down on Temple Hills Drive and Thalia Street. This climbing course will carry you high into the **Laguna Hills** with spectacular vistas along the entire coastline and into the interior valleys.

South on Route 1, called the Pacific Coast Highway in these parts, you will pass through **Dana Point.** This ultramodern enclave, with its manmade port and 2500-boat marina, has a history dating back to the 1830s when Richard Henry Dana immortalized the place. Writing in *Two Years Before the Mast*, the Boston gentleman-turned-sailor described the surrounding countryside: "There was a grandeur in everything around."

Today much of the grandeur has been replaced with condominiums, leaving little for the sightseer. There is the **Orange County Marine Institute** with a small sealife aquarium and a 130-foot replica of Dana's brig, *The Pilgrim*. They also lead evening cruises, for a fee, on weekends and selected weekdays. The Institute is closed on most major holidays, the aquarium is open only on weekends and *The Pilgrim* is shown on Sundays only. ~ 24200 Dana Point Harbor Drive; 714-496-2274.

The **Nautical Heritage Society**, a facsimile of an old beacon, serves as a nautical museum. Here you can view a collection of model sailing ships and other miniatures. Closed weekends. ~ 24532 Del Prado Avenue; 714-661-1001.

LODGING   Boasting 70 guest rooms, a pool, spa, and sundeck overlooking the sea, the **Inn at Laguna Beach** offers great ocean views from its blufftop perch. Rooms are small, the construction uneven, and the furnishings modern at this coastside property. ~ 211 North Coast Highway; 714-497-9722, 800-544-4479, fax 714-497-9972. DELUXE TO ULTRA-DELUXE.

Even if you never stay there, you won't miss the **Hotel Laguna.** With its octagonal bell tower and Spanish motif, this huge whitewashed building dominates downtown Laguna Beach. The oldest hotel in Laguna, it sits in the center of town, adjacent to Main Beach. In addition to 65 guest rooms there is a restaurant, lounge, and a casual lobby terrace. The place shows signs of age and suffers some of the ills characteristic of large old hotels. But for a place on the water *and* at the center of the action, it cannot be matched. ~ 425 South Coast Highway; 714-494-1151, fax 714-497-2163. MODERATE TO ULTRA-DELUXE.

The premier resting place in Laguna Beach is a sprawling 157-room establishment overhanging the sand. The **Surf & Sand Hotel** is a blocky 1950s-era complex, an architectural mélange of five buildings and a shopping mall. The accent here is on the ocean: nearly every room has a sea view and private balcony, the pool sits just above the sand, and the beach is a short step away. A full-service hotel, the Surf & Sand has two restaurants and an art deco lounge. Guest rooms are understated but attractive with raw-silk furnishings, unfinished woods, and sand-hued walls. ~ 1555 South Coast Highway; 714-497-4477, 800-524-8621, fax 714-494-2897. ULTRA-DELUXE.

Casa Laguna Inn, a hillside hacienda, has a dreamlike quality about it. The cottages and rooms are nestled in a garden setting complete with stone terraces and winding paths. Built in the 1930s, the Spanish-style complex features a courtyard, bell tower, and a swimming pool with an ocean view. The rooms are small, equipped with overhead fans, and furnished in antiques; many offer ocean views, though they also pick up noise from the highway. Continental breakfast and afternoon tea are served in the library. ~ 2510 South Coast Highway; 714-494-2996, fax 714-494-5009. DELUXE TO ULTRA-DELUXE.

◄ *HIDDEN*

It's not just the residential neighborhood that makes **The Carriage House** unique. The colonial architecture of the "New Orleans style" bed-and-breakfast inn also sets it apart. Within this historic landmark structure are six suites, each with a sitting room and separate bedroom. All face a luxurious brick courtyard filled with flowering plants and adorned with a tiered fountain. Certainly the Carriage House is one of the prettiest and most peaceful inns along the entire Orange Coast. ~ 1322 Catalina Street; 714-494-8945. DELUXE TO ULTRA-DELUXE.

Accommodations with kitchen facilities are hard to come by in Laguna Beach. You'll find them in most of the units at **Capri Laguna**, a multilevel motel situated on the beach. This 45-unit resting place provides contemporary motel-style furnishings, plus a pool, sauna, and sundeck with barbecue facilities. Continental breakfast is included in the price. ~ 1441 South Coast Highway; 714-494-6533, 800-225-4551, fax 714-497-6962. DELUXE TO ULTRA-DELUXE.

Holiday Inn Laguna Beach is one of those places destined to gain increasing renown. Fashioned in the style of the French Caribbean, it creates a luxurious atmosphere. The lobby is a breezy affair with provincial furnishings and hand-painted ceiling. The 54 guest rooms surround a lushly landscaped courtyard complete with swimming pool and patio. For a touch of the tropics right here in Laguna Beach, you can't go astray at this reasonably priced hotel. ~ 696 South Coast

Highway; 714-494-1001, 800-228-5691, fax 714-497-7107. MOD-ERATE.

HIDDEN ▶   Tucked into a secluded canyon is **Aliso Creek Inn and Golf Resort**, an appealing 83-acre resort complete with swimming pools, jacuzzi, Ben Brown's restaurant, lounge, and nine-hole golf course. Particularly attractive for families, every unit includes a sitting area, patio, and kitchen. Removed from the highway but within 400 yards of a beach, the resort is surrounded by steep hillsides which are populated by deer and raccoon. Tying this easy rusticity together is a small creek that tumbles through the resort. ~ 31106 South Coast Highway; 714-499-2271, 800-223-3309, fax 714-499-4601. DELUXE TO ULTRA-DELUXE.

The **Ritz-Carlton Laguna Niguel**, set on a 150-foot-high cliff above the Pacific, is simply the finest resort hotel along the California coast. Built in the fashion of a Mediterranean villa, it dominates a broad sweep of coastline, a 393-room mansion replete with gourmet restaurants and dark wood lounges. An Old World interior of arched windows and Italian marble is decorated with one of the finest hotel collections of 18th- and 19th-century American and English art anywhere. The grounds are landscaped with willows, sycamores, and a spectrum of flowering plants. Tile courtyards lead to two swimming pools, a pair of jacuzzis, four tennis courts, and a fitness and massage center. The guest rooms are equal in luxury to the rest of the resort. ~ 1 Ritz-Carlton Drive, Dana Point; 714-240-2000, 800-287-2706, fax 714-240-0829. ULTRA-DELUXE.

Most motels have a stream of traffic whizzing past outside, but the **Dana Marina Inn Motel**, situated on an island where the highway divides, manages to have traffic on both sides! The reason I'm mentioning it is not because I'm sadistic but because rooms in this 29-unit facility are inexpensive. The accommodations are roadside-motel style. ~ 34111 Coast Highway, Dana Point; 714-496-1300. BUDGET.

Four Sisters Inns, a bed-and-breakfast "chain" with several properties along the coast, has a 29-room property, **Blue Lantern Inn**, situated on an oceanside bluff in Dana Point. A contemporary building designed in classic Cape Cod–style, the bed and breakfast combines an ultramodern glass elevator with antique decor. Each room features a fireplace and jacuzzi as well as a hardwood armoire, and shuttered windows. Some rooms are furnished with four-poster beds. The sitting rooms are spacious and comfortable and the inn provides a well-done, though self-conscious, re-creation of a classic era. ~ 34343 Street of the Blue Lantern, Dana Point; 714-661-1304, 800-950-1236. ULTRA-DELUXE.

DINING   Laguna Beach is never at a loss for oceanfront restaurants. But somehow the sea seems closer and more intimate at **Laguna Village Cafe**, probably because this informal eatery was once entirely outdoors, with tables placed at the very edge of the coastal bluff (now they've added indoor seating warmed by a fireplace). The menu is simple: egg dishes in the morning, and a single menu with salads, sandwiches, and smoothies during the rest of the day. There are also house specialties like calamari, abalone, scallops amandine, teriyaki chicken, skewered shrimp, and Chinese-style chicken dumplings. ~ 577 South Coast Highway; 714-494-6344. BUDGET TO MODERATE.

The **Penguin Malt Shop** is from another era entirely. The 1950s to be exact. A tiny café featuring counter jukeboxes and swivel stools, as well as penguin memorabilia brought in by customers, it's a time capsule with a kitchen. Breakfast and lunch are all-American affairs from ham and eggs to hamburgers to pork chops. It's cheap, so what have you got to lose? Step on in and order a chocolate malt with a side of fries. ~ 981 South Coast Highway; 714-494-1353. BUDGET.

The **White House Restaurant** seems nearly as permanent a Laguna Beach fixture as the ocean. Dating to early in the century this simple wooden structure serves as bar, restaurant, and local landmark. The White House is lined with historic photos of Laguna Beach. You can drop by from early morning until late evening to partake of a menu that includes pasta, steak, chicken, and seafood dishes. ~ 340 South Coast Highway; 714-494-8088. MODERATE.

Choose one place to symbolize the easy elegance of Laguna and it inevitably will be **Las Brisas**. Something about this whitewashed Spanish building with arched windows captures the natural-living-but-class-conscious style of the Southland. Its cliffside locale on the water is part of this ambience. Then there are the beautiful people who frequent the place. Plus a dual kitchen arrangement that permits formal dining in a white-tablecloth room or bistro dining on an outdoor patio. The menu consists of Continental Mexican seafood dishes and other specialties from south of the border. Out on the patio there are sandwiches, salads, and appetizers. ~ 361 Cliff Drive; 714-497-5434. MODERATE TO DELUXE.

For people watching and swimming pool–sized cappuccinos, try **Cafe Zinc**. Here you'll find sidewalk seating complete with the obligatory umbrellas. They serve vegetarian fare that attracts a casual-intellectual crowd. No dinner. ~ 350 Ocean Avenue; 714-494-6302. BUDGET.

Five Feet Restaurant prepares contemporary Chinese cuisine. This "interpretation of modern Chinese cuisine" carries you from catfish to veal loin sautéed with sweet pepper. Also on the ever-changing and always unique bill of fare is blackened ahi, spring lamb in curry-cilantro sauce, and steak chinoise. Applying the principles of California cuisine to Chinese cooking and adding a few French flourishes, Five Feet has gained an impressive reputation. The decor is as avant-garde as the food. Dinner only. ~ 328 Glenneyre Street; 714-497-4955. MODERATE TO DELUXE.

Dizz's **As Is** represents one of those singular dining spots that should not be overlooked. Funk is elevated to an art form in this woodframe house. The tiny dining room is decorated with art deco pieces and 1930s-era tunes play throughout dinner. This studied informality ends at the kitchen door where a Continental cuisine that includes veal piccata, Cornish game hen, chicken stuffed with cheese and shallots, pasta with prawns, and cioppino is prepared by talented chefs. Dinner only. Closed Monday in winter. ~ 2794 South Coast Highway; 714-494-5250. DELUXE.

The most remarkable aspect of the **Cottage Restaurant** is the cottage itself, an early-20th-century California bungalow. The place has been neatly decorated with turn-of-the-century antiques, oil paintings, and stained glass. Meal time in this historic house is a traditional American affair. They serve classic eggs-and-bacon breakfasts starting at 7 a.m. Lunch consists of salads and sandwiches plus specials like top sirloin, fresh fish, and steamed vegetables. For dinner there is chicken fettuccine, top sirloin, broiled lamb, fresh shrimp, and swordfish as well as daily fresh fish specials. ~ 308 North Coast Highway; 714-494-3023. BUDGET TO MODERATE.

Ti Amo is a little jewel set on a coastal bluff. Situated in a former home, it offers intimate dining indoors or outside on the patio. The restaurant has renaissance decor with Italian-style murals and heavy draperies. In addition to ocean views, it offers a dinner menu that changes daily. On a typical evening you can expect such entrées as paella, fresh seafood, and fresh pastas. Dinner only. ~ 31727 Coast Highway, South Laguna; 714-499-5359. MODERATE TO DELUXE.

The **Harbor Grill**, located in spiffy Dana Point Harbor, lacks the view and polish of its splashy neighbors. But this understated restaurant serves excellent seafood dishes. The menu includes fresh swordfish and salmon with pesto sauce, but the real attraction is the list of

✔ **CHECK THESE OUT—UNIQUE DINING**

- *Budget to moderate:* Have a meal at a coastal institution, the historic **Harbor House Café**, where local folks have enjoyed the varied menu items since 1939, and continue to do so 24 hours a day, every day. *page 205*
- *Moderate:* Chow down at **Belisle's**, an old-fashioned joint that serves a two-pound steak and stays open late enough for you to finish it. *page 241*
- *Moderate to deluxe:* Feast on pasta and paella at **Ti Amo**, a cozy spot located on a bluff with ocean views. *page 222*
- *Moderate to ultra-deluxe:* Clam up at **The Quiet Woman**, where mesquite-grilled seafood is served and live music often breaks the silence. *page 214*

Budget: under $8   Moderate: $8–$16   Deluxe: $16–$24   Ultra-deluxe: over $24

daily specials. This might include sea bass with black bean sauce, gumbo, and other fresh fish dishes. Lunch, dinner, and Sunday brunch are served in a light, bright dining room with contemporary artwork. There is also patio dining. ~ 34499 Golden Lantern Street, Dana Point; 714-240-1416. MODERATE TO DELUXE.

If you'd prefer to dine alfresco overlooking the harbor, there's **Proud Mary's**, a little hole in the wall where you can order sandwiches, hot dogs, hamburgers, and a few chicken and steak platters, then dine on picnic tables outside. ~ 34689 Golden Lantern Street, Dana Point; 714-493-5853. BUDGET.

Japanese food in these parts is spelled **Gen Kai**. In addition to a trimly appointed dining room this chain restaurant features a sushi bar and comprehensive lunch and dinner menus. When I ate here the food was quite good. No lunch on Saturday and Sunday. ~ 34143 Coast Highway, Dana Point; 714-240-2004. MODERATE.

SHOPPING

Given its long tradition as an artist colony, it's little wonder that Laguna Beach is crowded with galleries and studios. In addition to painters and sculptors the town claims to support more goldsmiths and jewelers than any place in the country. Add a few designer clothing shops plus antique stores and you have one very promising shopping spot. The center of this action lies along Route 1 (Coast Highway) between Bluebird Canyon Drive and Laguna Canyon Road.

There are several art galleries clustered together which are particularly interesting. Foremost is **Redfern Gallery**, which specializes in early-American impressionist paintings. ~ 1540 South Coast Highway; 714-497-3356. The **Vladimir Sokolov Studio Gallery** presents works by Mr. Sokolov including a mixed media collage and other contemporary paintings. ~ 1540 South Coast Highway; 714-494-3633. **The Esther Wells Collection** features modern oil paintings and sculptures. ~ 1390 South Coast Highway; 714-494-2497.

Fine fashion is taken for granted at **Shebue**. This plush shop houses beautiful designer clothing for women. *Très chic* (and *très cher*). ~ 1555 South Coast Highway; 714-494-3148.

Chicken Little's bills itself as "The Museum of Modern Retail." Translation: they stock New Wave knickknacks like fish mugs and wacky greeting cards. ~ 574 South Coast Highway; 714-497-4818. Similar in spirit, though not in age, is **Tippecanoe's**, a vintage clothing store with a collection of antique knickknacks. ~ 648 South Coast Highway; 714-494-1200.

For imported goods there's **Khyber Pass**, dealing in rugs, statuary, and lapis lazuli pieces from Afghanistan. ~ 1970 South Coast Highway, 714-494-5021. For contemporary painting I particularly recommend **Diane Nelson Fine Art**, which displays the work of modern-day impressionist Marco Sassone and other artists. ~ 435 Ocean Avenue; 714-494-2440.

Laguna Beach's other shopping strip is Forest Avenue, a three-block promenade wall-to-wall with specialty stores. **Laura Downing** is here, a clothing store specializing in upscale sportswear, women's cowboy boots, and jewelry. ~ 241 Forest Avenue; 714-494-4300.

Thee Foxes Trot has an unpredictable inventory, a kind of cultural hodgepodge ranging from ethnic jewelry and clothing to African art. ~ 264 Forest Avenue; 714-497-3047.

> At **Sherwood Gallery**, they have a hilarious collection of soft sculptures portraying an odd assortment of frumpy people. ~ 460 South Coast Highway; 714-497-2668.

There are also two rustic, raw wood malls, **Forest Avenue Mall** at 332 Forest Avenue and **Lumberyard Plaza** at 384 Forest Avenue, which blend neatly into the background.

An important literary center, **Up Church Brown** is a great bookstore that hosts poetry readings every Friday night. There's a wonderful collection of new and used books. ~ #5 384 Forest Avenue; 714-497-8373.

Sounds foreboding, but **The Mole Hole** is a colorful and inviting gift shop specializing in limited-edition collectibles from around the world. David Winter cottages, hand-painted Limoges, Swarovski crystal, and original Tiffany lamps are part of the unusual selection. ~ 28121-G Crown Valley Parkway, Laguna Niguel; 714-362-3520.

NIGHTLIFE Admirers of art deco are bound to fall in love with the **Towers Lounge** in the Surf & Sand Hotel. This softly lit bar combines the ambience of the 1930s with wide-angle views of the ocean. Piano entertainment is available Wednesday through Saturday. Situated high atop Laguna Beach's finest hotel, it's one of the best watering holes along the Orange County coast. ~ 1555 South Coast Highway; 714-497-4477.

The White House Restaurant is a landmark 1917 building in downtown Laguna Beach. A long, narrow lounge with mirrored walls, it turns tradition upside down every night with live rock, reggae, and Motown. Cover. ~ 340 South Coast Highway; 714-494-8088.

One of Laguna Beach's hottest nightspots is also its most funky. **The Sandpiper** is a run-down club filled with dart boards and pinball machines. Often it is also filled with some of the finest sounds around. Rock, reggae, oldies, and other music is live nightly, sometimes preformed by well-known groups. Cover. ~ 1183 South Coast Highway; 714-494-4694.

Las Brisas, a sleek, clifftop restaurant overlooking the ocean, is a gathering place for the fast and fashionable. A wonderful place to enjoy a quiet cocktail, it features a tile bar as well as an open-air patio. ~ 361 Cliff Drive; 714-497-5434.

Laguna Beach's gay scene centers around the **Boom Boom Room** at the Coast Inn. This beachy, three-tiered discotheque one-half block from the beach boasts a dancefloor, pinball machines, and two bars. Weekend cover. ~ 1401 South Coast Highway; 714-494-7588.

There's a quieter gay scene at **Main Street,** which resembles *Cheers* with a predominantly male clientele. ~ 1460 South Coast Highway; 714-494-0056.

The ultimate evening destinations are located at the ultra-posh Ritz-Carlton Laguna Niguel. Here, along corridors of polished stone, is the **Club Grill and Bar,** a wood-paneled rendezvous decorated with 19th-century paintings of equestrian scenes. Also located in the Ritz-Carlton is **The Lounge,** an elegant two-tiered, glass-walled lounge with sweeping ocean views. The first offers a combo nightly and the latter features a solo pianist. ~ 1 Ritz-Carlton Drive, Dana Point; 714-240-2000.

The **Wind and Sea Restaurant,** on the waterfront in Dana Point Harbor, features sparkling views and entertainers nightly. ~ 34699 Golden Lantern Street, Dana Point; 714-496-6500.

CRYSTAL COVE STATE PARK This outstanding facility has a long, winding sand beach which is sometimes sectioned into a series of coves by high tides. The park stretches for over three miles along the coast and extends up into the hills. Grassy terraces grace the sea cliffs and the offshore area is designated an underwater preserve. Providing long walks along an undeveloped coastline and on upland trails in El Moro Canyon, it's the perfect park when you're seeking solitude. Facilities are limited to lifeguards and restrooms; restaurants and groceries are several miles away in Laguna Beach. Onshore fishing is permitted, and swimming is good. For surfing, try the breaks north of Reef Point in Scotchman's Cove. Day-use fee, $6. ~ Located along the Coast Highway between Corona del Mar and Laguna Beach. There are entrances at Pelican Point, Los Trancos, Reef Point, and El Moro Canyon; 714-494-3539.

▲ Environmental camping is permitted, a two-to-four-mile hike inland from El Moro Canyon entrance; $10 per night. At last report, no camping was permitted due to the Laguna Beach fire. Campsites are due to reopen.

CRESCENT BAY This half-moon inlet is flanked by a curving cliff upon which the fortunate few have parked their palatial homes. Down on the beach, the sand is as soft and thick as the carpets in those houses. Offshore stands Seal Rock, with barking denizens whose cries echo off the surrounding cliffs. This, to say the least, is a pretty place. You can swim, skindive, sunbathe, explore the rocks and tidepools, or venture up to the vista point that overlooks this natural setting. The beach has restrooms, and lifeguards in summer; restaurants and groceries are nearby. Fishing and swimming are good, and there's also very good bodysurfing and excellent skindiv-

BEACHES & PARKS

ing. ~ Entrances to the beach are located near the intersection of Cliff Drive and Circle Way.

SHAW'S COVE, FISHERMAN'S COVE, AND DIVER'S COVE

These three miniature inlets sit adjacent to one another, creating one of Laguna Beach's most scenic and popular sections of shoreline. Each features a white sand beach backdropped by a sharp bluff. Rock formations at either end are covered in spuming surf and honeycombed with tidepool pockets (particularly at the south end of Shaw's Cove). Well known to local residents, the beaches are sometimes crowded. There are lifeguards, but no other facilities; restaurants and groceries are nearby. Fishing is not permitted at Diver's Cove, and swimming, while generally good, can be hazardous at Fisherman's Cove because of rocks. Diver's Cove, in keeping with its name, is often awash with scuba divers, but skindiving is excellent along this entire shoreline. ~ All three coves rest along Cliff Drive. The walkway to Shaw's Cove is at the end of Fairview Street; the entrances to Fisherman's and Diver's are within 50 feet of each other in the 600 block of Cliff Drive.

HEISLER PARK, PICNIC BEACH, AND ROCK PILE BEACH

One of Laguna's prettiest stretches of shoreline lies along the clifftop in Heisler Park and below on the boulder-strewn sands of Picnic and Rock Pile beaches. The park provides a promenade with grassy areas and shade trees. You can scan the coastline from Laguna Beach south for miles, then meander down to the beach where sedimentary formations shatter the wave patterns and create marvelous tidepools. Picnic and Rock Pile form adjacent coves, both worthy of exploration. In addition to the tidepools, you'll find picnic areas, restrooms, lifeguards, and—get ready—shuffleboard; restaurants and groceries are located nearby. Fishing is excellent here and along most of the Laguna coast: perch, cod, bass, and halibut inhabit these waters. Swimming is permitted at Picnic Beach but not at Rock Pile Beach. Skindiving is also good at Picnic Beach, as the rocks offer great places to explore. For surfing, Rock Pile has some of the biggest waves in Laguna Beach. The best spots are at the south end. ~ Heisler Park is located along Cliff Drive. Picnic Beach lies to the north at the end of Myrtle Street; Rock Pile Beach is at the end of Jasmine Street.

MAIN BEACH

You'll have to venture north to Muscle Beach in Venice to find a scene equal to this one. It's located at the very center of Laguna Beach, with shopping streets radiating in several directions. A sinuous boardwalk winds along the waterfront, past basketball players, sunbathers, volleyball aficionados, little kids on swings, and aging kids on roller skates. Here and there an adventuresome soul has even dipped a toe in the wa-wa-water. In the midst of this humanity on holiday stands the lifeguard tower, an imposing glass-encased structure that looks more like a conning tower and has become a Laguna Beach icon. There are also restrooms, showers, picnic areas, a playground, and a grassy area. Fishing is good, and swimming is very good, as the beach is well-guarded. And because the Laguna Beach Marine Life Refuge lies just offshore, this a popular place for diving. ~ Located at Coast Highway and Broadway.

STREET BEACHES Paralleling downtown Laguna for nearly a mile is a single slender strand known to locals by the streets that intersect it. Lined with luxury homes, it provides little privacy but affords easy access to the town's amenities. There are lifeguards, and everything you want, need, or couldn't care less about is within a couple blocks. Swimming is good, and excellent peaks are created by a submerged reef off Brooks Street, making it a prime surfing and bodysurfing locale. The surf is also usually up around Thalia Street. ~ Off Coast Highway there are beach entrances at the ends of Sleepy Hollow Lane, and Cleo, St. Ann's, Thalia, Anita, Oak, and Brooks streets.

ARCH COVE Stretching for more than a half mile, bordered by a palisade of luxury homes and resort hotels, this sandy swath is ideal for sunbathers. A sea arch and blowhole rise along the south end of the beach; the northern stretch is more populated and not as pretty. Lifeguards are on duty, and swimming, although not as protected as the pocket beaches, is still okay. For surfing, there are sizeable breaks around Agate Street. Restaurants and groceries are nearby. ~ Entrances to the beach are at the ends of Cress Street, Mountain Road, Bluebird Canyon Drive, Agate Street, and Pearl Street. As a result, you will hear sections of the strand referred to as "Agate Beach," "Pearl Beach," etc.

WOOD'S COVE An S-shaped strand backed by Laguna's ever-loving shore bluff, this is another in the town's string of hidden wonders. Three rock peninsulas give the area its topography, creating a pair of sandy pocket beaches. The sea works in, around, and over the rocks, creating a tumultuous presence in an otherwise placid scene. Swimming is well protected by rock outcroppings, and skindiving is good off the rocks; lifeguards are on duty. When you get hungry, restaurants and groceries are nearby. ~ Steps from Diamond Street and Ocean Way lead down to the water. ◄ *HIDDEN*

MOSS POINT This tiny gem is little more than 50 yards long, but for serenity and simple beauty it challenges the giant strands. Rocky points border both sides and sharp hills overlook the entire scene. The sea streams in through the mouth of a cove and debouches onto a fan-shaped beach. The cove is well protected for swimming, and there is a lifeguard; the surrounding rocks also provide interesting areas for skindiving. Restaurants and groceries are nearby. ~ Located at the end of Moss Street. ◄ *HIDDEN*

HIDDEN ▶ **VICTORIA BEACH** 🏊 ⛵ 🚣 Known primarily to locals, this quarter-mile sand corridor is flanked by homes and hills. The rocks on either side of the beach make for good exploring and provide excellent tidepooling opportunities. Amenities are few, but that's the price to pay for getting away from Laguna's crowds. At least there's a lifeguard, and even volleyball; restaurants and groceries are nearby. Swimming is okay, but watch for the strong shore break and offshore rocks. Skindiving here is good. ~ From Coast Highway take Victoria Drive, then turn right on Dumond Street.

HIDDEN ▶ **ALISO CREEK BEACH PARK** 🏊 ⛵ 🎣 🚣 Set in a wide cove and bounded by low coastal bluffs, this park is popular with local folks. The nearby highway buzzes past and the surrounding hills are adorned with houses. A sand scimitar with rocks guarding both ends, the beach is bisected by a fishing pier. To escape the crowds

HIDDEN ▶ head over to the park's **southern cove**, a pretty beach with fluffy sand. Facilities include picnic areas, restrooms, showers, lifeguards, volleyball, and a snack bar. Restaurants and groceries are nearby, or, if you prefer free food, fishing is good from the pier. When swimming, beware of strong shore breaks. Bodysurfing is a better bet than board surfing at Aliso. ~ Along the Coast Highway in South Laguna; there's a public accessway to the southern cove along the 31300 block of Coast Highway.

HIDDEN ▶ **SOUTH LAGUNA COVES** 🏊 ⛵ 🎣 Hidden by the hillsides that flank South Laguna's waterfront are a series of pocket beaches. Each is a crescent of white sand bounded by sharp cliffs of conglomerate rock. These in turn are crowned with plate-glass homes. Two particularly pretty inlets can be reached via accessways called **1000 Steps** and **West Street**. Both beaches have lifeguards and restrooms. Restaurants and groceries are nearby. Swimming is good, and the bodysurfing is excellent in both coves. ~ Both accessways are on Coast Highway in South Laguna. 1000 Steps is at 9th Avenue; West Street is (surprise!) at West Street.

SALT CREEK BEACH PARK 🏊 ⛵ 🎣 🚣 This marvelous locale consists of two half-mile sections of beach divided by a lofty point on which the Ritz-Carlton Laguna Niguel Hotel stands. Each beach is a broad strip of white sand, backdropped by bluffs and looking out on Santa Catalina Island. The hotel above dominates the region like a palatial fortress on the Mediterranean. Though both beaches are part of Salt Creek, the strand to the south is also known as **Dana Strand**. It's possible to walk from one beach to the other. Both beaches have restrooms and lifeguards; at Salt Creek (north) there is also a snack bar. The swimming is good at either beach, but for fishing you're better off at Laguna Niguel. If you're hoping to hang ten, from Laguna Niguel you can surf "Dana Strand," located a short distance south. Salt Creek has two well-known breaks, "The Gravels," just north of the outcropping that separates the two beaches, and at "The Point" itself. ~ Laguna Niguel Beach Park is reached via a long stairway at the end of Selva Road. The staircase to Salt Creek is on Ritz-Carlton Drive. Both lie off Coast Highway in Laguna Niguel.

DOHENY STATE BEACH 🚲 ⛱ 🏊 🛶 This park wrote the book on oceanside facilities. In addition to a broad swath of sandy beach there is a five-acre lawn complete with private picnic areas, beach rentals, restrooms with changing areas, lifeguards, volleyball courts, and food concessions. The grassy area offers plenty of shade trees. Surfers work the north end of the beach and divers explore an underwater park just offshore. Dana Point Harbor, with complete marina facilities, borders the beach. For fishing, try the jetty in Dana Point Harbor. Swimming is good here, and surfing is comfortable for beginners, particularly on a south swell. Restaurants and groceries are nearby. Day-use fee, $5. ~ Located off Dana Point Harbor Drive in Dana Point; 714-496-6172.

▲ There are 121 sites for both tents and RVs, as well as 32 beach sites. Beach sites cost $22 per night, all other sites cost $17. For reservations call DESTINET at 800-444-7275.

San Juan Capistrano

When you're ready to flee Southern California's ultramodern coastline, Camino Capistrano is the perfect escape valve. At one time or another, almost everyone has heard the 1939 tune "When the Swallows Return to Capistrano." Like many other schmaltzy songs about California, it seems to remain eternally lodged in the brain whether you want it there or not. The lyrics, just to refresh your memory, describe the return of flocks of swallows every March 19. And return they still do, though in ever-decreasing numbers and not always on March 19. When you're ready to follow the swallows, head up Camino Capistrano to the mission and get out your telephoto lens—swallows are small and fast. They remain in the area until October, when winter's approach prompts them to depart for Argentina, where, blissfully, they are welcomed by no similar ditties. While you're here, take time to explore the beautiful mission and local architectural gems.

SIGHTS

Seventh in the state's chain of 21 missions, the **Mission San Juan Capistrano** was founded in 1776 by Father Junípero Serra. Considered "the jewel of the missions" it is a hauntingly beautiful site, placid and magical.

There are ponds and gardens here, ten acres of standing adobe buildings, and the ruins of the original 1797 stone church, destroyed by an earthquake in 1812. The museum displays American Indian crafts, early ecclesiastical artifacts, and Spanish weaponry, while an Indian cemetery memorializes the enslaved people who built this magnificent structure. There is also a living-history program (admission) on the last Saturday of every month, with costumed "characters" playing the role of Father Serra and others, and craftspeople showing how old-time crafts were made.

The highlight of the mission is not the swallows, which are vastly outnumbered by pigeons, but the chapel, a 1777 structure decorated with Indian designs and a baroque altar. Admission. ~ Located at Camino Capistrano and Ortega Highway; 714-248-2048.

> The oldest continually used building in California, the chapel at San Juan Capistrano is the only remaining church used by Father Serra.

At the **O'Neill Museum**, housed in a tiny 1870s Victorian, there are walking-tour maps of the town's old adobes. Within a few blocks you'll discover about a dozen 19th-century structures. The museum is furnished with Victorian decor. Closed Monday and Saturday. Admission. ~ 31831 Los Rios Street; 714-493-8444.

The **Capistrano Depot** appeared a little later in the century but is an equally vital part of the town's history. Converted into a restaurant, the beautifully preserved 1895 depot is still operating as a train station. Built of brick in a series of Spanish-style arches, the old structure houses railroad memorabilia. An antique Pullman, a brightly colored freight car, and other vintage cars line the tracks. ~ 26701 Verdugo Street; 714-488-7600.

Jolting you back to contemporary times are two nearby buildings, both constructed in the 1980s. The **New Church of Mission San Juan Capistrano**, a towering edifice next to the town's historic chapel, is a replica of the original structure. Spanish Renaissance in design, the new church even re-creates the brilliantly painted interior of the old mission. ~ 31522 Camino Capistrano.

Across the street rises the **San Juan Capistrano Regional Library**, an oddly eclectic building. Drawing heavily from the Moorish-style Alhambra in Spain, the architect, Michael Graves, also incorporated ideas from ancient Egypt and classical Greece. ~ 31495 El Camino Real; 714-493-1752.

DINING   One of San Juan Capistrano's many historic points, a 19th-century building, **El Adobe de Capistrano** has been converted into a restaurant. The interior is a warren of white-washed rooms, supported by *vigas* and displaying the flourishes of Spanish California. Stop by for a drink next to the old jail (today a wine cellar) or tour the building. (Counterpoint to all this dusty history is a display of Nixon memorabilia.) If you decide to dine, the menu includes lunch, dinner, and Sunday brunch. Naturally the cuisine is Mexican. ~ 31891 Camino Capistrano; 714-493-1163. BUDGET TO MODERATE.

Who can match the combination of intimacy and French and Belgian cuisine at **L'Hirondelle**? It's quite small, and conveys a French-country atmosphere. The restaurant offers a varied menu beginning with escargots, garlic toast, and crab crêpes. Entrées include roast duckling, rabbit in wine sauce, veal cordon bleu, bouillabaisse, sautéed sweetbreads, and daily fresh fish specials. No lunch on Sunday and Tuesday; closed Monday. ~ 31631 Camino Capistrano; 714-661-0425. MODERATE TO DELUXE.

Situated in a beautifully restored train depot, the **Capistrano Depot Restaurant** offers creative American cuisine at reasonable prices. Red satin and lace drapes add flourish, and guests can dine on lovely oak tables. Be sure to try the grilled black tiger shrimp with charred white corn and cilantro vinaigrette. Lovers of veggies should definitely not miss the chef's grilled vegetable Napoleon, which is served in an exquisite tomato broth. ~ 26701 Verdugo Street; 714-488-7600. MODERATE.

SHOPPING

The mission town of San Juan Capistrano has many shops clustered along its main thoroughfare, Camino Capistrano. Not surprisingly, the most common establishment in this two-century-old town is the antique store. In line with contemporary times, there are also pocket malls featuring boutiques, jewelers, and other outlets.

Particularly noteworthy is **The Old Barn,** a warehouse-size store filled to the rafters with antiques. ~ 31792 Camino Capistrano; 714-493-9144.

NIGHTLIFE

Swallows Inn is a hellbent Western bar with sawdust on the floors and ranch tools tacked to the walls. Every night you can kick up your heels to live country-and-western, except on Tuesday, when the music takes on a rock-and-roll, jazz, or blues feel. ~ 31786 Camino Capistrano; 714-493-3188.

BEACHES & PARKS

CAPISTRANO BEACH PARK This is a big rectangular sandbox facing the open ocean. Like many beaches in the area it offers ample facilities and is often quite crowded. Bounded by sedimentary cliffs and offering views of Dana Point Harbor, the beach is landscaped with palm and deciduous trees. The park is particularly popular with families and surfers, who all take advantage of the picnic areas, restrooms, showers, lifeguards, volleyball, and basketball court. Swimming is good here, but it's the surfing that's the big draw. "Killer Capo" breaks are about 400 yards offshore along the northern fringes of the beach (near Doheny State Park), and "Dody's Reef" breaks are about one-half mile to the south, but are not predictable. ~ Located along Coast Highway in Capistrano Beach.

San Clemente

If any place is the capital of Republican politics, it is San Clemente, a seaside town that sets the standard for Southern California's notorious conservatism because of one man. Richard Milhous Nixon, President of the United States from 1969 until his ignominious resignation during the Watergate scandal in 1974, established the Western White House on a 25-acre site overlooking the ocean.

SIGHTS

La Casa Pacífica, a magnificent Spanish-style home, was famous not only during Nixon's presidency, but afterwards when he retreated to San Clemente to lick his wounds. There are stories of Nixon, ever the brooding, socially awkward man, pacing the beach in a business suit and leather shoes.

The Nixon house is located off Avenida del Presidente in a private enclave called Cypress Shore. You can see it, a grand white stucco home with red tile roof, on the cliffs above San Clemente State Beach. Just walk south from the beach entrance about one-half mile toward a point of land obscured by palms; the house is set back in the trees.

Another point of interest (quite literally) is **San Clemente Municipal Pier**, a popular fishing spot and centerpiece of the city beach. There are food concessions, bait and tackle shops, and local crowds galore. ~ Foot of Avenida del Mar.

For more information on the area, call the **San Clemente Chamber of Commerce**. ~ 1100 North El Camino Real; 714-492-1131.

LODGING

Algodon Motel is a standard 18-unit facility several blocks from the beach. Some units have kitchens. Not much to write home about, but it is clean and affordable. ~ 135 Avenida Algodon; 714-492-3382. BUDGET TO MODERATE.

Cheaper still is the **Hostelling International—San Clemente Beach**, an AYH facility located in a stucco building on a residential street. The accommodations consist of bunk beds in dormitory rooms; one family room is also available in the summer. Visitors share a television room, kitchen, and small patio. ~ 233 Avenida Granada; 714-492-2848, 800-444-6111. BUDGET.

DINING

Center of the casual dining scene in San Clemente is along the beach at the foot of the municipal pier (end of Avenida del Mar). Several takeout stands and cafés are here. **The Fisherman's Restaurant and Bar**, a knotty-pine-and-plate-glass establishment, sits right on the pier, affording views all along the beach. With a waterfront patio it's a good spot for seafood dishes at lunch or dinner. There is also breakfast and Sunday brunch during the summer. ~ 611 Avenida Victoria; 714-498-6390. MODERATE TO DELUXE.

BEACHES & PARKS

SAN CLEMENTE CITY BEACH 🏊 🎣 ⚓ Running nearly the length of town this silver strand is the pride of San Clemente. Landlubbers congregate near the municipal pier, anglers work its waters, and surfers blanket the beachfront. There are railroad tracks and coastal bluffs paralleling the entire beach. Eden this ain't: San Clemente is heavily developed, but the beach is a pleasant place to spend a day. There are restaurants and other amenities at the municipal pier including picnic areas, restrooms, lifeguards, and a playground. The **Ole Hanson Beach Club** (105 Avenida Pico; 714-361-8207; admission) at the north end of the beach is a public pool with dressing rooms. Fishing is best from the pier, and surfing is good alongside of the pier. The beach is also good for swimming. ~ The pier is located at the foot of Avenida del Mar in San Clemente.

SAN CLEMENTE STATE BEACH 🏊 🚶 🛶 Walk down the deeply eroded cliffs guarding this coastline, and you'll discover a long narrow strip of sand that curves north from San Diego County up to San Clemente City Beach. There are camping areas and picnic plots on top of the bluff. Down below a railroad track parallels the beach and surfers paddle offshore. You can stroll north toward downtown San Clemente or south to President Nixon's old home. Beach facilities include lifeguards, picnic areas, and restrooms; restaurants and groceries are nearby in San Clemente. Surf fishing is best in spring, and surfers will find year-round breaks at the south end of the beach. Swimmers should beware of rip currents. Day-use fee, $6. ~ Located off Avenida Calafia in San Clemente; 714-492-3156.

▲ There are 160 sites for tents and RVs (72 with hookups); $17 for tents; $24 for hookups.

Moving away from the ocean, Orange County sprawls eastward towards and beyond the Santa Ana River, an ever-expanding region marked by constant sunshine and conservative politics. Like much of inland Orange County, Anaheim appears as a vast and bewildering plane of urbanization, an uninspiring amalgam of housing tracts and shopping centers.

Inland Orange County

But within this thickly populated and frenetic city lies the virtual epicenter of visitor appeal—**Disneyland**. Almost everyone, no matter how reclusive, regardless of age, race, creed, or religion, inevitably visits this colossal theme park.

SIGHTS

Cynics—who snicker at its fantasy formula, orderliness, ultra-cleanliness, cornball humor, and conservative overtones—nevertheless often seem to be swept away by the pure joy of Uncle Walt's fertile imagination.

When Walt Disney cleared away orange groves to open his dream park back in 1955, he provided 18 attractions and promised that Disneyland would never stop growing. Today the park features over 60 attractions, with plans afoot to add even more rides.

If at all possible, plan your Disneyland visit to avoid the peak summer months. Huge crowds mean long waiting lines. In any case, it's a good idea to arrive as the park opens and to go directly down Main Street (the park's entry corridor) to be among the first wave of visitors fanning out into the park's many theme lands.

The Magic Kingdom is divided into eight areas. *Main Street* portrays an all-American town at the turn of the century. *Adventure-*

land, a region of jungle rivers filled with hippos and crocodiles, is home to "Indiana Jones Adventure," one of Disneyland's most thrilling and popular rides.

With cactus, adobe buildings, and Western-style trading posts, *Frontierland's* main draw is "Big Thunder Mountain Railroad," which simulates a runaway mine train.

Iron-trellised balconies, winding streets, and sidewalk cafés make *New Orleans Square* one of the prettiest themed areas. Here are two perennial favorites: "Pirates of the Caribbean" and "The Haunted Mansion."

While absolutely nothing about it is "hidden," Disneyland can provide one of life's great escapes.

In *Critter Country* you can listen to a jamboree performed by mechanical bears or venture down the harrowing "Splash Mountain" log ride.

At the center of *Mickey's Toontown* is "Mickey's House," where you can visit with Mr. Mouse himself and view his personal possessions.

Sleeping Beauty's castle, Pinocchio's village, and the white-knuckle "Matterhorn Bobsleds" are only some of the highlights of *Fantasyland*.

Dedicated to the future and its limitless prospects, *Tomorrowland* uses rides, innovative films, and imaginative surroundings to portray technological wonders. "Star Tours" and "Space Mountain," Tomorrowland's most sensational rides, should be early on your agenda.

The list of things to see and do in Disneyland is staggering: take a jungle cruise, ride a Mississippi paddlewheeler, soar over the 85-acre park in a gondola, commute on a monorail, watch parades and live entertainment, eat at a mind-boggling array of restaurants, shop for just about anything, and have your picture taken with Mickey Mouse.

During off-peak periods, most adults can tour the park in a day. If you take children or visit during peak periods when lines are long, plan on a couple of days. Disneyland now employs the "Passport" type ticket, which includes park admission and unlimited use of rides and attractions. Two- and three-day passports are discounted but a family of four can figure on spending at least $150 a day, including meals, snacks, and souvenirs. Even at that, not many will argue the value of a day or two at the "Happiest Place on Earth." ~ 1313 South Harbor Boulevard, Anaheim; 714-999-4565.

California's second biggest tourist attraction, **Knott's Berry Farm**, lies just five miles away in Buena Park. While some have alluded to it as a country cousin to Disneyland, this 150-acre theme park with more than 165 rides and attractions is both larger and some 15 years older than its sophisticated neighbor. "The Farm," as it is known locally, actually began life back in 1920 when Walter and Cornelia Knott planted a ten-acre berry and rhubarb patch and opened a roadside stand. Eventually the stand evolved into a "Chicken Dinner Restaurant" to which Walter Knott added a mock California Gold Rush town, complete with narrow-gauge railroad.

The original restaurant still serves up Mrs. Knott's chicken dinners—at the rate of 1.5 million a year—and Walter's old *Ghost Town*, though rickety with age, looks much as it did in the beginning. To be sure, the park has grown right along with Disneyland, in a sort of symbiotic surge, meeting the demands of ever-increasing attendance.

Knott's *Wild Water Wilderness* resembles a 1900s California river wilderness park highlighted by "Mystery Lodge," an exploration of the traditions of the American Indians who lived on the Pacific Northwest Coast, and "Bigfoot Rapids," a wet and wild ride down California's longest manmade white-water river.

The area that was known as the Roaring 20s was revitalized in 1996 and reborn as *The Boardwalk*, a colorfully themed area designed to celebrate the vigor and vitality of Southern California's fabled beach culture. Besides the new thrill ride "Hammerhead," many of the park's old favorites are still here—"Boomerang," "Parachute Sky Jump," and "Kingdom of the Dinosaurs."

A south-of-the-border entertainment center, *Fiesta Village* is complete with California mission replicas, open markets, strolling mariachis, and two wild rides: "Montezooma's Revenge" and "Jaguar."

Geared toward young kids, *Camp Snoopy* is the official home of Charles Schultz's beloved "Peanuts" pals—Snoopy, Linus, Lucy, and Charlie Brown. Life-size versions of the popular cartoon characters roam the six-acre area hugging guests and posing for pictures. Modeled after the Sierra Nevada mountains, Camp Snoopy features a lake, waterfalls, petting zoo, animal show, and kiddie and family rides.

Indian Trails is the park's fifth theme area, a two-acre plot exhibiting the culture, entertainment, and crafts of American Indians. Admission. ~ 8039 Beach Boulevard, Buena Park; 714-827-1776.

Consult *Disneyland and Beyond: Southern California Family Attractions* (Ulysses Press) for further information on Southern California's theme parks.

Theme parks aren't the only visitor attractions in the inland reaches of Orange County. Their very existence, in fact, has spawned the growth of other travel destinations. The **Movieland Wax Museum**, with its collection of more than 200 wax figures of movie and television stars, has grown up right in the shadow of Knott's Berry Farm. Movie buffs and stargazers will either like or loath this wax mausoleum, which presents stars frozen in realistic scenes from their most famous movies and television programs. Admission. ~ 7711 Beach Boulevard, Buena Park; 714-522-1154.

Museums catering to broader interests include the **Anaheim Museum**, with exhibits depicting the city's meteoric growth from a 19th-century farm society. ~ 241 South Anaheim Boulevard, Anaheim; 714-778-3301. Also try the excellent **Bowers Museum of Cul-**

Text continued on page 238.

Orange County's Outback

To explore the last vestiges of Orange County's open country, plan to spend a day wandering the area's southeastern fringes. Along the ridges and valleys of the **Santa Ana Mountains** you'll find that all that remains of the county's undeveloped countryside. It's your final chance to catch a glimpse of Orange County as it looked back in 1769 when the Spanish first probed the region's rugged, chapparal-covered mountains. But at the rate new housing tracts are pushing into the region, you'd better hurry!

Simply point your steed south along Route 5, then turn east on El Toro Road (Route S18) toward those lovely mountains. Ride on to Live Oak Canyon Road, then turn right and you'll slip beneath a canopy of live oaks. This leafy tunnel into Orange County's distant past is also the way to **O'Neill Regional Park**. A perfect spot for a picnic lunch, the 3100-acre preserve is highlighted by Trabuco Creek Trail, which follows a bubbling stream well shaded by oak and cottonwood. ~ 714-858-9366.

Returning to El Toro Road, which becomes Santiago Canyon Road, the route curves up what locals call Modjeska Grade, leaving in its wake a spate of subdivision projects that spoil the view for solace seekers. Turn right on Modjeska Valley Road, another winding lane, then left at the junction of Modjeska Canyon and Foothill roads (there's a large tree forming an island between the two streets).

As you enter the rustic town of Modjeska, watch for the fire station on your left; across from it lies a small bridge leading to Hill Road. Once over the bridge, the first gate on the left belongs to one of Orange County's most important historic treasures, the **Modjeska House**. Formerly the retreat of the renowned Polish actress Madame Helena Modjeska, this white frame mansion, designed in the late 1880s by famed New York architect Stanford White, sits in disrepair. Surrounded by a forest of olive trees, the secluded home is officially closed to the public, but caretakers usually permit visitors to walk around the grounds.

A talented tragedienne, Madame Modjeska left the European stage to move to California with her venturesome husband, Count Karol Chlapowski. While the count tried unsuccessfully to develop a vineyard, Madame Modjeska began acting in the United States, achieving stardom in such roles as Mary Queen of Scots, Cleopatra, and Lady Macbeth. When the couple retired to Newport Beach, the estate was sold, becoming first a country club and later a private home. One can only hope that it will someday be restored to its original magnificence and opened to the public.

A mile further along Modjeska Canyon Road lies **Tucker Wildlife Sanctuary**. This 12-acre refuge is home to more than 170 species of birds and animals, which can be viewed along a series of short loop trails. Tucker is best known for its hummingbirds; all seven varieties known to exist in California can be seen here. An island of conservation in a sea of development, the preserve is also home to hawks and woodpeckers. Guided tours are available during the week only. ~ 714-649-2760.

Back on Santiago Canyon Road continue northwest to **Irvine Lake**, an 800-acre private lake. Stocked and maintained with the serious angler in mind, these waters have produced a state record 59-pound catfish as well as trophy-sized "super trout" (triploid rainbow) in the 20-pound range. Bass up to nearly 15 pounds have been caught and there are bluegill and white sturgeon as well. Admission. ~ 714-649-9111.

To wrap up this backcountry adventure, continue for four miles on Santiago Canyon Road to Chapman Avenue, turn left and go three miles to the Newport Freeway (Route 55), then proceed south to Route 5 or 405. Either will carry you back to the civilization from which you so recently departed.

tural Art, where cultural art exhibits include American Indian and Hispanic collections as well as displays from the Pacific Rim and Africa. Admission. ~ 2002 North Main Street, Santa Ana; 714-567-3600.

Located on a prehistoric fossil field that may be as extensive as the famed La Brea Tar Pits, **Ralph B. Clark Regional Park** has trained volunteers dig through centuries-old fossil beds while visitors look on. This unique facility also offers an interpretive center with fossil displays and a working paleontology lab. Providing marvelous educational opportunities, the digs and lab activities are structured as part of an organized tour program. Admission. ~ 8800 Rosecrans Avenue, Buena Park; 714-670-8045.

One of urban Orange County's most unusual edifices is the **Crystal Cathedral**, a spectacular glass cathedral that rises in the shape of a star to a height of 124 feet. The pipe organ, amplified by banks of speakers that would be the envy of any rock concert promoter, is one of the largest in the world. Through the cathedral's 10,661 panes of glass you can see both the steel tubing that forms the structure's skeleton and the cars that assemble every Sunday to attend "drive-in services" in the parking lot. ~ 12141 Lewis Street, Garden Grove; 714-971-4000.

For a sense of Orange County's cultural life, head down Costa Mesa way to the South Coast Plaza offices, across Bristol Street from South Coast Plaza Shopping Center. Here Japanese-American sculptor Isamu Noguchi has created **California Scenario**, a sculpture garden surrounded by office towers. An abstract expression of the Golden State, this stone-and-steel creation reflects the many faces of California.

The state's majestic redwoods are represented along Forest Walk, a curving path lined with granite. At the Energy Fountain, a stainless steel cone, resembling the nose of a rocket, symbolizes the space-age vitality of the state. The Desert Land section features an array of

---

DRIVE-THROUGH THEOLOGY

Unorthodox though it may seem, even for Southern California, drive-in religion was developed by the **The Crystal Cathedral's** pastor, Dr. Robert Schuller, when his hard-sell evangelism grew so rapidly during the 1950s that he had to conduct services at a local drive-in movie theater. Even today many of Schuller's penitents continue to prefer bucket seats to wooden pews. A massive glass door slides open during services so auto-bound worshippers can receive the word. Nor are they overlooked by ushers who glide like carhops from window to window with collection plates.

plants and cacti including the native tricereus, golden barrel cactus, and agave. The featured piece, Noguchi's tribute to the lima bean farmers who once worked this region, is a collection of 15 bronze-colored granite boulders, precisely cut and fit together to resemble a mound of the noble beans. ~ Costa Mesa; 714-435-2100.

LODGING

Covering 60 acres and containing 1138 rooms, 11 restaurants and lounges, 20 shops, and almost as many gimmicks as the Magic Kingdom itself, **Disneyland Hotel** is a self-contained world. Situated anywhere else it would rank as a full-blown destination. You can swim, play tennis, sun on a sandy "beach," feed koi fish, watch a light show, shop, dine, drink, dance—or even sleep here. And if that isn't enough, step out front to the monorail station and three minutes later you are at the real thing! ~ 1150 West Cerritos Avenue, Anaheim; 714-778-6600, fax 714-956-6582. ULTRA-DELUXE.

The **Disneyland Pacific Hotel** is situated on four-and-a-half acres of beautifully landscaped grounds including palm-fringed sidewalks and a koi pond. The Japanese theme continues in the 501 guest rooms, which are elegantly understated with light wood and warm earth tones. The tropical-style lobby is decorated with large over-sized chairs and has a glass-enclosed elevator. A swimming pool, spa, recreation area, two boutiques, and two restaurants are among the amenities. Located next door to the Disney monorail station, the hotel also provides its guests with special perks such as an early admission to Disneyland and other Disney deals. ~ 1717 South West Street, Anaheim; 714-956-6400, fax 714-956-6582. ULTRA-DELUXE.

The **Anaheim Marriott**, located two blocks from Disneyland, offers an outstanding luxury-hotel experience. Two towers, 19 and 17 stories in height, are centered on 15 acres of flower-filled grounds. The lobby reflects a soft, contemporary feel with a sunken sitting area. Framed by a tropical palm court with koi pond, the area has the atmosphere of a sunlit atrium. The hotel has a connecting indoor/outdoor pool, an outdoor pool, two whirlpools plus saunas and a Nautilus-equipped fitness center. Its 1033 rooms are medium-sized with small balconies, some with Disneyland views. ~ 700 West Convention Way, Anaheim; 714-750-8000, fax 714-748-2449. ULTRA-DELUXE.

Two blocks from Disneyland stands the cavernous, 1576-room **Anaheim Hilton**, a glass-enclosed monolith. The airy atrium lobby, set off by brass railings and blue and mauve tones, holds four restaurants, three lounges, a nightclub, and assorted shops, along with a pond and fountain. The modern guest rooms are individually decorated. ~ 777 Convention Way, Anaheim; 714-750-4321, 800-222-9923, fax 714-740-4737. ULTRA-DELUXE.

Like the little alpine lass who curtsies from her signboard perch above the entrance, the **Heidi Motel** is kind of cute. This 30-unit court was here even before Disneyland and occupies an ideal location nearby. Rooms are small but clean, well maintained, and trimly furnished. There's also a pool. ~ 815 West Katella Avenue, Anaheim; 714-533-1979, fax 714-776-2962. BUDGET.

One of the nicest of the hundreds of hotels and motels encircling the perimeter of Disneyland is **Best Western Park Place Inn**. Crisp, contemporary styling set it apart from many of its neighbors. Accommodations are fresh and colorful. There's a pool, sauna, and jacuzzi. You can walk to Disneyland, which is right across the street from the inn. ~ 1544 South Harbor Boulevard, Anaheim; 714-776-4800, 800-854-8175. MODERATE.

Best Western Raffles Inn offers a compromise between the huge highrise hotels and roadside motels in central Orange County. Just three stories high and sensibly sized (122 rooms), it actually conveys a bit of the "inn" feeling. It looks like one, too, with its tree-shrouded manor house facade. Rooms feature Early American furnishings and some contain kitchenettes. ~ 2040 South Harbor Boulevard, Anaheim; 714-750-6100, 800-654-0196, fax 714-740-0639. MODERATE.

Best of the old-time motels and "tourist courts" that line Beach Boulevard near Knott's Berry Farm is the **Silver Moon Motel**. It's been around since 1955; but nostalgia aside, the place is clean, carefully maintained, and offers 44 rooms, some with kitchens. Located one mile from Knott's Berry Farm, five from Disneyland. ~ 212 South Beach Boulevard, Anaheim; 714-527-1102. BUDGET.

A bit off the mainstream but still only a few blocks from Knott's Berry Farm is **Fullerton "A" Inn**. This 43-room motel may be the best low-cost lodging in close proximity to Knott's. Rooms are clean, air-conditioned, and nicely furnished in a contemporary mode. Pool, sauna, whirlpool, and exercise room. ~ 2601 West Orangethorpe Avenue, Fullerton; 714-773-4900. BUDGET.

Colony Inn is a rambling 128-room complex across the street from Knott's. It's clean, well maintained, and has a pair of pools and saunas in addition to efficiency units and suites. ~ 7800 Crescent Avenue, Buena Park; 714-527-2201, 800-982-6566. BUDGET TO MODERATE.

For visitors planning to bike Santiago Canyon Road, explore O'Neill Regional Park, or fish the Santa Ana River lakes, the nicest motel is **Sky Palm International Lodge**. It has 27 clean and spacious guest rooms, plus a pool with cabaña. ~ 210 North Tustin Avenue, Orange; 714-639-6602, 800-833-4477, fax 714-639-5581. BUDGET TO MODERATE.

Today, more than five million people visit Knott's Berry Farm each year.

DINING   Restaurants of every description surround Disneyland, most offering moderately priced but mediocre food. An exception, one of the area's best values for atmosphere and satisfying dining, is **Mr. Stox**, which boasts a versatile menu of steaks, rack of lamb, veal, pasta, and mesquite-broiled fresh seafood. Special touches include savory herbs and spices grown in a garden out back, plus homemade breads and desserts and an award-winning wine cellar. ~ 1105 East Katella Avenue, Anaheim; 714-634-2994. MODERATE TO DELUXE.

A full sushi bar in Disneyland? That's exactly what **Yamabuki** has to offer, as well as stir-fry dishes, tempura, and teriyaki. Laid out in a Japanese-style fashion, the dining area includes a traditional *tatami* room where guests are invited to take off their shoes, sit on cushion-covered straw mats and indulge in the culinary delights of authentic Japanese cuisine. No lunch on Saturday and Sunday. ~ Disneyland Pacific Hotel, 1717 South West Street, Anaheim; 714-239-5683. DELUXE TO ULTRA-DELUXE.

The top restaurant in these parts can be found at the Anaheim Marriott Hotel. **JW's** offers an outstanding Continental cuisine menu with such delicacies as antelope medallions with morels and roast saddle of wild boar. The candlelit ambience, attentive service and contemporary flourishes add to the experience. ~ 700 West Convention Way, Anaheim; 714-750-0900. DELUXE TO ULTRA-DELUXE.

Painted bright pink, **Belisle's Restaurant** is hard to miss. Once inside this converted house you'll find truck drivers, radically coifed coeds, and neat-as-a-pin Orange County families all shoveling away good old-fashioned country-style chow. There's a two-pound steak, "poke" chops, catfish 'n hushpuppies, and baked meatloaf. Belisle's is open late (midnight on weekdays, until two on weekends) and most everything on its voluminous menu is reasonably priced. ~ 12001 Harbor Boulevard, Garden Grove; 714-750-6560. MODERATE.

Somewhat distant from metropolitan Orange County is **La Vie En Rose**. Portraying a Norman farmhouse, complete with eight-sided steeple, it's an intimate dining room with French-country appointments. The theme of rural Normandy is carried to completion by waitresses who stream forth with hearty and authentic provincial dishes like *escalope de veau à la Normande* (sautéed veal scallopine with apple brandy cream sauce) and *carré d'agneau aux herbes fraîches* (rack of lamb with fresh herbs). Be sure to make reservations. ~ 240 South State College Boulevard, Brea; 714-529-8333. DELUXE.

Orange County's most original dining adventure is at **The Hobbit**. Here you'll be ushered into a gracious old 1930s hacienda for a magical evening of food and wine. Dinner begins with a tour of the wine cellar where guests select their favorite wines. For two or three hours you are tempted with a parade of hot and cold hors d'oeuvres, soup, salad, fowl, beef, and fish courses followed by sorbet and dessert. During "intermission" you can visit the chef in his immaculate kitchen or stroll in the art gallery and gardens. The menu is prix-fixe; reserve weeks in advance. ~ 932 East Chapman Avenue, Orange; 714-997-1972. ULTRA-DELUXE.

Antonello Ristorante, Orange County's best-decorated and most highly rated Italian eatery, is a re-creation of an actual Italian street setting. Window flower boxes give the place a genuine Old-Country feel. When it comes to cuisine, the nouvelle treatments of traditional Northern Italian dishes are outstanding. Pasta, breads, and desserts are made fresh daily and are quite good, but try something you won't find in run-of-the-mill Italian restaurants, like scampi *al anice* or raviolini stuffed with braised veal. Very highly recommended. Closed Sunday. ~ 1611 Sunflower Avenue, Santa Ana; 714-751-7153. DE-LUXE TO ULTRA-DELUXE.

For curry lovers there's Gandhi, an Indian restaurant with a decidedly British decor. Earth tones, wood panelling, English china, and heavy silver-plated tableware create a colonial atmosphere. The rich, exotic combination of herbs and spices that flavor the curried lamb, Muglai chicken, or *tandoori* treats make this award-winning restaurant a wise choice. ~ 1621 Sunflower Avenue, Santa Ana; 714-556-7273. MODERATE.

Flagship of a family fleet of popular Chinese restaurants is Mandarin Gourmet, a modern, sophisticated, and exciting restaurant. As the name implies, most dishes are from the northern provinces though there are samplings of Hunan, Beijing, and Szechuan cooking. The signature dish and almost everyone's favorite is aromatic shrimp. ~ 1500 Adams Avenue, Costa Mesa; 714-540-1937. MODERATE TO DELUXE.

To savvy diners, Chanteclair spells "enchantment." Entering the château along a brick walkway flanked by Italian terra cotta planters, you'll encounter a dining room furnished with antiques. Pure continental elegance, backed by fine food and consummate service, is almost taken for granted here. Filet Wellington with truffle sauce, veal Orloff, and a fabulous fresh lobster served over fettuccine lead the list of favorite dishes. Magnificent to the eye and palate, Chanteclair is one of Orange County's best (and most expensive) dining spots. Dressy by its very nature. ~ 18912 MacArthur Boulevard, Irvine; 714-752-8001. DELUXE TO ULTRA-DELUXE.

A high-tech Chinese restaurant? Lipstick reds and glossy blacks combine with lots of neon at Chinatown Restaurant and Bar. The list of entrées includes 20 original house specialties such as gunpowder scallops and veal Marco Polo. Exciting and different, Chinatown should not be overlooked. ~ 4139 Campus Drive, Irvine; 714-856-2211. BUDGET TO MODERATE.

Upscale, contemporary Prego packs 'em in both for tasty, authentic Italian food and a breathtaking interior scheme. Arched ceilings and a sizzling open-fire rotisserie greet the eye. Hardwood floors are accented by marbletop tables and black lacquered chairs. Aromas of saffron, oregano, and steaming pasta will quickly turn your attention to eating, however, and that's a real pleasure at Prego. The big surprise is Prego's pizza, superb pies baked in a huge woodburning oven.

Buon appetito! ~ 8420 Von Karman Avenue, Irvine; 714-553-1333. MODERATE.

Mandarin Taste Restaurant prepares traditional Mandarin fare. The oyster sauce, used to top a number of dishes, is especially good, as is the Chinese chicken salad. ~ 23600 Rockfield Boulevard, Lake Forest; 714-830-9984. MODERATE.

A lovely hideaway can be found at **La Ferme**, an intimate restaurant in the European country cottage tradition. Not surprisingly, its hallmark is French-country cuisine like crisp roasted duckling and fresh poached salmon in white wine served with tarragon cream sauce. Everything at La Ferme seems to taste better before a crackling fireplace, beside richly textured walls, and on tables bedecked in forest green linens and set with fine china and fresh flowers. ~ 28451 Marguerite Parkway, Mission Viejo; 714-364-6664. MODERATE TO DELUXE.

> Spend a day in a theme park and you've walked three to four miles. If you're not in good shape, better get moving!

Trabuco Oaks Steak House is popularly known as "the home of the two-pound cowboy steak." Don't be put off by its rundown facade or funky-rustic decor; nobody in Orange County turns out a bigger, tastier steak or better french fries (they're hand-cut daily). The dog-eared menu lists ribs, chicken, fish, and spaghetti as well, but you should stick to steak here. Leave your tie at home (they cut 'em and tack 'em to the walls), but be sure to bring a business card to add to the thousands plastered around the place. Dinner only. ~ 20782 Trabuco Oaks Drive, Trabuco Canyon; 714-586-0722. MODERATE TO DELUXE.

SHOPPING

Inland Orange County is a maze of suburban shopping centers large and small. Which is all right if you're really intent on buying but rather unappealing when you simply want to browse. For those charming little boutiques and artisan shops, stick to the beach area.

In spite of its discount-store facade, the **Crystal Factory** is a treasure trove of crystal and glassware. It's possible to spend from two bucks to two grand on everything from stemware to handblown crystal lamps. While browsing you can watch craftsmen engrave crystal items. ~ 8010 Beach Boulevard, Buena Park; 714-952-4135.

Fill a 16,000-square-foot building with 145 separate cubicles and you've got the **Old Chicago Antique Market**. Independent vendors sell wares ranging from fine old furniture to '50s memorabilia. ~ 18319 Euclid Street, Fountain Valley; 714-434-6487.

Hobby City looks like a miniature Knott's Berry Farm, anchored by a "perfect half-scale replica" of the White House. It also features an intriguing array of 24 specialized shops, each devoted entirely to the hobbyist and collector. Among them are stamp, coin, gem, antiques, and doll dealers. ~ 1238 South Beach Boulevard, Anaheim; 714-527-2323.

Biggest and best of the Orange County malls is **South Coast Plaza Shopping Center**. Some say this is the most distinguished retail address on the West Coast, loaded with sleek signature shops, showcase stores, and a host of lesser-known establishments. ~ 3333 South Bristol Street, Costa Mesa; 714-241-1700.

Orange County Market Place is the area's biggest flea market with some 1200 vendors displaying their wares each weekend at the Orange County Fairgrounds. ~ 88 Fair Drive, Costa Mesa.

Serious antique shoppers always head over to Orange where there's a gaggle of great shops. Considered the "antique capital of Southern California," **Orange Circle Antique Mall** is the biggest and one of the best. Housed in a refurbished 1909 brick building are some 120 independently operated booths, each offering something different. Tiffany lamps, toy soldiers, barber poles, mahogany armoires . . . you name it. ~ 118 South Glassell Street, Orange; 714-538-8160.

NIGHTLIFE   **Neon Cactus**, located in the Disneyland Hotel, is a fun nightspot with live rock-and-roll bands Friday through Sunday nights, DJ dancing Monday and Tuesday, and karaoke on Wednesday. ~ 1150 West Cerritos, Anaheim; 714-778-6600.

Cowboy Boogie is a nightclub where you can dance. Along with teaching you the cowboy cha-cha dance Tuesday through Saturday evenings, this nightspot features live country-and-western bands on Sunday. Cover. ~ 1721 South Manchester Avenue, Anaheim; 714-956-1410.

While original and creative forms of nightlife may be lacking in Orange County, it's through no fault of a couple of local residents who were just crazy enough to string together a laundromat, barbecue joint, and beer bar. Although the regulars begin by tossing in their dirty laundry, you may want to start out at **Brian's Beer & Billiards**. No worries about the wash, in case you brought yours—the bar has lights connected to the washers and dryers telling you exactly when your load is finished. ~ 1944 North Placentia Avenue, Fullerton; 714-993-1401.

It seems hokey at first: dining with your fingers in an imitation 12th-century castle while knights ride into battle. Actually, **Medieval Times** is a brilliant concept, a re-creation of a medieval tournament, complete with games of skill and jousting matches. It can get pretty wild when the knights—highly trained horsemen and stuntmen—perform dangerous jousting and sword-fighting routines. ~ 7662 Beach Boulevard, Buena Park; 714-521-4740.

Peppers is a colorful Mexican-themed restaurant that owes most of its popularity to its dancefloor rather than its food. Young singles dig the scene as deejays spin Top-40, hip-hop, and disco hits nightly. Male exotic dancers shake to the beat Thursday and Saturday. Cover. ~ 12361 Chapman Avenue, Garden Grove; 714-740-1333.

Happy Hour is a women's bar that features pool tables, video games, and deejay music. There's karaoke on Thursday and live music on weekends. Cover. ~ 12081 Garden Grove Boulevard, Garden Grove; 714-537-9079.

You can two-step to live country-and-western music at Crazy Horse Steak House & Saloon, Orange County's most popular and long-lived nightspot. Cover. ~ 1580 Brookhollow Drive, Santa Ana; 714-549-1512.

CLASSIC ENTERTAINMENT Grove Theater Center presents Shakespeare and other classical dramas, comedies, and musicals year-round. ~ 12852 Main Street, Garden Grove; 714-636-7213.

Orange County Performing Arts Center is one of Southern California's great cultural assets, a 2994-seat theater which regularly features the New York City Ballet and Joffrey Ballet, plus a host of visiting dance, opera, and musical companies. ~ 600 Town Center Drive, Costa Mesa; 714-556-2787.

Offering the best in classic and contemporary plays, South Coast Repertory Theatre has established itself as a major theatrical presence in California and nationwide. ~ 655 Town Center Drive, Costa Mesa; 714-957-4033.

Pacific Amphitheatre presents concerts by name performers in the largest outdoor concert setting on the West Coast. Closed during the winter. ~ Orange County Fairgrounds, 100 Fair Drive, Costa Mesa; 714-708-1870.

Irvine Meadows Amphitheatre features leading musical acts in a lovely outdoor amphitheatre. Closed during the winter. ~ 8808 Irvine Center Drive, Irvine; 714-855-4515.

BEACHES & PARKS

CANYON RV PARK AND CAMPGROUND 🚶🚴 Unique among Orange County parks, this one's only for camping. Situated in the heart of Santa Ana Canyon, it covers 90 acres, a fraction of which has been developed for campgrounds. The balance is a natural streamside wilderness which includes a nature trail flanked by cottonwood, oak, and willow trees. There are restrooms, showers, nature and bike trails, and a visitors center; restaurants and groceries are nearby. Day-use fee, $5. ~ Located at 24001 Santa Ana Canyon Road, Anaheim; 714-637-0210.

▲ There are 35 tent sites and 120 RV sites; $17.50 without hookups; $22.50 with hookups.

IRVINE REGIONAL PARK 🚶🚴🐎⛵ This 477-acre park offers more than ten miles of biking, hiking, and equestrian trails. There's a boating lagoon, petting zoo, and pony stables with rides for the kids. You'll find picnic areas, playground, bike and paddleboat rentals, restrooms, and a snack bar; restaurants and groceries are nearby. Day-use fee, $5. ~ Located at 1 Irvine Park Road, Orange; 714-633-8074.

O'NEILL REGIONAL PARK 🚶🚴🏇 Originally part of an 1841 Mexican land grant, this 3100-acre county park straddles Trabuco and Live Oak canyons in a delightfully undeveloped region of the Santa Ana Mountains. Topography varies from oak-lined canyon bottomlands and grassy meadows to chaparral-covered hillsides. There's a surprising variety of wildlife that can be spotted while hiking on the nature trails: opossum, raccoon, rabbit, and coyote are frequently seen, as are hawk, quail, dove, and roadrunner. Far more elusive, but ever present in the park, are mountain lion. Amenities include picnic areas, stables, restrooms, and showers; restaurants and groceries are nearby. Day-use fee, $2. ~ Located in southeastern Orange County at 30892 Trabuco Canyon Road, 18 miles east of Route 405 via El Toro Road exit; 714-858-9366.

▲ There are 90 tent/RV sites (no hookups); $12 per night.

RONALD W. CASPERS WILDERNESS PARK 🚶🚴🏇 A gem of a park, this is Orange County's largest preserve, covering 7600 acres of rugged mountain and canyonland bordering Cleveland National Forest. Within this vast domain are more than 30 miles of marked trails for hiking, biking, and horseback riding. There's a small museum, picnic areas, restrooms, and showers; groceries are several miles away. Note: No one under 18 is allowed to use the trails unless accompanied by a ranger. Day-use fee, $4. ~ Located at 33401 Ortega Highway (Route 74), San Juan Capistrano; 714-728-0235.

▲ There are 52 tent/RV sites and an equestrian camp with 30 sites; $12 per night.

▼▼▼▼▼▼▼▼▼▼▼▼▼
Outdoor Adventures

Whether you want to catch or watch, the Orange County coast offers plenty of possibilities.

FISHING & WHALE WATCHING

Davey's Locker offers sportfishing charters. ~ 400 Main Street, Balboa; 714-673-1434. Another Orange County outfit is Dana Wharf Sportfishing. ~ 34675 Golden Lantern Street, Dana Point; 714-496-5794. For those more interested in gazing at California's big grays, these companies also sponsor whale-watching cruises during the migratory season (late December through late March).

Inland you can fish at Irvine Lake, possibly landing a bluegill, "super trout," bass, or white sturgeon. ~ 714-649-2560.

DIVING

The coastal waters abound in interesting kelp beds rich with sea life; several companies are available to help you through the kelp.

To go below contact Aquatic Center. ~ 4537 West Coast Highway, Newport Beach; 714-650-5440. The center also operates a 24-hour surf and water condition line. ~ 714-650-5783. Laguna Sea Sports in Laguna Beach can also take care of your diving needs. ~ 925 North Coast Highway, Laguna Beach; 714-494-6965. If you're in Dana Point, try Beach City Scuba. ~ 34283 Coast Highway, Dana Point; 714-496-5891.

Orange County is surfer heaven, and, as the Bee Gees once sang, "nobody gets too much heaven no more." Right on. So when you're in the area, don't miss out on Orange County's wild waves. Grab a board from **Frog House** and head for the waves. ~ 6908 West Coast Highway, Newport Beach; 714-642-5690. In Dana Point, call **Hobie Sports**. ~ 24825 Del Parado, Dana Point; 714-496-1251. San Clemente's surf center is **Stewart Board Sports**. ~ 2102 South El Camino Real, San Clemente; 714-492-1085. For surf reports call 714-673-3371.

WIND-SURFING & SURFING

With elaborate marina complexes at Huntington Beach, Newport Beach, and Dana Point, this is a great area for boating. If you have the yearning to make some wake, call one of the outfits listed below.

SAILING

Sailboats and powerboats (including fishing skiffs) are available for rent at **Davey's Locker**. ~ 400 Main Street, Balboa; 714-673-1434. In Newport Beach, try **Marina Sailing**. ~ 600 East Bay Avenue, Suite B6, Newport Beach; 714-673-7763. Electric boats, motor boats, sailboats, kayaks, and waverunners are all available at **Balboa Boat Rentals**. ~ 510 Edgewater Avenue, Balboa; 714-673-7200. **Embarcadero Marina**, located at the public launch ramp, rents sailboats and fishing skiffs. ~ Embarcadero Place, Dana Point; 714-496-6177.

If you'd rather shake up the cellulite than the water, you can do it on Orange County's miles of beaches and running trails.

JOGGING

Mecca for Orange County runners is the **Santa Ana Riverbed Trail**, a smooth asphalt ribbon stretching 20.6 miles from Anaheim to Huntington Beach State Park. There are par courses and excellent running trails at both **Laguna Niguel Regional** and **Mile Square Regional** parks (see the "Beaches & Parks" section in this chapter). In Mission Viejo there's a beautiful two-and-a-half-mile trail around **Lake Mission Viejo**. And then there are the miles and miles of beaches for which Orange County is renowned.

◆◆

✔ CHECK THESE OUT—UNIQUE OUTDOOR ADVENTURES

- Serve and swing at one of the three public tennis courts in **San Clemente**, where you can take out any remaining Watergate rancor on the ball after visiting President Nixon's former home here. *page 248*
- Do the **Newport** thing by renting a sailboat and spending a day cruising on the bay. *page 247*
- Visualize whirled peace as you ride in the curl of a wave on **Huntington's** legendary coastline, where a rental board and a lesson can put you on top of the world—and the whirled! *page 247*
- Hike the oak-filled woodlands of Santa Ana on the Holy Jim Trail in **O'Neill Regional Park**. *page 250*

GOLF

The climate and terrain of Orange County make for excellent golfing. Take a break from Southern California freeways, and do some driving on the greens instead.

Tee up in Newport at **Newport Beach Golf Course.** ~ 3100 Irvine Avenue, Newport Beach; 714-852-8681. **Aliso Creek Golf Course** serves Laguna Beach. ~ 31106 Coast Highway, Laguna Beach; 714-499-1919. In Dana Point try **The Golf Links at Monarch Beach.** ~ 28341 Stonehill Drive, Dana Point; 714-240-8247. In San Clemente, head for **San Clemente Municipal Golf Course.** ~ 150 East Avenida Magdalena, San Clemente; 714-361-8384. Or try **Shorecliffs Golf Course.** ~ 501 Avenida Vaquero, San Clemente; 714-492-1177.

The inland sections of Orange County also feature numerous golf links. Among them are **Anaheim Municipal (H. G. "Dad" Miller) Golf Course.** ~ 430 North Gilbert Street, Anaheim; 714-774-8055. Anaheim is also home to **Anaheim Hills Golf Course.** ~ 6501 East Nohl Ranch Road, Anaheim; 714-637-7311. In Fullerton there's **Fullerton Golf Course.** ~ 2700 North Harbor Boulevard, Fullerton; 714-871-7411. And in Fountain Valley try **Mile Square Golf Course.** ~ 10401 Warner Avenue, Fountain Valley; 714-968-4556.

TENNIS

Even though public courts are hard to find in this area, who says Orange County is elitist? There are still many private clubs, and given the wonderful climate and the way you'll fit in wearing those white shorts and tennis sweaters, it's probably worth the club fee after all.

In Newport Beach, you can try the **Hotel Tennis Club.** ~ Marriott Hotel, 900 Newport Center Drive, Newport Beach; 714-729-3566. Laguna Beach's **Moulton Meadows Park** is open to the public. ~ Del Mar and Balboa avenues, Laguna Beach; 714-497-0716. **Laguna Niguel Regional Park** features four tennis courts. ~ 28241 La Paz Road, Laguna Niguel; 714-831-2791. In Dana Point **Dana Hills Tennis Center** is a good option. ~ 24911 Calle de Tenis, Dana Point; 714-240-2104. Strangely enough, San Clemente is the one Orange County town that does seem to have an abundance of public courts. **Bonito Canyon Park** offers two lighted courts. ~ El Camino Real and Calle Valle, San Clemente; 714-361-8264. There are four lighted courts at **San Luis Rey Park.** ~ Avenida San Luis Rey, San Clemente; 714-361-8264. **San Gorgonio Park** has two unlit courts. ~ Via San Gorgonio, San Clemente; 714-361-8264.

For courts around Anaheim try **Anaheim Tennis Center.** ~ 975 South State College Boulevard, Anaheim; 714-991-9090. In Buena Park visit **Ralph B. Clark Regional Park.** ~ 8800 Rosecrans Avenue, Buena Park; 714-670-8045.

BIKING

Wind and wheels are a perfect blend with Southern California's weather, and you can avoid adding to the smog and sitting in traffic by tooling around on a bike rather than in a car. Whether you like road riding or mountain biking, you'll find a suitable place to cycle in Orange County. **Route 1**, the Pacific Coast Highway, offers cyclists an opportunity to explore the Orange County coastline. The problem, of course, is the traffic. Along **Bolsa Chica State Beach**, however, a special pathway runs the length of the beach. Another way to avoid traffic is to mountain-bike; Moro Canyon in Crystal Cove State Park is a favorite off-road riding area.

Other interesting areas to explore are **Balboa Island** and the **Balboa Peninsula** in Newport Beach. Both offer quiet residential streets and are connected by a ferry which permits bicycles. A popular inland ride is along **Santiago Canyon Road**; leaving from Orange the route skirts Irvine Lake and Cleveland National Forest.

Bike Rentals   To rent bikes in Orange County try **Jack's Beach Concession**. ~ 2191 Pacific Coast Highway, Huntington Beach; 714-536-8328. In Seal Beach there's **Sandpiper Bicycle Repair**. ~ 231 Seal Beach Boulevard, Seal Beach; 310-594-6130. **Rainbow Bicycle Company** also rents bikes. ~ 485 North Coast Highway, Laguna Beach; 714-494-5806.

COASTAL ORANGE COUNTY   Though heavily developed, the Orange Coast still provides several outstanding trails. All are located near the beaches and offer views of private homes and open ocean. All distances listed are one way unless otherwise noted.

HIKING

The **California Coastal Trail** extends over 40 miles from the San Gabriel River in Seal Beach to San Mateo Point in San Clemente. Much of the route follows sandy beachfront and sedimentary bluffs. There are lagoons and tidepools, fishing piers, and marinas en route.

At the **Bolsa Chica Ecological Reserve Trail** (1.5 miles) you can say hello to birds traveling along the Pacific Flyway. A migratory rest stop, this lagoon features a loop trail which runs atop a levee past fields of cord grass and pickleweed.

Huntington Beach Paved Bike and Hike Trail (8.5 miles) parallels the Pacific from Bolsa Chica Lagoon to Beach Boulevard in Huntington Beach. Along the way it takes in Huntington Pier, a haven for surfers, and passes an army of unspeakably ugly oil derricks.

Newport Trail (2.5 miles) traces the ocean side of Balboa Peninsula from Newport Pier south to Balboa Pier, then proceeds to the peninsula's end at Jetty View Park. Private homes run the length of this pretty beach walk.

Back Bay Trail (3.5 miles) follows Back Bay Drive in Newport Beach along the shores of Upper Newport Bay. This fragile wetland, an important stop on the Pacific Flyway, is an ideal birdwatching area.

Crystal Cove Trail (3.2 miles) provides a pleasant seaside stroll. Starting from Pelican Point at the western boundary of Crystal Cove State Park, the paved path leads to the beach. The trail continues another mile to a cluster of cottages at Crystal Cove, then follows an undeveloped beach to Abalone Point, a 200-foot high promontory.

Aliso Creek Canyon Hiking Trail (1 mile) begins near the fishing pier at Aliso Beach County Park in South Laguna, leads north through a natural arch, and passes the ruins of an old boat landing.

INLAND ORANGE COUNTY Rising along the entire length of Orange County's eastern perimeter, the Santa Ana Mountains offer several challenging and surprisingly uncrowded trails.

Holy Jim Trail (8 miles) is a good Santa Ana sampler, with a creek, waterfall, oak woodland, and chaparral-covered slopes. It leads to Bear Springs where hikers can take a three-mile optional climb on **Main Divide Truck Trail** to the crest of 5687-foot Santiago Peak. The trail begins on Holy Jim Road, six miles from O'Neill Regional Park.

Bear Canyon Trail (5.5 miles) is a broad, well-graded and rather pleasant hike climbing through brush and meadow country to refreshing Pigeon Springs. Arrive at the spring early in the morning and you'll likely see deer, coyote, or even bobcat drinking from the cool waters. From Pigeon Springs there's an optional five-mile hike to Sitton Peak via **Verdugo and Sitton Peak Trail**. The trail is on Route 74, 20 miles east of Route 5.

Nearby **Chiquito Basin Trail** (9 miles) switchbacks past a sparkling waterfall and over oak-studded slopes to shady Lion Canyon. Don't be confused: the trailhead (just east of Bear Canyon trailhead) is signed San Juan Loop Trail, but Chiquito Basin Trail branches off a mile up.

Should you be city-bound during your visit to Orange County you can still get out and stretch the legs, thanks to the **Santa Ana Riverbed Trail** (28 miles). True to the name, it follows the Santa Ana River on a smooth asphalt surface from Imperial Highway in Anaheim south to Route 1 at Huntington Beach State Park. A great way to hike to the beach, it's also popular with joggers and bikers.

▼▼▼▼▼▼▼▼▼▼
Transportation

CAR

Several major highways crisscross Orange County. **Route 1**, known in this area as the Pacific Coast Highway, ends its long journey down the California Coast in Capistrano Beach. A few miles further inland, **Route 405** runs from Long Beach to Irvine, with feeder roads leading to the main coastal towns. Connecting Los Angeles and San Diego, **Route 5** follows an inland course through the heart of Orange County passing Anaheim and Santa Ana, then heads south to Dana Point and San Clemente.

AIR

John Wayne International Airport, located in Irvine, is the main terminal in these parts. Major carriers presently serving it include Alaska Airlines, American Airlines, America West, Continental Airlines, Delta Airlines, Northwest Airlines, Reno Airlines, Southwest Airlines, Trans World Airlines, United Airlines, and USAir.

Greyhound Bus Lines serves Orange County, stopping in Anaheim, Santa Ana, Seal Beach, Huntington Beach, Newport Beach, Corona del Mar, Dana Point, Laguna Beach, and San Clemente. Most stops are flag stops. However, a depot is located in Anaheim. ~ 100 West Winston Road; 714-999-1256. There's another in Santa Ana. ~ 1000 East Santa Ana Boulevard; 714-542-2215. Finally, there's the station in San Clemente. ~ 2421 South El Camino Real; 714-366-2646.

TRAIN

Amtrak's "San Diegan" travels between Los Angeles and San Diego, with Orange County stops at Fullerton, Anaheim Stadium, Santa Ana, San Juan Capistrano, and San Clemente. ~ 800-872-7245.

CAR RENTALS

Arriving at John Wayne International Airport, you'll find the following car rental agencies: **Avis Rent A Car** (714-852-8608, 800-331-1212), **Budget Rent A Car** (714-252-624, 800-527-0700), **Dollar Rent A Car** (714-756-6100, 800-800-4000), **Hertz Rent A Car** (714-756-8161, 800-654-3131), and **National Interrent** (714-852-1284, 800-227-7368). For less expensive (and less convenient) service, try **Enterprise Rent A Car** (714-851-7701, 800-325-8007).

PUBLIC TRANSIT

Orange County Transit Authority, or RIDE from southern Orange County, has bus service throughout Orange County, including most inland areas. Along the coast it stops at beach fronts including Seal Beach, Huntington Beach, Newport Beach, Corona del Mar, Laguna Beach, San Juan Capistrano, and San Clemente. ~ 714-636-7433.

In addition, **Los Angeles County Metropolitan Transit Authority** (MTA) serves some areas of Orange County including Fullerton, Disneyland, and Knott's Berry Farm. ~ 213-626-4455.

FIVE

San Diego

San Diego County's 4261 square miles occupy a Connnecticut-sized chunk of real estate that forms the southwestern corner of the continental United States. Geographically, it is as varied a parcel of landscape as any in the world. Surely this spot is one of the few places on the planet where, in a matter of hours, you can journey from bluff-lined beaches up and over craggy mountain peaks and down again to sun-scorched desert sands.

Moving east from the Pacific to the county's interior, travelers discover lush valleys and irrigated hillsides. Planted with citrus orchards, vineyards, and rows of vegetables, this curving countryside eventually gives way to the Palomar and Laguna mountains—cool, pine-crested ranges that rise over 6500 feet.

But it is the coast—some 76 sparkling miles stretching from San Mateo Point near San Clemente to the Mexican border—that always has held the fascination of residents and visitors alike.

When Portuguese explorer Juan Rodríguez Cabrillo laid eyes on these shores in 1542, he discovered a prospering settlement of Kumeyaay Indians. For hundreds of years, these native peoples had been living in quiet contentment on lands overlooking the Pacific; they had harvested the rich estuaries and ventured only occasionally into the scrubby hills and canyons for firewood and game.

Sixty years passed before the next visitor, Spanish explorer Sebastian Vizcaíno, came seeking a hideout for royal galleons beset by pirates. It was Vizcaíno who named the bay for San Diego de Alcala.

In 1769, the Spanish came to stay. The doughty Franciscan missionary Junípero Serra marched north from Mexico with a company of other priests and soldiers and built Mission San Diego de Alcala. It was the first of a chain of 21 missions and the earliest site in California to be settled by Europeans. Father Serra's mission, relocated a few miles inland in 1774, now sits incongruously amid the shopping centers and housing developments of Mission Valley.

California's earliest civilian settlement evolved in the 1820s on a dusty mesa beneath the hilltop presidio that protected the original mission. Pueblo San Diego quickly developed into a thriving trade and cattle ranching center after the ruling Spanish colonial regime was overthrown and replaced by the Republic of Mexico.

By the end of the century, new residents, spurred partly by land speculators, had taken root and developed the harbor and downtown business district. After the rails finally reached San Diego in 1885, the city flourished. Grand Victorian buildings lined 5th Avenue all the way from the harbor to Broadway and 1400 barren acres were set aside uptown for a city park.

After its turn-of-the-century spurt of activity, the city languished until World War II, when the U.S. Navy invaded the town en masse to establish the 11th Naval District headquarters and one of the world's largest Navy bases. San Diego's reputation as "Navytown USA" persisted well after the war-weary sailors went home. Some 130,000 Navy and Marine personnel are still based in San Diego and at Camp Pendleton to the north, but civilians now outnumber service types twenty to one and military influence has diminished accordingly.

The military has not been the only force to foster San Diego's growth. In the early 1960s, construction began on an important university that was to spawn a completely new industry. Many peg the emergence of the "new" San Diego to the opening of the University of California's La Jolla campus. Not only did the influx of 15,000 students help revive a floundering economy, it tended to liberalize an otherwise insular and conservative city.

Truth is, San Diego is no longer the sleepy, semitransparent little resort city it once was. Nowhere is the fact more evident than in the downtown district, where a building boom has brought new offices, condominiums, and hotels as well as a spectacular business and entertainment complex at Horton Plaza.

But for all the city's manmade appeal, it is nature's handiwork and an ideal Mediterranean climate that most delights San Diego visitors. With bays and beaches bathed in sunshine 75 percent of the time, less than ten inches of rainfall per year and average temperatures that mirror a proverbial day in June, San Diego offers the casual outdoor lifestyle that fulfills vacation dreams. There's a beach for every taste, ranging from broad sweeps of white sand to slender scimitars beneath eroded sandstone bluffs.

Situated a smug 120 miles south of Los Angeles on Route 5, San Diego is not so much a city as a collection of communities hiding in canyons and gathered on small shoulders of land that shrug down to the sea. As a result, it hardly seems big enough (just over 1.1 million) to rank as America's sixth largest city. Total county population is 2.7 million, and nine of ten residents live within 30 miles of the coast.

The city of San Diego is divided into several geographic sections. To the south lies Coronado, nestled on a peninsula jutting into San Diego Bay and connected to the mainland by a narrow sandbar known as the Silver Strand.

Although they are within the boundaries of the city of San Diego, the seaside communities of Ocean Beach, Mission Beach, Pacific Beach, and La Jolla have developed their own identities, moods, and styles.

"OB," as the first of these is known, along with Mission and Pacific beaches, exults in the sunny, sporty Southern California lifestyle fostered by nearby Mission Bay Park. These neighboring communities are fronted by broad beaches and an almost continuous boardwalk that is jammed with joggers, skaters, and cyclists. The beaches are saturated in the summer by local sun-seekers, but they have much to offer visitors.

Like a beautiful but slightly spoiled child, La Jolla is an enclave of wealth and stubborn independence that calls itself "The Village" and insists on having its own post office, although it's actually just another part of the extended San Diego family. Mediterranean-style mansions and small cottages shrouded by jasmine and hibiscus share million-dollar views of beaches, coves, and wild, eroded sea cliffs. Swank shops and galleries, trendy restaurants and classy little hotels combine in a Riviera-like setting that rivals even Carmel for chicness.

North County, a string of beach towns stretching from Oceanside south to Del Mar, has also been developing apace. Often stereotyped because it is the home of Camp Pendleton, the nation's largest Marine Corps base, Oceanside is struggling to shed its reputation as a rough-and-tumble military town. Its greatest strides have come along the beachfront, where a concrete pier and five-block promenade have brightened the scene.

The city of Carlsbad has pushed to the front of the North County pack in terms of sprucing up its image and attracting visitors. Along with its redeveloped downtown area and oceanfront lodging, Carlsbad includes the community of La Costa, a labyrinth of luxury homes and parks built around prestigious La Costa Resort & Spa.

Somnolent Leucadia remains the least developed of North County's beach communities. It's an uninspiring mix of old homes, new condominiums, and mom-and-pop commercial outlets, shaded by rows of towering eucalyptus. The place is a haven for artisans, musicians, vegetarians, triathletes (more of these iron types train in North County than anywhere else in the world), and others seeking lower rents and noise levels.

Encinitas, known as the "Flower Capital of the World," is home to some of the nation's largest growers. While they are slowly disappearing under pressure from housing developers, giant greenhouses and fields of flowers still dot the area.

Cardiff-by-the-Sea appears from the highway to be little more than a row of chain restaurants strung along an otherwise lovely beach.

That could also be said about Cardiff's southern neighbor, Solana Beach. There's no town center—no real focus—to this coastal community and that has always been Solana Beach's problem and charm. Visitors whiz through on Route 5 or Route 101 (the coastal highway that threads North County beaches from Oceanside to Del Mar) without even noticing the place or its excellent beaches, hidden from view by a string of condominiums and a dramatic sandstone bluff.

One gets the feeling that North County neighbor Del Mar would love to become another La Jolla. While it lacks the natural attributes of cliff and cove, it does attract the rich, famous, and hopeful to its thoroughbred racetrack.

It is safe to say that San Diego is not as eccentric and sophisticated as San Francisco, nor as glamorous and fast-paced as Los Angeles. But those who still perceive it as a laid-back mecca for beach bums—or as a lunch stop en route to Mexico—are in for a huge surprise.

▼▼▼▼▼▼▼▼▼▼▼▼▼▼▼▼▼
North San Diego County

Stretching along the coast above San Diego is a string of towns with a host of personalities and populations. Residents here range from the county's wealthiest folks in Rancho Santa Fe to Marine privates at Oceanside's Camp Pendleton to yogis in retreat at Encinitas.

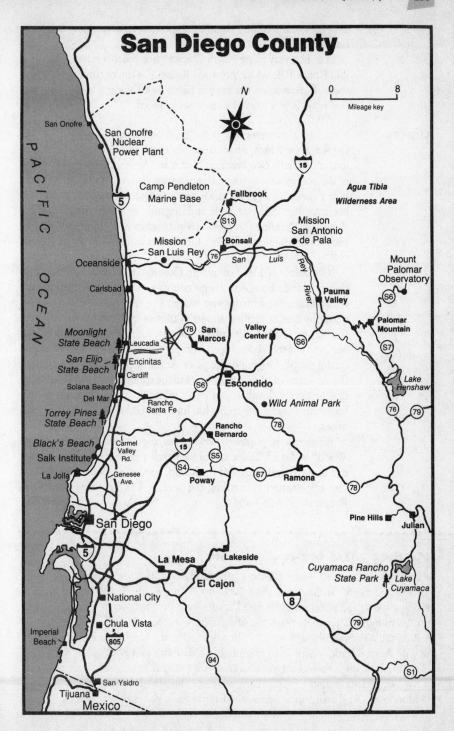

San Diego County

N

0   8
Mileage key

PACIFIC OCEAN

San Onofre

San Onofre
Nuclear
Power Plant

Camp Pendleton
Marine Base

Fallbrook

Agua Tibia
Wilderness Area

Mission
San Antonio
de Pala

S13

Mission
San Luis Rey

Bonsall

Oceanside

76 San   Luis   Rey   River

Mount
Palomar
Observatory

Carlsbad

Pauma
Valley

S6

Palomar
Mountain

Moonlight
State Beach

Leucadia

78 San
Marcos

Valley
Center

S6

S7

San Elijo
State Beach

Encinitas

Lake
Henshaw

Solana Beach

Cardiff

S6 Escondido

Del Mar

Wild Animal Park

76   79

Torrey Pines
State Beach

Rancho
Santa Fe

78

Black's Beach

Rancho
Bernardo

Salk Institute

Carmel
Valley
Rd.

15

S5

La Jolla

Genesee
Ave.

S4

Poway

67 Ramona

78

Pine Hills

Julian

San Diego

La Mesa

Lakeside

Cuyamaca Rancho
State Park

Lake
Cuyamaca

El Cajon

8

National City

Chula Vista

79

805

Imperial
Beach

94

S1

San Ysidro

Tijuana

Mexico

This part of the county really shines, however, in its many sparkling beaches.

The best way to see North County's fine beaches is to cruise along Old Route 101, which preceded Route 5 as the north–south coastal route. It changes names in each beach town along the way, but once you're on it you won't be easily sidetracked.

SIGHTS

Your first sightseeing opportunity in San Diego County is at **San Onofre State Beach**, about 16 miles north of Oceanside. Unique in that it's actually two beaches, North and South, this certainly is one of the county's most scenic beach parks. Its eroded sandstone bluffs hide a variety of secluded sandy coves and pocket beaches. But all this beauty is broken by an eerie and ungainly structure rising from the shoreline. Dividing the park's twin beaches is a mammoth facility, potent and ominous, the San Onofre nuclear power plant. Admission. ~ 714-492-4872.

Old Route 101 leads next into **Oceanside**, gateway to Camp Pendleton Marine Base. San Diego county's second largest city is busy renovating its beachfront and image. The refurbished fishing pier is a lengthy one, stretching almost 2000 feet into the Pacific.

Farther south, **Carlsbad** is a friendly, sunny beachfront town that has been entirely redeveloped, complete with cobblestone streets and quaint shops. Originally the place established its reputation around the similarity of its mineral waters to the springs of the original Karlsbad in Czechoslovakia. But don't waste your time looking for the fountain of youth, the spring has long since dried up. Go to the beach instead.

Encinitas is popularly known as the "Flower Capital of the World" and the hillsides east of the beach are a riot of colors. A quick call to the friendly folks at the local **Chamber of Commerce** will net you information concerning the area. ~ 138 Encinitas Boulevard, Encinitas; 619-753-6041.

✔ CHECK THESE OUT—UNIQUE SIGHTS

- Brown your buns at **Black's Beach**, where sunbathers bask *au naturel* while hang gliders soar overhead, getting the best view. *page 270*
- Enjoy the varied offerings of **Balboa Park**, from a five-star zoo to first-class museums, not to mention the Old Globe Theater. *page 296*
- Ride the monorail through the 2150-acre spread at the San Diego Zoo's **Wild Animal Park**, where lions roam in their savannas and gorillas galumph through their African rainforest. *page 311*
- Explore old adobes on a free walking tour and shop the Bazaar del Mundo at **Old Town San Diego State Historic Park**. *page 305*

Yogis, as well as those of us still residing on terra firma, might want to make a stop at Paramahansa Yogananda's **Self Realization Fellowship Center**. The gold-domed towers of this monastic retreat were built by an Indian religious sect in the 1920s and are still used as a retreat. Yogananda's house and the gardens inside the compound are beautifully maintained and open to the public on Sundays. The views, overlooking the famous "Swami's" surfing beach, are spectacular. ~ 215 K Street, Encinitas; 619-753-2888.

Although **Del Mar** is inundated every summer by "beautiful people" who flock here for the horse racing, the town itself has retained a casual, small-town identity. Its trim, Tudor-style village center and luxurious oceanfront homes reflect the town's subtle efforts to "keep up with the Joneses" next door (i.e., La Jolla).

On the east side of Route 5, about five miles inland on either Via de la Valle or Lomas Santa Fe Drive, is **Rancho Santa Fe**. If La Jolla is a jewel, then this stylish enclave is the crown itself. Residing in hillside mansions and horse ranches parceled out from an old Spanish land grant are some of America's wealthiest folks. Rancho Santa Fe is like Beverly Hills gone country. The area became popular as a retreat for rich industrialists and movie stars in the 1920s when Douglas Fairbanks and Mary Pickford built their sprawling **Fairbanks Ranch**. To make a looping tour of this affluent community, drive in on Via de la Valle, then return to Route 5 via Linea del Cielo and Lomas Santa Fe Drive.

Many of San Diego's best beaches lie to the north, between Ocean- ✓ **LODGING** side and Del Mar. Sadly, most of the good hotels do not. But don't worry, among those listed below all but two are either oceanfront or oceanview properties.

The **Southern California Beach Club** is a 44-suite Mediterranean-style time-share facility situated on the beach near Oceanside Pier. Each suite is graciously appointed with quality furnishings in contemporary hues of peach, heather, and blue. Kitchens are standard; other extras include a mini-gym, rooftop jacuzzis, and laundry facilities. ~ 121 South Pacific Highway, Oceanside; 619-722-6666, fax 619-722-8950. MODERATE TO DELUXE.

Every room is individually decorated at **Cardiff-by-the-Sea Lodge** with themes such as Old World, Southwest and Mediterranean, and many rooms have ocean views, fireplaces and in-room whirlpools. It's a bed and breakfast, but not of the converted-home variety; everyone has a private entrance and bath. Breakfast is served buffet-style in a center courtyard, but you can take it to your room or up to the rooftop garden and savor a panoramic view of the Pacific. ~ 142 Chesterfield Avenue, Cardiff; 619-944-6474, fax 619-944-6841. DELUXE TO ULTRA-DELUXE.

Carlsbad offers several nice oceanfront facilities, including **Tamarack Beach Resort**, a Spanish contemporary–style condominium.

Finished in peach and aqua hues, the Tamarack rents standard rooms as well as suites of all sizes. Most are smashingly decorated in upbeat tones and textures and incorporate sensitive touches like potted plants and photographic prints. Suites, though ultra-deluxe-priced, may be the best value on the North Coast. They have kitchens and private balconies. All guests can make use of the oceanfront restaurant, clubhouse, fitness center, jacuzzis, and activities program as well as enjoying the adjacent beach. ~ 3200 Carlsbad Boulevard, Carlsbad; 619-729-3500, 800-334-2199. DELUXE TO ULTRA-DELUXE.

Advertised as "a very special bed and breakfast," the **Pelican Cove Inn** is a lovely Cape Cod–style house with eight guest rooms. Each features a fireplace and is well furnished with antique pieces, including feather beds while some rooms have jacuzzis. Visitors share a sundeck and patio with gazebo. The inn is located just two blocks from the beach. ~ 320 Walnut Avenue, Carlsbad; 619-434-5995, fax 619-434-7649. DELUXE TO ULTRA-DELUXE.

Affordability and quiet are the order of the day at **Ocean Palm Beach Resort**. This tidy, 57-room mom-and-pop complex is so near the sea you can hear it, but a row of expensive beach houses blocks the view. Some sections of the rambling Ocean Manor date back to 1939, and "new" additions are 1950s vintage, so the general decor could best be described as Early-American Motel. An oldie but goodie in this case, however. The furniture may be oddly matched and a bit stodgy, but the place is clean and lovingly maintained and features a landscaped patio and pool area. All rooms have fully equipped kitchens. ~ 2950 Ocean Street, Carlsbad; 619-729-2493, 800-802-3224, fax 619-729-0579. MODERATE TO DELUXE.

There's not much to say about the **Beach Terrace Inn**. A 49-unit establishment with stucco facade and the feel of a motel, it is part of the Best Western chain. There's a pool, sauna, and jacuzzi, plus a single feature that differentiates the Beach Terrace from most other places hereabouts—it is located right on the beach. A broad swath of white sand borders the property, making the price for a room with kitchen a worthwhile investment. ~ 2775 Ocean Street, Carlsbad; 619-729-5951, 800-433-5415, fax 619-729-1078. DELUXE TO ULTRA-DELUXE.

Sporting a fresh look, the fabled **La Costa Resort & Spa** can justly claim to be one of the world's great "total" resorts. This luxurious 400-acre complex boasts 478 guest rooms, two 18-hole championship golf courses, 21 tennis courts (hard, clay, *and* grass), nine shops, four restaurants, and one of the country's largest and most respected spa and fitness centers. Simply put, the place is awesome. With rooms *starting* well up in the ethereal range, La Costa's appeal to the well-monied few is apparent. ~ 2100 Costa Del Mar Road, Carlsbad; 619-438-9111, 800-854-5000. ULTRA-DELUXE.

Located on a lofty knoll above the Pacific, **Radisson Inn Encinitas** is built on three levels and looks like a condominium. With a pool and jacuzzi, it has many of the same features. The 91 rooms are stylishly decorated in light pastel tones, with contemporary oak and bentwood furniture, and include private balconies overlooking the ocean. Continental breakfast is served at the poolside cabaña. ~ 85 Encinitas Boulevard, Encinitas; 619-942-7455, 800-333-3333. DELUXE.

The best reasonably priced lodging around the beach in Encinitas is **Moonlight Beach Motel**. This three-story, 24-unit family-run motel is tucked away in a residential neighborhood overlooking Moonlight Beach State Park. Rooms are modern as well as clean, and contain everything you'll need, including kitchenettes. Some of the accommodations on the upper two floors command ocean views. ~ 233 2nd Street, Encinitas; 619-753-0623, 800-323-1259, fax 619-944-9827. MODERATE.

◄ *HIDDEN*

It's all in the name when it comes to locating **Del Mar Motel on the Beach**, the only motel between Carlsbad and La Jolla on the beach. All 45 rooms in this plain stucco building are steps from the sand. That's undoubtedly where you'll spend your time because there is little about the rooms to enchant you. They are basic in design, equipped with refrigerators, color TVs, and air-conditioning. Because the hotel is at a right angle to the beach, only a few rooms have full views of the water. ~ 1702 Coast Boulevard, Del Mar; 619-755-1534, 800-223-8449, fax 619-259-5403. MODERATE TO DELUXE.

In the fall of 1997, the area code for North San Diego County will change from 619 to 760.

A two-story Spanish Mediterranean inn conveniently situated a few blocks from downtown Del Mar, **Les Artistes** honors several of the world's favorite artists: Diego Rivera, Georgia O'Keefe, Erté, Claude Monet, and Paul Gauguin. The owner, who is an architect from Thailand, designed each room in the style and spirit of the artist. Other architectural delights include a pond filled with water lillies and koi and other water features where guests can sit and listen to the soothing strumming of the guitar. ~ 944 Camino Del Mar; 619-755-4646, fax 619-794-7880. MODERATE TO DELUXE.

Built on the site of a once-famous Del Mar Beach getaway, **L'Auberge Del Mar** replicates the old hotel's nostalgic past of the '20s, '30s, and '40s. The Tudor/Craftsman inn was frequented by Hollywood greats such as Bing Crosby, Jimmy Durante, and Rudolph Valentino. Its rich lobby is dominated by a replica of the huge original brick fireplace. Along with 123 guest rooms and suites, the inn features a restaurant with patio dining, bar, full-service European spa, tennis courts, leisure and lap pools, shops, a park amphitheater, and partial ocean views. Each room has its own patio. ~ 1540 Camino del Mar, Del Mar; 619-259-1515, 800-323-1259, fax 619-755-4940. ULTRA-DELUXE.

On a hill overlooking Del Mar's village center and coastline is the romantic little **Rock Haus Inn**. One of the region's finest bed and breakfasts, it would be hard to top this sprawling Craftsman-style bungalow for location, charm, or quality. Built in 1910 and located two blocks from the beach, it saw action during Prohibition as a speakeasy and gambling den. Today its ten rooms, four with private baths, are thematically decorated and reflect considerable taste and talent. The little "Wren's Nest" has an ocean view and old-time iron twin beds; the "Huntsman's" suite features a fireplace. Guests assemble on the sunny veranda for a light breakfast. ~ 410 15th Street, Del Mar; 619-481-3764. DELUXE TO ULTRA-DELUXE.

For an elegant country inn consider **The Inn at Rancho Santa Fe.** Widely known among the world's genteel, it's a country inn comprised of Early California–style casitas on a wooded 20-acre site. Situated five miles inland from Solana Beach, the inn offers individually decorated guest rooms as well as one-, two-, and three-bedroom cottages. The latter generally feature private sun terraces, fireplaces, and kitchenettes. Furnishings, true to the understated theme, are old but durable, built from sturdy woods like chestnut and maple. Displayed in the homespun lobby is a priceless collection of antique hand-carved model ships. There are tennis courts, swimming pool, croquet, and two restaurants. ~ 5951 Linea del Cielo, Rancho Santa Fe; 619-756-1131, 800-654-2928, fax 619-759-1604. DELUXE TO ULTRA-DELUXE.

DINING ✓ In spite of its name, **Hamburger Heaven** is a great place for breakfast. Decorated with brightly colored murals, this eatery serves up innovative omelettes, buckwheat pancakes, and delicious home fries. For lunch, try the godfather burger topped with bell peppers, marinara sauce, and jack cheese. When dinner rolls along, the menu features chicken teriyaki, pasta dishes, and a special homemade meatloaf. Patio dining is also available. No dinner Sunday and Monday. ~ 714 North Coast Highway, Oceanside; 619-722-2254. BUDGET.

HIDDEN ► For a downright homey café, check out **Robin's Nest,** a country-style establishment with good eats and a gregarious chef. The menu features excellent omelettes, soups, and burgers. Daily early-bird dinner specials vary and might include prime rib, beef stew, and chicken or seafood gumbo. With a decor of soft blues and artwork by local artists, this place is quite popular with locals and has an outdoor patio that faces the harbor. ~ 280-A Harbor Drive South, Oceanside; 619-722-7837. BUDGET TO MODERATE.

La Costa Resort & Spa features four restaurants, including **Pisces,** a Mediterranean-style seafood restaurant (that serves formal dinners only), and **Ristorante Figaro,** specializing in northern Italian cuisine. **The Brasserie** offers American and Californian cuisine as well as low-calorie, low-cholesterol meals, designed to dovetail with La Costa's excellent spa programs; all are superbly prepared and colorfully presented. **Center Court,** a combination coffee bar and pastry shop, features a beautiful outdoor patio. ~ 2100 Costa del Mar Road, Carlsbad; 619-438-9111. MODERATE TO ULTRA-DELUXE.

Neiman's, an eye-catching Victorian landmark, hous
dining room and café/bar. My favorite for lunch or dinner i
where LeRoy Neiman lithographs hang on the walls and
includes trendy dishes such as rack of lamb, chicken D
smoked chicken with cheese quesadillas. It also has burgers, p
salads. The Sunday brunch in the sprawling turn-of-the-cen
Grill Restaurant is a definite "must," featuring a tremendo
assortment of breakfast and lunch items. ~ 2978 Carlsbad Boulevard, Carlsbad; 619-729-4131. MODERATE.

For light, inexpensive fare there's the **Daily News Café**. Breakfast
features eggs, pancakes, and French toast while the heartier lunch fare
includes an array of soups, salads, sandwiches, and burgers. ~ 3001-
A Carlsbad Boulevard, Carlsbad; 619-729-1023. BUDGET.

Pasta lovers should be sure to try the *penne* or *fusilli* in vodka-
tomato sauce at **When In Rome**. High ceiling, arched windows, and
an art-filled Roman decor provide the proper atmosphere, and the
Italian owners certainly know their trade. All the breads and pastas
are made fresh daily. Entrées include a variety of veal and seafood
items. ~ 1108 1st Street, Encinitas; 619-944-1771. MODERATE TO
DELUXE.

Most visitors to Encinitas never lay eyes on the **Potato Shack**   ◄ HIDDEN
Café, hidden away on a side street. But locals start packing its pine-
paneled walls at dawn to tackle North County's best and biggest
breakfast for the buck. There are great three-egg omelettes, including
a tasty cheese-and-tuna creation; but best of all are the home-style
taters and the old-fashioned biscuits and gravy. Lunch is also served,
but the Potato Shack is really a breakfast institution, and as such
serves breakfast until 2 p.m. ~ 120 West I Street, Encinitas; 619-436-
1282. BUDGET.

Another popular feeding spot is **Sakura Bana Sushi Bar**. The sushi here is heavenly, especially the *sakura* roll, crafted by Japanese
masters from shrimp, crab, scallop, smelt egg, and avocado. The bar
serves only sushi and sashimi, but table service will bring you such
treats as teriyaki, tempura, and shrimp *shumai*. No lunch Saturday
and Sunday; closed Monday. ~ 1031 1st Street, Encinitas; 619-942-
6414. BUDGET TO MODERATE.

Encinitas' contribution to the Thai food craze is an intimate café
called **Siamese Basil** set along the town's main drag. At lunch and
dinner this white-washed eatery serves up about six dozen dishes.
You can start with the spicy shrimp soup and satay, then graduate
to an entrée menu that includes noodle, curry, seafood, and vegetable
selections. House specialties include roast duck with soy bean and
ginger sauce, honey-marinated spare ribs, and barbecued chicken. ~
527 1st Street, Encinitas; 619-753-3940. BUDGET TO MODERATE.

Best of the beachfront dining spots in Cardiff is **Charlie's Grill
and Bar**, where the surf rolls right up to the glass. Here you can

choose from an innovative selection of fresh seafood items or an all-American menu of oak-smoked ribs and chicken, steak, and prime rib. Charlie's has a smartly decorated contemporary setting with a full bar, but still creates an easy and informal atmosphere. ~ 2526 South Route 101, Cardiff; 619-942-1300. MODERATE TO DELUXE.

For southern Mexican cuisine, try **Taco Auctioneers**, a roadside café with a deck overlooking the ocean. In addition to homemade tortillas and chips, you can feast on *arroz cabezon*, a barbecued pork and chicken dish. ~ 1951 San Elijo Road, Cardiff; 619-942-8226. BUDGET TO MODERATE.

Mille Fleurs tops everyone's list as San Diego's best French restaurant. The à la carte menu, which changes daily, provides exquisite appetizers, soup, and such entrées as rack of veal in garlic and rosemary, Norwegian salmon in pink grapefruit sauce, and whole Dover sole. A sophisticated interior features fireside dining, Portuguese tiles, and stunning *trompe l'oeil* paintings. There is also a Spanish courtyard for lunch as well as a piano bar. ~ 6009 Paseo Delicias, Rancho Santa Fe; 619-756-3085. ULTRA-DELUXE.

Celebrity chef Wolfgang Puck has made **Delicias** an instant and well-deserved success. The comfortable and spacious restaurant with adjoining bar is decorated in a mixture of antiques and wicker, accented by woven tapestries and flowers. The chefs in the open-view kitchen whip up pizza with smoked salmon, Chinese duck with ginger and orange essence, and grilled veal with a three-cheese polenta and marsala sauce. Delicious food, personable service. ~ 6106 Paseo Delicias, Rancho Santa Fe; 619-756-8000. DELUXE TO ULTRA-DELUXE.

HIDDEN ► Mention the words "Mexican food" in Solana Beach and the reply is sure to be **Fidel's**. This favored spot has as many rooms and patios as a rambling hacienda. Given the good food and cheap prices, all of them inevitably are crowded. Fidel's serves the best *tostada suprema* anywhere and the burritos, enchiladas, and *chimichangas* are always good. ~ 607 Valley Avenue, Solana Beach; 619-755-5292. BUDGET.

Il Fornaio, an Italian restaurant/bakery, boasts magnificent ocean views, outside dining terraces, elegant Italian marble floors and bar, *trompe l'oeil* murals, and an enormous exhibition kitchen. The place is packed with eager patrons ready to sample the pastas, pizzas, rotisserie, meats, and *dolci* (desserts); Sunday brunch. ~ 1555 Camino del Mar, Del Mar Plaza, Del Mar; 619-755-8876. MODERATE TO DELUXE.

Since life is lived outdoors in Southern California, **Pacifica Del Mar**, latest link in a restaurant mini-chain, features a terrace overlooking the ocean as well as a white tablecloth dining room. The accent here is on seafood, as in barbecued salmon with spicy Chinese mustard, sashimi ahi, and wok-charred catfish. ~ Del Mar Plaza, 1555 Camino del Mar, Del Mar; 619-792-0476. MODERATE TO DELUXE.

The place is mobbed all summer long, but **The Fish Marke** mains one of my favorite Del Mar restaurants. I like the noise, n cal atmosphere, oyster bar, affordable prices, on-the-run service the dozen or so fresh fish items. Among the best dishes are the sea yellowtail, orange roughy, and salmon, either sautéed or mes charbroiled. ~ 640 Via de la Valle, Del Mar; 619-755-2277. BUDGET TO MODERATE.

Scalini, housed in a classy new contemporary-style building with arched windows overlooking a polo field, is strictly star quality. The place has been decorated in a mix of modern and antique furnishings and wrapped in all the latest Southern California colors. But the brightest star of all is the menu. The Caesar salad and mesquite-broiled veal chops are exceptional, as is the duck à l'orange. There are many good homemade pasta dishes including lobster fettuccine, lasagna, linguine, and tortellini. Dinner only. ~ 3790 Via de la Valle, Del Mar; 619-259-9944. DELUXE TO ULTRA-DELUXE.

SHOPPING

Carlsbad has blossomed with a variety of trendy shops. You'll see many beach-and-surf-type shops, as well as a variety of specialty gift shops. **Alt Karlsbad Hanse Gift Shop**, ensconced in a German-style stone house, sells European art and collectibles, including steins, Hummels, and crystal pieces. ~ 2802 Carlsbad Boulevard, Carlsbad; 619-729-6912.

The Lumberyard is an attractive Victorian-style woodframe shopping village with a shaded courtyard on the former site of an old lumber mill. ~ On the east side of Route 101 between I and E streets, Encinitas; 619-634-3190.

Detouring, as every sophisticated shopper must, to Rancho Santa Fe, you'll find an assortment of chic shops and galleries along Paseo Delicias. One of my favorites is **Marilyn Mulloy Estate Jewelers**, with its stunning collection of old and new pieces. ~ 6024 Paseo Delicias, Rancho Santa Fe; 619-756-4010. Another one is **The Two Goats**, featuring designer fashions and exclusive gifts. ~ 6012 Paseo

TURF AND SURF

While seasonal, the **Del Mar Race Track** and companion **Fairgrounds** are the main attractions here. The track was financed in the 1930s by such stars as Bing Crosby, Pat O'Brien, and Jimmy Durante to bring thoroughbred racing to the fairgrounds. It was no coincidence that Del Mar, "where the turf meets the surf," became a second home for these and many other top Hollywood stars. Track season is from the end of July through mid-September. Admission. ~ Route 5 and Via de la Valle, Del Mar; 619-755-1141.

Delicias, Rancho Santa Fe; 619-756-1996. There are lots of million-aires per acre here, but bargains can still be found: **Carolyn's** is a con-signment shop boasting designer fashions from the closets of the community's best-dressed women. ~ 6033-J Paseo Delicias, Rancho Santa Fe; 619-756-2765.

Another place where the rich like to rummage is **Country Friends,** a charity-operated repository of antique furniture, silver, glass, and china priced well below local antique shops. ~ 6030 El Tordo, Ran-cho Santa Fe; 619-756-1192.

If little else, Solana Beach harbors an enclave of good antique stores. One of the best is the **Antique Warehouse,** with its collection of 101 small shops. ~ 212 South Cedros Avenue, Solana Beach; 619-755-5156.

A seacoast village atmosphere prevails along Del Mar's half-mile-long strip of shops. Tudor-style **Stratford Square,** the focal point, houses a number of shops in what once was a grand turn-of-the-cen-tury resort hotel. One of the most intriguing enterprises here is **Ocean Song,** a CD and cassette shop specializing in new age and internation-al music. ~ 1438 Camino del Mar, Del Mar; 619-755-7664. Equally intriguing is the adjoining **Earth Song Bookstore,** which offers an eclectic selection of books focusing on spiritual and psychological self-development. ~ 1440 Camino del Mar, Del Mar; 619-755-4254.

The stylized **Del Mar Plaza** is a welcome addition. Home to over 35 retail shops, this tri-level mall sells everything from sportswear to upscale Scandinavian fashions and has a host of eateries. ~ 1555 Ca-mino del Mar, Del Mar; 619-792-1555.

Flower Hill Mall, a rustic mall, has the usual fashion and special-ty shops. ~ 2720 Via de la Valle, Del Mar; 619-481-7131. But the real draw here is the **Bookworks** (619-755-3735) and an adjoining coffeehouse called **Pannikin Coffeehouse** (619-481-8007). Together they're perfect for a relaxed bit of book browsing and a spot of tea. ~ 2670 Via de la Valle, Del Mar.

NIGHTLIFE For a harbor view, cast an eye toward **Monterey Bay Canners.** ~ 1325 Harbor Drive North, Oceanside; 619-722-3474.

Try the **Grove Restaurant** for a place to hang your hat after din-ner. There's a dancefloor, cocktail lounge, and occasional live music on the weekend. The bar has a light sports motif and is decorated in dark wood and brass. ~ 3232 Mission Avenue, Oceanside; 619-757-7711.

First Street Bar is a neighborhood bar featuring live music on weekends. It was recently voted best neighborhood bar by locals. ~ 656 1st Street, Encinitas; 619-944-0233.

You can hear live blues or rock Thursday through Sunday nights at **Sharky's.** Cover on weekends. ~ 485 1st Street, Encinitas; 619-436-7397.

Solana Beach's low-profile daytime image shifts gears in the evening when the-little-town-that-could spotlights one of North County's hottest clubs. The **Belly Up Tavern** is a converted quonset hut that now houses a concert club and often draws big-name rock, reggae, jazz, and blues stars. Cover. ~ 143 South Cedros Avenue, Solana Beach; 619-481-9022.

Tucked away in the Flower Hill Mall, the **Pannikin Coffeehouse** brings a true taste of culture in the form of live jazz, classical guitarists, and poetry readings. ~ 2670 Via de la Valle, Del Mar; 619-481-8007.

SAN ONOFRE STATE BEACH San Diego County's northernmost beach is about 16 miles north of Oceanside, uneasily sandwiched between Camp Pendleton and the San Onofre nuclear power plant. It's well worth a visit if you're not put off by the nearby presence of atomic energy. Technically, San Onofre is two parks, North and South, separated by the power plant and connected via a public walkway along the seawall. The southern beach features a superb campground with trailer spaces and primitive tent sites, the only primitive campsite anywhere on San Diego County beaches. Eroded bluffs rumple down to the beach creating a variety of sandy coves and pockets. Gentle surf, which picks up considerably to the north, makes this a good swimming and bodysurfing spot. It is more than a rumor that some discreet nude sunbathing takes place at the end of beach path #6. The north side of the park is a favorite with surfers who flock to "Surf Beach," not far from famous "Trestles Beach," which is just beyond the park boundary. The swimming is good as is the surf fishing. You'll find picnic areas, restrooms, lifeguards, and hiking trails; restaurants and groceries are about five miles away in San Clemente. Parking fee, $6. ~ From Route 5, take Basilone Road exit and follow the signs to the beach; 714-492-4872 or 714-492-6060.

▲ There are 196 tent sites and 124 RV sites (no hookups); there are showers; $17 to $18 per night.

OCEANSIDE BEACHES Over three miles of clean, rock-free beaches front North County's largest city, stretching from Buena Vista Lagoon in the south to Oceanside Harbor in the north. Along the entire length the water is calm and shallow, ideal for swimming and bodysurfing. Lots of Marines from nearby Camp Pendleton favor this beach. The nicest section of all is around Oceanside Pier, a 1900-foot-long fishing pier. Nearby, palm trees line a grassy promenade dotted with picnickers; the sand is as clean as a pin. Added to the attractions is **Buena Vista Lagoon**, a bird sanctuary and nature reserve. Facilities include picnic areas, restrooms, lifeguards, basketball, and volleyball courts. Restaurants and groceries are located nearby. Try fishing from the pier, rocks, or beach. Swimming is good and surfing is reliable year-round. Day-use fee, $5. ~ Located

BEACHES
& PARKS

◄ *HIDDEN*

along The Strand in Oceanside; the pier is at the foot of 3rd Street; 619-722-8000.

▲ Limited to a few RV sites in a parking lot with no hookups; $15 per night.

CARLSBAD STATE BEACH ⚊ 🏊 🎣 Conditions here are about the same as at South Carlsbad (see below), a sand and rock beach bordered by bluffs. Rock and surf fishing are quite good at this beach and even better at the adjoining Encinas Fishing Area (at the San Diego Gas and Electric power plant), where Agua Hedionda Lagoon opens to the sea. **Carlsbad City Beach** connects to the north, extending another mile or so to the mouth of the Buena Vista Lagoon. Facilities include restrooms and lifeguards; restaurants and groceries nearby. The beach offers swimming, surfing, and skindiving. ~ The park entrance is at Tamarack Avenue, west of Carlsbad Boulevard, in Carlsbad; 619-438-3143.

SOUTH CARLSBAD STATE BEACH ⚊ 🏊 🎣 This is a big, bustling beachfront rimmed by bluffs. The pebbles strewn everywhere put towel space at a premium, but the water is gentle and super for swimming. The beach offers restrooms, lifeguards, showers, grocery, and beach rentals; restaurants are nearby. Swimming, fishing, surfing, and skindiving are popular activities. ~ Located west of Carlsbad Boulevard near Ponto Drive in Carlsbad; 619-438-3143.

▲ There are 226 sites for tents and RVs (no hookups), $17 to $22 per night. For reservations, call DESTINET at 800-444-7275.

LEUCADIA BEACH ⚊ 🏊 🎣 A broad sand corridor back-dropped by coastal bluffs, this beach has appeal, though it's certainly not North County's finest. The strand is widest at the north end, but the breakers are bigger at the south end, an area local surfers call "Beacon's Beach." Fishing, swimming, surfing, and skindiving are good. ~ There is a trail off the parking lot at Leucadia Boulevard and Neptune Avenue in Leucadia; 619-944-3398.

HIDDEN ► **STONE STEPS BEACH** ⚊ 🏊 Locals go there to hide away from the tourists. It is indeed stony and narrow to boot, but secluded and hard to find. Much like Moonlight to the south, its surf conditions are good for several types of water sports. ~ The staircase to the beach is located at South El Portal Street, off Neptune Avenue, in Leucadia.

MOONLIGHT STATE BEACH ⚊ 🏊 🎣 A very popular beach, Moonlight boasts a big sandy cove flanked by sandstone bluffs. Surf is relatively tame at the center, entertaining swimmers and bodysurfers. Volleyball and tennis courts are added attractions. Surfers like the wave action to the south, particularly at the foot of D Street. There are picnic areas, restrooms, lifeguards, a snack bar, equipment rentals, tennis courts and places to fish. ~ Located in Encinitas near 3rd Street and the end of C Street; 619-944-3398.

SWAMI'S PARK North County's most famous surfing beach derives its name from an Indian guru who founded the Self Realization Fellowship Temple here in the 1920s. The golddomed compound is located on the cliff-top just to the north of the park. A small, grassy picnic area gives way to stairs leading to a narrow, rocky beach favored almost exclusively by surfers, though divers and anglers like the spot as well. The reef point break here makes for spectacular waves. Facilities include restrooms, picnic areas, lifeguards, and a funky outdoor shower. ~ 1298 Old Route 101 in Encinitas about one mile south of Encinitas Boulevard; 619-944-3398.

SAN ELIJO STATE BEACH Although the beach is wide and sandy, low tide reveals a mantle of rocks just offshore and there are reefs, too, making this one of North County's most popular surf fishing and skindiving spots. Surfers brave big breakers at "Turtles" and "Pipes" reefs at the north end of the park. There is a campground atop the bluff overlooking the beach. Most amenities are located at the campground and include restrooms, showers, beach rentals, and grocery. Lifeguards and restaurants are found nearby. ~ Located off Old Route 101 north of Chesterfield Drive in Cardiff; 619-753-5091.

▲ There are 171 sites for tents and RVs (no hookups); $18 to $23 per night. For reservations, call DESTINET at 800-444-7275.

CARDIFF STATE BEACH This strand begins where the cliffs of Solana Beach end and where the town's most intriguing feature, a network of tidepools, begins. Popular with surfers because of the interesting pitches off its reef break, this wide, sandy beach is part of a two-mile swath of state beaches. At the beach there are restrooms, cold showers, and lifeguards. Restaurants and groceries are nearby. Fishing, swimming, and surfing are popular activities here. Day-use fee, $4. ~ Located off Old Route 101 in Cardiff directly west of San Elijo Lagoon; 619-753-5091.

FLETCHER COVE Lined by cliffs and carpeted with sand, this is a popular spot for water sports. There's a natural break in the cliffs where the beach widens and the surf eases up to allow comfortable swimming. Surfers gather to the north and south of Plaza Street where the beach is narrow and the surf much bigger. It's also a prime area for grunion runs. Facilities include restrooms, outdoor showers, lifeguards, basketball, and shuffleboard. Restaurants and groceries are nearby. ~ Located at the end of Plaza Street in Solana Beach; 619-755-1560.

DEL MAR BEACH Though rather narrow from Torrey Pines to about 15th Street, the beach widens further north. **Seagrove Park**, at the foot of 15th Street, is action central, with teens playing volleyball and frisbee while the elders read magazines beneath their umbrellas. Surfers congregate at the foot of 13th Street.

Quintessential North County! There are restrooms, showers, and lifeguards. Restaurants and groceries are nearby. Fishing is good, and there are regular grunion runs. There is typical beach surf with smooth peaks, year-round. ~ Easiest beach access is at street ends from 15th to 29th streets off Coast Boulevard, one block below Old Route 101 in Del Mar; 619-755-1556.

▼▼▼▼▼▼▼▼▼
La Jolla

A certain fascination centers around the origins of the name La Jolla. It means "jewel" in Spanish, but according to Indian legend it means "hole" or "caves." Both are fairly apt interpretations: this Mediterranean-style enclave perched on a bluff above the Pacific is indeed a jewel; and its dramatic coves and cliffs are pocked with sea caves. Choose your favorite interpretation but for goodness sake don't pronounce the name phonetically—it's "La Hoya."

La Jolla is a community within the city of San Diego, though it considers itself something more on the order of a principality—like Monaco. Locals call it "The Village" and boast that it's an ideal walking town, which is another way of saying La Jolla is a frustrating place to drive around. Narrow, curvy 1930-era streets are jammed with traffic and hard to follow. A parking place in The Village is truly a jewel within the jewel.

The beauty of its seven miles of cliff-lined sea coast is La Jolla's *raison d'être*. Spectacular homes, posh hotels, chic boutiques, and gourmet restaurants crowd shoulder to shoulder for a better view of the ocean. Each of the area's many beaches has its own particular character and flock of local devotees. Though most beaches are narrow, rocky, and not really suitable for swimming or sunbathing, they are the best in the county for surfing and skindiving.

SIGHTS

To get the lay of the land, wind your way up **Mount Soledad** (east on Nautilus Street from La Jolla Boulevard), where the view extends across the city skyline and out over the ocean. That large white cross at the summit is a memorial to the war dead and the setting for sunrise services every Easter Sunday.

Ah, but exploring The Village is the reason you're here, so head back down Nautilus Street, go right on La Jolla Boulevard, and continue until it leads into **Prospect Street**. This is La Jolla's hottest thoroughfare and where it intersects **Girard Avenue**, the town's traditional "main street," is the town epicenter. Here, in the heart of La Jolla, you are surrounded by the elite and elegant.

Although Girard Avenue features as wide a selection of shops as anyplace in San Diego, Prospect Street is much more interesting and stylish. By all means, walk Prospect's curving mile from the cottage shops and galleries on the north to the **Museum of Contemporary Art, San Diego** on the south. The museum, by the way, is a piece of art in itself. Its modern lines belie the fact it was designed as a private villa back in 1915, one of many striking contemporary structures in La Jolla by noted architect Irving Gill. The museum's highly regarded collection focuses on minimalist, California, pop, and other avant-garde developments in painting, sculpture, and photography. Closed Monday. Admission. ~ 700 Prospect Street; 619-454-3541.

During this stroll along Prospect Street, also visit the lovely **La Valencia Hotel**, a very pink, very prominent resting place nicknamed "La V." This pink lady is a La Jolla landmark and a local institution, serving as both village pub and town meeting hall. You can feel the charm and sense the rich tradition of the place the moment you enter. While "La V" has always been a haven for the gods and goddesses of Hollywood, the Gregory Peck and Olivia de Haviland gang of old has been replaced by a client roster of current stars like Cindy Crawford and Richard Gere. ~ 1132 Prospect Street; 619-454-0771.

Another center of interest lies at the northern end of La Jolla. The best beaches are here, stretching from the ritzy La Jolla Shores to the scientific sands at Scripps Beach. The latter strand fronts Scripps Institute of Oceanography, the oldest institution in the nation devoted to oceanography and the home of the **Stephen Birch Aquarium Museum**. Here you'll find 33 marine life tanks, a manmade tidepool, breathtaking exhibits of coastal underwater habitats, interactive displays for children and adults, and displays illustrating recent ad-

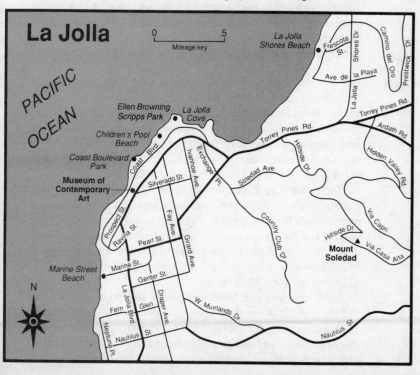

vances in oceanographic research. Admission. ~ 2300 Expedition Way; 619-534-3474.

Another research center, **The Salk Institute**, created by the man whose vaccine helped vanquish polio, is renowned not only for its research but its architecture as well. The surrealistic concrete structure was designed by Louis Kahn in 1960 to be an environment that would stimulate original thinking. It is a stunning site, perched on the lip of a high canyon overlooking the Pacific. ~ Crest of North Torrey Pines Road just north of the University of California—San Diego campus; tours information, 619-453-4100, ext. 200.

Next to the institute is the **Torrey Pines Glider Port** where you can watch hang-gliding masters soar over the waves from atop a 360-foot cliff. ~ 2800 Torrey Pines Scenic Drive; 619-452-9858.

HIDDEN ▶ Trails leading down to the notorious **Black's Beach** begin here. Black's is San Diego's unofficial, illegal, ever-loving nude beach. And a beautiful strip of natural landscape it is.

Bordering Black's on the north is **Torrey Pines State Beach and Reserve**, whose 1750-acre preserve was established to protect the world's rarest pine tree, the Torrey Pine. The tree itself is a gnarled and twisted specimen. Centuries ago these pines covered the southern coast of California; today they are indigenous only to Santa Rosa Island, off the coast of Santa Barbara, and to the reserve. A network of trails through this blufftop reserve makes hiking sheer pleasure. Among the rewards are the views, extending along the cliffs and ocean, and the chance to walk quietly among La Jolla's rare treasures. ~ Located west of North Torrey Pines Road, two miles north of Genesee Avenue.

LODGING Like a Monopoly master, La Jolla possesses the lion's share of excellent accommodations in the San Diego area. Understandably, there are no budget hotels in this fashionable village by the sea.

Sands of La Jolla is a small, 39-room motel on a busy thoroughfare. Rooms are not exactly designer showcases, but they are tastefully appointed and neatly maintained. ~ 5417 La Jolla Boulevard; 619-459-3336, 800-643-0530, fax 619-454-0022. DELUXE.

Tucked away on the north fringe of the village is **Andrea Villa Inn**, a classy looking 49-unit motel that packs more amenities than some resorts. There is a pool, jacuzzi, concierge, and continental breakfast service. The rooms are spacious and professionally decorated with quality furniture. Andrea Villa is one of La Jolla's best hotel buys. ~ 2402 Torrey Pines Road; 619-459-3311, 800-411-2141, fax 619-459-1320. DELUXE TO ULTRA-DELUXE.

Small, European-style hotels have always been popular in La Jolla, and the granddaddy of them all is the **Colonial Inn**. Established in 1913, the 75-room establishment features lavishly redecorated rooms that beautifully blend antique and contemporary furnishings. Oceanfront rooms provide matchless views. ~ 910 Prospect Street; 619-

454-2181, 800-826-1278 or 800-223-0888, fax 619-454-5679. DE-LUXE TO ULTRA-DELUXE.

More than just a hotel, **La Valencia** is a La Jolla institution and one of the loveliest hotels in San Diego. Resplendent in pink stucco and Spanish tile, it is perched on a breezy promontory overlooking the coves and sea cliffs of La Jolla. From the moment guests enter via a trellis-covered tile loggia into a lobby that could pass for King Juan Carlos' living room, they are enveloped in elegance. The private accommodations, however, don't always measure up to the hotel's image. Some of the 100 rooms are rather small and furnished in re-production antiques. Ah, but out back there's a beautiful garden ter-race opening onto the sea and tumbling down to a free-form swim-ming pool edged with lawn. Facilities include a gym, sauna, and three distinctive restaurants. ~ 1132 Prospect Street; 619-454-0771, 800-451-0772, fax 619-456-3921. ULTRA-DELUXE.

The **Sheraton Grande Torrey Pines**, adorned with marble and polished wood, is an equally spectacular white-glove establishment. Here, art deco visits the 21st century in a series of terraces that lead past plush dining rooms, multitiered fountains and a luxurious swim-ming pool. ~ 10950 North Torrey Pines; 619-558-1500, 800-325-3533, fax 619-597-6962. ULTRA-DELUXE.

Just as the village boasts San Diego's finest selection of small ho-tels, it can also claim a well-known bed and breakfast. **The Bed and Breakfast Inn at La Jolla**, listed as a historical site, was designed as a private home in 1913 by the renowned architect Irving Gill. The John Phillip Sousa family resided here in 1921. Faithfully restored by its present owners as a 16-room inn, it stands today as Gill's finest example of Cubist-style architecture. Impeccably decorated and ide-ally situated a block-and-a-half from the ocean, this inn is the essence of La Jolla. Each room features an individual decorative theme car-ried out in period furnishings. Some have fireplaces and ocean views.

✔ **CHECK THESE OUT—UNIQUE LODGING**

- *Budget:* Shed your armor at **Churchill's Castle**, a medieval manor in down-town San Diego. *page 287*
- *Moderate:* Park under the peaked roof of the Queen Anne **Keating House Inn**, a bed and breakfast convenient to Balboa Park. *page 299*
- *Deluxe:* Repose in antique elegance at downtown's **Horton Grand Hotel**, where a cheery fire in your own fireplace will make you want to curl up with a Jane Austen novel. *page 287*
- *Ultra-deluxe:* Try for a turret room at the landmark **Hotel del Coro-nado**, hostelry to movie stars, presidents . . . and ghosts. *page 300*

Budget: under $50   Moderate: $50–$90   Deluxe: $90–$120   Ultra-deluxe: over $120

All but one tiny sleeping room have private baths. ~ 7753 Draper Avenue; 619-456-2066, fax 619-456-1500. MODERATE TO ULTRA-DELUXE.

La Jolla's only true beachfront hotel is **Sea Lodge**. Designed and landscaped to resemble an old California hacienda, this 128-room retreat overlooks the Pacific on a mile-long beach. With its stuccoed arches, terra-cotta roofs, ceramic tilework, fountains, and flowers, Sea Lodge offers a relaxing south-of-the-border setting. Rooms are large and fittingly appointed with "rustic-Hispanic" furnishings. All feature balconies and the usual amenities: fitness room, sauna, jacuzzi, pool, and and tennis courts. ~ 8110 Camino del Oro; 619-459-8271. ULTRA-DELUXE.

DINING

Just as it is blessed with many fine hotels, La Jolla is a restaurant paradise. **George's at the Cove**, which based its climb to success on a knockout view of the water, a casual, contemporary environment, fine service, and a trendsetting regional menu. Daily menus incorporate the freshest seafood, veal, beef, lamb, poultry, and pasta available. Spicy Jamaican chicken quesadilla and rock shrimp with snow peas are two of my favorites. The food presentation alone is a work of art. There is also a café menu in the upstairs bar. ~ 1250 Prospect Place; 619-454-4244. DELUXE TO ULTRA-DELUXE.

Another important La Jolla dining place is **Cindy Black's**. Decorated with brightly painted murals and fresh flowers, this well-known establishment features French cuisine. You'll find chicken stew, roast rack of lamb, and steamed clams with cilantro. Dinner only. ~ 5721 La Jolla Boulevard; 619-456-6299. DELUXE TO ULTRA-DELUXE.

Manhattan, which successfully replicates a New York City family-style Italian restaurant (despite the palms and pink stucco), features a singing maître d'. The most popular dishes include zesty scampi *fra diavalo* over pasta, veal marsala, and rack of lamb. There are wonderful Caesar salads and *cannoli* desserts every night. ~ 7776 Fay Avenue; 619-554-1444. MODERATE TO ULTRA-DELUXE.

José's Court Room, a noisy, down-to-earth Mexican pub, is the best place in town for quick, casual snacks. They offer all the typical taco, tostada, and enchilada plates plus tasty sautéed shrimp and chicken ranchero dinners. ~ 1037 Prospect Street; 619-454-7655. BUDGET TO MODERATE.

HIDDEN ►

John's Waffle Shop is a traditional La Jolla stopping place for old-fashioned, counter-style breakfasts or lunches. Locals start their day here with golden waffles, cherry kiafa crêpes, or eggs Benedict. The best lunches are the country-fried steak and grilled tuna melt on sourdough. ~ 7906 Girard Avenue; 619-454-7371. BUDGET.

SHOPPING

Once a secluded seaside village, La Jolla has emerged as a world-famous resort community that offers style and substance. The shopping focuses on Girard Avenue (from Torrey Pines Road to Prospect Street) and along Prospect Street. Both are lined with designer boutiques, alluring specialty shops, and fabulous art galleries.

In La Jolla's numerous galleries, traditional art blends with contemporary paintings, and rare Oriental antiques complement 20th-century bronze sculpture. The **Tasende Gallery** has a small display area that packs in contemporary art by big names like Henry Moore and Marino Marini. The gallery concentrates on sculpture although it exhibits paintings and drawings as well. ~ 820 Prospect Street; 619-454-3691.

Simic New Renaissance Galleries has a fine selection of seascapes and master impressionist work. ~ 1205 Prospect Street; 619-456-4076.

Housed as it is in a landmark 1903 cottage covered with wisteria, **John Cole's Book Shop** provides a refuge from these slick, chic La Jolla shops. Its nooks and crannies are lined with books ranging from best sellers to rare editions. ~ 780 Prospect Street; 619-454-4766.

Located some distance south of the village center, **Capriccio** has made its mark in the world of women's fashions, having been numbered by *Women's Wear Daily* among the top three fashion stores in America. ~ 6919 La Jolla Boulevard; 619-459-4189.

NIGHTLIFE

The dark-paneled **Whaling Bar** attracts lots of La Jolla's big fish. A fine place to relax, listen to piano music, and nibble gourmet hors d'oeuvres. ~ La Valencia Hotel, 1132 Prospect Street; 619-454-0771.

Among the most romantic restaurants in town, **Top O' The Cove** features an equally romantic piano bar. ~ 1216 Prospect Street; 619-454-7779. A panoramic view of the ocean makes **Elarios** the perfect place to enjoy a mix of local and national jazz acts nightly. It features a special Latin jazz night on Thursday. Cover on weekends. ~ Summer House Inn, 7955 La Jolla Shores Drive; 619-459-0541.

The Comedy Store features comedians exclusively, many with national reputations. Cover plus minimum. ~ 916 Pearl Street; 619-454-9176.

WHERE THE FISH SHOP FOR SCALES

One of the oldest and most unusual shops in La Jolla guards the entrance to a sea cave and can actually be entered from land or sea. Dating to 1903, the **La Jolla Cave and Shell Shop** displays every kind of shell imaginable along with a variety of nautical gifts and tourist baubles. From inside the shop, 145 steps lead down a tunnel to the main chamber of Sunny Jim Cave. ~ 1325 Coast Boulevard; 619-454-6080.

The San Diego area finally got its own **Hard Rock Cafe**, where crowds line the streets just to get in. The main attraction here is the collection of rock-and-roll memorabilia; even the bar is modeled after Pete Townshend's guitar. ~ 909 Prospect Street; 619-454-5101.

HIDDEN ►   Hidden inside a nondescript building, **D. G. Wills Books** is a tiny literary haven featuring lectures and poetry readings, as well as an occasional jazz night. ~ 7461 Girard Avenue; 619-456-1800.

The **La Jolla Chamber Music Society** hosts summer and fall performances by such notables as the Isaac Stern, Yo-Yo Ma, and the Stuttgart Chamber Orchestra. ~ 619-459-3728. The prestigious **La Jolla Playhouse**, located on the University of California's San Diego campus, produces innovative dramas and musicals and spotlights famous actors. ~ 619-550-1070.

BEACHES & PARKS   **TORREY PINES STATE BEACH** 🏃 🏊 🎣 A long, wide, sandy stretch adjacent to Los Peñasquitos Lagoon and Torrey Pines State Reserve, this beach is highly visible from the highway and therefore heavily used. It is popular for sunning, swimming, surf fishing, volleyball, and sunset barbecues. Nearby trails lead through the reserves with their lagoons, rare trees, and abundant birdlife. The beach is unpatrolled so exercise caution in and out of the surf. Restrooms are available, however, restaurants and groceries are two miles away in Del Mar. Surfers might want to steer clear of this beach because there are powerful peaks. ~ Located just north of Carmel Valley Road in Del Mar; 619-755-2063.

HIDDEN ►   **BLACK'S BEACH** 🏊 One of the world's most famous nude beaches, on hot summer days it attracts bathers by the thousands, many in the buff. The sand is lovely and soft and the 300-foot cliffs rising up behind make for a spectacular setting. Hang-gliders soar from the glider port above to add even more enchantment. Swimming is dangerous; beware of the currents and exercise caution as the beach is infrequently patrolled. Surfing is excellent; one of the most awesome beach breaks in California. ~ From Route 5 in La Jolla follow Genesee Avenue west; turn left on North Torrey Pines Road, then right at Torrey Pines Scenic Drive. There's a parking lot at the Torrey Pines Glider Port, but trails to the beach from here are very steep and often dangerous. If you're in doubt just park at the Torrey Pines State Reserve lot one mile north and walk back along the shore to Black's.

SCRIPPS BEACH 🏃 With coastal bluffs above, narrow sand beach below, and rich tidepools offshore, this is a great strand for beachcombers. Two underwater reserves as well as museum displays at the Scripps Institute of Oceanography are among the attractions. There are museum facilities at Scripps Institute. ~ Scripps Institute is located at the 8600 block of La Jolla Shores Drive in La Jolla.

KELLOGG PARK–LA JOLLA SHORES BEACH The sand is wide and the swimming is easy at La Jolla Shores; so, naturally, the beach is covered with bodies whenever the sun appears. Just to the east is Kellogg Park, an ideal place for a picnic, swimming, and surfing. There are restrooms and lifeguards. Restaurants and groceries are nearby. ~ Off Camino del Oro and Costa Boulevard in La Jolla.

ELLEN BROWNING SCRIPPS PARK AND LA JOLLA COVE This grassy park sits on a bluff overlooking the cove and is the scenic focal point of La Jolla. The naturally formed cove is almost always free of breakers, has a small but sandy beach, and is a popular spot for swimmers and divers. It's also the site of the **La Jolla Ecological Reserve**, an underwater park and diving reserve. There are picnic areas, restrooms, shuffleboard, and lifeguards. Restaurants and groceries are nearby. Surfing: La Jolla's big wave action lies outside the cove so surfers should exercise caution. ~ Near Coast Boulevard and Girard Avenue in La Jolla.

CHILDREN'S POOL BEACH At the north end of Coast Boulevard Beach (see below) a concrete breakwater loops around a small lagoon. Despite its name, the beach's strong rip currents can make swimming hazardous. There are lifeguards and restrooms, and restaurants and groceries are nearby. Fishing is good from the surf. Seasonal rip tides can be hazardous to swimmers, so check with lifeguards. ~ Located off Coast Boulevard in La Jolla.

COAST BOULEVARD PARK After about a half-mile of wide sandy beach, the bluffs and tiny pocket beaches that characterize Windansea (see below) reappear at what locals call "Coast Beach." The pounding waves make watersports unsafe, but savvy locals find the smooth sandstone boulders and sandy coves perfect for reading, sunbathing, and picnicking. ~ Paths lead to the beach at several points along Coast Boulevard in La Jolla.

MARINE STREET BEACH Separated from Windansea to the south by towering sandstone bluffs, this is a much wider and more sandy strand, favored by sunbathers, swimmers, skindivers, and frisbee-tossing youths. The rock-free shoreline is ideal for walking or jogging. Restaurants and groceries are located nearby. The beach is good for board and bodysurfing; watch for rip currents and high surf. ~ Turn west off La Jolla Boulevard on Marine Street.

WINDANSEA BEACH This is surely one of the most picturesque beaches in the country. It has been portrayed in the movies and was immortalized in Tom Wolfe's 1968 nonfiction classic, *The Pumphouse Gang*, about the surfers who still hang around the old pumphouse (part of the city's sewer system), zealously protecting their famous surf from outsiders. Windansea is rated by experts as one of the best surfing locales on the West Coast. In the evenings, crowds line the Neptune Place sidewalk, which runs along the top of the cliffs, to watch the sunset. North of the pumphouse are several sandy nooks sandwiched between sandstone outcroppings. Romantic spot! There are lifeguards in the summer; restaurants and groceries are located nearby. ~ Located at the end of Nautilus Street in La Jolla.

HERMOSA TERRACE PARK 🏄 🏊 This beach is said to be "seasonally sandy," which is another way of saying it's rocky at times. Best chance for sand is in the summer when this is a pretty good sunning beach. The surfing is good. There are no facilities; restaurants and groceries are located nearby. ~ Located off Winamar Avenue in La Jolla; a paved path leads to the beach.

BIRD ROCK 🏄 🏊 Named for a large sandstone boulder about 50 yards off the coast, this beach is rocky and thus favored by divers. The surf rarely breaks here, but when it does this spot is primo for surfing; exercise caution. Fishing is also good. Facilities are nonexistent, but restaurants and groceries are located nearby. ~ Located at the end of Bird Rock Avenue in La Jolla.

SOUTH BIRD ROCK 🏊 Tidepools and good fishing are the attractions along this rocky, cliff-lined beach. Surfing is best in the summer. Restaurants and groceries are nearby. ~ From Midway or Forward streets in La Jolla follow paths down to the beach.

TOURMALINE SURFING PARK 🏊 A year-round reef break and consistently big waves make La Jolla one of the best surfing areas on the West Coast. Because of its narrow, rocky strand, Tourmaline has been designated a surfing-only beach. Skindiving is permitted, too, but no swimming. You'll find picnic areas and restrooms; restaurants and groceries are nearby in Pacific Beach. ~ Located at the end of Tourmaline Street in La Jolla.

▼▼▼▼▼▼▼▼▼▼▼▼▼▼
Mission Bay Park Area

Dredged from a shallow, mosquito-infested tidal bay, 4600-acre Mission Bay Park is the largest municipal aquatic park in the world. For San Diego's athletic set it is Mecca, a recreational paradise dotted with islands and lagoons and ringed by 27 miles of sandy beaches.

Here, visitors join with residents to enjoy swimming, sailing, windsurfing, waterskiing, fishing, jogging, cycling, golf, and tennis. Or perhaps a relaxing day of kite flying and sunbathing.

SIGHTS More than just a playground, Mission Bay Park features a shopping complex, resort hotels, restaurants, and the popular marine park, **Sea World**. This 150-acre park-within-a-park is the world's largest oceanarium. Admission. ~ Sea World Drive; 619-226-3901.

Among the attractions are performing killer whales; the largest penguin colony north of Antarctica; a "Forbidden Reef" inhabited by bat rays and over 100 moray eels; and "Rocky Point Preserve,"

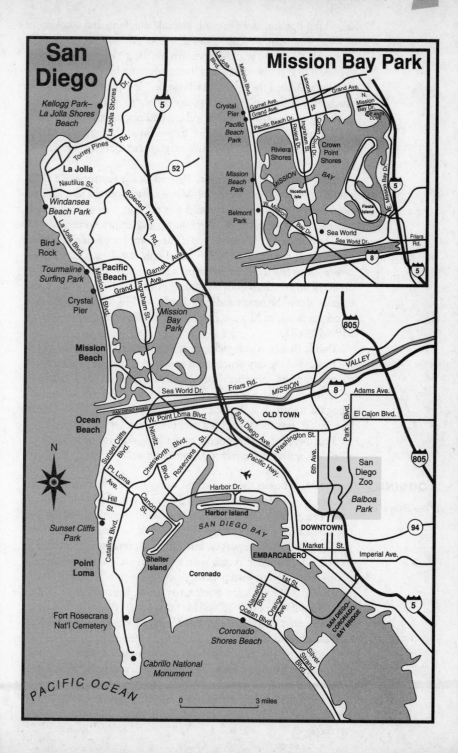

an exhibit boasting a wave pool, pettable dolphins, and a colony of Alaskan sea otters (rescued from the 1989 *Exxon Valdez* oil spill). The park also hosts world-class water-skiers, a Sky Tower that lifts visitors 320 feet above Mission Bay, and an underwater submarine simulator dubbed the "Bermuda Triangle." It's quality material, but much of it is wasted on me. I prefer simply to watch the penguins waddling about on a simulated iceberg and zipping around after fish in their glass-contained ocean, or to peer in at the fearsome makos at "Shark Encounter." The park's magnificent marine creatures are all the entertainment I need.

Down along the oceanfront, **Mission Beach** is strung out along a narrow jetty of sand protecting Mission Bay from the sea. Mission Boulevard threads its way through this eclectic, wall-to-wall mix of shingled beach shanties, condominiums, and luxury homes.

The historic 1925 "Giant Dipper" has come back to life after years of neglect at the **Belmont Park**. One of only two West Coast seaside coasters, this beauty is not all the park has to offer. There's also a carousel, video arcade, indoor swimming pool, and a host of shops and eateries along the beach and boardwalk. ~ 3146 Mission Boulevard or on the beach at Mission Boulevard and West Mission Bay Drive; 619-488-0668.

Pacific Beach, which picks up at the northern edge of the bay, is the liveliest of the city beaches, an area packed with high school and college students. Designer shorts, a garish Hawaiian shirt, strapped-on sunglasses, and a skate board are all you need to fit in perfectly along the frenetic boardwalk at "PB." Stop and see the 1920s **Crystal Pier** with its tiny motel built out over the waves. Or take a stroll along the boardwalk, checking out the sunbathers, skaters, joggers, and cyclists. ~ Located at the end of Garnet Avenue.

LODGING   Pacific Beach boasts the San Diego County motel with the most character of all. **Crystal Pier Motel** is a throwback to the 1930s. Fittingly so, because that's when this quaint-looking assemblage of 26 cottages on Crystal Pier was built. This blue-and-white woodframe complex, perched over the waves, features little cottages that are hardly more than huts. Each comes with a kitchen and patio-over-the-sea, not to mention your own parking place on the pier. A unique discovery indeed. ~ 4500 Ocean Boulevard, Pacific Beach; 619-483-6983, 800-748-5894, fax 619-483-6811. ULTRA-DELUXE.

There aren't many beachfront facilities along Pacific Beach, Mission Beach, and Ocean Beach, except for condominiums. One particularly pretty four-unit condominium, **Ventanas al Mar**, overlooks the ocean in Mission Beach. Its contemporary two- and three-bedroom units feature fireplaces, jacuzzis, kitchens, and washer-dryers. They sleep as many as eight people. ~ 3631 Ocean Front Walk, Mission Beach; 619-459-7125, 800-869-7858, fax 619-459-7125. ULTRA-DELUXE.

Just a few doors away is the family-oriented **Far Horizons**, a two-story gray frame fourplex. The one-bedroom apartments have ocean views and in summer rent by the week only. ~ 3643-45 Ocean Front Walk, Mission Beach; 619-459-7125, fax 619-459-7125. DELUXE.

Most of the hotels within sprawling Mission Bay Park are upscale resorts in the deluxe to ultra-deluxe price range. But there's budget-priced relief at the **Western Shores**, located just across the street from Mission Bay Golf Course. This is a quiet, newly refurbished 40-unit court that simply can't be matched for value anywhere in the area. ~ 4345 East Mission Bay Drive, Pacific Beach; 619-273-1121. BUDGET.

Another bargain is **Banana Bungalow**, a privately run hostel right on Mission Beach. Most of the accommodations are of the bunk-bed variety for the backpacking set who don't mind sharing rooms with strangers. A complimentary breakfast is served every morning. Accommodations are on a first-come, first-served basis. ~ 707 Reed Avenue, Mission Beach; 619-273-3060. BUDGET.

Only one Mission Bay resort stands out as unique—the **San Diego Princess**. Over 40 acres of lush gardens, lagoons, and white sand beach surround the villas and cottages of this 464-room resort. Except for some fancy suites, room decor is motel-modern, with quality furnishings. But guests don't spend much time in their rooms anyway. At the Princess there's more than a mile of beach, catamaran rentals, a fitness center, six tennis courts, five pools, three restaurants, two lounges, and an 18-hole putting course. A self-contained island paradise. ~ 1404 West Vacation Road, Mission Beach; 619-274-4630, 800-344-2626. DELUXE.

Critic's choice for the area's best omelettes is **Café Broken Yoke**. Choose from nearly 30 of these eggy creations or invent your own. If you can eat it all within an hour, the ironman/woman special—including a dozen eggs, mushrooms, onions, cheese, etc.—it costs only

DINING

✔ CHECK THESE OUT—UNIQUE DINING

- *Budget:* Sip margaritas on the patio at **Casa de Pico**, where the Mexican cuisine is a perfect way to top off a visit to Old Town. *page 306*
- *Budget to moderate:* Sample *pad thai* at **Celedon**, an elegant Thai eatery with curries and stir-fries that will make your mouth water. *page 293*
- *Moderate to deluxe:* Hum bars of "Bad Leroy Brown" to yourself as you peruse the international menu at **Croce's**, a bar/restaurant run by Jim Croce's widow, Ingrid. *page 289*
- *Ultra-deluxe:* Saunter into San Diego's best French restaurant, **Mille Fleurs**, where the à la carte menu changes daily. *page 262*

Budget: under $8   Moderate: $8–$16   Deluxe: $16–$24   Ultra-deluxe: over $24

$1.98. Faint or fail and you pay much more. Soups, sandwiches, and salads, too. No dinner. ~ 1851 Garnet Avenue, Pacific Beach; 619-270-0045. BUDGET.

The most creative restaurant in Pacific Beach is **Château Orleans**, one of the city's finest Cajun restaurants. Cajun, that is, with a delightfully different, delicate nouvelle twist. Tasty appetizers fresh from the bayous include Louisiana crab cakes and Southern-fried 'gator bites. Yes, indeed, they eat alligators down in Cajun country, and you should be brave enough to find out why. Seafood gumbo chocked with crawfish, pan-blackened prime rib, chicken sauce piquant, and colorful jambalaya are typical menu choices. Everything is authentic except the decor, which thankfully shuns board floors and bare bulbs in favor of carpets, classy furnishings, and a contemporary color scheme. Dinner only. ~ 926 Turquoise Street, Pacific Beach; 619-488-6744. MODERATE TO DELUXE.

The Mission is a casual neighborhood restaurant where folks are likely to chat with whoever is dining next to them. The ambience is funky, the furniture is eclectic, and the walls are enlivened with local art. Blending Asian and Latin influences, the cuisine emphasizes food that is healthy, tasty, and original. There are breakfast standards with a twist (the French toast, for example, is served on a broad plate with berries and intricate patterns of blueberry purée decorating the edges). If you're in the mood for something more Mexican, order the *plata verde con huevos* (slightly sweet tamales with eggs, roasted chile verde and cheese). For lunch and dinner there are such creations as Pacific Rim risotto, Baja shrimp burrito, and Thai chicken satay. You can also choose from several soups, salads, and sandwiches. ~ 3795 Mission Boulevard, San Diego; 619-488-9060. BUDGET.

HIDDEN ► Hidden away in Ocean Beach is a cottage restaurant called **The Belgian Lion**. Nobody in San Diego provides lustier, tastier European provincial fare than the folks here, who prepare French onion soup, braised rabbit, crispy confit of duck, sea scallops with braised Belgian endives, turnip soufflé, and steaming cassoulets in the classic manner. Home-grown herbs and spices delight both the sauces and the senses. But go easy when you order; the portions are meant to satisfy a Flemish farmer. Service here is especially personalized. Dinner is served only on Thursday, Friday, and Saturday. ~ 2265 Bacon Street, Ocean Beach; 619-223-2700. DELUXE.

SHOPPING Commercial enterprises in the beach communities cater primarily to sun worshipers. Beachie boutiques and rental shops are everywhere. A new shopping center on the beach, **Belmont Park** has a host of shops and restaurants. ~ 3190 Mission Boulevard, Mission Bay Park; 619-488-0668.

The Promenade at Pacific Beach, a modern, Mediterranean-style shopping complex, houses around 12 smartly decorated specialty shops. ~ Located on Mission Boulevard between Pacific Beach Drive and Reed Street, Pacific Beach; 619-490-9097.

Blind Melons, on Crystal Pier, is best described as a Chicago beach bar featuring live blues music. Wednesday is reggae night. Cover. ~ 710 Garnet Avenue, Pacific Beach; 619-483-7844.

The **Cannibal Bar** features a variety of live music nightly, including blues and classic rock. Cover. ~ Catamaran Hotel, 3999 Mission Boulevard, Pacific Beach; 619-488-1081.

Moose McGillycuddy's is a popular nightclub where recorded music keeps the crowd active. ~ 1165 Garnet Avenue, Pacific Beach; 619-274-2323.

The Pennent is a Mission Beach landmark where local writers and beachies congregate en masse on the deck to get rowdy and watch the sunset. The entertainment here is the clientele. ~ 2893 Mission Boulevard, Mission Beach; 619-488-1671.

Delta Six is frequented by a mostly twentysomething crowd that enjoys the live jazz and blues played on the weekends. If you're lucky, you'll get to hear Tom "Cat" Courtney, a real-life legend who has played and sung the blues here every Thursday night for some 17 years. He strummed guitar with the likes of T-Bone Walker, Lightnin' Hopkins, and Freddie King. Cover. ~ 4970 Voltaire Street, Ocean Beach; 619-222-6895.

PACIFIC BEACH PARK 🚲 🏄 🏃 At its south end, "PB" is a major gathering place, its boardwalk crowded with teens and assorted rowdies, but a few blocks north, just before Crystal Pier, the boardwalk becomes a quieter concrete promenade that follows scenic, sloping cliffs. The beach widens here and the crowd becomes more family oriented. The surf is moderate and fine for swimming and bodysurfing. North of the pier Ocean Boulevard becomes a pedestrian-only mall with a bike path, benches, and picnic tables. Facilities include restrooms, lifeguards, and restaurants. ~ Located near Grand Avenue and Pacific Beach Drive.

MISSION BAY PARK 🏄 🏊 One of the nation's largest and most diverse city-owned aquatic parks, Mission Bay has something to suit just about everyone's recreational interest. Key areas and facilities are as follows: **Dana Landing** and **Quivira Basin** make up the southwest portion of this 4600-acre park. Most boating activities begin here, where port headquarters and a large marina are located. Adjacent is **Bonita Cove**, used for swimming, picnicking and volleyball. There is a softball field at **Marina's Point**. Mission Boulevard shops, restaurants, and recreational equipment rentals are within easy walking distance. **Ventura Cove** houses a large hotel complex but its sandy beach is open to the public. Calm waters make it a popular swimming spot for small children.

Vacation Isle and Ski Beach are easily reached via the bridge on Ingraham Street, which bisects the island. The west side contains public swimming areas, boat rentals, and a model yacht basin. Ski Beach is on the east side and is the favorite spot in the bay for waterskiing. Fiesta Island is situated on the southwest side of the park. It's ringed with soft sand swimming beaches and laced with jogging, cycling, and skating paths. A favorite spot for fishing from the quieter coves and for kite flying.

Over on the East Shore, you'll find landscaped picnic areas, playgrounds, a physical fitness course, a sandy beach for swimming, and the park information center. De Anza Cove, at the extreme northeast corner of the park, has a sandy beach for swimming plus a large private campground. Crown Point Shores provides a sandy beach, picnic area, nature study area, physical fitness course, and a waterski landing.

Sail Bay and Riviera Shores make up the northwest portion of Mission Bay and back up against the apartments and condominiums of Pacific Beach. Sail Bay's beaches aren't the best in the park and are usually submerged during high tides. Riviera Shores has a better beach with waterski areas.

Santa Clara and El Carmel Points jut out into the westernmost side of Mission Bay. They are perfect for water sports: swimming, snorkeling, surfing, waterskiing, windsurfing, and boating. Santa Clara Point is of interest to the visitor with its recreation center, tennis courts, and softball field. A sandy beach fronts San Juan Cove between the two points.

Just about every facility imaginable can be found somewhere in the park. There are also catamaran and windsurfer rentals, playgrounds and parks, frisbee and golf, and restaurants and groceries. ~ Located along Mission Boulevard between West Mission Bay Drive and East Mission Bay Drive; 619-221-8900.

▲ The finest and largest of San Diego's commercial campgrounds is Campland On The Bay (2211 Pacific Beach Drive; 800-422-9386), featuring 600 hook-up sites for RVs, vans, tents, and boats; $26 to $52 per night.

MISSION BEACH PARK 🚲 ⚓ 🏊 🚶 The wide, sandy beach at the southern end is a favorite haunt of high schoolers and college students. The hot spot is at the foot of Capistrano Court. A paved boardwalk runs along the beach and is busy with bicyclists, joggers, and roller skaters. Farther north, up around the old Belmont Park roller coaster, the beach grows narrower and the surf rougher. The crowd tends to get that way, too, with heavy-metal teens, sailors, and bikers hanging out along the sea wall, ogling and sometimes harassing the bikini set. This is the closest San Diego comes to Los Angeles' colorful but funky Venice Beach. Facilities include restrooms, lifeguards, and a boardwalk lined with restaurants and beach rentals.

Surfing is popular along the jetty. ~ Located along Mission Boulevard north of West Mission Bay Drive.

San Diego's beautiful harbor is a notable exception to the rule that big-city waterfronts lack appeal. Here, the city embraces its bay and presents its finest profile along the water.

▼▼▼▼▼▼▼▼▼▼▼▼

San Diego Harbor

SIGHTS

The best way to see it all is on a harbor tour. A variety of vessels dock near Harbor Drive at the foot of Broadway. **San Diego Harbor Excursion** provides leisurely trips around the 22-square-mile harbor, which is colorfully backdropped by commercial and naval vessels as well as the dramatic cityscape. Admission. ~ 1050 North Harbor Drive; 619-234-4111. My favorite sunset harbor cruises are aboard the 151-foot schooner *Invader*. Admission. ~ 1006 North Harbor Drive; 619-234-8687.

All along the cityside of the harbor from the Coast Guard Station opposite Lindbergh Field to Seaport Village is a lovely landscaped boardwalk called the **Embarcadero**. It offers parks where you can stroll and play, a floating maritime museum, and a thriving assortment of waterfront diversions.

The **Maritime Museum of San Diego** is composed of three vintage ships: most familiar is the 1863 *Star of India*, the nation's oldest iron-hulled merchant ship still afloat. Visitors go aboard for a hint of what life was like on the high seas more than a century ago. You can also visit the 1898 ferry *Berkeley*, which helped in the evacuation of San Francisco during the 1906 earthquake, and the 1904 steam yacht *Medea*. Admission. ~ 1306 North Harbor Drive; 619-234-9153.

Nautical buffs or anyone concerned about American naval power will be interested in the huge **U.S. Navy** presence in San Diego harbor. As headquarters of the 11th Naval District, San Diego hosts one of the world's largest fleets of fighting ships—from aircraft carriers to nuclear submarines. Naval docks and yards are off-limits but you'll see the sprawling facilities and plenty of those distinctive gray-hulled ships during a harbor cruise. Naval vessels moored at the Broadway Pier hold open house on weekends.

Both Navy and Marine centers present colorful **military reviews** most Fridays. Marching ceremonies begin at exactly 1 p.m. at the Naval Training Center (619-524-1101) and at 10 a.m. at the Marine Corps Recruiting Depot (619-524-1772). ~ Both centers may be reached from downtown by going north on Pacific Highway to Barnett Avenue, then left to Gate 1.

Near the south end of the Embarcadero sits the popular shopping and entertainment complex known as **Seaport Village**. Designed to replicate an Early California seaport, it comprises 14 acres of bayfront parks and promenades, shops, and galleries. ~ Pacific Highway and Harbor Drive; 619-235-4013. On the south side, overlooking the water, is the 45-foot-high **Mukilteo Lighthouse**, official symbol of the village, a recreation of a famous lighthouse located in Washington state. Nearby is the Broadway Flying Horses Carousel, a hand-carved, turn-of-the-century model that originally whirled around on Coney Island.

One of the latest additions to the city skyline, the **San Diego Convention Center** looks like an erector set gone mad. An uncontained congeries of flying buttresses, giant tents, and curved glass, it is fashioned in the form of a ship, seemingly poised to set sail across San Diego Harbor. This architectural exclamation mark is certainly worth a drive by or a quick tour. ~ 111 West Harbor Drive; 619-525-5000.

▼▼▼▼▼▼▼▼▼▼▼▼▼▼▼
Downtown San Diego

At one time downtown San Diego was a collection of porn shops, tattoo parlors, and strip-tease bars. Billions of dollars invested in a stunning array of new buildings and in the restoration of many old ones have changed all that.

Within the compact city center there's Horton Plaza, an exciting experiment in avant-garde urban architecture, and the adjacent Gaslamp Quarter, which reveals how San Diego looked at the peak of its Victorian-era boom in the 1880s.

SIGHTS

Horton Plaza is totally unlike any other shopping center or urban redevelopment project. It has transcended its genre in a whimsical, rambling paths, bridges, towers, piazzas, sculptures, fountains, and live greenery. Mimes, minstrels, and fortune tellers meander about the six-block complex performing for patrons.

Horton Plaza was inspired by European shopping streets and districts such as the Plaka of Athens, the Ramblas of Barcelona, and Portobello Road in London. ~ The Plaza is bounded by Broadway and G Street and 1st and 4th avenues.

The **Gaslamp Quarter** is one of America's largest national historic districts, covering a 16-block strip along 4th, 5th, and 6th avenues from Broadway to the waterfront. Architecturally, the Quarter reveals some of the finest Victorian-style commercial buildings constructed in San Diego during the 50 years between the Civil War and World War I. It was this area, along 5th Avenue, that became San Diego's first main street. The city's core began on the bay where Alonzo Horton first built a wharf in 1869.

It was this same area that later fell into disrepute as the heart of the business district moved north beyond Broadway. By the 1890s, prostitution and gambling were rampant. Offices above the street level were converted into bordellos and opium dens. The area south of Market Street became known as the "Stingaree," an unflattering reference coined by the many who were stung by card sharks, con men, and of course, con ladies.

Rescued by the city and a dedicated group of preservationists, the area not only survived but played a major role in the massive redevelopment of downtown San Diego. The city has added wide brick sidewalks, period street lamps, trees, and benches. In all, more than 100 grand old Victorian buildings have been restored to their original splendor.

History buffs and lovers of antique buildings should promptly don their walking shoes for a tour of the Gaslamp Quarter. One way to do this is to join a walking tour (see the "Transportation" section in this chapter). Or head out on your own, accompanied by a map available at the **William Heath Davis House Museum**. Admission. ~ 410 Island Avenue; 619-233-4692.

The Quarter includes 153 buildings so I couldn't hope to describe them all, but let me take you on a mini-tour of the most important structures. Begin at the aforementioned William Heath Davis House, a well-preserved example of a prefabricated "salt box" family home, dating to about 1850. Framed on the East Coast, it was shipped to San Diego by boat around Cape Horn and represents the oldest structure in the Quarter.

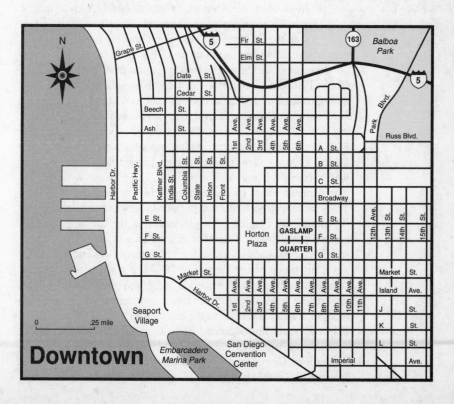

Just across the street is the **Royal Pie Bakery**. Almost unbelievably, a bakery has been on this site since 1871. Around the turn of the century the bakery found itself in the middle of a red-light district. It never stopped turning out cakes and pies, though a notorious bordello operated on the second floor. ~ 554 4th Avenue.

Go back down Island Avenue to 5th Avenue and turn left. Not only was this block part of the Stingaree, as hinted by the old 1887 hotel by the same name on your left, at 542 5th Avenue, but it was San Diego's Chinatown. **Nanking Café** was built in 1912 and retains the atmosphere of the past. ~ 467 5th Avenue.

The nearby **Timken Building**, notable for its fancy arched brick facade, was erected in 1894. ~ Located at 5th Avenue and Market Street. Across the street is the **Backesto Building**, a beautifully restored late-19th-century structure.

The tall, Romanesque Revival **Keating Building** was one of the most prestigious office buildings in San Diego during the 1890s, complete with such modern conveniences as steam heat and an elevator. ~ 5th Avenue and F Street. Next door is the **Ingersoll Tutton Building**. When this 90-foot-long structure was built in 1894 for $20,000 it was the most expensive building on the block! ~ 832 5th Avenue.

Fourteen different styles, ranging from Renaissance to Post Modern, are employed in the design of Horton Plaza.

Most of the block on the other side of 5th Avenue, from F up to E streets, represents the most architecturally significant row in the Gaslamp Quarter. From south to north, there's the **Marston Building** on the corner of F Street. Built in 1881, it was downtown San Diego's leading department store. Next is the 1887 **Hubbell Building**, originally a dry goods establishment. The **Nesmith-Greeley Building** next door is another example of the then-fashionable Romanesque Revival style with its ornamental brick coursing. With twin towers and intricate Baroque Revival architecture, the 1888 **Louis Bank of Commerce** is probably the most beautiful building in the Quarter. It originally housed a ground-floor oyster bar that was a favorite haunt of Wyatt Earp. The famous Western lawman-cum-real-estate speculator resided in San Diego from 1886 to 1893. Be sure to go to the fourth floor to see the beautiful skylight.

Though it's situated a few blocks east of the Gaslamp Quarter, make a point to visit **Villa Montezuma**. This ornate, Queen Anne-style Victorian mansion, magnificently restored, was constructed by a wealthy group of San Diegans in 1887 as a gift to a visiting musician. Culture-hungry civic leaders actually "imported" world-famous troubadour Jesse Shepard to live in the opulent dwelling as something of a court musician to the city's upper crust. Shepard stayed only two years but decorated his villa to the hilt with dozens of stained-glass windows and elaborate hand-carved wood trim and decorations. Open Saturday and Sunday only. Admission. ~ 1925 K Street; 619-239-2211.

Providing contrast to all this preserved history is the new **Museum of Contemporary Art**, adjacent to the American Plaza Trolley Transfer Station. Two floors and four galleries showcase an internationally renowned collection and temporary exhibits featuring cutting-edge contemporary art. Educational tours and a well-stocked bookstore complement the exhibits. Closed Monday. Admission. ~ 1001 Kettner Boulevard at Broadway; 619-234-1001.

LODGING

Among the few decent downtown budget overnight spots, **Churchill's Castle** is about the cleanest and most livable. Billed as "small, quaint, and unique," this venerable seven-story, 92-room hotel is mostly quaint. Built in 1915, it was somewhat tastelessly remodeled to "depict an authentic medieval English castle." In an equally schmaltzy decorative scheme, 30 of the Churchill's better rooms are done up in different thematic motifs such as "Hawaiian Sunset" and "American Indian." Bedspreads and wall murals are the only difference. To really save money during a downtown stay, ask for one of the rooms with a shared bathroom. ~ 827 C Street; 619-236-1673. BUDGET.

Chain hotels are normally not included in these listings, but because of the lack of good, low-cost lodgings downtown, I'm compelled to tell you about **Super 8 Bayview**. This 98-room property offers pleasant, affordable rooms downtown. Queen-sized beds complement a bright, functional, and contemporary environment. ~ 1835 Columbia Street; 619-544-0164, 800-800-8000, fax 619-237-9940. MODERATE.

A recommended midtown hotel is the **Best Western Bayside Inn**. Small enough (122 rooms) to offer some degree of personalized service, this modern highrise promises nearly all the niceties you would pay extra for at more prestigious downtown hotels, including a harbor view. Furnishings and amenities are virtually at par with those found in the typical Hilton or Sheraton. There is a pool and spa, plus a restaurant and cocktail lounge. ~ 555 West Ash Street; 619-233-7500, 800-528-1234. MODERATE.

On the more charming side are San Diego's guesthouses, bed and breakfasts, and historic hotels. **Harbor Hill Guest House** overlooks the harbor in a centrally located area known as "Banker's Hill." This elegant 1920 home once belonged to the city's mayor. Six smartly decorated rooms are arranged on three levels. Each level offers a kitchen-dining area and sitting room. There is also a lovely garden and redwood deck. ~ 2330 Albatross Street; 619-233-0638. MODERATE.

No downtown hotel has a more colorful past than the **Horton Grand Hotel**. This 132-room Victorian gem is actually two old hotels that were disassembled piece by piece and resurrected a few blocks away. The two were lavishly reconstructed and linked by an atrium-lobby and courtyard. The 1880s theme is faithfully executed, from the hotel's antique-furnished rooms (each with a fireplace) to its period-costumed staff. Such amenities as a concierge and afternoon tea combine with friendly service and perfect location to make it one of the city's best hotel values. ~ 311 Island Avenue; 619-544-1886, 800-542-1886, fax 619-239-3823. ULTRA-DELUXE.

Built in 1910 in honor of the 18th president by his son Ulysses S. Grant, Jr., the **U. S. Grant Hotel** reigned as downtown San Diego's premier hotel for decades. The U.S. Grant is a showcase boasting 280 rooms, a restaurant, and a lounge. It is quite possibly the most elegant and certainly the most beautifully restored historic building in the city. There's a marble-floored lobby with cathedral-height ceilings and enormous crystal chandeliers. Rooms are richly furnished with mahogany poster beds, Queen Anne–style armoires, and wing-back chairs. ~ 326 Broadway; 619-232-3121, fax 619-236-3626. ULTRA-DELUXE.

DINING

A couple of San Diego's better restaurant finds lie "uptown" just east of Route 5. **Fifth and Hawthorn** is a neighborhood sensation, but not many tourists find their way to this chic little dining room. The owners present an array of tasty dishes, specializing in fresh seafood ranging from sea bass with ginger to fresh salmon baked in shredded potato. Usually available is filet mignon with green peppers and cabernet sauce. ~ 5th Avenue and Hawthorn Street; 619-544-0940. MODERATE TO DELUXE.

As its name suggests, **Liason** is an intimate, casual bistro with beautiful French doors, a wood-burning fireplace, and a patio with a waterfall. Add candlelight and superb French cuisine, and you're talking about the perfect place for a rendezvous. The five-course, prix-fixe dinner varies and may include lamb curry served with rice, medallions of filet mignon with béarnaise sauce, and salmon served in a crayfish butter sauce. For a romantic dinner, this place comes highly praised. Reservations are recommended. No lunch Saturday, Sunday, and Monday. ~ 2202 4th Avenue; 619-234-5540. DELUXE TO ULTRA-DELUXE.

History, atmosphere, and great cooking combine to make dining at **Ida Bailey's Restaurant** a memorable experience. Located in the Horton Grand Hotel, Ida's was once a brothel, operated back in the 1890s by a madam of the same name. Things are tamer now, but the rich Victorian furnishings serve as a reminder of San Diego's opulent past. The chef serves a varied menu highlighted by old-fashioned American fare, including Victorian pot roast, rack of lamb, and tenderloin. Dinner only. ~ 311 Island Avenue; 619-544-1886. MODERATE TO DELUXE.

Visitors to Horton Plaza are bombarded with dining opportunities. But for those who can resist the temptation to chow down on pizza, french fries, and enchiladas at nearby fast-food shops, there is a special culinary reward. On the plaza's top level sits **Panda Inn**. Here the plush, contemporary design alludes only subtly to Asia with a scattering of classic artwork. But the menu is all-Chinese. Three dishes stand out: orange-flavored beef with asparagus, lemon scallops, and chicken with garlic sauce. Lunch and dinner menus together present more than 100 dishes. Dine on the glassed-in veranda for a great view of the harbor. ~ 506 Horton Plaza; 619-233-7800. MODERATE TO DELUXE.

Situated in a fine, historic 1907 building in the Gaslamp Quarter, **Johnny M's 801** is truly a work of art. It has handsome crown molding and a magnificent stained-glass dome from Greece. The menu features burgers and steaks as well as Maryland soft-shell crab. ~ 801 4th Avenue; 619-233-1131. MODERATE.

For Mexican food head to **El Indio** in the Gaslamp Quarter. Dressed in a pink-and-white color scheme, this self-service café has chimichangas, shredded beef burritos, and a host of other south-of-the-border dishes. Closed Sunday. ~ 409 F Street; 619-239-8151. BUDGET.

Fans of the late Jim Croce ("Bad Leroy Brown," "Time in a Bottle") will surely enjoy a visit to **Croce's Restaurant**. This bar and restaurant in the heart of the Gaslamp Quarter is managed enthusiastically by Jim's widow, Ingrid Croce, and features an eclectic mix of dishes served in a friendly cabaret setting. Daily specials for lunch and dinner vary and are best described as a mixed international home-style ranging from sandwiches and exotic salads to pastas, beef, chicken, and fresh fish dishes. Live music from **The Jazz Bar**, loaded with Croce memorabilia, filters in to the restaurant. They also serve Saturday and Sunday brunch. ~ 802 5th Avenue; 619-233-4355. MODERATE TO DELUXE.

Next door at **Ingrid's Cantina** Ingrid serves up Tex-Mex chow Santa Fe–style: painted desert pasta, grilled mahimahi, and chile rellenos. ~ 619-233-3660. MODERATE TO DELUXE.

You'd be remiss to visit San Diego without enjoying a fresh seafood feast at a spot overlooking the harbor. Why not go first class at **Anthony's Star of the Sea Room**? This place wears more awards than a Navy admiral. Dramatically set over the water and elegantly decorated, Anthony's presents a remarkable menu including abalone, broad-bill swordfish, and lobster pasta. Reservations and coat and tie are recommended. ~ 1360 North Harbor Drive; 619-232-7408. DELUXE TO ULTRA-DELUXE. If your budget can't handle the "Star," check out the other Anthony's next door—the **Fish Grotto**. ~ 619-232-5103. MODERATE.

For decades, San Diegans have enjoyed the authentic Mexican dishes at **Chuey's**. Nestled in the shadow of Coronado Bridge, it draws crowds with its great tacos, made the authentic way, crammed with juicy string beef and heaped with grated Mexican cheese. ~ 1894 Main Street; 619-234-6937. BUDGET.

◄ HIDDEN

SHOPPING   No other shopping center in the county is quite like **Horton Plaza**. More than 140 individually designed stores are situated here. Anchored by four department stores, a flood of specialty and one-of-a-kind shops complete the picture. Along the tiled boulevard are shops and vendors offering whimsical items—everything from saltwater taffy to psychic readings. ~ Between Broadway and G Street, 1st and 4th avenues; 619-239-8180.

Clever designs distinguish many of the shops, such as **Adventure 16**, where a split-log cabin facade invites you in to shop for outdoor and adventure travel apparel, books, and accessories. ~ 619-234-1751. Nearby on the same level is **Banana Republic**, a popular emporium for casual clothes, footwear, and bath accessories. ~ 619-238-0080. There are men's apparel shops, shoe stores, jewelry shops, art galleries, and women's haute couture boutiques, dozens of stores in all. Worth a special visit is **Horton Plaza Farmers Market**, where 25,000 square feet of fresh produce and specialty food products are beautifully displayed. ~ 619-696-7766.

If Horton Plaza doesn't have what you're looking for, try across the street at the **Paladion**. The "bill of fare" at this 23-shop plaza includes clothes, jewelry, and a wealth of other consumer goodies, most in the upper price range. ~ 777 Front Street; 619-232-1627.

The **Gaslamp Quarter**, along 5th Avenue, is a charming 16-square-block assemblage of shops, galleries, and sidewalk cafés in the downtown center. Faithfully replicated in the quarter are Victorian-era street lamps, red-brick sidewalks, and window displays thematic of turn-of-the-century San Diego. Stroll down the **G Street Arts Corridor** to the **International Gallery**, where you'll find a dazzling collection of contemporary crafts combined with primitive and folk art. Wander this wood-and-brick warehouse and let your eyes feast on the brilliant array of Kilim rugs from North Africa, the Middle East, and Central Asia. ~ 643 G Street; 619-235-8255.

A favorite spot for antique lovers is **The Olde Cracker Factory**, which offers a 20-store selection in the restored 1913 Bishop Cracker Factory. Legend has it that a resident ghost named "Crunch" shuffles through mounds of broken crackers here searching for a small brass cookie cutter. ~ 448 West Market Street; 619-233-1669.

A perfect place to stock up for a picnic is the **Farmers Bazaar**, a down-to-earth produce market. ~ 245 7th Avenue; 619-233-0281.

Seaport Village was designed to capture the look and feel of an Early California waterfront setting. Its 65 shops dot a 14-acre village and include the usual mix of boutiques, galleries, clothing stores, and gift shops. ~ Foot of Pacific Highway and Harbor Drive.

On Thursday through Sunday, **Kobey's Swap Meet** converts the parking lot of the San Diego Sports Arena into a giant flea market where over 1000 sellers hawk new and used wares. ~ Sports Arena Boulevard; 619-226-0650.

NIGHTLIFE

The sun is certainly the main attraction in San Diego, but the city also features a rich and varied nightlife, offering the night owl everything from traditional folk music to high-energy discos. There are piano bars, singles bars, and a growing number of jazz clubs.

Call the **San Diego Theater League** for its monthly arts calendar and information about inexpensive events. ~ 619-238-0700. KIFM Radio (98.1 FM) hosts **Lights Out Jazz**, a 24-hour hotline, that provides the latest in jazz happenings. ~ 619-458-9898.

THE BEST BARS   An elegant Old World setting of marble, brass, and leather makes **Grant Grill Lounge** *the* place for the elite to meet. Live jazz keeps the wingtips tapping on the weekend. ~ U.S. Grant Hotel, 326 Broadway; 619-232-3121.

Johnny M's in the Gaslamp Quarter is a favored place to bend an elbow with live blues and rock most nights. Cover charge. ~ 801 4th Avenue; 619-233-1131.

For a good-time bar try **Kenny's Steak Pub**. This beautifully appointed mahogany-and-glass bar is accented by green shamrock carpets. Kenny's draws the after-work crowd and is enlivened on weekends with a jazz-fusion ensemble. Closed Sunday. ~ 939 4th Avenue; 619-231-8500.

At **Croce's** fans of the immortal Jim Croce will love the bar built as a memorial to the late singer-songwriter by his wife, Ingrid. Family mementos line the walls in tribute to a talented recording artist. ~ 802 5th Avenue; 619-233-4355. Just next door, **Croce's Top Hat Bar and Grill** is a snazzy New Orleans–style club featuring live rhythm-and-blues. Cover on weekends. ~ 818 5th Avenue; 619-233-6945.

Karl Strass' Old Columbia Brewery and Grill may well have the best beer in town. This newcomer in the old Gaslamp Quarter has been well-greeted by San Diegans. ~ 1157 Columbia Avenue at B Street; 619-234-2739.

It's easy to spot the shocking pink, neon-lit facade of **Fat City**. Art deco styling marks the exterior, but the bar features an authentic Victorian decor. It's not a meat market, but Fat City is a favorite among friendly young singles and hosts a variety of musical styles Friday and Saturday. ~ 2137 Pacific Highway; 619-232-0686.

Plaza Bar, at the distinctive Westgate Hotel, is a graceful period French lounge where prominent locals and visitors enjoy classy piano entertainment nightly. ~ 1055 2nd Avenue; 619-238-1818.

Mr. A's is the critics' choice for "best drinking with a view." The atmosphere at this elegant restaurant and piano bar is one of monied luxury, and gentlemen are expected to wear jackets. ~ 2550 5th Avenue, 12th floor; 619-239-1377.

For '50s fun, go to the **Corvette Diner, Bar and Grill**. Great oldies keep this joint jumpin'. ~ 3946 5th Avenue; 619-542-1001.

If you're a culture vulture with a limited pocketbook, try **ArtTix**, a 24-hour recording listing half-priced theater, music, and dance tickets. ~ 619-497-5000.

There's a wonderful view of San Diego Bay from the Seaport Village restaurant, **Luigi Lamara**, where a tropical setting creates a relaxed atmosphere. ~ 861 West Harbor Drive; 619-232-7581.

THEATER In addition to performances of the San Diego Opera, the **San Diego Civic Theater** presents a variety of entertainment ranging from pop artists to plays to dance performances. ~ 202 C Street; 619-236-6510.

The **San Diego Repertory Theatre** performs dramas, comedies, and musicals. ~ 79 Horton Plaza; 619-235-8025.

OPERA, SYMPHONY, AND DANCE With performances at the San Diego Civic Theater, the **San Diego Opera** presents such international stars as Ramon Vargas, Deborah Riedel, and Jeffrey Black. The season runs from January through May, with some additional recitals in the spring and fall. ~ 202 C Street; 619-232-7636.

Performing in the historic 1929 Spanish Renaissance–style Copley Symphony Hall, the **San Diego Symphony Orchestra** offers an array of guest conductors and artists. ~ 1245 7th Avenue; 619-699-4205. During the summer, the SDSO presents outdoor performances at the Embarcadero Marina Park South. ~ 5th Street and Harbor Boulevard.

California Ballet Center presents a diverse repertoire of contemporary and traditional ballets. ~ 202 C Street; 619-560-5676.

BEACHES & PARKS

EMBARCADERO MARINA PARK The center city's only real waterfront park is a breezy promenade situated on the bay and divided into two sections. The northern part has a nicely landscaped lawn and garden, picnic tables, and benches. The southern half features a fishing pier, basketball courts, and an athletic course. Restrooms are available, and restaurants and groceries are nearby. ~ Enter at the southern end at Harbor Drive and 8th Street; at the northern end, from Seaport Village Shopping Center; 619-686-6200.

SPANISH LANDING PARK This is a slender sandy beach with walkways and a grassy picnic area that's situated close to San Diego International Airport. Overlooks Harbor Island Marina and offers lovely views of the bay and city. Restrooms are available, and restaurants and groceries are nearby. ~ Located just west of the airport on North Harbor Drive; 619-686-6200.

▼▼▼▼▼▼▼▼▼▼▼▼▼▼▼

San Diego Gay Scene

Though not as dynamic—or as expensive—as the Castro district in San Francisco, Hillcrest holds its own as San Diego's gay and lesbian neighborhood. The '50s architecture and neon also give the area a campy feel (a neon sign, which is sometimes burned out, hangs across University Avenue and signals entrance into Hillcrest). Bookstores, trendy boutiques, and coffeeshops line University Avenue, 5th

Avenue, and Robinson Street—all within easy walking distance of one another. And because Hillcrest boasts some of the best movie houses and restaurants in San Diego, you'll see everyone there: gay yuppies, leather-clad lesbians, and Ozzie and Harriet lookalikes.

LODGING

Although only 16 percent of its guests hail from outside the U.S., the **Hillcrest Inn Hotel** considers itself an international hotel. Right in the hub of Hillcrest activity, the 45 modestly furnished rooms, outfitted with microwaves and refrigerators, provide its gay guests with a comfortable stay. Fatigued wayfarers will appreciate the sun patio and jacuzzi after long days (and nights) of sightseeing. ~ 3745 5th Avenue; 619-293-7078, 800-258-2280, fax 619-293-3861. MODERATE.

The **Balboa Park Inn** is a very popular caravansary with gays. Like Balboa Park nearby, the four-building inn was built in 1915 for the Panama–California Exposition. Its 26 rooms are decorated in different themes; you can choose to luxuriate in *Gone With the Wind's* "Tara," get sentimental in 1930s Paris, or go wild in Greystoke. Some suites boast jacuzzis, kitchens, and fireplaces, and *everyone* can request a continental breakfast served in bed. A courtyard and sun terrace round out the facilities of this winsome getaway. ~ 3402 Park Boulevard; 619-298-0823, fax 619-294-8070, 800-938-8181. MODERATE TO ULTRA-DELUXE.

Not located in Hillcrest but catering to an exclusively gay clientele, **Dmitri's Guesthouse** offers five rooms away from the hubbub in a residential area on the opposite side of Balboa Park. Each suite comes with a ceiling fan and a refrigerator (some include a full kitchen). Feel free to shed your clothing on the sundeck and immerse yourself in the hot tub or swimming pool. Situated in a century-old house, Dmitri's serves a continental breakfast poolside every morning. ~ 931 21st Street; 619-237-1789. BUDGET TO MODERATE.

DINING

If you're looking for a really hot time in Hillcrest, there is nothing better than a plate of *poo ja* followed by a spicy serving of *gang ped*. Enjoy these and other wonderful Thai favorites at **Celedon**. Mild or spicy, Celedon's curried and stir-fried specialties are delicious. The stylish art nouveau surroundings, nicely appointed with original Thai brassworks and tapestries, add to the graceful flair of this eatery. ~ 3628 5th Avenue; 619-295-8800. BUDGET TO MODERATE.

Judging by the name itself, you'd think **Hamburger Mary's** was a typical burger joint. It peddles burgers, yes, but with washboards, surfboards, and murals decorating the walls, it definitely ain't typical. Besides hamburgers, you'll find steak and halibut dinners, vegetarian plates, and salads, which can be eaten outdoors on the patio. Afterward, you'll want to join the festivities at Kickers, the gay country-western bar in the same building. Sunday brunch. ~ 308 University Avenue; 619-491-0400. BUDGET.

HIDDEN ▶ Bread lovers will think they have landed in paradise when they enter **Bread & Cie**. The aroma of fig, jalapeño, cheese, and rosemary breads lingers in this amazing bakery, which also serves lunch and cappuccinos. ~ 350 University Avenue; 619-683-9322.

Attracting attention has never been a problem for the **Corvette Diner, Bar, and Grill**. Although it's usually crammed full of families and high school kids, the decor is not to be missed. Cool 1950s music, a soda fountain (complete with resident jerks), rock-and-roll memorabilia, dancing waitresses, and a classy Corvette have proven a magnetic formula for this Hillcrest haven. The place is jammed for breakfast, lunch, and dinner. Simple "blue-plate" diner fare includes meatloaf, chicken-fried steak, and hefty burgers named for 1950s notables like Annette, Eddie, and Kookie. ~ 3946 5th Avenue; 619-542-1001. BUDGET.

Located in the middle of the Rainbow Block, **California Cuisine** offers sumptuous dishes for your discriminating palate. Beef tenderloin and New Zealand lamb loin are among the many items on their ever-changing menu, as are pasta, salads, and vegetarian fare. You also get a taste of promising local artists whose original work adorns the walls. Closed Monday. ~ 1027 University Avenue; 619-543-0790. DELUXE.

SHOPPING   **Obelisk** carries gay, lesbian, and bisexual reading material, as well as gift items to tickle your fancy—jewelry, shirts, and cards—to name a few. ~ 1029 University Avenue; 619-297-4171.

Searching high and low for that Betty Page calendar? How about some sweater-girl paper dolls? **Babbette Schwartz**, the local drag queen, has a store that carries '50s paraphernalia and other eclectic gifts, including lava lamps and Barbie dolls. ~ 421 University Avenue; 619-220-7048.

Enter the **Blue Door Bookstore** and browse through the extensive collection of gay and lesbian fiction, poetry, and philosophy. It stocks contemporary, classical, and modern literature, too. ~ 3823 5th Avenue; 619-298-8610.

California Man is a modern-day haberdashery, catering to the needs of an active '90s man. You'll find some casual wear for shopping in, beach wear to sunbathe and swim in, dressy wear for more formal affairs, and body-conscious club wear for a night out on the town. ~ 3930 5th Avenue; 619-294-9108.

Unlike other antique stores in the area, **Circa a.d.** offers anything but American antiques. It proudly displays a vast assortment of Asian, Spanish, African, and European artwork, textiles, and pottery. It even carries bonsai trees. ~ 3867 4th Avenue; 619-293-3328.

NIGHTLIFE   The **Brass Rail**, which opened in 1958, is San Diego's oldest gay bar. The bartenders' famed congeniality keeps the primarily male clientele coming back year after year for more—more drinks and more dancing (which is in full swing Tuesday through Sunday). Monday and Tuesday are hosts to a comedy drag show, while Thursday is Latino night. You can watch the go-go boys doing their thing on Wednesday and Saturday. ~ 3796 5th Avenue; 619-298-2233.

A few doors down from the Brass Rail and across the street from the Hillcrest Inn Hotel is **David's Place**. Designed to look like a living room with a couch and antique furniture, this popular coffeehouse is a home away from home for travelers and locals alike. Aside from knocking back espresso and admiring the passing scenery, you engage your neighbor with a board game. David's Place is a nonprofit establishment that donates its proceeds to local AIDS organizations. ~ 3766 5th Avenue; 619-294-8908.

Also in this same stretch of 5th Avenue, **The Loft** is a gay bar offering jukebox music and pool playing. ~ 3610 5th Avenue; 619-296-6407.

The short trek up to University Avenue brings you to Hamburger Mary's restaurant, home of **Kickers**. This country-and-western bar keeps gay, lesbian, and straight folks kickin' with free line dancing and two-step lessons Monday through Friday. On Saturday and Sunday patrons are left to fend for themselves on the dancefloor. ~ 308 University Avenue; 619-491-0400.

The real action on University Avenue is over at the Rainbow Block. First there's **Flicks**, a video bar that flashes visual stimuli on its four big screens while playing dance and progressive music. Pool, pinball, and darts are also on the menu for the young gay men who frequent this joint. ~ 1017 University Avenue; 619-297-2056.

At the far end of the block, **Rich's** heats up Thursday through Sunday with high energy dancing till 2 a.m. The DJ-mixed music sets the beat: groove, techno, house, and tribal rhythms. The music isn't the only thing to stimulate your senses; your eyes will be dazzled by the specially created visual effects. Each night has a different theme. Thursday is Club Hedonism (enough said). On Friday nights Rich's go-go boys "work it." On Saturday the go-go boys give way to erotic dancers. To finish off the weekend, there is Rich's Tea and Me on Sunday with the doors opening at 7 p.m., two hours earlier than other nights. Cover. ~ 1051 University Ave; 619-295-2195.

Perfectly situated between the hotspots Rich's and Flicks, **Euphoria** is *the* place to take a breather from dancing and barhopping. Their espresso drinks and sugar-enriched pastries are a sure way to re-energize. Euphoria, which displays local artistic talent on its walls, maintains a cozy, mellow atmosphere from early morning until late in the evening. The sidewalk tables are a prime spot to check out the Rainbow Block scene. ~ 1045 University Avenue; 619-295-1769.

Beyond the Rainbow Block you can take a pleasant stroll along the north side of Balboa Park to **The Flame**. Touted as "San Diego's hottest women's nightclub," this postmodern apocalypse features a dancefloor, pool tables, and a video bar. Although men are always welcome here, Tuesday is officially "Boys Night." Dancing runs seven nights a week with Deejays spinning everything from salsa rhythms to disco delights. Drag shows and gogo dancers entertain on Friday night. No cover Thursday. ~ 3780 Park Boulevard; 619-295-4163.

While most of the gay bars are located in the Hillcrest neighborhood, there is a place down by the beach. **Matador,** one block from Mission Beach, features taped music, a pool table, and video games. ~ 4633 Mission Boulevard; 619-483-6943.

There's an older, yuppie, all-woman crowd that enjoys an endless line-up of activities at **Club Bombay.** Along with weekday happy hour and Sunday barbecue, which can be savored inside or out on the patio, the women enjoy Monday pool tournaments, Tuesday dart contests, and Wednesday and Saturday karaoke. On Friday, the deejay takes a spin at roiling up the dancefloor. ~ 3175 India Street; 619-296-6789.

Other gay bars around town include **Bourbon Street,** a comfortable piano bar that features an outdoor patio. ~ 4612 Park Boulevard; 619-291-0173. The action at the **Chee Chee Club,** a local cruise bar, revolves around listening to video music, shooting pool, and playing pinball. ~ 929 Broadway; 619-234-4404. Similarly, **Shooter's,** a popular sports bar, boasts three large-screen televisions, seven pool tables, pinball, video games, and a video jukebox. ~ 3815 30th Street; 619-574-0744.

▼▼▼▼▼▼▼▼▼▼▼▼▼▼▼
Balboa Park and the San Diego Zoo

History is unclear as to whether it was intelligent foresight or unbridled optimism that prompted the establishment of Balboa Park. Certain that a fine neighborhood would flourish around it, city fathers in 1868 set aside 1400 acres of rattlesnake-infested hillside above "New Town" as a public park. The park's eventual development, and most of its lovely Spanish Baroque buildings, came as the result of two world's fairs—The Panama–California Exposition of 1915–16 and the California–Pacific International Exposition of 1935–36.

Today Balboa Park ranks among the largest and finest of America's city parks. Wide avenues and walkways curve through luxurious subtropical foliage leading to nine major museums, three art galleries, four theaters, picnic groves, the world's largest zoo, a golf course, and countless other recreation facilities. Its verdant grounds teem with cyclists, joggers, skaters, picnickers, weekend artists, and museum mavens.

SIGHTS
The main entrance is from 6th Avenue onto Laurel Street, which becomes El Prado as you cross Cabrillo Bridge. Begin your visit at the **Balboa Park Visitors Center,** located on the northeast corner of Plaza

de Panama. They provide plenty of free pamphlets and maps on the park. Balboa Park's museums charge an admission fee but every Tuesday select museums can be visited free. ~ 619-239-0512.

From here you can stroll about, taking in Balboa Park's main attractions. To the right, as you head east on the pedestrian-only section of El Prado, is the newly rebuilt Casa de Balboa. It houses the **San Diego Model Railroad Museum** (619-696-0199), which features the largest collection of mini-gauge trains in the world. Closed Monday. Here, too, is the San Diego Historical Society's extensive collection of documents and photographs spanning the urban history of San Diego. Closed Monday and Tuesday. Upstairs, the **Museum of Photographic Arts** (619-239-5262) has exhibits of internationally known photographers. Sports fans will want to take in the **Hall of Champions Sports Museum** (619-234-2544) in Casa de Balboa. It houses a Hall of Fame and exhibits featuring world-class San Diego athletes from more than 40 sports. Admission. ~ 1649 El Prado.

Continuing east to the fountain, you'll see the **Reuben H. Fleet Space Theater and Science Center** on your right. Among the park's finest attractions, it features one of the largest planetariums and most impressive multimedia theaters in the country. The hands-on Science Center features various exhibits and displays dealing with modern phenomena. Admission. ~ 619-238-1233.

Across the courtyard is the **Natural History Museum** with displays devoted mostly to the environment of Southern California. Admission. ~ 619-232-3821.

Going back along El Prado, take a moment to admire your reflection in the Lily Pond. With the old, latticed **Botanical Building** in the background, the scene is a favorite among photographers. The fern collection inside is equally striking.

Next is the **Timken Museum of Art**, considered to have one of the West Coast's finest collections of European and Early American paintings. The displays include works by Rembrandt and Copley, as well as an amazing collection of Russian icons. ~ 619-239-5548.

Right next door on the plaza is the **San Diego Museum of Art**, with an entrance facade patterned after the University of Salamanca in Spain. The museum treasures a permanent collection of Italian Renaissance, Dutch, and Spanish Baroque paintings and sculpture, a display of Asian art, a gallery of Impressionist paintings, contemporary California art, and a contemporary American collection. Admission. ~ 619-232-7931.

The grandest of all Balboa Park structures, built as the centerpiece for the 1915 Panama–California Exposition, is the 200-foot Spanish Renaissance **California Tower**. The **Museum of Man**, at the base of the tower, is a must for anthropology buffs and those interested in American Indian cultures. Admission. ~ 619-239-2001.

Another museum not to be missed is the **San Diego Aerospace Museum**, several blocks south of the plaza. It contains over 65 aircraft including a replica of Charles Lindbergh's famous *Spirit of St. Louis*, the original of which was built in San Diego. Admission. ~ 619-234-8291.

En route you'll pass the **Spreckels Organ Pavilion**. Those 4416 pipes make it the world's largest outdoor instrument of its kind.

You'll want to attend a play at the **Old Globe Theatre** to absorb the full greatness of this Tony Award-winning stage, but for starters you can stroll around the 581-seat theater, famed for its Shakespearean presentations. Located in a grove on the north side of California Tower, the Old Globe is part of the trio of theaters that includes the **Cassius Carter Centre Stage** and the outdoor **Lowell Davies Festival Theatre**. Admission. ~ 619-239-2255.

On display at the Aerospace Museum is Black Bird, the world's fastest plane.

North of the Balboa Park museum and theater complex is **San Diego Zoo**, which needs no introduction. It quite simply is the world's top-rated zoo. The numbers alone are mind-boggling: 3900 animals, representing 800 species, spread out over 100 acres. Most of these wild animals live in surroundings as natural as man can make them. Rather than cages there are many moated enclosures where lions roam free on grassy islands and multihued birds fly through tropical rainforests. All around is a manmade jungle forest overgrown with countless species of rare and exotic plants.

Of particular merit is "Polar Bear Plunge." Here you can watch the polar bears as they gracefully swim underwater in their deep saltwater bay. At "Hippo Beach," Funani and Jabba delight all with their infamous underwater hippo ballet. The zoo's state-of-the-art primate exhibit, the "Gorilla Tropics," is a two-and-a-half acre African rainforest that is home to six lowland gorillas and hundreds of jungle birds. Within this area is "Pygmy Chimps at Bonobo Road," home to frolicsome troupes of pygmy chimps and Angolan colobus monkeys. At the nearby "Sun Bear Forest," an equatorial rainforest, you'll encounter sun bears and lion-tailed macaques. For a bird's-eye view of the entire zoo, you can take the "Skyfari" aerial tramway. At the **Children's Zoo**, where there are just as many adults as kids, you can watch baby chicks peck out of their shells in the hatchery. Don't miss the pygmy marmosets. They are the world's smallest monkeys, weighing in at only four ounces when full grown. Admission. ~ 619-234-3153.

LODGING   The best value for your dollar among reasonably priced hotels in the area is the 67-room **Comfort Inn**. They feature wood furniture, designer color schemes, and high-grade carpeting. The inn has a pool-sized jacuzzi and serves a continental breakfast. Conveniently located next to Balboa Park just a few blocks from the city center. ~ 719 Ash Street; 619-232-2525, 800-221-2222, fax 619-687-3024. MODERATE.

My vote for the prettiest and most hospitable of San Diego's bed and breakfasts goes to the **Keating House Inn**. This historically designated 1888 Victorian home in a sunny hillside residential neighborhood between Balboa Park and downtown offers eight comfy-cozy rooms in the moderate category. With its gabled roof, octagonal window turret, and conical peak, this beautifully restored Queen Anne is every bit as nice inside, where quality period furnishings and accessories round out the decor. A nice garden completes the homey scene. ~ 2331 2nd Avenue; 619-239-8585, 800-995-8644, fax 619-239-5774. MODERATE.

Situated on the stunning Florida Canyon on the edge of Balboa Park, **Katy's Herbs & Things** is a true bed and breakfast. There are two one-bedroom suites featuring a kitchenette and private patio overlooking the herb garden. Every morning, the owner will treat you to a lovely continental breakfast consisting of homemade breads and jams, locally grown fruit, and fine coffee or tea. The proprietress is also an enthusiastic storyteller, drawing in her listeners as she weaves mythic tales on the history of herbs. For a delightful sojourn, this place comes highly praised. ~ 2818 Juniper Street; 619-544-0375, 800-544-0568, fax 619-696-6877. BUDGET TO MODERATE.

DINING

When you're visiting the San Diego Zoo, consider **Albert's Restaurant**. Named for the gorilla who once occupied the area, this sit-down eatery offers a variety of salads, sandwiches, fresh pastas, and fish and meat entrées. ~ 2920 Zoo Drive, The San Diego Zoo; 619-685-3200. MODERATE.

NIGHTLIFE

The **Simon Edison Theatre Centre for the Performing Arts** presents classic and contemporary plays in three Balboa Park theatres. ~ Balboa Park; 619-239-2255.

▼▼▼▼▼▼▼▼▼▼
Coronado

An isolated and exclusive community in San Diego Bay, Coronado is almost an island, connected to the mainland only by the graceful San Diego–Coronado Bay Bridge and by a long, narrow sandspit called the Silver Strand. Long a playground of the rich and famous, the city's hotels reflect this ritzy heritage.

SIGHTS

Once known as the "Nickel Snatcher," the Coronado Ferry for years crossed the waters of San Diego Harbor between the Embarcadero and Coronado. All for five cents each way. That's history, of course, but the 1940-vintage, double-deck *Silvergate* still plies the waters. The **San Diego Bay Ferry** leaves from the Bay Café on North Harbor Drive at the foot of Broadway on the hour and docks 15 minutes later at the Old Ferry landing on the Coronado side. ~ 619-234-4111.

The town's main attraction is the **Hotel del Coronado**, a red-roofed, Victorian-style, wooden wonder, a century-old National Historic Landmark. Explore the old palace and its manicured grounds, discovering the intricate corridors and cavernous public rooms. It was Elisha Babcock's dream, when he purchased 4100 acres of barren, wind-blown peninsula in 1888, to build a hotel that would be the "talk of the Western world." Realizing Babcock's dream from the beginning, it attracted such famous guests as Thomas Edison, Robert Todd Lincoln, and Henry Ford. ~ 1500 Orange Avenue; 619-435-6611.

> At least a dozen United States presidents have bedded down at the "Hotel Del."

Although shadowed by its noted neighbor, the **Glorietta Bay Inn** is a worthy landmark in its own right. It was built in 1908 as the private mansion of sugar scion John D. Spreckels. From here you can cruise the quiet neighborhood streets that radiate off Orange Avenue between the bay and the ocean, enjoying the town's handsome blend of cottages and historic homes. ~ 1630 Glorietta Boulevard; 619-435-3101.

LODGING

El Cordova Hotel is in the heart of Coronado. Originally built as a private mansion in 1902, El Cordova's moderate size (40 rooms) and lovely Spanish-hacienda architecture make it a relaxing getaway spot. A pool and patio restaurant are added niceties. ~ 1351 Orange Avenue; 619-435-4131, 800-229-2032, fax 619-435-0632. DELUXE TO ULTRA-DELUXE.

Nothing can detract from the glamour of the **Hotel del Coronado**. With its turrets, cupolas, and gingerbread facade, it is one of the great hotels of California. The last in a proud line of extravagant seaside resorts, the Hotel del Coronado has long been the resting place of United States presidents and Hollywood stars. Remember, however, this celebrated 108-year-old Victorian landmark is a major tourist attraction, so in addition to guests, who usually fill its 692 rooms to capacity, thousands of visitors crowd the lobby, grounds, and shops every day. Be aware, too, that many rooms are in a high-rise wing adjacent to the original building and though more comfortable are not the real thing. "Hotel Del" has two pools, a long stretch of beach, five tennis courts, a first-class health club, and a gallery of shops. ~ 1500 Orange Avenue; 619-522-8000, 800-468-3533, fax 619-522-8238. ULTRA-DELUXE.

Across the street rises the **Glorietta Bay Inn**, the 1908 Edwardian mansion of sugar king John D. Spreckels which has been transformed into an elegant 98-room hotel. Suites here reflect the grandeur of Spreckels' time, but ordinary rooms are, in fact, rather ordinary. Continental breakfast, ladies and gentlemen, is served on the mansion terrace. ~ 1630 Glorietta Boulevard; 619-435-3101, 800-283-9383, fax 619-435-6182. DELUXE TO ULTRA-DELUXE.

The **Coronado Victorian House** is quite possibly the only hotel anywhere to include dance, exercise, and gourmet cooking classes in a night's stay. Located in a historic building near the beach and down-

town Coronado, the decor of this eight-room bed and breakfast includes oriental rugs, stained-glass windows, claw-foot tubs, and jacuzzis. Those guests not interested in the extracurricular activities are
invited to relax and enjoy such home-cooked specialties as baklava,
stuffed grape leaves, homemade yogurt, and potato casserole. ~ 1000
8th Street; 619-435-2200, fax 619-435-4760. ULTRA-DELUXE.

DINING

Visitors crossing over to Coronado invariably tour the famous Hotel
del Coronado, and many are lured into the **Crown-Coronet Room.**
Its grand Victorian architecture and enormous domed ceiling set a
tone of elegance and style unmatched anywhere on the Pacific Coast.
The place is so magnificent the food seems unimportant. Most critics, in fact, assert that dinner in the hotel's **Prince of Wales Room** is
better, but breakfast, lunch, dinner, or Sunday brunch at the Crown
Room will never disappoint. ~ 1500 Orange Avenue; 619-435-6611.
DELUXE TO ULTRA-DELUXE.

Locals looking to avoid the crowds at "Hotel Del" usually head
for **Chez Loma.** Located in a charming 1889 Victorian house, it
serves a lovely French dinner—excellent *canard roti façon Chez Loma* (traditional roast duckling with Montorency cherry port wine
sauce and lingon berries)—plus Sunday brunch. Dine inside or out.
A cozy *salon du vin* upstairs features appetizers, light meals, desserts,
beer, and wine. ~ 1132 Loma Avenue; 619-435-0661. DELUXE.

Peohe's, located at the Old Ferry Landing, is primarily praised for
its panoramic views of San Diego Bay and for its tropical decor. The
aqua-accented dining room features green palms and rushing cascades of water flowing into ponds of live fish. The dinner menu is
mostly fresh fish plus lobster, shrimp, and a daily featured "catch."
There is also prime rib and lamb. I prefer the lunch, with a tasty
soup/salad/sandwich combo at an affordable price. Sunday brunch.
~ 1201 1st Street; 619-437-4474. MODERATE TO DELUXE.

SHOPPING

Coronado's fancy Orange Avenue in the village center harbors six
blocks of unusual shops and a mini-mall in the **El Cordova Hotel.** ~
1351 Orange Avenue; 619-435-4131.

The **Ferry Landing Marketplace** is a modern shopping area complete with boutiques, specialty shops, galleries, and eateries. ~ 1201
1st Street; 619-435-8895.

The **Hotel del Coronado** is a city within a city and home to many
intriguing specialty shops, such as **Ribbons and Roses,** which has an
interesting selection of pins, hats, and other Victorian accessories. ~
1500 Orange Avenue; 619-435-9270.

NIGHTLIFE

If you're out Coronado way, stop for a cocktail in the famed Hotel
del Coronado's **Ocean Terrace Lounge.** The Del's **Palm Court** offers
live piano music in a palm-studded lounge. ~ 1550 Orange Avenue;
619-435-6611.

Check out the boisterous Irish scene at **McP's,** a full swinging bar and grill with shamrock-plastered walls and a bartender with the gift of gab. Entertainment includes live rock and jazz bands on a nightly basis. ~ 1107 Orange Avenue; 619-435-5280.

THEATER The historic Spreckels Building in Coronado is a vintage-1917 opera house (more lately a rundown warehouse) that is being restored to a 340-seat venue, the **Lamb's Players Theatre.** ~ 1317 Ynez Avenue; 619-437-0600.

BEACHES & PARKS

CORONADO SHORES BEACH 🏖 🏊 ⛵ It's the widest beach in the county but hardly atmospheric, backed up as it is by a row of towering condominiums. Still, crowds flock to this roomy expanse of clean, soft sand where gentle waves make for good swimming and surfing. The younger crowd gathers at the north end, just past the Hotel del Coronado. Restaurants and groceries are nearby. ~ Located off Ocean Boulevard in Coronado.

CORONADO CITY BEACH 🏖 🏊 ⛵ That same wide sandy beach prevails to the north. Here the city has a large, grassy picnic area known as **Sunset Park** where frisbees and the aroma of fried chicken fill the air. Facilities include restrooms and lifeguards; restaurants and groceries nearby. The beach offers good fishing and swimming. Surfing is generally safe, but be wary of unpredictable breaks. ~ On Ocean Boulevard north of Avenue G in Coronado.

▼▼▼▼▼▼▼▼▼▼▼▼
Point Loma Area

The Point Loma peninsula forms a high promontory that shelters San Diego Bay from the Pacific. It also provided Juan Rodríguez Cabrillo an excellent place from which to contemplate his 16th-century discovery of California. For those of us today interested in contemplating life—or just zoning out on a view—Point Loma peninsula presents the perfect opportunity.

SIGHTS

Naturally, **Cabrillo National Monument,** featuring a statue of the navigator, stands facing his landing site at Ballast Point. The sculpture itself, a gift from Cabrillo's native Portugal, isn't very impressive but the view is outstanding. With the bay and city spread below, you can often see all the way from Mexico to the La Jolla mesa. The visitors center includes a small museum. The nearby **Old Point Loma Lighthouse** guided shipping from 1855 to 1891. Admission. ~ 1800 Cabrillo Memorial Drive; 619-557-5450.

On the ocean side of the peninsula is **Whale Watch Lookout Point** where, during winter months, you can observe the southward migration of California gray whales. Close by is a superb network of tidepools.

To reach Point Loma from San Diego, go southwest on Rosecrans Street and follow the signs. You'll enter the monument through the U.S. Navy's Fort Rosecrans, home to a variety of sophisticated military facilities and the haunting **Fort Rosecrans National Cemetery**. Here, thousands of trim, white markers march down a grassy hillside in mute testimony to San Diego's fallen troops and deep military roots.

When you leave the monument, follow Catalina Boulevard to Hill Street and go left. At water's edge turn right onto Sunset Cliffs Boulevard and enjoy one of San Diego County's most dramatic coastlines. Continue north a bit to **Ocean Beach**, whose reputation as a haven for hippie hold-outs is not entirely undeserved.

LODGING

Ensconced in a plain vanilla, two-story former church building, the **Elliot International Hostel** is filled with 60 economy-minded guests almost every night during the summer. Comfortable bunk beds are grouped in 13 rooms housing from two to eight persons in youth-hostel fashion. Family rooms are also available, and there is a common kitchen and dining area. ~ 3790 Udall Street; 619-223-4778, fax 619-223-5217. BUDGET.

A rare beachfront find in residential Point Loma is the **Ocean Manor Hotel**. This trim, white, two-story, 25-room apartment hotel sits right on the seaside cliffs. Rooms are neat and clean but very basic. There are also bachelor and studio apartments (with kitchenettes) available for rent. ~ 1370 Sunset Cliffs Boulevard; 619-222-7901. BUDGET TO MODERATE.

Manmade Shelter and Harbor Islands jut out into San Diego Bay, providing space for several large resorts. For a relaxing, offbeat alternative to these mammoth hotels try **Humphrey's Half Moon Inn**. Surrounded by subtropical plants, this nautical 182-room complex overlooks the yacht harbor and gives the feeling of staying on an island. The rooms are tastefully decorated with a Polynesian theme. There is a pool, spa, putting green, and restaurant. ~ 2303 Shelter Island Drive; 619-224-3411, 800-345-9995, fax 619-224-3478. DELUXE TO ULTRA-DELUXE.

DINING

A marine view and whirling ceiling fans at **Humphrey's** suggest Casablanca. Italian fish specialties and Eastern-style "shore dinners" are popular. ~ Adjacent to the Half Moon Inn, 2241 Shelter Island Drive; 619-224-3577. DELUXE TO ULTRA-DELUXE.

At Fisherman's Village in Point Loma you'll find **The Blue Crab Restaurant**. Appealing Cape Cod decor and terrific bay views set the mood for fresh seafood, including Maryland blue and soft-shell crabs. There's great mesquite-broiled swordfish. Prime rib and steak satisfy the landlubbers. ~ 4922 North Harbor Drive; 619-224-3000. DELUXE.

◀ HIDDEN

San Diego's best soup-and-salad bar and my personal favorite for healthy budget dining is **Souplantation**, featuring two bars loaded with the prettiest produce this side of the farmer's market. Included are over 60 items to heap on your plate. Six tasty soups are made from scratch daily, and a variety of muffins are served hot from the oven. Fresh fruit rounds out this wholesome fare. It's a comfortable wood-paneled environment. ~ 3960 West Point Loma Boulevard; 619-222-7404. BUDGET.

NIGHTLIFE   For the mellow crowd interested in enjoying cocktails, yummy appetizers, and conversation while overlooking a picturesque marina, there's **Hurricanes**. ~ 2051 Shelter Island Drive; 619-223-2572.

Even musicians head outdoors during San Diego summers. **Humphrey's** hosts the city's most ambitious series of jazz and mellow rock shows, which include an impressive lineup of name artists in a beautiful bayside lawn setting. ~ 2241 Shelter Island Drive; 619-224-3577.

Aside from being a popular restaurant and lounge, **Tom Ham's Lighthouse** is a real lighthouse and the official Coast Guard–sanctioned beacon of Harbor Island. This scrimshaw-filled nautical lounge is a piano bar Wednesday through Friday, then a karaoke bar, later in the evening, Thursday through Saturday. ~ 2150 Harbor Island Drive; 619-291-9110.

BEACHES & PARKS   **HARBOR ISLAND** There are no sandy beaches on this manmade island, but there is a walkway bordered by lawn and benches along its entire length. You'll get fabulous views of the city, and there's great fishing here. Facilities here include restrooms and restaurants. ~ Located south of San Diego International Airport on Harbor Island Drive.

SHELTER ISLAND Like Harbor Island, its neighbor to the northeast, Shelter Island functions primarily as a boating center, but there's a beach facing the bay that is popular for swimming, fishing, and picnicking. A landscaped walkway runs the length of the island. There are picnic areas, restrooms, a fishing pier, and restaurants. ~ Located on Shelter Island Drive near Rosecrans Street.

SUNSET CLIFFS PARK The jagged cliffs and sandstone bluffs along Point Loma peninsula give this park a spectacular setting. High-cresting waves make it popular with expert surfers, who favor the rocky beach at the foot of Ladera Avenue. Tidepools evidence the rich marine life that attracts many divers. Winding staircases (at Bermuda and Santa Cruz avenues) and steep trails lead down to some nice pocket beaches. Restaurants and groceries are located nearby. ~ Off of Sunset Cliffs Boulevard south of Ocean Beach; 619-531-1527.

OCEAN BEACH Where you toss down your towel at "OB" will probably depend as much on your age as your interests. Surfers, sailors, and what's left of the hippie crowd hang out around the pier; farther north, where the surf is milder and the beach wider, families and retired folks can be found sunbathing and strolling. There are picnic areas, restrooms, and restaurants. Fishing is good from the surf or the fishing pier. Swimming and surfing is very popular here. ~ Take Ocean Beach Freeway (Route 8) west until it ends; turn left onto Sunset Cliffs Boulevard, then right on Voltaire Street; 619-531-1527.

Old Town and Mission Valley

Back in 1769, Spanish explorer Gaspar de Portolá selected a hilltop site overlooking the bay for a mission that would begin the European settlement of California. A town soon spread out at the foot of the hill, complete with plaza, church, school, and the tile-roofed adobe casas of California's first families. Through the years, Spanish, Mexican, and American settlements thrived until an 1872 fire destroyed much of the town, prompting developers to relocate the commercial district nearer the bay.

SIGHTS

Some of the buildings and relics of the early era survived, however, and have been brought back to life at **Old Town San Diego State Historic Park**. Lined with adobe restorations and brightened with colorful shops, the six blocks of Old Town provide a lively and interesting opportunity for visitors to stroll, shop, and sightsee. ~ Park headquarters, 4002 Wallace Street; 619-220-5423.

The park sponsors a free walking tour at 2 p.m. daily, or you can easily do it on your own by picking up a copy of the *Old San Diego Gazette*. The paper, which comes out once a month and includes a map of the area, is free at local stores. You can also hop aboard the **Old Town Trolley** for a delightful two-hour narrated tour of Old Town and a variety of other highlights in San Diego and Coronado. Admission. ~ 4040 Twiggs Street, 619-298-8687.

As it has for over a century, everything focuses on **Old Town Plaza** (sometimes called Washington Square). Before 1872 this was the social and recreational center of the town: political meetings, barbecues, dances, shootouts, and bullfights all happened here.

Casa de Estudillo is the finest of the original adobe buildings. It was a mansion in its time, built in 1827 for the commander of the Mexican Presidio. Admission. ~ Located at the Mason Street corner of the plaza.

Casa de Bandini was built in 1829 as a one-story adobe but gained a second level when it became the Cosmopolitan Hotel in the

OLD TOWN VICTORIANA

On the outskirts of Old Town lies **Heritage Park**, an area dedicated to the preservation of the city's Victorian past. Seven historic 1880-era houses and an old Jewish temple have been moved to the hillside site and beautifully restored. ~ At Juan and Harney streets.

late 1860s. ~ At Mason and Calhoun streets. **Seeley Stables** next door is a replica of the barns and stables of Albert Seeley, who operated the stage line. Nowadays it houses a collection of horse-drawn vehicles and Western memorabilia. Admission.

Casa de Altamirano was Old Town's first frame building and the site where the *San Diego Union* was first printed in 1868. It has been restored as a 19th-century printing office. ~ Located at San Diego Avenue and Twiggs Street. Adjacent to the old newspaper office is **Dodson's Corner**, a collection of shops finished with Old West–style falsefronts.

Shoppers seem to gravitate in large numbers toward the north side of the plaza to browse the unusual shops comprising **Bazaar del Mundo**. Built in circular fashion around a tropical courtyard, this complex also houses several restaurants.

The original mission and Spanish Presidio once stood high on a hill behind Old Town. This site of California's birthplace now houses **Junipero Serra Museum**, a handsome Spanish Colonial structure containing an excellent collection of American Indian and Spanish artifacts from the state's pioneer days and relics from the Royal Presidio dig sites. Admission. ~ Presidio Drive; 619-297-3258.

Within five years after Father Serra dedicated the first of California's 21 missions, the site had become much too small for the growing numbers it served. So **Mission San Diego de Alcala** was moved from Presidio Hill six miles east into Mission Valley. Surrounded now by shopping centers and suburban homes, the "Mother of Missions" retains its simple but striking white adobe facade topped by a graceful campanile. There's a museum containing mission records in Junípero Serra's handwriting and a lovely courtyard with gnarled pepper trees. ~ 10818 San Diego Mission Road; 619-281-8449.

LODGING   Best bet in the lower price categories is the appropriately named **Old Town Inn**. Strolling distance from Old Town, this spiffy little 84-room family-owned motel has small rooms but adds amenities like full kitchens in some units and a guest laundry. ~ 4444 Pacific Highway; 619-260-8024. BUDGET TO MODERATE.

For the romantic, **Heritage Park Bed & Breakfast Inn**, a storybook 1889 Queen Anne mansion with a striking turret, is an enchanting bed and breakfast. Set on a grassy hillside, it provides a tranquil escape. Choose from nine distinctive chambers (all with private baths), each furnished with museum-quality antiques. Most feature ornate brass or four-poster canopy beds and old-fashioned quilts. ~ 2470 Heritage Park Row; 619-295-7088, 800-995-2470, fax 619-299-9465. DELUXE TO ULTRA-DELUXE.

DINING   Mexican food and atmosphere abound in Old Town, especially in the popular Bazaar del Mundo. Here two restaurants lure a steady stream of diners into festive, flowered courtyards. **Casa de Pico** is my favorite place to sit and munch cheese nachos and sip margaritas. Mexican entrées are served outside or in one of the hacienda-style dining rooms. ~ 2754 Calhoun Street; 619-296-3267. BUDGET.

Next door, in a magnificent 1829 hacienda, **Casa de Bandini,** you will find the cuisine a bit more refined. Seafood is good here, especially the crab enchiladas. Mariachis often play at both restaurants. ~ 619-297-8211. BUDGET TO MODERATE.

Two Old Town charmers provide satisfying diversions from a Mexican diet. **Berta's** is new to the area and specializes in Latin American cuisine. *Vatapa* (coconut sauce over mahimahi, scallops, and shrimp) and *bandeja pixa* (a plate of pinto beans, rice, salsa, avocado, onions, and green salad with tomatoes) are wonderfully prepared. ~ 3928 Twigg Street; 619-295-2343. MODERATE.

Café Pacífica rates equally high marks for a creative menu of fresh fish specialties including Hawaiian ahi tuna with shiitake mushrooms in a ginger butter sauce. Stylish but comfortable environs include a patio under a removable roof and a friendly bar. No lunch Monday. ~ 2414 San Diego Avenue; 619-291-6666. MODERATE TO DELUXE.

Less than a mile from Old Town lies a pair of excellent ethnic take-out shops that few visitors ever find. **El Indio** opened in 1940   ◄ HIDDEN
as a family-operated *tortillería*, then added an informal restaurant serving quesadillas, enchiladas, tostadas, burritos, tacos, and taquitos (or "little tacos"). Quality homemade Mexican food at Taco Bell prices; you can sit indoors, out on the patio, or order to go. ~ 3695 India Street; 619-299-0333. BUDGET.

Another one-of-a-kind fast-food operation with an equally fervent following, **Saffron Chicken** turns out zesty Thai-grilled chicken on a special rotisserie. The aroma is positively exquisite and so is the chicken served with jasmine rice, Cambodian salad, and the five tangy sauces. Eat on an adjacent patio or take a picnic to the beach. ~ 3731-B India Street; 619-574-0177. BUDGET.

Historic Old Town is blessed with several exciting bazaars and shopping squares. By far the grandest is the **Bazaar del Mundo,** Old Town's version of the famous marketplaces of Spain and Mexico. Adobe casitas house a variety of international shops. ~ Calhoun Street between Twigg and Juan streets; 619-296-3161. Here **Fabrics and Finery** unfurls cloth, beads, and craft accessories from around the world, and **Ariana** features wearable art. ~ 619-296-4989.

SHOPPING

Walk down San Diego Avenue and take a gander at **Dodson's Corner.** The cactus-lined courtyard and bougainvillea-laced cottages lend an authentic feel of yesteryear to the souvenir shops. ~ 2611 San Diego Avenue; 619-220-5423.

A haven for art lovers is **Spanish Village Center.** Over 35 studios are staffed by artists displaying their work. For sale are original paintings, sculpture, photographs, ceramics, jewelry, and gems. ~ 1770 Village Place, near the San Diego Zoo entrance; 619-233-9050.

NIGHTLIFE   The prevailing culture in Old Town is Mexican, as in mariachis and margaritas. The **Old Town Mexican Café y Cantina**, a festive, friendly establishment, has a patio bar. ~ 2489 San Diego Avenue; 619-297-4330.

O'Hungry's, a nearby restaurant, features an acoustic guitarist nightly. ~ 2547 San Diego Avenue; 619-298-0133.

For country-and-western, try **In Cahoots**, featuring live bands on Sunday. Cover. ~ 5373 Mission Center Road; 619-291-8635.

▼▼▼▼▼▼▼▼▼▼▼▼▼▼▼▼▼▼▼
South San Diego County

Linking downtown with the Mexican border city of Tijuana, 20 miles south, a string of seaside cities straddle Route 5. While thriving as manufacturing, commercial, and residential communities, Imperial Beach, Chula Vista, and National City are beginning to develop as tourist industries.

SIGHTS   Along this southern stretch, **Border Field State Park** features a two-mile-long stretch of sandy beach. ~ 619-575-3613. The adjoining **Tijuana Slough National Wildlife Refuge** comprises the county's largest and most pristine estuarine sanctuary. For nature lovers, this haven of salt marsh and sand dunes is a must-see diversion. Trails lead to the beach and wildlife refuge at this fascinating wetland (see the "Beaches & Parks" and "Hiking" sections for more information).

LODGING   Among all those identical motels grouped around the freeway exits in Chula Vista, **The Traveler Motel** is your best bet. Conveniently located just a block from the highway, this family-owned 85-unit motel is early Holiday Inn throughout, but its rates hark back to 1960s. Not that you would really expect them, but extras include two pools, laundry facilities, and color cable TV. ~ 235 Woodlawn Avenue, Chula Vista; 619-427-9170, fax 619-427-5247. BUDGET.

The **Seacoast Inn** is the only hostelry located directly on the sands of Imperial Beach. Recently remodeled and decked out with a heated outdoor pool and hot tub, this 38-room complex looks good inside and out. Beachside units are especially nice and have full kitchens. Summer reservations should be made a year in advance. ~ 800 Seacoast Drive, South Imperial Beach; 619-424-5183, 800-732-2627, fax 619-424-3090. DELUXE.

DINING   **La Bella Pizza Garden** is like an annex to Chula Vista's town hall, and owner Kitty Raso is known as the "Mayor of Third Avenue." But the food will interest you far more than the latest political gossip. Besides pizza, there's great lasagna, rigatoni, and ravioli. La Bella features tender veal dishes, too, from a menu that amazingly rarely strays beyond budget prices. Best Italian food for the money in San Diego. ~ 373 3rd Avenue, Chula Vista; 619-426-8820. BUDGET.

Another good bet for low-cost dining with an international twist lies just up the *strasse* at **House of Munich**. Here the traditional German dishes include wienerschnitzel, potato pancakes, sauerbraten, potato dill soup, and bratwurst. For dessert, try the traditional apple strudel! With its lace tablecloths and European feel, this eatery is wonderfully authentic. Closed Monday. ~ 230 3rd Avenue, Chula Vista; 619-426-5172. MODERATE.

Plaza Bonita in National City is a modern mall with four department stores and a range of smaller outlets. ~ 3030 Plaza Bonita Road; 619-267-2851.

SHOPPING

Chula Vista's newly renovated downtown is highlighted by **Park Plaza in the Village Shopping Plaza**. Here 20 stores, including fashion and specialty shops, cluster around a central court. In addition, the shopping district on 3rd Avenue between E and H streets is a charming mix of long-standing family businesses and quality shops. ~ 310 3rd Avenue, Chula Vista; 619-282-6814.

If you're looking for nighttime entertainment in these areas, you'll probably want to consider a trip to the city. Otherwise be content with scattered restaurant bars and local pubs. There's a notable exception: **J. J.'s** and **Marisol's Million Dollar Club**. Actually two clubs under one roof, the music offered here spans the spectrum from salsa and Top-40 to hip hop and techno. Cover. ~ 1862 Palm Avenue, Imperial Beach; 619-429-1161.

NIGHTLIFE

SILVER STRAND STATE BEACH 🏊🚣 This two-mile strip of fluffy white sand fronts a narrow isthmus separating the Pacific Ocean and San Diego Bay. It was named for tiny silver sea shells found in abundance along the shore. The water here is shallow and fairly calm on the ocean side, making it a good swimming beach. Things are even calmer and the water much warmer on the bay shore. Silver Strand State Beach is also popular for surf fishing and shell hunting. Facilities include picnic areas, restrooms, lifeguards, showers, and equipment rentals; restaurants and groceries are several miles away in Imperial Beach. Day-use fee, $4. ~ Located on Route 75 (Silver Strand Boulevard) and Coronado Caves Boulevard between Imperial Beach and Coronado; 619-435-5184.

BEACHES & PARKS

▲ There are 122 sites for RVs and trailers (no hookups); $14 to $16 per night.

IMPERIAL BEACH 🏊🎣🏄 A wide, sandy beach, popular at the south end with surfers; boogie-boarders and swimmers ply the waters between the two jetties farther north, just past the renovated fishing pier. The crowd is mostly young with many military personnel. Each July Imperial Beach hosts the annual U.S. Open Sandcastle Competition, attracting huge crowds. There are restrooms and lifeguards. There is also a deli nearby. Surfing is very popular on both sides of the pier and rock jetties. ~ Take Palm Avenue exit west off Route 5 all the way to the water.

BORDER FIELD STATE PARK 🚶🐎 True to its name, this ocean-front park actually borders on Mexico. It features a two-mile-long stretch of sandy beach, backed by dunes and salt marshes studded with daisies and chaparral. Equestrian and hiking trails crisscross this unsullied wetlands area which adjoins a federal wildlife refuge at the mouth of the Tijuana River. Sounds idyllic except for the constant racket from Border Patrol helicopters and the ever-present threat of untreated sewage drifting north from Mexico. There are restrooms available. Restaurants and groceries are miles away in San Ysidro or Imperial Beach. Fishing and swimming are not recommended because of pollution. Open Thursday through Sunday only. ~ Take the Dairy Mart Road exit off Route 5 and go west. The name changes to Monument Road about a mile before reaching the park entrance; 619-575-3613.

▼▼▼▼▼▼▼▼▼▼▼▼▼▼▼▼▼
Inland San Diego County

Touring Inland San Diego County's rugged backcountry means wandering through a landscape filled with rambling hills, flowering meadows, and rocky peaks. There are old missions and gold mines en route, as well as farms and ranches. More than anything else, exploring this region consists of driving over miles of silent country road.

SIGHTS

Beginning in the county's northwest corner, Route 76 will carry you to **Mission San Luis Rey**. Known as the "King of the Missions," this beautifully restored complex was originally constructed in 1789 and represents the largest California mission. Today you can visit the museum chapel and cemetery while walking these historic grounds. ~ San Luis Rey; 619-757-3651.

Guajome Park, a 569-acre playground, offers a variety of natural, historical, and recreational opportunities. The park is centered around Guajome Adobe, considered one of the region's best examples of early Spanish architecture. Just steps away is a 25-acre fishing lake. Hiking trails thread the property, and there are picnic areas and a playground. ~ On Guajome Lake Road about seven miles east of Route 5, Oceanside; 619-565-3600.

Farther inland lies **Mission San Antonio de Pala**. An *asistencia*, or branch of the larger mission, it has been conducting mass since it was built in 1816. The original chapel and bell tower have been faithfully restored, and the long, low walls of the church interior are still decorated with primitive Indian frescoes. Located on the Pala Indian Reservation, it is the only mission primarily serving Indians. ~ Pala Mission Road, Pala; 619-742-3317.

Rockhounds will be interested in **Gems of Pala**, which has exhibits and retail displays of some of the world's finest tourmaline. These pink gems are extracted from the nearby Stewart Mine. ~ Route 76 and Magee Road, Pala; 619-742-1356.

There's no finer wildlife sanctuary in the country than the San Diego Zoo's remarkable **Wild Animal Park**. This 2150-acre spread, skillfully landscaped to resemble Asian and African habitats, houses over 3000 animals. Among them are several endangered species not found in zoos elsewhere. Many of the animals roam free while you view them from monorails and elevated walkways. After visiting the fearsome lions and gorillas, you can follow that line of children to the "Petting Kraal," where the kids can fluff up a lamb or tug on a friendly billy goat. Admission. ~ 15500 San Pasqual Valley Road, Escondido; 619-234-6541.

Two miles east of the animal park is **San Pasqual Battlefield State Historic Park**, where an interpretive center tells the story of a strange and little-known battle. It seems that during the Mexican War in 1846 about 100 U.S. Dragoons, including the famous scout Kit Carson, suffered an embarrassing defeat at the hands of the California Mexicans. Today a small monument here marks the battle site. ~ 15808 San Pasqual Valley Road, Escondido; 619-220-5430.

On a more modern note, **Lawrence Welk Resort**, an elaborate resort complex, contains a museum featuring the famous "one-ana-two" entertainer's memorabilia. High camp at its most bizarre. ~ 8860 Lawrence Welk Drive, Escondido; 619-749-3000.

One of the fastest growing places in California, Escondido is also home to one-tenth of the state's 70,000 acres of avocados. Planted in neat rows, they climb the hillsides north and east of town.

Progress continues to intrude upon this once-rustic region, but you can still chat with the folks at **Ferrara Winery** and stroll around the vineyards. A small family enterprise, the winery has been producing vintages for three generations. ~ 1120 West 15th Avenue, Escondido; 619-745-7632.

Another Escondido vintner is **Bernardo Winery**, the oldest operating winery in the county. ~ 13330 Paseo del Verano Norte, Escondido; 619-487-1866. The **Deer Park Winery** offers tastings of wines from its Napa and Escondido vineyards and displays a fine collection of vintage automobiles. ~ 29013 Champagne Boulevard, Escondido; 619-749-1666.

From Escondido, you can drive northeast along scenic Route S6 to Pauma Valley, and then pick up Route 76, which will carry you from a verdant region of citrus groves up into the pine-rimmed high country of Cleveland National Forest.

A spiraling road leads to that great silver dome in the sky, **Mount Palomar Observatory**. With a clear shot heavenward from its 6100-foot-high perch, one of the world's largest reflecting telescopes scans the night skies for celestial secrets. Staffed by scientists and astronomers from the California Institute of Technology, this is an active research facility and, only reluctantly, a tourist attraction. You can glimpse the 200-inch Hale Telescope from the visitor's gallery, view a movie on how research is conducted, and look at photos in the museum, but there's little else to see or do. Unless of course you have the time and the legs to hike around the mountain (see the "Hiking" section at the end of this chapter). ~ At the end of Route 56; 619-742-2119.

Southeast of Mount Palomar, Route 76 ends at Route 79, which then courses through backcountry to the tiny town of Santa Ysabel. **Mission Asistencia de Santa Ysabel**, where a 20th-century church stands on the site of an 18th-century branch mission, lacks the appeal of its sister missions. ~ Santa Ysabel; 619-765-0810.

Most of the pilgrims in these parts are bound not for the chapel but for **Dudley's Bakery**, where dozens of kinds of bread, including a delicious jalapeño loaf, come steaming from the oven. ~ Routes 78 and 79, Santa Ysabel; 619-765-0488.

HIDDEN ►   Down the road in **Julian** you'll come upon the belle of Southern California mountain mining towns. During the 1890s, the local mines employed 2000 miners, who hauled up $15 million in gold ore. Today the region produces red apples rather than gold nuggets and Julian, with its dusty aura of the Old West, has become a major tourist attraction.

Some of the falsefront stores along **Main Street** are 19th-century originals. Have a look, for instance, at the 1897 **Julian Hotel**, and don't miss the **Julian Drug Store**, an old-style soda fountain serving sparkling sarsaparilla and conjuring images of boys in buckskin and girls in bonnets. The white clapboard **Town Hall** still stands, and over at the **Julian Museum**, the townsfolk have turned an old brewery into a charming hodgepodge of local collectibles. Admission. ~ 2811 Washington Street, Julian; 619-765-0227.

The first hard-rock mine in Julian, **Washington Mine** is a state historic site. Although the tunnels have long since collapsed, the Julian Historical Society displays mining memorabilia depicting the mining era. ~ 9917 2nd Street, Julian; 619-765-0174.

Operations closed in 1942, but the **Eagle and High Peak Mines** still offer tours of the tunnels and an opportunity to pan for gold. What seems certain to be a "tourist trap," is actually an interesting and educational experience. Admission. ~ At the end of C Street, Julian; 619-765-0036.

But remember, these days apples are actually the main business in Julian and dozens of orchards drape the hillsides below town. The countryside all around is quilted with pear and peach orchards as well, and there are Appaloosa ranches and roadside stands selling fruits and jams.

Route 79 points south from Julian along a densely forested ridge of the Laguna Mountains to **Cuyamaca Rancho State Park**. Isolated Indian country that was turned into a Spanish rancho in the 19th century, this alpine sanctuary rests amid rugged mountain terrain. The vistas reach from desert to ocean and the park is rich in wildlife.

After exploring the shores of lovely Lake Cuyamaca, take in the Indian museum at **park headquarters**. ~ 619-765-0755. Exhibits here portray the tragic clash between Westerners and indigenous Diegueño tribes. The **Stonewall Mine** site, representing a later era, consists of old building foundations and rusting mine equipment.

> In the fall of 1997, the area code for Northern Inland San Diego County will change from 619 to 760.

Near Lake Cuyamaca, Route S1 (Sunrise Highway), leads southeast to **Mount Laguna**, a region rich in recreational areas and desert views. You can continue your backcountry adventure by following the highway (which becomes Buckman Springs Road) south toward the Mexican border. This is rough, arid, scrub country, but you'll find an oasis at **Lake Morena**, where an oak-shaded park borders a fishing lake. Farther south lies the high desert outpost of **Campo**, with its sun-baked streets and 19th-century ruins. From here you can head south across the border or west toward the seaside metropolis of San Diego.

LODGING

San Luis Rey Downs is a casual little resort nestled along the San Luis Rey River. There are only 26 rooms, neat, clean, and basic, in a two-story woodframe lodge overlooking the golf course. But this inviting hideaway also offers a restaurant, lounge, pool, spa, and tennis courts. ~ 31474 Golf Club Drive, Bonsall; 619-758-3762, 800-783-6967, fax 619-940-8509. ULTRA-DELUXE.

Pine Tree Lodge is clearly the nicest of the reasonably priced motels in Escondido. Family owned and operated, it is sparkling clean and well maintained. Some of the 38 rooms have kitchens and fireplaces; pool and sundeck. ~ 425 West Mission Avenue, Escondido; 619-745-7613, fax 619-745-3377. BUDGET TO MODERATE.

One of the county's leading resorts is **Rancho Bernardo Inn**. World-class golf and tennis aside, this handsome hacienda-style complex is a gracious country retreat. Rooms here, however, are rather ordinary considering the high rent. ~ 17550 Bernardo Oaks Drive, Rancho Bernardo; 619-487-1611, 800-542-6096, fax 619-675-6501. ULTRA-DELUXE.

Overnighting in the Mount Palomar area is limited to camping, except for the **Lazy H Ranch**. When the proprietor said the place "dates back to the '40s," I wondered which '40s—it has the look and feel of an early California homestead. The 11 rooms include amenities you'd expect from a budget-priced establishment. But here you can adjourn to the Spanish-style patio, stroll through a garden with

Text continued on page 316.

South of
the Border

Tijuana, a favorite day-trip destination for San Diego visitors, has been amazingly transformed in recent years from a bawdy bordertown to a modern, bustling city of almost two million people. Gone, or very well hidden, are the borderline attractions that once lured sailors and marines. In their place is a colorful center of tourism suitable for the entire family.

A major revitalization effort brought highrise buildings, broad boulevards, huge shopping centers, and classy shops and restaurants. But don't get the idea Tijuana has become completely Americanized. It still retains much of its traditional Mexican flavor and offers visitors an exciting outing and some surprising cultural experiences.

Perhaps the most impressive attraction, ideal for learning about Mexico, is the **Centro Cultural Tijuana**. Here the striking 85-foot-high Omnimax Space Theater is a silvery sphere held up by a stylized hand that symbolizes the earth housing a world of culture. Inside, the giant 180° screen carries viewers on a journey through Mexico. The complex, designed by Pedro Ramírez Váquez, architect of Mexico City's famous Anthropological Museum, houses four exhibit halls and a multi-level cultural and historical museum. ~ Paseo de los Héroes and Calle Mina; 52-66-84-11-11.

Spectator sports are an exciting and popular pastime for Tijuana visitors, including thoroughbred and greyhound racing at **Caliente Race Track**. ~ Boulevard Agua Caliente, 52-66-81-78-11 in Tijuana; 619-231-1919 from San Diego. Catch a colorful bullfight at **El Toreo**. ~ Boulevard Agua Caliente. Or try **Plaza Monumental**. ~ Located six miles west via Highway 1D. Call **Five Star Tours** for tickets and information. ~ 619-232-5049.

Jai alai fans crowd **Frontón Palacio**, the oldest building in Tijuana, for the fastest moving sport in the world (the ball travels at speeds in excess of 160 miles per hour). ~ Avenida Revolución and Calle 7a; 52-66-85-25-24. Call the **Baja Visitors Information** at 619-298-4105 for information about all events.

No doubt a major reason to visit "TJ" is to shop. The central shopping district is downtown, along Avenida Revolución, where arcades, stalls, and hawkers line the boulevard promoting the usual selection of tourist trinkets, piñatas, colorful flowers, serapes, pottery, and lace. There are numerous shops featuring quality merchandise such as leather goods, designer clothes, perfumes, artwork, and jewelry at incredible savings. **Sara's Imports** has ladies designer fashions and perfumes. ~ Avenida Revolución No. 635 at Calle 4a; 52-66-85-76-85. **Tolan-Arte de México** offers authentic Mexican folk art and fashions. ~ Avenida Revolución No. 1471; 52-66-88-36-37, 706-688-3637.

American currency is accepted everywhere but small bills are recommended since getting change can sometimes be a problem. U.S. residents receive a duty and federal tax exemption on the first $400 in personal goods purchased in Mexico. One liter of alcoholic beverage is allowed for those 21 years and older.

Tijuana has some exceptional restaurants. **La Costa** serves succulent seafood in a quiet, comfortable atmosphere. ~ Calle 7a between Avenida Revolución and Avenida Constitución; 52-66-85-40-52. **Fiesta Mexicana** has an interesting and enticing menu of nouvelle and Mexican cuisine. ~ Calle 7a No. 8186; 52-66-85-07-44. **Tía Juana Tilly's** is a great spot to sit on the patio, sip margaritas, munch on tacos, and listen to mariachis. ~ Avenida Revolución, No. 701 and Calle 7a; 52-66-85-60-24. The **Tijuana Chamber of Commerce** will provide visitors with information on the city's shops and restaurants. ~ 52-66-85-84-72.

Should you decide to stay longer than a day, enjoy Tijuana's stylish hotel, **The Grand Hotel Tijuana**. This 422-room luxury complex boasts dramatic city views from its 32-story glass towers and offers four restaurants, three bars, a disco, a gallery of shops, tennis courts, and a health club. ~ Boulevard Agua Caliente No. 4500, 52-66-81-70-00, 706-681-7000 in Tijuana; 800-472-6385 in San Diego. MODERATE.

Just a little further south of Tijuana, located right along the coast, the small towns of Rosarito Beach and Ensenada provide a less commercial glimpse of Mexico. A modern highway makes the trip easy and comfortable.

lemon trees, or take a dip in the pool. ~ Route 76, Pauma Valley; 619-742-3669. BUDGET.

HIDDEN ►   One of Southern California's oldest hostelries, the 1897 **Julian Hotel Bed and Breakfast** is a Victorian charmer. Even though most of its 18 rooms share European-style baths, the place is often full, particularly on weekends, so reserve in advance. Two charming cottages and the rooms are done in period fashion with plenty of brass, lace, porcelain, and mahogany. In addition to a historic building, guests share a lovely sitting room. ~ Main and B streets, Julian; 619-765-0201, 800-734-5854. DELUXE TO ULTRA-DELUXE.

The 23-room **Julian Lodge**, designed after a 19th-century hotel, is a new woodframe structure that nicely recaptures the original. The rooms are small but well decorated with period-style furnishings. The breakfast parlor is also quite homey, with oak tables and an inviting fireplace. ~ 4th and C streets, Julian; 619-765-1420, 800-542-1420. MODERATE TO DELUXE.

HIDDEN ►   **Shadow Mountain Ranch**, a large, attractive country house near Julian, provides the area's most unique lodging in its "enchanted cottage," complete with pot-bellied stove, and the "grandma's attic cottage," containing all of granny's antiques. For the adventurous, they even have a tiny treehouse with built-in toilet. And there is one room in the main house as well. Full breakfast is included in the price. ~ 2771 Frisius Road, Pine Hills; 619-765-0323. MODERATE TO DELUXE.

Also consider **Pine Hills Lodge**, a wonderfully rustic complex with a lodge and cabins that date back to 1912. Surrounded by pines and cedars, this cozy retreat features six European-style rooms (with shared bath) in the lodge. The 12 equally countrified cabins are woodframe structures complete with clawfoot tubs. Located at 4500 feet elevation, Pine Hills is a mini-resort featuring a restaurant, bar, and dinner theater. ~ 2960 La Posada Way, Pine Hills; 619-765-1100. MODERATE TO DELUXE.

Can't get a room in Julian? Don't despair, go to the **Ramona Valley Inn**. It's a 39-room roadside motel, clean and comfortable, located 22 miles west of Julian. Pool; kitchenettes in some rooms. ~ 4th and Main streets, Ramona; 619-789-6433. BUDGET TO MODERATE.

Magnolia Travel Lodge is the nicest of a gaggle of affordable motels lining Route 8. You won't confuse its Spanish stucco styling with the Alhambra, but you will find the attractively furnished rooms quite comfortable. Pool. ~ 471 North Magnolia Avenue, El Cajon; 619-447-3999. BUDGET TO MODERATE.

It's not listed or advertised anywhere, but if you need clean, cozy, low-cost lodgings, check out the **St. Francis Motel**. This trim 37-room court offers small, simply decorated rooms, some with kitchens. Pool. ~ 1368 East Main Street, El Cajon; 619-444-8147. BUDGET.

DINING   Whatever you do during your North County visit, don't pass up the chance to dine at **El Bizcocho**. Tucked away in the upscale Rancho

Bernardo Inn, an Early California–style resort, this award-winning restaurant rates among greater San Diego's best. Two distinct menus with different personalities are featured here. First, there's the traditional French haute cuisine menu, which includes a nice balance of beef, veal, fish, and fowl dishes. Then, there's the lighter fare menu with a Northern Italian/Mediterranean twist. Try the roast duckling for two or indulge in the creamy lobster bisque. Dinner only. ~ 17550 Bernardo Oaks Drive, Rancho Bernardo; 619-487-1611. DELUXE TO ULTRA-DELUXE.

Peg Henry's is a favorite among smart locals and savvy travelers.   ◄ HIDDEN
The tasty Mexican-American fare includes huge servings of enchiladas, tostadas, tacos, and quesadillas. On the gringo side of the menu, there's a less interesting roster of steak, chicken, and seafood dishes. The rustic interior is paneled with pine. Closed Sunday. ~ 16220 Route 76, Pauma Valley; 619-742-8986. BUDGET TO MODERATE.

The **Lazy H Ranch** serves up steaks, prime rib, chicken, and fish dishes in a family-style dining room set in the leafy environs of a six-acre orchard. Closed Sunday. ~ Route 76, Pauma Valley; 619-742-3669. MODERATE.

Hikers will appreciate **Palomar Mountain General Store**, whose adjacent vegetarian café serves hearty soups, salads, sandwiches, and hot entrées at lunch and dinner. Closed Tuesday and Wednesday. ~ Routes S6 and S7, Palomar Mountain; 619-742-3496. BUDGET.

The Julian Grill, situated in a 1920-vintage house, is cozy and folksy, especially around the living room fireplace. The menu emphasizes such hearty mountain fare as steaks, prime rib, scampi, and chicken breast. They also feature sophisticated chef's specials like chicken Jerusalem. ~ 2224 Main Street, Julian; 619-765-0173. MODERATE TO DELUXE.

At **Romano's Dodge House** you will feel like a Romano family   ◄ HIDDEN
guest. This intimate Italian restaurant, with its homespun ambience, dishes out delicious chicken cacciatore, lasagna, and authentic Sicilian pizza. At reasonable prices, Romano's is hard to beat. ~ 2718-B Street, Julian; 619-765-1003. BUDGET TO MODERATE.

At least a dozen places in Julian prepare the local specialty, apple pie. But buyer beware: all pies are not created equal: some are definitely better than others. The pies at the **Julian Pie Company**, for instance, always have flaky crusts and just the right mix of apples, cinnamon, and sugar. ~ 2225 Main Street, Julian; 619-765-2449. BUDGET

For buffalo burgers and local gossip, the townsfolk all head over to **Kendall's Korner**. This friendly café, with its all-American cuisine   ◄ HIDDEN
and Early American decor serves up a standard-fare breakfast and lunch menu weekdays, with special dinner plates like steak and potatoes on the weekend. ~ 2603-B Street, Julian; 619-765-1560. BUDGET.

Ask anyone in Julian where to find a good restaurant, and two out of three times they'll tell you **Kozak's**. The city's all-purpose eatery, it offers a 24-hour coffee shop up front and a classy dining room in back. The food is good, all-American fare, with budget prices at the coffee shop and moderate to deluxe tabs out back. ~ 401 West Main Street, Julian; 619-442-7768. BUDGET TO DELUXE.

For a touch of Europe, consider **Dansk**. Here both the food and the mood are traditional Scandinavian. Belgian waffles, Swedish pancakes, and Danish sausage are favorites at breakfast, while Swedish meatballs top the lunch menu. *Karré* (tenderloin of pork with prunes and apples) and *alte rullader* (beef roll) are dinner favorites. ~ 8425 La Mesa Boulevard, La Mesa; 619-463-0640. BUDGET.

SHOPPING

Jewelry is a high art form at **The Collector**, where every piece is crafted by hand. The owners go right to the source for the best gems—Colombia for emeralds, Sri Lanka for rubies, and Africa for diamonds. ~ 912 South Live Oak Park Road, Fallbrook; 619-728-9121.

Mega-malls are popping up all around San Diego these days, but few match Escondido's **North County Fair**. This 83-acre complex has a half-dozen major department stores and a host of independent shops. ~ Via Rancho Parkway and Route 15, Escondido; 619-489-2344.

Collectibles are a way of life at **Family Affair Gift Galleries**. The plates, lithographs, figurines, and ornaments assembled here from around the world are hand-numbered, limited-edition items. ~ 13330 Paseo del Verano Norte, Rancho Bernardo; 619-485-5850.

Even if you're not in the market for nuts, dried fruit, or candy, a visit to **Bates Nut Farm** is mandatory. Name the nut and they have it—walnuts, cashews, pistachios, pecans, almonds, and peanuts—attractively displayed with an equally amazing variety of dried and glazed fruits, jellies, honey, and candy. ~ 15954 Woods Valley Road, Valley Center; 619-749-3334.

Main Street in Julian is lined with dozens of antique, gift, clothing, and curio shops. Among the more intriguing ones are the **Antique Boutique**, with an especially nice selection of furniture and collectibles. ~ 2626 Main Street; 619-765-0541. **Julian's Toy Chest** features unusual educational toys and children's books. ~ 2116 Main Street; 619-765-2262. **Quinn Knives** is where you can buy anything from a sword to a Swiss Army knife. ~ 2116 Main Street; 619-765-2230. Nearby is **Applewood & Company**, a popular emporium for antiques and home accessories. ~ 2804 Washington Street; 619-765-1185.

Harvest Ranch Market is an epicure's delight. Deli items, farm-fresh produce, international gourmet foods, picnic supplies, and rack after rack of fine wines are available at this pleasant country store. ~ 759 Jamacha Road, El Cajon; 619-442-0355.

La Mesa Boulevard, the center of La Mesa's revitalized downtown, looks like an all-American hometown business district circa 1930. Old storefronts have been refurbished and filled with specialty shops, making it a great street to stroll and shop.

J. P.'s Lounge, a classy and contemporary watering hole at Pala Mesa Resort, is one of the region's top nightclubs. You can count on a sophisticated crowd and live entertainment on the weekend. ~ 2001 South Route 395, Fallbrook; 619-728-5881.

NIGHTLIFE

Built in 1926 as a training camp for Jack Dempsey, **Pine Hills Lodge** uses the champ's old ring as a dinner theater stage. And it looks as though they've scored a knockout. A dedicated and talented local company performs light plays and musicals on Friday and Saturday only. ~ 2960 La Posada Way, Pine Hills; 619-765-1100.

Theatre East is the cultural flagship of the region, offering everything from chamber music to Mel Torme. The cultural calendar here includes orchestras, dance companies, and repertory theater groups. ~ 210 East Main Street, El Cajon; 619-440-2277.

P.J.'s Country Connection, a hot Western club, cooks up a live batch of country-and-western music five nights a week. Cover. ~ 1013 Broadway, El Cajon; 619-444-7443.

The **Lamplighter Community Theatre** presents a year-round series of stage plays by a local theater group. ~ 8053 University Avenue, La Mesa; 619-464-4598.

CLEVELAND NATIONAL FOREST 🚶🚲🐎🚗 A major mountain preserve, this sprawling retreat is divided into three districts, two of which encompass more than 400,000 acres in San Diego County. Northernmost is the Palomar District, covering 189,000 acres around the famous observatory and stretching south beyond Lake Henshaw. Its main feature is the rugged Agua Tibia Wilderness Area, with several excellent trails. Horseback riding is permitted in the Boulder Oaks Equestrian Area. Farther south, the 216,000-acre Descanso District adjoins Cuyamaca Rancho State Park. Here the Mount Laguna Recreation Area offers camping, picnicking, and hiking. There are picnic areas and restrooms. Day-use fee, $8. ~ Access to the Palomar District is via Routes 79, S6, and S7; the Descanso District and the Mount Laguna Recreation Area are located on Route S1 (Sunrise Highway) a few miles north of Route 8; 619-445-6235.

PARKS

▲ There are five campgrounds in the Palomar District, three of which accommodate RVs (no hookups); $7 to $8 a night. There are six campgrounds in the Descanso District, all of which accommodate both tents and RVs (no hookups); $12 to $19.50 a night. Reservations may be made by calling DESTINET (800-280-2267).

PALOMAR MOUNTAIN STATE PARK 🚶🐎🎣 Thick forests of pine, fur, and cedar combine with rambling mountain meadows to create a Sierra Nevada-like atmosphere. The average elevation here on the side of Mount Palomar is 5500 feet, so the evenings are cool and heavy snow is common in the winter. Doane Pond is stocked with trout for good fishing in fall and winter. Facilities include picnic areas, restrooms, and showers. Restaurant and groceries are nearby at Palomar General Store. Day-use fee, $5. ~ Located on Route S7 on top of Mount Palomar; 619-742-3462.

▲ There are 31 sites; 12 accommodate both tents and RVs (no hookups); $14 a night. Reservations are required for weekend stays; call DESTINET at 800-444-7275.

HIDDEN ▶ **WILLIAM HEISE PARK** 🚶🐎 Beautifully situated in a forest of pines and oaks, this preserve rests at 4200-foot elevation in the Laguna Mountains near Julian. The park is largely undeveloped and provides more than 900 acres of hiking and riding trails. It's also one of the few county parks where the snowfall is sufficient for winter recreation. There are picnic areas, restrooms, and showers. Groceries and restaurants are about five miles away in Julian. Day-use fee, $2. ~ From Route 79 (one mile west of Julian) go south on Pine Hills Road for two miles, then east on Frisius Road for two more miles; 619-565-3600.

▲ There are 100 tent/RV sites (no hookups); $11 a night.

CUYAMACA RANCHO STATE PARK 🚶🚴🐎 Broad meadows, forests of pine and oak, and numerous streams make the Cuyamaca Peninsular Range one of Southern California's most beautiful areas. Encompassing 25,000 acres (including 13,000 acres of wilderness), the park provides a habitat for deer, coyote, fox, bobcat, and mountain lion, as well as over 100 species of birds. Hike or ride your horse on 120 miles of open trails. Facilities include a museum, picnic areas, restrooms, and showers. Restaurants and groceries are nearby in Descanso and Julian. Day-use fee, $5. ~ Located on Route 79 about ten miles south of Julian; 619-765-0755.

▲ There are 166 tent/RV sites (no hookups); $15 to $16 a night. For reservations, call DESTINET at 800-444-7275.

HIDDEN ▶ **LAKE MORENA PARK** 🚶🐎�️🚤⛵ As its name suggests, the highlight of this hideaway is a 1000-acre lake renowned for its bass, crappie, bluegill, and catfish. Located near the Mexican border, the park covers a total of 3250 acres, which range from flat terrain to low hills covered with oak and scrub. There are picnic areas, restrooms, and showers. Fishing facilities and boat rentals are available. Groceries are nearby. Day-use fee, $5. ~ Located off Route 8 (Buckman Springs Road) in the southeast corner of San Diego County; 619-565-3600.

▲ There are 80 tent/RV sites; 50 have hookups; $10 to $12 a night.

LOS PEÑASQUITOS CANYON PRESERVE 🚶 This 2200-acre parcel, a canyonland wilderness several miles from the coast, features narrow rock gorges, mesa plateaus, and streamside woodlands. There are hiking trails as well as historic adobe houses to explore. Restrooms are available. ~ Located off Black Mountain Road near Mira Mesa.

The lure of sport and bottom fishing attracts thousands of enthusiasts to San Diego every year. Albacore and snapper are the close-in favorites, with marlin and tuna the prime objectives for longer charters.

▼▼▼▼▼▼▼▼▼▼▼▼▼▼
Outdoor Adventures

SPORT-FISHING

For deep-sea charters, see **Helgren's Sportfishing.** ~ 315 Harbor Drive South, Oceanside; 619-722-2133. In Mission Bay try **Seaforth Sportfishing.** ~ 1717 Quivira Road, Mission Bay; 619-224-3383. Or you can also try **Islandia Sportfishing.** ~ 1551 West Mission Bay Drive, Mission Bay; 619-222-1164. **Coronado Boat Rental** serves the Coronado area. ~ 1715 Strand Way, Coronado; 619-437-1514. If you are in the Point Loma area try **H & M Sportfishing Landing.** ~ 2803 Emerson Street, Point Loma; 619-222-1144. In San Diego the place to call is **Fish N' Cruise.** ~ 1231 Shafter Street, San Diego; 619-224-2464. Try calling the **Point Loma Sportfishing Association.** ~ 1403 Scott Street, Point Loma; 619-223-1627. Or, also in Point Loma is **Fisherman's Landing.** ~ 2838 Garrison Street, Point Loma; 619-222-0391.

Spearfishing is very popular off La Jolla beaches, especially south of La Jolla Cove. Contact **San Diego Divers Supply** for supplies, tours, and information. ~ 5701 La Jolla Boulevard, La Jolla; 619-459-2691. Note: Spearfishing is not allowed in protected reserves from La Jolla Cove north.

WHALE WATCHING

Seeing our fellow mammalian creatures in migration is a wonderful sight to behold.

For whale-watching tours contact **Helgren's Sportfishing.** ~ 315 Harbor Drive South, Oceanside; 619-722-2133. **Islandia Sportfishing** serves the Mission Bay area. ~ 1551 West Mission Bay Drive, Mission Bay; 619-222-1164. In Point Loma try **H & M Sportsfishing Landing.** ~ 2803 Emerson Street, Point Loma; 619-222-1144. Or you can call the **Point Loma Sportfishing Association.** ~ 1403 Scott Street, Point Loma; 619-223-1627. **San Diego Harbor Excursion** provides whale-watching tours during winter. ~ 1050 Harbor Drive North; 619-234-4111. A free whale-watching station at Cabrillo National Monument on Point Loma offers a glassed-in observatory from which to spot whales.

DIVING

San Diego offers countless spots for skindiving. The rocky La Jolla coves boast the clearest water on the California coast. Bird Rock, La Jolla Underwater Park, and the underwater Scripp's Canyon are ideal havens for scuba and skindivers. In Point Loma try the colorful tidepools at Cabrillo Underwater Reserve; at "No Surf Beach" (Sunset Cliff Boulevard) pools and reefs are for experienced divers only.

For diving rentals, sales, instruction, and dive tips contact **Underwater Schools of America.** ~ 707 Oceanside Boulevard, Oceanside; 619-722-7826. In San Diego, **Ocean Enterprises** is the place to call.

~ 7710 Balboa, San Diego; 619-565-6054. Or call **Diving Locker**. ~ 405 North Route 101, Solana Beach; 619-755-6822. In La Jolla, dive with **San Diego Diver's Supply**. ~ 5701 La Jolla Boulevard, La Jolla, 619-459-2691; and 4004 Sports Arena Boulevard, San Diego, 619-224-3439. In Pacific Beach try **Diving Locker**. ~ 1020 Grand Avenue, Pacific Beach; 619-272-1120. Or try calling **Buhrow Into Surf and Dive** for diving equipment and information. ~ 4114 Madier Street, Mission Bay; 619-275-3212.

SURFING & WIND-SURFING

Surf's up in the San Diego area. Pacific, Mission, and Ocean beaches, Tourmaline Surfing Park, and Windansea, La Jolla Shores, Swami, and Moonlight beaches are well-known hangouts for surfers. Sailboarding is concentrated within Mission Bay. Oceanside is home to annual world-class boogie-board and surfing competitions.

For surfboard rentals try **Mitch's**. ~ 631 Pearl Street, La Jolla; 619-459-5933. For more surfing tips, call **Hanson's**. ~ 1105 First Street, Encinitas; 619-753-6595. Or you can also try **Hobie Oceanside**. ~ 1909 South Coast Highway, Oceanside; 619-433-4020.

BOATING & SAILING

You can sail under the Coronado Bridge, skirt the gorgeous downtown skyline, and even get a taste of open ocean in this Southern California sailing mecca. Several sailing companies operate out of Harbor Island West in San Diego, including **Harbor Sailboats**. ~ 2040 Harbor Island Drive, Suite 104, San Diego; 619-291-9568. For boat rentals try the **San Diego Yacht Charters**. ~ 1880 Harbor Island Drive, San Diego; 619-297-4555. You can also try contacting the **San Diego Sailing Club and School**. ~ 1880 Harbor Island Drive, San Diego; 619-298-6623.

Other motor boat and sail rentals can be found at **C. P. Sailing Sports**. ~ 1775 East Mission Bay Drive, Mission Bay; 619-276-4010. Another one to try is the **Mission Bay Sportscenter**. ~ 1010 Santa Clara Place, Mission Bay; 619-488-1004. In Coronado, the **Coronado Boat Rental** is the place to try. ~ 1715 Strand Way, Coronado; 619-437-1514. In Mission Bay sail with **Seaforth Mission Bay Boat Rental**. ~ 1641 Quivira Road, Mission Bay; 619-223-1681.

Yacht charters are available through **Hornblower Dining Yachts**. ~ 2825 Fifth Avenue, San Diego; 619-234-8687.

GLIDING

Torrey Pines Flight Park, Inc. is an expert-rated hang gliding site, located atop a towering sandstone bluff overlooking Black's Beach. If you're not yet an expert, there is a great vantage point to watch from. ~ 2800 Torrey Pines Scenic Drive, La Jolla; 619-452-9858. Contact **The Hang Gliding Center** for rentals, sales, and instruction. ~ 15263 Golda Odessa Lane, Lakeside; 619-561-1009.

BALLOON RIDES

Hot-air ballooning is a romantic pursuit that has soared in popularity in the Del Mar area. A growing number of ballooning companies offer spectacular dawn and sunset flights, most concluding with a traditional champagne toast. **A Beautiful Morning** is a ballooning company that flies out of Del Mar. ~ 3142 Camino Del Mar, Del Mar; 619-481-6225. Also contact **A Skysurfer Balloon Company**. ~ 1221 Camino Del Mar, Del Mar; 619-481-6800. Or try **Del Mar Balloons** for a high flying adventure. ~ 3142 Camino Del Mar, Del Mar; 619-259-3115.

For the golfing set there's **Emerald Isle Golf Course**. ~ 660 El Camino Real, Oceanside; 619-721-4700. Tee off at **Oceanside Golf Course**. ~ 825 Douglas Drive, Oceanside; 619-433-1360. Try **Rancho Carlsbad Golf Course**. ~ 200 El Camino Real, Carlsbad; 619-438-1772. In Rancho Sante Fe try playing at **Morgan Run Golf Course**. ~ 5690 Cancha de Golf, Rancho Santa Fe; 619-756-2471. The beautiful **Torrey Pines Municipal Golf Course** is famous for its greens. ~ 11480 North Torrey Pines Road, La Jolla; 619-570-1234. **Balboa Park Municipal Golf Course** is a duffer's delight. ~ Golf Course Drive, Balboa Park; 619-235-1184. Try also the **Coronado Golf Course**. ~ 2000 Visalia Row, Coronado; 619-435-3121. Another course to play is at **Mission Bay Golf Resort**. ~ 2702 North Mission Bay Drive, Mission Bay; 619-490-3370.

GOLF

For the Inland San Diego County area, consider **Fallbrook Golf and Country Club**. ~ 2757 Gird Road, Fallbrook; 619-728-8334. Try your luck at **San Luis Rey Downs Golf Resort & Country Club**. ~ 31474 Golf Club Drive, Bonsall; 619-758-3762. The **Lake San Marcos Executive Course** in San Marcos is open to the public. ~ 1556 Camino del Arroyo, San Marcos. 619-744-9092. Tee off at the **Lawrence Welk Resort Village Golf Courses**. ~ 8860 Lawrence Welk Drive, Escondido; 619-749-3000. Head to **Rancho Bernardo Inn Golf Course** to play a round. ~ 17550 Bernardo Oaks Drive, Rancho Bernardo; 619-487-0700. In El Cajon try **Singing Hills Golf Courses**. ~ 3007 Dehesa Road, El Cajon; 619-442-3425.

North County suffers from a lack of public tennis courts; however, Del Mar has free courts located off 22nd Street between Camino del Mar and Jimmy Durante Boulevard.

TENNIS

San Diego has many private and public courts open to traveling tennis buffs. For information call **Balboa Tennis Club**. ~ 2221 Morley Field Drive, San Diego; 619-295-9278. The **Cabrillo Recreation Center** also has courts available. ~ 3051 Cañon Street, Point Loma; 619-531-1534. More courts are found at **Mission Valley YMCA**. ~ 5505 Friars Road, Mission Valley; 619-298-3576. In Ocean Beach try **Peninsula Tennis Club**. ~ 2525 Bacon Street, Ocean Beach; 619-226-3407. Also try your serve at the **La Jolla Recreation Center**. ~ 615 Prospect Street, La Jolla; 619-552-1658.

In Coronado call the **Coronado Tennis Center** for information on courts. ~ 1501 Glorietta Boulevard; 619-435-1616.

For Inland San Diego County, try **Pala Mesa Resort**. ~ 2001 Old Route 395, Fallbrook; 619-728-5881. In Bonsall try **San Luis Rey Downs Resort**. ~ 31474 Golf Club Drive, Bonsall; 619-758-3762. **Kit Carson Park** in Escondido also has courts available. ~ 3333 Bear Valley Parkway, Escondido; 619-741-4691. Visit **Lindo Lake Park** and try their courts. ~ Lindo Lane, Lakeside; 619-565-5928. In El Cajon try **Parkway Tennis Club**. ~ 444 Broadway, El Cajon; 619-442-9623.

RIDING STABLES

An area just outside Imperial Beach is one of the few places in the county where you can ride on the beach. **Hilltop Stable** rents mounts for rides at Border Field State Beach. ~ 2671 Monument Road, San Diego; 619-428-5441.

San Diego's backcountry, on the other hand, boasts hundreds of miles of riding trails. Cleveland National Forest, Palomar Mountain Park, William Heise Park, and Cuyamaca Rancho State Park all feature fine mountain riding. **Holidays on Horseback** offers a variety of day and multiday rides around Cuyamaca Rancho State Park; reservations required. ~ 24928 Viejas Boulevard, Descanso; 619-445-3997.

BIKING

North County's **Old Route 101** provides almost 40 miles of scintillating cycling along the coast from Oceanside to La Jolla. Traffic is heavy but bikes are almost as numerous as autos along this stretch. Bike lanes are designated along most of the route.

Cycling has skyrocketed in popularity throughout San Diego County, especially in coastal areas. **Balboa Park** and **Mission Bay Park** both have excellent bike routes (see the "Balboa Park and the San Diego Zoo" and "Mission Bay Park Area" sections of this chapter).

Inland, **Julian** makes a good base for bicycling the hilly country roads such as the nine-mile loop to Wynola. Mountain bikers can enjoy many miles of traffic-free riding in **Cuyamaca State Park**.

Bike Rentals   To rent a bicycle in downtown San Diego, contact **Pennyfarthings**. ~ 314 G Street; 619-233-7696. In the Mission Bay area, go to **Rent A Bike**. ~ 1st and Harbor streets, across from the Marriott Hotel; 619-232-4700. Another bike outlet is **Holland's Bicycles**. ~ 977 Orange Avenue at 10th Street, Coronado; 619-435-3153.

HIKING

Most of the San Diego County coastline is developed for either residential or commercial purposes, limiting the hiking possibilities. There are some protected areas set aside to preserve remnants of the county's unique coastal chaparral communities and tidelands. These reserves offer short hiking trails. Inland San Diego County, particularly in the Palomar and Laguna mountains, also provides backpacking opportunities. All distances listed are one way unless otherwise noted.

Serious hikers might also consider taking on the San Diego section of the **California Coastal Trail**. It follows the shoreline, as much as possible, from the Mexican border all the way to San Onofre State Beach.

NORTH SAN DIEGO COUNTY Three Lagoons Trail (5 miles) originates on the beach in Leucadia and heads north along the sand past three saltwater lagoons, ending in Carlsbad. Best place to begin is at the beach parking lot at Grandview Street in Leucadia.

LA JOLLA La Jolla Coastal Walk (1 mile), a dirt path atop La Jolla Bluffs, affords some of the most spectacular views anywhere on the San Diego County coastline. It begins on Coast Boulevard just up the hill from La Jolla Cove and continues past a sea cave accessible from the trail.

Without a doubt, the 1750-acre **Torrey Pines State Park and Reserve** offers the county's best hiking. It was named for the world's rarest pine tree *(Pinus torreyana)* which the reserve was established to protect. An estimated 6000 of the gnarled and twisted trees cling to rugged cliffs and ravines, some growing as tall as 60 feet.

Several major trails offer hikers a variety of challenges and natural attractions. Most are easily walked loops through groves of pines, such as **Guy Fleming Trail** (.6 mile), which scans the coast at South and North overlooks, and **Parry Grove Trail** (.4 mile), which passes stands of manzanita, yucca, and other shrubs. There are more strenuous treks such as the **Razor Point Trail** (.6 mile), which follows the Canyon of the Swifts, then links up with the **Beach Trail** (.8 mile); and the **Broken Hill Trail** (1.3 miles), which zigzags to the coast past chamiso and scrub oak.

Del Mar Beach Trail (3 miles) leads from the Del Mar Amtrak Station along the beach past flatrock tidepools and up to the bluffs of Torrey Pines State Reserve.

POINT LOMA AREA Cabrillo National Monument offers the **Bayside Trail** (1 mile). It begins at the Old Point Loma Lighthouse, beautifully restored to its original 1855 condition, and meanders through the heart of a scenic coastal chaparral community. A wide variety of

---

✔ **CHECK THESE OUT—UNIQUE OUTDOOR ADVENTURES**

- Lift a glass of champagne over the **Del Mar Valley** in a hot-air balloon as the sun sinks into the Pacific. *page 323*
- Soar out over the ocean from a bluff at **Torrey Pines**, where the buffeting breezes make conditions prime for hang gliding pros. *page 322*
- Peer into the clearest water on the California coast when you dive in the **La Jolla** coves, where world-class oceanographers train. *page 321*
- Hike the beautiful Bayside Trail in **Cabrillo National Monument**, which leads from the restored Old Point Loma Lighthouse through rolling coastal terrain with sweeping vistas. *page 325*

native plants including prickly pear cactus, yucca, buckwheat, and Indian paintbrush grow along the path. In addition to stunning views of San Diego, there are remnants of the coastal defense system built here during World Wars I and II. ~ 619-557-5450.

SOUTH SAN DIEGO COUNTY Hiking trails crisscross the dunes and marshes of the largely undeveloped **Border Field State Park**, which forms the coastal border between the United States and Mexico. Trails lead through dunes anchored by salt grass, pickleweed, and sand verbena. The marshy areas, especially those in an adjacent federal wildlife refuge around the Tijuana River estuary, provide feeding and nesting grounds for several hundred species of native and migratory birds, including hawks, pelicans, plovers, terns, and ducks.

Border Field to Tijuana River Trail (1.5 miles) is a level beach walk past sand dunes and the Tijuana River Estuary.

INLAND SAN DIEGO COUNTY Rising along San Diego County's northern border, the Palomar Mountain Range provides a number of demanding trails. Well-protected and maintained within Cleveland National Forest, they offer hikers a prime wilderness experience. ~ 619-595-3693.

Observatory Trail (4 miles) is one of the area's easiest treks and rewards the hiker with a view of that famous silver hemisphere, the Mount Palomar Observatory.

The Agua Tibia Wilderness Area in the northwest corner of Cleveland National Forest is the setting for rugged **Dripping Springs Trail** (13 miles). Ascending the side of Agua Tibia Mountain, the trail leads through precipitous canyons to vista points with views of the Pacific, more than 40 miles away.

Scott's Cabin Trail (1 mile) loops through varied terrain in Palomar State Park. The trail passes the remains of a homesteader's cabin, descends into a fir forest, and climbs to a lookout tower.

Cuyamaca Rancho State Park, located further south in the Laguna Mountains, offers nearly a dozen trails covering more than 100 miles. **Cuyamaca Peak Trail** (5 miles) ascends a 6512-foot mountain, traversing forests of oak, pine, and fir. The views from the top of the trail extend from the Pacific to Mexico.

Stonewall Peak Trail (4.4 miles) takes you to the summit of 5730-foot Stonewall Peak, with views of an 1870-era mine site along the way. Nearby **Azalea Glen Trail** (3 miles) loops through open meadows as well as forests of oak and pine. **Paso Nature Trail** (.8 mile) is a self-guided loop designed to introduce visitors to the local flora.

▼▼▼▼▼▼▼▼▼▼
Transportation

CAR

Even though it is located in California's extreme southwest corner, San Diego is the hub of an elaborate highway network. The city is easily reached from north or south via Route 5; Route 8 serves drivers from the east; and Route 15 is the major inland freeway for travelers arriving from the mountain west.

Route 76 runs inland from Oceanside to the Palomar Mountains, then becomes **Route 79**, which leads to Julian. From Carlsbad, **Route 78** connects the coast with inland communities like Escondido.

San Diego International Airport (Lindbergh Field) lies just three miles northwest of downtown San Diego and is easily accessible from either Route 5 or Route 8. The airport is served by most major airlines, including Alaska Airlines, American Airlines, America West Airlines, Continental Airlines, Delta Airlines, Northwest Airlines, Reno Air, Skywest, Southwest Airlines, United Airlines, USAir, and Wardair Canada.

AIR

Taxis, limousines, and buses provide service from the airport. **San Diego Transit System** bus #2 carries passengers to downtown destinations. ~ 619-233-3004. Or try the **Coast Shuttle** which travels to major points in the city as well as to Orange County and Los Angeles. ~ 619-231-1123.

Greyhound Bus Lines services San Diego from around the country. The terminal is downtown at 120 West Broadway and 1st Avenue (619-239-3266). Greyhound also carries passengers inland from San Diego to Escondido (700 West Valley Parkway; 619-745-6522) and El Cajon (250 South Marshall Avenue; 619-444-2591).

BUS

Chugging to a stop at historic Santa Fe Depot, at Kettner Boulevard and Broadway downtown, is a nice and convenient way to arrive in San Diego. **Amtrak** offers several coast-hugging roundtrips daily between Los Angeles and San Diego, with stops at Oceanside and Del Mar. ~ 800-872-7245.

TRAIN

Much like the rest of Southern California, San Diego is spread out over a wide area and is best seen by car. Car rental companies abound. Most major rental agencies have franchises at the airport. These include **Avis Rent A Car** (619-231-7171, 800-831-2847), **Dollar Rent A Car** (619-234-3388, 800-800-4000), **Hertz Rent A Car** (619-283-7161), and **National Interrent** (619-231-7100, 800-227-7368).

CAR RENTALS

For better rates (but less convenient service) try agencies located near the airport that provide pick-up service: **Aztec Rent A Car** (619-232-6117, 800-231-0400), **Thrifty Car Rental** (619-233-9333, 800-367-2277), **Rent A Wreck** (619-223-3300, 800-535-8391), and **Budget Rent A Car** (619-229-2900, 800-527-0700).

North County Transit District, or NCTD, covers the general area from Camp Pendleton to Del Mar along the coast. NCTD operates numerous North County bus routes that service the communities of Oceanside, Carlsbad, Encinitas, Leucadia, Cardiff, Rancho Santa Fe, Solana Beach, and Del Mar. ~ 619-743-6283.

PUBLIC TRANSIT

Several modern and efficient public transportation systems operate throughout San Diego. Information and schedules are available for all systems by calling **Regional Transit.** ~ 619-233-3004.

The Regional Transit bus system is the city's largest public transportation network, with lines linking all major points. All Regional Transit stops are marked with a blue triangle.

The city's newest and most venturesome mode of public transportation is the **San Diego Trolley.** The light rail system's line operates daily from the Santa Fe Depot to the Mexican border. Understandably, this line is known as the "Tijuana Trolley," but it also serves the south bay cities of National City, Chula Vista, and Imperial Beach. The East Line, also departing from the Santa Fe Depot, serves southeastern San Diego and inland communities to El Cajon. ~ 619-233-3004.

National City Transit serves National City. ~ 619-474-7505. **Chula Vista Transit** serves Bonita and the city of Chula Vista. ~ 619-691-5260. **ATC/Vancom** runs from downtown San Diego to National City and Chula Vista and on to the San Ysidro international border. In addition, ATC/Vancom runs from Coronado along the Silver Strand to Imperial Beach. ~ 619-427-5660.

For Inland San Diego, NCTD provides bus service from Escondido to Ramona. **Northeast Rural Bus System** takes passengers from El Cajon to Julian, Santa Ysabel, and Cuyamaca Rancho. ~ 619-767-4287.

TAXIS

In North County (La Jolla to Carlsbad), you can call **Bill's Cab** (619-755-6737) or **Oceanside Yellow Cab** (619-722-4217).

San Diego is not a taxi town in the usual big-city sense, but there's a cab if you need it—just a telephone call away. Leading companies include **Silver Cabs** (619-280-5555), **Yellow Cab** (619-234-6161), **Orange Cab** (619-291-3333), and **USA Cab** (619-231-1144).

WALKING TOURS

Several San Diego organizations and tour operators offer organized walks: **Gaslamp Foundation** conducts walking tours of the restored downtown historic district. ~ 410 Island Avenue; 619-233-5227. Walking tours of Old Town State Historic Park are offered through **Old Town Walking Tours.** ~ 3977 Twiggs Street; 619-296-1004. Join **Coronado Touring** for a leisurely guided stroll through quaint Coronado. ~ 1110 Isabella Avenue, Coronado; 619-435-5993, 619-435-4444.

SIX

Central Coast

To call any one section of the California Coast the most alluring is to embark upon uncertain waters. Surely the Central Coast, that 200-mile swath from Ventura to San Simeon, is a region of rare beauty. Stretching across Ventura, Santa Barbara, and San Luis Obispo counties, it embraces many of the West's finest beaches.

Five of California's 21 missions—in Ventura, Santa Barbara, Lompoc, San Luis Obispo, and further inland in Solvang—lie along this stretch. Chosen by the Spanish in the 1780s for their fertile pastures, natural harbors, and placid surroundings, they are a historic testimonial to the varied richness of the landscape.

The towns that grew up around these missions, evocative of old Spanish traditions, are emblems of California's singular culture. Santa Barbara, perhaps the state's prettiest town, is a warren of whitewashed buildings and red tile roofs, backdropped by rocky peaks and bounded by a five-mile palm-fringed beach.

Ventura and San Luis Obispo represent two of California's most underrated towns. In addition to a wealthy heritage, Ventura possesses beautiful beaches and San Luis Obispo is set amid velvet hills and rich agricultural areas. Both are less expensive than elsewhere and offer many of the same features without the pretensions.

Offshore are the Channel Islands, a 25-million-year-old chain and vital wildlife preserve. Sandblasted by fierce storms, pristine in their magnificence, they are a china shop of endangered species and unique life forms. While the nearby reefs are headstones for the many ships that have crashed here, the surrounding waters are crowded with sea life.

Together with the rest of the coast, the islands were discovered by Juan Rodríguez Cabrillo in 1542. The noted explorer found them inhabited by Chumash Indians, a collection of tribes occupying the coast from Malibu to Morro Bay. Hunters and gatherers, the Chumash were master mariners who built woodplank canoes called *tomols*, capable of carrying ten people across treacherous waters to the Channel Islands. They in turn were preceded by the Oak Grove Tribes, which inhabited the region from 7000 to 3000 B.C.

Once Gaspar de Portolá opened the coast to Spanish colonialists with his 1769 explorations, few Indians from any California tribes survived. Forced into servitude and religious conversion by the padres, the Chumash revolted at Santa Barbara Mission and Mission de la Purísima Concepción in 1824. They held Purísima for a month before troops from Monterey overwhelmed them. By 1910 the Westerners who had come to save them had so decimated the Indians that their 30,000 population dwindled to 1250.

It took Cecil B. De Mille and over 1000 workers to build the set for the epic 1923 movie *The Ten Commandments* at Nipomo Sand Dunes.

By the mid 1800s these lately arrived white men set out in pursuit of any sea mammal whose pelt would fetch a price. The Central Coast was a prime whale-hunting ground. Harpooners by the hundreds speared leviathans, seals, and sea lions, hunting them practically to extinction. Earlier in the century American merchants, immortalized in Richard Henry Dana's *Two Years Before the Mast*, had combed the coast trading for cattle hides.

The land that bore witness to this colonial carnage endured. Today the Central Coast and its offshore islands abound in sea lions, harbor seals, Northern fur seals, and elephant seals. Whales inhabit the deeper waters and gamefish are plentiful. The only threats remaining are those from developers and the oil industry, whose offshore drilling resulted in the disastrous 1969 Santa Barbara spill.

The Central Coast traveler finds a Mediterranean climate, dry and hot in the summer, tempered by morning fog and winds off the ocean, then cool and rainy during winter months. Two highways, Routes 1 and 101, lead through this salubrious environment. The former hugs the coast much of the way, traveling inland to Lompoc and San Luis Obispo, and the latter, at times joining with Route 1 to form a single roadway, eventually diverges into the interior valleys.

Almost as much as the ocean, mountains play a vital part in the life of the coast. Along the southern stretches are the Santa Monica Mountains, which give way farther north to the Santa Ynez Mountains. Below them, stretching along the coastal plain, are the towns of Oxnard, Ventura, Santa Barbara, and Goleta.

Both mountain systems are part of the unique Transverse Range, which unlike most North American mountains, travels from east to west rather than north and south. They are California's Great Divide, a point of demarcation between the chic, polished regions near Santa Barbara and the rough, wild territory around San Luis Obispo.

Arriving at the ocean around Point Conception, the Transverse Range separates the curving pocket beaches of the south and the endless sand dunes to the north. Here the continent takes a sharp right turn as the beaches, facing south in Santa Barbara, wheel about to look west across the Pacific.

Amid this geologic turmoil lies Lompoc, the top flower seed producing area in the world, a region of agricultural beauty and color beyond belief, home to 40 percent of the United States' flower crop. To the north are the Nipomo Sand Dunes, extending 18 miles from Point Sal to Pismo Beach, one of the nation's largest dune systems. A habitat for the endangered California brown pelican and the California least tern,

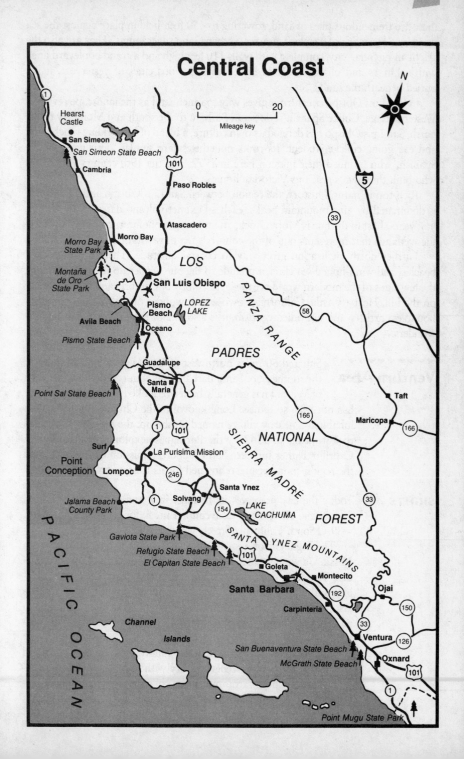

Central Coast

0   20
Mileage key

N

①

Hearst
Castle
● San Simeon
San Simeon State Beach
Cambria

101

Paso Robles

Atascadero

Morro Bay
State Park
Morro Bay
LOS
Montaña
de Oro
State Park
San Luis Obispo
PANZA RANGE
Pismo
Beach
LOPEZ
LAKE
Avila Beach
58
Oceano
Pismo State Beach
PADRES
Guadalupe
Point Sal State Beach
Santa
Maria
Taft
166
NATIONAL
Maricopa
166
Surf
101
①
La Purisima Mission
SIERRA
Point
Conception
Lompoc
246
MADRE
33
Jalama Beach
County Park
①
Solvang
Santa Ynez
154
LAKE
CACHUMA
FOREST
Gaviota State Park
SANTA YNEZ MOUNTAINS
Refugio State Beach
El Capitan State Beach
101
Goleta
Montecito
Ojai
Santa Barbara
192
150
Carpinteria
Channel
33
Ventura
Islands
126
San Buenaventura State Beach
Oxnard
McGrath State Beach
101
PACIFIC OCEAN
①
Point Mugu State Park

these are tremendous piles of sand, towering to 450 feet, held in place against the sea wind by a lacework of ice plant, grasses, verbena, and silver lupine. They are also the site of an Egyptian city, complete with walls 110 feet high and a grand boulevard lined with sphinxes and pharaohs. Today, like other glorious cities of yesteryear, it lies buried beneath the sand.

In San Luis Obispo oceanfront gives way to ranch land as the landscape reveals a Western visage. Unlike Spanish-style Santa Barbara to the south and Monterey to the north, San Luis Obispo has defined its own culture, a blend of hard-riding ranch hand and easygoing college student. Its roots nonetheless are similar, deriving from the Spanish, who founded their mission here in 1772, and the 19th-century Americans who built the town's gracious Victorian homes.

Rich too in natural history, the region between San Luis Obispo and Morro Bay is dominated by nine mountain peaks, each an extinct volcano dating back 20 million years. Last in the line is Morro Rock, an imposing monolith surrounded by a fertile wetlands that represents one of the country's ten most vital bird habitats.

Further north civilization gives way to coastal quietude. There are untracked beaches and wind-honed sea cliffs, a prelude to Big Sur further up the coast. Among the few signs of the modern world are the artist colony of Cambria and that big house on the hill, Hearst Castle, California's own eighth wonder of the world. Symbol of boundless artistry and unbridled egotism, it is also one of the Central Coast's many wonders.

▼▼▼▼▼▼▼▼▼▼

Ventura Area

Situated 60 miles northwest of Los Angeles and 30 miles to the southeast of Santa Barbara, the 18th-century mission town of Ventura has generally been overlooked by travelers. History has not been so remiss. Long known to the Chumash Indians, who inhabited a nearby village named Shisholop, the place was revealed to Europeans in 1542 by the Portuguese explorer Juan Rodríguez Cabrillo. Father Junípero Serra founded a mission here in 1782 and the region soon became renowned for its fruit orchards.

SIGHTS

Today the city preserves its heritage in a number of historic sites. Stop by the **Visitors and Convention Bureau** for brochures and maps. ~ 89-C South California Street, Ventura; 805-648-2075.

The highlight of a stroll through Ventura is **San Buenaventura Mission**, a whitewash and red tile church flanked by a flowering garden. The dark, deep chapel is lined with Stations of the Cross paintings and features a Romanesque altar adorned with statues and pilasters. My favorite spot is the adjacent garden with its tile fountain and stately Norfolk pines. Admission. ~ 211 East Main Street, Ventura; 805-643-4318.

Just down the street, the **Ventura County Museum of History and Art** traces the region's secular history with displays of Chumash Indian artifacts and a farm implement collection. The art gallery features revolving exhibits of local painters and photographers. There's a collection of 20,000 photos depicting Ventura County from its origin to the present. Closed Monday. ~ 100 East Main Street, Ventura; 805-653-0323.

Then stroll across to the **Albinger Archaeological Museum** and view an archaeological dig that dates back 3500 years. A small museum displays the arrowheads, shell beads, crucifixes, and pottery uncovered here. At the dig site itself you'll see the foundation of an 18th-century mission church, an ancient earth oven, and a remnant of the Spanish padres' elaborate aqueduct system. Closed Monday and Tuesday. ~ 113 East Main Street, Ventura; 805-648-5823.

Further along sits the **Ortega Adobe,** a small, squat home built in 1857. With its woodplank furniture and bare interior it provides a strong example of how hard and rudimentary life was in that early era. Closed Monday and Tuesday. ~ 215 West Main Street, Ventura; 805-648-5823.

Backtrack to San Buenaventura Mission and wander down **Figueroa Plaza,** a broad promenade decorated with tile fountains and flowerbeds. This is the site of the town's old Chinatown section, long since passed into myth and memory.

Figueroa Street continues to the waterfront, where a **promenade** parallels the beach. This is a prime area for water sports, and countless surfers, with their blond hair and black wetsuits, will be waiting offshore, poised for the perfect wave. Along the far end of the esplanade, at the **Ventura Pier,** you'll encounter one more Southern California species, the surf fisherman.

Another local wonder is the **Ventura County Courthouse,** a sprawling structure designed in Neo-Classical style. The place is a mélange of Doric columns, bronze fixtures, and Roman flourishes. But forget the marble entranceway and grand staircase, what makes it memorable is the row of friars' heads adorning the facade. Where else but in Southern California would a dozen baroque priests stare out at you from the hall of justice? ~ 501 Poli Street.

✔ CHECK THESE OUT—UNIQUE SIGHTS

- Overwhelm your senses with grandeur at **Hearst Castle,** the monumental estate of publishing magnate William Randolph Hearst. *page 378*
- Do the Danish thing in **Solvang,** where you can munch pastries amongst the windmills and peaked-roof buildings of this Scandinavian village. *page 364*
- Admire adobes as you stroll the 14-block **Red Tile Tour** in Santa Barbara, watching California history unfold with each step. *page 344*
- Look down on Shangri-La, otherwise known as the **Ojai Valley,** from the vantage point used in *Lost Horizon* while savoring fruit from local farmers. *page 338*

By contrast, the **Olivas Adobe** is a spacious hacienda surrounded by flowering gardens. This two-story gem, with balconies running the full length of the upper floor, is a study in the Monterey-style architecture of 19th-century California. The rooms are furnished in period pieces and there is a museum adjacent to the house, providing a window on the world of California's prosperous Spanish settlers. Open daily; tours are available on the weekends. ~ 4200 Olivas Park Drive, Ventura; 805-644-4346.

LODGING

For something spacious, plush, and formal consider the **Bella Maggiore Inn.** Set in downtown Ventura, this 28-room hostelry follows the tradition of an Italian inn. There are European appointments and antique chandeliers in the lobby and a Roman-style fountain in the courtyard. The accommodations I saw were painted in soft hues and decorated with pastel prints. The furniture was a mixture of cane, washed pine, and antiques. ~ 67 South California Street, Ventura; 805-652-0277. MODERATE TO ULTRA-DELUXE.

Up the hill, overlooking Ventura and the ocean, sits **La Mer European Bed & Breakfast.** The flags decorating the facade of this 1890 house illustrate the inn's international theme. Each of the five guest rooms is decorated after the fashion of a European country—England, Austria, Norway, Germany, and France. All with private baths and entrances, they vary from the Norwegian "Captain's Cove," decorated nautically, to the French "Madame Pompadour," with its bay window. ~ 411 Poli Street, Ventura; 805-643-3600. MODERATE TO ULTRA-DELUXE.

DINING

Up at the Fisherman's Wharf complex in Oxnard you'll find another low-priced eatery, the **Captain's Galley**, which offers breakfast dishes as well as hamburgers, sandwiches, and salads. ~ 3900 West Channel Islands Boulevard, Oxnard; 805-985-7754. BUDGET.

Joe Daddy's is housed in a 1914 Victorian home that's decorated in a New Orleans style. Specializing in Cajun cooking, this spot features great ribs and chicken from the oak barbecue, as well as gumbo,

RELIVING THE REAGAN YEARS

Outside Ventura in the suburban town of Simi Valley lies the **Ronald Reagan Presidential Library**. Here you'll find a visual history of Reagan's 1980s-era presidency in the form of film clips, videos, artifacts, and photos. There's a piece of the Berlin Wall, a re-creation of the White House cabinet room, a replica of the Oval Office, and, re-creating Reagan's earlier years, memorabilia from his boyhood and Hollywood career. Admission. ~ 40 Presidential Drive, Simi Valley; 805-522-8444.

crawfish, and blackened catfish. Closed Monday. ~ 211 East Santa
Clara Street, Ventura; 805-643-3264. MODERATE.

Or try **Eric Ericsson's Fish Company**, a small snuggery done in
casual California style. At lunch they could be serving fish chowder,
seafood pasta, poached shrimp, or fresh fish tacos. Then for dinner
they might charbroil mahimahi, salmon, swordfish, or sea bass, depending on the season. Located near the beach this understated
restaurant is a good place for fresh fish. ~ 668 Harbor Boulevard,
Ventura; 805-643-4783. MODERATE TO DELUXE.

Franky's Restaurant is a trip. The place resembles a mini-art gallery, decorated with paintings, mobiles, murals, and statuary. All the
artwork is for sale, so the decorative scheme is ever-changing. The
interior is liable to be adorned with marble busts and Modernist
canvases. Moving from palette to palate, the lunch menu contains
omelettes and salads, plus pita bread sandwiches and croissants
stuffed with chicken salad, shrimp, or tuna. Dinner is served Friday
and Saturday only; lunch is served seven days a week. ~ 456 East
Main Street, Ventura; 805-648-6282. BUDGET TO MODERATE.

If it's live blues you're after, check out **Joe Daddy's** on Friday or   **NIGHTLIFE**
Saturday nights. Cover. ~ 211 East Santa Clara Street, Ventura; 805-
643-3264.

Bombay Bar & Grill offers live entertainment nightly with a musical medley that changes frequently. The South Seas–style bar, with
overhead fans and oak-and-mirror decor, features piano plunkers,
while the room in back hosts live dance bands weekends only. Cover
on weekends. ~ 143 South California Street, Ventura; 805-643-4404.

Check out the dance scene at **The Metro**. There's live entertainment and deejay music ranging from disco to alternative. Cover
Wednesday through Sunday. ~ 317 East Main Street; 805-653-2882.

Scene of scenes in the seaside community of Ventura is the **Ventura
Theatre**, a refurbished movie house. With its intricate gold fixtures,
stained-glass windows, and ornamental molding, this 1928 structure
has been redone in grand style and converted into a restaurant/con-
cert hall. The club frequently draws top-name entertainers and offers a cultural mix that includes jazz, rock, reggae, and blues. Cover.
~ 26 South Chestnut Street, Ventura; 805-648-1936.

Vallanta de Cantina draws a Spanish-speaking crowd for salsa,
cumbia, and merengue dancing on the weekends. ~ 2485 East Main
Street, Ventura; 805-653-9194.

POINT MUGU STATE PARK 🏃🚴🐎🛶 This outstanding   **BEACHES
& PARKS**
facility extends along four miles of beachfront and reaches back six
miles into the Santa Monica Mountains. Much of the landscape is
characterized by hilly, chaparral-cloaked terrain. Vegetation is plentiful, and the campgrounds are very open. The beaches—which in-

clude **Sycamore Cove Beach, Thornhill Broome,** and **Point Mugu Beach**—are wide and sandy, with rocky outcroppings and a spectacular sand dune. To the interior, the park rises to 1266-foot Mugu Peak and to Tri-Peaks, 3010 feet in elevation. There are two large canyons as well as wide, forested valleys. Over 70 miles of hiking trails lace this diverse park. Facilities include picnic areas, restrooms, and lifeguards. Restaurants and groceries are within a few miles. Swimming and bodysurfing are popular but watch for rip currents. There is good surf a few miles south of the park at **County Line Beach.** ~ On Route 1 ten miles south of Oxnard. Information center at Sycamore Cove, 818-880-0350.

▲ There are three separate campgrounds in the park. At Sycamore Canyon there are 56 sites for tents and RVs (no hookups); $14 to $18 per night. Thornhill Broome Beach has 63 sites for tents and RVs (no hookups); $7 to $11 per night. And La Jolla Valley has 12 sites (hike-in only) and costs $3 per person per night. Reservations only; call DESTINET (800-444-7275).

MCGRATH STATE BEACH 🚲 ⚓ 🏊 ⛵ This long, narrow park extends for two miles along the water. The beach is broad and bounded by dunes. A lake and wildlife area attract over 200 bird species. The Santa Clara River, on the northern boundary, is home to tortoises, squirrels, muskrats, weasels, and other wildlife. Together the lake and preserve make it a great spot for camping or daytripping at the beach. There are restrooms, showers, and lifeguards. Restaurants and groceries are nearby in Ventura. Swimming and surfing is recommended for strong swimmers only; watch for rip currents. Day-use fee, $5. ~ 2211 Harbor Boulevard in Oxnard; 805-654-4610.

▲ There are 174 sites for tents and RVs (no hookups); $14 to $18 per night.

SAN BUENAVENTURA STATE BEACH 🚲 ⚓ 🏊 ⛵ In the world of urban parks this 114-acre facility ranks high. The broad sandy beach, bordered by dunes, extends for two miles to the Ventura pier. Since the pier is a short stroll from the city center, the beach provides a perfect escape hatch after you have toured the town. Facilities include picnic areas, restrooms, showers, dressing rooms, snack bar, lifeguards; groceries and restaurants nearby in Ventura. The breakwaters here provide excellent swimming. Surfing is popular at **Surfer's Point Park,** foot of Figueroa Street; and at **Peninsula Beach,** at the north end of Spinnaker Drive. Fishing from the 1700-foot pier is good, and anglers may catch bass, shark, surf perch, corbina, and halibut. The nearby rock jetties are a haven for crabs and mussels. Day-use fee, $5. ~ Located along Harbor Boulevard southeast of the Ventura Pier in Ventura; 805-654-4610.

EMMA WOOD STATE BEACH 🚶 🚲 ⚓ 🏊 ⛵ Sandwiched between the ocean and the Southern Pacific railroad tracks, this slender park measures only 116 acres. The beach consists almost entirely of rocks, making it undesirable for swimmers and sunbathers. There is a marsh at one end inhabited by songbirds and small mammals. Considering the fabulous beaches hereabouts, I rank this one pretty low. Restrooms are available and groceries are nearby in Ventura. Cabezon, perch, bass, and corbina are caught here. Day-use fee, $5. ~ Located on the northwest boundary of Ventura just off Route 101; 805-654-4610.

▲ There's camping nearby along the small, rocky beaches north of Emma Wood State Beach at three different campgrounds. **Emma Wood–North Beach** has 61 sites for tents and RVs (no hookups); $12 per night; for information, call 805-654-4610. **Faria County Park** is a bit smaller with 42 sites for tents and RVs (no hookups); $13 to $16 per night. **Hobson County Park** is smaller still with 31 sites for tents and RVs (no hookups); $13 to $16 per night. For information on the latter two parks, call 805-654-3951.

Ojai Area

To Chumash Indians the word ojai signified the nest. And to the generations of mystics, health aficionados, artists, and admirers who have settled here, the place is indeed a secluded abode. Geographically it resembles its Chumash namesake, nestling in a moon-shaped valley girded by the Topa and Sulphur Mountains.

A town of 7900 souls, Ojai is an artist colony crowded with galleries and studios. The site is also a haven for the health conscious, with spas and hot springs. To the metaphysically minded it is a center for several esoteric sects.

Ever since the 1870s, when author Charles Nordhoff publicized the place as a tourist spot, it has been popular with all sorts of visitors. The cultural life of the town focuses around an annual music festival that runs from May to October and ranges in style from classical to country-and-western to blues. For sport there is nearby Lake Casitas, Los Padres National Forest, 4500-foot mountains, and a network of hiking trails extending over 400 miles.

Inland just 14 miles from Ventura, Ojai is a valley so extraordinary it was used as the setting for Shangri-La in the movie *Lost Horizon* (1937). Sun-bronzed mountains rise in all directions, fields of wildflowers run to the verge of forested slopes, and everywhere there is tranquility, making it clear why the region is a magnet for mystics.

SIGHTS

Set on top of a hill overlooking Ojai Valley is the **Krotona Institute of Theosophy**. This 118-acre forested estate is a center for "students of Theosophy and the ancient wisdom." A spiritual-philosophical movement that developed early in the 20th century, Theosophy combines science with religion and draws from the classic philosopher Pythagoras. Visitors can tour the library, shop in the bookstore, and enjoy the grounds, which are beautifully landscaped. ~ 2 Krotona Hill, Ojai; 805-646-2653.

Another sect, the **Krishnamurti Foundation**, has an equally secluded library in the hills on the other side of town. ~ 1130 McAndrew Road, Ojai; 805-646-4948. At nearby **Meditation Mount**, where the grounds and meditation rooms are open daily, there are special meditative sessions to celebrate the full moon. ~ 10340 Reeves Road, Ojai; 805-646-5508.

Before venturing to these ethereal heights, stop off at the **Ojai Valley Chamber of Commerce**, which has maps and brochures of the area. ~ 150 West Ojai Avenue, Ojai; 805-646-8126. The 1917 Mission Revival **Post Office** is also downtown. ~ 201 East Ojai Avenue, Ojai. While you are there, visit the Spanish-style **City Hall**. ~ 401 South Ventura Street, Ojai; 805-646-5581.

To capture the spirit of Ojai, hike, bicycle, or drive the back roads and mountain lanes. **Grand Avenue loop** will carry you past orange orchards and horse ranches to the foot of the mountains. It leads along thick stone walls built by Chinese laborers during the 19th century. ~ Take Ojai Avenue, Route 150, east from town; turn left on Reeves Road, left again on McAndrew Road, left on Thatcher Road, and left on Carne Road. This returns to Route 150, completing the ten-mile loop.

East End drive follows Route 150 west past palm trees and farmhouses. Three miles from town, on a promontory with a stone bench inscribed "The Ojai Valley," is the overlook from which actor Ronald Colman gazed down on Shangri-La in *Lost Horizon*. With deep green orchards below and sharp gold mountains above, it truly evokes that fictional utopia.

Near Ojai, especially along Route 150 east of town and off Route 33 around Oakview, are farms where visitors can pick fresh fruits and vegetables—oranges, melons, pumpkins, nuts, grapefruit, lemons, peaches, and a host of other products.

HIDDEN ►

The path to the mountains surrounding town lies along Route 33. Leading north it passes rows of orchards and cuts into a narrow canyon before arriving at the luxurious spa at **Wheeler Hot Springs**. The private rooms here are pine-paneled affairs with skylights and hot and cold tubs. There are massage rooms, a spring-fed swimming pool, and a lodge housing a fine restaurant. ~ Route 33, six miles from Ojai; 805-646-8131.

The highway winds higher into the sun-scorched mountains past forests of pine and oak. Paralleling the Sespe River, Route 33 bisects rocky defiles and skirts 7500-foot Reyes Peak. For 60 miles the road tracks through the mountains until it meets Route 166, where the alternatives are heading east to the Central Valley or west toward the coastline.

Another Ojai sightseeing jaunt follows Route 150 west as it snakes down from the hills. The valleys are covered with scrub growth and small farms and the heights support lofty forests. The road skirts **Lake Casitas**, whose 60-mile shoreline is a labyrinth of coves and inlets. Ten miles from Ojai it joins Route 192, which leads to Santa Barbara. This meandering country road, in the hills above Carpinteria, traverses pretty pastureland. All around lies a quiltwork of orchards, fields, and tilled plots. Shade trees overhang the road and horses graze in the distance.

LODGING

The premier mountain resort hereabouts is **Ojai Valley Inn**, a 200-acre retreat with tennis courts, two swimming pools, and 18-hole golf course. Set on a ridge top with spectacular mountain vistas, the complex has been refurbished and modernized. Rooms, which are on a full European plan, are quite spacious, imaginatively decorated, and share the resort's oh-so-incredible views. There is an ample lobby for lounging plus such amenities as a croquet court, putting green, hiking trails, and dining room. ~ Country Club Road, Ojai; 805-646-5511, 800-422-6524, fax 805-646-7969. ULTRA-DELUXE.

For less lavish accommodations consider **Ojai Rancho Motel**. It's an 18-unit affair with large, attractive rooms, paneled entirely in knotty cedar and carpeted wall-to-wall. Some rooms have fireplaces and some are equipped with kitchenettes; all have refrigerators, microwaves, and coffeemakers. Guests can use the pool, jacuzzi, and sauna. ~ 615 West Ojai Avenue, Ojai; 805-646-1434. MODERATE TO DELUXE.

For bed-and-breakfast accommodations try **Ojai Manor Hotel**, set in a vintage 1874 schoolhouse. The facility contains six rooms; a typical guest room is small but attractively decorated with throw rugs across the softwood floor and a wrought-iron bed. Guests share bathrooms and can use the living room, porch, and side yard. ~ 210 East Matilija Street, Ojai; 805-646-0961. MODERATE TO DELUXE.

Because of its surrounding mountains Ojai is extremely popular with the health conscious. One of the region's leading resorts, **The**

◆◆◆

✔ CHECK THESE OUT—UNIQUE LODGING

- *Budget:* Score a room with a kitchen at **La Casa del Sol**, where you'll be close to Carpinteria's classic beach. *page 348*
- *Moderate to deluxe:* Hide away at the rustic **Cambria Pines Lodge**, where the lobby's stone fireplace will keep you warm on chilly nights. *page 379*
- *Moderate to ultra-deluxe:* Tell your friends you stayed at the **Madonna Inn**, a famous roadside spectacle that's been doing its thing longer than the Material Girl. *page 372*
- *Ultra-deluxe:* Relax at the **Ojai Valley Inn**, where you can enjoy golf, hiking, croquet—and panoramic ridgetop views. *page 339*

Budget: under $50 Moderate: $50–$90 Deluxe: $90–$120 Ultra-deluxe: over $120

Oaks at Ojai, caters to this interest. It provides a full menu of physical activity including aerobic exercise, weight training, yoga classes, body conditioning, and massage. Guests take all their meals—low-calorie vegetarian, fish, or poultry plates—at the resort. The accommodations include comfortable, spacious rooms in the lodge and in multiunit cottages. Included in the tab are three meals, fitness classes, and use of the pool, saunas, jacuzzi, and other health facilities. ~ 122 East Ojai Avenue, Ojai; 805-646-5573. ULTRA-DELUXE.

DINING Everyone's favorite Ojai restaurant is the **Ranch House**. Little wonder since this dining terrace rests in a tranquil garden surrounded by ferns, bamboo, and rose bushes. A flowering hedge shelters one side while a statue of Buddha gazes out from the other. Nearby, a graceful footbridge curves across a koi pond. Dinner includes Indonesian-style beef, Boston scrod, flaked crab, and veal in cream sauce. Desserts come from the restaurant's bakery, as do the three varieties of bread served with each meal. At lunch they feature those same delicious baked goods, plus Greek dolmas, spanakopita, and chicken in coconut milk. Open Wednesday through Sunday for dinner (two seatings on Saturday, four on Sunday). A must. Lunch is served from May through September. ~ South Lomita Avenue, Ojai; 805-646-2360. DELUXE TO ULTRA-DELUXE.

For fine French-Belgian dining **L'Auberge**, a venerable old house replete with brick fireplace and chandeliers, sets the tone. You can also dine on the terrace, choosing from a menu that includes scampi, frogs' legs, poached sole, tournedos, pepper steak, sweetbreads, and duckling in orange sauce. Lunch is on weekends only and features almost a dozen different crêpes. ~ 314 El Paseo Road, Ojai; 805-646-2288. MODERATE TO DELUXE.

Healthful dishes at moderate prices could well be the slogan at **Roger Keller's Restaurant**. Here you can dine on fresh soups, salads, a fish of the day selection, pasta dishes, and fresh-baked bread. Or if you'd prefer to let your culinary desires run wild they also feature hamburgers, espresso, and a host of other sinful offerings. ~ 331 East Ojai Avenue, Ojai; 805-646-7266. MODERATE.

HIDDEN ► If Ojai is a mountain hideaway then **The Restaurant at Wheeler Hot Springs** is a retreat from a retreat. Set creekside in the mountains above town, the century-old lodge features a stone fireplace surrounded by blond wood furniture and potted palms. The Mediterranean menu changes seasonally. Dinner in this intimate environment might start with appetizers such as a wild mushroom polenta made with fresh seasonal mushrooms, award-winning bouillabaisse, and Italian sea bass served in a pink peppercorn sauce over mashed potatoes. Dinner only, plus Saturday and Sunday brunch. Meal-and-hot-tub packages are available. ~ Route 33, six miles north of Ojai; 805-646-8131. MODERATE TO DELUXE.

The center of the shopping scene in the mountain resort town of Ojai   **SHOPPING**
is **Arcade Plaza,** a promenade between Ojai Avenue and Matilija
Street that extends from Montgomery Street to Signal Street. Within
this tile-roofed warren and along surrounding blocks are crafts
stores and galleries. Many are operated by the community of artisans which has grown over the years in Ojai.

An even more extensive collection of pottery is on display at the
Human Arts Gallery. There are also wallhangings, handblown glass
pieces, and handwrought jewelry items. ~ 310
East Ojai Avenue, Ojai; 805-646-1525.

The bookstore of bookstores is
Bart's Books, which is almost
entirely outdoors. Browsers
can soak up the sun, enjoy
mountain breezes, and
wander a maze of used
books. ~ 302 West Mati-
lija Street; 805-646-3755.

For women's fashions consider **Priscilla,** specializing in casual chic clothing for professional
women. ~ 320 East Ojai Avenue, Ojai; 805-646-
9782. For stylish fashions, visit the **Barbara Bow-
man** shops, owned by the well-known designer. ~
125 and 133 East Ojai Avenue, Ojai; 805-646-2970.

Quite a collection it is at **The Antique Collection:**
it seems that a number of dealers gathered together,
formed a collective, and combined their stock, filling an
entire warehouse with room after room of heirlooms. ~ 236 West
Ojai Avenue, Ojai; 805-646-6688.

An important gathering place for the spiritual movement in Ojai
is the **Heart of Light Bookstore** with its collection of mystical works,
crystals, and religious paraphernalia. ~ 451 East Ojai Avenue, Ojai;
805-646-3812.

For museum-quality traditional pottery, head east from town to
The Pottery. Otto Heino has been working in porcelain and stone-
ware for over 40 years. After browsing the showroom visitors can
wander the landscaped grounds viewing the carp pond, cactus garden, and peacocks. ~ 971 McAndrew Road, Ojai; 805-646-3393.

Further outside town, in a hilltop estate flanked by gardens, is
the **Beatrice Wood Studio,** a place that you absolutely must visit.
Beatrice Wood, whose autobiography is entitled *I Shock Myself*, is a
regional institution. Tremendously talented, she has been a potter for
six decades. Her work is more like sculpture than pottery. Pieces are
wrought as figurines of people and animals: vases feature forms in
bas-relief; pitchers are shaped as people, their arms pouring spouts;
couples are cast in bed or standing forlornly. Open by appointment
only. ~ 8560 Route 150, Ojai; 805-646-3381.

Up at the posh **Ojai Valley Inn** you can order a drink, relax, and enjoy   **NIGHTLIFE**
a mountain view from The Club. ~ Country Club Drive, Ojai; 805-
646-5511.

Deer Lodge Tavern & Restaurant, a jukebox-and-pool-table bar,
has dancing to rhythm-and-blues and rock bands every Friday and
Saturday. ~ 2261 Route 33, Ojai; 805-646-4256.

PARKS

LAKE CASITAS RECREATION AREA 🚶🚲🚤🐟⛵ This is a 6200-acre park surrounded by forested slopes and featuring a many-fingered lake. No swimming is permitted since Casitas is a reservoir, but fishing and boating are encouraged. Outlying mountains and the proximity of Ojai make it a particularly popular locale. Facilities include picnic areas, restrooms, showers, snack bar, bait and tackle shop, and grocery store. For bike rentals and boat rentals, call 805-649-2043. Bass, trout, and channel catfish are caught in these waters. Day-use fee, $5. ~ 11311 Santa Ana Road about ten miles east of Ventura; 805-649-2233.

▲ There are 450 sites in total, 140 with hookups. Camping costs $18 with hookups, $12 without.

▼▼▼▼▼▼▼▼▼▼▼▼▼▼

Santa Barbara Area

From Ventura, Route 101 speeds north and west to Santa Barbara. For a slow-paced tour of the shoreline, take the Old Pacific Coast Highway instead. Paralleling the freeway and the Southern Pacific Railroad tracks, it rests on a narrow shelf between sharply rising hills and the ocean. The road glides for miles along sandy beaches and rocky shoreline, passing the woodframe communities of Solimar Beach and Seacliff Beach.

Past this last enclave the old road ends as you join Route 101 once more. With the Santa Ynez Mountains looming on one side and the Pacific extending along the other, you'll pass the resort town of Carpinteria. The temperature might be 80 with a blazing sun overhead and a soft breeze off the ocean. Certainly the furthest thing from your mind is the North Pole, but there it is, just past Carpinteria—the turnoff for Santa Claus Lane.

SIGHTS

Santa Claus Lane? It's a block-long stretch of trinket shops and toy stores with a single theme. A giant rooftop Santa Claus with a waistline measuring maybe 30 feet oversees the New England–style village. It's one of those places that's so tacky you feel like you've missed something if you pass it by. If nothing else, you can mail an early Christmas card. Just drop it in the mailbox at **Toyland** and it will be postmarked (ready for this?) "Santa Claus, California." ~ 3821 Santa Claus Lane, Carpinteria; 805-684-3515.

Tucked between a curving bay and the Santa Ynez Mountains lies one of the prettiest places in all California. It's little wonder that the Spanish who settled **Santa Barbara**, establishing a presidio in 1782 and a mission several years later, called it *la tierra adorada*, the beloved land.

Discovered by a Portuguese navigator in 1542, it was an important center of Spanish culture until the Americans seized California in the 19th century. The town these Anglo interlopers built was an early-20th-century community. But a monstrous earthquake leveled

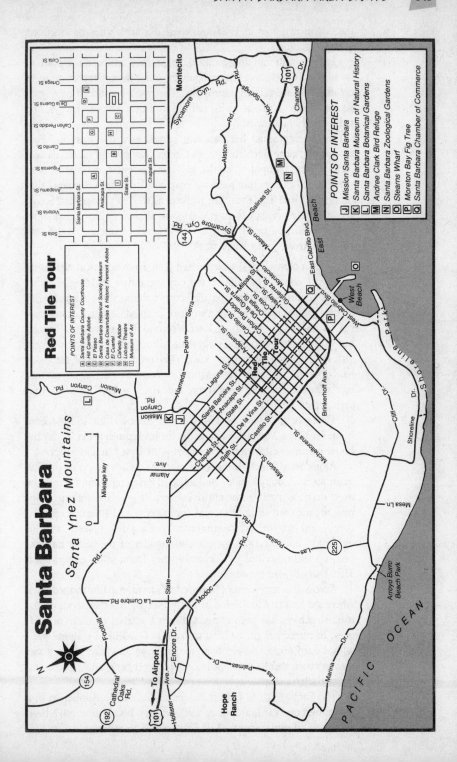

Santa Barbara

Santa Ynez Mountains

Montecito

Red Tile Tour

POINTS OF INTEREST

- Ⓐ Santa Barbara County Courthouse
- Ⓑ Hill-Carrillo Adobe
- Ⓒ El Paseo
- Ⓓ Santa Barbara Historical Society Museum
- Ⓔ Casa de Covarrubias & Historic Fremont Adobe
- Ⓕ El Cuartel
- Ⓖ Cañedo Adobe
- Ⓗ Lobero Theatre
- Ⓘ Museum of Art

POINTS OF INTEREST

- Ⓙ Mission Santa Barbara
- Ⓚ Santa Barbara Museum of Natural History
- Ⓛ Santa Barbara Botanical Gardens
- Ⓜ Andree Clark Bird Refuge
- Ⓝ Santa Barbara Zoological Gardens
- Ⓞ Stearns Wharf
- Ⓟ Moreton Bay Fig Tree
- Ⓠ Santa Barbara Chamber of Commerce

Hope Ranch

To Airport

Mileage key

0   1

PACIFIC OCEAN

the downtown area in 1925 and created a *tabla rasa* for architects and city planners.

Faced with rebuilding Santa Barbara, they returned the place to its historic roots, combining Spanish and Mission architecture to create a Mediterranean metropolis. The result is modern day Santa Barbara with its adobe walls, red tile roofs, rounded archways, and palm-lined boulevards.

Sightseeing Santa Barbara is as simple as it is rewarding. First stop at the **Santa Barbara Visitors Center**. The myriad materials here include more pamphlets, books, and booklets than you ever want to see. The most important piece is a map entitled "Santa Barbara" that outlines a "Red Tile Tour" for walkers as well as a lengthier "Scenic Drive." Together they form two concentric circles along the perimeters of which lie nearly all the city's points of interest. ~ 1 Santa Barbara Street, Santa Barbara; 805-965-3021.

RED TILE TOUR The 14-block **Red Tile Tour** begins at the **Santa Barbara County Courthouse**, the city's grandest building. This U-shaped Spanish–Moorish "palace" covers almost three sides of a city block. The interior is a masterwork of beamed ceilings, arched corridors, and palacio tile floors. On the second floor of this 1929 courthouse are murals depicting California history. The highlight of every visit is the sweeping view of Santa Barbara at the top of the clock tower. From the Santa Ynez Mountains down to the ocean all that meets the eye are palm trees and red tile roofs. ~ 1100 block of Anacapa Street; 805-962-6464.

Two blocks down, the **Hill Carrillo Adobe** is an 1826-vintage home built by a Massachusetts settler for his Spanish bride. Today the house is furnished with period pieces. ~ 11 East Carrillo Street.

Along State Street, the heart of Santa Barbara's shopping district, many stores occupy antique buildings. **El Paseo** represents one of the most original malls in the entire country. It is a labyrinthine shopping arcade consisting of several complexes. ~ 814 State Street. Incorporated into the architectural motif is **Casa de la Guerra**, a splendid house built in 1827 for the commander of the Santa Barbara presidio and described by Richard Henry Dana in his classic book *Two Years Before the Mast*.

Across the street rests **Plaza de la Guerra**, a palm-fringed park where the first city hall stood in 1875. Nearby, another series of historic structures has been converted into a warren of shops and offices. In the center of the mall is **Presidio Gardens**, a tranquil park with a carp pond and elephant-shaped fountains that spray water through their trunks. ~ On de la Guerra Street between Anacapa and Santa Barbara streets.

The **Santiago de la Guerra Adobe** and the **Lugo Adobe**, set in a charming courtyard, are other 19th-century homes that have been converted to private use. ~ 110 East de la Guerra Street.

The **Santa Barbara Historical Museum** certainly looks its part. Set in an adobe building with tile roof and wrought-iron window bars, the facility sits behind heavy wooden doors. Within are fine art displays and a series depicting the Spanish, Mexican, and early American periods of Santa Barbara's history, including memorabilia from author Richard Henry Dana's visits. There is a pleasant courtyard in back with a fountain and shade trees, a perfect place for a sightseer's siesta. ~ 136 East de la Guerra Street; 805-966-1601.

A right turn on Santa Barbara Street carries you to **Casa de Covarrubias**. Most places in town are a little too neatly refurbished to provide a dusty sense of history. But this L-shaped house, and the adjacent **Historic Fremont Adobe,** are sufficiently wind-blasted to evoke the early 19th century. The former structure, dating to 1817, is said to be the site of the last Mexican assembly in 1846; the latter became headquarters for Colonel John C. Fremont after Americans captured the town later that year. ~ 715 Santa Barbara Street.

Turn back along Santa Barbara Street and pass the **Rochin Adobe**. This 1856 adobe, now covered with clapboard siding, is a private home. ~ 820 Santa Barbara Street.

It's a few steps over to **El Presidio de Santa Barbara State Historic Park**, which occupies both sides of the street and incorporates some of the city's earliest buildings. Founded in 1782, the Presidio was one of four military fortresses built by the Spanish in California. Protecting settlers and missionaries from Indians, it also served as a seat of government and center of Western culture. Today only two original buildings survive. **El Cuartel**, the guards' house, served as the soldiers' quarters. The **Canedo Adobe**, also built as a military residence, is now the offices of the Santa Barbara Trust for Historic Preservation. Most interesting of all is the **Santa Barbara Presidio Chapel**, which re-creates an early Spanish church in its full array of colors. Compared to the plain exterior, the interior is a shock to the eye. Everything is done in red and yellow ochre and dark blue. The altar is painted to simulate a great cathedral. Drapes and columns, difficult to obtain during Spanish days, have been drawn onto the walls. Even the altar railing is painted to imitate colored marble. ~ 123 East Cañon Perdido Street; 805-966-9719. The last stop on this walking tour will carry you a step closer to the present. The **Lobero Theatre** was constructed in 1924. It is a three-tiered design that ascends to a 70-foot-high stage house. The original Lobero dates back to 1872, Santa Barbara's first theater. ~ 33 East Cañon Perdido Street; 805-963-0761.

SCENIC DRIVE The **Scenic Drive** around Santa Barbara, a 21-mile circular tour, incorporates several of the sites covered along the Red Tile Tour. To avoid repetition begin at the **Santa Barbara Museum of Art** with its collection of American paintings, Asian art, and classical sculpture. Admission. ~ 1130 State Street; 805-963-4364.

Then head up to **Mission Santa Barbara**, which sits on a knoll overlooking the city. Founded in 1786 and restored in 1820, this twin-towered beauty, known as the "Queen of the Missions," follows a design from an ancient Roman architecture book. The interior courtyard is a colonnaded affair with a central fountain and graceful flower garden. The chapel itself is quite impressive with a row of wrought-iron chandeliers leading to a multicolored altar. There are also museum displays representing the original Indian population and early-19th-century mission artifacts. Also visit the Mission Cemetery, a placid and pretty spot where frontier families and about 4000 Chumash Indians are buried in the shade of a Moreton Bay fig tree. Mission Santa Barbara is the only California mission that has been continuously used by Franciscan fathers throughout its 200-year history. Admission. ~ 2201 Laguna Street; 805-682-4713.

Farther uphill at the **Santa Barbara Museum of Natural History** are successive rooms devoted to marine, plant, vertebrate, and insect life. Excellent for kids, it also features small exhibits of Indian tribes from throughout the United States. You'll recognize the museum by the 72-foot skeleton of a blue whale out front. There is also a planetarium with a space lab. Admission. ~ 2559 Puesta del Sol Road; 805-682-4711.

HIDDEN ►   Nearby Mission Canyon Road continues into the hills for close-up views of the rocky Santa Ynez Mountains and a tour of **Santa Barbara Botanic Garden**. The five and one-half miles of trails here wind past a desert section carpeted with cactus and a meadow filled with wildflowers. Near the top of the park, beyond the ancient Indian trail, where the forest edges down from the mountains, is a stand of cool, lofty redwood trees. Admission. ~ 1212 Mission Canyon Road; 805-682-4726.

Backtrack to Alameda Padre Serra and cruise this elite roadway past million-dollar homes with million-dollar views. From this thoroughfare a series of side roads leads through the exclusive bedroom community of **Montecito**. Here a variety of architectural styles combine to create a luxurious neighborhood. After exploring the town's shady groves and manicured lawns, you can pick up **Channel Drive**, a spectacular street that skirts beaches and bluffs as it loops back toward Santa Barbara.

From this curving roadway you'll spy oddly shaped structures offshore. Looking like a line of battleships ready to attack Santa Barbara, they are in fact **oil derricks**. Despite protests from environmentalists and a disastrous 1969 oil spill, these coastal waters have been the site of drilling operations for decades. Those hazy humps further out past the wells are the **Channel Islands**.

The **Andree Clark Bird Refuge** is a placid lagoon filled with geese and other freshwater fowl. There are three tree-tufted islands in the center and a trail around the park. ~ 1400 East Cabrillo Boulevard;

805-564-5437. Upstaging all this is the adjacent **Santa Barbara Zoological Gardens** with its miniature train ride and population of monkeys, lions, elephants, giraffes, and exotic birds. Admission. ~ 500 Niños Drive; 805-962-5339.

Cabrillo Boulevard hugs the shore as it tracks past **East Beach**, Santa Barbara's longest, prettiest strand. With its rows of palm trees, grassy acres, and sunbathing crowds, it's an enchanting spot.

For a taste of sea air and salt spray walk out along **Stearns Wharf**. From the end of this wooden pier you can gaze back at Santa Barbara, realizing how aptly author Richard Henry Dana described the place: "The town is finely situated, with a bay in front, and an amphitheater of hills behind." Favored by local anglers, the wharf is also noted for the **Sea Center**, a marine museum with an aquarium, underwater photographs, computerized learning center, a 37-foot replica of a gray whale and calf, and a touch tank filled with local marine life. Admission. ~ At the foot of State Street, 211 Stearns Wharf; 805-962-0885.

The **Moreton Bay Fig Tree**, another local landmark, is a century-old giant with branches that spread 160 feet. This magnificent specimen stands as the largest tree of its kind in the United States. ~ Chapala and Montecito streets.   ◄ *HIDDEN*

Back along the waterfront, Cabrillo Boulevard continues to the **Yacht Harbor** where 1200 pleasure boats, some worth more than homes, lie moored. The walkway leads past yawls, ketches, sloops, and fishing boats to a breakwater. From here you can survey the fleet and take in the surrounding mountains and ocean. ~ West Cabrillo Boulevard and Castillo Street.

To continue this seafront excursion, follow Shoreline, Cliff, and Marina drives as they parallel the Pacific, past headlands and beaches, en route to **Hope Ranch**. Santa Barbara is flanked by two posh communities: Montecito in the east and this elite enclave to the west. It's a world of country clubs and cocktail parties, where money and nature meet to create forested estates.

If you tire of walking, remember that Stearns Wharf is the departure point for the Santa Barbara Trolley, an old-fashioned vehicle that carries visitors along the waterfront, through the downtown area, and out to the mission. ~ 805-965-0353.

NORTH OF SANTA BARBARA Route 101 streams northwest past a series of suburban communities, including Goleta and Isla Vista, where the **University of California—Santa Barbara** is located. Cutting a swath between mountains and ocean, the road passes a series of attractive beach parks, then turns inland toward the mountains and interior valleys. ~ 805-893-8000.

About 35 miles from Santa Barbara Routes 101 and 1 diverge. For a rural drive past white barns and meandering creeks, follow **Route 1**. En route to Lompoc it passes farmlands, pastures, and rolling hills. About five miles south of Lompoc, you can follow

HIDDEN ▶   **Jalama Road,** a country lane that cuts through sharp canyons and graceful valleys on a winding 15-mile course to the ocean, ending at a beach park.

This journey becomes a pilgrimage when Route 1 approaches **La Purísima Mission.** The best restored of all 21 California missions, this historic site has an eerie way of projecting you back to Spanish days. There's the mayordomo's abode with the table set and a pan on the oven, or the mission store, its barrels overflowing with corn and beans. The entire mission complex, from the sanctified church to the tallow vats where slaughtered cattle were rendered into soap, is re-created. Founded nearby in 1787, the mission was re-established at this site in 1813. Today you can tour the living quarters of priests and soldiers, the workshops where weaving, leathermaking, and carpentry were practiced, and the mission's original water system. Admission. ~ 2295 Purisima Road, Lompoc; 805-733-3713.

In spring and summer the hills around **Lompoc** dazzle with thousands of acres of cultivated flowers. The countryside is a rainbow of color throughout the season. Then in fall fields of poppies, nasturtiums, and larkspurs bloom.

LODGING   South of Santa Barbara in Carpinteria, the **Eugenia Motel** has ten rooms (four with kitchens). Each is small, carpeted, and clean. The furniture is comfortable though nicked. The baths have stall showers. ~ 5277 Carpinteria Avenue, Carpinteria; 805-684-4416. BUDGET TO MODERATE.

Because of its excellent beach, Carpinteria is very popular with families. Many spend their entire vacation here, so most facilities rent by the week or month. Among the less expensive spots for overnighters is **La Casa del Sol Motel.** This multiunit complex has 211 rooms (including eight with kitchens). The one I saw was paneled in knotty pine and trimly furnished. Small pool. ~ 5585 Carpinteria Avenue, Carpinteria; 805-684-4307. BUDGET.

To provide an idea of the full range of accommodations available in the Santa Barbara area there are two centralized reservation agencies in town. One is **Accommodations in Santa Barbara.** ~ 1 Santa Barbara Street, Santa Barbara; 805-687-9191. **Santa Barbara Hotspots** can also give information on prices and availability. ~ 36 State Street, Santa Barbara; 805-564-1637. Since room rates in Santa Barbara fluctuate by season and day of the week, it's advisable to check.

For modest-priced accommodations within a block or two of the beach, check out **Cabrillo Boulevard.** This artery skirts the shoreline for several miles. Establishments lining the boulevard are usually a little higher in price. But along the side streets leading from Cabrillo are numerous generic motels.

From these you can generally expect rooms that are small but tidy and clean. The wall-to-wall carpeting is industrial grade, the fur-

niture consists of naugahyde chairs and formica tables, and the artworks make you appreciate minimalism. There's usually a swimming
pool and surrounding terrace, plus a wall of ice machines and soda
dispensers. There are two such places located a block from Santa
Barbara's best all-around beach. **Pacific Crest Motel** has 26 units
renting at affordable prices. ~ 433 Corona del Mar Drive, Santa Barbara; 805-966-3103, fax 805-568-0673. BUDGET TO MODERATE.
Next door, that generic facility, **Motel 6**, has 51 rooms. ~ 443 Corona
del Mar Drive, Santa Barbara; 805-564-1392, 800-466-8356, fax
805-963-4687. BUDGET TO MODERATE.

Over in the West Beach area, **Beach House Inn** has 12 units located two blocks from the beach. Rooms here are larger than usual
and most have kitchens, but there's no pool. ~ 320 West Yanonali
Street, Santa Barbara; 805-966-1126. MODERATE TO DELUXE.

L-Rancho Motel, a block farther away, has 23 units. Ask for a
room with a kitchen. No pool. No reservations; it's on a first-come,
first-served basis. ~ 316 West Montecito Street, Santa Barbara; 805-
962-0181. BUDGET TO MODERATE.

For chic surroundings there is **Villa Rosa**. Built during the 1930s
in Spanish palazzo fashion, it was originally an apartment house.
Today it is an 18-room inn with raw wood furnishings, pastel walls,
and private baths. There's a pool and spa in the courtyard. Guests
co-mingle over continental breakfast and afternoon wine and cheese,
then settle into plump armchairs around a tile fireplace with port and
sherry in the evening. The spacious rooms, some with fireplaces, are
pleasantly understated and located half a block from the beach. ~ 15
Chapala Street, Santa Barbara; 805-966-0851, fax 805-962-7159.
DELUXE TO ULTRA-DELUXE.

The **California Hotel** has one thing going for it: location. It sits
on the main street in Santa Barbara just a block from the beach. The
hotel is in a blocky, four-story building with a restaurant and bar
downstairs. Popular with Europeans; the rooms are trimly appointed.
If you can get an oceanside room on the fourth floor it could be
worth it, otherwise keep on reading. ~ 35 State Street, Santa Barbara;
805-966-7153, fax 805-962-9781. MODERATE.

The **Eagle Inn** is an attractive Mediterranean-style apartment
house converted into a 23-room hotel. Just two blocks from the beach,
most of the rooms are studio units with living rooms, some with
kitchens. Check out the room with the cheerful sunflower theme. ~
232 Natoma Avenue, Santa Barbara; 805-965-3586, 800-767-0030,
fax 805-966-1218. MODERATE TO DELUXE.

Small and intimate as bed and breakfasts tend to be, the **Simpson
House Inn** is even more so. Close to downtown, it resides along a
quiet tree-lined block secluded in an acre of English gardens complete with fountains and intimate sitting areas. The century-old
Victorian inn features 14 guest rooms, restored-barn suites, and gar-

den cottages—all decorated with antiques, fine art, and English lace. Some feature private decks or patios, fireplaces, and jacuzzis. A gourmet breakfast is served on the veranda or to private patios or rooms; beverages are served in the afternoon, and hors d'oeuvres and wine are provided in the evening. Bikes and croquet complete the package. ~ 121 East Arrellaga Street, Santa Barbara; 805-963-7067. ULTRA-DELUXE.

The **Old Yacht Club Inn** is two inns in one. The main facility is a 1912 California Craftsman–style house with five rooms. There's a parlor with piano downstairs and a decorative motif throughout that brings back cheery memories of grandmother's house. Next door, in a 1927 vintage stucco, are four guest rooms with private baths tabbed deluxe. Each has been decorated by a different family and features their personal photographs and other heirlooms. The inn is just one block from East Beach, serves a full breakfast and provides bikes, beach chairs, and towels to guests. Three Saturdays a month, owner Nancy Donaldson offers an elegantly prepared five-course gourmet dinner to guests. The Inn books far in advance on these nights, but it's well worth the wait. ~ 431 Corona del Mar Drive, Santa Barbara; 805-962-1277, 800-549-1676, fax 805-962-3989. DELUXE TO ULTRA-DELUXE.

The **Glenborough Inn** is laid out in similar fashion. The main house is a 1906 California Craftsman design with extensive wood detailing and period furniture. A suite in the main house is decorated in turn-of-the-century nouveau style with a fireplace, private entrance, garden, patio, and bath. The second house is an 1880-era cottage with rooms and suites enjoying private baths. The theme in both abodes is romance. The rooms are beautifully fashioned with embroidered curtains, inlaid French furniture, canopied beds, crocheted coverlets, and needlepoint pieces. There's a garden and three hot tubs at the main house and a patio beside the cottage. Guests enjoy a gourmet breakfast brought to their door and afternoon hors d'oeuvres; they also share a cozy living room with tile fireplace. ~ 1327 Bath Street, Santa Barbara; 805-966-0589, 800-966-0589, fax 805-564-8610. DELUXE TO ULTRA-DELUXE.

Down the road at the **Bath Street Inn** you'll encounter a Queen Anne Victorian constructed in 1890. It's an attractive house with an equally charming hostess, Susan Brown. Enter along a garden walkway into a warm living room with marble-trimmed fireplace. The patio in back is set in another garden. Rooms on the second floor feature the hardwood floors and patterned wallpaper which are the hallmarks of California bed and breakfasts. The third floor has a cozy sloped-roof and a television lounge for guests. Rooms include private baths, breakfast, and evening refreshments. ~ 1720 Bath Street, Santa Barbara; 805-682-9680, 800-341-2284, fax 805-569-1281. DELUXE TO ULTRA-DELUXE.

Personally, I prefer the **Upham Hotel**, "the oldest cosmopolitan hotel in continuous operation in Southern California." Established in 1871, it shares a sense of history with the country inns, but enjoys the lobby and restaurant amenities of a hotel. Victorian in style, the two-story clapboard is marked by sweeping verandas and a cupola. While not as personalized as the bed-and-breakfast guest rooms, the accommodations are nicely appointed with hardwood and period furnishings. Around the landscaped grounds are garden cottages, some with private patios and fireplaces, and a carriage house with five Victorian-style rooms. Continental breakfast and afternoon wine and cheese are included. ~ 1404 De la Vina Street, Santa Barbara; 805-962-0058, 800-727-0876, fax 805-963-2825. DELUXE TO ULTRA-DELUXE.

John and Jackie Kennedy spent part of their honeymoon at San Ysidro Ranch.

Santa Barbara's two finest hotels dominate the town's two geographic locales, the ocean and the mountains. **Four Seasons Biltmore Hotel** is a grand old Spanish-style hotel set on spacious grounds beside the beach. It's the kind of place where guests play croquet or practice putting on manicured lawns, then meander over to the hotel's Coral Casino Beach and Cabaña Club. There are several dining rooms as well as tennis courts, swimming pools, and a complete spa. The refurbished rooms are quite large and have an airy feel heightened by white plantation shutters, light wood furnishings, and full marble baths. Many are located in multiplex cottages and are spotted around the magnificent grounds which have made the Biltmore one of California's most famous hotels since it opened back in 1927. ~ 1260 Channel Drive, Santa Barbara; 805-969-2261, 800-332-3442, fax 805-565-1602. ULTRA-DELUXE.

El Encanto sits back in the Santa Barbara hills and is a favorite hideaway among Hollywood stars. The hotel's 83 rooms are set in cottages and villas that dot this ten-acre retreat. The grounds are beautifully landscaped and feature a lily pond, tennis court, and swimming pool. The ocean views are simply spectacular. Rooms are very spacious with attached sitting rooms, plus extra features like room service, refrigerator, and terrycloth bathrobes. Some have private patios. The decor is French country with a lot of brass and etched-glass fixtures. ~ 1900 Lasuen Road, Santa Barbara; 805-687-5000, 800-346-7039, fax 805-687-3903. ULTRA-DELUXE.

The **Miramar Hotel-Resort** is billed as "the only hotel right on the beach" in the Santa Barbara area. Indeed there is 500 feet of beautiful beachfront. It also is right on noisy Route 101. Not to worry—the Miramar is still the best bargain around. Where else will you find dining facilities, room service, two swimming pools, tennis courts, health spa, and shuffleboard at desirable prices? Granted that will place you in a plainly appointed room closer to motor city than the beach, but you can be oceanfront for a deluxe price. Wherever you choose, you'll be in a lovely 15-acre resort inhabited by blue-roofed cottages and tropical foliage. ~ 1555 South Jameson Lane, Montecito; 805-969-2203, 800-322-6983, fax 805-969-3163. MODERATE TO DELUXE.

In the Santa Ynez foothills above Montecito sits another retreat where the rich and powerful mix with the merely talented. **San Ysidro Ranch** sprawls across 540 acres, most of which is wilderness traversed by hiking trails. There are tennis courts, pool, bocci ball court, complete fitness facilities, and a driving range. The grounds vie with the Santa Barbara Botanic Garden in the variety of plant life: there are meadows, mountain forests, and an orange grove. The Stonehouse Restaurant serves gourmet dishes and the complex also features sitting rooms and lounges. Privacy is the password: all these features are shared by guests occupying just 45 units. The accommodations are dotted around the property in cottages and small multiplexes. Rooms vary in decor, but even the simplest are trimly appointed and spacious with hardwood furnishings, wood-burning fireplaces, king-size beds, and a mountain, ocean, or garden view. ~ 900 San Ysidro Lane, Montecito; 805-969-5046, 800-368-6788, fax 805-565-1995. ULTRA-DELUXE.

DINING

At **The Palms** you cook your own steak or halibut dinner, or have them prepare a shrimp or scallop meal. A family-style restaurant with oak chairs and pseudo-Tiffany lamps, it hosts a salad bar and adjoining lounge. Dinner only. ~ 701 Linden Avenue, Carpinteria; 805-684-3811. BUDGET TO MODERATE.

A step upscale at **Clementine's Steak House** they feature filet mignon, fresh fish dishes, vegetarian casserole, steak teriyaki, and Danish-style liver. It's dinner only here, but the meal—which includes soup, salad, vegetable, starch dish, homemade bread, and pie—could hold you well into the next day. The interior has a beamed ceil-

✔ CHECK THESE OUT—UNIQUE DINING
- *Budget to moderate:* Linger over croissant and cappuccino at **Franky's Restaurant**, which is adorned with artwork galore. *page 335*
- *Moderate:* Savor the gastronomic delights at **Cafe del Sol**, where you can dine on lamb shanks and enchiladas. *page 354*
- *Deluxe:* Kick open the swinging saloon doors and sit down to a buffalo burger at **F. McLintock's Saloon & Dining House.** *page 373*
- *Deluxe to ultra-deluxe:* Find spiritual and culinary nirvana dining under Buddha's gaze on the eclectic offerings at Ojai's **Ranch House.** *page 340*

Budget: under $8   Moderate: $8–$16   Deluxe: $16–$24   Ultra-deluxe: over $24

ing and patterned wallpaper. Lean back in a captain's chair and enjoy some home-style cooking. Closed Monday. ~ 4631 Carpinteria Avenue, Carpinteria; 805-684-5119. MODERATE TO DELUXE.

For a scent of Santa Barbara salt air with your lunch or dinner, **Brophy Brothers Restaurant & Clam Bar** is the spot. Located out on the Breakwater, overlooking the marina, mountains, and open sea, it features a small dining room and patio. If you love seafood, it's heaven; if not, then fate has cast you in the wrong direction. The clam bar serves all manner of clam and oyster concoctions, and the restaurant is so committed to fresh fish they print a new menu daily to tell you what the boats brought in. When I was there the daily fare included fresh snapper, shark, scampi, salmon, sea bass, halibut, mahi-mahi, redfish, and butterfish. ~ 119 Harbor Way, Santa Barbara; 805-966-4418. MODERATE.

One of the more romantic restaurants in Santa Barbara is the **Wine Cask**, where you can dine outside in a lovely courtyard or indoors under the colorful hand-painted ceiling mural that dates from the 1920s. Among the innovative entrées are grilled pesto-stuffed swordfish and herb-crusted Colorado lamb loin, as well as chicken, beef and pastas. Appetizers are equally creative and tempting. ~ 813 Anacapa Street, Santa Barbara; 805-966-9463. MODERATE TO DELUXE.

Best of Santa Barbara's low-priced restaurants is **La Tolteca**. This tortilla factory contains an informal, self-order café serving delicious Mexican food. Almost everything is fresh, making it *the* place for tacos, tostadas, burritos, and enchiladas. You can sit at one of the few tables inside or out near the sidewalk. Early dinner only. ~ 614 East Haley Street, Santa Barbara; 805-963-0847. BUDGET.

Another south-of-the-border favorite is **La Super Rica**. The menu includes banana-leaf-wrapped tamales, *alambre de pechuga* (marinated chicken strips fried with peppers and onions on a warm tortilla), and chile rellenos. The homemade salsa is recommended. ~ 622 North Milpas Street, Santa Barbara; 805-963-4940. BUDGET.

Santa Barbara natives have been eating at **Joe's Café** for 60 years. Crowds line the coal-black bar, pile into the booths, and fill the tables. They come for a meat-and-potatoes lunch and dinner menu that stars prime rib. This is where you go for pork chops, lamb, and steak. The walls are loaded with mementos and faded photographs; softball trophies, deer antlers, and a buffalo head decorate the place; and the noise level is the same as the Indy 500. Paradise for slummers. ~ 536 State Street, Santa Barbara; 805-966-4638. MODERATE.

Santa Barbara Shellfish Company ain't fancy: just a takeout stand with a few picnic tables. But they serve fresh crab and shrimp cocktails, chowder, crab Louie, and hot seafood platters. Even better, they're located way out on Stearns Wharf where you can enjoy the open waterfront. ~ 230 Stearns Wharf, Santa Barbara; 805-963-4415. BUDGET TO MODERATE.

Downey's, a small, understated dining room, numbers among Santa Barbara's premiere restaurants. The dozen tables here are set amid peach-colored walls lined with local artwork. The food is renowned: specializing in California cuisine, Downey's has a menu that changes daily. A typical evening's entrées are salmon with forest mushrooms, lamb loin with grilled eggplant and chiles, sea bass with artichokes, duck with fresh papaya chutney, and scallops with tomato salsa. There is a good wine list featuring California vintages. Very highly recommended. Closed Monday. ~ 1305 State Street, Santa Barbara; 805-966-5006. DELUXE.

The graphics on the wall tell a story about the cuisine at **The Palace Café.** Portrayed are jazz musicians, catfish, redfish, and scenes from New Orleans. The message is Cajun and Creole, and this informal bistro is very good at delivering it. This restaurant prepares soft-shelled crab, blackened filet mignon, crawfish *étouffée,* and jambalaya. For dessert, honey, we have key lime pie and bread pudding soufflé. Dinner only. ~ 8 East Cota Street, Santa Barbara; 805-966-3133. MODERATE TO DELUXE.

If you prefer your bistros French, there's an excellent place a few doors up called **Mousse Odile.** Blue tablecloths and French art create an easy lunch ambience here. For dinner, out come the white and blue linens. Menu selections includes couscous, mushrooms on pastry shell, and veal in basil cream; lunch features *ficelles,* those foot-long Parisian sandwiches, as well as quiche and stuffed croissants. Even the breakfasts have a French flair. Modest but well managed, Mousse Odile is quite popular with local residents. Closed Sunday. ~ 18 East Cota Street, Santa Barbara; 805-962-5393. MODERATE TO DELUXE.

Hanging out in coffeehouses is my favorite avocation. There's no better spot in Santa Barbara than **Sojourner Coffeehouse.** Not only do they serve espresso and cappuccino, but lunch and dinner as well. Everyone seems to know everyone else in this easygoing café. They come to kibitz and enjoy the tostadas, rice-and-vegetable plates, and stuffed baked potatoes. The accent is vegetarian so expect daily specials like Szechuan peanut pasta or *spanakopita,* a Greek spinach and egg pastry. They also serve fresh fish and chicken dishes like African-style chicken with couscous. ~ 134 East Cañon Perdido, Santa Barbara; 805-965-7922. BUDGET TO MODERATE.

HIDDEN ► For truly prodigious breakfasts, locals know that the nondescript **Esau's** is *the* place. Pancakes, omelettes, homemade hash, and scrambles are nicely prepared and served in generous portions. If there's a queue (usually the case on weekends), look for a stool at the counter. ~ 403 State Street, Santa Barbara; 805-965-4416. BUDGET.

Cafe del Sol is the rarest of creatures, an upscale "Santa Barbara–style" restaurant. Enter this Cabo San Lucas–style eatery, where you'll find a tortilla deli/bar. Here you can sample tapas, Mexican appetizers, and margaritas. A large bank of windows allows dining room guests a view of the Andree Clark Bird Refuge while they dine on a menu varying from lamb shanks to enchiladas. ~ 30 Los Patos Way, Santa Barbara; 805-969-0448. MODERATE.

Dining at **El Encanto** is pleasurable not only for the fine California and French cuisine but the sweeping vistas as well. The restaurant resides in a hillside resort overlooking Santa Barbara. There's a luxurious dining room and a terrace for dining outdoors. Dinner is a gourmet experience. Changing weekly according to harvest and catch, the menu could include sautéed sea bass with a tarragon crust, roast tenderloin of beef with garlic mashed potatoes, or angelhair pasta with roasted garlic and organic red and yellow tomatoes. The appetizers and desserts are equally outrageous, as are the breakfast and lunch courses. ~ 1900 Lasuen Road, Santa Barbara; 805-687-5000. DELUXE TO ULTRA-DELUXE.

On the beach at Arroyo Burro Country Park is the **Brown Pelican**. It's a decent restaurant with great ocean views—what more need be said? Sandwiches, salads, hamburgers, and several fresh seafood and pasta dinners are served. Trimly appointed and fitted with a wall of plate glass, it looks out upon a sandy beach and tawny bluffs. ~ 2981 Cliff Drive, Santa Barbara; 805-687-4550. MODERATE TO DELUXE.

The **Stonehouse Restaurant**, located at the legendary San Ysidro Ranch, serves breakfast, lunch, dinner, and Sunday brunch with a classic American flavor. You can begin with barbecued duck tacos with tomatillo salsa, then indulge in the salmon or aged New York steak. Top off the meal with baked custard and fresh berries in a chocolate phyllo shell. ~ 900 San Ysidro Lane, Montecito; 805-969-5046. DELUXE.

SHOPPING

Since Santa Barbara's shops are clustered together, you can easily uncover the town's hottest items and best bargains by concentrating on a few key areas. The prime shopping center lies along State Street, particularly between the 600 and 1300 blocks. **Paseo Nuevo** is, literally, a new *paseo*—a mall, really, with department stores, chain shops and a few homegrown merchants lining a tastefully designed

SMALL CRAFT WARNING

For over 20 years Santa Barbara County artists and craftspeople have turned out for the **Arts & Crafts Show**. Every Sunday and holiday from 10 a.m. until dusk they line East Cabrillo Boulevard. The original artwork for sale includes paintings, graphics, sculptures, and drawings. Among the crafts are macrame, stained glass, woodwork, textiles, weaving, and jewelry. If you are in town on a Sunday make it a point to stop by.

Spanish-style pedestrian promenade. ~ On State Street between Ortega and Canon Perdido streets, Santa Barbara; 805-963-2202.

El Paseo, a famous promenade, is one of the most imaginative malls I've ever seen. It consists of a historic adobe house and surrounding buildings combined and converted into a succession of stores. This is a middle- and high-ticket complex: the art galleries, jewelry stores, and designer dress stores number among the best, but there are also curio shops and toy stores. ~ 814 State Street, Santa Barbara; 805-965-1616.

Pier 1 Imports looks like a Hong Kong warehouse. It's stuffed to the rafters with wickerware, glassware, scented candles, wood carvings, ethnic rugs, ceramics, and cotton fabrics. ~ 928 State Street, Santa Barbara; 805-965-0118.

La Arcada Court is another spiffy mall done in Spanish style. The shops, along the upper lengths of State Street, are more chic and contemporary than they are elsewhere. **Santa Barbara Baggage Company** (805-966-1669) sells luggage, handbags, wallets, business bags and gifts. ~ 1114 State Street, Santa Barbara.

A favorite Santa Barbara bookstore is **Earthling Bookshop**, a spacious store with a friendly staff and tasteful selection of hardbacks and paperbacks, as well as a full-blown coffeehouse within the store. Can you identify the literati on the café's mural wall? ~ 1137 State Street, Santa Barbara; 805-965-0926.

Antiques in Santa Barbara are spelled Brinkerhoff Avenue. This block-long residential street conceals a half-dozen antique shops. My favorite, **Carl Hightower Galerie**, is crowded with jewelry, ceramics, and everything else imaginable under the sun. ~ 528 Brinkerhoff Avenue, Santa Barbara; 805-965-5687.

Near the corner of State and Cota streets is the center for vintage clothing. **Yellowstone Clothing** features Hawaiian shirts and other old-time favorites. ~ 527 State Street, Santa Barbara; 805-963-9609. Also try **Pure Gold**, which has everything from early exotic to late lamented. ~ 625 State Street, Santa Barbara; 805-962-4613.

NIGHTLIFE The Palms features local rock-and-roll bands every Thursday, Friday, and Saturday night. There's a small dancefloor here for footloose revelers. ~ 701 Linden Avenue, Carpinteria; 805-684-3811.

The State Street strip in downtown Santa Barbara offers several party places. **Zelo**, a video nightclub, has dancing to DJ music. Cover. ~ 630 State Street, Santa Barbara; 805-966-5792.

Up at **Acapulco Restaurant**, in La Arcada Court, you can sip a margarita next to an antique wooden bar or out on the patio. Every Friday they feature live Spanish music. Cover on Friday only. ~ 1114 State Street, Santa Barbara; 805-963-3469.

If for no other reason than the view, **Harbor Restaurant** is a prime place for the evening. A plate-glass establishment, it sits out on a pier with the city skyline on one side and open ocean on the other. The bar upstairs features surf videos. ~ 210 Stearns Wharf, Santa Barbara; 805-963-3311.

For sunset views, nothing quite compares to **El Encanto Lounge**. Located in the posh El Encanto Hotel high in the Santa Barbara hills, it features a split-level terrace overlooking the city and ocean. ~ 1900 Lasuen Road, Santa Barbara; 805-687-5000.

You can also consider the **Lobero Theatre**, which presents dance, drama, concerts, and lectures. Closed Sunday. ~ 33 East Cañon Perdido Street, Santa Barbara; 805-963-0761.

Or head into the mountains about 27 miles outside Santa Barbara and catch a show at the **Circle Bar B Dinner Theater**. This well-known facility offers a menu of comedies, musicals, and light dramas. Open weekends only. ~ 1800 Refugio Road, 27 miles north of Santa Barbara; 805-965-9652.

Part of the gay scene in Santa Barbara is represented by **Gold Coast**, which features pinball, a pool table, and a small dancefloor. ~ 30 West Cota Street, Santa Barbara; 805-965-6701.

RINCON BEACH COUNTY PARK Wildly popular with nudists and surfers, this is a pretty white sand beach backed by bluffs. At the bottom of the wooden stairway leading down to the beach, take a right along the strand and head over to the seawall. There will often be a bevy of nude sunbathers snuggled here between the hillside and the ocean in an area known as **Bates Beach**, or **Backside Rincon**. Be warned: nude sunbathing is illegal. Occasionally the sheriff *will* crack down on nudists. Surfers, on the other hand, turn left and paddle out to Rincon Point, one of the most popular surfing spots along the entire California coast. There are picnic areas and restrooms. Restaurants and groceries are two miles away in Carpinteria. ~ Located two miles southeast of Carpinteria; from Route 101 take the Bates Road exit.

CARPINTERIA STATE BEACH This ribbon-shaped park extends for nearly a mile along the coast. Bordered to the east by dunes and along the west by a bluff, the beach has an offshore shelf that shelters it from the surf. As a result, Carpinteria provides exceptionally good swimming and is nicknamed "the world's safest beach." Wildlife here consists of small mammals and reptiles as well as seals and many seabirds. It's a good spot for tide-pooling; there is also a lagoon here. The Santa Ynez Mountains rise in the background. Facilities include picnic areas, restrooms, dressing rooms, showers, and lifeguards (during summer only). Restaurants and groceries are nearby in Carpinteria. Swimming is excellent, and skindiving is good along the breakwater reef, a habitat for abalone and lobsters. Surfing is very good in the "tar pits" area near the east end of the park. If you are into fishing, cabezon, corbina, and barred

BEACHES & PARKS

perch are caught here. Day-use fee, $5. ~ Located at the end of Palm Avenue in Carpinteria; 805-684-2811.

▲ There are 262 sites for tents and RVs, about half have hookups and prices vary, depending on the type of site and its location, from $17 to $28 per night.

SUMMERLAND BEACH 🏃🐎 ⚓🛶🏄🚤 Part of this narrow strip of white sand is a popular nude beach. It's backed by low-lying hills, which afford privacy from the nearby freeway and railroad tracks. The favored skinny-dipping spot is on the east end between two protective rock piles. Gay men congregate farther down the beach at Loon Point. There are no facilities here, but nearby **Lookout Park** (805-969-1720) has picnic areas, restrooms, and playground. Restaurants and groceries are nearby in Summerland. Swimming is popular, and there is good bodysurfing here. ~ Located in Summerland six miles east of Santa Barbara. Take the Summerland exit off Route 101 and get on Wallace Avenue, the frontage road between the freeway and ocean. Follow it east for three-tenths of a mile to Finney Road and the beach.

EAST BEACH 🚲⚓🏊🚤 Everyone's favorite Santa Barbara beach, this broad beauty stretches more than a mile from Montecito to Stearns Wharf. In addition to a fluffy sand corridor there are grassy areas, palm trees, and a wealth of service facilities. Beyond the wharf the strand continues as **West Beach**. The area known as "Butterfly Beach" at the far east end is frequented by nude sunbathers. Facilities include restrooms, showers, lifeguards, playground, and volleyball courts. Fishing and swimming are recommended. **Cabrillo Pavilion Bathhouse** (1118 East Cabrillo Boulevard, Santa Barbara; 805-965-0509) provides lockers, showers, and a weight room for a small daily fee. There's a restaurant next door. Other facilities are at Stearns Wharf. ~ In Santa Barbara along East Cabrillo Boulevard between the Andree Clark Bird Refuge and Stearns Wharf. Butterfly Beach can be reached by following East Cabrillo Boulevard east past the Cabrillo Pavilion Bathhouse until the road turns inland. From this juncture continue along the beach on foot. Although sunbathers use the beach as a clothing-optional area, this spot, just beyond the Clark Mansion, is sometimes patrolled by the sheriff to discourage nudity.

LEADBETTER BEACH 🚲⚓🏄🚤 A crescent of white sand, this beach rests along a shallow cove. While it is quite pretty here, with a headland bordering one end of the strand, it simply doesn't compare to nearby East Beach. There are picnic areas, restrooms, lifeguards (during summer only), and a snack bar. Restaurants and groceries are nearby. Surfing is good west of the breakwater. ~ Located along the 800 block of Shoreline Drive in Santa Barbara.

SHORELINE PARK 🚲⚓ The attraction here is not the park but the beach that lies below it. The park rests at the edge of a high bluff;

at the bottom, secluded from view, is a narrow, curving length of white sand. It's a great spot to escape the Santa Barbara crowds while enjoying a pretty beach. Stairs from the park lead down to the shore. Topside in the park are picnic areas, restrooms, and a playground. Restaurants and groceries are within a mile in Santa Barbara. ~ Located in Santa Barbara along Shoreline Drive.

MESA LANE BEACH 🐦 🏄 🏊 This is the spot Santa Barbarans ◄ *HIDDEN* head when they want to escape the crowds at the better-known beaches. It's a meandering ribbon of sand backed by steep bluffs. You can walk long distances along this secluded strand. Surfing is good. There are no facilities; restaurants and groceries are several miles away in Santa Barbara, so be sure to pack a snack. ~ There's a stairway to the beach at the end of Mesa Lane, off Cliff Drive in Santa Barbara.

ARROYO BURRO BEACH PARK 🚶 🐎 🐦 🏊 🛶 This 13-acre facility is a little gem on summer days. The sandy beach and surrounding hills are packed with locals, who often refer to is as "Hendry's Beach." If you can arrive at an uncrowded time you'll find beautiful scenery along this lengthy strand. There are picnic areas, volleyball courts, restrooms, lifeguards, restaurant, bar, and a snack bar. Swimming and fishing here is good and surfing is excellent west of the breakwater. ~ 2981 Cliff Drive, Santa Barbara; 805-687-3714.

MORE MESA 🏊 According to nude beach aficionado Dave ◄ *HIDDEN* Patrick, this is the region's favorite bare-buns rendezvous. Thousands of sunbathers gather at this remote site on a single afternoon. "On a hot day," Patrick reports, "the beach almost takes on a carnival atmosphere, with jugglers, surfers, world-class frisbee experts, musicians, dancers, joggers, and volleyball champs." A scene that should not be missed. ~ Located between Hope Ranch and Goleta, three miles from Route 101. Take the Turnpike Road exit from Route 101; follow it south to Hollister Avenue, then go left; from Hollister turn right on Puente Drive, right again on Vieja Drive, then left on Mockingbird Lane. At the end of Mockingbird Lane a path leads about three-quarters of a mile to the beach.

EL CAPITAN STATE BEACH 🚶 🐦 🏄 🏊 🛶 Another one of Southern California's sparkling beaches, El Capitan stretches along three miles of oceanfront. The park is 168 acres and features a nature trail, tidepools, and wonderful opportunities for hiking along the beach. El Capitan Creek, fringed by oak and sycamore trees, traverses the area. Seals and sea lions often romp offshore and in winter gray whales cruise by. Swimming is good. Surfing is good off El Capitan Point. This beach is also a good place to catch grunion. Facilities include picnic areas, restrooms, showers, store, and seasonal lifeguard. Day-use fee, $5. ~ Located in Goleta off Route 101 about 20 miles north of Santa Barbara; 805-968-3294.

Text continued on page 362.

The
Channel
Islands

Gaze out from the Ventura or Santa Barbara shoreline and you will spy a fleet of islands moored offshore. At times fringed with mist, on other occasions standing a hand's reach away in the crystal air, they are the Channel Islands, a group of eight volcanic islands.

Situated in the Santa Barbara Channel 11 to 40 miles from the coast, they are a place apart, a wild and storm-blown region of sharp cliffs, rocky coves, and curving grasslands. Five of the islands—Anacapa, Santa Cruz, Santa Rosa, San Miguel, and Santa Barbara—comprise Channel Islands National Park while the surrounding waters are a marine sanctuary.

Nicknamed "North America's Galapagos," the chain teems with every imaginable form of life. Sea lions and harbor seals frequent the caves, blowholes, and offshore pillars. Brown pelicans and black oystercatchers roost on the sea arches and sandy beaches. There are tidepools crowded with brilliant purple hydrocorals and white-plumed sea anemones. Like the Galapagos, this isolated archipelago has given rise to many unique life forms, including 40 endemic plant species and the island fox, which grows only to the size of a house cat.

The northern islands were created about 14 million years ago by volcanic activity. Archaeological discoveries indicate that they could be among the oldest sites of human habitation in the Americas. When explorer Juan Cabrillo revealed them to the West in 1542 they were populated with thousands of Chumash Indians.

Today, long since the Chumash were removed and the islands given over to hunters, ranchers, and settlers, the Channel Islands are largely uninhabited. Several, however, are open to hikers and campers. At the mainland-based **Channel Islands National Park Visitors Center** there are contemporary museum displays, an indoor tidepool, and an excellent 25-minute movie to familiarize you with the park. ~ 1901 Spinnaker Drive, Ventura; 805-658-5730.

Next door at **Island Packers** you can arrange transportation to the islands. This outfit schedules regular daytrips by boat to Anacapa, Santa Barbara, Santa Cruz, Santa Rosa, and San Miguel islands. ~ 1867 Spinnaker Drive, Ventura; 805-642-1393. **Horizons West** can arrange camping trips on the islands or will book you into a room at the 19th-century Scorpion Ranch on Santa Cruz Island. ~ 800-430-2544.

The **Nature Conservancy** also leads seasonal tours of Santa Cruz, the largest and most diverse of the islands. Here you will find an island just 24 miles long that supports 600 species of plants, 130 types of land birds, and several unique plant species. There are Indian middens, earthquake faults, and two mountain ranges to explore. To the center lies a pastoral valley while the shoreline is a rugged region of cliffs, tidepools, and offshore rocks. ~ 213 Stearns Wharf, Santa Barbara; 805-962-9111.

Anacapa Island, the island closest to shore, is a series of three islets parked 11 miles southwest of Oxnard. There is a nature trail here. Like the other islands, it is a prime whale-watching spot and is surrounded by the giant kelp forests that make the Channel Islands one of the nation's richest marine environments.

Whether you are a sailor, swimmer, daytripper, hiker, archaeologist, birdwatcher, camper, tidepooler, scuba diver, seal lover, or simply an interested observer, you'll find this amazing island chain a place of singular beauty and serenity.

▲ There are 140 sites for tents and RVs (no hookups) in the park near the beach; $18 per night. There is also a private campground, **El Capitan Ranch Park** (11560 Calle Real, Goleta; 805-685-3887), about one-half mile inland. It is a sprawling 100-acre complex with picnic areas, restrooms, showers, store, pool, playground, game areas, and outdoor theater.

REFUGIO STATE BEACH 🏃 ⛱ 🏄 🎣 🏊 ⛵ This is a 39-acre park with over a mile of ocean frontage. You can bask on a sandy beach, lie under palm trees on the greensward, and hike or bicycle along the two-and-a-half-mile path that connects this park with El Capitan. There are also interesting tidepools. Facilities include picnic areas, restrooms, showers, seasonal lifeguard, and a store. Fishing, swimming, and surfing are good. Day-use fee, $5. ~ Located on Refugio Road in Goleta, off Route 101 about 23 miles north of Santa Barbara; 805-968-1033.

▲ There are 80 sites for tents and RVs (no hookups); $18 per night.

HIDDEN ▶ **SAN ONOFRE BEACH** 🏃 ⛱ This nude beach is a rare find indeed. Frequented by few people, it is a pretty white sand beach that winds along rocky headlands. There's not much here except beautiful views, shore plant life, and savvy sun bathers. Wander for miles past cliffs and coves. Restaurants and groceries are two miles away in Gaviota. ~ Located off Route 101 about 30 miles north of Santa Barbara and two miles south of Gaviota. Driving north on Route 101 make a U-turn on Vista del Mar Road; drive south on Route 101 for seven-tenths of a mile to a dirt parking area. Cross the railroad tracks; a path next to the railroad light signal leads to the beach.

GAVIOTA STATE PARK 🏃 ⛱ 🏄 🎣 🏊 🚤 🚣 ⛵ This mammoth 2776-acre facility stretches along both sides of Route 101. The beach rests in a sandy cove guarded on either side by dramatic sedimentary rock formations. A railroad trestle traverses the beach and a fishing pier extends offshore. On the inland side a hiking trail leads up to **Gaviota Hot Springs** and into Los Padres National Forest. Facilities include picnic areas, restrooms, showers, lifeguards, and fishing pier. Day-use fee, $5. ~ The beach is located off Route 101 about 33 miles north of Santa Barbara. To get to the hot springs take Route 101 north from the beach park; get off at Route 1 exit; at the end of the exit ramp turn right; turn right on the frontage road and follow it a short distance to the parking lot. The trail from the parking lot leads several hundred yards to the hot springs; 805-968-3294.

▲ There are 52 sites for tents and RVs (no hookups are available); $16 per night. The vegetation is sparse from the forest fires a few years ago, and there is no drinking water, so bring your own.

JALAMA BEACH COUNTY PARK ⛱ 🏄 🎣 🏊 ⛵ This remote park sits at the far end of a 15-mile long country road. Nevertheless,

in summer there are likely to be many campers here. They come because the broad sandy beach is fringed by coastal bluffs and undulating hills. Jalama Creek cuts through the park, creating a wetland
frequented by the endangered California brown pelican. Point Conception lies a few miles to the south, and the area all around is undeveloped and quite pretty (though Vandenberg Air Force Base is situated north of the beach). This is a good area for beachcombing as
well as rock-hounding for chert, agate, travertine, and fossils. Facilities
include picnic areas, restrooms, hot showers, store, snack bar, and
playground. Swimming is not recommended here because of dangerous rip currents. Surfing is good at Tarantula Point about one-
half mile south of the park. You can surf fish for perch or fish from
the rocky points for cabezon and rock fish. Day-use fee, $3.50. ~
From Lompoc take Route 1 south for five miles; turn onto Jalama
Beach Road and follow it 15 miles to the end; 805-736-3504.

▲ There are 110 sites for tents and RVs (15 with electrical
hookups); $13 to $16 per night.

POINT SAL STATE BEACH ◢ This is one of the most secluded and   ◀ *HIDDEN*
beautiful beaches along the entire Central Coast. Access is over a nine-
mile country road, part of which is unpaved and impassable in wet
weather. When you get to the end of this steep, serpentine monster
there are no services available. The scenery, however, is magnificent.
A long crescent beach curves out toward Point Sal, a bold headland
with a rock island offshore. The Casmalia Hills rise sharply from the
ocean, creating a natural amphitheater. Sea birds roost nearby and
the beach is a habitat for harbor seals. There is surf fishing from the
beach and rocks. ~ From Route 1 three miles south of Guadalupe
turn west on Brown Road, then pick up Point Sal Road. Together
they travel nine miles to a blufftop overlook. Steep paths lead to the
beach; 805-733-3713.

The mountain road from Santa Barbara, Route 154,   ▼▼▼▼▼▼▼▼▼▼▼
curves up into the Santa Ynez Mountains past forests of   **Santa Ynez Valley**
evergreen and oak. All along the roadside are rocky
promontories with broad views back toward the city and out over
the ocean. Along the way, you can visit the charming Danish town
of Solvang. Oenophiles will enjoy exploring the burgeoning wineries in the Santa Ynez Valley.

Turn off onto Stagecoach Road, head downhill a mile and rein in at   **SIGHTS**
Cold Spring Tavern. Back in the 1880s this squat wood structure
served as a rest stop for stagecoaches coming through San Marcos
Pass. Next door is a split-log cabin with stone fireplace. ~ 5995 Stagecoach Road, Santa Barbara; 805-967-0066.

Beyond the mountain pass, amid striated hills and rolling ranch
country, lies **Lake Cachuma.** Fed by creeks from Los Padres National

Forest, this eight-mile-long lake is a jewel to the eye. Boating and fishing facilities lie nearby, and hiking trails lead into the nearby wilderness. ~ 805-688-4658.

For visitors, wandering around Solvang means catching a ride on a horse-drawn Danish streetcar, then popping into a Danish bakery for hot pretzels or *aebleskiver*, a tasty Danish pastry.

Thirty miles from Santa Barbara the mountains open onto the Santa Ynez Valley. Here a string of sleepy towns creates a Western-style counterpoint to California's chic coastline. **Santa Ynez** is a false-front town. Downtown **Ballard** is one block long; the town was settled in 1880 and features the **Ballard School**, a little red schoolhouse that was constructed a few years later. ~ 2425 School Street.

Nearby **Los Olivos** is complete with a white steeple church that dates back to 1897. It is also home to **Mattei's Tavern**. This former stagecoach inn, constructed in 1886, is a fine old wood-frame building with a trellised porch. ~ Route 154, Los Olivos; 805-688-4820.

The valley's other town, the most famous of all, does not resemble any of the others. It doesn't really resemble anything in California. **Solvang** is a town that looks like it was designed by Walt Disney. The place is a Danish village complete with cobblestone walks, gas-lights, and stained-glass windows. Steep-pitched roofs with high dormers create an Old World atmosphere here. Stores and homes reveal the tall, narrow architecture of Scandinavia and windmills dominate the view. What saves the place from being a theme park is that Solvang actually is a Danish town. Emigrants from Denmark established a village and school here in 1911.

Bethania Lutheran Church illustrates Danish provincial architecture. The model of a fully rigged ship hanging from the ceiling is traditional to Scandinavian churches. ~ At Atterdag Road and Laurel Avenue.

To further confuse things, the centerpiece of Solvang in no way fits the architecture of the town. **Mission Santa Inés** does, however, meet the building style of the rest of California. Founded in 1804, the mission church follows the long, narrow rectangular shape traditional in Spanish California. The altar is painted brilliant colors and the colonnaded courtyard is ablaze with flowers. A small museum displays 18th-century bibles and song books and one chapel contains a 17th-century statue of polychromed wood. ~ On Mission Drive.

HIDDEN ► To escape the bustle of Solvang, take a ride out Alisal Road. After six miles this rustic road arrives at **Nojoqui Falls**. There's a picnic park here and a short hiking trail up to hillside cascades.

The Santa Ynez Valley is horse country. Stud farms and working ranches dot the countryside and thoroughbreds graze in the meadows.

It's also a prime winegrowing region with several dozen wineries scattered around the valley on picturesque back roads. The **Santa**

Ynez Valley Winery, housed in an old dairy building, is a 110-acre spread specializing in chardonnay and pinot noir. With vines dating to 1969, it claims to be the oldest commercial vineyard in the valley, indicating just how recent winegrowing is to the area. ~ 343 North Refugio Road, Santa Ynez; 805-688-8381.

For a long country ride, travel out Zaca Station and Foxen Canyon roads in Los Olivos. A string of wineries begins with the most elegant. **Firestone Vineyard** is set in stone-trimmed buildings and features a courtyard with fountain and picnic tables. The largest winery in the valley, it offers several estate-grown varietal wines. ~ 5017 Zaca Station Road, Los Olivos; 805-688-3940.

Zaca Mesa Winery sits about nine miles from Route 101. Set in a modern woodframe building with an attractive tasting room, it's a beautiful winery with vineyards lining Foxen Canyon Road. Other wineries lie further along the road and elsewhere throughout the Santa Ynez Valley. ~ 6905 Foxen Canyon Road, Los Olivos; 805-688-3310.

LODGING

Up in the Santa Ynez Valley, tucked between the Santa Ynez and San Rafael mountains, lies **Alisal Guest Ranch**. A 10,000-acre working cattle ranch, Alisal represents one of the original Spanish land grants. Part of the ranch is an exclusive resort featuring 73 units, two 18-hole golf courses, swimming pool, spa, tennis courts, and dining room. Guests ride horseback through the property and fish and sail on a mile-long lake. Square dances, hay rides, and summer barbecue dinners add to the entertainment. Breakfast and dinner are included. ~ 1054 Alisal Road, Solvang; 805-688-6411, 800-425-4725, fax 805-688-2510. ULTRA-DELUXE.

Inexpensive lodging in the Santa Ynez Valley usually means finding a place in Solvang. This Danish town has numerous motels, many of which line Route 246. Be sure to reserve in advance; they fill up fast, particularly in summer and on weekends.

One I recommend is **Solvang Gaard Lodge**. Designed in old Danish style, it's a standard motel with basic facilities. ~ 293 Alisal Road, Solvang; 805-688-4404. BUDGET.

If they are booked solid, try the **Denmark Motel** next door. ~ 279 Alisal Road, Solvang; 805-688-6813. BUDGET.

DINING

A vestige of the Old West, **Cold Spring Tavern** is a former stagecoach stop dating back to the 19th century. The floors tilt, the bar is wood plank, and the walls are stained with a century of use; a cow head with antlers decorates the stone fireplace. Dinner in this roughhewn time capsule features marinated rabbit, steak, pork back ribs, and fresh seafood. The evening special might be elk or buffalo, but that is a rare occasion. At lunch you can order a venison steak sandwich, *chile verde*, or a buffalo burger. Make a point of stopping by. Dinner reservations are recommended. ~ 5995 Stagecoach Road off Route 154, Santa Barbara; 805-967-0066. MODERATE TO DELUXE.

There's another stagecoach-stop-turned-restaurant in the Santa Ynez Valley. **Mattei's Tavern** is a mammoth old building that served as an inn back in the 1880s. Today you can dine in a rustically decorated room or out on the patio. Dinner features steaks, prime rib, pasta, and fresh seafood dishes. For a sense of history and a good meal, it's a safe bet. Lunch is served only on Saturday and Sunday. ~ Route 154, Los Olivos; 805-688-4820. DELUXE.

Finger foods are part of the fun in dining around Solvang. Stop by **The Front Yard** for sandwiches or hot pretzels smothered in cheddar cheese. ~ 475 1st Street, Solvang; 805-688-7674.

This Danish town is also famous for its bakeries. **Solvang Bakery** has excellent Danish pastries and other Scandinavian treats. ~ 460 Alisal Road, Solvang; 805-688-4939. BUDGET.

SHOPPING   The Danish town of Solvang is a choice spot to shop for imported products from Northern Europe. Walk the brick-paved streets and you'll encounter everything from cuckoo clocks to lace curtains. Many of the shops line **Copenhagen Drive**.

There are Danish handknit sweaters, music boxes, tiles, and pewter items. The toy stores are designed to resemble doll houses and shops throughout town feature the tile roofs and high gables of Scandinavian stores.

In the nearby town of **Los Olivos** several art galleries and antique shops will help round out your shopping spree.

NIGHTLIFE   Carousing at **Cold Spring Tavern**, a log cabin set high in the mountains outside Santa Barbara, is like being in an old Western movie. Every Friday through Sunday you can pull up a stool and listen to the rock, country-and-western, and rhythm-and-blues bands that ride through. ~ 5995 Stagecoach Road, off Route 154, Santa Barbara; 805-967-0066.

AJ Spurs hosts live music every Friday and Saturday night. This is an elegant Western saloon with log walls, stone fireplace, and frontier artifacts. ~ 350 Route 246, Buellton; 805-686-1655.

And don't forget the **Solvang Theaterfest**, one of the West's oldest repertory groups. Performing during summer months in an open-air theater, they present musicals and dramas. ~ 420 East 2nd Street, Solvang; 805-922-8313.

PARKS   **LAKE CACHUMA COUNTY PARK** 🚶🚴🛶🚤🎣 Surrounded by the 4000-foot Santa Ynez Mountains and 6000-foot San Rafael Mountains, this is one of the prettiest lakes along the entire Central Coast. Oak forests and fields of tall grass border much of the shoreline. There are full facilities for camping, boating, bicycling, and hiking. A great place for families and people exploring the backcountry above Santa Barbara. Facilities here include picnic areas, restrooms, swimming pool, snack bar, store, nature center (805-688-4515), boat launch and rentals (805-688-4040), seasonal bike rentals, par course, game field, and hiking trails. Swimming is not permitted in lake, but there is a pool here. The lake has trout, perch, bass, bluegill, crappie, and catfish. Day-use fee, $5. ~ Located on Route 154 north of Santa Barbara; 805-688-4658.

▲ There are 50 tent sites ($13 per night), 25 partial hookups ($16 per night), and 50 full hookups ($18 per night).

▼▼▼▼▼▼▼▼▼▼▼▼▼▼
San Luis Obispo Area

This stretch of rugged coastline attracts an increasing number of residents as well as visitors, both of whom are drawn by the beautiful beaches, nearby mountains, and temperate climate of the region. San Luis Obispo itself (don't call attention to yourself as a tourist by saying "San Louie"—locals pronounce the "s") is home to California Polytechnic State University, the state system's only polytechnic school. Known far and wide as Cal Poly, the university is the focal point for a growing student population. In contrast with the business- and technology-oriented atmosphere that the students bring to San Luis Obispo, many of the smaller surrounding communities still retain their bohemian character.

SIGHTS

PISMO BEACH An unattractive congeries of mobile homes and beach rental stands, Pismo Beach is a nondescript town that has a single saving grace—its dunes. They are sand castles in the air, curving, rolling, ever-changing hills of sand. Wave after wave of them parallel the beach, like a crystalline continuation of the ocean.

Otherwise, this town of 8000 people is a tacky tourist enclave known for an annual clam festival and for the migrating monarch butterflies that land just south of the town pier every year from late-November to March. Traveling north, you reach Pismo Beach after Route 1 completes its lengthy inland course through Lompoc and Guadalupe, then rejoins Route 101 and returns to the coast.

Those vaunted sand piles comprise the most extensive coastal dunes in California. From Pismo Beach the sand hills run six miles south where they meet the 450-foot-high **Guadalupe dunes** (see "Beaches & Parks" section), forming a unique habitat for wildflowers and shorebirds.

Back in the 1930s and 1940s a group of bohemians, the "Dunites," occupied this wild terrain. Comprised of nudists, artists, and mystics, the movement believed that the dunes were a center of cosmic energy. Today the area is filled with beachcombers, sunbathers, and off-highway vehicles.

Stop by the **Pismo Beach Chamber of Commerce & Visitors Bureau** for brochures and maps of the San Luis Bay region. ~ 581 Dolliver Street, Pismo Beach; 805-773-2055. Of the three seaside communities lining this harbor—Pismo Beach, Shell Beach, and Avila Beach—the prettiest of all is **Avila Beach**. Here you can comb a white sand beach or walk out along three fishing piers. At the far end of town a dramatic headland curves out from the shoreline, creating a crescent-shaped harbor where sailboats bob at their moorings.

There are hot springs in the hills around Avila Beach. **Sycamore Mineral Springs Resort** has tapped these local waters and created a lovely spa with hotel units, volleyball courts, and a swimming pool. The real attractions here, however, are the redwood hot tubs. Very private, they are dotted about on a hillside and shaded by oak and sycamore. Admission. ~ 1215 Avila Beach Drive, Avila Beach; 805-595-7302.

HIDDEN ►

From the Pismo Beach–Avila Beach strip, you can buzz into San Luis Obispo on Route 101 or take a quiet country drive into town via **See Canyon Road**. The latter begins in Avila Beach and corkscrews up into the hills past apple orchards and horse farms. Along its 13-mile length, half unpaved, you'll encounter mountain meadows and ridgetop vistas. During the fall harvest season you can pick apples at farms along the way.

SAN LUIS OBISPO   San Luis Obispo, a pretty jewel of a town, lies 12 miles from the ocean in the center of an expansive agricultural region. Backdropped by the Santa Lucia Mountains, the town focuses around an old Spanish mission. Cowboys from outlying ranches and students from the nearby campus add to the cultural mix, creating a vital atmosphere that has energized San Luis Obispo's rapid growth.

For a sense of the region's roots, pick up information at the **San Luis Obispo Chamber of Commerce**. ~ 1039 Chorro Street, San Luis Obispo; 805-781-2777. A self-guided tour of this historic town logically begins at **Mission San Luis de Tolosa**. Dating to 1772, the old Spanish outpost has been nicely reconstructed, though the complex is not as extensive as La Purísima Mission in Lompoc. There's a museum re-creating the American Indian, Spanish, and Mexican eras as well as a pretty church. Mission Plaza, fronting the chapel, is a well-landscaped park. ~ Chorro and Monterey streets, San Luis Obispo; 805-543-6850.

The **County Historical Museum** continues the historic overview with displays from the Chumash, pre-Hispanic, Spanish, and American periods. Closed Monday and Tuesday. ~ 696 Monterey Street, San Luis Obispo; 805-543-0638. Across the street at the **San Luis Obispo Art Center** are exhibits of works by the area's artists. Closed Monday. ~ 1010 Broad Street, San Luis Obispo; 805-543-8562.

St. Stephen's Episcopal Church is a narrow, lofty, and strikingly attractive chapel. Built in 1867, it was one of California's first Episcopal churches. ~ Nipomo and Pismo streets, San Luis Obispo.

The **Dallidet Adobe**, constructed by a French vintner in 1853, is another local architectural landmark. ~ On Toro Street between

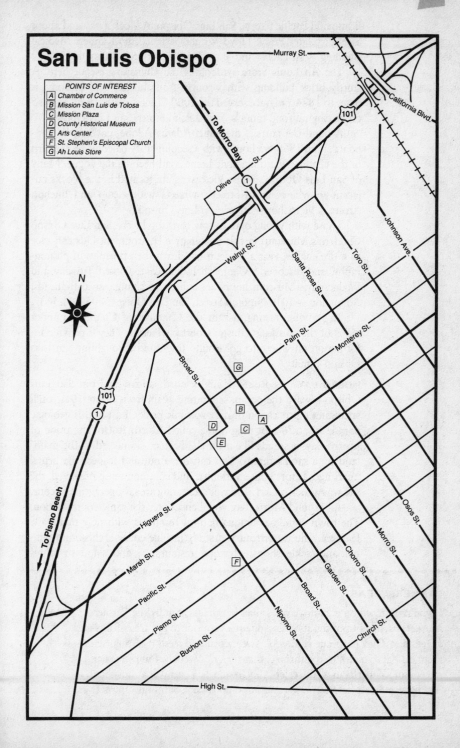

San Luis Obispo

POINTS OF INTEREST
- A Chamber of Commerce
- B Mission San Luis de Tolosa
- C Mission Plaza
- D County Historical Museum
- E Arts Center
- F St. Stephen's Episcopal Church
- G Ah Louis Store

Pismo and Pacific streets, San Luis Obispo. A block away and about a century later Frank Lloyd Wright designed the **Kundert Medical Building**. ~ At Pacific and Santa Rosa streets, San Luis Obispo.

The **Ah Louis Store** symbolizes the Chinese presence here. A sturdy brick building with wrought-iron shutters and balcony, it dates to 1874 and once served the 2000 Chinese coolies who worked on nearby railroad tunnels. ~ 800 Palm Street, San Luis Obispo.

Around the corner, the **Sauer-Adams Adobe**, covered in clapboard, is an 1860-era house with a second-story balcony. By the turn of the century, Victorian-style homes had become the vogue. Many of San Luis Obispo's finest Victorians are located in the blocks adjacent to where Broad Street intersects with Pismo and Buchon streets. ~ 964 Chorro Street, San Luis Obispo.

Those with young ones in tow can stop by the **San Luis Obispo Children's Museum**. In this imaginative environment kids can race to a fire engine, visit a planetarium, learn the principles of photography, and discover a Chumash Indian cave. Closed Tuesday and Wednesday. (Museum hours are subject to change, so call ahead.) Admission. ~ 1010 Nipomo Street, San Luis Obispo; 805-544-5437.

To go wine tasting, ask at the Chamber of Commerce about maps of the San Luis Obispo County wineries. They'll provide information on where to go around town and throughout San Luis Obispo County.

MORRO BAY   As Route 1 angles north and west from San Luis Obispo toward the ocean, separating again from Route 101, you'll encounter a procession of nine volcanic peaks. Last in this geologic parade is a 576-foot plug dome called **Morro Rock**. The pride of Morro Bay, it stands like a little Gibraltar, connected to the mainland by a sand isthmus. You can drive out and inspect the brute. Years ago, before conservationists and common sense prevailed, the site was a rock quarry. Today it's a nesting area for peregrine falcons.

All around Morro Bay you'll encounter the same contradiction. The town combines unique natural resources with ugly manmade features. The waterfront is a study in blue-collar architecture with bait-and-tackle shops, plywood restaurants, and slapdash stores

FARMERS' FEAST

If you're in town on a Thursday evening, be sure to stop by the **Farmers Market**. Farmers from the surrounding area turn out to sell fresh fruits and vegetables. They barbecue ribs, cook sweet corn and fresh fish, then serve them on paper plates to the throngs that turn out weekly. Puppeteers and street dancers perform as the celebration assumes a carnival atmosphere. ~ At Higuera Street between Osos and Nipomo streets, San Luis Obispo.

everywhere; and dominating the skyline, vying with the great rock itself, are three monstrous concrete smokestacks.

Turn your back on this travesty and you are in a bird sanctuary. Extending for miles out toward Morro Rock is a dramatic **sandspit**, a region of sand dunes and a tranquil estuary teeming with birds and sea life. **Kayaks of Morro Bay** rents kayaks and canoes. ~ 699 Embarcadero, Morro Bay; 805-772-1119. For something more formal, **Tiger's Folly** sponsors harbor cruises in an old-fashioned paddle-wheeler. ~ 1205 Embarcadero, at the Harbor Hut Restaurant, Morro Bay; 805-772-2257.

Back on terra firma, visit the **Morro Bay State Park Museum** with its displays of local history and wildlife. The museum itself is unimpressive, but it is located at White Point, a rock outcropping in which Indian mortar holes are still evident. From this height there are views of the sandspit, Morro Bay, and Morro Rock. The nearby estuary, a habitat for 250 migratory and resident bird species, is one of the largest salt marshes in California. Admission. ~ Morro Bay State Park Road, Morro Bay; 805-772-2694.

Lodging in the Pismo Beach–Shell Beach–Avila Beach area generally means finding a motel. None of these seaside towns has expanded more than a few blocks from the waterfront, so wherever you book a room will be walking distance from the beach.

LODGING

Adams Motel is a 20-unit hostelry (14 with kitchenettes) priced similarly. The furniture and decoration is standard motel. ~ 1000 Dolliver Street, Pismo Beach; 805-773-206. MODERATE TO DELUXE.

It's a step up and a lot nearer the water at **Dolphin Cove Lodge**. This place is right above the beach and each of its 21 units has an ocean view. ~ 170 Main Street, Pismo Beach; 805-773-4706, fax 805-773-4214. MODERATE TO DELUXE.

If it's panoramic Pacific Coast views you are after, try **The Best Western Shore Cliff Lodge**. Perched on the cliffs just off Route 101, the hotel offers spacious, although conventional, rooms with private balconies and expected amenities. There is a restaurant, lounge, pool, spa, sauna, and tennis courts. Rooms aren't cheap, but what a view! ~ 2555 Price Street, Pismo Beach; 805-773-4671, 800-441-8885, fax 805-773-2341. DELUXE TO ULTRA-DELUXE.

The **Beachcomber Inn** also has rooms with ocean views. Each is decorated with floral prints and wicker furniture. ~ 541 Cypress Street, Pismo Beach; 805-773-5505, fax 805-773-0880. DELUXE.

Surfside Motel & Apartments is located directly across the street from lovely Avila Beach. Here rooms come with or without kitchenettes. ~ 256 Front Street, Avila Beach; 805-595-2300. BUDGET TO MODERATE.

For a different type of vista at a different kind of price, try the **Adobe Inn**. Here the rooms are simple but comfortable with double or queen-size beds and rocking chairs. The view is of the surrounding hills, and a night's stay includes a trip to the inn's bounteous breakfast buffet. ~ 1473 Monterey Street, San Luis Obispo; 805-549-0321, fax 805-549-0383. MODERATE TO DELUXE.

Where else but the Madonna Inn does a waterfall serve as the men's room urinal?

Sycamore Mineral Springs Resort reposes on a hillside one mile inland from Avila Beach. Situated in a stand of oak and sycamore trees are 26 motel-style rooms and 24 suites. Each has a private spa and patio; there are also redwood hot tubs scattered about in the surrounding forest; swimming pool. The rooms are decorated in contemporary style. ~ 1215 Avila Beach Drive, San Luis Obispo; 805-595-7302, 800-234-5831, fax 805-781-2598. DELUXE.

Heritage Inn Bed & Breakfast is a San Luis Obispo anomaly. There aren't many country inns in town and this one is not even representative of the species. It sits in a neighborhood surrounded by motels and a nearby freeway. What's more, the house was moved—lock, stock, and bay windows—to this odd location. Once inside, you'll be quite pleased. There's a warm, comfortable sitting parlor and seven guest rooms, all furnished with antiques. The beds are brass or oak; and some accommodations include window seats and terraces. All but three of the rooms in this 1902 home share baths and four rooms have fireplaces. Full breakfast is included. ~ 978 Olive Street, San Luis Obispo; 805-544-7440. MODERATE TO DELUXE.

The **Garden Street Inn** is a beautifully restored, 1887 Victorian that has 13 rooms and suites. Each is individually decorated in such themes as "Walden," "Amadeus," and "Emerald Isle." Some rooms honor local history; others are filled with family mementoes. A full breakfast is served family-style in the bay-windowed morning room. ~ 1212 Garden Street, San Luis Obispo; 805-545-9802, fax 805-781-7469. DELUXE TO ULTRA-DELUXE.

The **Apple Farm Inn** represents another example of a classic country inn set in a neighborhood of drive-in motels. The carefully landscaped property, including a stream that runs by the old Victorian-style buildings, takes you away from the hubbub of Monterey Street and into Old America complete with apple pies fresh from the Inn's bakery and a working, water-powered mill. ~ 2015 Monterey Street, San Luis Obispo; 805-544-2040, 800-374-3705, fax 805-546-9495. ULTRA-DELUXE. The adjoining **Trellis Court** has all the advantages of the Apple Farm Inn but its smaller rooms are more affordably priced. While no two rooms are the same in either accommodation, they all have working gas fireplaces. MODERATE.

The most outlandish place in town is a roadside confection called the **Madonna Inn**. Architecturally it's a cross between a castle and a gingerbread house, culturally it's somewhere between light opera and heavy metal. The lampposts are painted pink, and the gift shop contains the biggest, gaudiest chandeliers you've ever seen. Personally, I wouldn't be caught dead staying in the place, but I would never miss an opportunity to visit. If you prove more daring than I, there are 109 rooms, each decorated in a different flamboyant style. ~ 100 Madonna Road, San Luis Obispo; 805-543-3000, 800-543-9666, fax 805-543-1800. MODERATE TO ULTRA-DELUXE.

There are countless motels to choose from in Morro Bay, ranging across the entire spectrum in price and amenities. For information on availability contact the **Morro Bay Chamber of Commerce.** ~ 880 Main Street, Morro Bay; 805-772-4467 or 800-231-0592.

Fashionable but casual, **The Inn at Morro Bay** is a waterfront complex with the amenities of a small resort: restaurant, lounge, swimming pool, and an adjacent golf course. It sits on ten acres overlooking Morro Bay and contains 96 guest rooms. French country in decor, many have brass beds, shuttered windows, and oak armoires. ~ 60 State Park Road, Morro Bay; 805-772-5651, 800-321-9566, fax 805-772-4779. DELUXE TO ULTRA-DELUXE.

Fish-and-chip joints are everywhere on the Central Coast, but **Pismo Fish & Chips** is special—mainly because it's good, but also because it's a local institution. The fish is fresh, the portions generous, and the service friendly. Closed Monday. ~ 505 Cypress Street, Pismo Beach; 805-773-2853. BUDGET TO MODERATE.

DINING

◄ *HIDDEN*

At **The Old Custom House Restaurant** ask for a table out on the patio. It's a garden arrangement with umbrellas shading the tables. Quite nice, and besides, the indoor dining area is just a counter and a series of plain formica tables. Serving three meals daily, they specialize in seafood (what else?) and steak. Dinners are prepared on an oak pit barbecue; breakfast features 20 different omelettes. ~ 324 Front Street, Avila Beach; 805-595-7555. MODERATE.

If you missed the swinging doors in the saloon you'll get the idea from the moose head trophies and branding irons. "Taste the Great American West" is the motto for **F. McLintock's Saloon & Dining House.** This is the place where on Sundays you can get an 18-ounce steak for breakfast. Every evening, when the oak pit barbecue really gets going, there are a dozen kinds of steak and ribs, seafood, buffalo burgers, and grilled veal liver. If popularity means anything, this place is tops. It's always mobbed. So dust off the Stetson and prepare to chow down. ~ 750 Mattie Road, Shell Beach; 805-773-1892. MODERATE TO DELUXE.

Sick of seafood by now? Tired of saloons serving cowboy-sized steaks? Happily, San Luis Obispo has several ethnic restaurants. Two are located in The Creamery, a turn-of-the-century dairy plant that has been transformed into a shopping mall. **Tsurugi Japanese Restaurant** features a sushi bar and dining area decorated with Oriental screens and wallhangings. At lunch and dinner there are shrimp tempura, chicken teriyaki, *nigiri*, and other Asian specialties. The atmosphere is placid and the food quite good. No lunch on Saturday and Sunday. ~ 570 Higuera Street, San Luis Obispo; 805-543-8942. MODERATE TO DELUXE.

Next door at **Tortilla Flats** they've fashioned an attractive restaurant from the brick walls, bare ducts, and exposed rafters of the old creamery. It's lunch, dinner, and Sunday brunch at this Mexican eatery where the bar serves pitchers of margaritas. ~ 1051 Nipomo Street, San Luis Obispo; 805-544-7575. BUDGET TO MODERATE.

If you can get past the garish red and yellow sign at **Golden China Restaurant**, there's an array of standard Chinese dishes printed on a menu that continues for pages. ~ 675 Higuera Street, San Luis Obispo; 805-543-7576. BUDGET TO MODERATE.

Italy enters the picture with **Cafe Roma**, a delightful restaurant decorated in country Tuscan style. Copper pots as well as portraits from the old country decorate the walls. Lunch and dinner include Italian sausage, veal marsala, steak *fiorentina*, and several daily specials. There are also assorted pasta and antipasto dishes, an extensive Italian wine list, and homemade ice cream for dessert. Run by an Italian family, it serves excellent food; highly recommended. Closed Monday. ~ 1819 Osos Street, San Luis Obispo; 805-541-6800. MODERATE TO DELUXE.

HIDDEN ► For a low-priced meal in a white-tablecloth restaurant with views of the surrounding hills, beat a path to the California Polytechnic campus. **Vista Grande Restaurant** serves Cal Poly students as well as the public in a comfortable plate-glass dining room. Open for lunch, dinner, and Sunday brunch, it features veal parmesan, pasta, meat or vegetarian dishes, and fish and chips. There are also several different salads and a host of sandwiches. Closed Saturday from June through August. ~ Grand Avenue, San Luis Obispo; 805-756-1204. BUDGET.

Outside town there's a particularly good Western-style restaurant. (You didn't think I'd let you off scot-free, did you?) **This Old House** is another oak pit grill serving steak and ribs, plus lobster, sweetbreads, barbecued chicken, and fresh halibut. The decor is early Western with oxen yokes, cowboy boots, and branding irons on the wall. With its unique barbecue sauce and rib-sticking meals, This Old House merits a visit. Dinner only. ~ 740 West Foothill Boulevard, San Luis Obispo; three and one-half miles west of Route 1; 805-543-2690. MODERATE TO DELUXE.

You needn't cast far in Morro Bay to find a seafood restaurant. Sometimes they seem as frequent as fishing boats. One of the most venerable is **Dorn's Original Breakers Café**. It's a bright, airy place with a postcard view of the waterfront. While they serve all three meals, in the evening you better want seafood because there are about two dozen fish dishes and only a couple of steak, chicken, and

If you're in the mood to explore the water in a semisubmersible vessel, contact Sub-Sea Tours. ~ 699 Embarcadero, Morro Bay; 805-772-9463.

veal platters. ~ 801 Market Street, Morro Bay; 805-772-4415. MOD-
ERATE TO DELUXE.

Fine California cuisine is the order of the day at **The Inn at Morro
Bay**. Situated in a waterfront resort, the dining room looks out over
Morro Bay. In addition to great views and commodious surroundings, it features an enticing list of local and French entrées. All three
meals are served, but the highlight is dinner. The menu might include
home-smoked salmon with crème frâiche caviar, roast duckling, and
fresh fish in a mustard-chive butter. ~ 60 State Park Road, Morro
Bay; 805-772-5651. DELUXE.

In the old Spanish town of San Luis Obispo, the best stores are located along the blocks surrounding Mission Plaza. Stroll the two
blocks along Monterey Street between Osos and Chorro streets, then
browse the five-block stretch on Higuera Street from Osos Street to
Nipomo Street. These two arteries and the side streets between form
the heart of downtown.

SHOPPING

The **Natural Selection** is a unique shop dedicated to nature and
science. The posters, books, toys, jewelry, telescopes, binoculars, and
greeting cards all follow a similar theme. So if you've been searching
everywhere for that moon map, rain gauge, or *T-rex* T-shirt, look no
further. ~ 737 Higuera Street, San Luis Obispo; 805-541-6755.

The **Network Mall** is a collection of crafts shops and small stores.
~ 778 Higuera Street, San Luis Obispo. Also consider **The Creamery**,
an old dairy plant converted into an ingenious shopping center. ~
Higuera and Nipomo streets, San Luis Obispo; 805-541-0106.

Ready for a Western saloon? Stone fireplace, antlers on the wall,
etc.? It's called **F. McLintock's Saloon & Dining House**. Unlike its
rowdier counterparts, this lounge is low key. The music, seven nights
a week, is by solo guitarists playing soft rock and country. ~ 750
Mattie Road, Shell Beach; 805-773-1892.

NIGHTLIFE

There's live entertainment on Friday and Saturday nights in the
lounge at **The Inn at Morro Bay**. Appointed with bentwood furniture and pastel paneling, it's a beautiful bar. The most striking feature of all is the view, which extends out across the water to Morro
Rock. ~ 60 State Park Road, Morro Bay; 805-772-5651.

GUADALUPE DUNES BEACH 🏃 🎣 ⚓ The Sahara Desert has noth-
ing on this place. The sand dunes throughout the area are spectacu-
lar, especially 450-foot Mussel Rock, the highest dune on the West
Coast. The dunes provide a habitat for California brown pelicans,
California least terns, and other endangered birds and plants. The
Santa Maria River, which empties here, forms a pretty wetland area.
Fishing is very popular here. Restaurants and groceries are located
five miles away in Guadalupe. ~ From Route 1 in Guadalupe, follow

**BEACHES
& PARKS**

Main Street west for five miles to the beach. Windblown sand some-times closes the road, so call beforehand; 805-545-9925.

PISMO STATE BEACH 🏃 🏊 🎣 🚣 🐚 ⚓ This spectacular beach runs for six miles from Pismo Beach south to the Santa Maria River. Along its oceanfront are some of the finest sand dunes in California, fluffy hills inhabited by shorebirds and tenacious plants. Also home to the pismo clam, it's a wonderful place to hike and explore. There are picnic areas here, and restrooms at one campground. Restaurants and groceries are nearby in Pismo Beach. Fishing for cod and red snapper is good from the Pismo Pier (at the end of Hinds Avenue, Pismo Beach). You can also dig for pismo clams along the beach (check for local restrictions). ~ The park parallels Route 1 in Pismo Beach; 805-489-1869.

▲ There are tent/RV sites (limited hookups); $18 to $20 per night. There is also camping at **Oceano Memorial County Park** (near Mendel Drive and Pier Avenue, Oceano; 805-781-5219) on 23 tent/RV sites (full hookups); $20 per night. Reservations can be made by calling DESTINET at 800-444-7275.

HIDDEN ► **PIRATE'S COVE OR MALLAGH LANDING** 🏊 This crescent-shaped nude beach is a beauty. Protected by 100-foot cliffs, it curves for a half mile along a placid cove. At one end is a rocky headland pock-marked by caves. Restaurants and groceries are in Avila Beach. Swimming and skindiving are very good because the beach is in a sheltered area. ~ Located ten miles south of San Luis Obispo in Avila Beach. From Route 101 take Avila Beach Drive west for two miles; turn left on Cave Landing Road (the road travels immediately up-hill); go six-tenths of a mile to a dirt parking lot; crude stairs lead down to the beach.

MONTAÑA DE ORO STATE PARK 🏃 🚴 🐎 🏊 ⛵ 🎣 🐚 🐟 ⚓ This 9000-acre facility is one of the finest parks along the entire Central Coast. It stretches over a mile along the shore, past a sandspit, tidepools, and sharp cliffs. There are remote coves for viewing seals, sea otters, and migrating whales and for sunbathing on hidden beaches. Monarch butterflies roost in the eucalyptus-filled canyons and a hiking trail leads to Valencia Peak, with views scan-ning almost 100 miles of coastline. Wildlife is abundant along 50 miles of hiking trails. Chaparral, Bishop pine, and coast live oak cover the hills; in spring wildflowers riot, giving the park its name, "Mountain of Gold." You can go fishing or clamming, but swim-ming is not recommended because of dangerous undertow. Surfing is good around Hazard Canyon. There are picnic areas and rest-rooms; restaurants and groceries are several miles away in Los Osos. ~ Located on Pecho Valley Road about ten miles south of Morro Bay; 805-528-0513.

▲ There are 50 tent/RV sites (no hookups); $11 per night.

MORRO BAY STATE PARK 🚶🚲🏊🛶⛺⛺🚐🚤⚓ Located amid one of the biggest marshlands along the California coast, this 2435-acre domain is like an outdoor museum. The tidal basin attracts over 250 species of sea, land, and shore birds. Great blue herons roost in the eucalyptus trees. There's a marina where you can rent canoes or kayaks to explore the salt marsh and nearby sandspit, and a natural history museum with environmental displays. Camping is in an elevated area trimmed with pine and other trees. Since the park fronts the wetlands, there is no beach here, but you can reach the beach at **Morro Bay State Park Sand Spit** by car or private boat. Facilities include picnic areas, restrooms, and showers. Fishing is good. Restaurants and groceries are a mile away in Morro Bay. Day-use fee, $6. ~ On State Park Road in Morro Bay; 805-772-7434.

▲ There are 135 tent/RV sites (limited hookups); $18 to $24 per night.

MORRO STRAND STATE BEACH 🚤🏊🛶⛺⚓ Another of the Central Coast's long, skinny parks, this sandy beach stretches almost two miles along Morro Bay. Private homes border one side, but in the other direction there are great views of Morro Rock. It's a good place for beachcombing, fishing, and clamming. There are restrooms Restaurants and groceries are nearby in Morro Bay. ~ Located parallel to Route 1 north of Morro Bay; park entrance is along Yerba Buena Street; 805-772-8812.

▲ There are 100 tent/RV sites (no hookups); $14 to $18 per night.

LOS PADRES NATIONAL FOREST 🚶🚲🐎🚤⛺⚓ The southern section of this mammoth park parallels the coast from Ventura to San Luis Obispo. Rising from sea level to almost 9000 feet, it contains the Sierra Madre, San Rafael, Santa Ynez, and La Panza mountains. Characterized by sharp slopes and a dry climate, only one-third of the preserve is forested. But there are Coast redwoods, ancient bristlecone pines, and amazingly diverse plant life. The rare California condor, which with its nine-foot wingspan is the largest land bird in North America, has recently been reintroduced to Los Padres. Among the animals still remaining are golden eagles, quail, owls, woodpeckers, wild pig, mule deer, black bear, and desert bighorn sheep. The northern and southern sectors of the national forest contain over 1500 miles of hiking trails, almost 500 miles of streams, and a ski trail on Mt. Pinos. For information and permits contact forest headquarters at 6144 Calle Real, Goleta, CA 93117. Day-use fees range throughout the different districts from $3 to $6. ~ Route 33 cuts through the heart of Los Padres. Route 101 provides numerous access points; 805-683-6711.

▲ There are 82 tent/RV sites (no hookups); prices vary from free to $16 per night.

▼▼▼▼▼▼▼▼▼
Cambria Area

It seems only appropriate that your introduction to the coastal region around Cambria is through an antique village called Harmony that boasts a population of 16 souls. Cambria itself is a seaside town that was originally settled in the 1860s and later expanded into a major seaport and whaling center. As the railroad replaced coastal shipping, Cambria declined, only to be resurrected during the past few decades as an artist colony and tourist center.

SIGHTS

One of the first places you'll happen upon in this rural region is the **Cambria Chamber of Commerce** office. ~ 767 Main Street, Cambria; 805-927-3624. Start wandering around and you'll find that it's a pretty place, with ridgetop homes, sandy beaches, and rocky coves. But like many of California's small creative communities, Cambria has begun peering too long in the mirror. The architecture along Main Street has assumed a cutesy mock-Tudor look and the place is taking on an air of unreality.

Still, there are many fine artists and several exceptional galleries here. It's a choice place to shop and seek out gourmet food. While you're at it, head up to **Nit Wit Ridge**. That hodgepodge house on the left, the one decorated with every type of bric-a-brac, was the home of Art Beal, a.k.a. Captain Nit Wit, who died in 1992. He worked on this folk-art estate, listed in the National Register of Historic Landmarks, from 1928 until his death. ~ Hillcrest Drive just above Cornwall Street.

Then take a ride along **Moonstone Beach Drive**, a lovely oceanfront corridor with vista points and tidepools. It's a marvelous place for beachcombers and daydreamers.

Funny thing about travel, you often end up visiting places in spite of themselves. You realize that as soon as you get back home friends are going to ask if you saw this or that, so your itinerary becomes a combination of the locales you've always longed to experience and the places everyone else says you "must see."

The world-renowned **Hearst Castle** is one of the latter. Built by newspaper magnate William Randolph Hearst and designed by architect Julia Morgan, the Hearst San Simeon State Historical Monument includes a main house that sports 37 bedrooms, three guest houses, and part of the old Hearst ranch, which once stretched 40 miles along the coast.

The entire complex took 27 years to build. Back in the 1930s and 1940s, when Hearst resided here and film stars like Charlie Chaplin, Mary Pickford, Clark Gable, and Cary Grant frequented the place, the grounds contained the largest private zoo in the world.

An insatiable art collector, Hearst stuffed every building with priceless works. Casa Grande, the main house, is fronted by two cathedral towers and filled with Renaissance and Gothic art. To see it is overwhelming. There is no place for the eye to rest. The main sitting room is covered everywhere with tapestries, bas-relief works, 16th-century paintings, Roman columns, and a carved wood ceiling. The walls are fashioned from 500-year-old choir pews, the French fireplace dates back 400 years; there are hand-carved tables and silver candelabra (I am still describing the same room), overstuffed furniture, and antique statuary. It is the most lavish mismatch in history.

Ninety species of wild animals—including lions, tigers, yaks, and camels—roamed about Hearst Castle.

Hearst Castle crosses the line from visual art to visual assault. The parts are exquisite, the whole a travesty. And yet, as I said, you must see the place. It's so huge that four different two-hour tours are scheduled daily to various parts of the property. Since over one million people a year visit, the guided tours are often booked solid. I recommend that you reserve in advance and plan on taking Tour 1, which covers the ground floor of Casa Grande, a guest house, the pools, and the gardens. Reservations are made through DESTINET at 800-444-4445.

Ultimately you'll find that in spite of the pomp and grandiosity, there is a magic about the place. In the early morning, when tour shuttles begin climbing from sea level to the 1600-foot-elevation residence, fog feathers through the surrounding valleys, obscuring everything but the spiked peaks of the Santa Lucia Mountains and the lofty towers of the castle. The entire complex, overbearing as it is, evokes a simpler, more glamorous era, before the Depression and World War II turned the nation's thoughts inward, when without blinking a man could build an outlandish testimonial to himself. Admission. ~ Route 1, San Simeon; 805-927-2000.

Beyond Hearst Castle, Route 1 winds north past tidepools and pocket beaches. There are pretty coves and surf-washed rocks offshore. To leeward the hills give way to mountains as the highway ascends toward the dramatic Big Sur coastline. Over two hundred miles farther north sits the city that Hearst made the center of his publishing empire, an oceanfront metropolis called San Francisco.

LODGING

In the coastal art colony of Cambria is an 1873 bed and breakfast called the **Olallieberry Inn**. The Greek Revival clapboard house contains nine guest rooms, done in Victorian style with 19th-century antiques. The rose-colored carpet and curtains, together with the carefully selected linens, add an element of luxury to this well-appointed establishment. The sitting room is attractively furnished with oak wood. ~ 2476 Main Street, Cambria; 805-927-3222, 888-927-3222, fax 805-927-0202. MODERATE TO ULTRA-DELUXE.

If you would prefer a more rustic atmosphere, head up to **Cambria Pines Lodge**. Set amid 25 acres of Monterey pines, are rambling split-rail lodges with additional cabins dotted about the property. The main building offers a spacious lobby with stone fireplace plus a restaurant and lounge; other amenities include a swimming pool, sauna, and jacuzzi. ~ 2905 Burton Drive, Cambria; 805-927-4200, 800-445-6868, fax 805-927-4016. MODERATE TO DELUXE.

North of Hearst Castle, where Route 1 becomes an isolated coastal road with few signs of civilization, are two hostelries. **Piedras Blancas Motel** has 14 standard motel-type rooms. Most of the units have ocean views. ~ Route 1, seven miles north of Hearst Castle; 805-927-4202. MODERATE TO DELUXE.

Farther along, on a ridge poised between the highway and ocean, sits the more appealing **Ragged Point Inn**. This 19-unit facility has attractive rooms furnished with contemporary hardwood furniture. Another compelling reason to stay is the beautiful ocean view from this clifftop abode. Despite the inn's proximity to the road, it's peaceful and quiet here; fox and raccoon wander near the rooms and sea sounds fill the air. A steep trail leads down to a rock-and-sand beach. ~ Route 1, 15 miles north of Hearst Castle; 805-927-4502, fax 805-927-8862. DELUXE.

DINING

Ethnic and vegetarian food lovers will fare well at **Robin's**. Set in a 1930s Mexican-style house, it serves homemade lunches and dinners. Selections range from burritos to sweet-and-sour prawns to stir-fried tofu. It's an eclectic blend with the accent on Italian and Asian cuisine. Patio seating is available. No dinner on Sunday. ~ 4095 Burton Drive, Cambria; 805-927-5007. BUDGET TO MODERATE.

For fine California cuisine try **Ian's Restaurant**. The decor is contemporary, featuring floral prints on pastel-shaded walls, blond wood furniture, and upholstered banquettes. Ian's seasonal menu draws upon local fresh produce, herbs, and seafood. Also among the specialties are salmon, veal, and lamb. Dinner nightly. ~ 2150 Center Street, Cambria; 805-927-8649. MODERATE TO DELUXE.

SHOPPING

Located a few miles south of Hearst Castle, the seaside enclave of Cambria has developed into an artist colony and become an important arts-and-crafts center, with numerous galleries and specialty shops. Several antique shops are also here; like the crafts stores, they cluster along Main Street and Burton Drive.

Among the foremost galleries in here is **Seekers Collection & Gallery**. It's a glass menagerie inhabited by contemporary, one-of-a-kind vases, goblets, and sculptures. ~ 4090 Burton Drive, Cambria; 805-927-8626.

The Soldier Factory is a journey back to childhood. Part toy store and part aviation gallery, it serves as headquarters for thousands of hand-painted toy soldiers. Some of these antiques are deployed in battle formation, re-enacting clashes from the Civil War and other engagements. Many of the pewter pieces are made in the adjacent "factory." This unique shop has been featured in the *Wall Street Journal*. ~ 789 Main Street, Cambria; 805-927-3804.

For a journey into another world visit **Victoriana**. This diminutive store sells miniatures of Victorian house furnishings. ~ Arlington Street near Main Street, Cambria; 805-927-3833.

Camozzi's Saloon is a century-old bar with longhorns over the bar, wagon wheels on the wall, and a floor that leans worse than a midnight drunk. The place is famous. Besides that, it has a rock band every Friday and Saturday and karaoke on Tuesday. ~ 2262 Main Street, Cambria; 805-927-8941.

SAN SIMEON STATE PARK This wide sand corridor reaches for about two miles from San Simeon Creek to Santa Rosa Creek. It's a wonderful place to wander and the streams, with their abundant wildlife, add to the enjoyment. Unfortunately, Route 1 divides the beach from the camping area and disturbs the quietude. Other parts of the park are very peaceful, especially the **Moonstone Beach** section in Cambria, known for its moonstone agates and otters. There are picnic areas, restrooms, and showers. Restaurants and groceries are nearby in Cambria. ~ On Route 1 in Cambria; 805-927-2020.

▲ There are two campgrounds in the park. San Simeon Creek has 134 sites for tents and RVs (no hookups); $14 to $18 per night. At Washburn there are 70 sites for tents and RVs (no hookups); $7 to $11 per night. Camping reservations can be made by calling DESTINET at 800-444-7275.

WILLIAM R. HEARST MEMORIAL STATE BEACH Located directly below Hearst Castle, this is a placid crescent-shaped beach. The facility measures only two acres, including a grassy area on a rise above the beach. There is a 1000-foot-long fishing pier. Scenic San Simeon Point curves out from the shoreline, creating a pretty cove and protecting the beach from surf. Swimming and fishing is very good, and there are charter boats leaving from San Simeon Landing. Facilities include picnic areas and restrooms. Restaurants and groceries are nearby in San Simeon. Day-use fee, $3. ~ On Route 1 opposite Hearst Castle; 805-927-2020.

▼▼▼▼▼▼▼▼▼▼▼▼▼▼

Outdoor Adventures

Albacore, barracuda, bonito, bass, halibut, yellowtail, and marlin are just some of the fish that ply the waters off the Central Coast and the Channel Islands. If you're interested in a fishing cruise, contact **Cisco's Sportfishing**. ~ Jack's Landing, 4151 South Victoria Avenue, Oxnard; 805-985-8511. **Sea Landing Aquatic Center** offers half- and full-day cruises. ~ 301 West Cabrillo Boulevard, Santa Barbara; 805-963-3564. **Virg's Fish'n** specializes in fishing trips for rock cod and salmon. They also offer long trips ranging from two to three days. ~ 1215 Embarcadero, Morro Bay; 805-772-1222. **Avila Beach Sport-**

fishing has three boats, ranging from 55 to 65 feet. ~ Pier 3, Avila Beach; 805-595-7200.

WHALE WATCHING

If you're in the mood for a whale-watching excursion during the annual migration, contact **Cisco's Sportfishing**. ~ Jack's Landing, 4151 South Victoria Avenue, Oxnard; 805-985-8511. For humpbacks and blue whales, call **Captain Don's**. ~ Stearns Wharf, Santa Barbara; 805-969-5217. **Sea Landing Aquatic Center** will also take you on whale-watching excursions from January through April. ~ The Breakwater, Santa Barbara; 805-963-3564. **Virg's Fish'n** offers skipper-led tours. Sometimes they'll take you out on a small boat for an up-close look at those wonderful creatures. ~ 1215 Embarcadero, Morro Bay; 805-772-1222. **Avila Beach Sportfishing** also operates daily whale-watching trips from the end of December through March. ~ Pier 3, Avila Beach; 805-595-7200.

SEA KAYAKING

A unique way to explore the "aquatic garden" of Morro Bay is by kayak. **Good Clean Fun** offers rentals and instruction. ~ 136 Ocean Front, Cayucos; 805-995-1993. **Kayaks of Morro Bay** provides exciting tours that let you hobnob with seals and local birds. In addition to kayaks, they have a 25-foot American Indian war canoe which seats up to 14 people. ~ Morro Bay; 805-772-1119. You can rent a kayak or arrange a one-day guided paddling trip to the sea caves of Santa Cruz Island through **Aquasports**. ~ 111 Verona Avenue, Goleta; 805-968-7231.

DIVING

For those more interested in watching fish, several outfits in the Central Coast area sponsor dive boats and also offer scuba diving rentals and lessons.

In the Ventura area try **Ventura Dive and Sport** for diving rentals and equipment. ~ 1559 Spinnaker Drive #108, Ventura; 805-650-6500. In Santa Barbara call **Anacapa Dive Center** for scuba instruction, rentals, and exotic warm-water trips. ~ 22 Anacapa Street, Santa Barbara; 805-963-8917. Dive charters to local waters are arranged by **Sea Landing Aquatic Center**. ~ The Breakwater, Santa Barbara; 805-963-3564.

SURFING

Hang ten with surfboard rentals from the following enterprises. **Harbor Water Sports** rents wetsuits, surfboards, and boogie boards. ~ 117 Harbor Way, Santa Barbara; 805-962-4890. **Good Clean Fun** rents boogie boards and wetsuits. ~ 136 Ocean Front, Cayucos; 805-995-1993. **Wavelengths Surf Shop** also offers wetsuits and surfboards to surfers ready to take on the waves. ~ 998 Embarcadero, Morro Bay; 805-772-3904.

BOATING & SAILING

To sail the Pacific or visit the Channel Islands, contact **Sailing Center of Santa Barbara** for boat rentals. They have 40 boats, ranging from

21 to 42 feet. ~ The Breakwater, Santa Barbara; 805-962-2826. **Sea Landing Aquatic Center** offers coastal cruises and charters. ~ The Breakwater, Santa Barbara; 805-963-3564.

GOLF

Golf enthusiasts will enjoy the weather as well as the courses along the Central Coast. In the Oxnard-Ventura area try the wide open 18-hole **River Ridge**. ~ 2401 West Vineyard Avenue, Oxnard; 805-983-4653. **Olivas Park** is a flat 18-hole course complete with driving range and putting green. ~ 3750 Olivas Park Drive, Ventura; 805-642-4303. **San Buenaventura** is lined with eucalyptus, spruce, and pine trees. ~ 5882 Olivas Park Drive, Ventura; 805-485-3050.

In the Santa Barbara area try **Santa Barbara Golf Club**, which is dotted with oaks, pines, and sycamores. ~ Las Positas Road and McCaw Avenue, Santa Barbara; 805-687-7087. **Twin Lakes Golf Course** is a nine-hole field that meanders around two lakes. ~ 6034 Hollister Avenue, Goleta; 805-964-1414. Two miles north is **Sandpiper Golf Course**, an 18-hole championship course right on the ocean. ~ 7925 Hollister Avenue, Goleta; 805-968-1541. A meandering creek passes through **Ocean Meadows Golf Course**, which is a nine-hole, relatively flat playing field. ~ 6925 Whittier Drive, Goleta; 805-968-6814.

The San Luis Obispo area has **Pismo State Beach Golf Course**. ~ 25 Grand Avenue, Grover City; 805-481-5215. **Laguna Lake Golf Course** is a nine-hole field surrounded by beautiful mountains. ~ 11175 Los Osos Valley Road, San Luis Obispo; 805-781-7309. **Avila Beach Resort Golf Course** is dotted with trees, and the driving range overlooks the beach area. ~ Avila Beach Road, Avila Beach; 805-595-2307. **Morro Bay Golf Course** is an 18-hole field lined with lofty pine trees. Part of the course overlooks the ocean. ~ State Park Road, Morro Bay; 805-772-4560. **Sea Pines Golf Course** offers gently rolling hills speckled with mature pine trees. ~ 250 Howard Avenue, Los Osos; 805-528-1788.

◆◆

✔ **CHECK THESE OUT—UNIQUE OUTDOOR ADVENTURES**

- Cruise the **Channel Islands** with one of the local sportfishing companies in search of barracuda, bass, and other big ones. *page 381*
- Paddle a sea kayak on the protected waters of **Morro Bay**, where seals cavort and seabirds play. *page 382*
- Climb Gaviota Peak for the view, then take a dip in natural hot springs on the way down, when you hike the aptly-named **Gaviota Hot Springs and Peak Trail**. *page 386*
- Bike the beautiful seven-mile **Atascadero Recreation Trail** to Goleta Beach, where you can bask in the sun and play in the surf. *page 384*

TENNIS

Tennis anyone? Courts are available at the following sites: **Moranda Park Tennis Complex** has eight lighted courts situated in a beautiful park setting. ~ 200 Moranda Parkway, Port Hueneme; 805-986-6584. **Santa Barbara Municipal Courts** has four facilities with a total of 22 courts; 14 have lighting. ~ Contact the Santa Barbara Recreation Department; 805-564-5418. **Cuesta College** has eight courts which are periodically available to the public. ~ Route 1, San Luis Obispo; 805-546-3207. **Sinsheimer Park** has six courts. ~ 900 Southwood Drive, San Luis Obispo; 805-781-7300. Additional courts are on Price Street near Shore Cliff Lodge, where you can play tennis and watch the waves break. There are four more courts at Shell Beach and Florin roads.

RIDING STABLES

Riding opportunities are available in the Central Coast. **Circle Bar B Stables** takes riders through a ranch and then up to a vista point overlooking the Channel Islands. ~ 1800 Refugio Road, Goleta; 805-968-3901. To ride right along the ocean, contact **The Livery Stable**. ~ 1207 Silverspur Place, Oceano; 805-489-8100.

BIKING

Bicycling the Central Coast can be a rewarding experience. The coastal route, however, presents problems in populated areas during rush hour.

The town of **Ventura** offers an interesting bicycle tour through the historical section of town with a visit to the county historical museum and mission. Another bike tour of note, off of Harbor Boulevard, leads to the Channel Islands National Monument and Wildlife Refuge Visitors Center. A bike map is available at the **Ventura Visitors Bureau**. ~ 89-C South California Street, Ventura; 805-648-2075.

The Goleta Valley bikeway travels from Santa Barbara to Goleta along Cathedral Oaks Road.

Santa Barbara is chock full of beautiful bicycle paths and trails. Two notable beach excursions are the **Atascadero Recreation Trail**, which starts at the corner of Encore Drive and Modoc Road and ends over seven miles later at Goleta Beach, and **Cabrillo bikeway**, which takes you from Andree Clark Bird Refuge to Leadbetter Beach. Also, the **University of California–Santa Barbara** has many bike paths through the campus grounds and into Isla Vista.

Up the coast, a stunning, three-mile bike path links **El Capitan** and **Refugio** state beaches.

Exploring the shores of Morro Bay is popular with cyclists. For the hardy biker a ride up **Black Mountain** leads to sweeping views of the Pacific Ocean.

Bike Rentals   For bicycles in Ventura and Santa Barbara try **Beach Rentals**, which offers tandem and mountain bikes. ~ 901 San Pedro Drive, Ventura, 805-641-1932; and 22 State Street, Santa Barbara, 805-966-2282.

Kites Galore rents tandems, four-wheeled surreys, and traditional bikes in Morro Bay. ~ 1108 Front Street; 805-772-8322.

HIKING

With its endless beaches and mountain backdrop, the Central Coast is wide open for exploration. Shoreline paths and mountain trails crisscross the entire region. All distances listed are one way unless otherwise noted.

First among equals in this hiker's dreamland is the **California Coastal Trail**, the 600-mile route that runs the entire length of the state. Here it begins at Point Mugu and travels along state beaches from Ventura County to Santa Barbara. In Santa Barbara the trail turns inland toward the Santa Ynez Mountains and Los Padres National Forest. It returns to the coast at Point Sal, then parallels sand dunes, passes the hot springs at Avila Beach, and continues up the coast to San Simeon.

VENTURA AREA Bounded by the Santa Monica and Santa Ynez mountains and bordered by 43 miles of shoreline, Ventura County offers a variety of hiking opportunities. (Note, however, that some trails were damaged in the 1993 Southern California fires.) For more information on hiking trails in the area, contact the City of Ventura Community Services Department at 805-658-4733.

Ventura River Trail (3 miles) is a lovely shore hike from the Emma Wood State Beach to Seaside Wilderness Park; popular with birders.

River's Edge Trail (.75 mile) is a great hike for exploring the riparian woodlands along the Ventura River.

Located near Seaside Wilderness Park, **Ocean's Edge Trail** leads you past coastal dunes, a cobblestone shoreline, and wetland vegetation. From here you can go all the way to the Ventura River Estuary.

OJAI AREA Nine miles east of Ojai, **Santa Paula Canyon Trail** (3.5 miles) provides an easy hike to Santa Paula Creek. The path leads to waterfalls and a camp situated in a lovely area.

In Matilija Canyon the **Middle Matilija Trail** (3.1 miles) offers a moderately difficult backpacking hike in a stunning oak-filled area.

Near Ojai, the **Murietta Trail** (1.5 miles) is a good place to bring the kids for an easy trek.

SANTA BARBARA AREA What distinguishes Santa Barbara from most of California's coastal communities is the magnificent Santa Ynez mountain range, which forms a backdrop to the city and provides excellent hiking terrain.

A red steel gate marks the beginning of **Romero Canyon Trail** (5.75 miles) on Bella Vista Road in Santa Barbara. After joining a fire road at the 2350-foot elevation, the trail follows a stream shaded by oak, sycamore, and bay trees. From here you can keep climbing or return via the right fork, a fire road that offers an easier but longer return trip.

San Ysidro Trail (4.5 miles), beginning at Park Lane and Mountain Drive in Santa Barbara, follows a stream dotted with pools and waterfalls, then climbs to the top of Camino Cielo ridge. For a different loop back, it's only a short walk to Cold Springs Trail.

Also located in the Santa Ynez Mountains is Rattlesnake Canyon Trail (3 miles). Beginning near Skofield Park, the trail follows Mission Creek, along which an aqueduct was built in the early 19th century. Portions of the waterway can still be seen. This pleasant trail offers shaded pools and meadows.

Cold Springs Trail, East Fork (4.5 miles) heads east from Mountain Drive in Santa Barbara. The trail takes you through a canyon covered with alder and along a creek punctuated by pools and waterfalls. It continues up into Hot Springs Canyon and crosses the flank of Montecito Peak.

Cold Springs Trail, West Fork (2 miles) leads off the better known East Fork. It climbs and descends along the left side of a lushly vegetated canyon before arriving at an open valley.

Tunnel Trail (4 miles) is named for the turn-of-the-century tunnel through the mountains which brought fresh water to Santa Barbara. The trail begins at the end of Tunnel Road in Santa Barbara and passes through various sandstone formations and crosses a creek before arriving at Mission Falls.

San Antonio Creek Trail (3.5 miles), an easy hike along a creek bed, starts from the far end of Tucker's Grove County Park in Goleta. In the morning or late afternoon you'll often catch glimpses of deer foraging in the woods.

Thirty-five miles of coastline stretches from Stearns Wharf in Santa Barbara to Gaviota State Beach. There are hiking opportunities galore along the entire span.

Summerland Trail (2.5 miles), starting at Lookout Park in Summerland, takes you along Summerland Beach, past tiny coves, then along Montecito's coastline to the beach fronting the Biltmore Hotel.

Goleta Beach Trail (3.5 miles) begins at Goleta Beach County Park in Goleta and curves past tidepools and sand dunes en route to Goleta Point. Beyond the dunes is Devereux Slough, a reserve populated by egrets, herons, plovers, and sandpipers. The hike also passes the Ellwood Oil Field where a Japanese submarine fired shots at the mainland United States during World War II.

Gaviota Hot Springs and Peak Trail (2.5 miles) begins in Gaviota State Park. The first stop on this trek is the mineral pools at Gaviota Hot Springs (about a half mile from the trailhead). After a leisurely dip you can continue on a somewhat strenuous route into Los Padres National Forest, climbing to Gaviota Peak for a marvelous view of ranch land and the Pacific.

Santa Barbara's backcountry offers an inexhaustible number of hiking opportunities ranging from day hikes to week-long treks.

A favorite hiking spot among college students is the **Sespe Hot Springs Trail** (17.5 miles). This steep trail follows a river bed to a hot springs favored by nude bathers. This trip is a two- to three-day trek.

Southern Wilderness Loop (64.5 miles) is a seven- to ten-day back-packer's delight. This strenuous hike leads along creeks and through pine forests, canyons, and chaparral country. Overnight stopovers can be made at any of several camps.

For those interested in a less arduous trek, try **Reyes Peak to Piedra Blanca Trail** (14.5 miles), a two-day trek down Reyes Peak along Piedra Blanca Creek Road. Three Mile Camp and Lion Campground offer inviting overnight respites.

An easy hike for backpackers is the **Blue Canyon Trail** (7.7 miles), located on the far side of the Santa Ynez Mountains from Santa Barbara. This serene canyon country is ideal for exploration.

SAN LUIS OBISPO AREA   The San Luis Obispo area, rich in wildlife, offers hikers everything from seaside strolls to mountain treks. Many of the trails in this area are in the Los Padres National Forest (for information, call 805-925-9538).

Guadalupe-Nipomo Dunes Preserve (2.5 miles) is especially rewarding for dune lovers. This wetland area is a habitat for many endangered birds. The boardwalk trail passes a freshwater lake, a willow community, and many dunes, ending at Pismo Beach. At Oso Flaco Lake there's an entrance kiosk with trail and hiking information. ~ 805-545-9925.

The **Point Sal Trail** (6 miles) offers an excellent opportunity to hike in a forgotten spot along the coast. (But beware, it's not for inexperienced hikers or those afraid of heights.) Alternating between cliffs and seashore, the trail takes you past tidepools, pelicans, cormorants, and basking seals. An excellent whale-watching area, the trail ends near the mouth of the Santa Maria River.

The golden mustard plants and poppies along the way give **Montaña de Oro Bluffs Trail** (2 miles) its name ("Mountain of Gold"). This coastal trail takes you past Spooner's Cove (a mooring place for bootleggers during Prohibition). You'll pass clear tidepools, sea caves, basking seals, otters, and ocean bluffs.

For an interesting hike along the sandspit that separates Morro Bay from Estero Bay, try the **Morro Bay Sandspit Trail** (4 miles). The trail leads past sand dunes and ancient Chumash shell mounds. Stay on the ocean side of the sandspit if you want to avoid the muck.

Several trails in the vicinity of **Lopez Lake Recreational Area** offer opportunities to see the region's flora and fauna. Deer, raccoon, fox, and wood-rats predominate, along with a variety of birds species (not to mention rattlesnakes and poison oak.) ~ 805-489-8019.

At the entrance to the park, **Turkey Ridge Trail** (1.1 miles) climbs steeply through oak and chaparral and offers splendid views of the lake and the Santa Lucia Mountains.

Two Waters Trail (1.3 miles) connects the Lopez and Wittenberg arms of Lopez Lake. It offers marvelous views. The trailheads are located at Encinal or Miller's Cove.

Blackberry Spring Trail (1 mile) commences at upper Squirrel campground and passes many plant species used by the Chumash Indians. This is a moderate hike with a 260-foot climb which connects with High Ridge Trail.

Little Falls Creek Trail (2.75 miles) begins along Lopez Canyon Road (High Mountain Road) and ascends 1350 feet up the canyon past a spectacular waterfall. Views of the Santa Lucia wilderness await you at the top of the mountain.

▼▼▼▼▼▼▼▼▼▼
Transportation

CAR

As it proceeds north from the Los Angeles area, coastal highway Route 1 weaves in and out from Route 101. The two highways join in Oxnard and continue as a single roadway until a point 30 miles north of Santa Barbara. Here they diverge, Route 1 heading toward the coast while Route 101 takes an inland route. The highways merge again near Pismo Beach and continue north to San Luis Obispo. Here Route 1 leaves Route 101 and begins its long, beautiful course up the coast past Morro Bay and San Simeon.

AIR

Santa Barbara and San Luis Obispo have small airports serving the Central Coast. Several airlines stop at the Santa Barbara Municipal Airport, including American Eagle, America West Express, Sky West Airlines, United Airlines, United Express, and USAir Express.

The Santa Barbara Airbus can be scheduled to meet arrivals at the airport; it otherwise goes to Carpinteria, Goleta, and downtown Santa Barbara, as well as Los Angeles International Airport. ~ 805-964-7759. There are also a number of taxi companies available. For the disabled, call Easy Lift Transportation. ~ 805-568-5114.

San Luis Obispo Municipal Airport is serviced by West Air, Wings West, and Sky West Airlines. ~ 805-781-5205.

Ground transportation from San Luis Obispo Municipal Airport is provided by Yellow Cab. ~ 805-543-1234. Or try Yellow Cab of Five Cities. ~ 805-489-1155.

BUS

Greyhound Bus Lines (800-231-2222) has continual service along the Central Coast from both Los Angeles and San Francisco. The Ventura bus terminal is located at 291 East Thompson Boulevard (805-653-0164). Santa Barbara has one at Carrillo and Chapala streets (805-965-3971). The terminal in San Luis Obispo is at 150 South Street (805-543-2123).

For a funky communal "trip" by bus, book reservations with Green Tortoise. This alternative company has once-a-week service from Los Angeles or San Francisco. ~ 800-867-8647.

For those who want spectacular views of the coastline, try Amtrak's **TRAIN** "Coast Starlight." This train hugs the shoreline, providing rare views of the Central Coast's cliffs, headlands, and untracked beaches. Amtrak stops in Oxnard, Santa Barbara, and San Luis Obispo on its way north to Oakland and Seattle. ~ 800-872-7245.

The larger towns in the Central Coast have car rental agencies; check **CAR** the Yellow Pages to find the best bargains. **RENTALS**

To pick up a car in the Oxnard-Ventura area, try **Avis Rent A Car** (805-339-2260, 800-331-1212), **Budget Rent A Car** (805-647-3536, 800-527-0700) or **Hertz Rent A Car** (805-985-0911, 800-654-3131).

At the airport in Santa Barbara try **Avis Rent A Car** (805-964-4848, 800-331-1212), **Budget Rent A Car** (805-964-6791, 800-527-0700), **Hertz Rent A Car** (805-967-0411, 800-654-3131), or **National Interrent** (805-967-1202, 800-227-7368). Agencies located outside the airport with free pick-up include **Dollar Rent A Car** (805-683-1468, 800-800-4000) and **Enterprise Rent A Car** (805-683-0067, 800-325-8007).

In San Luis Obispo, car-rental agencies at the airport include **Avis Rent A Car** (805-544-0630, 800-331-1212), **Budget Rent A Car** (805-541-2722, 800-527-0700), **Hertz Rent A Car** (805-543-8843, 800-654-3131) and **Thrifty Car Rental** (805-544-3777, 800-367-2277). Among those with free pickup service, try **Enterprise Rent A Car** (805-541-4811, 800-325-8007).

Public transportation in the Central Coast is fairly limited. In the **PUBLIC** Ventura area you'll find **South Coast Area Transit**, or SCAT, which **TRANSIT** serves Oxnard, Port Hueneme, Ojai, and Ventura. ~ 805-487-4222.

In the Santa Barbara area, the **Santa Barbara Metropolitan Transit** stops in Summerland, Carpinteria, Santa Barbara, Goleta, and Isla Vista. ~ Carrillo and Chapala streets; 805-683-3702.

The San Luis Obispo area has **San Luis Obispo Transit**, or SLO, which operates on weekdays during daylight hours and even less frequently on weekends. ~ 805-541-2877.

SEVEN

Low Desert

East of metropolitan Los Angeles lies a land of brilliant greens and dusty browns, scorched flats and snow-thatched mountains. The Colorado Desert, the hottest, driest desert in the country, covers a broad swath of California's southeastern quarter. Here winter, with daily highs in the 70s and 80s, attracts sun worshippers, while summer brings withering heat waves.

It's a place where visitors can swim and ski in the same day. Little wonder that its entertainment capital, Palm Springs, has become a celebrity playground. Ever since 1930, when silent film stars Ralph Bellamy and Charlie Farrell began buying up desert land at $30 an acre, Hollywood has been vacationing in Palm Springs. The racquet club that Bellamy and Farrell initiated soon attracted Humphrey Bogart, Ginger Rogers, and Clark Gable. Latter-day luminaries like Bob Hope, Frank Sinatra, and Kirk Douglas continue to strengthen the spot's celebrity cachet.

Only 400 feet above sea level, the town nestles beneath mountains two miles high. Today Palm Springs is the golf capital of the world, sponsoring over 100 tournaments every year. In addition to dozens of golf courses, the region boasts hundreds of tennis courts and a swimming pool for every five residents. Together with satellite towns like Rancho Mirage and Palm Desert, it has become an opulent enclave in which billboards are prohibited, buildings are limited to heights of 30 feet, and manicured lawns are more common than cactus plants.

It was the Agua Caliente Indians who inhabited the area originally and discovered the desert's hot mineral baths. These American Indians hunted and gathered in the surrounding mountains and attributed magical healing powers to the natural springs. Eventually the United States government divided the entire territory into alternating squares of real estate, giving the odd-numbered sections to the Southern Pacific Railroad and deeding the rest to the Agua Calientes.

Today much of this valuable Indian property is leased to tourist res
just 100 miles from Los Angeles, the desert has become a major travel d
Visitors arrive not only to soak in the sun and spas of Palm Springs, but also
the palm groves of Indio. The date-growing center of the country, this bland ag
tural town is a date palm oasis, with gardens reaching from road's edge to the fri
of the mountains. Little Indio's day in the sun arrives every February when it hosts
the Riverside County Fair & National Date Festival, a gala celebration complete with
ostrich and camel races, Arabian Nights pageantry, and booths displaying over 100
varieties of dates.

Farther south lies the Salton Sea, California's largest lake, a briny trough which sits
astride the notorious San Andreas Fault. Nearby Anza–Borrego Desert State Park
stretches across parts of three counties and encompasses a half-million acres of gem-like
springs, rock promontories, and sandstone chasms. Created about 150 million years ago
by an earthquake fault system, the region includes the Jacumba Mountains, a granite
jumble filled with eerie rock formations. Named for Juan Bautista de Anza, the Spanish
explorer who trekked through in 1774, and *borrego*, the desert sheep which inhabits its
hillsides, Anza–Borrego was a vital route for 1850-era stagecoaches and mail wagons.

Joshua Tree National Park, the area's other major park, lies astride the Low and
High deserts, rising from the scorching Colorado Desert to the cooler climes and higher
elevations of the Mojave. Noted for its cactus gardens and stands of Joshua trees, this
vast preserve was formerly home to the Chemehuevi Indians. Miners entered the territory following the Civil War, striking gold in 1873. Within a few years, cattle ranchers also arrived, creating vast ranges and driving the Indians from the land.

Rising between Los Angeles and Palm Springs, creating a gateway to the Low
Desert, is a rapidly developing region known as the Inland Empire. Bounded to the
north by the San Bernardino Mountains, which rise over 11,000 feet and embrace the
popular resort areas of Lake Arrowhead and Big Bear Lake, it is bordered on the east
by the San Jacinto Mountains.

A Spanish explorer named Pedro Fage uncovered the Inland Empire during a 1772
expedition and in the 1830s missionaries began colonizing the region. By the next
decade powerful Spanish families had transformed the territory into sprawling cattle
and horse ranches.

Then in 1851 a party of Mormons settled here, staying for only six years but leaving an indelible legacy. They planted wheat, harvested lumber, and founded the city
of San Bernardino.

Located at the foot of Cajon Pass along a vital route between Los Angeles and the
East Coast, the area expanded in importance. The railroad arrived in 1875; and during the same decade Luther and Eliza Tibbetts planted three orange saplings shipped
across the country from Washington, D.C., giving birth to the Inland Empire's
vaunted citrus industry.

Together with Riverside and Redlands, San Bernardino sprouted with orange and
lemon trees. Growth slackened during the first half of the 20th century, but began to
accelerate again in the 1950s. Today the Inland Empire, with its trim orchards, burgeoning cities, and mountain lakes, is one of California's fastest growing regions, a
fitting entranceway to the increasingly popular Low Desert.

UCTION

391

orts. Located
estination.
to tour
ricul-
ge

▼▼▼▼▼▼▼
ountains

One of the highest ranges in California, the San Bernardinos rise to over 11,000 feet elevation. Together with the San Ga- west, they provide a pine-rimmed barrier between the Basin and Mojave Desert. A popular winter and water the mountains are encompassed within San Bernardino est and offer a string of alpine lakes and lofty peaks.

During the 1860s prospectors combed the area in search of gold. After their luck petered out, loggers and cattle ranchers took over the territory. Later in the century, as dams created the mountain lakes, herds of tourists began roaming the landscape.

Today a single highway, Route 18, nicknamed "Rim of the World Drive," courses through the entire region. Beginning in Crestline, north of San Bernardino, it winds east to Big Bear Lake, offering postcard vistas of the San Bernardino region.

SIGHTS

Before departing on this mountaintop cruise, follow Route 138 from Crestline out to **Silverwood Lake**, the least developed of this region's mountain pools. Here a state recreation area provides opportunities to fish, boat, swim, and explore the secluded fringes of the lake (see the "Beaches & Parks" section in this chapter). Admission. ~ 619-389-2303.

The prettiest and most precious of these alpine gems is **Lake Arrowhead**, a socially exclusive enclave encircled by private homes. Popular with Hollywood notables and Los Angeles business executives, the lake has public facilities along the south shore. The closest most people come to the remaining shoreline is aboard the **Arrowhead Queen**, a 65-passenger paddlewheeler that tours the lake. Admission. ~ Lake Arrowhead Village; 909-336-6992.

About the only thing you'll encounter on Route 18 between Lake Arrowhead and Big Bear Lake, except for panoramic views, is **Santa's Village**. A theme park for little ones, this mock-North-pole outpost features a puppet theater, petting zoo, pony ride, and other attractions. (It's advisable to call ahead to confirm that the village is open.) Admission. ~ 909-337-2481.

HIDDEN ►

A short distance further east lies the **Heaps Park Arboretum**. Here a three-quarter-mile loop trail meanders past ponderosa pines, cypresses, ferns, quaking aspens, and young sequoia trees. The views from this ridge sweep south toward San Bernardino and north across the Mojave Desert.

Larger, friendlier, and less formal than Lake Arrowhead, **Big Bear Lake** stretches for seven miles at a 7000-foot altitude. Lined with resort facilities, it is generally less expensive and less private than its counterpart to the west. Created in the 1880s by a single arch dam, Big Bear is a popular ski area in winter. During summer months it offers a full array of aquatic amenities.

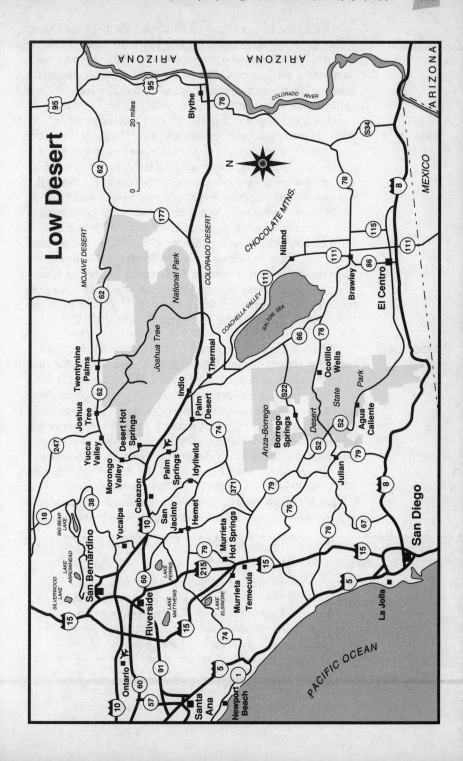

To tour the lake, you can climb aboard the **Big Bear Queen.** Admission. ~ Big Bear Marina, Big Bear Lake; 909-866-3218. While on board, the most unusual place you'll pass will be that stark white dome on the north shore. Called the **Big Bear Solar Observatory,** the telescope is a research station for scientists from Cal Tech. No boat tours are available from June to September.

HIDDEN ▶

Miners nicknamed part of this territory "Starvation Flats," but a few of them struck it rich in **Holcomb Valley.** During the 1860s this conifer-studded region boasted a boom town that rivaled Los Angeles in size. Today rough dirt roads lead to the last vestiges of those golden days. From Fawnskin on the north shore of Big Bear Lake, you can pick up Poligue Canyon Road and other well-marked roads, which bump for five miles past Wilber's Grave, the log remains of Two-Gun Bill's Saloon, Hangman's Tree, and an old log cabin.

A favored destination for children is **Moonridge Animal Park.** Featuring animals indigenous to the San Bernardino Mountains, the zoo contains bobcats, mountain lions, timber wolves, and black bears. Open daily May through October and weekends during the winter (weather permitting). Admission. ~ On Moonridge Road two miles south of Route 18, Big Bear Lake; 909-866-0183.

LODGING

Saddleback Inn beautifully plays the role of mountain lodge. The vintage 1920 structure, complete with steep-pitched roof, gables, and stone chimney, holds 34 comfortable units. The architecture is a mix of formal and country styles and the location is just a few blocks from Lake Arrowhead. A restaurant and lounge round out the amenities in the main building, but the true attraction is the cluster of cottages dotting the property. Similar to the lodge rooms, they feature washed pine furniture, Laura Ashley designs, fireplaces, and tile baths with jacuzzi tubs. ~ 300 State Route 173, Lake Arrowhead; 909-336-3571, 800-858-3334, fax 909-337-4277. DELUXE TO ULTRA-DELUXE.

The **Storybook Inn** is a 1940s-vintage mansion converted to a bed and breakfast, with ten theme-decorated rooms ("Anne of Green

◆◆◆

✔ CHECK THESE OUT—UNIQUE SIGHTS

Gables," "Shangri-La," etc.). Each is filled with antiques and has a private bath. There's an Oriental garden here with oak trees, pagoda, and hot tub, overlooking the valley. The inn is three miles from Lake Arrowhead and, should it matter to anyone, a quarter-mile from Santa's Village. ~ 28717 Route 18, Skyforest; 909-336-1483. DELUXE TO ULTRA-DELUXE.

For reasonably priced accommodations, head uphill about a mile from the lake. **Arrowhead Tree Top Lodge**, an attractive woodframe motel, has 20 units available. Paneled in knotty pine, they are carpeted wall to wall and equipped with veneer furniture. There are also suites with kitchens at deluxe cost. Pool. ~ 27992 Rainbow Drive, Lake Arrowhead; 909-337-2311, 800-358-8733. MODERATE.

For a true bed-and-breakfast experience, stay at **Truffles: A Special Place**. Situated on approximately one acre, this quaint establishment offers five rooms with private baths. Each room is decorated in an English-country style and features antique pieces. Rose, green, and burgundy dominate the color scheme. There's a spacious sitting room with a fireplace where you can spend a cold winter's day chatting with other visitors. Attention to detail is a way of life here. You'll find a fresh bowl of fruit in your room along with truffles and an inviting turned-down bed in the evening. A full breakfast is served every morning. ~ 43591 Bow Canyon Road, Big Bear Lake; 909-585-2772. DELUXE TO ULTRA-DELUXE.

For a location right on Big Bear Lake, you need look no further than **Shore Acres Lodge**. Here 11 woodframe cabins rest in the shade of a pine grove. Each is a full-facility unit with living room, bedroom, and kitchen; several feature two bedrooms and can easily sleep a family. The interiors are bland but quite trim and contemporary. Located away from the main road, Shore Acres is a quiet, private enclave with a pool, jacuzzi, dock, and swings. ~ 40090 Lakeview Drive, Big Bear Lake; 909-866-8200, 800-524-6600, fax 909-866-1580. MODERATE TO DELUXE.

Located "on the quiet side of the lake," the **Quail Cove Lodge** features six rustic cabins with full kitchens, wood-burning fireplaces, and private baths. The whole property borders a bay on one side and a creek on the other, where kids swim all summer long. There's boat access, and the fishing is prime. Other amenities include porches and barbecues. ~ 39117 North Shore Drive, Fawnskin; phone/fax 909-866-5957, 800-595-2683. MODERATE TO DELUXE.

DINING

◄ HIDDEN

At the **Cedar Glen Inn**, there's a simple, wood-paneled café, where they serve breakfast until 3 p.m. at inexpensive prices. There is a sandwich lunch menu and they serve dinner as well, but the bargain here is eggs, eggs, eggs. No dinner on Tuesday. ~ 28942 Hook Creek Road, Cedar Glen; 909-337-8999. BUDGET.

Praised by critics far and wide as Big Bear Lake's finest restaurant, the **Iron Squirrel** is a class act indeed. It's quite a delight to find escargots, duckling in orange sauce, and scrumptious dessert pastries at a restaurant deep in the mountains. But here it is, a fine French-country dining room. No lunch on Monday. ~ 646 Pine Knot Boulevard, Big Bear Lake; 909-866-9121. DELUXE.

Fresh wild game is the order of the day at **Stillwell's**, an exquisite restaurant located in the Northwood Resort. Adorned with stenciled leaf murals, antler chandeliers, and old photos of Big Bear Valley, this dining room recalls the glorious season of autumn. Three gourmet chefs preside over the menu, which includes fresh pastas, wild game, vegetarian entrées, homemade soups, and salads. ~ 40650 Village Drive, Big Bear Lake; 909-866-3121. MODERATE TO DELUXE.

SHOPPING　**Lake Arrowhead Village**, a mock mountain chalet shopping complex, contains dozens of shops. Located directly on Lake Arrowhead, the mall includes boutiques, galleries, sporting goods stores, and sundries shops. ~ Route 189 at Route 173, Lake Arrowhead.

At **Big Bear Lake** the stores are concentrated along Pine Knot Avenue and Big Bear Boulevard (Route 18). Here you'll find crafts shops and knickknack stores. My favorite is a must-see destination called **Sugarloaf Cordwood Co.** The chain-saw carvings of bears and Indians are as big as totem poles, and the shop is cluttered with thousands of ingenious carvings. ~ 42193 Big Bear Boulevard, Big Bear Lake; 909-866-2220.

NIGHTLIFE　The Milky Way will provide most of your evening entertainment in the San Bernardino Mountains. There are a few lounges around Lake Arrowhead and Big Bear Lake, particularly at the **Lake Arrowhead Resort**, but most are little more than pool-table bars. ~ Route 189, Lake Arrowhead; 909-336-1511.

Country-and-western describes the music and the setting at **Defazio's**. This cowboy bar kicks up live entertainment Thursday through Sunday. ~ 28314 Winchester Road, Winchester; 909-926-1057.

PARKS　**SAN BERNARDINO NATIONAL FOREST** 🚶🚴🏇♨️⛺🦌🛶 The most popular national forest in the country, this 670,000-acre park encompasses Lake Arrowhead, Big Bear Lake, and a half-dozen ski areas. It's divided into two sections, one covering the San Bernardino Mountains and the eastern section of the San Gabriel Mountains, the other extending across the San Jacinto Mountains. Topographically, the preserve reaches from desert to mountains, Joshua trees to Jeffrey pines. There are six peaks over 10,000 feet high, six wilderness areas, and 538 miles of hiking trails (as well as a 200-mile section of the Pacific Crest Trail). The park's lakes and 110 miles of streams teem with trout, crappie, bluegill, and small-mouth bass. Skiers, anglers, and boaters will also find complete amenities. Facilities include picnic areas, restrooms, and showers. Restaurants and groceries are located in nearby towns. ~ Off Route 18 north of San Bernardino is the main highway through the national forest's northern section. Routes 74 and 243, between Hemet and Palm Springs, lead through the southern portion; 909-383-5588.

▲ There are 60 campgrounds including 45 sites with hookups. Campgrounds have developed sites for tents and RVs. $10 per night for developed sites; $20 per night for sites with hookups.

SILVERWOOD LAKE STATE RECREATION AREA 🏃 🚲 🏊 🎣
🚣 🛥 🚤 A 976-acre lake and 13 miles of hiking trails make this park a prime destination. It's located at 3355 feet elevation in the San Bernardino Mountains. Except for the recreation area and marina, Silverwood remains undeveloped, a great place to swim and fish. Almost 130 species of birds have been spotted here; coyotes, bobcats, and black bears range the forested slopes that encircle the lake. Facilities include restrooms, picnic areas, snack bar, store, boat rentals, and lifeguards. Trout, bass, bluegill, crappie, catfish, and other fish inhabit the lake. Day-use fee, $6. ~ Located on Route 138 about 30 miles north of San Bernardino; 619-389-2303.

▲ There are 136 campsites that accommodate tents and RVs (no hookups). $18 per night; reservations required.

▼▼▼▼▼▼▼▼▼▼▼▼
The Inland Empire

Extending south from the San Bernardino Mountains, California's Inland Empire encompasses the cities of San Bernardino, Redlands, and Riverside. Once a cattle-ranching region and later a prime citrus-growing area, this interior belt is presently being developed at a mind-boggling rate. For travelers it provides several possibilities: you can tour the San Bernardino Mountains, seek out sites in Riverside and Redlands, or continue further south to the Murrieta Hot Springs and the pine forests of Mt. San Jacinto.

Blessed with water from Big Bear Lake, the town of Redlands became a prime citrus-growing region during the 1880s. By the turn of the century wealthy Easterners seeking mild winters began building mansions amid the orange groves. Today the town numbers about 350 period homes, from tiny California-style bungalows to gaudy Victorian estates.

SIGHTS

Among the most spectacular is **Kimberly Crest**, constructed in 1897. An overweening assemblage of turrets, gables, arches, and fountains, this hilltop château is surrounded by five acres of Italian gardens. The grounds are open daily and there are tours of the house every Thursday through Sunday from 1 to 4 p.m. Admission. ~ 1325 Prospect Drive, Redlands; 909-792-2111.

Redlands also takes pride in its public buildings. Several brick stores line Orange Street (just north of Redlands Boulevard), a commercial strip highlighted by the Grecian-style **Santa Fe Railroad Station**.

The **A. K. Smiley Public Library** is a Moorish structure dramatized by carved sandstone friezes, stained-glass windows, and elaborate woodwork. ~ 125 West Vine Street, Redlands; 909-798-7565. Behind this 1898 edifice stands the **Lincoln Memorial Shrine**, a small but noteworthy museum devoted to Abraham Lincoln. Built of polished limestone in 1932, the octagonal building displays marvelous WPA-type murals. Closed Sunday and Monday.

San Bernardino County Museum, one of the region's major historical facilities, has three floors of changing exhibits. There's an anthropology hall with Indian artifacts and covered wagons, plus an excellent mineral collection. It also features the largest bird egg collection in North America. Around the grounds you'll find orange groves and antique mining equipment as well as odds and ends from the golden age of the railroad. Closed Monday. Admission. ~ 2024 Orange Tree Lane, Redlands; 909-798-8570.

Whitewashed adobe buildings surround a tranquil courtyard at **Asistencia Misión de San Gabriel**. Built in 1830 as an outpost of the San Gabriel Mission, the entire site was used during later years as a rancho. The tree-shaded plaza is a wonderful place to sit and ponder; to divert your attention, there are two small museums re-creating the era of padres and pioneers. Closed Monday and Tuesday. ~ 26930 Barton Road, Redlands; 909-793-5402.

The **Yucaipa Adobe** in neighboring Yucaipa dates to 1859. As the oldest standing two-story adobe in San Bernardino County, the house is a showcase of antiques from the era. With overhanging trees and rusting farm implements, the surrounding yard is another throwback to California's colonial era. Closed Monday and Tuesday. ~ 32183 Kentucky Street, Yucaipa; 909-795-3485.

HIDDEN ▶   A **country drive** out on Oak Glen Road will carry you past orange groves and into apple country. Orchards, blossoming each spring and heavy with fruit in autumn, blanket the landscape. Between Yucaipa and Cherry Valley the road winds through foothills, passing cider mills and roadside stands.

En route are two small county museums, unique but often overlooked. The **Mousley Museum of Natural History** claims to have the largest sea shell collection west of the Mississippi. This appealing little showroom also displays fossils, minerals, and glowing rocks.

FOLKLORIC THEATER

Hemet is home to the **Ramona Pageant**, an annual re-enactment of Helen Hunt Jackson's fabled love story of an Indian maiden. The Ramona Bowl, a natural amphitheater where the play is presented, is set in the foothills of Mt. San Jacinto and utilizes the rocky terrain as its stage. ~ 27400 Ramona Bowl Road, San Jacinto; 909-658-3111.

Closed Monday through Wednesday. ~ 35308 Panorama Drive, Yucaipa; 909-790-3163.

Equally imaginative is the **Edward–Dean Museum of Decorative Arts**, with a rare selection of fine furniture, porcelain, and crystal. The museum has gathered one of the country's best collections of Far Eastern bronzes. The beautifully landscaped grounds are also a pleasure to visit. Closed Monday and the month of August. Admission. ~ 9401 Oak Glen Road, Cherry Valley; 909-845-2626.

Two cities, San Bernardino and Riverside, dominate the Inland Empire. While the former has few noteworthy attractions, the latter provides visitors with several opportunities. Riverside's chief landmark is 1337-foot **Mount Rubidoux**, a rocky prominence on the west side of town. Capped by a memorial cross and peace tower, the cactus-coated hill affords a full-circle vista of the Inland Valley. A narrow thoroughfare, Mount Rubidoux Drive, corkscrews to the summit. (Cars are no longer allowed on Mount Rubidoux Drive. You can walk all the way up to the top.)

Pride of the city is the **Riverside County Court House**, a Beaux-Arts beauty built in 1903. The community also boasts several museums. ~ 4050 Main Street, Riverside. The **Riverside Art Museum**, set in a 1929 Mediterranean-style building designed by Julia Morgan, hosts changing exhibits and special events. Closed Sunday. Admission. ~ 3425 Mission Inn Avenue, Riverside; 909-684-7111.

At the nearby **Riverside Municipal Museum**, housed in the equally inviting 1912 Post Office building, cultural exhibits portray American Indian crafts and trace the history of citrus growing in the region. Among the natural history displays are fossils, minerals, and dioramas illustrating local animal life in its native habitat. ~ 3580 Mission Inn Avenue, Riverside; 909-782-5273.

A seven-year, $55-million renovation was completed in December 1992 at Riverside's most historic site. The **Mission Inn**, one of California's most famous hotels, dates to the 1880s when Frank Miller began expanding his family's adobe house to accommodate guests. The home eventually became a palace with room keys, sprawling across an entire city block and entertaining four United States presidents. (Teddy Roosevelt helped Miller dedicate the structure in 1902, the Nixons were wed here, and the Reagans honeymooned here.) Built in Mission Revival fashion, with Moorish and Oriental elements, Miller's dream became a labyrinth of alcoves and art galleries, balconies and terraces, and patios. More than a hotel, the building incorporates a museum displaying an extensive collection of artifacts from around the world, including Craftsman-period furniture and Tiffany stained glass. But really, the entire building is an antique-filled museum. You can arrange a docent-guided walking tour (fee) by calling the Mission Inn Foundation at 909-788-9556. ~ 3649 Mission Inn Avenue, Riverside; 909-784-0300.

If you tour the campus of the University of California at Riverside, located at the east end of University Avenue, be sure to take in the **Botanic Gardens**. Extending across 39 acres of rugged terrain, it contains cactus, rose, and iris gardens as well as a fruit orchard. The preserve specializes in plants from California, Australia, and southern Africa. ~ 909-787-4650.

Down in Perris, a town better known as a center for hot-air ballooning, the **Orange Empire Railway Museum** displays freight and passenger cars, cabooses, and trolleys. A kind of junkyard for trains, this outdoor museum also contains steam engines, a station house, and several antique buildings. The facility is rather disorganized, however, with exhibits scattered across a sprawling railyard. On weekends and minor holidays, when they muster enough volunteers, the museum provides train and trolley rides. Admission for rides. ~ 2201 South A Street, Perris; 909-657-2605.

The century-old town of **San Jacinto**, rapidly developing in all directions, preserves its heritage along Main Street, where falsefront buildings line several blocks.

HIDDEN ►

The American Indians portrayed in the Ramona extravaganza once occupied the entire area. An outstanding example of their artistry is evident at the **Maze Stone** outside Hemet. This large, perfectly preserved pictograph, carved into a hillside boulder, presents a detailed labyrinth. To get there, take Route 74 about five miles west from Hemet; turn north on California Avenue; turn left on Tres Cerritos Avenue and follow for two and two-tenths miles; then turn right on Reinhardt Canyon Road.

Numerous manmade lakes dot the Inland Empire, including **Lake Elsinore**, a resort destination bordering Cleveland National Forest. While the lake offers a full array of water sports, the town of Lake Elsinore provides all the amenities needed for boating, fishing, and swimming. Among its historic buildings are hotels, restaurants, and shops. ~ Near the intersection of Routes 15 and 74.

A geologic hot spot, the Inland Empire contains some of California's finest spas. At **Glen Ivy Hot Springs** you can down a platter of nachos from the snack bar while relaxing in a jacuzzi, sauna, or mineral pool. The favorite spot, one for which Glen Ivy has gained its nickname, is the red clay mud bath. Guests plop down into this caramel-colored ooze, smear it across their ever-loving bodies, then bask in the sun till it hardens. Human mud pies. ~ 25000 Glen Ivy Road, Corona; 909-277-3529.

Like many towns in transition throughout the Inland Empire, **Temecula** is an Old West community that is simply exploding with development. Falsefront stores still line Front and Main streets, with wooden sidewalks leading to antique stores. And the **Temecula Valley Museum**, located within eyeshot of shopping complexes and housing developments, preserves the village's early history. Closed Monday and Tuesday. ~ 41950 Main Street, Temecula; 909-676-0021.

The Temecula Valley is a prime winegrowing region. Travel east from Temecula along Rancho California Road and you'll discover nearly a dozen vineyards. **Callaway Vineyard & Winery**, largest of the lot, produces premium wines from its 720-acre spread. ~ 32720 Rancho California Road; 909-676-4001. At **Mount Palomar Winery** there are shady picnic areas amid 100 acres of vineyards as well as a full-service Mediterranean deli. ~ 33820 Rancho California Road; 909-676-5047. **Maurice Carrie Vineyard and Winery**, with 113 acres and a contemporary tasting room, offers free tastings. Most of the other local wineries now charge a minimal tasting fee. ~ 34225 Rancho California Road; 909-676-1711. **Thornton Winery**, in addition to the winery tour, offers a champagne bar where, for a fee, you can sample a variety of champagnes, freshly baked breads, and goat cheese inside or on a patio overlooking its 20 acres of vineyards. ~ 32575 Rancho California Road; 909-699-0099.

LODGING

Other than being the second largest city in the Inland Empire, San Bernardino has little to recommend it. Since the intersection of Routes 10 and 215 lies along the edge of town, many desert travelers use San Bernardino as a jumping off point, though few remain more than one night. One of the most convenient motel strips is Hospitality Lane, a frontage road adjacent to Route 10. **La Quinta Motor Inn**, a representative sample, has 153 units. ~ 205 East Hospitality Lane, San Bernardino; 909-888-7571, 800-531-5900, fax 909-884-3864. MODERATE.

In neighboring Redlands, the **Morey Mansion Bed & Breakfast Inn**, with its French mansard roof and onion dome, is nothing short of spectacular. An 1890-era Victorian, the inn is garnished with Italianate balustrades, Gothic arched windows, beveled glass from Belgium, stained glass from France, and hand-carved oak. The sitting rooms are museum-quality examples of the age of Victorian archi-

---

✔ CHECK THESE OUT—UNIQUE LODGING

- *Budget:* Save money for soaking in hot springs at **Linda Vista Lodge**, a motel in Desert Hot Springs with mineral pools. *page 411*
- *Moderate to deluxe:* Stroll through the pines and oaks at the cozy **Strawberry Creek Inn**, where country living goes a long way. *page 404*
- *Deluxe to ultra-deluxe:* Retreat to the **Saddleback Inn**, a vintage lodge near the shores of Lake Arrowhead. *page 394*
- *Ultra-deluxe:* Pretend you're not looking for celebrities at the elegant **Ingleside Inn**, where many of the antique-filled rooms include fireplaces, terraces, and private steambaths. *page 409*

Budget: under $50 Moderate: $50–$90 Deluxe: $90–$120 Ultra-deluxe: over $120

tecture and the five upstairs bedrooms are embellished with rare fixtures and antique furnishings. ~ 190 Terracina Boulevard, Redlands; 909-793-7970, fax 909-793-7870. DELUXE TO ULTRA-DELUXE.

The **Mission Inn** is the region's most luxurious hotel and one of the most famous hostelries in the country. Originally constructed in the 19th century, the hotel has been completely renovated to preserve its elegant and original design. A veritable palace, the Mission Inn features an arched entranceway that extends a full city block, Oriental gardens, and a cloister complete with music room and museum. The rotunda curves upward to a gallery where there are now meeting rooms and retail outlets. There are 248 rooms, an Olympic-sized pool, health club, massage room, two restaurants, two lounges, and a museum that houses artifacts from around the world including Tiffany furniture, 19th- and 20th-century paintings, and historical pieces from the Far East. ~ 3649 Mission Inn Avenue, Riverside; 909-784-0300, 800-843-7755, fax 909-784-5528. DELUXE TO ULTRA-DELUXE.

If you want to indulge in the spa treatments at Glen Ivy Hot Springs, be sure to spend the night at the **Country Side Inn**. The place offers French-country atmosphere in the Low Desert. There are 100 guest rooms decorated with four-poster beds and colorful prints. Complimentary breakfast buffet is offered every morning. ~ 2260 Griffin Way, Corona; 909-734-2140, 800-448-8810, fax 909-734-4056. MODERATE TO DELUXE.

At long last there's a proper bed and breakfast in the scenic Temecula Valley wine country. **Loma Vista Bed and Breakfast** is a classy, Mission-style hilltop home overlooking vineyards. It offers a choice of six spacious designer rooms, each done in a different decorative motif. Guests share a lovely living room with a fireplace and take breakfast family-style in a formal dining room. ~ 33350 La Serena Way, Temecula; 909-676-7047, fax 909-676-0077. DELUXE.

DINING   If you're in San Bernardino, check out **GuadalaHarry's**, a hacienda-style Mexican restaurant. With its brilliantly colored walls, interior balcony, and serape decor, the place evokes a sense of the high life in Old Mexico. Despite the ironwork and handcarved beams, this multichambered establishment is reasonably priced. The menu presents a medley of *chimichanga* and taco dishes as well as *favoritos Mexicanos* like fajitas and flautas. ~ 280 East Hospitality Lane, San Bernardino; 909-889-8555. BUDGET.

Ask for a table in the vault at **The Bank** and withdraw your favorite Mexican dishes. Housed in the 1913 First National Bank of Temecula building, this is the town's most unusual restaurant. The enchiladas, quesadillas, fajitas, and tacos, served at lunch and dinner, make it the area's favorite Mexican eatery. ~ 28645 Front Street, Temecula; 909-676-6160. BUDGET.

Café Champagne is ideally located overlooking the vineyards at the Thornton Winery. The elegant California-style decor makes this the perfect spot to sip champagne or wine. Entrée choices vary but typically include angelhair primavera and mesquite salmon. They even serve a gourmet burger for lunch and dinner. ~ 32575 Rancho California Road, Temecula; 909-699-0088. MODERATE TO DELUXE.

Big-name rock and pop acts play at **Glen Helen Blockbuster Pavilion**, an outdoor arena in a natural setting. Closed in winter. ~ Glen Helen Regional Park, Devore; 909-886-8742.

NIGHTLIFE

GLEN HELEN REGIONAL PARK 🚶 🚴 ⛵ 🎣 🏊 There are 500 acres of shady groves and chaparral-coated hills here at the foot of the San Bernardino Mountains. Two lakes stocked with trout and catfish, a one-mile nature trail through a marsh, and ample playground and picnic areas are among the features. Facilities include restrooms, showers, boat rentals, waterslide, and other swimming equipment; restaurants and groceries are nearby in Devore. Day-use fee, $5. ~ Located at 2555 Devore Road in Devore (near the intersection of Routes 15 and 215); 909-880-2522.

PARKS

▲ There are 60 tent sites; $10 per night. Camping is also available at **Yucaipa Regional Park** (33900 Oak Glen Road, Yucaipa; 909-790-3127), which has 9 tent sites and 26 RV sites (13 with full hookups); $17 per night for hookups, $11 per night without.

LAKE PERRIS STATE RECREATION AREA 🚶 🚴 🏇 ⛵ 🎣 🏊 🚤 Another of the Inland Empire's attractive lakes, Perris is bounded by the Russell Mountains and Bernasconi Hills. It features rock-climbing areas, a sandy beach for swimming, boat rentals, and a ten-mile bike trail around the lake. More than 100 bird species have been spotted here, including ducks and geese, and the eastern shore is open seasonally to hunters. Everything from lizards to mule deer inhabits the surrounding sage scrub countryside. Facilities include picnic areas, restrooms, showers, lifeguards, marina, and waterslide. If you fish, try for bass, trout, catfish, and bluegill. Day-use fee, $6. ~ 17801 Lake Perris Drive in Perris; 909-657-0676.

▲ There are 177 tent sites and 254 RV sites with hookups; $22 per night for hookups, $16 per night without.

LAKE ELSINORE RECREATION AREA 🚶 🚴 🏇 ⛵ 🎣 🏊 🚤 Bounded by a large lake on one side and lofty mountains on another, this popular park is inevitably filled with anglers, boaters, and aquatic enthusiasts of all stripes. Far from idyllic, the recreation area consists of a sprawling parking lot fringed with palm trees and campsites. Lake Elsinore offers a picnic area, restrooms, showers, and a playground. Restaurants and groceries are nearby. Fishing is good when the water level is high. Day-use fee, $5. ~ Located on Route 74 two miles southwest of the intersection with Route 15; 909-674-3177.

▲ There are 325 sites with hookups and 25 sites without; $17.50 per night for hookups, $13.50 per night without.

▼▼▼▼▼▼▼▼
Idyllwild

Bordering the Inland Empire to the east are the San Jacinto Mountains, a spectacular chain of 10,000-foot peaks dividing the region from Palm Springs and the Low Desert. Routes 243 and 74 climb into this alpine environment from the north and west respectively.

SIGHTS

At the center of the chain sits the mile-high town of **Idyllwild**. Tucked beneath bald granite peaks, this pine-tufted community is surrounded by San Bernardino National Forest. Once inhabited by Cahuilla Indians, the area now is a major tourist destination. In addition to restaurants and shops, Idyllwild has a host of secluded cabins for rent. For information on trails and campgrounds throughout the region, stop by the **Idyllwild County Park Nature Center**. ~ Off Route 243 one mile north of Idyllwild; 909-659-3850.

LODGING

Strawberry Creek Inn is a rambling old mountain home nestled among the pines and oaks of the San Jacinto Mountains. Country-decorated and carefully maintained, it offers a cozy, cabin-in-the-woods atmosphere within walking distance from Idyllwild's busy village center. Guests can choose from several original rooms in the main house or newer ones in an added wing at the rear. A full gourmet breakfast is served in a bright, cheery wraparound dining porch. ~ 26370 Route 243, Idyllwild; 909-659-3202, 800-262-8969, fax 909-659-4707. MODERATE TO DELUXE.

A place with a name like **Knotty Pine Cabins** could easily devolve into a self-parody. But there they are, eight woodframe cabins nestled in a conifer grove. Nicely secluded yet still within walking distance of town, the units feature fireplaces, homespun decorations, and knotty-pine walls. Most offer a living room, bedroom, and kitchen, and price in the moderate to deluxe range; one cabin, the "Sleepy Pine," is a single room without kitchen at a budget price. ~ 54340 Pine Crest Drive, Idyllwild; 909-659-2933. MODERATE TO DELUXE.

You can also rent houses and cabins in Idyllwild through a local agency, **Associated Idyllwild Rentals**. ~ P.O. Box 43, Idyllwild, CA 92349; 909-659-5520.

DINING

The local gathering place up in the mile-high town of Idyllwild is **Jan's Red Kettle**. Homey as a log cabin, it's a knotty-pine café with lace curtains. Breakfast items fill about half the menu and include *huevos rancheros*, "old-fashioned oatmeal," omelettes, and biscuits with gravy. Completing the daily offerings are soups, salads, hamburgers, pastas, and sandwiches. No dinner on Monday, Tuesday, and Wednesday. ~ 54220 North Circle Drive, Idyllwild; 909-659-4063. MODERATE.

Among Idyllwild's finest restaurants is **Restaurant Gastrognome**, a pretty woodframe place with a stone fireplace and beam ceiling. The selections are diverse, portions plentiful, and the food delicious. Beef tournedos, Australian lobster, and rack of lamb head the menu; also included are calamari, chicken Kiev, and a variety of seafood pasta dishes and fresh fish. ~ 54381 Ridgeview Drive, Idyllwild; 909-659-5055. MODERATE TO DELUXE.

Idyllwild offers numerous arts and crafts shops. Several country roads near the village center are dotted with cabins converted into small stores.

SHOPPING

Kountry Collectibles typifies the homespun theme pervading most of these shops. Here you will find quilts, decorative wreaths, and stitchery. ~ 54380 North Circle Drive, Idyllwild; 909-659-4498.

Epicurean, by contrast, demonstrates that the elite influence of Palm Springs is filtering into this remote mountain town. Among its offerings are rare wines, gourmet specialties, and sleek decorative accessories. ~ 54791 North Circle Drive, Idyllwild; 909-659-5251.

MOUNT SAN JACINTO STATE PARK 🚶🚴🏇🛶 Extending from Idyllwild in the west to Palm Springs in the east, this magnificent preserve encompasses a broad swath of the San Jacinto Mountains. It features mountain meadows and subalpine forests as well as granite peaks 10,000 feet high. The park itself covers about 3500 acres and an adjacent wilderness area extends across 10,000 acres. Facilities include picnic areas, restrooms, and showers. Day-use fee, $5. ~ Located on Route 243 in Idyllwild; the park can also be reached via the aerial tramway in Palm Springs; 909-659-2607.

PARKS

▲ About 125 sites are spread out over several campgrounds and hike-in camps and include 25 RV sites without hookups. Camping costs $12 to $15 per night, depending on site and location. There is also camping at **Idyllwild County Park** (909-684-0196, reservations; 909-659-2656, information).

Take a desert landscape thatched with palm trees, add a 10,000-foot mountain to shade it from the sun, then place an ancient mineral spring deep beneath the ground. What you have is a recipe for Palm Springs. It's a spot where the average daily temperature swings from an invigorating 55 to a toasty 85.

▼▼▼▼▼▼▼▼▼▼▼▼
Palm Springs Area

Little wonder that the town represents the nation's desert showplace, one of the few Western locales where winter brings the best weather. A fashionable health spa and celebrity playground, Palm Springs is the ultimate destination for sunning, swimming, and slumming. Many attractions close or have limited hours during the hot summer months. It's advisable to call in advance.

To direct you, divert you, and help you determine an itinerary for touring the town, there are two local agencies. You may try the **Palm Springs Desert Resorts Convention and Visitors Bureau**, which is

SIGHTS

closed on weekends. ~ Atrium Building, Route 111, Rancho Mirage; 619-770-9000. Printed information and friendly advice is also available at the **Palm Springs Chamber of Commerce**. ~ 190 West Amado Road, Palm Springs; 619-325-1577.

They'll inevitably point you toward the **Palm Springs Desert Museum**, one of California's great regional art centers. Contained in a dynamic and contemporary structure with stone facade, the museum combines desert art, culture, and natural history. There are dioramas illustrating local animal life, a wing devoted to Death Valley, exhibits of basketry by indigenous Cahuilla Indians, and stark black-and-white photos of the American West. Backed against the mountains in an exclusive section of Palm Springs, the complex includes works of contemporary art as well as a section devoted to Western American art. The most appealing places of all are the sculpture gardens—lovely, restful plots with splashing fountains and native palms. A 22,000-square-foot addition with new art galleries and an education center opens in November 1996. Closed Monday. Admission. ~ 101 Museum Drive, Palm Springs; 619-325-7186.

In the fall of 1997, the area code for the Palm Springs Area will change from 619 to 760.

If it's local history you're after, the **Village Green Heritage Center** will do quite nicely. Incongruously located amid a row of luxury shops are three antique buildings. Each seems to have been restored a bit too efficiently, making this downtown attraction look more like a mock-antique mall than a museum. Open mid-October to May. ~ 221 South Palm Canyon Drive, Palm Springs; 619-323-8297.

The interiors, however, encapsulate the entire sweep of local history. In the **McCallum Adobe Museum** you'll find tools, clothes, paintings, and books from Palm Springs' early years. Constructed in 1884, the town's oldest building, it's also filled with photos of Hollywood stars, including one of Groucho Marx without his trademark moustache. Admission.

Neighboring on the old McCallum place is **Cornelia White's House**, the 1893 home of a pioneer woman. Fabricated from railroad ties, it displays 20th century appurtenances, including a wrought-iron wood stove and Palm Springs' first telephone. Admission.

Had Cornelia lived longer, she could have patronized **The 1930s General Store Museum**. A re-creation of a 1930-era general store, this marvelous museum is literally lined with tins of Chase & Sanborn coffee, boxes of Rinso Detergent, and an entire wall of apothecary jars. One of the most complete collections of its kind, it contains an inventory of over 6000 items, almost all filled with their original contents. The Store has penny gumball machines, nickel candy bars, and, yes, Prince Albert in a can. Open weekends only during the summer and Thursday through Sunday the rest of the year. Admission. ~ 619-327-2156.

One of the most luxuriant labyrinths you will ever traverse is a place called the **Moorten Botanical Garden**. The result of a 50-year effort by the Moorten family, this living monument to the desert displays over 3000 varieties of desert plants. There are prickly pears, agaves, and a cactarium with a desert's worth of cacti in a single greenhouse. It's an enchanted garden, inhabited by birds and turtles, dotted with petrified trees, and filled with dinosaur fossils. Admission. ~ 1701 South Palm Canyon Drive, Palm Springs; 619-327-6555.

Renowned as a retreat for millionaires and movie stars, Palm Springs for centuries was the private domain of the Agua Caliente Indians. A band of the Cahuilla Indian group, the Agua Calientes roamed the territory, seeking out the cool canyons of the San Jacinto Mountains in summer, then descending during winter months to the warmth and healing mineral springs of the desert floor.

Among the most scenic parcels are the **Indian Canyons,** a string ◄ *HIDDEN* of four lush mountain valleys that reach from desert bottomlands deep into the San Jacinto Mountains. Visitors can spend the day hiking, exploring, and picnicking in these preserves:

Andreas Canyon, a spectacular mountain gorge, contains Indian rock art as well as mortar holes left by Indian women pounding beans and acorns into meal. A stream tumbles through the valley, cutting the canyon walls and watering the 150 plant species that parallel its course. From here a one-mile trail leads to **Murray Canyon,** where more than 750 palm trees cluster around deep pools and small waterfalls. Mountain sheep and wild ponies roam this remote chasm.

Palm Canyon stretches for 15 miles and contains more than 3000 Washingtonia palm trees, some as old as 2000 years. An island of palms in a desert sea, it displays exotic rock formations and mountain pools. Admission. ~ Four miles south of Palm Springs, off South Palm Canyon Road; 619-325-5673.

If hiking 14 miles up Palm Canyon is really a bit much, you can soar into the San Jacinto Mountains on the **Palm Springs Aerial Tramway.** Climbing at a teeth-clattering 50-degree angle and ascending more than a mile to 8516 feet elevation, this mountain shuttle makes Mr. Toad's wild ride seem like a cakewalk. Admission. ~ Tramway Road, Palm Springs; 619-325-1391.

The reward for those white knuckles is a view of the Coachella Valley from Joshua Tree to the Salton Sea. On a clear day you might not see forever, but you will spot a mountain peak near Las Vegas, 175 miles away.

In addition to the usual snack bar/souvenir shop amenities, there are several trails at the top, including a three-quarter-mile nature loop. The nearby **ranger station,** which serves this section of Mount San Jacinto State Park, has information on longer hikes. ~ 619-327-0222. From mid-November to mid-April, snow permitting, the Nordic Ski Center is open for cross-country skiing.

Cabot's Old Indian Pueblo, the home of a feisty desert pioneer, is a four-story adobe built in the fashion of the Hopi Indians. With 35 rooms, 150 windows, and walls two feet thick, this maze-like building is a testament to the strange vision of a single individual. Cabot Yerxa, who arrived in the desert in 1913, spent more than 20 years building his house. A personal museum, it is filled with pioneer relics, Indian artifacts, and turn-of-the-century photographs of the great tribes. Today the carefully preserved pueblo is open to anyone with an interest in this pioneer spirit. Closed Tuesday. Admission. ~ 67-616 East Desert View Avenue, Desert Hot Springs; 619-329-7610.

You can take a 20-minute mule ride (summer only) around the slopes of Mt. San Jacinto before descending on the Palm Springs Aerial Tramway.

South of Palm Springs lie **Rancho Mirage** and **Palm Desert**, two extraordinarily wealthy bedroom communities. Parked in the middle of the desert, these havens for the rich and retired display so many country clubs, palm trees, and landscaped estates as to create a kind of release from reality. They name streets after people like Bob Hope and Frank Sinatra and use water everywhere—for fountains, cascades, golf greens—in a splendid display of excess.

The ultimate expression of this profligacy is **Marriott's Desert Springs Resort and Spa**, a 400-acre resort with hanging gardens, five-tiered waterfalls, and a lagoon with motorboats. Here white desert sands slope down to crystalline lakes and one of the swimming pools is a 12,000-square-foot extravaganza. To combine such unrestrained decadence with so much water, the Romans would have had to build Venice. ~ 74-855 Country Club Drive, Palm Desert; 619-341-2211.

Aptly named indeed is **The Living Desert**, a 1200-acre nature park that presents a raw and realistic picture of desert life. This grand outdoor zoo contains bighorn sheep, gazelles, and Arabian oryx from the deserts of Africa. Bats, rattlesnakes, and screech owls inhabit a special display that simulates the desert at night; and a walk-through aviary houses finches, green herons, and hermit thrushes. The Eagle Canyon section, a wildlife exhibit and endangered species breeding center, is home to mountain lions, wolves, and golden eagles among other animals. There are also botanical gardens planted with vegetation from eight of the world's deserts, and hiking trails that wind for more than six miles into nearby foothills. Ponds re-create the life of desert oases and special lizard and tortoise exhibits present some of the region's most familiar creatures. Culturally speaking, this exceptional park is an oasis in itself. Open daily from October to mid-June; closed August. Open irregular hours the rest of the year, so call ahead. Admission. ~ 47-900 Portola Avenue, Palm Desert; 619-346-5694.

For an overview of the entire area, head up Route 74 on the **Palms to Pines Tour**, which will carry high into the Santa Rosa Mountains. Desert ironwood trees and creosote bushes front the road, giving way at higher elevations to manzanita and mountain mahogany. As the highway climbs to lofty heights, dramatic vistas of the Coachella Valley open to view. If you're ambitious, it's possible to connect with

Routes 243, 10, and 111 on a 130-mile loop trip through the San Jacinto Mountains and back to Palm Springs.

Indio may be flat, dry, and barren, but it has one homegrown product that puts the place on everyone's map—dates. The only region in the United States where the fruit is grown, Indio boasts 3000 acres of date palms. Tall, stately trees with fan-shaped fronds, they transform a bland agricultural town into an attractive oasis.

At Shield's Date Gardens they serve date shakes and date ice cream. Unfortunately, the best thing about their movie, *The Romance and Sex Life of the Date*, is the title. ~ 80-225 Route 111, Indio; 619-347-0996. Here or at Jensen's Date & Citrus Garden you can wander through a date orchard. ~ 80-653 Route 111, Indio; 619-347-3897.

If you still haven't had your fill, the Coachella Valley Museum and Cultural Center features displays on local agriculture. This small regional showplace also contains an Indian room with artifacts from the Cahuilla tribe and a collection of heirlooms donated by local residents. Closed Monday and Tuesday. Admission. ~ 82-616 Miles Avenue, Indio; 619-342-6651.

LODGING

Travelers interested in rubbing elbows with show-biz types should consider the elegant little Ingleside Inn. Garbo slept here, they say, and Sinatra, Schwarzenneger, and Shields. And why not? The double rooms, villas, and minisuites are cozy, charming, and laden with unusual antiques. Extras include fireplaces, private steambaths, and terraces, but everyone gets the same old-fashioned (i.e., attentive) service here. ~ 200 West Ramon Road, Palm Springs; 619-325-0046, 800-772-6655, fax 619-325-0710. ULTRA-DELUXE.

The Mira Loma Hotel, a conservatively styled complex, has 14 rooms surrounding a pool. The interior patio is lined with flagstones and planted with citrus trees, creating an attractive desert environment. Laid out in the fashion of a motel, Mira Loma's guest rooms are very spacious; most have dressing areas and some are equipped with kitchens. ~ 1420 North Indian Canyon Drive, Palm Springs; 619-320-1178, fax 619-320-5308. MODERATE TO DELUXE.

The private villas at La Mancha Private Villas and Court Club are the last word in romantic escapism. Spanish-Moroccan architecture, high arched windows, and massive ceiling beams give the 54 accommodations an almost castlelike ambience. All the villas have private courtyards; many have private pools. Spa and in-room dining are among the amenities. ~ 444 North Avenida Caballeros, Palm Springs; 619-323-1773, 800-255-1773, fax 619-323-5928. ULTRA-DELUXE.

Out on the southern edge of Palm Springs, Tiki Spa Hotel is a 28-unit facility occupying almost two acres. Polynesian in style, it offers jacuzzis, saunas, swimming pool, game room, and a restaurant. The accommodations vary from hotel rooms to apartment units, with

the latter featuring kitchens and private patios. ~ 1910 South Camino Real, Palm Springs; 619-327-1349. DELUXE.

La Serena Villas is one of those places people come back to year
after year. A colony of semi-detached houses, it offers guests a homelike atmosphere with yards, flowerbeds, and two
swimming pools. While some units resemble standard
hotel rooms, others are one-bedroom apartments with
kitchens and patios. Located in a residential neighborhood, La Serena, true to its claim, is "clean, quaint, and
quiet." Closed July and August. ~ 339 South Belardo
Road, Palm Springs; 619-325-3216. MODERATE TO DELUXE.

According to local lore, Al
Capone turned the Two
Bunch Palms oasis into
a fortress, constructing
a stone house with a
lookout turret and
secret escape tunnel.

Desert House Inn, one block away, rests within shouting
distance of the San Jacintos. Another small, personalized hotel, its five guest rooms are situated around a swimming pool.
Each room is slightly different in decor and all have kitchens. The
grounds are tenderly maintained, with flower gardens, palm trees,
and poolside umbrellas. ~ 200 South Cahuilla Road, Palm Springs;
619-325-5281. MODERATE.

Casa Cody Hotel bills itself as "a country bed and breakfast inn."
The second oldest hostelry in Palm Springs, Casa Cody has a hideaway feel that recalls the early gentility of Palm Springs. Its 23 guest
rooms have been refurbished in a Southwest-chic decor. Many have
kitchens and some have fireplaces. Breakfast is served poolside. ~
175 South Cahuilla Road, Palm Springs; 619-320-9346, 800-231-
2639, fax 619-325-8610. MODERATE TO DELUXE.

With its overweening wealth, Palm Springs inevitably possesses
numerous luxury resorts. Unlike many, Villa Royale Inn displays its
richness in an understated, personalized fashion. The owners spent
six years buying antiques in Europe and shipping them home to fur-
nish their sumptuous bed-and-breakfast inn. Every room of this
walled-in complex follows an individual theme, reflecting the art and
culture of a different European country. Many have kitchens, fireplaces, and private patios. Covering more than three acres, the inn's
grounds are a series of interior courtyards framed by pillars and
planted in bougainvillea. Amid brick footpaths and asymmetrical
gardens are two swimming pools, jacuzzis, and a restaurant. Room
tabs here in Eden are moderate to deluxe for standard rooms and
ultra-deluxe for larger rooms with private outdoor patio spas and
suites. ~ 1620 Indian Trail, Palm Springs; 619-327-2314, 800-245-
2314, fax 619-322-3794. MODERATE TO ULTRA-DELUXE.

The hot mineral pools that the Agua Caliente Indians originally
discovered are today part of the Spa Hotel Resort and Mineral
Springs. Bubbling from the ground at 106 and containing 32 trace
minerals, the waters made Palm Springs famous. They have also made
the Spa Hotel a unique resort. On the grounds are two Roman-style
tubs, an outside swimming pool, and spa facilities including inhala-

tion rooms, dry saunas, and mineral baths. Lodgers can also enjoy herbal wraps and massages or join in exercise classes in the gymnasium. The entire hotel is lavishly appointed with pastel-hued carpets and contemporary decor. A pictorial history of the Agua Caliente tribe adorns the lobby walls. Guest rooms are equally fashionable. ~ 100 North Indian Canyon Drive, Palm Springs; 619-325-1461, 800-854-1279, fax 619-325-3344. ULTRA-DELUXE.

If you listen to their publicity agents, many resorts are destinations unto themselves, providing everything a traveler could possibly desire. **Two Bunch Palms** is an entire oasis unto itself, a world of hot mineral baths surrounded by ancient palm trees. This exclusive 45-acre retreat, with its guarded entrance, serves as a hideaway for Hollywood celebrities. They've been visiting since the 1930s, when mobster Al Capone reputedly built the place. The gangster's gambling casino has given way to a gourmet restaurant and his ultra-secure hideout has become an informal resort. Guests soak in the hot mineral pool, utilize a spa facility with saunas and massage therapists, and wander an estate which includes lawns, tennis courts, swimming pool, nude sunbathing areas, and koi ponds. ~ 67-425 Two Bunch Palms Trail, Desert Hot Springs; 619-329-8791, 800-472-4334, fax 619-329-1317. DELUXE TO ULTRA-DELUXE.

Desert Hot Springs also offers lower-priced facilities, many of which are parked along Hacienda Drive. **Linda Vista Lodge** is a motel-style establishment with 42 rooms clustered around two hot mineral pools. There are also saunas, jacuzzis, and an outdoor swimming pool. ~ 67-200 Hacienda Drive, Desert Hot Springs; 619-329-6401, 800-334-7200. BUDGET.

Guests at any of the 240-plus accommodations at the **Ritz-Carlton Rancho Mirage** have only to open the french doors to their patio or balcony to enjoy a commanding view of the entire Palm Springs area. Located on a 650-foot-high plateau in the Santa Rosa Mountain foothills, this is a 24-acre hotel and tennis resort. Fine artwork, custom fabrics, antiques, crown moldings, and luxury-level amenities are standard in the rooms; the suites are truly elegant. ~ 68-900 Frank Sinatra Drive, Rancho Mirage; 619-321-8282, 800-241-3333, fax 619-321-6928. ULTRA-DELUXE.

DINING

Everybody's favorite lunch counter is **Louise's Pantry**, a landmark café so popular with the local gentry that people are inevitably lined up outside the door. This is a plastic-and-formica eatery providing standard American fare. Settle into a booth or pull up a counter stool and dine on meatloaf, pork chops, or filet of sole. ~ 124 South Palm Canyon Drive, Palm Springs; 619-325-5124. BUDGET TO MODERATE.

A spacious hacienda with murals, fountains, and inlaid tile, **Las Casuelas Terraza** is a classic Hispanic dining room. Pass through the archways and you'll discover hanging plants and exquisite wrought-iron decorations throughout. A step above other Mexican restaurants, the establishment serves *pollo asado* (marinated chicken), *pescado greco* (fish filet in garlic and wine), and *camarones florencio* (shrimp in salsa), as well as the standard south-of-the-border entrées. ~ 222 South Palm Canyon Drive, Palm Springs; 619-325-2794. MODERATE.

If you do nothing but admire the stained glass at **Lyon's English Grille**, it will prove worth the price of admission. This grand British dining room also displays a museum-quality collection of plates, Toby jugs, and art pieces from Olde England. The bill of fare at this enchanting establishment includes steak-and-kidney pie, braised lamb shank, roast duckling, prime rib, calf's liver, and fresh seafood. Dinner only. ~ 233 East Palm Canyon Drive, Palm Springs; 619-327-1551. MODERATE TO DELUXE.

For entertainment with your dinner, make reservations at **Moody's Celebrity Room**. You'll dine at Liveri's Italian restaurant and choose from a bill of fare including *osso buco*, angelhair primavera, and shrimp scampi. An ensemble with six vocalists and a pianist will perform songs from Broadway musicals and, at the conclusion of this festive but relaxed evening, the waiter will present you with an extravagant dinner tab. ~ 350 South Indian Canyon Drive, Palm Springs; 619-323-1806. ULTRA-DELUXE.

Melvyn's is one of those famous establishments with as many awards on the wall as items on the menu. Among the toniest addresses in town, it's a classic Continental restaurant complete with mirrors, crystal chandeliers, and wooden upholstered chairs. Celebrities have frequented the place for years. Among its other attributes is an inventory of entrées that features Maryland crab cakes, grilled fish, and châteaubriand. ~ 200 West Ramon Road, in the Ingleside Inn, Palm Springs; 619-325-2322. DELUXE TO ULTRA-DELUXE.

Le Vallauris is an enclave of country French cuisine and decor just off the main drag. A piano bar sets the tone in this converted

---

✔ CHECK THESE OUT—UNIQUE DINING

- *Budget:* Cash in on tasty Mexican meals at **The Bank**, an eatery housed a 1913 bank, where the food is good and the local interest rate is high. *page 402*
- *Budget to moderate:* Line up outside **Louise's Pantry**, a landmark lunch counter in Palm Springs serving standard American fare. *page 411*
- *Deluxe:* Scurry over to the **Iron Squirrel**, where you can savor French country cuisine in the heart of the mountains at Big Bear Lake. *page 395*
- *Deluxe to ultra-deluxe:* Step into the Ingleside Inn for filet dijonnaise and salmon hollandaise at the award-winning **Melvyn's**. *page 412*

Budget: under $8   Moderate: $8–$16   Deluxe: $16–$24   Ultra-deluxe: over $24

private residence for rich dishes such as duck and foie gras and New Zealand venison. Velvet armchairs and a garden of ficus trees and blooming cyclamen warm up this attractive two-room restaurant. ~ 385 West Tahquitz Canyon Way, Palm Springs; 619-325-5059. DE-LUXE TO ULTRA-DELUXE.

Kam Lum, a Chinese eatery set in a mini-mall, serves Cantonese dishes such as orange beef and shrimp with lobster sauce, as well as a dozen specialty dishes. Closed Monday. ~ 66610 8th Street, Desert Hot Springs; 619-251-1244. BUDGET.

El Gallito Café is a cheap, funky, bare-bones Mexican restaurant with good food at even better prices. There are piñatas and hokey paintings on the walls and some talented people back in the kitchen. The crowd is local, and the menu is solid and predictable. ~ 68-820 Grove Street, Cathedral City; 619-328-7794. BUDGET.

◄ *HIDDEN*

Beef, beef, and more beef is the item of choice at **Côte de Boeuf.** Elegantly furnished with soft kerosene lighting, this restaurant is a great place to try 34 different varieties of beef. A typical entrée might include grilled steak with green beans and garlic mashed potatoes. Dinner only. ~ 69-620 Route 111, Rancho Mirage; 619-328-9000. MODERATE TO DELUXE.

Palm Desert Cedar Creek Inn is a little old-fashioned, which might be the reason it's so popular with local residents. White walls, flowery curtains, and oak booths are a trademark here. The cuisine, accordingly, is American, with such entrées as fresh salmon, New York steak, beef medallions, and rack of lamb. ~ 73-445 El Paseo, Palm Desert; 619-340-1236. MODERATE TO DELUXE.

For upscale French dining, saunter into **Club 74.** The brass-rail, hardwood decor accentuates an Old World motif that includes live piano music, impeccable service and exquisitely prepared dishes. Here the local elite packs the small dining room, each personally greeted by the gregarious owner, Ali Baba (no kidding). Try the succulent duck specials. ~ 73-061 El Paseo, Palm Desert; 619-568-2782. DELUXE TO ULTRA-DELUXE.

Palm Canyon Drive, the Main Street of Palm Springs, contains the region's greatest concentration of shops. There are almost as many signature stores as palm trees along this swank boulevard. The center within the center is **Desert Fashion Plaza,** a stone-floor-and-splashing-fountain labyrinth, which wends past jewelers, designer boutiques, and department stores. ~ Between Tahquitz Way and Amado Road, Palm Springs; 619-320-8282.

SHOPPING

Adagio Galleries down the street has a fine collection of Southwestern art. The inventory not only includes colorful oil paintings but American Indian ceramics as well. ~ 193 South Palm Canyon Drive, Palm Springs; 619-320-2230.

Across the street at **B. Lewin Galleries,** you'll find what is reputedly the world's largest collection of paintings by Mexican masters.

Some of the works here are little short of magnificent. ~ 210 South Palm Canyon Drive, Palm Springs; 619-325-7611.

Cathedral City has several shops that will delight any budget-minded shopper. **Pier 1 Imports** stocks a full range of decorative items and clothing styles. ~ Located at Fred Waring Drive and Town Center Way, Cathedral City; 619-321-6622. At **Little Baja** you'll find Mexican pottery, wall masks, statuary, and pre-Columbian idols. ~ 34-750 Date Palm Drive, Cathedral City; 619-328-3708.

Consumer central in Palm Desert is the **Palm Desert Town Center**, a large mall offering several department stores and a host of small shops. ~ 72-840 Route 111 at Route 74, Palm Desert; 619-346-2121.

The region's more elegant stores line **El Paseo**, a multiblock extravaganza that runs through the heart of Palm Desert. Among the galleries lining this well-heeled boulevard is **Icings**, displaying items crafted from wood, metal, fiber, clay, and glass. ~ 73-425 El Paseo, Palm Desert; 619-568-1224.

Also stop by **The Tortoise Shelf**, the gift shop at the Living Desert Reserve. They have an excellent collection of books, prints, jewelry, and gift items, all relating to the desert. ~ 47-900 Portola Avenue, Palm Desert; 619-346-5694.

NIGHTLIFE   A growing Palm Springs tradition of recent vintage is **Villagefest**, a weekly night street fair on Palm Canyon Drive that features food booths, live music, and 150 artists and craftspersons. The fair takes place every Thursday evening throughout the year.

The center of action in downtown Palm Springs is **Zelda's**, a rocking disco with video screens, two dancefloors, and eight bars. Contests and fashion shows punctuate sets of deejay music. Cover. ~ 169 North Indian Canyon Drive, Palm Springs; 619-325-2375.

The place to view and be viewed in this celebrity-conscious town is **Melvyn's**. The lounge at this fashionable Continental restaurant offers piano bar music and a small dancefloor. ~ 200 West Ramon Road, Palm Springs; 619-325-0046.

Over at the Wyndham Palm Springs Hotel, **The Lobby Bar** is a pleasant spot for a quiet drink. ~ 888 East Tahquitz Way, Palm Springs; 619-322-6000.

Cactus Corral features live country music and will even teach you to dance western-style. Cover. ~ 67501 Route 111, Cathedral City; 619-321-8558.

State-of-the-art and ultra-fashionable, the **McCallum Theatre for the Performing Arts** represents the desert showplace for symphonies, dramas, and concerts. This 1140-seat theater is the cultural capital of the Palm Springs area. ~ 73-000 Fred Waring Drive, in the Bob Hope Cultural Center, Palm Desert; 619-346-6505.

PARKS   **LAKE CAHUILLA COUNTY PARK**
Stark is the word for this place. It's a manmade lake with dirt banks,

very little vegetation, and bald mountains looming in every direction. One section of the park has been landscaped with lawns and palm trees; the rest is as dusty as the surrounding desert. Since the lake is stocked with trout and catfish, most people come to fish, swim, or camp. The park offers picnic areas, a swimming pool, restrooms, showers, lifeguards, and a playground. Restaurants and groceries are several miles away in Indio. In the summer the park is only open Friday through Monday. Day-use fee, $2. ~ Located at 58-075 Jefferson Street in La Quinta; 619-564-4712.

▲ There are 60 RV sites, all with hookups, and 88 primitive sites; $16 for hookups, $12 for primitive sites. This park is locked at 10 p.m., so campers cannot go in or out until 6 a.m.

▼▼▼▼▼▼▼▼▼▼▼▼▼▼▼▼▼

Palm Springs Gay Scene

Gay travelers are heartily welcomed throughout this desert resort community. Since the first exclusively gay resort opened in the 1970s, Palm Springs has grown to be a popular gay getaway. Today the lively scene is as much a part of Palm Springs as are golf courses; there are over two dozen gay resorts as well as numerous restaurants, nightspots, and shops, owned by gays and catering to gay visitors.

Much of the scene revolves around the resorts, so selecting one that reflects your personal taste is an important part of planning your trip. Once you arrive you'll need a car to get to all the hot spots, but finding your way around is easy. Most visitors overlook the fact that having a car provides the opportunity to enjoy the wilderness areas around Palm Springs, and while I don't recommend you try to reenact the hiking scene from *Priscilla Queen of the Desert*, I do suggest you consider escaping town for a picnic and a stroll on a desert trail (see "Beaches & Parks" sections throughout this chapter).

LODGING

With almost 30 resorts and hotels serving a gay clientele, Palm Springs is a major vacation destination for both gay men and women. Lodgings range from small bed-and-breakfast inns to deluxe resorts that serve singles, couples, or a mix of both.

Alexander Resort offers eight garden rooms, five of which are equipped with kitchenettes. Tastefully appointed, these guest rooms surround landscaped grounds, a spa, and swimming pool. Two of the rooms have individual patios. The resort affords complete privacy and allows nude sunbathing. Men only. ~ 598 Grenfall Road, Palm Springs; 619-327-6911, 800-448-6197. MODERATE.

Harlow Club Hotel bills itself as "a civilized Eden." Surrounded by tropical gardens, it features Spanish-style 1930s-era bungalows. Guest rooms, designed in award-winning style, include fireplaces and private patios. There's also a gymnasium, spa, and rooftop sundeck for guests. Men only. ~ 175 East El Alameda, Palm Springs; 619-323-3977, 800-223-4073, fax 619-320-1218. DELUXE TO ULTRA-DELUXE.

The **Abbey West** is a flashback to the old days in Palm Springs, when movie stars and starlets slipped away from Hollywood for some private sun time in the desert. Sixteen handsome rooms form a low-rise horseshoe around a landscaped pool and outdoor spa. Custom-designed furniture, whimsical framed artwork, private patios, and kitchenettes make these accommodations comfortable for a week-long stay. Although this establishment is gay-friendly, it caters to a mixed clientele. ~ 772 Prescott Drive; 619-416-2654, 800-223-4073, fax 619-323-5719. DELUXE TO ULTRA-DELUXE.

The **Hot Desert Knights** plays host to gay men. Each of the eight studio units comes with a kitchen and private patio, and there is a swimming pool in a garden setting. ~ 435 Avenida Olancha, Palm Springs; 619-325-5456, 800-256-7938. MODERATE.

Debuting in 1975 as Palm Springs' first gay resort, **El Mirasol Villas** was built by Howard Hughes back in the '40s for Elizabeth Taylor's mum. This lavish resort offers one- and two-bedroom suites equipped with kitchens; some have private patios. Trees and other lush landscapes surround the two pools and the jacuzzi. Fountains, statues, and umbrellas abound. Breakfast and lunch are served poolside. ~ 525 Warm Sands Drive, Palm Springs; 619-327-5913, 800-327-2985, fax 619-325-8931. DELUXE TO ULTRA-DELUXE.

Spread across two acres, **Hacienda En Sueño** is an upscale retreat with seven one-bedroom apartments. There are gardens, trees, and grassy areas at this refined getaway. Men only. ~ 586 Warm Sands Drive, Palm Springs; 619-327-8111, 800-359-2077. ULTRA-DELUXE.

A women-only establishment, **Bee Charmer Inn** offers 13 rooms decorated in a Southwestern style. All units feature French doors overlooking a swimming pool and garden. ~ 1600 East Palm Canyon Drive, Palm Springs; 619-778-5883. MODERATE.

Delilah's Enclave, a women-only inn, serves complimentary breakfast to its boarders. Its 11 rooms are touched with a homey, Southwestern flair. The king suites are very cozy; they feature private patios and full kitchens. A misting system over the pool and jacuzzi keeps things cool, as does the clothing-optional rule. ~ 641 San Lorenzo Road, Palm Springs; 619-325-5269, 800-621-6973, fax 619-320-9535. MODERATE.

DINING

The **Rainbow Cactus Cafe** has a large gay clientele and keeps it loyal with good homecooking: chicken and dumplings, liver and onions, and New York steak. Lunch consists of egg dishes, salads, and sandwiches. A piano bar swings into action at night. Brunch on Sunday. ~ 212 South Indian Canyon Drive, Palm Springs; 619-325-3868. BUDGET TO MODERATE.

With mauve brocade booths and a giant granite slab for a bar, gay-owned **Shame on the Moon** is both elegant and modern. Despite its debonair standards, "desert-casual" wear is heartily welcomed.

Diners may feast on the special dinner entrées whipped up each evening, usually Continental dishes ranging from baked filet of salmon with a fresh horseradish crust to sautéed calf's liver. Dinner only. Open Thursday through Sunday in the summer; closed Monday the rest of the year. ~ 69-950 Frank Sinatra Drive, Rancho Mirage; 619-324-5515. MODERATE TO DELUXE.

R & R Menswear stocks contemporary, stylish clothing for the guy on the go. Beach wear, sports jackets, active wear, and club-geared garb can all be found here at moderate prices. ~ 333 North Palm Canyon Drive, Palm Springs; 619-320-3007.   **SHOPPING**

Quench your thirst for glamour at **Patsy's Clothes Closet**, where you can find high-end designer styles and movie costumes (Brad Pitt's *Interview With a Vampire* raiments were sold here for a pretty penny). ~ 4121 East Palm Canyon Drive, Palm Springs; 619-324-8825.

For novelty gifts and gags, try **Paper Lilli**. ~ 114 North Palm Canyon Drive, Palm Springs; 619-327-3373. **Moonlighting** is equally wacky and includes T-shirts in its selection as well. ~ 307 East Arenas Road, Cathedral City; 619-323-8830.

The friendly atmosphere of **Streetbar** explains why it's so popular among the locals and tourists. Although the clientele is primarily men, women also receive a hearty welcome. The knocking of billiard balls and pinballs keeps things active, and if you happen to be here on the right day at the right time, you might catch a drag show or a diva captivating the crowd. Otherwise, take a seat inside or on the outdoor patio, have a drink, and relax. ~ 224 East Arenas Road, Palm Springs; 619-320-1266.   **NIGHTLIFE**

Despite its dark, gloomy interior, **The Tool Shed** is a spirited watering hole. The graffiti on the painted black walls changes once a year at the bar's anniversary party. In the meantime, the guys pass the time by downing a few drinks, learning how to throw a dart properly, and cuing up the stick until it's a perfect sky blue. ~ 600 East Sunny Dunes Road, Palm Springs; 619-320-3299.

More low-key and appealing to both gay men and women is **Gloria's**, a cozy piano bar. ~ 2400 North Palm Canyon Drive, Palm Springs; 619-322-3224.

Furnished with antiques and bric-a-brac, the **Sweetwater Saloon** is a restaurant/bar where you can eat and drink until it closes. The piano bar swings into action Monday through Thursday and is accompanied by a lounge singer who belts out more than lounge music: country, big band, and jazz. When the live music comes to an end, the jukebox picks up. ~ 2420 North Palm Canyon Drive, Palm Springs; 619-320-8878.

With high energy dancing in the compound, fresh air and cool conversation on the patio, plus pool tables and a video bar in the connections room, **Choices** certainly lives up to its name. However, the real action takes place on the big dancefloor. Arrive early on Thursdays to stake out a good seat for the male strip show. On Sunday nights the club hosts a popular celebrity lookalike contest featuring a new celebrity each month—call ahead so you can pack the right outfit and wig. Cover. ~ 68352 Perez Road, Cathedral City; 619-321-1145.

Also in Cathedral City is **CC Construction Co.** This sprawling club boasts two bars—a dance bar and a country-and-western bar. Cover on weekends. ~ 68-449 Perez Road, Cathedral City; 619-324-4241.

For women's night out, check out **Delilah's.** This combination sportsbar and nightclub gives the predominantly female crowd plenty to do: dancing in the glow of the disco ball (Thursday through Sunday), watching sports on one of a dozen TV screens, or competing in the weekly pool tournament. ~ 68-657 Route 111, Cathedral City; 619-324-3268.

▼▼▼▼▼▼▼▼▼▼▼▼▼▼▼
Joshua Tree National Park Area

It's only about 50 miles from Palm Springs to Joshua Tree, but in the course of the journey you will pass from the heart of California's hot, windblown Low Desert to the edge of its rugged and diverse High Desert. In the course of this transition, the road rises from 400 feet above sea level to over 4000 feet. Even more dramatic is the change in the flora and fauna as you pass from one biological zone to another.

SIGHTS
No, that's not a hallucination on Route 10 west of Palm Springs. Those really are dinosaurs at **Dinosaur Delights** looming above the highway. Or dinosaur replicas anyway: an *Apatosaurus* 45 feet high and 150 feet long, and his companion, a *Tyrannosaurus rex* that stands 65 feet high. Each weighs more than 40 tons and has interior viewing platforms. The *Apatosaurus* even contains a gift shop and petting zoo. ~ 5800 Seminole Drive, Cabazon; 909-849-8309.

Bridging the gap between the High and Low desert areas is **Big Morongo Canyon Wildlife Preserve,** a 3900-acre facility managed by the Nature Conservancy and the Bureau of Land Management. This oasis, with several springs and one of the region's few year-round streams, features several nature trails. Bobcat and bighorn sheep inhabit the area, which is also prime birdwatching territory. The bird population here is about 100 times as plentiful as elsewhere in the desert. Varying from a cottonwood-rimmed stream to desert washes, the canyon is also a place of rare beauty. ~ Located on East Drive, Morongo Valley; 619-363-7190.

In addition to dramatic rock formations, the town of Yucca Valley, a stopover on the way to Joshua Tree, possesses two points of interest. **Desert Christ Park**, at the north end of Mohawk Trail, created by one man during the last nine years of his life, portrays several biblical scenes. Among the outsize sculptures are a 16-ton statue of Christ and a tableau of the Last Supper. The town's **Hi-Desert Nature Museum** exhibits fossils, rocks and minerals, and Indian artifacts. They also have a small zoo with desert animals and reptiles. Closed Monday. ~ 57116 Twentynine Palms Highway, Yucca Valley; 619-369-7212.

One of the great inland destinations, **Joshua Tree National Park** is an awesome 793,000-acre sanctuary straddling California's High and Low deserts. Its northern region, of greater interest to visitors, rests at about 4000 feet elevation in the Mojave. To the south, where Joshua trees give way to scrub vegetation, lies the arid Colorado Desert. Admission.

The main entrance to the park, off Route 62 in Twentynine Palms, leads to the **Oasis Visitors Center**, a full-facility stop with a museum and ranger station. The best place to chart a course through the preserve, it rests in the Oasis of Mara, a grove of palms once used by Indians and prospectors. ~ 619-367-7511.

Black Rock Canyon Visitors Center, featuring a ranger station and small exhibit, lies about 30 miles farther west of the Oasis Visitors Center. ~ 619-365-9585.

As you proceed south and west into the heart of the park, weathered granite, smoothed by the elements, rises in fields of massive boulders. In the foreground, Joshua trees, their branches like arms raised heavenward, stand against a cobalt sky. Many of the rocks are carved and hollowed to create skulls, arches, and whatever shapes the imagination can conjure. With such an abundance of rock, it's no wonder that Joshua Tree is one of the world's top rock-climbing destinations. Especially in winter, you'll see lizard-people all over the park, scaling sheer faces with impossible grace.

FICTIONAL GHOST TOWN

Fiction, it seems, has become reality in **Pioneertown**. This unusual hamlet was built in 1947 as a film set for Westerns. Somehow the producers never managed to start the cameras rolling and the place became an ersatz ghost town. Then people began moving in, converting falsefront buildings into a general store, post office, private homes, and even a bowling alley. Today several of the old raw wood structures survive and you can tour the neighborhood, exploring a fictional ghost town that returned to life. ~ Located four miles northwest of Yucca Valley on Pioneertown Road.

The Joshua trees that complement this eerie landscape are giant yucca plants, members of the agave family, which grow to heights of almost 50 feet. They were named in the 1850s by Mormon pioneers, who saw in the stark, angular trees the figure of the prophet Joshua pointing them further westward.

West of Jumbo Rocks Campground, **Geology Tour Road**, a dirt track (four-wheel-drive vehicles recommended), leads for nine miles past unusual rock sculptures, alluvial fans, and desert washes. **Squaw Tank**, an ancient Indian campsite, contains Indian bedrock mortars and a concrete dam built by ranchers early in the century. A pamphlet available from the information centers will also help locate petroglyphs, mine shafts, and magnificent mountain vistas.

A paved route from the main roadway deadends at **Keys View**. The finest panorama in the park, it sweeps from 11,485-foot Mt. San Gorgonio across the San Jacinto Mountains to the Salton Sea, and takes in Palm Springs, the Colorado River Aqueduct, and Indio. The full sweep of the Coachella Valley lies before you, a dusty brown basin painted green with golf courses and palm groves.

Desert Queen Ranch, one of the few outposts of civilization in Joshua Tree, was built early in the century by William F. Keys, a former sheriff, prospector, and Rough Rider. On a ranger-led tour you can visit this ghost village complete with ranch house, school, corral, and barn.

The unique transition zone between the Mojave and Colorado deserts becomes evident when you proceed toward the southern gateway to the park. As the elevation descends and temperatures rise, plant life becomes sparser.

Yet here, too, the inherent beauty of the park is overwhelming. **Cholla Cactus Garden**, a forest of cactus that is a pure delight to walk through, is one of Joshua Tree's prettiest places. With their soft, bristly branches, these Bigelow cactus live in a region that rarely receives more than four inches of rain a year.

Beyond this natural garden the road passes through a landscape of long, lithe ocotillo plants. Then you'll journey past the parched, dust-blown Pinto Basin to the **Cottonwood Visitors Center**, the southern gateway to Joshua Tree National Park.

LODGING   A desert traveler could not ask for more than a rustic, family inn in a palm oasis. Located in a natural setting within eyeshot of Joshua Tree National Park headquarters, **29 Palms Inn** has 12 adobe cottages and four renovated old frame cottages. With fireplaces, country decor, and sturdy old furniture, they bear personalized names like "Ghost Flower" and "Fiddle Neck." This marvelous inn, encompassing 70 acres, was founded in 1928 and has been in the same family for four generations. Pool, restaurant, and lounge. ~ 73950 Inn Avenue, Twentynine Palms; 619-367-3505, fax 619-367-4425. MODERATE TO DELUXE.

Near the northern entrance to Joshua Tree National Park, **29 Palms Inn** is a homespun restaurant with a friendly staff and family photos on the walls. Situated in a rustic hotel, it serves American cuisine at lunch and dinner. There's grilled halibut, steak, stir-fry vegetables, and several daily specials. ~ 73950 Inn Avenue, Twentynine Palms; 619-367-3505. MODERATE.

DINING

JOSHUA TREE NATIONAL PARK 🚶🚲 Covering 793,000 acres, most of it wilderness, this famous preserve lies on the border of California's High and Low deserts. It possesses characteristics of both the Mojave and Colorado deserts, ranging from Joshua tree forests at 4000 feet to ocotillo and cholla cactus at lower elevations. The preserve's granite hills offer sport for rock climbers, while its miles of hiking trails attract day-hikers and wilderness enthusiasts alike. The desert life includes tarantulas, roadrunners, sidewinders, golden eagles, and coyotes, but it is the desert plants that make the sanctuary truly special. Facilities include picnic areas, restrooms, and museums; restaurants and groceries are located in towns outside of the park; there are three information centers. ~ Entrances are located off Route 62 in Joshua Tree and Twentynine Palms and off Route 10 east of Indio; 619-367-7511.

PARKS

▲ There are five primitive campgrounds with free camping. (Bring your own water.) The two developed campgrounds, Black Rock and Cottonwood, cost $10 and $8 per night respectively. No hookups are available at either campground but RVs may use the developed sites. All vehicles must pay a $5 park entrance fee.

▼▼▼▼▼▼▼▼▼▼▼▼▼▼

The largest state facility in the United States, Anza–Borrego Desert State Park, which extends across a broad swath of the Colorado Desert, reaches almost to the Mexican frontier. Within its borders lie desert sinks, sculpted rocks, and multicolored badlands. Bighorn sheep roam the mountains and desert life abounds in the lowlands.

Anza–Borrego Desert State Park

Borrego Springs, the only sizeable town in the entire preserve, contains an excellent **visitors center**. Here are nature trails, a cactus garden, and a small museum with displays and a slide show. ~ End of West Palm Canyon Drive; 619-767-4205.

SIGHTS

For a **vantage point** overlooking this magnificent territory, follow Route S22 west toward Culp Valley. Sharply ascending into the mountains, the road looks out across the Borrego Badlands to the Salton Sea. To the north rise the Santa Rosa Mountains and in the south, deep brown against the blue sky, are the Vallecito Mountains.

Font's Point, one of the park's most popular vistas, will provide a close-up view of the Borrego Badlands. A truly spectacular spot, it overlooks rock formations painted brilliant colors and chiseled by wind and water. This heavily eroded area reveals remnants of the prehistoric Colorado River delta. To reach Font's Point, follow Route S22 for about 12 miles east from Borrego Springs, then turn south for four miles onto a marked road. This rough, sandy track lies at the bottom of a wash, so take care not to become mired in the sand.

The entire stretch of Route S22 from Borrego Springs east to the Salton Sea is nicknamed **Erosion Road**. Along its 30-mile length are countless sandstone hills, brilliant red in color and carved into myriad shapes. Many are banded with sedimentary layers containing marine fossils.

Perhaps one even contains the lost gold mine of "Pegleg" Smith. Thomas Long "Pegleg" Smith, it seems, was a prospector with a talent for tall tales. The nickname, he claimed, resulted from an 1827 Indian battle from which he emerged missing one leg. A few years later Pegleg passed through California, discovering a small amount of gold, which in the alembic of his imagination was eventually transformed into an entire mine.

Even a prospector needs a public relations man. Pegleg's publicity agent came along a century later when Harry Oliver, a Hollywood director, created the **Pegleg Monument**. Drawing a circle on the ground, Oliver urged everyone hoping to discover Pegleg's lost gold mine to fill the area with rocks. Today the monument is a huge pile of stones to which you are obliged to contribute. Good luck! ~ Route S22 and Henderson Canyon Road, eight miles east of Borrego Springs.

HIDDEN ► Along the eastern border of the park, near Ocotillo Wells, lie the **Split Mountain/Fish Creek**. Sculpted by water, these heights have been transformed into a variety of textures and compositions. Each level presents a different color, as if the hills had been deposited layer by layer from on high. To get there, follow Split Mountain Road south from Route 78 for 12 miles; turn right onto the road to Fish Creek campground and follow it for about two-and-one-half miles (until it becomes impassable). When the road is in good condition, you can drive right into the gap in the mountain created by geologic forces.

South of Borrego Springs, Route S3 traverses Yaqui Pass. From the roadside (near the 2.0 mile sign), a .25-mile trail leads to **Kenyon Overlook**, with views of Sunset Mountain and surrounding canyons.

Farther south in Anza–Borrego, Route S2 parallels the historic Southern Emigrant Trail. At **Box Canyon Monument**, a path leads to a point overlooking the old trail. It was here in 1847 that the Mormon Battalion hewed a track wide enough for wagons. ~ Nine miles south of Scissors Crossing.

The **Vallecito Stage Station**, built in 1852, served the Butterfield and other lines for years. Today an adobe reconstruction of the building stands in Vallecito County Park. With its plentiful water supply, this site was also an important campground for the gold prospectors coming overland to Northern California mines in 1849. ~ Route S2, 19 miles south of Scissors Crossing.

The Salton Sea

One of California's strangest formations lies deep in the southern section of the state, just 30 miles from the Mexican border. The Salton Sea, a vast inland waterway 36 miles long and 15 miles wide, may be the biggest engineering blunder in history.

Situated 234 feet below sea level, directly atop the San Andreas Fault, the area has been periodically flooded by the Colorado River for eons. From six million until two million years ago forests covered the hillsides and local hollows were filled with lakes and streams. But as the region became increasingly arid, the lakes dried up, and for two million years the basin was desert.

Then in 1905 the irrigation system for the Imperial Valley went amok, the Colorado River overflowed its banks, and a flood two years in duration inundated the land. The Salton Sea was reborn. Because of present-day evaporation as well as minerals left by earlier seas, the water is ten percent saltier than the Pacific.

California's largest lake, it continues even today to grow from agricultural runoff. As you approach it from the north, this vast sea, ringed by palms and seeming to extend endlessly, resembles the ocean itself. Lying at the confluence of the Imperial and Coachella valleys, one of the lushest agricultural regions in the world, the Salton Sea possesses rare beauty. Along its northwest shore on Route 86, rows of date palms run to the water's edge and citrus orchards create a brilliant green landscape backdropped by chocolate-brown mountains. Other sections of shore, given over to trailer parks, mud flats, and alkali deposits, are astonishingly ugly.

The best place to fish and enjoy sandy beaches is at the **Salton Sea State Recreation Area**. Long and narrow, this amazing park extends for 18 miles along the northeast shore. Since the lake represents California's richest inland fishery, there are great opportunities to fish for sargo, tilapia, corbina, and gulf croaker. Swimming is popular at each of the park's five campgrounds, but is best at Mecca Beach. Admission. ~ On Route 111; 619-393-3059.

The Salton Sea supports 350 bird species, so birdwatchers also flock here in significant numbers. The best places to birdwatch are at Sneaker Beach, the marshes around Salt Creek Campground, and between the campgrounds at park headquarters and Mecca Beach.

Farther south lies the **Salton Sea National Wildlife Refuge**. This preserve is a prime avian habitat as some 371 bird species have been sighted here, including stilts, pintails, green-winged teal, and the endangered Yuma clapper rail. The rising of sea level has diminished the park's land area from 35,000 to 20,000 acres, but you're still liable to see great blue herons wading along the shore and snow geese arriving for the winter. ~ Entrances from Sinclair Road west of Calipatria and Vendel Road north of Westmorland; 619-348-5278.

For a dramatic idea of the terrain confronting these pioneers, continue to **Carrizo Badlands Overlook**. In all directions from this windswept plateau, the landscape is an inhospitable mix of mountain peaks and sandy washes. Heavy erosion has worked its magic here, creating stone sculptures and hills banded with color. ~ Route S2, 36 miles south of Scissors Crossing.

LODGING

Anza–Borrego's premier hostelry is **La Casa del Zorro**, a desert hideaway in a garden setting. Spread across several acres, the resort is a collection of Spanish-style buildings positioned around several swimming pools and jacuzzis. There are tennis courts, a restaurant, and a cozy lounge. The Southwestern-theme lobby contains spacious sitting rooms finished with washed pine. Guest rooms vary from small traditional motel rooms at deluxe prices in high season to lavish suites and casitas with fireplaces, private patios, and desert accoutrements. ~ 3845 Yaqui Pass Road, Borrego Springs; 619-767-5323, 800-824-1884, fax 619-767-4782. DELUXE TO ULTRA-DELUXE.

The **Oasis Motel** is a small, seven-unit establishment. Set amid palm trees and offering views of the mountains, it has rooms with or without kitchens. ~ 366 Palm Canyon Drive (West Route S22), Borrego Springs; 619-767-5409. MODERATE.

DINING

With whitewashed walls, *viga* ceilings, and candle sconces, the dining room at **La Casa del Zorro** is Southwestern in atmosphere. Part of a lavish resort complex, the restaurant serves three meals daily, offering guests a traditional selection of dishes. Among the entrées are scampi, Alaskan salmon, chicken piccata, veal chops, prime rib, and rack of lamb. ~ 3845 Yaqui Pass Road, Borrego Springs; 619-767-5323. DELUXE.

Out toward the eastern border of Anza–Borrego Desert State Park, **Burro Bend Restaurant** provides café-type meals at low cost. You've seen the place in a thousand locales—ham and eggs in the morning, burgers for lunch, and roast beef and spaghetti at dinner. Dinner only on weekends. ~ Route 78 near Ocotillo Wells; 619-767-5970. BUDGET.

NIGHTLIFE

For blues and jazz in Borrego Springs, check out the scene at La Casa del Zorro's **Fox Pub**. Overlooking the hotel's swimming pool and featuring a dancefloor and fireplace, this evening retreat is a special place. ~ 3845 Yaqui Pass Road, Borrego Springs; 619-767-5323.

PARKS

ANZA–BORREGO DESERT STATE PARK 🚶🚲🐎 Spreading across 600,000 acres of the Colorado Desert, this dusty behemoth is the largest state park in the contiguous United States. It's a tumbling region of jagged mountains, hidden springs, and deep sandstone canyons. The tree life ranges from palms at sea level to pines at 5000 feet; over 150 bird species have been sighted here. Hiking trails lead along the

desert floor, through multihued valleys, and up into the mountains.
Facilities include picnic areas, restrooms, and showers, Restaurants,
groceries, and lodging are nearby in Borrego
Springs. There is also a visitors center and museum. ~ Routes 78 and S22 lead into the park from
both the east and west; 619-767-5311.

In 1857, the first transcontinental mail service passed
through the Box Canyon
region; soon afterwards
the Butterfield Overland
Stage Line began trans-
porting passengers.

▲ There are several campgrounds throughout
the park. In the Borrego Palm Canyon Campground
there are 52 RV sites with hookups and 65 developed
tent sites; in Tamarisk Grove Campground there are 12
semiprivate sites; and in Horse Camp there are 9 sites
with corrals. Camping costs $22 per night for sites with
hookups, $16 per night for all other sites.

AGUA CALIENTE COUNTY PARK 🚶🚴 Surrounded by Anza–Borrego Desert State Park, this scenic desert reserve measures 910 acres.
It's located at 1300 feet elevation on the eastern slope of the Tierra
Blanca Mountains. The greatest attraction here is the system of natural waters—four springs, one cool and pure, the others warm and
sulfurous, percolate to the surface. As a result, the park has two
pools—an outdoor wading area and an indoor pool complete with jacuzzi jets. The park offers picnic areas, restrooms, a store, and hiking
trails. Day-use fee, $2. ~ Located on Route S2, 23 miles south of Scis-
sors Crossing; Vallecito Park is four miles north of Agua Caliente;
619-694-3049.

▲ There are 104 sites with hookups ($12 to $14 per night) and
36 developed tent sites ($10 per night). Camping is also permitted at
Vallecito County Park (619-565-3600). There are 45 developed tent
and RV (no hookups) sites; $8 per night.

Outdoor Adventures

SPORT-FISHING

Lakes in the Inland Empire and Low Desert areas
offer a variety of fishing opportunities. Alpine Trout
Lakes, Silverwood Lake State Recreation Area, Lake
Perris State Recreation Area, Lake Arrowhead, Big Bear Lake, and
the Salton Sea are stocked with an assortment of fish, including trout,
bass, catfish, bluegill, corbina, croaker, sargo, and tilapia.

For fishing boat and equipment rentals contact **Silverwood Lake
State Recreation Area Marina.** ~ Silverwood Lake; 619-389-2320.
Big Bear Marina has 23 fishing boats, 13 pontoon boats, canoes, kayaks, and pedal boats. ~ Lakeview Drive, Big Bear; 909-866-3218. To
spend your day idling away on the water looking for bear and deer,
contact **Pleasure Point Landing.** ~ 603 Landlock Landing Road,
South Shore, Big Bear Lake; 909-866-2455. For night dock fishing,
call **Gray's Landing.** ~ North Shore, Big Bear Lake; 909-866-2443.

WATER SPORTS

For boating and canoeing expeditions on mountain lakes and the
Salton Sea, try **Pine Knot Landing.** ~ 439 Pine Knot Avenue, Big Bear

Lake; 909-866-2628. For rentals try **Pleasure Point Landing**. ~ 603 Landlock Landing Road, South Shore, Big Bear Lake; 909-866-2455.

RIDING STABLES

In Palm Springs, **Smoke Tree Stables** offers guided rides through stunning desert terrain. Closed during the hot summer months. ~ 2500 Toledo Avenue; 619-327-1372. **Covered Wagon Tours** hosts pioneer-style desert tours. ~ La Quinta; 619-347-2161.

BALLOON RIDES

You can soar through the desert skies in a balloon manned by **American Balloon Charters**. ~ Palm Springs; 619-327-8544. For unmatched views of open desert terrain, call **Sunrise Balloons** in Palm Springs, Borrego Springs, and Temecula; 800-548-9912. **Desert Balloon Charters** offers two balloon rides a day from October until May. ~ Palm Desert; 619-346-8575.

GOLF

Golfers in the San Bernardino Mountains can try **El Rancho Verde Country Club**, which is an 18-hole flat course studded with eucalyptus trees. ~ Country Club Drive, Rialto; 909-875-5346. For outstanding views of the San Bernardino Mountains, go to **Shandin Hills Golf Club**. ~ 3380 North Little Mountain Drive, San Bernardino; 909-886-0669. Around Big Bear Lake you'll have to settle for the nine-hole **Bear Mountain Golf Course**. ~ 43100 Clubview Drive, Moonridge; 909-585-8002.

In Palm Springs, on the other hand, golfers will think they have died and gone to heaven. This desert oasis is chockablock with courses open to the public, including **Tahquitz Creek Resort**. ~ 1885 Golf Club Drive, Palm Springs; 619-328-1005. **Canyon South Golf Course** is an 18-hole course overlooking the San Gregorio mountains. ~ 1097 Murray Canyon Drive, Palm Springs; 619-327-2019. **Mesquite Country Club** is an 18-hole course surrounded by mesquite trees and featuring spectacular mountain views. ~ 2700 East Mesquite Avenue, Palm Springs; 619-323-1502.

Desert Falls Country Club is an 18-hole course dotted with majestic palm trees. ~ 1111 Desert Falls Parkway, Palm Desert; 619-341-4020. At **Oasis Country Club** the playing field meanders around 22 lakes and ponds. ~ 42-300 Casbah Way, Palm Desert; 619-345-2715. To play with palm trees swaying in the breeze, be sure to visit **Palm Desert Resort Country Club**. ~ 77-333 Country Club Drive, Palm Desert; 619-345-2791. Surrounded by mature olive and eucalyptus trees, **De Anza–Palm Springs Country Club** is a choice spot. ~ 36-200 Date Palm Drive, Cathedral City; 619-328-1315.

In Indio, try **Indio Municipal Golf Course**, which is a relatively flat 18-hole course. ~ 83-040 Avenue 42; 619-347-9156.

TENNIS

Around Big Bear Lake, three lighted public courts are located at **Meadow Park**. ~ Park Avenue. For more information, call the park district at 909-866-0130.

In Palm Springs, public courts are located at **Demuth Park**, which offers four lighted courts. ~ 4365 Mesquite Avenue; 619-323-8272. At **Palm Springs Tennis Center**, there are nine courts available to the public. ~ 1300 East Baristo Road; 619-320-0020. **Ruth Hardy Park** features eight courts. ~ Tamarisk Road and Avenida Caballeros; 619-342-6582. In Desert Hot Springs, try **Wardman Park**, which features two public tennis courts. ~ 66150 8th Street. Courts in Indio are available at **South Jackson Park**. ~ Jackson Street and Date Avenue; 619-347-3484. You can also try **Miles Avenue Park**. ~ Miles Avenue.

Also, check local papers for information on weekly events and activities sponsored by private clubs.

BIKING

Cycling is popular throughout the Inland Empire and Low Desert. There's mountain riding in the San Bernardino Mountains, desert cycling around Palm Springs, Joshua Tree, and Anza–Borrego, and recreational riding in the regional park areas.

Many of the regional and national parks listed in the "Parks" sections of this chapter have miles of bicycle trails, including **Silverwood Lake State Recreation Area** and **Lake Perris State Recreation Area**. Riding in Anza–Borrego and Joshua Tree is also very good.

Mountain riding is popular around **Lake Arrowhead** and **Big Bear Lake,** especially on forest service roads. The north shore of Big Bear Lake is a popular route, as is **Skyline Drive** (Route 2N10), a graded road that travels past Snow Summit to the Goldmine Ski area. **Snow Summit** sells all-day passes that allow mountain bikers access to the ski lift and a honeycomb of mountain trails. Passes are available at Team Big Bear at Snow Summit (see "Bike Rentals" below). Another graded thoroughfare, **Sand Canyon Road** (Route 2N27) in the Moonridge district, is also a lovely ride.

Thirty-five miles of bike routes encircle **Palm Springs**. Popular riding spots include the luxurious residential neighborhoods, the Mesquite Country Club area, the Indian Canyons, and around the

---

✔ CHECK THESE OUT—UNIQUE OUTDOOR ADVENTURES

- Play pioneer and rediscover the West when you cross the burning desert outside **Palm Springs** on a covered wagon tour. *page 426*
- Paddle your own canoe in the mountain paradise of **Big Bear Lake**, where the altitude ensures you an aerobic workout. *page 425*
- Fill your water bottle before attempting the 11,499-foot summit of Mt. San Gorgonio, where the view awaits at the top end of the eight-mile **Mt. San Gorgonio Trail**. *page 428*
- Let the ski lift haul you and your mountain bike up **Snow Summit**—when there's no snow, of course—and fly down a double black-diamond trail, if you dare. *page 427*

local parks. A notable trail is the ten-mile long **White Water Wash**, which begins in Palm Springs and extends into Palm Desert. Check with bike rental shops for more tour information.

Bike Rentals For bike rentals, as well as maps and information on mountain biking throughout the San Bernadinos, stop in at **Big Bear Bikes**. ~ 41810 Big Bear Boulevard, Big Bear Lake; 909-866-2224. For competitive mountain-bike racing, call **Team Big Bear**. ~ 880 Summit Boulevard, Big Bear Lake; 909-866-4565. Also try **Skyline Ski and Sports**, which offers rentals and repairs. ~ 653 Pine Knot Boulevard, Big Bear Lake; 909-866-3501. For guided bike tours to Indian Canyon, call **Big Horn Bike Rentals and Tours**. ~ 302 North Palm Canyon, Palm Springs; 619-325-3367.

HIKING

SAN BERNARDINO MOUNTAINS Hikers will delight in the San Bernardino Mountains trails, with their sweeping views of valleys and surrounding peaks. All distances are one way unless otherwise noted.

Pacific Crest Trail covers the entire length of the chain. It passes through pine forests, overlooks Big Bear Lake, and continues on to Lake Arrowhead before turning north toward Deep Creek.

Just above Mount Baldy Village, **Icehouse Canyon to Cuca-monga Peak via Icehouse Saddle Trail** (7.3 miles) is an arduous hike through subalpine wilderness to an 8859-foot summit. The views are worth the struggle.

Another ascent, **San Bernardino Peak Trail** (8 miles) leads up the jagged slope of its 10,624-foot namesake, providing breathtaking vistas.

Serious hikers should not miss **Mt. San Gorgonio Trail** (8 miles). The highest peak in this range, 11,499-foot Mt. San Gorgonio, presents an extraordinary challenge. The trail leads through meadows and past lakes to a summit high above the world.

The strenuous **Siberia Creek Trail** (7 miles) passes the largest known lodgepole pine, Champion Lodgepole, then continues through coniferous forest to the edge of a picturesque meadow. Here the route crosses Siberia Creek and descends Lookout Mountain to Siberia Creek Group Camp.

Near Lake Arrowhead, **Arboretum Trail** (.8 mile) offers a fascinating loop tour through deciduous and coniferous forests.

IDYLLWILD Rising high above the desert, the 10,000-foot **San Jacinto Mountains** present endless alpine hiking opportunities.

From Idyllwild County Park Visitors Center, **Deer Springs Trail** (3.8 miles) crosses Marion Ridge and travels past oak and pine forests to Suicide Rock (7510 feet), a granite monolith that offers spectacular views.

From Mountain Station at the top of the Palm Springs Aerial Tramway, there's an exhilarating hike along **Mt. San Jacinto Trail**

(6.3 miles) to the 10,804-foot summit. A shorter, two-and-a-half mile trek leads through pine and white fir forest to Round Valley.

PALM SPRINGS AREA For those uninterested in playing golf or lolling about in swimming pools, the desert environs of Palm Springs offer numerous hiking adventures.

In Palm Springs, the **Museum Trail** (1 mile) ascends the mountain behind the Palm Springs Desert Museum. Markers along this nature trail describe the plant life and other features of the terrain.

For a splendid view of Palm Springs and the Coachella Valley, climb the **Shannon Trail** (3.5 miles), a steep hike that ascends 1522-foot Smoke Tree Mountain.

At the eastern end of the Living Desert Reserve sits **Eisenhower Mountain Trail** (3 miles). The path carries across a wash and up the mountain slope for sweeping views of the Coachella Valley.

Bear Creek Canyon Trail (2 miles), located near La Quinta, also probes a desert valley. In the spring after rains this lovely area is alive with golden poppies and a bubbling creek.

Another vantage point is reached via **Edom Hill Trail** (3 miles). In the center of the Coachella Valley, this 1610-foot promontory offers panoramic views of Mt. San Jacinto, Mt. San Gorgonio, and the Salton Sea.

In Mecca Hills, **Painted Canyon Trail** (3 miles) explores a beautifully sculpted canyon.

JOSHUA TREE NATIONAL PARK AREA Joshua Tree National Park is an area where the High Desert meets the Low Desert, providing marvelous hikes through both environments.

Ryan Mountain Trail (1.5 miles) is a prime place to view both the Joshua trees and granite outcroppings for which the park is renowned. This difficult trail, which leads to the top of Mt. Ryan (5470 feet), also offers views of several valleys.

Another sweeping vista is reached along **Mastodon Peak Trail** (1.5 miles). Atop the 3371-foot promontory, the Hexie Mountains, Pinto Basin, and the Salton Sea extend before you.

Hidden Valley Trail (1 mile), beginning near Hidden Valley Campground, is a twisting loop through boulder-strewn desert to a legendary cattle rustler's hideout.

From Canyon Road, **Fortynine Palms Oasis Trail** (1.5 miles) is a moderate hike to a refreshing desert oasis. Near Cottonwood Visitors Center, **Lost Palms Oasis Trail** (4 miles) leads through a canyon to another oasis, which sports the largest group of fan palms in the park.

Lost Horse Mine Trail (2 miles) takes you to an old gold mine. It's a moderately strenuous hike that should be avoided in hot weather—there is no shade or water en route. A less taxing trip for anyone intent on exploring abandoned diggings is the **Desert Queen Mine Trail** (.8 mile), located north from Geology Tour Road (four-wheel drive only).

The **Cottonwood to Morton Mill Trail** (.5 mile) leads to a gold-refining mill.

For the hearty hiker, **Boy Scout Trail** (7.8 miles) leaves from Indian Cove and traverses the western edge of Wonderland of Rocks.

Ideal for families, **Arch Rock Nature Trail** (.5 mile) in White Tank Campground wanders through intriguing rock formations while interpreting the geology of the region.

ANZA–BORREGO DESERT STATE PARK   An arid landscape filled with desert wonders awaits hikers in Anza–Borrego. As with all desert hiking, you'll need plenty of water, protection from the sun, and a map of the area.

The most popular trail in Anza–Borrego Desert State Park is the **Borrego Palm Canyon Nature Trail** (3 miles). This short route leads to a palm grove and cool stream. If you're in good shape, you can continue up the canyon on **Borrego Palm Canyon Trail** (3 miles). There's a lot of boulder hopping, but the rewards are a palm-studded and colorful route.

In the Split Mountain area, rare elephant trees are the highlight of **Elephant Trees Discovery Loop Trail** (1.5 miles round-trip).

A steep climb along **Marshal South Home Trail** (1 mile) leads to ruins of a writer's home on top of Ghost Mountain. The trailhead is in the Blair Valley area.

Also in Blair Valley, **Morteros Trail** (.2 mile) leads to a field of large granite boulders used by Indians as bedrock mortars.

Nearby **Pictograph Trail** (1 mile) guides you to rocks painted by Diegueño Indians, then continues to a vista point above Vallecito Valley.

California Riding and Hiking Trail (6 miles) courses down a chaparral-covered mountain to the desert below. Lovely views of the Borrego Desert are seen from the ridge between Hellhole and Dry canyons. The trailhead is in the Culp Valley camp area.

From the Bow Willow area, **Mountain Palm Springs Canyon, North Fork** (1.3 miles) leads to a natural bowl ringed with more than 100 palm trees. **Mountain Palm Springs Canyon, South Fork** (1.5 miles) explores a pygmy palm grove and stand of elephant trees.

▼▼▼▼▼▼▼▼▼▼
Transportation

CAR

Route 10, the San Bernardino Freeway, travels east from Los Angeles through the heart of the Inland Empire and Low Desert. Near San Bernardino you can pick up **Route 18** (Rim of the World Drive), which runs along the entire length of the San Bernardino Mountains.

Further east, **Route 62** departs Route 10 and leads northeast to Joshua Tree National Park, while **Route 111** courses southeast through Palm Springs and down to the Salton Sea.

From San Diego, **Route 8** goes east along the southern fringes of the Low Desert near the Mexican border. The main roads in Anza–

Borrego Desert State Park are **Routes S22** and **78**, which travel east and west through the preserve.

Two facilities, **Ontario International Airport** and **Palm Springs Regional Airport**, serve this region. Carriers flying into Ontario include Alaska Airlines, American Airlines, America West Airlines, Continental Airlines, Delta Air Lines, Northwest Airlines, Skywest Airlines, Southwest Airlines, TWA, United Airlines, and USAir.

AIR

Carriers into Palm Springs Regional Airport currently include Air 21, Alaska Airlines, American Airlines, America West Express, Delta Air Lines, Reno Air, Skywest Airlines, United Airlines, and USAir Express.

Greyhound Bus Lines offers service to San Bernardino (596 North G Street; 909-884-4796), Riverside (3911 University Avenue; 909-686-2345), Perris (412 East 4th Street; 909-657-7813), Palm Springs (311 North Indian Avenue; 619-325-2053), and Indio (45-524 Oasis Street; 619-347-3020).

BUS

All aboard. **Amtrak** has two passenger trains to San Bernardino, the "Desert Wind" and "Southwest Chief." Another train, the "Sunset," stops at the railroad platform on Jackson Street in Indio. From here Greyhound Bus Lines connects to Palm Springs. ~ 1170 West 3rd Street; 909-884-1307; 800-872-7245.

TRAIN

Located at Ontario International Airport are the following rental agencies: **Avis Rent A Car** (909-983-3689, 800-331-1212), **Budget Rent A Car** (909-983-9691, 800-527-0700), **Hertz Rent A Car** (909-986-2024, 800-654-3131), and **National Interrent** (909-988-7444, 800-227-7368).

CAR RENTALS

Less expensive car rentals in the Ontario area include **Alamo Rent A Car** (909-983-2733, 800-327-9633), **American Eagle Rent A Car** (909-984-5551), and **Thrifty Car Rental** (909-988-8581, 800-367-2277). These agencies are located outside the airport but most provide pickup service.

Several agencies are located at the Palm Springs terminal: **Avis Rent A Car** (619-327-1353, 800-331-1212), **Budget Rent A Car** (619-327-1404, 800-527-0700), **Dollar Rent A Car** (619-325-7333, 800-800-4000), **Hertz Rent A Car** (619-778-5100, 800-654-3131), and **National Interrent** (619-327-1438, 800-227-7368). For used cars try **Foxy Wheels Rent A Car** (619-320-7055). If you're looking for a jeep, contact **Aztec Rent A Car** (477 South Palm Canyon Drive; 619-325-2294).

For local bus service in San Bernardino, Redlands and points in between call **OmniTrans**. ~ 909-889-0811. Riverside is served by the **Riverside Transit Agency**. ~ 909-682-1234.

PUBLIC TRANSIT

In the Palm Springs area, **Sun Bus** carries passengers to destinations throughout the Coachella Valley. ~ 619-343-3451. From Palm Springs, **Desert Stage Lines** provides transportation to Twentynine Palms. ~ 619-367-3581.

From inland San Diego County, **Northeast Rural Bus System** takes passengers to Borrego Springs. ~ 619-765-0145.

TAXIS   To hail a cab in Palm Springs, call **Desert Cab**. ~ 619-325-2868.

EIGHT

High Desert

Picture an endless expanse of basin and range, desert and mountain, a realm guarded by the sharp teeth of the Sierra Nevada and the gaping maw of Death Valley. California may be known for glittering cities and postcard beaches, but along its southeastern shoulder the Golden State unveils a different face entirely. Here the Mojave Desert reaches from Los Angeles County across an awesome swath of territory to Arizona and Nevada.

The sky in these parts is immense, and the landscape is so broad that mountains are like islands on its surface. The Mojave is a region of ancient lakebeds and crystalline sinks, ghost towns and deserted mines. When Jedediah Smith, one of the West's great explorers, trekked through in 1826, he declared the desert "a country of starvation."

Even today it seems desolate and unyielding. Winters are cold here, the summers hot. Rainfall, which dwindles from six inches in the western Mojave to less than two inches around Death Valley, comes only during winter. But plants proliferate and the area is alive with reptiles and small mammals—and, increasingly, people. Edwards Air Force Base and the NASA space shuttle make the Mojave a strategic aerospace center. Its western reaches around Antelope Valley are rapidly filling with developments spilling over from the Los Angeles Basin.

Foreign and unforgiving though it might be, the Mojave Desert has always possessed particular importance in the history of California. In 1774, Yuma Indians guided Juan Bautista de Anza and other Spanish explorers through this wasteland. By 1831 the vital Santa Fe Trail was open from Santa Fe to Los Angeles. Later in the century the U.S. Army converted other Indian paths into roads, opening them to wagon trains and stage coaches.

The land Jedediah Smith labeled "a complete barrens" proved rich in minerals. For four decades beginning in the 1870s, the Mojave was a major thoroughfare for 20-mule teams laden with borax and miners weighted down with gold, silver, zinc, and tungsten. The towns of Mojave and Barstow became important railroad centers; even now they remain essential crossroads, oases with amenities.

At the northern edge of the Mojave, in a land the Indians knew as "Tomesha" or "ground on fire," lies Death Valley. Measuring 120 miles long and varying in width from four to sixteen miles, it is among the hottest places on earth, second only to the Sahara. During summer the *average* daily high temperature is 116°.

This long narrow valley is itself only a small part of Death Valley National Park, the most recent addition to our national park system. In 1995, Death Valley was "upgraded" from a national monument to a national park, affording it a higher degree of protection and an additional 1.3 million acres. The 3.3 million-acre park is now the largest in the continental United States.

A museum without air conditioning, Death Valley is a giant geology lab displaying salt beds, sand dunes, and an 11,000-foot elevation climb. Its multitiered hills contain layers that are windows on the history of the earth. One level holds Indian arrowheads, another Ice Age fish, and beneath these deposits lies Precambrian rock.

At the end of the Pleistocene, when warming temperatures melted glaciers atop the Sierra Nevada, this desiccated domain was covered by a vast inland sea. Today mud playas and the shadows of ancient shores are all that remain. Instead of water, the lowlands are filling with rock debris from the neighboring Black and Panamint mountains.

One of the most hauntingly beautiful places in the world, Death Valley received its ominous name in 1849 when a party of pioneers, intent on following a shortcut to the gold fields, crossed the wasteland, barely escaping with their lives. Later, prospectors stayed to work the territory, discovering rich borax deposits during the 1880s and providing the region with a home industry.

Testament to the diversity of the High Desert, Death Valley contains the lowest spot in the contiguous U.S. (Badwater, 282 feet below sea level), yet rests within 60 miles of the highest place (Mt. Whitney, 14,495 feet above sea level). Its snow-rimmed neighbor, the Sierra Nevada, is the largest single mountain range in the country, a solitary block of earth 430 miles long and 80 miles wide. A mere child in the long count of geologic history, the Sierra Nevada rose from the earth's surface a few million years back and did not reach its present form until 750,000 years ago. During the Pleistocene epoch, glaciers spread across the land, grinding and cutting at the mountains. They carved river valleys and deep canyons, and sculpted bald domes, fluted cliffs, and stone towers.

The glaciers left a landscape dominated by ragged peaks where streams number in the thousands and canyons plunge 5000 feet. There are cliffs sheer as glass that compete with the sky for dominance. It is, as an early pioneer described it, a "land of fire and ice."

On the western flank of this massive range lie Sequoia and Kings Canyon national parks. Within eyeshot of the brine pools and scrub growth of Death Valley, they contain more than 1000 glacial lakes and boast rich stands of giant sequoia trees, the largest living things on earth.

Unlike its western face, which slopes gently down into California's verdant Central Valley, the eastern wall of the Sierra Nevada falls away in a furious succession of granite cliffs to the alkali floor of the Owens Valley.

Folded between three mountain ranges, with 14,000-foot peaks on either side, the long, slender Owens Valley was discovered by Joseph Walker in 1834. Indians had occupied the territory for perhaps 40,000 years, even during the period up to 10,000 years ago when the canyon floor was an immense lake. Paiutes later dominated the region, subsisting on rabbits, birds, and nuts, and perfecting the art of basket weaving.

During the 1860s gold and silver miners flooded the area, discovering rich deposits in Cerro Gordo, Darwin, and elsewhere. By the turn of the century, Owens Valley was a prime ranch and farm region planted in corn, wheat, and alfalfa. A population of 4500 settlers lived in an area dominated by Owens Lake, a 30-foot-deep lake that stretched across 100 square miles.

Then in 1905 agents from water-hungry Los Angeles began buying up lands and riparian rights. Two years later Los Angeles voters passed a multi-million-dollar aqueduct bond. When the 223-mile conduit was completed in 1913, the destruction of Owens Valley commenced. Over the next few decades, as Los Angeles systematically drained the basin, trees withered, ranchers sold out, and farms went unwatered. Outraged residents rebelled, dynamiting the water works and pleading their case in Washington.

Today bristlecone pines, the oldest living things on earth, still occupy the nearby White Mountains, as they have for 4000 years. The Mammoth Lakes region to the north, with its alpine forests and glacial lakes, remains a favorite ski area. But Owens Valley itself is a dusty testament to the needs of a distant metropolis. A place of unconquerable beauty, bounded by granite mountains and visited with hot winds, it has in the end become a manmade extension of the great Mojave Desert.

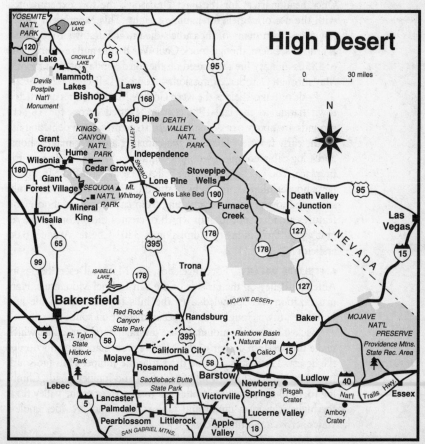

▼▼▼▼▼▼▼▼▼▼
Mojave Desert

Stretching from Los Angeles County all the way to Arizona and Nevada, the Mojave Desert is a region of daunting distance. Sightseeing this open range means driving hundreds of miles between points of interest. As a result, the descriptions below are organized by geographic region, some covering extremely extensive areas.

Bakersfield actually lies west of the Mojave but incorporates much of its history and culture. Antelope Valley sits in the desert's western corner just south of the town of Mojave. The "Barstow area" extends south from the town of Barstow for 35 miles and east for over 100 miles. Death Valley, actually part of the Mojave Desert, is treated as a separate destination.

SIGHTS

BAKERSFIELD AREA   Up in Grapevine Canyon, where Tejon Pass cuts a notch in the Tehachapi Mountains, the U.S. Army built an outpost in 1854 to keep American Indian tribes on their reservations. At **Fort Tejon State Historic Park**, a few restored and reconstructed adobe structures stand, set against a backdrop of curving mountains. Once headquarters for the First Dragoons, the fort experimented with the use of camels for hauling freight. This experiment failed, however, when many of the camels died near Barstow. Today there is little to see here, though mock Civil War battles and re-enactments of 1850s military life are staged on the third Sunday of each month, May through October. Admission. ~ Route 5, Lebec; 805-248-6692.

Pride of Bakersfield is the **Kern County Museum**, a reconstructed town dating to the late-19th century. Dotted across the 16-acre grounds are about five dozen Western structures, each depicting life on the early frontier. There are watchmaker and dressmaker shops, and a log cabin complete with photographs of Abe Lincoln over the fireplace. You can step up to the Fellows Hotel, visit old Mr. Pinckney's house, and tour the railway station. An excellent outdoor museum, the town contains everything from caboose to calaboose and features an adjacent museum which re-creates the history of the region's vital farm industry. Admission. ~ 3801 Chester Avenue, Bakersfield; 805-861-2132.

ANTELOPE VALLEY   For Angelenos, the Mojave Desert begins in **Antelope Valley** on the far side of the San Gabriel Mountains. Here urbanization has sprawled over the hills to create Palmdale and Lancaster, towns long on aerospace and short on soul.

HIDDEN ►

Backed against the mountains are several natural attractions which make this western corner of the Mojave a dramatic introduction to the desert. The first is a scenic drive into the **Juniper Hills** (go south from Pearblossom along 106th Street East and Juniper Road). Climbing to 4600 feet, this loop trades the Joshua trees of the valley floor for higher-elevation piñon and juniper trees and provides endless views across a multihued desert.

Connect with Route N6 and you'll arrive at **Devil's Punchbowl County Natural Area.** This wedge-shaped canyon, paralleled on two fronts by earthquake faults, has been crushed between opposing geologic forces. On either side sedimentary rocks have been thrust upward to create vertical walls reaching up to 300 feet that are folding in upon each other like the pages of a closing book. Hiking trails lead through these angular sandstone slabs, passing stands of juniper, piñon, and manzanita. Admission. ~ 28000 Devil's Punchbowl Road, Pearblossom; 805-944-2743.

Unique is too timid a term to describe the **Antelope Valley Indian Museum.** With displays of bone tools, arrowheads, kachina dolls, and basketry, the museum offers a cross section of American Indian life in California. But the truly impressive element is the museum building itself. Built directly into the rocks that backdrop the complex, it's a chalet-style house with two gabled turrets and seven different roof levels. Constructed in the 1930s as a private home, the facility contains walls of wood and natural bedrock. One room has a rock floor with huge boulders rising in the center. These natural formations combine with brilliant murals and colorfully painted ceilings to create a striking desert setting. Call for tour reservations; closed from June through August. Admission. ~ 15701 East Avenue M, Lancaster; 805-942-0662.

In the fall of 1997, the area code for the High Desert will change from 619 to 760.

On the other side of Lancaster's sprawling metropolis, more than 20 miles away, lies the **Antelope Valley California Poppy Reserve.** From March until May, when California's state flower blooms, these slopes are transformed into a wildflower wonderland. In addition to the bright-hued countryside, there is an architecturally noteworthy visitors center, with three sides built into the earth for insulation against desert extremes. ~ 15101 West Lancaster Road, Lancaster; 805-724-1180.

To find out whether the poppies are blooming and for general information on the Antelope Valley area, contact the **Lancaster Chamber of Commerce.** ~ 554 West Lancaster Boulevard, Lancaster; 805-948-4518.

Most of the gold mines which once flowered in Antelope Valley have long since died. **Burton's Tropico Gold Mine,** shut down and closed to the public, can still be seen from afar in its hillside setting. Amid slag heaps and the detritus of a bygone era stand the mining buildings. Formerly one of Southern California's richest strikes, it is now a cluster of tin structures and woodframe houses ravaged by desert wind. ~ From Route 14 in Rosamond, take Rosamond Boulevard west four miles, then turn right on Mojave Tropico Road for one mile.

MOJAVE AREA   One of nature's most impressive desert displays is **Red Rock Canyon State Park,** a photogenic badlands that resembles a miniature Grand Canyon. As you enter through the sheer-walled gorge that leads into the valley, the landscape opens into a succession of accordion-pleated cliffs. Eroded by water, the rockfaces are carved into minarets, spires, and crenelated towers. Nearby walls of sandstone have been formed by weather to create columnar structures resembling stalagmites.

This 10,000-acre park rests in a biologic transition zone between the Mojave and the Sierra Nevada and is alive with flora and fauna from both areas. The canyon also sits on a geologic cusp between the Mojave and the Great Basin, making it a kind of outdoor museum. Little wonder that everyone from early American Indians to modern-day movie makers has been attracted to the region. Admission. ~ Route 14 about 20 miles north of Mojave; 805-942-0662.

Desert Tortoise Natural Area is a unique habitat housing the largest known concentration of desert tortoises. This 16,000-acre preserve serves as sanctuary for a reptile that can live up to 100 years. Measuring only 15 inches, the desert tortoise digs communal burrows which are often 20 feet long. Since they hibernate in winter and stay underground to avoid summer heat, the best time to see them is from March to June in the morning and late afternoon. ~ Three miles northeast of California City along Randsburg–Mojave Road (graded). For more information, contact the Desert Tortoise Preserve Committee at P.O. Box 2910, San Bernardino, CA 92406.

The "living ghost town" of **Randsburg**, as well as neighboring **Johannesburg** and **Red Mountain**, is rich in minerals and history. Together these frontier communities formed a mining district that boomed first from gold deposits, then tungsten and silver. Of course that was a century ago, but today Randsburg still retains an aura of the 1890s. Many of the houses in town are stripped of paint and seem ready to fall to the next desert wind; others are restored and occupied. There's a gravity-feed gas pump, wooden sidewalk, and an

✦✦✦

✔ CHECK THESE OUT—UNIQUE SIGHTS

- Drive over, under, and through giant Sequoia trees—literally, for they've been hollowed out with car-sized tunnels—in **Sequoia National Park**. *page 445*
- Leave only footprints as you climb 300-foot sand dunes for a view of **Death Valley National Park** at sunset. *page 465*
- Sing a carol under the boughs of **General Grant**, the nation's Christmas Tree, in Kings Canyon National Park. *page 448*
- Peer down at the hexagonal pillars of rock that form **Devils Postpile National Monument**—and keep your eyes peeled for the views on the drive in and out. *page 460*

outhouse with a crescent moon carved in the door. You'll pass a white-steepled church and a succession of tin-roof stores whose signs have long since faded into indecipherable blurs.

The **Randsburg General Store** still has its antique soda fountain and grizzled clientele. And over at the **Desert Museum** (Butte Avenue) you can view such mining-era artifacts as a miniature five-ton steam locomotive (which seems more like a toy train for big kids than a real machine). Open weekends. ~ 35 Butte Avenue, Randsburg; 619-374-2418.

BARSTOW AREA   Crossroads of the Mojave is the sun-baked community of Barstow. An important railroad town, Barstow is the converging point for the Union Pacific and Santa Fe railways. It's also the intersection of Routes 58, 15, and 40, which together cover much of the California desert.

Communications central for this region is the **California Desert Information Center**. This hilltop museum features displays reflecting the area's flora and fauna. There are also pamphlets, maps, an information desk, and a bookstore. ~ 831 Barstow Road, Barstow; 619-255-8760.

The nearby **Mojave River Valley Museum** has a more complete collection of artifacts and memorabilia. Dedicated to the preservation of local history and culture, it contains discoveries from the Calico Early Man Site and specimens of desert minerals and gems. Other displays re-create the era of Spanish explorers and the recent advent of the space industry. ~ 270 East Virginia Way, Barstow; 619-256-5452.

Surprisingly, just a few miles from the drab streets of Barstow you'll discover folded and faulted mountains that are layer cakes of color. Drive out to **Rainbow Basin Natural Area** and encounter a deep canyon surrounded by striped cliffs of sedimentary rock. Rich in fossil deposits, the adjacent hills were created over eons and contain the remains of mastodons, rhinos, and camel-type creatures.

Even more impressive is the bald beauty of the place. These are hills the color of dawn built in a myriad of shapes that change character with the light. The three-mile road that loops through this rock preserve passes zebra-striped buttes, boulders formed into fists, and tortuously twisted formations. To explore the basin from Barstow follow Irwin Road north for five miles from Route 58, then turn left on Fossil Bed Road for three miles to the loop drive.

The commercial outlets are as numerous as the memories at **Calico Ghost Town San Bernardino Regional Park**. This old mining center has been transformed into a kind of windblown theme park complete with narrow-gauge railroad rides, a hall of illusions, and a hokey Western playhouse. Native charm endures despite it all. There are stone houses built into the surrounding mountain and woodframe stores bent with time. Mining paraphernalia lies scattered everywhere; and the town's cemetery and open mines remain prime exploring sites. Camping is permitted. Admission. ~ Ghost Town Road, ten miles northeast of Barstow; 619-254-2122.

It was 1881 when prospectors struck it rich and Calico boomed to life with over 20 saloons, a temperance society, and its own Chinatown. More than $86 million in gold, silver, and other minerals was mined from the multihued "calico" mountains before the town went bust. Eventually Walter Knott, of Knott's Berry Farm fame, restored the ramshackle town and turned it over to the local government.

Perhaps 200,000 years before Calico Ghost Town was even conceived, hunters roamed the **Calico Early Man Archaeological Site**. Back in those Pleistocene times the landscape was lush with junipers, live oaks, and pines. The climate was temperate and a large body of water, Lake Manix, attracted mammoths, sloths, and saber-toothed cats.

Don't miss viewing Roy Rogers' faithful horse Trigger, mounted, in a display case, fully saddled and ready to ride.

This scientifically important site was a tool factory where early man rendered local deposits of chert and chalcedony into choppers, picks, and scrapers. Directed for several years by Dr. Louis S. B. Leakey, famed discoverer of Africa's Olduvai Gorge, the site is so ancient it upset earlier theories that man was in the New World for only 10,000 or 20,000 years. In fact Calico Early Man might not have been a *Homo sapiens* at all, but a now-extinct species such as *Homo erectus* or *Homo sapiens neandertalensis*.

Today, either on a guided or self-guided tour, you can view the archaeological pits, see early stone tools, and wander back in your mind to an age of ice when the desert was in bloom. To get your body to the place from which your mind can wander, take Route 15 for about 15 miles east from Barstow, get off at the Minneola exit, and go north three miles. Closed Monday and Tuesday; for information call the California Desert Information Center. ~ 619-255-8760.

North of the San Bernardino Mountains, where the hills descend to meet the Mojave Desert, lie the Lucerne and Apple valleys. Characterized by dry lake beds and granite heights, the region is 35 miles south of Barstow.

Victorville, the chief town hereabouts, is known primarily as a stop along Route 15, the golden road that whisks Angelenos to the promised land of Las Vegas. This unassuming crossroads is also a point of pilgrimage for buckaroos everywhere, home to the **Roy Rogers–Dale Evans Museum**. You'll thrill to the diorama of Roy and Dale as well as the photos of Roy's mom and dad and of the cowboy as a lad back in Duck Run, Ohio. Roy's African safari heads are here, as well as Dale's dining room table and Roy's decorative saddles. There are awards galore and an entire section filled with religious mementoes (Christian, of course). (Don't forget to stop at the Happy Trails Gift Shop on the way out.) Admission. ~ 15650 Seneca Road; 617-243-4547.

Two long, lonesome highways, Routes 40 and 15, travel east from Barstow deeper into the desert. Along Route 40, which tracks due east toward Arizona and New Mexico, chocolate brown mountains crowd the horizon in every direction.

About 35 miles from town **Pisgah Crater**, a 250-foot cinder cone, rises to the south. Another young volcano, **Amboy Crater**, lies along old Route 66 (National Trails Highway), which diverts from Route 40 in Ludlow. A curving black figure against a mountain backdrop, the volcano is surrounded by a vast lava field. To the southeast this lava flow gives way to **Bristol Dry Lake**, an ancient freshwater lake that now supports an extensive chloride works.

The vast area between Routes 40 and 15, east of Barstow and west of Needles, appears to the interstate traveler to offer very little, but the **Mojave National Preserve** easily rivals Death Valley, Anza–Borrego and Joshua Tree for desert beauty. In the heart of the scenic area is **Hole-in-the-Wall**, where volcanic rock solidified into all sorts of unusual formations, ideal for rock scrambling and framing funny pictures. ~ To reach Hole-in-the-Wall campground, take Route 40 east from Barstow for 100 miles, go eight miles north on Essex Road, then another eight miles on Black Canyon Road; 619-255-8801.

◄ HIDDEN

From Hole-in-the-Wall, you can make a circle tour of other highlights of the area. First, go north on Black Canyon Road to Midhills, where juniper and piñons provide shade and relief from the prevailing scrub of the desert. Then turn left on Cedar Canyon Road, and left again on the paved Kelso-Cima Road. This leads to Kelso Depot, a surprisingly gracious, abandoned Spanish-style train depot that may one day be restored as a visitors center.

Then continue to the marked turnoff for **Kelso Dunes**. A three-mile approach road leads to the tallest dunes in the California desert. An intriguing phenomenon here results from the wind, which shifts around the dunes in circular fashion, causing the tall grasses to etch round tracks in the sand with their tips. If you hike the dunes, watch for these telltale marks and for the lizards inhabiting this forlorn but beautiful spot. ~ To get there from Route 40, travel 80 miles east of Barstow, then go north 15 miles on Kelbaker Road; turn left onto a marked road (just past the power line). This rough dirt road leads three miles to a parking lot.

◄ HIDDEN

From Kelso Dunes, return to Kelbaker Road, go south to Route 40, and once again take the Essex Road exit. This time stay on Essex Road and go 16 miles northwest to **Providence Mountains State Recreation Area**. This island of state land within the Scenic Area rests sidesaddle on the slopes of a rugged mountain. From the visitors center, perched at 4300 feet, you can gaze across 300 square miles of desert to mountains 125 miles away in Arizona. Buttes, dunes, and broad desert valleys extend in a 180° panorama.

◄ HIDDEN

The park's most remarkable feature, however, lies not upon the earth but within it. Carved deep into the Providence Mountains are the **Mitchell Caverns**, limestone caves filled with elaborate rock formations. Touring El Pakiva and Tecopa caves, you'll see delicate stalactites and monstrous stalagmites in a natural cathedral. The bones of a Pleistocene ground sloth were uncovered here. Cavern tours are scheduled weekdays at 1:30 p.m. and on weekends and holidays at 10 a.m., 1:30 p.m., and 3 p.m.; no weekday tours are offered in summer. Tour reservations should be made several weeks in advance. Admission. ~ To reach the park take Route 40 east from Barstow for 100 miles, then go 16 miles northwest on Essex Road; 619-928-2586.

LODGING

Towns in the Mojave Desert are little more than corridors for cars. Lined with neon, they resound with the shudder and drone of passing trucks. The larger communities have standard motel accommodations, catering to truck drivers, desert rats, and itinerant salesmen. Bed-and-breakfast inns, it seems, are rare as rain out here.

Lancaster, located at the western fringe of the desert in Antelope Valley, has numerous resting places. **EZ-8 Motel** is a clean, trim facility with carpeted, neatly furnished rooms. With a pool and jacuzzi, it's a good deal considering the inexpensive rates. There are similar motels crowded along Routes 58 and 14 in Mojave. ~ 43530 17th Street West, Lancaster; 805-945-9477, 800-326-6835 ext. 99, fax 805-726-9426. BUDGET.

For about 500 years the Chemehuevi Indians used Mitchell Caverns, blackening the walls with campfires.

The crossroads town of Barstow, where Routes 58, 14, and 40 converge, is another neon enclave. Here the sleeper's strip lies along Main Street, where you'll find the **Sunset Inn**. Among the amenities are a pool, jacuzzi, and cluster of adequately appointed rooms. ~ 1350 West Main Street, Barstow; 619-256-8921, fax 619-296-5829. BUDGET.

The nicest place in town is **Barstow Holiday Inn**, a 148-unit hotel with adjoining restaurant, pool, and jacuzzi. Ultramodern in design, it's clean to the point of being sterile. Rooms are finished in blond woods and nicely appointed. They are fairly spacious, well carpeted, and include room service. The ample lobby area is decorated with fabric paintings and furnished with plump, irresistible armchairs. ~ 1511 East Main Street, Barstow; 619-256-5673, fax 619-256-5917. MODERATE.

DINING

If you caught the delightfully quirky film *Bagdad Café*, you'll enjoy **The Sidewinder**, where the movie was filmed. Pictures of the stars and scenes from the movie are on the walls, and souvenir T-shirts are on sale, but the eatery hasn't gone highfalutin on us. It retains its original name and serves good-quality, no-nonsense grub: chicken-fried steak, liver and onions, hamburgers, and made-before-your-eyes milkshakes. ~ 46548 National Trails Highway/Old Route 66, Newberry Springs; 619-257-3101. BUDGET.

Chain restaurants and fast-food outlets proliferate throughout Antelope Valley. In Lancaster, the largest town in this western Mojave region, you'll encounter **Marie Callender's**, a sterile brass-and-hardwood-style restaurant known more for its homemade pies than gourmet dinners. The menu includes fresh pasta dishes as well as vegetable casserole, meatloaf, hamburgers, and chicken dishes. ~ 1649 West Avenue K, Lancaster; 805-945-6958. BUDGET.

For Mexican fare consider **Casa de Miguel**, a contemporary hacienda-style restaurant with high-back chairs and outsize metal chandeliers. The menu is elaborate, offering the standard medley of Mexican dishes plus specialties like red snapper, sirloin tips, New York steak, and broiled chicken. Lunch, dinner, and Sunday brunch. ~ 44245 North Sierra Highway, Lancaster; 805-948-0793. BUDGET TO MODERATE.

Idle Spurs Steak House is Barstow's gathering place, a common denominator destination for locals and outlanders alike. A Texas-size establishment with a lounge and two dining rooms, it's Western in style. The menu is a reasonably priced steak-and-seafood affair with prime rib, pork ribs, sautéed chicken, scallops, lobster, and halibut. Lunch and dinner are served weekdays; dinner only on weekends. ~ 29557 West Route 58, Barstow; 619-256-8888. MODERATE.

When in doubt, cover all bases: that seems to be the motto at **Canton Restaurant**. Ostensibly a Chinese restaurant, it offers egg rolls, sweet and sour pork, *chow yuk*, and other Asian standards. But the switch-hitting eatery also serves breakfast all day and prepares sandwiches, steaks, rainbow trout, fried scallops, and fried chicken on toast. On toast? Closed the last two weeks in December. ~ 1300 West Main Street, Barstow; 619-256-9565. BUDGET.

The year-round Christmas lights add to the local color at **Peggy Sue's Nifty 50's Diner**, a jukebox and soda-fountain joint that serves burgers, sandwiches, and all-American lunches and dinners. Meatloaf, honey-dipped chicken, roast beef, and chicken-fried steak are specialties. For decor there are photos of '50s celebrities as well as period pieces from the early era of rock-and-roll. ~ Yermo and Ghost Town roads, Yermo; 619-254-3370. BUDGET.

SHOPPING

Somehow the desert seems an unlikely place to find fine art and contemporary fashions. There are stores in Mojave and Barstow, but most serve the local populace.

Calico Ghost Town, a kind of antique theme park in the mountains ten miles northeast of Barstow, has several shops. These are located in the town's 1880-era buildings and include a confectionery, spice shop, pottery store, and rock shop. The Old West town also features the obligatory general store, which in this case generally sells tourist items.

NIGHTLIFE

Out in the railroad town of Barstow, the **Idle Spurs Steak House** has live entertainment every Friday and Saturday. This lounge also features a dancefloor. ~ 29557 West Route 58; 619-256-8888.

PARKS

SADDLEBACK BUTTE STATE PARK 🚶🏇 Sprinkled with Joshua trees and backdropped by its 3651-foot namesake, this desert facility gazes out toward distant mountains. Roadrunners, desert tortoises, kit fox, and rattlesnakes inhabit these 2875 acres. Trails lead up the granite butte and through the state park. There are picnic areas here; restaurants and groceries are four miles away in Lake Los Angeles or 17 miles to Lancaster. Day-use fee, $5. ~ Located on East Avenue J, 17 miles east of Lancaster; 805-942-0662.

▲ There are 50 sites for RVs and tents (no hookups) available on a first-come, first-served basis; $10 per night.

RED ROCK CANYON STATE PARK 🚶🚴🏇 This 10,000-acre facility, situated amid sculpted cliffs, is a major sightseeing destination. Its deposits of red sandstone, white clay, lava, and pink tuff have been uplifted and then eroded to create a dramatic landscape. Joshua trees, desert holly, and creosote bushes abound and wildlife is plentiful. The recently built Visitors Center displays wildlife and geology as well as gold mining, American Indian, and film histories. There's a small store in Cantel, about eight miles away. Restaurants and groceries are 20 miles away in Mojave. Day-use fee, $5. ~ Located on Route 14 about 20 miles north of Mojave; 805-942-0662.

The opening scenes of the 1993 hit *Jurassic Park* were filmed at Red Rock Canyon State Park.

▲ There are 50 family campsites. Tent/RV sites available (no hookups); $7 per night.

MOJAVE NARROWS REGIONAL PARK 🚶🚴🏇🎣 Sitting astride an old riverbed, this 880-acre park boasts two lakes and an intaglio of waterways. There are broad meadows and stately stands of willow and cottonwood. Renowned for its fishing (permits required and can be obtained at park), the park also offers riding stables and hiking trails. Facilities include restrooms, picnic areas, a snack bar, and a bait shop; restaurants and groceries are in Victorville. Day-use fee, $5. ~ From Route 15, take the Ridgecrest exit which turns into Yates Road. Located at 18000 Yates Road in Victorville; 619-245-2226.

▲ There are 38 sites with hookups and 50 tent sites; $15 for hookups, $10 for tent sites.

MOJAVE NATIONAL PRESERVE 🚶🚴🏇 Featuring volcanic rock formations and a variety of cacti, as well as shady groves of juniper and piñons, this remote area showcases the diverse beauty of the desert. People come here primarily for the camping. The petroglyph-covered rock walls of Hole-in-the-Wall campground open up into Box Canyon with great views of Wild Horse Mesa. The Midhills campground is surrounded by trees and populated by bobcats, coyotes, and foxes. Hiking trails wind through both campgrounds. There are pit toilets and picnic areas. Stock up before you arrive—restaurants and groceries are dozens of miles away. See the "Mojave Desert" sights section above for more details. ~ From Barstow take Route 40 east for 100 miles, go eight miles north on Essex Road, then another eight miles on Black Canyon Road. Continue past Hole-in-the-Wall campground to reach Midhills campground; 619-255-8801.

▲ Each campground has from 25 to 35 sites for tents and RVs (no hookups) on a first-come, first-served basis; $5 to $10 per night.

PROVIDENCE MOUNTAINS STATE RECREATION AREA 🏃 This 5900-acre park, set on a mountain slope overlooking a vast desert panorama, is remarkably beautiful. Hiking trails lead into the hills; and Mitchell Caverns, a series of spectacular limestone formations, provide sightseeing opportunities. You have to go with a guide to see Mitchell Caverns (closed weekdays during summer; for more information, call 619-942-0662). Bighorn sheep, wild burros, coyotes, and bobcats traverse the area and yucca and cacti cover the hillsides. You'll find restrooms and a picnic area. As with the Mojave National Preserve, restaurants and groceries are dozens of miles away. See the "Mojave Desert" sightseeing section above for further details. Day-use fee, $5. ~ From Barstow go east on Route 40 for 100 miles; then northwest on Essex Road for 16 miles; 619-928-2586.

▲ There are six sites for tents and RVs (no hookups) on a first-come, first-served basis; $12 per night.

AFTON CANYON 🏃🚴🐎 One of the rare places in the Mojave Desert to have year-round running water, this valley has been carved for millennia by the Mojave River. The result is a remarkable series of eroded cliffs, brilliantly colored and reminiscent of the Grand Canyon. There are remote gorges to explore and ancient Indian trails nearby. The railroad runs through the center of this scenic wonder, with a steel trestle crossing one span. The place also has limited off-road-vehicle access, so in some places you have to weigh the beauty against the intrusions. Restrooms and picnic areas are the facilities here; restaurants and groceries are about 35 miles away in Barstow. ~ From Barstow take Route 15 east for 38 miles, then go south for three miles on Afton Road.

▲ There are 22 campsites for tents and RVs (no hookups) on a first-come, first-served basis; $6 per night.

Sequoia & Kings Canyon

Two of California's finest parks, Sequoia and Kings Canyon, lie next to each other along the western slopes of the Sierra Nevada range. Encompassing 14,000-foot peaks, alpine lakes, and stands of giant sequoia trees, they provide a lush counterpoint to the flat, dry Mojave. These natural wonders provide a stunning landscape where the mountains extend into the sky, and the sky knows no limit.

SEQUOIA NATIONAL PARK Prelude to the park is the drive to Mineral King, a remote mountain hamlet that boomed as a silver mining

SIGHTS

center during the 1870s and quickly went bust. The 25-mile Mineral King Road, branching from Route 198 a few miles before the park entrance, leads to a remote and particularly pretty section of Sequoia National Park. (Mineral King Road is usually closed in winter.)

Though paved along most stretches, the road winds through the mountains in maddening fashion, tracing the random course of the Kaweah River. En route are sharp canyons, switchbacks that jack-knife above sheer cliffs, and a lone arched bridge.

Mule deer and black bear inhabit the region. Along the precipitous slopes ponderosa pines and quaking aspens give way to white fir, incense cedar, and sequoia. At **Atwell Mill**, a late-19th-century logging center, there are Indian bedrock mortars as well as an old steam engine. Here you'll also see the ever-present sequoia stumps that are a legacy of the logging era. Further along lies **Cold Springs**, a mountain village studded with numerous log cabins, each braced against the winter wind by the chimney stem of a woodburning stove.

HIDDEN ▶   At **Mineral King** there's a campground, ranger station, a cluster of cozy cottages, and a lovely subalpine meadow. All around are the mountains, rock-ribbed ranges that leap up and outward from the town, leaving far behind on their shoulders waterfalls, talus slides, and rivers that are silver pennants fluttering down the canyons. And everywhere there are hiking trails, which radiate from Mineral King like spokes from a hub.

Generals Highway, the road through Sequoia and Kings Canyon, is a continuation of Route 198, which enters the park at Ash Mountain. The nearby **visitors center** (209-565-3134) provides maps, books, and information, but your symbolic entrance into this world of granite mountains and giant trees comes a few miles further as you pass beneath **Tunnel Rock**. The roadway here has been cut from a monstrous boulder which serves as a stone portal.

At **Hospital Rock**, a granite outcropping near the turnoff to Buckeye Flats, there are pictographs from an early tribe of Indians. These painted designs, red stains against gray rock, were a vital element in local American Indian culture. Of a more practical nature are the nearby mortar holes, ground into the resistant bedrock by Indian women pounding acorns into meal.

Generals Highway is menacingly steep, ascending 4700 feet in 16 miles between Ash Mountain and Giant Forest, and numbering in its serpentine course some 230 curves. Each switchback reveals a succession of ridges folded against one another. Domes and spires of granite dominate the horizon; from the valleys stands of conifers run along the hillsides, vaulting upward and then falling back just short of the peaks. As you ascend into the heart of the park, this mix of scrub vegetation and tall pine surrenders to stately groves of sequoia. Generals Highway is usually closed for road cleanup after snowstorms from November through April.

Giant Forest Village, a mountain complex complete with lodge and cafeteria, lies at the center of Sequoia National Park. Round Meadow, located just below the lodge, is a flowering glade with a one-mile loop trail that passes regal stands of sequoia.

Starting at the village, Crescent Meadow Road curves through the woods past several points of interest. Auto Log, a giant tree that fell in 1917, has been dug out to form a driveway. If for some unspeakable reason you long to wheel your car onto a sequoia, this is your only chance. The Parker Group, a pretty grove of sequoias, lies further up the road, as does Tunnel Log, a felled sequoia under which you can drive (having already driven *over* another of the brutes).

From here, noble explorers, it's on to Crescent Meadow, an overgrown marsh surrounded by sequoia trees and filled (in spring and summer) with wildflowers. Continue four-fifths of a mile along the meadow trail and you'll arrive at Tharp's Log, a fallen hollow sequoia which was converted into a log cabin (in the literal sense of the term).

A fork from Crescent Meadow Road runs past Hanging Rock, a granite boulder poised uneasily above a deep chasm, and Moro Rock, where a steep quarter-mile staircase ascends a magnificent dome. The views from this 6725-foot summit reach along the Great Western Divide, a chain of 12,000-foot peaks. In the dizzying depths 4000 feet below, the Middle Fork of the Kaweah River carves a stone channel en route to the San Joaquin Valley.

In the summer months one-hour tours of Crystal Caves are available. The hike down to these beautiful caverns is steep and requires sturdy shoes. Once beneath the earth you'll encounter temperatures of 48°, so bring along extra clothing.

Next, you can follow Generals Highway up to the central attraction of the entire park. Surrounded by conifers that appear little more than children, stands the General Sherman Tree. The largest living thing on earth, this leviathan weighs 1385 tons, measures 102 feet around, and rises 275 feet high. About 2500 years old, the tree is as tall as a 27-story building. Even statistics so overwhelming fall short in conveying the magnificence of this colossus.

To truly appreciate the General Sherman Tree, stand for a few minutes in his lengthy shadow and then explore the adjacent Congress Trail. This two-mile loop passes several awesome stands of sequoias, including one grove named for the United States Senate and another honoring the House of Representatives.

Generals Highway climbs and weaves from Sequoia to Kings Canyon. There are groves of the big trees along the way, as well as broad vistas of the Sierra Nevada mountains. At Lodgepole Visitors Center you can gain your bearings at the information desk, tour a mini-museum, and watch a slide show on the region. ~ Located on Generals Highway five miles north of Giant Forest Village; 209-565-3782.

KINGS CANYON NATIONAL PARK   Near the park entrance, **Big Stump Trail**, a one-and-one-half mile nature loop, demonstrates some of the natural and manmade disasters that can befall giant trees. Within its narrow ambit the path crosses a sequoia scarred by lightning, another shattered into unusable pieces by clumsy loggers, and a third sequoia that was reduced to sawdust piles big as giant anthills. The most striking specimen is the Mark Twain Stump, a 24-foot-wide behemoth felled as a display piece for the American Museum of Natural History in New York City.

Headquarters in Kings Canyon National Park for sightseers, rangers, hikers, and assorted others is Grant Grove. This mountain village, a few miles from the park entrance, offers a small grocery, restaurant, lodge, and gift shop. The **Grant Grove Visitors Center** provides information, maps, books, and wilderness permits. There is also a small museum dedicated to the sequoia tree. ~ 209-335-2856.

Pride of the park is the **General Grant Grove**, a forest of giants dating back more than 2000 years. Here a short loop leads past a **twin sister sequoia** (on the left at the end of the parking lot), formed when two trunks grew from a single base. Nearby lies the **Fallen Monarch**, the proverbial tree that crashed in the forest when there was no one around to record its demise. A 120-foot-long hollow log, it has served as a loggers' shelter, saloon, and stable. Today this natural tunnel makes a unique corridor for inquisitive hikers.

The Civil War is still being fought here in Grant Grove. Among these sentinel-straight sequoias is the **Robert E. Lee Tree**, rising 254 feet above the forest floor. The **General Grant Tree** is a gnarly giant tattooed with woodpecker holes and adorned with thick, stubby branches that twist upward. Proclaimed the Nation's Christmas Tree, it is the site of special services every year. Needless to say, the General Grant outstrips its Confederate counterpart, topping out at 267 feet and boasting a diameter (40 feet) greater than any other sequoia tree.

POETRY OF STONE

From Grant Grove a mountain road corkscrews up to **Panoramic Point**. Situated at 7520 feet, this lookout could soon be at sea level considering the peaks that rise above it. Stretched along the horizon in a kind of granite amphitheater is a line of bald domes, cresting at 13,000- and 14,000-foot heights. Each bears a name resonant of the simple poetry of stone— Kettle Dome, Marble Mountain, Eagle Peaks, and Thunder Mountain. Cradled beneath them, an aquamarine glint in a forest of green, is Hume Lake. Roads leading to Panoramic Point close in winter.

In the shadow of this leviathan sits the **Gamlin Cabin**, a log house built in 1872 by an early settler. Looking as sturdy as the trees around it, the structure was used at one time by U.S. Cavalry patrols.

Follow Route 180 from Grant Grove down into Kings Canyon itself. Along this 35-mile mountain road, which twists and curves as it descends the canyon walls, are countless vista points. You can peer down sharp rockfaces, gaze out at massive ridges, and take in the rivers which rumble into the San Joaquin Valley.

A side road diverges to **Hume Lake**, a small mountain lake which reflects in its glassy surface the faces of surrounding peaks. Then Route 180 (usually closed from November through April) descends through lofty mountains that break the sunlight into shafts and splinters. As you spiral further and further into this shadowy canyon, the granite walls edge closer and climb more steeply. Eventually the landscape narrows to a sharp defile and then reopens to reveal a tumbling river strewn with boulders, the South Fork of the Kings River.

Here, where road meets river, sits **Boyden Cavern**. Formed over a 300,000-year period, this marble cave descends past rock pools, massive stalagmites, cave pearls, and ornate stalactites. Among these marvelous underground formations are sights named Upside Down City, The Wedding Cake, Christmas Tree Room, and the Drapery Room. Closed from November through April. Admission. ~ 209-736-2708.

Route 180 continues along the river past **Cedar Grove**, where civilization rises in the form of a lodge with grocery store and snack bar. Just beyond this oasis lies **Roaring River Falls**, a cascade that rolls down from the mountains, crashes through a granite chasm, and debouches into an emerald pool.

Nearby **Zumwalt Meadow** is awash with color in spring when the wildflowers bloom. For an even more intimate view of the natural surroundings, drive or hike the **Motor Nature Trail**, which bumps for three miles along a dirt road, paralleling the river and passing rich marshland.

Here, deep in the canyon, you will find the river loud in your ears. Sounds echo off the surrounding walls, ricocheting upward along flinty rockfaces and vertiginous cliffs. Vying with Yosemite in grandeur, the valley is more than 8000 feet beneath the surrounding mountains, the deepest canyon in the United States.

LODGING

Accommodations in both Sequoia and Kings Canyon national parks fall into several categories. There are "rustic cabins," available only in summer, which lack bathrooms and decoration, utilize oil or wood stoves, often have canvas roofs, and price in the budget range. The "cabins," on the other hand, are trim woodframe structures with pine furniture, private baths, decorative posters, and thermostat heaters. These are moderately priced and quite comfortable.

Both parks also offer "motel rooms." Tabbed in the moderate category, they are roadside-style accommodations with veneer furniture, wall-to-wall carpeting, decorative appointments, and private baths. The central number for reservations to most facilities is 209-335-5500. Remember, large sections of the parks are closed during the winter.

The main complex in Sequoia National Park is **Giant Forest Lodge**. Located along Generals Highway, it is part of a village layout that includes a restaurant, cafeteria, market, and lounge. Accommodations include cabins and motel rooms. Closed in winter. ~ 209-335-5500. BUDGET TO MODERATE.

Stony Creek, located on Generals Highway between Sequoia and Kings Canyon, features a lodge with motel-type accommodations. There's a dining room, gift shop and market here as well as a lobby with stone fireplace. Closed in winter. ~ 209-561-3314. MODERATE.

Grant Grove Lodge, the central facility in Kings Canyon National Park, sits in a village that features a restaurant, grocery, gift shop, and information center. Facilities at Grant Grove include rustic and developed cabins. ~ 209-335-5500. BUDGET TO MODERATE.

Cedar Grove, located on Route 180 deep within Kings Canyon, is a mountain lodge idyllically set in a grove of tall trees beside a river. There are motel rooms here, as well as a snack bar, market, and gift shop. Closed in winter. ~ 209-335-5500. MODERATE.

HIDDEN ▶ Sequoia National Park's **Bearpaw Meadow Backcountry Camp** offers rustic cabins. Extremely popular, this mountain hideaway lies at the end of an 11-mile trail along which guests hike in. The accommodations include breakfast and dinner. ~ 209-335-5500. DELUXE.

For a full-facility mountain resort, you'll be hard pressed to find anything quite like **Montecito Sequoia Lodge**. Located at 7500 feet elevation along Generals Highway between Sequoia and Kings Can-

▲▲

✔ CHECK THESE OUT—UNIQUE LODGING

- *Budget:* Sleep in the shadow of the great mountains at **Winnedumah Country Inn**, a 1927 building with antique-furnished rooms. *page 457*
- *Budget to moderate:* Enjoy Mammoth's outdoor offerings from a base camp at the **North Village Inn**. *page 462*
- *Moderate to deluxe:* Repair to the lakeside mountain resort of **Montecito Sequoia Lodge**, where breakfast is included in the price. *page 450*
- *Ultra-deluxe:* Give in to temptation in the desert by staying at **Furnace Creek Inn**, where you'll find an oasis of luxury set against the beautifully harsh backdrop of Death Valley. *page 471*

Budget: under $50　Moderate: $50–$90　Deluxe: $90–$120　Ultra-deluxe: over $120

yon national parks, it's a family vacation camp with rustic cabins and a lodge. The complex rests next to a lake on 38 acres and offers a pool, tennis courts, basketball, volleyball, canoeing, waterskiing, archery, horseback riding and cross-country skiing in the winter. There's a dining room with a stone fireplace, an ample recreation room, and a bar. Guest rooms in the lodge are priced in the deluxe range and include breakfast (ultra-deluxe with dinner included). The cabins rent in the deluxe range but include all meals. They are closed in winter; lodge rooms are open year-round. ~ 209-565-3388, 800-227-9900, fax 209-565-3223. DELUXE TO ULTRA-DELUXE.

On the road down into Kings Canyon, surrounded by rough-hewn mountains, lies **Kings Canyon Lodge**. This way station, with its homemade bar and grill and gravity-feed gas pumps, contains a cluster of simple woodframe cottages. They are basic accommodations, with knotty-pine walls and uninspired furnishings. Located just off the highway, some have kitchen facilities. Closed in winter. ~ 67751 Route 180; 209-335-2405, fax 209-335-2310. MODERATE.

Also serving the national parks are several affordable motels in the nearby town of Three Rivers. Located along Route 198 within a few miles of Sequoia National Park is the **Lazy J Ranch Motel**, a 16-unit facility with plain rooms; some rooms come with kitchens. ~ 39625 Sierra Drive, Three Rivers; 209-561-4449, 800-341-8000. BUDGET TO MODERATE.

Nearby, **The River Inn** has standard rooms at reasonable prices. ~ 45176 Sierra Drive, Three Rivers; 209-561-4367. MODERATE.

DINING

You can scale granite cliffs in Sequoia and Kings Canyon, shoot white-water rapids, and return unscathed. What will kill you is the food. Nowhere is the "good enough for government work" philosophy more closely followed than in the kitchens of these national parks. Note: At press time, some of Sequoia National Park's dining and nightlife facilities were being revamped.

The **Village Cafeteria** ladles out steam-tray food for all three meals. Closed in winter. ~ 209-335-5500. BUDGET.

At **Lodge Pole**, a deli serves up barbecued ribs, fried chicken and an assortment of sandwiches, burgers and hot dogs. Closed in winter. ~ 209-335-5500. BUDGET.

The **Grant Grove Coffee Shop** is located at Grant Grove Village, adjacent to the information center. A simple mountain eatery, the coffee shop offers a menu of soups, salads, and sandwiches. Daily specials feature such entrées as ravioli, fettuccine, fish and chips, and steak. ~ 209-335-5500. BUDGET.

The decor consists of stuffed game animals and wilderness photos. The bar is hewn from pine, and the dining room is filled with oil-cloth tables. Otherwise **Kings Canyon Lodge**, set deep in the mountains, is just your average backcountry café. The menu features standard breakfast fare and sandwiches and hamburgers for lunch and dinner. ~ 67751 Route 180; 209-335-2405. MODERATE.

PARKS

SEQUOIA AND KINGS CANYON NATIONAL PARKS
These adjoining facilities, together covering more than 850,000 acres, are discussed at length elsewhere in this chapter. For wilderness enthusiasts they offer 800 miles of trails, 14,500-foot peaks, and opportunities for horseback riding and cross-country skiing. There are streams and lakes throughout both parks, with many good trout pools. Fishing licenses are required. Swimming is permitted in certain spots, but do not take any chances when the river is high. Facilities include restrooms, picnic areas, restaurants, cabins, and museums. ~ Route 198 leads into Sequoia from the southwest and Route 180 (General's Highway) connects the two parks; 209-565-3341 or Kings Canyon Visitors Center, 209-335-2856.

▲ In the two parks, there's camping in 13 campgrounds that offer 350 sites in Sequoia and 700 sites in Kings Canyon, most of which are closed in winter. Prices range from $5 to $12 per night; RV sites are available (no hookups). Reservations are required for Lodgepole Campground (the largest of the campgrounds with 225 sites); call DESTINET (800-365-2267). All others are on a first-come, first-served basis. Wilderness camping is very popular. Lodgepole Campground is located four miles north of Giant Forest Village.

SEQUOIA NATIONAL FOREST   Located at the southern edge of the Sierra Nevada, this facility boasts more than 38 sequoia groves. It also includes several resort spots like Kern Canyon, popular with weekend refugees from Los Angeles. Climbing from 1000 to 12,000 feet, the preserve contains six wilderness areas. About 1200 miles of streams and several dozen high-country lakes offer ample opportunities to drop a line. Day-use fee, $5. ~ Access is via Routes 178, 155, and 190; 209-784-1500.

▲ There are 47 campgrounds with about 1946 sites; $8 to $22 per night. Most campgrounds accommodate RVs (no hookups).

SIERRA NATIONAL FOREST
Tucked between Kings Canyon and Yosemite national parks, this 1,300,000-acre preserve climbs from 1000 to 14,000 feet elevation and ranges from rolling chaparral country to bald peaks. There are two groves of sequoias and 1100 miles of trails. More than one-half of the forest is wilderness. About 1200 miles of streams and more than 1000 lakes (including Bass Lake) provide excellent trout, bass, and kokanee salmon fishing. ~ Access is via Routes 168 and 41; 209-297-0706.

▲ There are 61 campgrounds, most of which are closed in winter; $6 to $12 per night. RV sites are available in most campgrounds.

The backbone of the Eastern Sierra is Route 395, which runs
north past black lava hills, red cinder cones, and other volcanic
outcroppings. The land all about is a morass of sand divided
in random fashion by arroyos, a dust bowl with a rim of mountains.
This is the Owens Valley, bled dry by Los Angeles, which has di-
verted its once plentiful water. Today only the mountains remain—
to the east the Inyos, Panamints, and Whites, in the west the Sierra
Nevada. From them the valley, victimized by a metropolis hundreds
of miles away, derives its identity and maintains its dignity.

▼▼▼▼▼▼▼▼▼▼
Owens Valley

At **Fossil Falls**, 20,000-year-old lava flows have solidified to create
dramatic cascades of black rock. ~ On Route 395 for three miles
north of Little Lake; go east one-half mile on Cinder Road; turn right
on the dirt road and proceed three-quarters of a mile to a parking
lot; hike one-quarter mile to the falls; a second set of falls lies several hundred yards farther south.

SIGHTS

Route 395 continues past miles of sage brush in a landscape that
is broken only occasionally by a solitary and spindly cactus. **Owens
Lake Bed**, once part of a rich string of intermountain lakes, stretches
for miles to the west—a dry, salt-caked expanse.

To understand the allure of Owens Valley, stop by the **Eastern
Sierra InterAgency Visitors Center**. A valuable resource, the information center has a good selection of maps and pamphlets and an
excellent collection of books on California's mountain and desert regions. ~ Route 395 one mile south of Lone Pine; 619-876-6222.

In the neon town of Lone Pine you can pick up Whitney Portal
Road (one of America's greatest byways), which climbs from 4000
to 8300 feet elevation in its 13-mile course. Passing streams shaded
by cottonwood trees, it cuts through the **Alabama Hills**, a unique
formation of weathered granite whose reddish colors contrast brilliantly with the gray backdrop of the Sierra Nevada.

Then Whitney Portal Road rides out of this rolling range land,
trading the soft contours of the Alabamas for the cold granite world
of the Sierra Nevada. These latter mountains are young (geologically) and roughhewn, with adze-like slopes that lift away from the
road in vertical lunges. Far from embracing admirers, the surrounding heights seem to dare people to ascend them. Even the pine trees,
which grow in crowded groves along the early slopes, quit the climb
half way up.

When the road itself quits at **Whitney Portal**, base camp for
climbers, you find above you Mount Whitney, at 14,495 feet the
tallest mountain in the contiguous United States. In the giant's
shadow stand six other peaks, all topping 14,000 feet. It is a scene
of unpronounceable beauty, fashioned from dark chasms and stone
minarets, almost two miles above the floor of Owens Valley.

HIDDEN ►
On the slopes of a 9000-foot peak outside Lone Pine lie the rusting remains of **Cerro Gordo**. One of the High Desert's best-preserved ghost towns, its story begins in 1865 when rich silver deposits were discovered. Within a few years almost 2000 miners had arrived, hauling out as much as 5300 tons of bullion each year. Among the ruins is a store, two-story house, and other tumbledown buildings constructed in 1871. Later structures, dating to 1916, are dotted around the property. Cerro Gordo is now privately owned, but the public is welcome. The owners ask that you check in with them at their home to sign a liability waiver before entering. ~ To get there, pick up Route 136 just south of Lone Pine and follow it twelve-and-one-half miles; turn left on Cerro Gordo Road and proceed for five miles along this graded but *very* steep road.

Proceeding north along Route 395 from Lone Pine (particularly in early morning and late afternoon), pull over about four miles outside town and gaze eastward toward the river bottom. A herd of **tule elk**, whose ancestors once inhabited California's Central Valley, roams the area.

Farther outside town, with the Sierra Nevada looming in the background like an impenetrable wall, stands **Manzanar**. In 1942, when panic over Pearl Harbor pervaded the country, 10,000 Americans of Japanese ancestry were interned here. Perceived as potential spies and saboteurs, they were uprooted from their West Coast homes and "relocated" to concentration camps like Manzanar. Today little remains to commemorate their tragedy other than two guard stations, fashioned, almost insultingly, like pagodas. There is also a plaque imploring that "the injustices and humiliation suffered here as a result of hysteria, racism, and economic exploitation never emerge again."

HIDDEN ►
Even more overwhelming in its moral ramifications is the **Manzanar cemetery**, where internees were buried. The place inspires sadness and remorse, and also a sense of terror. It is not so much the stark white monument set against the unyielding Sierra Nevada that

COWBOY COUNTRY

If the Alabama Hills seem a bit too familiar, little wonder: they have served as the setting for countless Westerns. At one time they were almost as important to the movie industry as the Hollywood Hills. Hopalong Cassidy, Gene Autry, and the Lone Ranger all rode this range. For a close-up of cowboy country, turn right on Movie Road. A network of dirt roads leads past **Movie Flat**, where many sequences were shot, then continues into this badlands of humpbacked boulders. ~ On Movie Road, off Whitney Portal Road three miles from Route 395.

evokes this final response, but the cemetery itself. Running in a double line around the burial ground, dividing it dramatically from the countryside, indeed from the country itself, is a barbed wire fence. ~ Continue on Route 395 north for four-fifths of a mile, turn left on the dirt road; when it forks after one mile, bear left to the cemetery.

The **Eastern California Museum** in nearby Independence contains photographs and news clips retracing the story of Manzanar. There are snapshots of the tarpaper barracks and wooden sentry towers as well as personal belongings of the internees. This excellent regional facility also contains such Indian artifacts as arrowheads, baskets, and beadwork. Tools of the trade from cowboy days include branding irons, a mule pack canteen, leather chaps, and even a spittoon. The handwoven quilts, antique telephones, and accordion cameras of the region's more genteel set are also presented. Out back, a few of the town's original buildings—weather-beaten, woodframe structures—still stand. Closed on Tuesday. ~ 155 Grant Street; 619-878-0258.

The **Mount Whitney Fish Hatchery** raises brood stock (egg-producing) trout. The resultant fingerlings are used for stocking backcountry streams, making this area one of the most popular freshwater fishing regions in the state. Breeding rainbow, brook, brown, and golden trout, the facility offers an opportunity to watch gamefish hatching and to glimpse fat but spirited adult fish. The building alone, a stone structure with Tudor flourishes and a red tile roof, built in 1916, makes the visit worthwhile. ~ Off Route 395 about two miles north of Independence; 619-878-2272.

East of the little town of Big Pine, Route 168 connects with a side road that leads up into the White Mountains. Climb this backcountry byway and a dazzling 180° **mountain panorama** of the Sierra Nevada Mountain Range will open to view. The mountains seem to wrap around you, forming an amphitheater of stone and snow. Within this ring of 13,000-foot peaks rests **Palisade Glacier**, the southernmost glacier in North America. For more information, contact the White Mountains Ranger Station. ~ 619-873-2500.

Then the road ascends to over 10,000 feet elevation and—in a kind of high altitude riddle—enters a territory where the living reside next to the dead and the dead are often half alive. The denizens of this mysterious locale are over 4000 years old, the world's most ancient living things, dating back to the days of the Egyptian pyramids.

The site is an **Ancient Bristlecone Pine Forest**, where short, stunted trees with needles like fox tails grow on an icy, windblown landscape. Sculpted by the elements, they resemble living driftwood; many of the trees are partially dead, sustained by a thin strip of bark carrying water and nutrients.

In the forest's **Schulman Grove**, where the oldest trees survive, you can follow a one-mile loop trail past Pine Alpha, a 4300-year-old tree. Here you will also find the **Edmond P. Schulman Visitors Center** (open from June 15 to November 15), which has exhibits and demonstrative trails on the region's natural history. From here a sometimes impassable dirt road continues for 12 miles along the lip of the world, through a lunar landscape, and past ever-thinning forest to The **Patriarch Grove**, a second stand of bristlecones located at 11,000 feet.

Bishop is one of those towns that exist not in and for themselves but for what is around them. The **Bishop Chamber of Commerce** serves as the local information center, a good place to plan an exploration of the area. ~ 690 North Main Street, Bishop; 619-873-8405.

Dedicated to American Indian traditions, **The Owens Valley Paiute Shoshone Indian Cultural Center** has outstanding displays of basketry, leathercrafts, and beadwork. There are also showcases filled with petroglyphs and arrowheads. Centerpiece of the showroom is a circular house of cane, replicating the traditional homes of Owens Valley tribes. ~ 2300 West Line Street, Bishop; 619-873-4478.

Route 168 buzzes west from Bishop for about 20 miles into the high country of the Sierra Nevada. Here **Lake Sabrina** and **South Lake**, favored fishing holes, are like crystal inlaid in a setting of granite.

Directly north of Bishop, the **Volcanic Tablelands** rise above the valley floor, ascending to 7912-foot Casa Diablo Mountain. Built from a series of lava flows, this sparse plateau is cut by sharp, narrow canyons. Gleaming red against the gray walls of the Sierra Nevada and White Mountains, it's a desolate but enchanting region, particularly pretty around dawn and dusk. ~ Pick up Five Bridges Road at the north end of Bishop and take it to the end, where it continues as Casa Diablo Road, a dirt road that climbs all the way to Casa Diablo Mountain.

The nearby town of Laws, a major railroad stop during the 1880s, is re-created at the **Laws Railroad Museum and Historical Site**. Combining the town's original buildings with antique structures relocated from other parts of the valley, it conveys an atmosphere of the Old West.

The general store is here with its lard buckets and spice canisters; tumblers still turn in the mailbox locks at the post office; and the surgical tools in the doctor's office look as threatening as they did back when. In addition, the original Bishop Catholic Church has been converted into a library, museum and art gallery and the Wells Fargo office now displays rock crystals and Indian artifacts.

But the centerpiece of the exhibit is still the railroad yard. Here the station, with its waiting room, telegraph office, and loading dock, has been nicely preserved. Resting just down the track is old Southern Pacific Engine Number Nine, with a line of freight cars and a bell whose clangs still echo across the valley. ~ Route 6 about four miles northeast of Bishop; 619-873-5950.

Artifacts of a much earlier era, **Indian petroglyphs,** lie off the ◄ HIDDEN beaten track north of Laws. Etched into volcanic rocks, these ancient drawings portray people, deer, snakes, and insects. Possibly left by ancestors of local Paiutes, the figures carry significant symbolic meaning. Since they occur along old deer trails, one theory holds they were intended to bring the blessing of good hunting. For maps and directions to the petroglyphs, contact the Bureau of Land Management. ~ Route 395, 785 North Main Street, Suite E, Bishop; 619-872-4881.

The neon strip along Route 395 serves as motel row in Lone Pine. **LODGING** Several resting places line the highway, each providing adequate accommodations. The **Dow Villa Hotel and Motel** features a modern motel attached to a 1920s-era hotel. The complex includes a lobby, pool, and spa. Rooms in the hotel are time-worn but tidy; the motel rooms are more modern and very comfortable. ~ 310 South Main Street, Lone Pine; 619-876-5521, 800-824-9317, fax 619-876-5643. BUDGET TO MODERATE.

Another important find is **Winnedumah Country Inn,** an imposing two-story edifice across the street from the Inyo County Court House on Route 395 in Independence. Built in 1927, its spacious lobby greets guests with a stone fireplace, beam ceiling, and cozy armchairs. The accommodations are bright, friendly rooms with quilts and original furnishings. ~ 211 North Edward Street, Independence; 619-878-2040. BUDGET TO MODERATE.

Bishop also has its share of roadside motels, strung like lights along Route 395. **High Sierra Lodge** is a two-story complex with a pool and spa. Among the 52 units are guest rooms with or without kitchens; each is spacious, carpeted, and well maintained. ~ 1005 North Route 395, Bishop; 619-873-8426, 800-824-9317, fax 619-876-5643. MODERATE.

That pretty place at the edge of town, the historic house with lace curtains and porches on both floors, is a bed and breakfast. The **Matlick House,** with its handmade quilts and beveled-mirror armoires, is known for miles around. Each of the four guest rooms has been decorated with a flourish: there are overhead fans, iron beds, turn-of-the-century settees and other antiques. Guests enjoy a full breakfast and evening hors d'oeuvres. ~ Two miles north of Bishop on Route 395; 619-873-3133, 800-898-3133. MODERATE.

Up at 8500 feet elevation, socked in by mountains and graced with a stream and natural pool, is **Cardinal Village Resort.** Part of an old mining claim, this retreat consists of a cluster of cabins dating to 1906. Attractive houses, they combine such old-fashioned amenities as wooden counters with new-fangled conveniences like tile baths. Blended into the nearby aspen grove are the general store and café as well as a lodge complete with stone fireplace and library.

All nine units contain kitchens. Closed in winter. ~ Route 168 about 16 miles west of Bishop; 619-873-4789. MODERATE.

DINING

Dining on the east side of the Sierra Nevada is as grand a gourmet experience as in Sequoia and Kings Canyon. Somehow the love of the good life in this area has never been translated to the dinner table. All the towns located along Route 395 are lined with restaurants, but most are cafés unworthy of note.

At **The Seasons**, the atmosphere is decidedly rustic. Landscape paintings by local artists line the walls adding a mountain-country flavor. The menu includes rack of lamb with fresh rosemary, filet mignon with green peppercorn sauce, and grilled chicken breast with a tropical fruit sauce. If you're otherwise inclined, they offer a few fish entrées plus some pasta dishes. Closed Tuesday and Wednesday during winter. ~ 206 South Main Street, Lone Pine; 619-876-8927. MODERATE.

Over at **Margie's Merry-Go-Round** they specialize in steaks, pork chops, barbecue dishes, and grilled seafood. This small, friendly restaurant attracts a local crowd. ~ 212 South Main Street, Lone Pine; 619-876-4115. MODERATE.

If local crowds are any indication, **Bishop Grill** is the best place in Bishop to eat. It's certainly the cheapest: the low budget prices at this café are vintage 1960s. The cuisine is straight Americana from the ham dinners to the pork chops to the breaded trout. Meat and potato entrées extend to steak, veal, and sausage. The breakfast and lunch menus can be derived by deduction. ~ 281 North Main Street, Bishop; 619-873-3911. BUDGET.

Then there's the place that offers the world's strangest Sunday champagne brunch special—all the Chinese food you can eat. Hopefully you won't be stopping at **Imperial Gourmet Chinese Restaurant** on your way to church. Instead I recommend lunch and din-

---

✔ **CHECK THESE OUT—UNIQUE DINING**

- *Budget:* Slide over to **The Sidewinder** and feast on diner chow while perusing photos from the movie *Bagdad Cafe*, which was filmed here. *page 442*
- *Moderate:* Sample ecclectic Asian offerings in a simple, Japanese-style environment at **Matsu**. *page 463*
- *Deluxe:* Sentence yourself to dinner at **The Restaurant at Convict Lake**, where the rustic ambience enhances the superb cuisine. *page 462*
- *Ultra-deluxe:* Wash off that desert dust and spruce up for a candlelight dinner at the **Inn Dining Room**, where the price is fixed and the selection is almost limitless. *page 472*

Budget: under $8 Moderate: $8–$16 Deluxe: $16–$24 Ultra-deluxe: over $24

ner, when you'll find enough Asian atmosphere and a variety of Chinese dishes for an enjoyable meal. ~ 785 North Main Street, # K, Bishop; 619-872-1144. MODERATE.

In sharp contrast to the dust-blown basin of Owens Valley is the green Mammoth Lakes region. Here on the eastern face of the Sierra Nevada, volcanoes and earthquakes have wracked the region, leaving a legacy of lakes.

Mammoth Lakes

Among the most lovely lakes in the region is **Convict Lake**, a mountain jewel formed by receding glaciers. Bounded by precipitous cliffs and multihued rocks, the lake was the scene of a famous 1871 gun battle between a sheriff's posse and a band of fugitives. ~ Convict Lake Road about two miles west of Route 395.

SIGHTS

Hot Creek, a beautiful stream set deep in a rock-rimmed canyon, is one of Mammoth Lakes most deceptive and alluring spots. One section, peaceful as a babbling brook, is popular with fly fishermen. Farther downstream, there are hot springs that warm the water to perfect spa temperatures. Then, within a 100 yards of this popular pool, the creek erupts in low geysers and dramatic steam vents. Light concentrations of chemicals and dangers of scalding prompted local authorities to post "swimming not recommended" signs. Visitors, however, generally ignore them, opting to soak in the emerald moss-filled creek. Vapors percolate from gray mud holes and pungent bubbles rise out of the depths. ~ Located six miles south of Mammoth Lakes. From Route 395 turn east on the road next to Mammoth–June Lakes Airport and follow the signs for three and one-half miles to the parking lot; then its a short hike down to the creek.

◄ HIDDEN

The facts and figures concerning Mammoth Lakes are found at two locations. The **Mammoth Visitors Center** offers information on hiking, camping, and other outdoor activities. ~ Route 203 just outside Mammoth Lakes; 619-924-5500. At **Mammoth Lakes Visitors Bureau** they provide details on local hotels, restaurants, and other amenities; this facility will also help with reservations. ~ Village Center Mall along Route 203, Mammoth Lakes; 619-934-2712.

A thumbnail introduction to the history of this former mining region awaits along Old Mammoth Road. Back in 1878, after gold and silver were uncovered, Mammoth City developed into a boom town with 22 saloons, two breweries, 13 stores, and two newspapers. The place went bust within a year, but a few artifacts from the glory days remain.

During summer months the **Mammoth Museum**, housed in a log cabin, traces the region's story from the days of mining and ranching to the current era. About a mile from the top of Old Mammoth Road, the grave of one Mrs. J. E. Townsend, deceased 1882, rests in a shaded grove. Further along, across from a state historical marker, are the remains of a log cabin and the ill-fated mine.

Lake Mary Road climbs past a chain of beautiful glacial lakes. **Twin Lakes**, a wasp-waisted body of water that was once two separate lakes, sits in a granite bowl. Just beyond here a half-mile trail leads to **Panorama Dome**, a volcanic rock with outstanding views of the surrounding lakes and the White Mountains.

The loop around **Lake Mary**, largest of this glacial group, diverts to **Lake George**, a crystal pool dominated by a single granite shaft. During early summer, meadows along the nearby hiking trails are filled with flowers.

Spilling down from **Lake Mamie** are the **Twin Falls**, which cascade 300 feet along a granite bed into Twin Lakes. **Horseshoe Lake**, the only lake where swimming is permitted, sits near the top of the road at 8950 feet elevation. To explore the alpine waters that rest beyond Horseshoe Lake, you'll have to don hiking boots.

A number of sights lie along Minaret Road (Route 203), which ascends from the town of Mammoth Lakes into the mountains. Unsettling evidence of Mammoth Lakes' dramatic geology lies along the sharp walls of the **earthquake fault**. A nature trail wends along the sides of this fracture, where the earth has opened to create a deep fissure. The rocks on either side fit perfectly into their counterparts, providing a graphic illustration of how an earthquake can split the globe like a ripe fruit.

Minaret Vista, with its views of the Ansel Adams Wilderness, is otherworldly. The San Joaquin River winds through the deep canyon below; and the stark peaks of the Ritter Range loom above, a setting in which the top of the world seems to have been ripped away, leaving a jagged line of needle-point peaks and razor-edge ridges.

But enough mere beauty. At **Devils Postpile National Monument**, where Devils Postpile Road (Route 203) reveals its final surprise, physical beauty is combined with the magic of geology. Here layer on layer of angular shafts, some vertical, others twisted into curving forms, create a 60-foot-high cliff with smooth-sided columns.

Volcanic forces molded this rare formation when surface cracks appeared during the cooling of molten lava. The surface breaks extended vertically through the rock, creating the polygonal posts. Then glaciers flowed over the fractured mass 10,000 years ago, pol-

RIDE HIGH

At Mammoth Mountain Ski Area farther uphill from the earthquake fault, you can take a **gondola ride** to the 11,053-foot summit of Mammoth Mountain. Of course if it's winter and the area has been graced with the white powder for which locals pray, you can ski back down. Admission. ~ Minaret Road (Route 203); 619-934-2571.

ishing the tops of the posts and leaving a geometric surface resembling a tile floor (which can be viewed from atop Devils Postpile).

Along the trail at the bottom you can gaze at this unique wall of pillars, some of which curve toward the mountain, seeming to support the posts behind, while others lean free and appear about to collapse. Directly below them, like splinters from a magnificent sculpture, lie piles of fallen columns.

Mammoth Scenic Loop, branching from Minaret Road one mile outside Mammoth Lakes, contains within its ambit several points of interest. **Inyo Craters** is a string of three volcanic cavities created by violent eruptions. Part of the volcanic ridge that runs between Mammoth Mountain and Mono Lake, these craters and their lakes are mere babies in geologic terms, dating back perhaps 1500 years. ~ One mile down a dirt side road and one-quarter mile up a trail.

En route to June Lake, another string of glacial lakes, the local geology shows another of its many faces. **Obsidian Dome** is a glass mountain composed entirely of obsidian. This black volcanic glass, created during the cooling of molten lava, was used by local Indians to fashion arrowheads. ~ Follow Route 395 about 11 miles north of Mammoth Lakes, then turn west for one and one-half miles on Glass Flow Road.

June Lake Loop (Route 158), a mountain road 15 miles north of Mammoth Lakes, curves past June Lake and three other pools. Each is an alpine beauty, a shimmering blue lake bounded by forest and lofty peaks. Popular for fishing, camping, and hiking, the region is also crowded with skiers in winter. June Mountain is situated at the head of the horseshoe-shaped loop.

As the loop closes upon Route 395, with Mono Lake in the distance, a series of volcanic mountains rise in the east. These are the **Mono Craters**, which reach elevations of about 2700 feet. Built of lava, the craters contain rich deposits of obsidian along their flanks.

LODGING

Convict Lake Resort, located near one of the region's prettiest lakes, features a colony of cabins bounded by an aspen grove. Built of pine, they are plain mountain lodgings with wall heaters and full kitchens. Set at 7600 feet, the resort includes a restaurant, store, and marina. ~ Convict Lake Road about two miles west of Route 395, nine miles south of Mammoth Lakes; 619-934-3800, 800-992-2260, fax 619-934-0396. MODERATE.

Mammoth Mountain Inn is a modern hotel with a distinct rustic-mountain atmosphere. Located across the road from Mammoth Mountain Ski Area, the inn is primarily a ski lodge, but its easy proximity to Devils Postpile and other natural features makes it popular year-round. There are restaurants, lounges, spas, and shops here as well as a wood-and-stone lobby, which is decorated with antler chandeliers. The hotel rooms are moderate to deluxe. Condos, with kitchen facilities, are deluxe to ultra-deluxe during peak periods. ~

Minaret Road, Mammoth Lakes; 619-934-2581, 800-228-4947, fax 619-934-0701. MODERATE TO ULTRA-DELUXE.

One of the prettiest and most secluded spots in Mammoth Lakes is **Tamarack Lodge Resort**. A classic mountain lodge with split log walls and stone fireplace, it sits on Twin Lakes in the shadow of the mountains. The lobby is a cheery alpine room inevitably filled with guests warming themselves by a roaring fire. There are small rooms (with shared and private baths) in the lodge, sentimentally decorated and paneled in knotty pine. More than 25 cabins, ranging from studios to three-bedroom extravaganzas, also dot the six-acre grounds. While these are traditional woodframe structures, the interiors of many are modern in design with wall-to-wall carpeting, stall showers, and contemporary kitchens. Most offer partial views of the lake. Located at 8600 feet, the resort is in a major nordic ski area, with trails radiating in all directions. It also features a restaurant. Depending on the season, lodge rooms with shared baths are budget to moderate; cabins range from moderate to ultra-deluxe, also depending on the season. ~ Twin Lakes Road, just off Lake Mary Road, Mammoth Lakes; 619-934-2442, 800-237-6879, fax 619-934-2281. BUDGET TO ULTRA-DELUXE.

> At **Rainbow Falls** the San Joaquin River plunges 100 feet over volcanic rock to an alpine pool, creating multi-hued patterns in the mist. This spot is particularly pretty in the afternoon. ~ Off Reds Meadow and along a 1.3 mile trail.

North Village Inn, a small mountain motel on the north end of town, features standard rooms as well as accommodations with kitchens. The place is located on a main road but is set amid trees and offers partial mountain views. Many of the rooms are furnished in knotty pine and have carpets and wall prints. One- and two-bedroom facilities with kitchens are also available. ~ 103 Lake Mary Road, Mammoth Lakes; 619-934-2525, 800-934-4042, fax 619-934-1466. MODERATE TO DELUXE.

For assistance booking reservations in the Mammoth Lakes region, contact **Mammoth Lakes Resort Association**. ~ 619-934-2522. Or try **The Mammoth Line**. ~ 619-934-2712, 800-367-6572.

Over in June Lake, **Big Rock Resort** has eight cabin units. These are attractive duplexes with kitchens and knotty-pine interiors. Some have fireplaces. Nicely situated on the lake, the complex includes a tackle shop and marina. It's a convenient locale if you want to fish, swim, boat, or gaze out at the mountains. Dinner is served year-round; lunch is only served in the summer. ~ 1 Big Rock Road, June Lake; 619-648-7717, 800-769-9831, fax 619-648-1067. MODERATE.

DINING   One of the area's prime dining rooms is not on Mammoth Lakes at all, but a few miles south near a neighboring lake. **The Restaurant at Convict Lake** is a plush but rustic place. A fireplace with copper hood dominates the main room and the adjoining lounge has a wood-burning stove. But the menu is the true drawing card at this critically acclaimed establishment. The chef prepares a California cuisine–style menu of rack of lamb, beef Wellington, duck breast sauté, homemade gravlox, stuffed chicken breast, and a nightly fresh fish special like salmon. Dinner only. ~ Convict Lake Road about two miles west of Route 395; 619-934-3803. DELUXE.

Shogun Japanese Restaurant may be parked in a shopping mall, but it still provides marvelous views of the mountains. Equipped with a sushi bar and adjoining lounge, the restaurant features sukiyaki, *tonkatsu*, tempura, and teriyaki dishes. Dinner only. ~ Sierra Centre Mall, Old Mammoth Road, Mammoth Lakes; 619-934-3970. MODERATE.

Matsu Restaurant, a small wood-paneled place, offers an Asian grab bag. The entrées cover a lot of geography, ranging from Filipino-style *pansit* (shrimp and pork sautéed with onions and noodles) to teriyaki dishes from Japan to Chinese courses like sweet and sour chicken. Dinner only. ~ Route 203, Mammoth Lakes; 619-934-8277. MODERATE.

Pine plank walls and hand-stitched decorations make **La Sierra's Mexican Restaurant and Cantina** a charming spot for a meal. They prepare a full array of dishes from south of the border and some Italian and American food. The restaurant serves lunch and dinner, with a champagne brunch on Sunday. ~ 3789 Route 203, Mammoth Lakes; 619-934-8083. MODERATE.

With its Swiss alpine atmosphere, the **Matterhorn Restaurant** is one of Mammoth Lakes' most congenial dining places. The Continental dinner menu begins with smoked salmon, escargots, and onion soup. Among the entrées are more than a dozen dishes—champagne-poached salmon, rainbow trout, rack of lamb, pepper steak, scampi, grilled chicken, wienerschnitzel, and veal *médaillons*. Add a wine list plus dessert tray and you have an excellent opportunity to feast. Dinner only. Closed in spring and fall. ~ 6080 Minaret Road, Mammoth Lakes; 619-934-3369. MODERATE TO DELUXE.

Informal, inexpensive café dining is the specialty of the house at **Blondie's Kitchen and Waffle Shop.** Famous for its waffles and homemade specialties, this unassuming spot is favored by a local crowd. Breakfast, served all day, includes granola and oatmeal, omelettes, *machacas* (shredded beef and eggs), and blueberry pancakes. Lunch features cheeseburgers, a "veggie" sandwich with cream cheese, avocado, and sprouts, plus burritos and homemade soup. No dinner. ~ 3599 Main Street, Mammoth Lakes; 619-934-4048. BUDGET.

It's a far stretch from the sea, but **Ocean Harvest Restaurant** has an impressive selection of broiled seafood dishes. This establishment also offers steaks, chicken dishes, and baby back ribs in a comfortable setting. Dinner only. ~ Corner of Old Mammoth and Sierra Nevada roads, Mammoth Lakes; 619-934-8539. MODERATE.

The **Sierra Inn Restaurant**, near the center of town in June Lake, performs double duty. Part of the complex is a coffee shop serving standard breakfast, lunch and dinner items. In the evening the dining room opens, providing fresh seafood dishes as well as steaks, lasagna, pizza, and chicken dinners. With a high-beamed ceiling and full lounge, the dining room overlooks June Lake. Closed in November and for two weeks in April. ~ 2588 Boulder Drive, June Lake; 619-648-7774. MODERATE.

Who would have guessed that a place called **Carson Peak Inn** would be right there at the base of Carson Peak offering spectacular views of the mountain. In addition to plate-glass vistas this restaurant serves up steaks and seafood as well as pork ribs and vegetarian dishes. Dinner only. ~ Two miles west of June Lake on Route 158; 619-648-7575. MODERATE TO DELUXE.

NIGHTLIFE   In Mammoth Lakes, where the ski crowd livens up the territory, there are several nightspots worthy of note. During summer and winter, the bar at **Slocums Italian American Grill** is a popular watering hole. ~ Route 203; 619-934-7647.

During the winter months there's dancing to live bands Tuesday through Sunday at **La Sierra's Mexican Restaurant and Cantina**. This club has one of the largest dancefloors in town. Cover for live music. ~ 3789 Route 203, Mammoth Lakes; 619-934-8083.

Nevados features a spiffy, modern-style lounge complete with metallic silver bar and European bistro atmosphere. There are sports on the screen and contemporary sounds in the air. Closed for a couple of weeks in June and for a couple of weeks in October. ~ Minaret Road and Main Street, Mammoth Lakes; 619-934-4466.

For a quiet drink and a view of June Lake, try the lounge at **Sierra Inn Restaurant** near the center of town in June Lake. ~ 2588 Boulder Drive, June Lake; 619-648-7774.

PARKS   **INYO NATIONAL FOREST** 🏃🚵🐎🎿🚠🏊🎣🛶 🚤 This sprawling giant encompasses the high-country crest of the Sierra and plunges 150 miles into the eastern Sierra region. It contains within its domain the Ansel Adams Wilderness (formerly Minarets Wilderness), Mammoth Lakes, the John Muir Wilderness, Devils Postpile, the White Mountains, Mono Lake, the Ancient Bristlecone Forest, and Mount Whitney. Numbering 500 lakes and 100 streams, it is traversed by 1150 miles of trails, including the John Muir Trail. There's excellent angling in trout streams and well-stocked lakes. ~ Access points are generally located off Route 395 in the Owens Valley and Mammoth Lakes areas; 619-873-2500.

▲ Camping is permitted in 67 campgrounds; most take RVs (no hookups) and most are closed in winter. Prices range from $5 to $11 per night.

Set between the lofty Black and Panamint ranges, Death
Valley is a place renowned for exquisite but merciless
terrain. A region of vast distances (the national park is
half as large as Delaware) and plentiful plant life (over 900 plant species subsist here, 22 of them growing only in this area), Death Valley
holds a magician's bag of surprises.

▼▼▼▼▼▼▼▼▼▼▼▼▼
Death Valley Area

SIGHTS

BAKER TO DEATH VALLEY AREA   A fitting prelude to dusty, desiccated Death Valley lies along the southern gateway to this fabled destination. Here, stretching north along Route 127 from the town of
Baker, is a chain of **dry lakes.** Once part of Lake Mojave, an ancient
body of water which drained over 3500 square miles, they are now
flat expanses baked white in the sun. Silver Dry Lake, which appears
to the west four miles outside Baker, was an Indian habitat over
10,000 years ago.

To the east rise the Silurian Hills, backdropped by the Kingston
Range. If there is a snow-domed mountain in the far distance, it's
probably 11,918-foot Charleston Peak, 60 miles away in Nevada.
Those pretty white hills with the soft curves are the Dumont Dunes,
30 miles north of Baker.

Beyond Ibex Pass, as the road descends into another ancient lake
bed, you'll pass **Tecopa Lake Badlands**, where erosion has carved
fascinating formations from soft sedimentary rock.

A side road leads several miles to **Tecopa Hot Springs**, a series of
rich mineral baths once used by Paiute Indians. Today this natural
resource has been transformed into a bizarre tourist attraction.

If there is a last outpost before the world ends, this will be the
place. A white mineral patina covers the ground everywhere, as if salt
had been shaken across the entire desert. Water sits in stagnant pools.
Wherever you look—backgrounded by rugged, stark, glorious mountains—there are trailers. Hundreds of trailers, metal refuges against
the Mojave sun, painted white like the earth and equipped with satellite dishes. In a kind of desert monopoly game, if you collect enough
mobile homes you can hang a sign out front and call it a motel.

The species that inhabits these tin domiciles is on permanent vacation. This is, after all, a health resort; people walk about clad in
bathrobes. They wander from the private baths at the trailer parks
and "motels" to the public baths, which, in the single saving grace
to this surreal enclave, are free. ~ 619-852-4264.

DEATH VALLEY NATIONAL PARK   Better times lie ahead. Picking
up Route 178 as it leads into Death Valley National Park (admission) and maintaining a steady composure despite the raw landscape
and signs that threaten "No Roadside Services Next 72 Miles," you
will enter the most famous desert in the United States.

Due to the extreme summer temperatures (average July highs of
116°!), travel to the valley is not recommended in summer months.

The best time to see the park is from November through April. In late February and March (average highs of 72°, dropping to a cool 45° average at night) the desert comes alive with the spring blossoms of Death Valley sage, rock *mimulus*, and Panamint daisies if sufficient winter rains fall.

Crossing two low-lying mountain passes as it travels west, Route 178 (Badwater Road) turns north upon reaching the floor of Death Valley. Within a couple miles lie the ruins of **Ashford Mill**, built during World War I when gold mining enjoyed a comeback. The skeletons of a few buildings are all that remain of that early dream.

A nearby vista point overlooks **Shoreline Butte**, a curving hill marked by a succession of horizontal lines. Clearly visible to the naked eye, they trace the ancient shorelines of Lake Manly, which covered the valley to a depth of 600 feet and stretched for 90 miles. Formed perhaps 75,000 years ago when Pleistocene glaciers atop the Sierra Nevada began melting, the lake dried up about 10,000 years ago.

For a close-up of a cinder cone, follow nearby West Side Road, a graded thoroughfare, downhill for two miles. That reddish-black mound on your left is **Cinder Hill**, residue from an ancient volcano.

The main highway continues through the heart of the region to **Mormon Point**. From here northward Death Valley is one huge salt flat. As you traverse this expanse, notice how the Black Mountains to the east turn from dark colors to reddish hues as gray Precambrian rocks give way to younger volcanic and sedimentary deposits.

Then continue on to that place you've been reading about since third grade geography, **Badwater**, 282 feet below sea level, the lowest point in the western hemisphere. Legend has it the place got its name from a surveyor whose mule refused to drink here, inspiring him to scratch "bad water" on the map he was charting.

Take a stroll out onto the salt flats and you'll find that the crystals are joined into a white carpet which extends for miles. Despite the brackish environment the pool itself supports water snails and other invertebrates. Salt grass, pickleweed, and desert holly also endure here. Out on the flats you can gaze west at 11,049-foot **Telescope Peak** across the valley. Then be sure to glance back at the cliff to the west of the road. There high in the rocks above you a lone sign marks "Sea Level."

The water that carved **Natural Bridge** was quite unlike those stagnant pools on the valley floor. Indeed, it cascaded from the mountains in torrents, punched a hole in the underlying rock, and etched this 50-foot-high arch. Behind the bridge, you can still see the lip of this ancient waterfall. Also notice the formations along the canyon walls that were left by evaporating water and bear a startling resemblance to dripping wax. ~ Off Route 178 about two miles along a bumpy gravel road and up a half-mile trail.

Another dirt side road travels one mile to the **Devil's Golf Course**. Rather than a sand hazard, this flat expanse is one huge salt trap, complete with salt towers, pinnacles, and brine pools. The salt deposits here are three to five feet thick. They were formed by a small lake that evaporated perhaps 2000 years ago; below them earlier deposits from larger lakes reach over 1000 feet beneath the surface.

Artists Drive, a nine-mile route through the Black Mountains, is one of Southern California's most magnificent roads. The hills all around are splashed with color—soft pastels, striking reds, creamy browns—and rise to sharp cliffs. En route at **Artists Palette**, the hills are colored so vividly they seem to pulsate. It's a spot admired by photographers from around the world, a place where the rainbow meets the badlands.

If you'd like a scientific explanation for all this beauty—the artistic medium is oxidation: chloride deposits create the green hues,

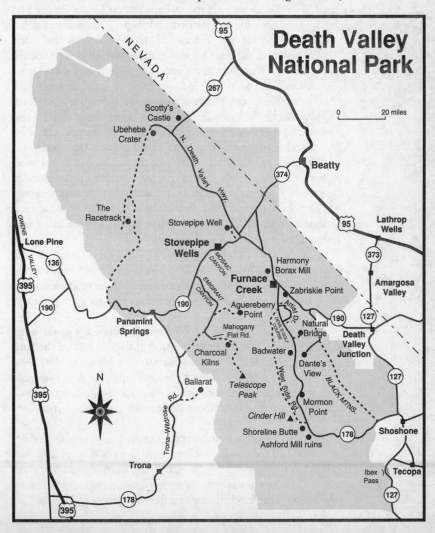

manganese oxides form the blacks, and the reds, yellows, and oranges are shades of iron oxide. These contrasting colors are most
spectacular during late afternoon.

Mushroom Rock, the sculptor's answer to Artists Palette, rises
on the right several hundred yards after you regain Route 178. A
boulder of basalt lava, it was carved by windblown particles.

Up in **Golden Canyon**, erosion has chiseled chasms into the bright
yellow walls of a narrow gorge. Climb the three-quarter-mile trail
and you arrive in a natural amphitheater, named for the iridescent
quality of the canyon walls, which are the embodiment of sunlight.

In this entire wasteland of wonders the only major center of civilization is **Furnace Creek**, where a gas station, campground, restaurants, and two hotels create a welcome oasis. The
Death Valley National Park Visitors Center is a good resource for information and maps. It houses a museum
re-creating the history of American Indians and early
prospectors. There are also mineral displays, descriptions of
Death Valley flora and fauna, and an oversize relief map of
the valley. ~ 619-786-2331.

The sodium chloride
at Devil's Golf
Course is 95 per-
cent pure, com-
parable to table
salt.

The nearby **Borax Museum** features the oldest house in Death
Valley, a sturdy 1883 structure built by a borax miner. There's also
a wonderful collection of stage coaches as well as a huge Rube Gold-
berg contraption once used to extract gold deposits from rock.

While the yellow metal symbolizes the romance of desert pros-
pecting, the lowly borax mineral proved of much greater value to
Death Valley miners. Important as a cleaning agent, the white crystal
was first discovered in 1881. Eventually it inspired its own romantic images, with 20-mule teams hauling 36-ton wagonloads across
180 miles of desert to the railhead in Mojave.

A two-and-a-half-mile trail climbs from Golden Canyon to **Zabriskie Point**, but most folks follow Route 190, which leads southeast from Furnace Creek. In any case, everyone inevitably arrives at
this place, as though it were a point of pilgrimage for paying homage
to nature.

What else can a mortal do, confronted with beauty of this mag-
nitude? In the east amber-hued hills roll like waves toward the horizon. To the west lies a badlands, burnished by blown sand to fierce
reds and soft pastels. All around, the landscape resembles a sea gone
mad, waves of sand breaking in every direction, with a stone tsuna-
mi, Manly Beacon, high above the combers, poised to crash into
Death Valley.

Prosaic though it sounds, these mustard-colored hills are dry
mud, lake-bed sediments deposited 2 to 12 million years ago, then
uplifted to their present height. In the early morning and late afternoon, when the place is suffused with color, Zabriskie Point demonstrates that humble origins are of little consequence.

For a close-up view of those mud hills, follow the nearby dirt road through **Twenty Mule Team Canyon**. It winds almost three miles through a former borax-mining region.

Then to get above it all, venture on to **Dante's View**, a 5475-foot perch with a 360° vista. From this vantage point, the salt flats and trapped pools of Death Valley are like a bleak watercolor. Though the Panamint Mountains wall off the western horizon, a steep half-mile trail (up the knoll north of the parking lot) leads to a point where you can gaze beyond them to Badwater and the snow-thatched Sierra Nevada.

Backtracking to Furnace Creek, Route 190 proceeds north toward the upper end of Death Valley. The history of the region's most valuable mineral is further revealed at the **Harmony Borax Works**. Surrounded by the ruins of Death Valley's most successful borax plant is an original 20-mule team rig.

At the very end of Death Valley, when you've gone as far north as you can without bumping fenders with the Nevada border, you'll find the strangest feature in the entire park—a castle in the desert. It's a place called **Scotty's Castle**, though Scotty never owned it. In fact Scotty swindled the fellow who did own it, then became his life-long friend. Sound preposterous? Perhaps.

It seems that one Walter "Death Valley Scotty" Scott, a former trick rider in Buffalo Bill's Wild West Show, once convinced a Chicago millionaire, one Albert Johnson, to invest in a nonexistent gold mine. Johnson traveled west to see the mine, discovered that the dry desert clime helped his fragile health, forgave Scotty, and decided during the 1920s to build a mansion in the sand.

The result was a $2 million Moorish castle, a wonderfully ridiculous building with wrought-iron detailing, inlaid tile, carved-beam ceilings, expensive antiques, and nothing for miles around. Scotty, the greatest story teller in Death Valley history, told everyone it was his castle. Hence the name. Somehow it reminds me of Hearst Castle in San Simeon, a place too gaudy to appreciate but too outrageous to ignore. Admission.

Ubehebe Crater, eight miles from Scotty's lair, is another of the park's natural wonders. One-half mile in diameter and reaching a depth of 500 feet, this magnificent landmark was created by a single explosion. The force of the volcanic steam scattered debris over a six-square-mile area and blew the crater walls so clean that one side retains its original sedimentary colors. Whether the crater dates back 10,000 years or is only a few hundred years old is currently being debated by geologists. They do agree that other nearby craters have been formed in the last few centuries.

From the crater a winding gravel road leads 27 miles to **The Racetrack**, another of nature's magic acts. This two-mile mud playa, set at the bottom of a dry lake, is oval shaped like a racecourse. In

◄ HIDDEN

fact an outcropping at the north end of the valley is dubbed The Grandstand. The racers, oddly enough, are rocks, ranging in size from pebbles to boulders. Pushed by heavy winds across the mud-slick surface, they leave long, faint tracks that reveal the distances they have "raced."

Stovepipe Wells, Death Valley's other village, is even smaller than Furnace Creek. A motel, restaurant, store, gas station, and campground comprise the entire town. It was here at **Burned Wagons Point** (historic marker) that a desperate party of '49ers killed their oxen and dried the meat by burning their wagons.

Six miles east of Stovepipe, a graded road departs Route 190 and travels four miles past **sand dunes** before joining North Death Valley Highway, the road to Scotty's Castle. The tallest dunes are over 300 feet, and take deceptively long to reach. Alive with greenery, they support many plant species, including creosote bushes, mesquite, and pickleweed. Coyotes hunt prey in these undulating sandhills and there are kit fox, lizards, kangaroo rats, and beetles. All of these creatures leave their fascinating tracks in the sand, making the dunes a paradise for children and wildlife lovers, as well as photographers.

Further along rests the old **Stovepipe Well** from which the village derived its name. Used by prospectors crossing Death Valley, the well was fitted with a tall stovepipe so travelers could see it even when sand blanketed the area.

DEATH VALLEY TO TRONA AREA   Stovepipe Wells marks the western gateway to Death Valley. From here Route 190 travels out of the valley southwest through Towne Pass in the Paramint Range. An alternative route leaving the park is Trona–Wildrose Road that winds south through Emigrant Canyon. This route, leading to Trona, passes several intriguing spots.

Aguereberry Point, a 6433-foot overlook, lies at the end of a six-mile-long side road. From atop this crag you gaze back at Death Valley and enjoy a circular view of the Black Mountains and the Sierra Nevada. (Despite a sign advising four-wheel drive, the road is graded and usually passable by two-wheel-drive vehicles. It's advisable to inquire about road conditions at the ranger station.)

Another detour onto Mahogany Flat Road (partially paved) leads seven miles to a startling site. As you round a bend, ten beehives, 25

R.I.P.

One person found neither well nor stovepipe at Stovepipe Well. **Val Nolan's grave**, a simple resting place within crawling distance of the well, consists of a pile of stones and a wooden marker. Carved into the grave is an epitaph that graphically reveals Val Nolan's last days: "A Victim of the Elements."

feet high, line the road. At least they look like beehives; in fact these stone-sided cones are **Charcoal Kilns**, used to create fuel for nearby silver smelters.

Meanwhile Trona–Wildrose Road descends into the Panamint Valley, a sun-parched plain bounded by the Panamint and Argus ranges. Here another side road cuts east for four miles to **Ballarat**, a ghost town dating to 1897. The wood and adobe ruins are remnants of a mining supply center which flourished until 1905. In its heyday this desolate spot boasted a stagecoach stop, three general stores, a school, Wells Fargo office, and hotel.

◄ HIDDEN

Near the southeast corner of Death Valley, in the postage-stamp town of Shoshone, the **Shoshone Inn** has standard motel rooms. There is a tree-shaded courtyard, nearby swimming pool, restaurant and bar, and the Shoshone is conveniently placed for exploring the southern stretches of Death Valley. ~ Route 127, Shoshone; 619-852-4335, fax 619-852-4107. BUDGET.

LODGING

Furnace Creek, the main village in Death Valley, features two facilities. **Furnace Creek Ranch** is a 175-unit resort sprawling across several acres. In addition to three restaurants, a saloon, and general store, the ranch contains a swimming pool, horseback riding facilities, a golf course, tennis courts, and a playground. Guest accommodations include duplex "cabins," fully furnished but lacking extra amenities; and standard rooms, which are plusher, more spacious, and feature televisions and refrigerators. ~ Route 190, Furnace Creek; 619-786-2345, fax 619-297-3175. MODERATE TO DELUXE.

The poshest place for many miles is **Furnace Creek Inn**, a 68-room hotel set on a hillside overlooking Death Valley. This Spanish Moorish–style building, built of stone and adobe, is surrounded by flowering gardens. Palm trees shade the grounds and a stream feeds three koi ponds. There are two restaurants, a swank lobby, tennis courts, jacuzzi, and a spring-fed swimming pool. Guest rooms are trimly appointed and quite comfortably furnished. They offer such features as tile baths with brass fittings; most have fireplaces. Closed in summer. ~ Route 190, Furnace Creek; 619-786-2345, fax 619-786-2423. ULTRA-DELUXE.

Stovepipe Wells Village is an attractive 82-unit motel about 25 miles up the road. With a pool, lounge, restaurant, general store and gas station, it's as well-equipped as you could expect. If your heroes have always been cowboys, you'll sleep well here; some of the rooms are decorated Western-style with oxen yokes attached to the headboards and steer heads carved into the light fixtures. ~ Stovepipe Wells; 619-786-2387, fax 619-786-2389. MODERATE.

Not far from the southern entrance to Death Valley, there's a café where water is served in Mason jars and red-checkered curtains cover every window. The **Red Bugg** offers sandwiches, Mexican dishes,

DINING

and standards such as steak, pork chops, fried chicken and trout filet. ~ Shoshone; 619-852-9908. BUDGET TO MODERATE.

Eat heartily because the next facilities are 72 miles away in Furnace Creek off Route 190. Here you'll find six restaurants, all of which can be reached at 619-786-2345.

The least expensive food in all Death Valley, except for dishes you cook on your campfire, is in the **Wrangler Buffet** at Furnace Creek Ranch. Open for breakfast and lunch, this steam-tray emporium serves an all-you-can-eat buffet of American food classics. Atmosphere is nonexistent and the food has invariably been warming for hours before it hits your plate, but oh, those inexpensive prices! In the evening, the Wrangler Buffet becomes the **Wrangler Steak House**, serving steak, chicken, and seafood entrées. ~ MODERATE TO DELUXE.

The **49er Coffee Shop** next door has omelettes, hot sandwiches, burgers, and a selection of dinners ranging from pork chops and steak to calf's liver. With woodplank walls and ranch atmosphere, it's a good place for a reasonably priced meal. Open October through May. ~ MODERATE.

The **Coyote International** serves up a variety of food including Sicilian chicken, Chinese stir-fries, broiled New York steak, and Mexican chimichangas. Cozy and informal, the place consists of an unassuming room decorated with Mexican rugs. Closed June through September. ~ MODERATE.

The fine dining places are up at Furnace Creek Inn. At **L'Ottimos** you can feast on shrimp scampi, veal scallopine, and pasta primavera. Dinner only. Closed June through September. ~ MODERATE TO DELUXE.

Upstairs at the **Inn Dining Room**, candlelight and a beamed ceiling create a more formal atmosphere. It's a five-course meal, and the menu is a fixed price. You can choose from among nearly 40 entrées including lobster del mar and tournedos Rossini. Breakfast and lunch menus are standard. ~ ULTRA-DELUXE.

In Stovepipe Wells you'll find a spacious **Dining Room** embellished with Indian rugs and paintings of the Old West. The cuisine matches the ambience, an all-American menu featuring filet mignon, fried chicken, steak, prawns, and halibut. ~ Route 190, Stovepipe Wells; 619-786-2604. MODERATE.

NIGHTLIFE   In Death Valley, the Furnace Creek Inn includes the **Oasis Lounge** among its elegant facilities. Featuring live acts on occasion, it's a lovely spot to enjoy a quiet evening. ~ Furnace Creek; 619-786-2345.

The **Badwater Saloon** in Stovepipe Wells also hosts jukebox dancing. With Western-style decor and a dancefloor, it's a night owl's oasis. ~ Stovepipe Wells; 619-786-2608.

The finest entertainment for many miles is at the **Amargosa Opera House**. This amazing show is the creation of Marta Becket, who performs dance pantomimes in a theater that she herself decorated with colorful murals. Performances run every Friday and Monday in February, March, April, and November and every Saturday in October and May. Locally renowned, she's extremely popular, so call for reservations. ~ Death Valley Junction; 619-852-4441.

DEATH VALLEY NATIONAL PARK 🚶🚴 Extending across more than three million acres and rising from below sea level to over 11,000 feet, this park is a land unto itself, varied and full of possibility. It contains 550 square miles of salt flats, 30 square miles of sand dunes, and several mountain ranges. Death Valley itself covers only a small part of the facility.

In addition to standard sightseeing spots there are hiking trails and 300 miles of jeep tracks leading to obscure high desert locales. Over 350 bird species are found here, together with desert tortoises, rattlesnakes, mountain lions, bobcats, mule deer, and bighorn sheep. There's an information center and museum, as well as hotels, restaurants, picnic areas, restrooms, and limited groceries. For complete information see the "Sights" and "Hiking" sections in this chapter. Day-use fee, $5. ~ Located in the northern Mojave Desert along Routes 178 and 190. Furnace Creek Campground is located one-quarter of a mile north of the Furnace Creek Visitors Center. Mesquite Springs Campground is at the north end of the desert near Scotty's Castle; 619-786-2331.

▲ Permitted in nine campgrounds; Furnace Creek has 30 tent/RV sites (no hookups); $10 per night; three low-elevation facilities are open from October to April; and three high-elevation campgrounds are open from April to October. Located at about 2500 feet, Mesquite Springs (open year-round) has 30 tent/RV sites; $6 per night.

PARKS

▼▼▼▼▼▼▼▼▼▼▼▼▼
Outdoor Adventures

The Kern and Kings rivers in Sequoia and Kings Canyon national parks offer trout fishing. The Mammoth Lakes area is also an angler's delight.

FISHING & BOATING

For fishing gear rentals, tackle, and friendly information, contact **Ernie's Tackle and Ski Shop**. ~ 2604 Route 158, June Lake; 619-648-7756. If you'd like to try fly fishing, **Western Waters Fly Fishing** offers instruction. Closed during winter. ~ 343 Hillside Drive, Mammoth Lakes; 619-934-4897.

A few places rent fishing boats, including **Kaweah Marina**. ~ 34467 Sierra Drive, Lemon Cove; 209-597-2526. There is also **June Lake Marina**. Open April through October. ~ End of Brenner Street, June Lake; 619-648-7726. Or try **Lake Sabrina Boat Landing**. ~ Bishop Creek, Bishop; 619-873-7425.

WATER SPORTS

Water sports are nearly as popular as skiing in Mammoth Lakes. Windsurfing, waterskiing, and sailing are available through **Alpine Adventures**. ~ Mammoth Lake; 619-934-7188. There is no waterskiing on June Lake, but windsurfing is permitted.

RIVER RUNNING

Shooting the rapids on the Kern and Kings rivers is great sport. Several California tour companies offer exciting adventures on rubber rafts, and some offer kayaking. Among them is **Sierra South**. ~ 11300 Kernville Road, Kernville; 619-376-3745. There is also **Spirit Whitewater**. ~ 1849 Crane Lane, Squaw Valley; 209-332-2227. Contact **Zephyr River Expeditions** for a trip down the rivers. ~ P.O. Box 510, Columbia; 209-532-6249. Or try **Whitewater Voyages**. ~ P.O. Box 20400, El Sobrante, CA 94820; 510-222-5994.

BALLOON RIDES & GLIDING

Soaring in a hot air balloon is all part of a day's work at **High Sierra Ballooning and Alpine Adventures**. Advance reservations are required for winter rides. ~ Mammoth Lakes; 619-934-7188.

Another way to sail through the air is in a glider: contact **Crystal Soaring**. Closed Monday and Tuesday. ~ 32810 North 165th Street East, Llano; 805-944-3341.

RIDING STABLES & PACK TOURS

Out here in the High Desert you can saddle up and ride into the American past. To rent horses around Victorville try **Mojave Narrows Riding Stables**. Open weekends only during summer. ~ 619-244-1644. In Sequoia and Kings Canyon national parks there are stables at **Wolverton Pack Station**. Open from June through mid-October. ~ 209-565-3445. You can also ride at **Grant Grove**. Open May through September. ~ 209-565-3464; **Cedar Grove** is open from June through mid-October. ~ 209-565-3464. Also try **Mineral King**. Open from July through September. ~ 209-561-4142.

Pack trips in the Sierra Nevada often combine horseback riding with fishing expeditions. If you prefer something less adventurous, most outfits offer full-day or half-day excursions as well as longer treks. Keep in mind that most pack stations close in winter, so call in advance. Among the outfitters to choose from is **Bishop Pack Outfitters**. ~ 247 Cataract Road, Aspendell; 619-873-4785. Also try **Red's**

▲▼▲

✔ CHECK THESE OUT—UNIQUE OUTDOOR ADVENTURES

- Raft the infamous boat-bouncing rapids along the Forks of the **Kern River** through the giant trees in Sequoia National Park. *page 474*
- Sail up, up, and away in a balloon over the Sierra and the desert from a liftoff point at **Mammoth Lakes** or **Quartz Hill**. *page 474*
- Get high as you ascend the **Mount Whitney Trail** to the highest point in the continental U.S., which is—not to deter you—14,495 feet above sea level. *page 478*
- Let a mule do the grunt work when you take a pack tour into the **Sierra** to fish a mountain lake. *page 474*

Meadow Resort Pack Train. ~ Mammoth Lakes; 619-934-2345. **Frontier Pack Train** also gives pack tours. ~ June Lake; 619-648-7701 in summer; 619-873-7971 in winter. Contact **Mineral King Pack Station.** ~ Three Rivers; 209-561-4142. Or you can also call **Cedar Grove Pack Station.** ~ Three Rivers; 209-565-3464.

In Death Valley, **Furnace Creek Ranch** offers wagon and carriage rides (winter only). ~ 619-786-2345.

The desert may be one huge sand trap, but golf enthusiasts won't find many greens in these parts. Among the exceptions is the **Victorville Municipal Golf Course.** ~ 14144 Green Tree Boulevard, Victorville; 619-245-4860. In Mojave try **Camelot Golf Course.** ~ Camelot Boulevard, Mojave; 805-824-4107. Also contact **Three Rivers Golf Course.** ~ 41117 Sierra Drive, Three Rivers; 209-561-3133. Near Lone Pine you can golf at **Mount Whitney Golf Course.** ~ Route 395, south of Lone Pine; 619-876-5795. Tee off at **Bishop Country Club.** ~ South Highway 395, Bishop; 619-873-5828. In the valley try **Furnace Creek Golf Course.** Closed July and August. ~ Highway 190, Death Valley; 619-786-2301.

GOLF

The Eastern Sierra is a prime place for mountain riding. In Mammoth Lakes, the **Mammoth Scenic Loop** (off of Minaret Road) offers a lovely, though hilly, overview of this majestic area. Another picturesque ride is the **June Lake Loop** (Route 158), an easy 16-mile route around the base of the mountains and along the lake shore. The **Mammoth Mountain Ski Area** is a mountain bike mecca in summer. Riders can take the gondola to the top of the mountain and descend on the ski area's extensive service roads. For experienced bike riders, the road from **Tom's Place** to **Rock Creek Winter Lodge** is nine miles of uphill pedaling through a stunning canyon. Think of the fun you'll have coming back.

BIKING

Death Valley may seem like the last place to ride a bicycle, but it's actually quite pleasant from October to April. The main road in the park is paved and there's little traffic. The side roads to some of the sights are dirt or gravel, however, and require a mountain bike.

Furnace Creek is a good starting point: it's an easy ride from here to Badwater and Artists Drive, though the latter destination requires uphill pedaling. For an even more challenging ride you can venture up, up, uphill to Dante's View; plan on an all-day effort and bring provisions (especially water!).

Excellent mountain biking can be found in most of the canyons off the West Side Road—they'll all be challenging uphills for as long as you can stand it, and downhill thrills on the way out. If you have two cars—or a big thumb and a nice smile—you can ride Titus Canyon, a one-way downhill; it's a stunning run through a deep gorge that is, in places, hardly wide enough for a car.

Text continued on page 478.

Ski the
Southland

As a travel destination, Southern California offers everything. Even during winter, when rain spatters the coast and fog invades the valleys, the Southland has one more treat in its bottomless bag—snow.

No sooner has the white powder settled than skiers from around the world beeline to the region's high altitude resort areas. They come to schuss through fir forests in the San Gabriel Mountains, challenge the runs above San Bernardino, and breathe the beauty of Mammoth Lakes at Christmas.

The season begins in late fall and sometimes lasts until May. During those frosty months dozens of alpine areas offer both downhill and cross-country skiing.

Within Los Angeles County itself, Angeles National Forest features both **Kratka Ridge** (818-449-1749) and **Mt. Waterman** (818-790-2002) ski areas plus five nordic ski trails. For further information, contact the local ranger station at 818-790-1151. One of Southern California's most popular ski areas is **Mt. Baldy** (909-981-3344), a 10,064-foot peak just 45 minutes from the city. With a vertical drop of 2140 feet, the facility provides 24 runs, four lifts, a lodge, and a ski school.

The neighboring San Bernardino Mountains, which rise to over 11,000 feet, offer several alpine ski areas. Located along Route 18 between Lake Arrowhead and Big Bear Lake, these resorts include **Snow Valley** (909-867-2751), **Snow Summit** (909-866-5766), and **Bear Mountain Ski Resort** (909-585-2519).

Even Palm Springs, California's vaunted warm-weather hideaway, gives spa-goers a chance to challenge the surrounding slopes. The Palm Springs Aerial Tramway carries desert dwellers to over 8000 feet elevation in **Mount San Jacinto State Park** (619-327-0222), where a nordic center rents cross-country gear, and two loop trails circle through backcountry wilderness. Permit required and obtainable at the station.

This more demanding nordic-style skiing is gaining increased popularity around the state. It's the adventurer's way to explore the slopes—fill a daypack, strap on skis, and take off across the mountains. In the pack are extra clothes, food, water, flashlight, knife, map, compass, blanket, matches, equipment repair tools, and a first-aid kit.

Unrestricted by ski lifts and marked runs, cross-country skiers venture everywhere that geography and gravity permit. Their sport is tantamount to hiking on skis, with the entire expanse of the mountain range their domain. Some skiers disappear into the wilderness for days on end, emerging only when supplies run low.

If you prefer a base of operations from which to experience the wild, several nordic ski centers operate in Sequoia and Kings Canyon national parks. The Giant Forest and Lodgepole/Wolverton sections of Sequoia, for instance, feature 35 miles of trails and offer rentals, lessons, and other recreational activities. Giant Forest Village contains restaurants and motel accommodations; nearby **Sequoia Ski Touring** (209-565-3435) assists skiers in making arrangements.

Grant Grove in Kings Canyon National Park has five marked trails, varying in difficulty, and offers lessons and rentals through **Grant Grove Ski Touring** (209-335-2348). Like Sequoia National Park, Kings Canyon sits amid a network of High Sierra cross-country trails. Miles of these alpine paths extend in every direction, leading through forests of giant sequoia trees. There are frozen lakes to explore, extraordinary mountain vistas, and secluded warming huts.

Many resorts, on the other hand, focus on downhill and alpine-style skiing and provide complete facilities for their athletic guests. Some, like those around Mammoth Lakes in the eastern Sierra, are self-contained villages with every amenity imaginable. Such resorts often have boutiques, galleries, pools, tennis courts, groceries, restaurants, and après-ski spots. There are instructors for beginners and intermediate skiers alike, snow schools for children, and enough diversions to keep even a non-skier content.

For Angelenos, the Mammoth/June Lakes region represents skier heaven. Located high in the Sierra Nevada chain, about 300 miles from the streets of Los Angeles, **Mammoth Mountain** (619-934-2571) is one of the largest ski areas in the United States. A major center for both alpine and nordic skiers, it boasts mountain lodges, craggy peaks, and enough white powder to create an aura of the Alps right here in sun-drenched Southern California.

Bike Rentals   Up around Mammoth Lakes try **Mammoth Sporting Goods** for bike rentals. ~ Old Mammoth Road; 619-934-3239. Or try **Footloose** for mountain bikes. ~ 6175 Minaret Road; 619-934-2400.

HIKING

A special note: As tempting as mountains waters look, don't drink from them unless you have brought water-purification equipment: the intestinal parasite *Giardia* is widespread in this area. Also, when possible, avoid trails used by pack trains. All distances listed are one way unless otherwise noted.

SEQUOIA AND KINGS CANYON   Sequoia and Kings Canyon national parks offer miles of serene trails amid towering sequoia trees and tumbling waterfalls.

Mist Falls Trail (4.5 miles), near Zumwalt Meadow, leads north past a massive stone face called The Sphinx, then continues on toward its namesake, a cascade so light it resembles mist.

A moderate hike along **Sugarbowl–Redwood Canyon–Hart Tree Loop Trail** (6 miles) takes you through some of the most beautiful country in Grant Grove. Beginning on Sugarbowl Trail, then connecting with Redwood Canyon Trail and Hart Tree Trail, the loop passes the 209-foot Hart Tree. The trailhead is located at Redwood Saddle. (Check ahead with the ranger, the area is sometimes closed.)

For a 360° view of the Sierra Crest, Kings Canyon, and the sequoias of Redwood Canyon, hike **Buena Vista Peak** (1 mile), one of the highest points west of Generals Highway. (The trailhead is south of Kings Canyon Overlook.)

Another majestic view lies along **Little Baldy Trail** (1.7 miles). From here on a clear day you can see the San Joaquin Valley. Begin this trail at Little Baldy Saddle, located 11 miles north of Giant Forest Village on Generals Highway.

Ever-popular **Muir Grove Trail** (2 miles), which begins near Dorst campground contains magnificent sequoias in a lovely setting.

An easy hike along the **Tokopah Falls Trail** (1.7 miles) leads through Tokopah Valley, where the Marble Fork of the Kaweah Ri-

A VIEW WITH ROOM

The most famous climb in the Sierra is along **Mount Whitney Trail** (10.7 miles) to the 14,495-summit. The lure of ascending the highest peak in the "lower 48" is irresistible to many. Camping is permitted at Outpost Camp (3.5 miles) and Trail Camp (6 miles). Wilderness permits good from March 1 to May 31 are available from Mount Whitney Ranger District, P.O. Box 8, Lone Pine, CA 93545; 619-876-6200. There is a quota, so applications are picked by lottery. Day-use permits are available at the trailhead.

ver flows between soaring granite cliffs. The trailhead is located at Lodgepole campground.

From the same campground, **Pear Lake Trail** (6.7 miles), a moderate climb, carries past Emerald Lake and through an area rich in wildlife and wildflowers to Pear Lake. The trail ends in a granite-bound basin amid a dozen tiny lakes and crystal creeks.

Of the many trails crossing Mineral King, several offer day-excursions. **Tar Gap Trail** (2.2 miles), rising quickly from Cold Spring campground, crosses several creeks and provides views of Sawtooth Peak, Empire Mountain, and Timber Gap.

Timber Gap Trail (2.2 miles), which begins near the end of the road in Mineral King, passes through a red fir forest, crosses a summit, then dips into the flower-strewn meadows of Timber Gap Creek.

Sawtooth Pass Trail (5.5 miles), beginning at the same trailhead as Timber Gap, follows Monarch Creek upward through manzanita cover to Groundhog Meadow. Here Monarch Lakes Trail continues across the creek and zigzags up through open pine and fir stands to Monarch Lakes.

From the road's end in Mineral King, **Eagle Lake Trail** (3.4 miles) follows Eagle Creek through fragrant sagebrush and colorful wildflowers. The path ascends 2000 feet before reaching Eagle Lake, which nestles below White Chief Peak in a granite bowl.

OWENS VALLEY   The Sierra Nevada offer the finest hiking in California, attracting adventurers from all over the world. Along Route 395 in the Owens Valley, roads leading to major trailheads branch off in nearly every town.

Sparkling lakes, wildflowers, cascades, and encircling peaks await when you climb the **Kearsarge Pass to Flower Lake Trail** (2.5 miles). The trailhead is at the end of Onion Valley Road, outside the town of Independence.

West of Bishop, Lake Sabrina and South Lake are important trailheads for serious backpackers. Backdropped by glacier-bearing peaks, **South Lake to Treasure Lakes Trail** (5 miles) climbs 1000 feet through mixed coniferous forest to the south fork of Bishop Creek.

Lake Sabrina to Dingleberry Lake Trail (5 miles) ascends 1500 feet to an alpine lake and presents a panorama of lakes, forests, and lofty Sierra crests.

MAMMOTH AND JUNE LAKES   The Mammoth and June lakes region is a key entranceway to the Ansel Adams (formerly Minarets) and John Muir wilderness areas. From here there is easy access to the Pacific Crest and John Muir trails. The John Muir Trail, which extends from Lake Tahoe to Mount Whitney, is a 200-mile-long portion of the Pacific Crest Trail. (Permits are required for these wilderness areas and should be obtained well in advance.)

Day-hikes up Coldwater Creek and Mammoth Creek from Lake Mary offer great outings. Try **Mammoth Creek to Duck Lake Trail**

(5.5 miles) with its many lakes, vistas, and flowering meadows. Duck Lake is an ideal trout-fishing spot.

An easy hike along **Mammoth Rock Trail** (3 miles) leads east past its namesake, a fossil-embedded marble and limestone monolith. The trail, which begins from Old Mammoth Road, also skirts the largest Jeffrey pine forest in the world.

It's a beautiful hike along the **Sherwin Creek Canyon Trail** (3 miles) to the five small Sherwin Lakes. Switchbacks ease the 800 foot climb. Once here, you can ascend further along **Valentine Lake Trail** (4.5 miles) to a forest-fringed lake squeezed into a glaciated cirque. Sherwin Creek Canyon trailhead is located one mile west of Sherwin Creek campground.

Lake George to Crystal Lake Trail (1 mile) treks through mountain hemlock to a serene lake at the base of Crystal Crag. For sweeping views, continue up to the top on **Mammoth Crest Trail** (2 miles).

You'll experience a touch of wilderness with little effort along **Lake George–Lake Barrett–T. J. Loop Trail** (1.5 miles). It starts at Lake George campground and follows the lake shore before veering uphill through flowering meadows and stands of alder and pine.

From the June Lake Loop, **Agnew Lake Trail** (2 miles) departs near Silver Lake and rises 1300 feet to a picnic area and cold mountain lake.

Another hike leaving the Silver Lake area is **Fern Creek Trail** (1.5 miles), which climbs nearly 2000 feet en route to Fern Lake. A branch trail travels another three miles to Yost Lake.

Convict Creek Trail (10 miles) is a long but rewarding trek from Convict Lake past three alpine lakes, well-stocked with fish, over a 10,000-foot ridge. The trail then switchbacks down to Laurel Canyon Road.

Horseshoe Lake to Reds Meadow Trail (6.5 miles) passes through pine-hemlock forest, skirts McCloud Lake, and crosses the Sierra Crest. The trail then descends to the old John Muir Trail where a side trip leads to Red Cones, a formation of geologically young cinder cones. The main trail continues through red-fir forests to Reds Meadow campground with its refreshing hot springs.

DEATH VALLEY AREA Rugged hiking in the desert and mountains is a favorite sport around Death Valley. Special precautions, however, must be taken throughout this area: be sure to carry plenty of water; watch for rattlesnakes; do not enter mine shafts and tunnels; and avoid desert hiking between May and October. Maps of more than 20 hiking trails are available at the ranger station.

The **Salt Creek Interpretive Trail** (.5 mile), near the sand dunes at Stovepipe Well, provides a glimpse of the salt-tolerant grasses and rare pupfish of Salt Creek. Arriving at dawn you will see the tracks left by numerous nocturnal animals.

West of Stovepipe Wells Village, a short dirt road heads south to **Mosaic Canyon Trail** (2 miles). Formed by a fault zone, the canyon's walls are polished by wind and water. The multicolored rock debris deposited here gives the canyon its name.

For a view from the highest peak for miles around, park your car at Mahogany Flat and climb **Telescope Peak Trail** (7 miles). Summer and fall are the best seasons for this moderate ascent. Once atop this 11,049-foot peak you can gaze east across Death Valley and west to the Sierra Nevada.

A less ambitious trip is up **Wildrose Peak Trail** (4 miles) from Charcoal Kilns. Here you'll find wide vistas and a variety of animals and plants, including bristlecone pines.

Hikers who are history buffs or ghost town enthusiasts should consider a journey to **Panamint City** (5 miles), a once-booming mining center dating from the 1870s. Located on the west side of the Panamint range at the top of Surprise Canyon, the remains of the town include a brick chimney several stories high—part of the original lumber mill—plus several cabins, some of which date from later booms in the 1920s and '30s. To reach the mouth of Surprise Canyon, take the Wildrose-Trona Road to Ballarat Road. After passing through the ghost town of Ballarat, take the second turnoff on your right—the road should be in noticably better shape than the others along this stretch—and follow it up the large alluvial fan as far as you can. Park at the encampment of trailers, where you'll see forbidding signs inaccurately admonishing hikers that Panamint City is "ten miles on foot"; these are the work of modern-day prospectors who try to dissuade others from exploring the canyon.

The hike up Surprise is wonderful, wild, and may be a little wet, depending on the time of year. Some climbing is involved in the lower section, where the canyon is steep and narrow; above the narrows it's a four-wheel-drive road all the way. Above Panamint City, the trail continues up to Panamint Pass, from which you can view Death Valley and Johnson Canyon. Carrying a topographic map is a good idea during any hike in Death Valley, and is essential if you intend to continue above Panamint City.

▼▼▼▼▼▼▼▼▼▼

Transportation

CAR

The California desert is a region of Texas-style proportions. In this chapter it is divided into several large slices—the Mojave Desert, Sequoia and Kings Canyon national parks, Owens Valley, Mammoth Lakes, and Death Valley.

In crossing the Mojave Desert, **Route 58** leads from Bakersfield to Barstow, the hub of this entire area. From here **Route 40** travels east to Arizona and **Route 15** buzzes northeast toward Las Vegas.

Two highways lead into Sequoia and Kings Canyon national parks, which are located on the western slopes of the Sierra Nevada:

Route 198 from Visalia and Route 180 from Fresno. The Generals Highway, generally closed in winter, connects the parks.

From Route 15, Route 127 proceeds north and links with Route 178 and Route 190, which wind through Death Valley National Park.

Route 395, the desert's major north–south thoroughfare, runs the entire length of the Owens Valley, then continues north to Mammoth Lakes.

There are several important points to remember when driving in the desert. Stay on the main roads unless you have inquired about the conditions of side roads. Turn back if a road becomes too difficult to navigate. Be sure to keep your radiator and gas tank filled and make sure the cooling system is in good condition. Also, carry spare water, food, and gas in your vehicle. If stranded in the summer heat, do not leave the shade of your car. Happy trails!

AIR

Airports in these areas are rare and regularly scheduled flights are even scarcer. A few small airlines provide flights from various California locations. For air travel to Sequoia and Kings Canyon national parks you'll have to fly into Fresno, then pick up ground transportation.

For information about charter service, contact Mammoth Airport Information (619-934-3825). Sierra Mountain Air (800-224-6359) and Mountain Air Express (310-595-1011) fly into Mammoth–June Lakes Airport.

Death Valley visitors usually fly to Las Vegas, then drive from there.

BUS

Bus service here is almost as scarce as air transportation. To visit Owens Valley and the Mammoth Lakes area, try Greyhound Bus Lines, which stops in Lone Pine and Mammoth Lakes (Mammoth Tavern Road). ~ 619-872-2721, 800-231-2222.

TRAIN

The nearest Amtrak station servicing Sequoia and Kings Canyon is in Fresno, 65 miles west of the parks. From here you'll have to hike, hitch, or rent a car.

For service to Death Valley, the closest stops are Barstow and Las Vegas. Two trains, the "Desert Wind" and the "Southwest Chief," arrive in Barstow. The "Desert Wind" also stops in Las Vegas. Both towns offer car rental agencies. ~ 800-872-7245.

CAR RENTALS

In Barstow, call Avis Rent A Car (619-256-8614, 800-331-1212). There's an Auto Rental (619-872-1730) in Bishop. Around Mammoth Lakes, try You Save Auto Rental (619-934-4999, 800-272-8728) or Mammoth Car Rental (619-934-8111).

Lodging Index

Dining Index

Index

HIDDEN GUIDES
Adventure travel or a relaxing vacation?—"Hidden" guidebooks are the only travel books in the business to provide detailed information on both. Aimed at environmentally aware travelers, our motto is "Adventure Travel Plus." These books combine details on unique hotels, restaurants and sightseeing with information on camping, sports and hiking for the outdoor enthusiast.

THE NEW KEY GUIDES
Based on the concept of ecotourism, The New Key Guides are dedicated to the preservation of Central America's rare and endangered species, architecture and archaeology. Filled with helpful tips, they give travelers everything they need to know about these exotic destinations.

ULTIMATE FAMILY GUIDES
These innovative guides present the best and most unique features of a family destination. Quality is the keynote. In addition to thoroughly covering each destination, they feature short articles and one-line "teasers" that are both fun and informative.

Order Form

Ulysses Press books are available at bookstores everywhere. If any of the following titles are unavailable at your local bookstore, ask the bookseller to order them. Or you can order them directly from Ulysses Press (P.O. Box 3440, Berkeley, CA 94703; 510-601-8301, 800-377-2542).

HIDDEN GUIDEBOOKS

____ Hidden Boston and Cape Cod, $9.95
____ Hidden Carolinas, $15.95
____ Hidden Coast of California, $15.95
____ Hidden Colorado, $13.95
____ Hidden Florida, $15.95
____ Hidden Florida Keys and Everglades, $9.95
____ Hidden Hawaii, $16.95
____ Hidden Idaho, $13.95
____ Hidden Maui, $12.95
____ Hidden Montana, $12.95

____ Hidden New England, $16.95
____ Hidden Oregon, $12.95
____ Hidden Pacific Northwest, $16.95
____ Hidden Rockies, $16.95
____ Hidden San Francisco and Northern California, $15.95
____ Hidden Southern California, $16.95
____ Hidden Southwest, $16.95
____ Hidden Tahiti $15.95
____ Hidden Wyoming $12.95

THE NEW KEY GUIDEBOOKS

____ The New Key to Belize, $14.95
____ The New Key to Cancún and the Yucatán, $14.95
____ The New Key to Costa Rica, $16.95

____ The New Key to Ecuador and the Galápagos, $15.95
____ The New Key to Guatemala, $14.95

ULTIMATE FAMILY GUIDEBOOKS

____ Disneyland and Beyond, $12.95

____ Disney World and Beyond, $12.95

Mark the book(s) you're ordering and enter the total cost here ⇨ [ ]

California residents add 8% sales tax here ⇨ [ ]

Shipping, check box for your preferred method and enter cost here ⇨ [ ]

❑ BOOK RATE   FREE! FREE! FREE!

❑ PRIORITY MAIL $3.00 First book, $1.00/each additional book

❑ UPS 2-DAY AIR $7.00 First book, $1.00/each additional book   [ ]

Billing, enter total amount due here and check method of payment ⇨ [ ]

❑ CHECK   ❑ MONEY ORDER

❑ VISA/MASTERCARD _____ EXP. DATE _____

NAME _____ PHONE _____

ADDRESS _____

_____

CITY_____ STATE _____ ZIP _____

MONEY-BACK GUARANTEE ON DIRECT ORDERS PLACED THROUGH ULYSSES PRESS.

ABOUT THE AUTHOR

RAY RIEGERT is the author of eight travel books, including *Hidden San Francisco and Northern California*. His most popular work, *Hidden Hawaii*, won the coveted Lowell Thomas Travel Journalism Award for Best Guidebook. In addition to his role as publisher of Ulysses Press, he has written for the *Chicago Tribune*, *Saturday Evening Post*, *San Francisco Examiner and Chronicle*, and *Travel & Leisure*. A member of the Society of American Travel Writers, he lives in the San Francisco Bay Area with his wife, co-publisher Leslie Henriques, and their son Keith and daughter Alice.

ABOUT THE ILLUSTRATOR

TIMOTHY CARROLL worked as a graphic designer before turning his talents to illustration. He has illustrated several other Ulysses Press guidebooks, including *Hidden Florida* and *Hidden New England*. His artwork has also appeared in *Esquire*, *GQ*, the *Boston Globe*, *San Francisco Focus*, *Premiere*, and the *Washington Post*.